D1232115

WITHDRAWN

ANATOMY
OF VICTORY

ANATOMY OF VICTORY

Why the United States Triumphed in World War II, Fought to a Stalemate in Korea, Lost in Vietnam, and Failed in Iraq

John D. Caldwell

ROWMAN & LITTLEFIELD
Lanham • Boulder • New York • London

Published by Rowman & Littlefield
An imprint of The Rowman & Littlefield Publishing Group, Inc.
4501 Forbes Boulevard, Suite 200, Lanham, Maryland 20706
www.rowman.com

Unit A, Whitacre Mews, 26-34 Stannary Street, London SE11 4AB, United Kingdom

Distributed by NATIONAL BOOK NETWORK

British Library Cataloguing in Publication Information Available

Library of Congress Cataloging-in-Publication Data
Names: Caldwell, John Dean, 1940– author.
Title: Anatomy of victory : why the United States triumphed in World War II, fought to a
    stalemate in Korea, lost in Vietnam, and failed in Iraq / John D. Caldwell.
Description: Lanham : Rowman & Littlefield, [2019] | Includes bibliographical references
    and index.
Identifiers: LCCN 2018017886 (print) | LCCN 2018034665 (ebook) | ISBN
    9781538114780 (ebook) | ISBN 9781538114773 | ISBN 9781538114773 (cloth : alk.
    paper)
Subjects: LCSH: United States—History, Military—20th century. | United States—
    History, Military—21st century.
Classification: LCC E745 (ebook) | LCC E745 .C28 2019 (print) | DDC
    355.00973/0904—dc23
LC record available at https://lccn.loc.gov/2018017886

♾™ The paper used in this publication meets the minimum requirements of
American National Standard for Information Sciences—Permanence of Paper
for Printed Library Materials, ANSI/NISO Z39.48-1992.

Printed in the United States of America

To the Armed Forces of the United States

CONTENTS

ILLUSTRATIONS

MAPS

FIGURES

PHOTO INSERTS

TABLE

PREFACE

Writing about the armed forces of the United States and their allies is a humbling experience. Studying the accounts of expeditionary operations during World War II and the Korean, Vietnam, and Iraqi Wars reveals extraordinary levels of duty, courage, patriotism, and sacrifice. These four major conflicts into which eleven presidents since 1941 committed our forces to fight convinces me that I was lucky to have been born an American. There is no other country in the world capable of fielding such forces to bear the international burdens that Americans in December 1941 found themselves assuming globally. Whether one regards American participation in the postwar conflicts as wise or unwise, our forces did not make that choice. Presidents did. Our fighting forces carry out military direction from duly constituted national executive authority regardless of whether Congress goes through the constitutional formality of declaring war.

The original impetus for this book began almost fifty years ago in my salad days as I was beginning my first real job in Saigon in the middle of a war. In March 1968, I met Jeffrey Race for the first time. A US Army first lieutenant, he had already served two combat tours in Vietnam and returned to Saigon as a civilian to begin research for a book about the war. Within minutes of my first encounter with Jeffrey, he told me, "John, we are going to lose the Vietnam War." I was shocked. The Tet Offensive was barely a month old. It seemed to me that we were winning, or at least holding our own. What astonished me even more was the scale of the American way of war—the sheer size of our military commitment to the theater and logistically how lavishly it was being supplied. American manpower was at its peak in 1968: more than a half million men—twelve divisions—supported by a large naval fleet offshore in the South China Sea and 1,700 combat aircraft dedicated to the theater. Large combat bases seemed to be everywhere, especially in the Saigon area. How could we lose? Jeffrey put it very simply: our enemies have a "theory of victory and we don't." That compelling phrase has resonated with me over half a lifetime.

After I retired from a four-decade career in defense think tanks and aerospace companies, I thought I might be ready to address Jeffrey's assertion about what has happened over the course of our lifetimes: theories of victory that neither succeeded the way World War II did nor produced outcomes that satisfied the American people. My work experience has been a learning one, about war fighting, leadership, technology, weapons systems, and the people who design, build, and use them.

One thing that made a powerful early impression on me was meeting combat soldiers and military advisors in Vietnam. The officers, NCOs, and enlisted men and women I encountered, officially and unofficially, over a lifetime in the business of the "military-industrial complex" uniformly impressed me as implacably honest, well-informed, and, in many cases, extraordinarily well-educated people, who took their military responsibilities and duties very seriously, often in life-threatening circumstances. I learned much from them, as well as from my aerospace colleagues, many of whom are military veterans themselves. I am particularly grateful to my colleagues with whom I worked starting in 1982 at TRW's Defense Systems Group as an advanced systems manager and, later, in 1989, in TRW Proposal Operations (Northrop Grumman Aerospace Systems after NG acquired TRW in 2002). Proposal Ops was an organization founded and led by the late Sam Petralia. Sam's able successors—Mr. Stephen C. Hart, Dr. Robert Goldstein, and Mr. Greg Davidson—continued his legacy that excellence wins. From all of them, I learned how rigorous, disciplined thought processes make writing easier. Proposals, of course, are about winning and losing. My colleagues may recognize that I still use some of the vernacular, particularly the very useful analytical distinction between discriminators and differentiators and the value of Dr. Goldstein's canon that assertion of a feature without hard evidence of a proof (preferably with quantitative data) is meaningless. I long ago became a student of geopolitics and war and read widely.

The idea of winning and losing was at the center of how I began researching and writing this work. World War II has long been the historical paradigm for winning—because there has never been any doubt in any informed mind about who won. I imagine that is one of the reasons why the reading public's appetite for any book about World War II makes for good sales in the marketplace. Another reason is demographic: virtually everyone in the 1940s and in the generations that followed knew of a family member or friend who served in the armed forces of the United States, so there is abiding curiosity about the war.

I thought that if I began with World War II as a "benchmark," some lessons might emerge about how to think about the postwar conflicts. That indeed turned out to be the case. There is much to be learned from what the Allies did in World War II that could have informed how the United States fought in Korea, Vietnam, and Iraq.

That is the reason I have dedicated this work to the millions of our countrymen in the US Armed Forces who were sent to fight in these conflicts—especially to those who never came home.

I have been profoundly impressed with Professor Eliot Cohen's *Supreme Command* and the five critical functions of leadership he identifies virtually on the first page of his seminal book. Whether friend or foe, combatant political and military leaders have to set direction, pick winning generals, plan and execute effectively, accommodate critical domestic and international constituencies, and communicate convincingly to wartime publics. The substantive definition and performance of these functions constitutes a strategic architecture. How well combatant statesmen and generals perform these functions determines conflict outcomes.

The outcomes in Korea, Vietnam, and Iraq by no means have been satisfying for Americans, not after the exhilaration of victory in fighting and winning a long, brutal, and total war in 1945. Explaining the outcomes in all these conflicts against the common framework of a strategic architecture is what this work is about.

All errors and misjudgments are mine.

ACKNOWLEDGMENTS

Many have helped me write a better manuscript. My deep gratitude goes out to the late Joann Bowen, who read early sections of the World War II and Korean draft; Jake Butts, who read early sections of the draft and offered much encouragement; the late Thomas F. Cave, colonel, USMC (Ret.), my first real boss in Saigon, who was a wonderful mentor in the ways the armed forces function and operate; Stanley H. Cochran, Korean War naval veteran and former TRW colleague, who read parts of the draft and offered helpful comments and suggestions; Larry Crandall, a Vietnam CORDS veteran, who offered helpful pointers; David W. P. Elliott, professor emeritus, Pomona College, who read the Vietnam chapter; Andrew R. Finlayson, colonel, USMC (Ret.), a Vietnam veteran and published scholar, who read the Vietnam chapter and shared many valuable insights, including his two superb books about his service in Vietnam; Leo J. Flynn, professor emeritus, Pomona College, who introduced me to the importance of Dallas Isom's Midway writing; George B. Forgie, professor, University of Texas, who read the manuscript and told me it needed more "connective tissue"—he was right; John P. Hamilton, who read an entire early draft and whose editing improved many passages; Stephen C. Hart, a former and venerable TRW boss, who read the entire draft multiple times and applied his formidable editing skills to the manuscript—Steve is the best there is; David J. Harbison, retired teacher, Cate School, Department of History, who offered helpful guidance; Peter Haslund, professor emeritus, Santa Barbara City College, a Vietnam veteran who served as a USAF intelligence officer and provided helpful operational insights into the execution of the *Igloo*

White program; Mark Helprin, who read the entire manuscript and offered helpful guidance; Steve Hunnisett, who researched and found valuable World War II photographs at the Imperial War Museum in London; the late William B. Hussey, captain, USNR (Ret.), a World War II veteran whose private published memoir is cited in this work; Rodney P. Katz, retired reference librarian, Library of Congress, who answered many arcane questions—he is truly a national resource; R. DeWitt "Kyle" Kirwan, an army captain in Vietnam who commanded a USMC/US Army Mobile Advisory Team in I Corps in 1969; H. R. McMaster, PhD, lieutenant general, US Army (Ret.), a decorated Iraq and Afghanistan veteran of multiple tours and published scholar, who reviewed an early version of the entire manuscript and clarified important details about his service in Iraq and Afghanistan—General McMaster's comments enabled me to improve the strategic architecture framework significantly; William P. Mac-Kinnon, member of the Montecito History Forum, for leading me to the little-known official and unofficial histories of the extensive American Lend-Lease route to Russia via the rail and truck "Persian Corridor" in Iran between 1942 and 1945; Carter Malkasian, director, Operations Team 3, Bureau of Conflict and Stabilization Operations (CSO), Department of State, who reviewed parts of the Iraq chapter, particularly with respect to his own service in the Garmser district of Helmand Province in Afghanistan; Frank Martini, cartographer, US Military Academy, Department of History, who was most helpful in navigating the department's excellent atlases, available online, many maps of which have been downloaded and modified for inclusion in this work; Michael S. Melnyk, Northrop Grumman colleague, who introduced me to the little-known Hideyoshi, the Japanese shogun who invaded Korea in the sixteenth century and discovered the perils of advancing to the Yalu River 450 years before General MacArthur did; A. E. Keir Nash, professor emeritus, UCSB, who read some of the World War II sections and offered helpful corrections; W. C. "Peter" Naylor, professor, Santa Barbara City College, Korean War veteran, who read much of the early draft; the late Hon. Ralph H. Nutter, lieutenant colonel, USAAF, who flew with General Curtis LeMay in the 8th Air Force and 20th Bomber Command as his lead navigator in both the Europe and Pacific theaters and reminded me what a superb air commander LeMay was; Douglas M. Pell, TRW–Northrop Grumman colleague, who convinced me that Midway made no sense as a stand-alone narrative without inclusion of Guadalcanal and the naval battles fought in the Lower Solomons in 1942 and who offered trenchant critiques of the strategic architecture thesis; Jeffrey Race, PhD, lieutenant colonel, US Army Reserve (Ret.), a Vietnam veteran who read the entire manuscript multiple times, offered superb edits, and is the author of the best book on the Vietnam War; Thomas S. Schrock, professor emeritus, UCSB, who read multiple parts of the draft and offered excellent suggestions; Terry R. Schultz, cataloging librarian (until 2012); Carla I. Garcia, assistant librarian; Molly

Krill Schlesinger, director of libraries (until 2016); and Kate Parker, director of library services, of the McBean Library, Cate School—Terry, Carla, Molly, and Kate were astonishingly resourceful in finding scores of academic titles and obscure documents; Robert V. Schwartz, colonel, USAF (Ret.), decorated Vietnam veteran, friend of many years, and former TRW colleague, who read the Vietnam chapter and provided helpful comments; Jay A. Stout, lieutenant colonel, USMC (Ret.), a Persian Gulf War combat veteran, F-18 fighter pilot, Northrop Grumman colleague, and published authority on the strategic bombing offensive, whose expert editing of this chapter made it much more accurate and readable; Elizabeth W. Woodworth, librarian and archivist emerita, Cate School, who read the entire draft and offered constant encouragement.

I am deeply grateful to my publisher, Rowman & Littlefield, for accepting my manuscript for publication. I especially want to thank Susan McEachern, senior editor and vice president, who recognized that the work of an unknown, unproven neophyte might be worthy of publication. I also want to express gratitude to her colleagues, Katelyn Turner and Janice Braunstein, for their expert guidance in introducing me to the rigorous process of turning a manuscript into this handsome volume.

I am particularly grateful to my wife, Karen L. Sketch, a professional graphic designer, who created or adapted all the many maps in this work, improved the graphics and numerous photo illustrations, and designed the cover image.

PART I

STRATEGIC ARCHITECTURES: INTRODUCTION

In the past seventy-five years, the United States has engaged in four major conflicts: World War II and the Korean, Vietnam, and Iraqi Wars.* Victory in World War II was marked by spontaneous, tumultuous, public celebrations. But there were no victories for Americans to celebrate at the end of the Korean, Vietnam, and Iraqi Wars. Why and how did the United States win World War II as part of a global coalition, fight to a stalemate in Korea, lose in Vietnam, and fail in Iraq?

World War II overshadows the three postwar conflicts in terms of scale, destruction, and lethality. It marks the last time the armed forces of the United States participated in a coalition that defeated an enemy coalition totally and completely, resulting in unconditional surrenders of the major Axis powers of Italy, Germany, and Japan. The three subsequent wars were "limited." But they were hard to limit or stop because escalation proved easier than termination as leaders struggled to maintain initiative, define effective policies, or contain conflict expansion and risk.

If World War II is used as the benchmark of success, examining the outcomes of the three principal post-1945 conflicts is difficult because none of them produced incontrovertible victories. Unlike the definitive close of World War II, they did not end with the signing of surrender documents. The definition of geopolitical success is much more complex and may not be

---

*Afghanistan could also be classified as a major conflict, but the final outcome remains uncertain. A brief discussion of the Afghanistan War after 9/11 fits within the strategic architecture analysis of the Iraqi War chapters.

defined in terms of simply winning or losing. But despite being smaller in scale, these conflicts bear similarities to World War II. The Korean, Vietnam, and Iraqi Wars all required enormous national commitments. They resulted in American deaths approaching a third of World War II levels—nearly three hundred thousand combat deaths in World War II versus one hundred thousand deaths for Korea, Vietnam, and Iraq combined. The post-1945 conflicts also required massive expenditures measured in trillions of dollars and produced bitter political controversies.

This book comprehensively examines the four wars against the conceptual framework of a *strategic architecture*. Its core focus is analyzing and explaining how and why the outcomes were so different.

Success or failure of the combatant strategic architectures in the four wars can be expressed as a straightforward thesis: strategic architectures are more likely to succeed when policy, strategy, and operations are in alignment. Alignment is the key concept, signaling that these three elements are arranged proportionally so that resulting operations can be designed and executed to achieve a successful geopolitical result. Alignment is the rigorous integration of policy, strategy, and operations; it is the essential thread that runs through the elements of an effective strategic architecture.

A strategic architecture consists of continually evolving policies, strategies, and operations by which combatant states endeavor to achieve a desired end state. Policy defines the high-level goals of the end state a nation seeks to achieve once it initiates a conflict or finds itself drawn into one. Statesmen direct a broad course of action and strive to control the initiative. When they make decisions, they have to respond to unforeseen conditions to guide and determine future decisions. Effective statesmen are skilled at organizing the constituencies they need to succeed and communicating to them convincingly. Strategy means employing whatever resources are available to achieve policy goals in situations that are dynamic because conflicts can change quickly over time. Operations are the actions that occur when statesmen, soldiers, and diplomats execute plans. At any given time, a state's strategic architecture is constrained by its capabilities, but it can develop more robust capabilities, allowing implementation of more ambitious policies and operations.

We might well ask why the concept of a strategic architecture is more useful than a definition of strategy. Lawrence Freedman cogently defines strategy as "maintaining a balance between ends, ways, and means; about identifying objectives; and about the resources and methods available for meeting such objectives." His seminal treatise acknowledges that this definition is well established, "although not in such a way to capture the dynamic interaction between ends, ways, and means. . . . That dynamic explains why strategy is the central political art. It is about getting more out of a situation than the starting balance of power would suggest. It is the art of creating power."[1]

The concept of a strategic architecture provides a framework to examine the dynamics of creating power that Freedman finds so interesting. Combatant success or failure in the four conflicts resulted from the beneficial or adverse effects of policy, strategy, and operations at various stages of each conflict. The strategic architecture concept integrates these three levels of thought and action. Policy defines the end states combatants hope to achieve. Strategy encompasses more than the overall planning and directing of armed forces. It is the expression of all the political, economic, psychological, and military capabilities of a nation to achieve goals. Operations are what statesmen and generals undertake to get the most out of a given situation and move on to the next stage of a conflict.

Strategy may well require coping with a crisis or preventing a dire situation from getting worse, as was the case for Great Britain in 1940. As Freedman puts it, "the first requirement might be one of survival."[2] Strategy demands the appointment of people who can effectively formulate and execute plans. Effective operational execution creates systems of accountability to monitor the performance of people, allocate resources, and make changes to both.

A strategic architecture is thus not a static blueprint per se but a dynamic vision of how a state can prevail in a conflict. It is a framework that allows us to study the tasks performed by competing statesmen, generals, and diplomats on the levels of policy, strategy, and operations. Examining how leaders in combatant states perform these multilevel tasks before, during, and after conflicts is a way to illuminate conflict outcomes.

In Eliot A. Cohen's formulation, "leaders at the top have some roughly similar tasks: setting direction, picking [effective] subordinates, monitoring performance, handling constituencies, and inspiring achievement."[3] A strategic architecture is thus a unifying concept to enable an analyst to assess why and how a state either succeeds or fails to achieve its goals in both peace and war by examining the interaction of policy, strategy, and operations. Leaders function within different cultures and ideologies, where governance can enhance or constrain their abilities to achieve successful outcomes.[4]

Cohen, who considers Winston Churchill "the greatest war statesman" of the twentieth century, wrote that Churchill "would have found the notion that one could produce a blueprint for victory at any time before, say, 1943 an absurdity bred of unfamiliarity with war itself." He quotes from notes the prime minister prepared for his first meeting with President Roosevelt in December 1941 after Pearl Harbor:

> War is a constant struggle and must be waged from day to day. It is only with some difficulty and within limits that provision can be made for the future. . . . Nevertheless, there must be a design and theme for bringing the war to a victorious end in a reasonable period. All the more is this necessary when under

modern conditions no large-scale offensive operation can be launched without
the preparation of elaborate technical apparatus.[5]

As the early chapters about World War II will show, the prime minister's
war statesmanship

> struck a middle position between those who would deny any possibility of
> strategy (as opposed to mere military opportunism . . .) and those who would
> reduce it to a blueprint. . . . Churchill believed that the formulation of strategy
> in war did not consist merely in drawing up state documents sketching out a
> comprehensive view of how the war would be won, but also in a host of detailed
> activities which, when united and dominated by a central conception, would
> form a comprehensive picture.[6]

I draw on two additional analytical distinctions to explain whether strategic architectures succeed or fail: the difference between discriminators and
differentiators and the difference between front-to-back and back-to-front
strategic planning.

Each combatant in the four conflicts had to create and effectively use discriminators or differentiators that enabled their armed forces to win battles.
Discriminators are attributes, qualities, or resources that are exclusive and
unique to a single combatant. Germany, for example, produced and deployed
discriminators during World War II such as exoatmospheric rockets with advanced propulsion and guidance systems and jet aircraft that flew in combat
months before the end of the war. However, in a failure of leadership, Hitler
was unable to take advantage of the discriminators to alter the outcome of
the war. In August 1945, American use of two atomic bombs to destroy two
Japanese cities was the strategic discriminator that ended the Pacific war and
obviated the need to invade the Japanese home islands, potentially saving
hundreds of thousands of American lives and probably millions of Asian lives.
The postwar controversies that erupted over American use of nuclear weapons continue to the present day. As we will discover in chapter 10, historical
debate persists over whether the atomic bombs were decisive or unnecessary
and immoral because of Russia's intervention against the Japanese Kwantung
Army in Manchukuo on the Asian mainland and the continued application of
overwhelming Allied conventional military and naval power against the home
islands. Together these operations would have produced mass Japanese and
Asian starvation in the fall of 1945. Debate centers on the magnitude of the
deaths resulting from the destruction of Hiroshima and Nagasaki, which are
known, and the deaths from the intensification of conventional power against
Japan, which historians have estimated.

Differentiators are attributes, qualities, or resources that are commonly
available to all combatants but of which one combatant has a greater supply,

such as more or better soldiers or matériel, and is able to use them effectively, such as employing smarter tactics. However, the creation of discriminators or differentiators per se does not guarantee combat success.

Frederick W. Kagan introduces the second analytical overlay on strategic outcomes: front-to-back versus back-to-front strategic planning.[7] In front-to-back planning, a combatant focuses on near-term requirements over the course of a conflict and does not think through the complete offensive chain of events needed to accomplish the strategic objective. Kagan's striking example of the inadequacy of front-to-back planning is the *Wehrmacht* reaching Moscow in December 1941 without the combat power to capture the city. Conversely, back-to-front planning requires the combatant to first assess the resources needed to win the final battle and then create a campaign plan that secures and marshals those resources toward the final objective. Given a choice, back-to-front planning is the better approach. One might think of back-to-front planning the way engineers conceive of "reverse engineering."[8] Kagan's front-to-back/back-to-front distinction is a powerful analytical tool, as we will see in the chapters that follow.

Back-to-front planning may not be possible in a defensive battle where a combatant is weaker and is forced to react to an enemy's offensive initiative, does not have an overarching plan, or lacks enough military resources to mount a strategic offensive until some future event, such as when Hitler's surprise invasion of Russia thirteen months after Churchill assumed office changed the balance of power favorably for the Allies. Churchill had to react and plan front-to-back during the Battle of Britain and initially during the Battle of the Atlantic. The US Navy's front-to-back planning before and after the Battle of Midway exploited strategic intelligence to attack the Japanese Combined Fleet sailing to invade Midway. After the Midway victory, the American recovery of the naval initiative enabled US Marine forces to invade Guadalcanal in the Lower Solomon Islands. This Solomon Islands campaign enabled the successful island-hopping campaign between 1943 and 1945.

Formal treatises on warfare have influenced the substance and exercise of supreme leadership for centuries. Among the writers on war in the Western canon, Carl P. G. von Clausewitz is dominant. Passages from *On War* permeate the strategic, doctrinal, and historical literature of most World War II and postwar combatants. The most widely quoted dictum that "war is merely the continuation of policy by other means"[9] is an Aristotelian recognition of the distinction between ends and means.[10]

By contrast, from the Eastern canon, Sun Tzu is the more venerable authority but less widely studied and followed by Western militaries. His Taoist tract antedated Clausewitz by more than two millennia and commands attention because he does not regard war as an instrument of rationally thought-out high policy. War simply happens, and when it does, "it is a matter of life or death."[11]

That is the second sentence in Sun Tzu's *The Art of War*, what Martin van Creveld describes as "the product of stern necessity."[12]

While Clausewitz was emphasizing maximum force through the state's monopoly on the means of organized violence to achieve political goals, the Chinese were recommending minimum force. The Oriental emphasis on minimum force leads to an obvious corollary, the use of trickery and deception of every sort over the application of brute strength. The former enables one to manipulate an adversary, neutralize his strengths, and turn one's own weaknesses to advantage. Brute strength encourages "stupidity and barbarism."[13]

Principles from both of these martial traditions are present in how statesmen and military leaders performed Cohen's tasks in World War II and the three postwar conflicts. Those who failed to grasp the principles in either canon were at a disadvantage.

Clausewitz's concepts dominated the conduct of World War II. Sun Tzu's concepts of less force, more use of stratagem and trickery, the value of patience, and the asymmetry between the powerful and the weak guided the behaviors of the enemy combatants in Korea, Vietnam, and Iraq. Clausewitz and Sun Tzu agree that war is an extension of national policy. Both accept the concept that national objectives should determine the wisdom of using military power and should guide and control its application. Clausewitz advocates clarity and caution: "No one starts a war—or rather, no one in his senses ought to do so—without first being clear in his mind what he intends to achieve by that war and how he intends to conduct it."[14] Both recognize the need for military genius. Neither discusses the value of allies in terms of the political leverage or force multiplier that alliances can create.[15]

Machiavelli's sixteenth-century handbook for rulers offered intelligent and realistic guidance to Churchill and Roosevelt on the necessity of alliances.

> Here let it be noted that a Prince should be careful never to join with one stronger than himself in attacking others, unless, as already said, he be driven to it by necessity. For if he whom you join prevails, you are at his mercy; and Princes, so far as in them lies, should avoid placing themselves at the mercy of others. . . . But when an alliance cannot be avoided, a Prince . . . must take a side. Nor let it be supposed that any State can choose for itself a perfectly safe line of policy. . . . Prudence therefore consists in knowing how to distinguish degrees of disadvantage, and in accepting a less evil as a good.[16]

After Hitler's surprise attack on the Soviet Union on June 22, 1941, Churchill wasted little time in trying to ally Britain with the Soviet Union. His private secretary, John R. Colville, before his first radio broadcast, reminded him of the irony of allying himself with the same Bolshevik enemy he had sought to "strangle in its cradle."[17] Churchill retorted with Machiavellian realism: "If Hitler invaded hell I would make at least a favourable reference to the devil in the House of Commons."[18]

Where Sun Tzu and Clausewitz differ is over the latter's preference for comprehensive warfare, concentration of force, and fighting the "decisive battle" to destroy an enemy's armed forces. Sun Tzu argues that while it is true that when war comes, a nation must mobilize its resources to prevail, a country should not necessarily seek total war in which the objective is complete destruction of the enemy. The survival of one's own nation may be put at risk. Sun Tzu's strategic principles of war place less emphasis on brute-force violence.[19] He considered the art of war to be getting what you want at the lowest possible price: win all without fighting; achieve the objective without destroying it; avoid strength, attack weakness; deceive the enemy with fore-knowledge; shape the enemy; use speed and prepare carefully; lead through character-based qualities; reinforce success, starve failure.

Whether combatant leaders in the four conflicts we are considering actually read Clausewitz or Sun Tzu or were directly influenced by their ideas is less important than analytically studying how nations and armies during all four conflicts acted as if Clausewitz or Sun Tzu had influenced their doctrines and preparations for war. Clausewitz's and Sun Tzu's approaches to war led to significant differences and emphases. The differences are noted to show how and why leaders favored maneuver versus attrition, attacked weakness rather than strength, emphasized leadership over management, or tried to exploit advanced technology.

The eleven chapters in part II outline how the strategic architecture of World War II evolved and why it ended in an Allied victory. The later chapters on Korea, Vietnam, and Iraq examine these conflicts in considerable detail against the strategic architecture framework to illuminate what went right and what went wrong. Each chapter examines combatant policy, strategy, and operations. The assessments and conclusions draw mainly from canonical secondary works, with probes into archival documents where warranted.

How might successful outcomes have been defined differently in order to produce better strategic architectures in Korea, Vietnam, and Iraq that aligned policy, strategy, and operations more coherently?

The five chapters in part III on Korea demonstrate that General Douglas MacArthur could have used the decisive military advantage he created after his brilliant counterstroke at Inchon in November–December 1950 to restore the sovereignty of South Korea, force the North Korean army to move back north of the 38th parallel, and reinstall the preexisting governmental authority in South Korea. A strong military presence might have buttressed South Korea in defending itself from any future invasion by North Korea. All of these criteria were met by the armistice in 1953. Could MacArthur's stunning military success at Inchon have avoided Chinese intervention, two and a half more years of attrition combat, and tens of thousands more casualties? Could MacArthur's brief meeting with President Truman on Wake Island in October 1950 have addressed a strategic architecture in detail about how the war could end in 1950 instead of 1953?

The seven chapters in part IV on Vietnam identify how a more realistic strategic architecture against the communist revolutionary movement might have been the creation of a stronger governing regime that could draw sufficient legitimacy from urban and rural constituencies to exercise its authority nationally and administer Vietnam's provinces and rural districts with competent military, paramilitary, and law enforcement organizations. Such a regime might have attracted enough popular support to counteract the highly disciplined, ruthless, and well-led communist revolutionary movement attempting to overthrow the government and the society underpinning it.

The six chapters in part V on Iraq identify how geopolitical success might be defined as the formulation of a strategic architecture to create and support an effective governing regime backed by Iraq's three major population groups, Shias, Sunnis, and Kurds. Such a regime could defend itself against interference by neighboring states and defeat Sunni insurgent or jihadist Islamic movements that use violence and terror to undermine the regime's authority. Indeed, these criteria are explicit in current American policy. However, Iraq has been a continuing challenge for American governments for a quarter century. It leaves open the question of whether a succession of US governments has the resolution and capability to sustain a strategic architecture where a long game is required.

The Iraqi Wars underscore a weakness in the exercise of American military power, as did the wars in Korea and Vietnam. The strategic architectures in all of these postwar conflicts reveal an American deficiency in terminating conflicts without a well-planned successful endgame.

Part VI summarizes the success or failure of the strategic architectures in the four wars and describes what can be learned in the form of four simple imperatives that future practitioners might profitably consider, whether they are statesmen, soldiers, or diplomats. Statesmen who know or can learn how to translate these imperatives into a realistic alignment of policies, strategies, and operations can design much more effective—in some cases winning—strategic architectures.

PART II

WORLD WAR II

Examination of the Allied World War II victory unpacks ten selected major battles or campaigns into their geopolitical and military details. These were battles that the Allies had to fight and win, and certainly could not afford to lose. The rationale for their selection emerges from the way the strategic architectures for each of the principal combatants evolved and changed over time, often in response to events that could not possibly have been predicted.

Chapters are designed to explain how the Axis dictators in Germany and Japan began the war with flawed strategic architectures, wildly unrealistic expectations on how the war would evolve, and equally unrealistic preparations for what turned out to be a very long global war. For example, Hitler found himself surprised at British resolution after learning of the Chamberlain government's declaration of war on September 3, 1939. Glaring at his foreign minister, Joachim von Ribbentrop, he asked, "What now?"[1]

The operational narratives show how and why the major combatants' strategic architectures had to change over time in response to actions by their enemies. It is in the comparative analysis of the evolving Allied and Axis strategic architectures that the war's final outcome can be better understood. Germany believed after its early blitzkrieg successes in Poland and the Low Countries that the string of quick victories would continue. Japan believed that the shock of the surprise attack on the US Pacific Fleet at Pearl Harbor would compel America to reach an accommodation with Japan in the Pacific, preoccupied as it soon would be fighting Germany. These early Axis successes turned out to be illusory. By the middle years of the war, the Allies were performing their strategic architecture tasks better than their Axis enemies. They set strategic direction, selected military leaders, executed military plans, and communicated with their vital constituencies well enough to start winning.

The selected battles show how the range of forces grew and evolved over time, how the balance of forces changed hands, how the Axis powers failed in the end to exploit their early military advantages, how German and Japanese military thinking fell behind Allied learning and innovation, and how each side created critical outcome-producing discriminators or differentiators. Focusing on how the discriminators and differentiators affected military outcomes yields insights that illuminate the Allied victory.

Chapters 1 through 5 explain six defensive battles: the Battle of Britain, the Battle of the Atlantic, the invasion of Russia (Operation *Barbarossa*), and the Battles of El Alamein, Midway, and Guadalcanal, where the Allies fought to resist Axis expansion. These battles were fought with reactive, front-to-back plans where a comprehensive, war-winning strategy for the Allies was not yet ready for realistic execution.

Chapter 1 discusses Churchill's strategic problem in June 1940: to demonstrate that Britain could persevere credibly as a viable combatant against the Axis powers. As long as Fighter Command could fly interception missions against the *Luftwaffe*, Germany could not achieve air supremacy over southern England and the English Channel.

Chapter 2 establishes that fighting the Battle of the Atlantic was a necessary condition for Britain's survival as a viable belligerent. The Allied navies and merchant fleets sustained appalling losses until effective execution of an antisubmarine strategy defeated the U-boats.

Chapter 3 describes Germany's surprise invasion of Russia. Operation *Barbarossa* changed the balance of forces among the combatants. Examining selected *Barbarossa* battles shows why it was to Anglo-American strategic advantage to help the Red Army kill more Germans on the Continent. Indeed, by the end of the war, the Soviets had sustained 95 percent of the combat casualties. Democracy was saved by the enormous sacrifices and military effort of soldiers and citizens of the Soviet Union fighting on behalf of communism.[2] Nearly twenty-seven million Soviet citizens lost their lives during the war, twelve million of them military personnel.[3]

Chapter 4 shows that Churchill, to win the Battle of El Alamein, took risky decisions during the first three years of the war to reinforce British forces in the Middle East. He needed military success in the North African desert by 1942 because of the imperatives of coalition warfare—keeping both Americans and Russians convinced that Britain could bear its share in defeating Axis armies.

Chapter 5 presents the Battle of Midway as an early decisive victory in June 1942 for the US Navy. The surprise naval upset at the Battle of Midway enabled the US Navy and Marine Corps to go on the offensive in the Lower Solomon Islands where a series of fleet engagements were fought over a period of seven months in which the Imperial Japanese Navy ultimately lost and found itself on the defensive in the Pacific for the rest of the war.

Chapters 6 through 10 explain five more battles that were proactive and offensive: the strategic bombing offensive over Europe, the Italian campaign, D-Day and the battle for Normandy, the battle for the Rhine, and the invasion of Okinawa and the atomic bombing of Japan. These battles and campaigns marked shifts in the Allied-Axis balance of forces in which the Allies regained the military initiative, eventually decisively. *Decisive* in this World War II context connoted more than simply military defeat in the field; it also meant one side winning the war and the other surrendering, formally acknowledging defeat. Victory was not the result of the execution of a single grand plan, particularly in the early years of the war. Allied strategy between 1939 and 1942 was reactive and front-to-back. It became proactive and back-to-front, more offensively oriented, by late 1942 and early 1943. Total global victory very much depended on executing a sequence of major operations and campaigns on multiple continents and then sustaining and expanding the capability to fight and win a long series of battles of attrition.

Chapter 6 analyzes the evolving strategic architecture of the Anglo-American strategic bombing offensive over Europe, which began in 1940 and continued until the last weeks of the war. The evidence points to decisive if unintended strategic benefits for the Allies. By late 1942–1943, Allied air forces began to execute an offensive bombing campaign to strike at German industrial and urban targets. They destroyed Germany's sixty largest cities. When they started attacking single-point failure targets like Germany's ball-bearing plants, they came tantalizingly close to destroying Germany's war-fighting infrastructure, but they could not sustain the campaign because of the appalling losses to their air wings. Only when they realized that bombers could not fly offensive missions without long-range fighter escorts could they achieve the necessary air supremacy to ensure the success of the Second Front.

Chapter 7 explains why the outcome of high-level strategic debates among Anglo-American leaders resulted in the invasion of Italy. The Allied strategic architecture of an early invasion to liberate the overrun countries of northwest Europe was not viable in 1943. Churchill succeeded in convincing his American ally that deferring the invasion until mid-1944 was the only realistic strategic option after victory in North Africa. Meanwhile, American and Allied forces already deployed to the Mediterranean theater invaded Italy because they could.

Chapter 8 examines the invasion of Normandy and the sanguinary land battles that followed. The D-Day execution of Operation *Overlord* resolved more than two and a half years of often acrimonious Anglo-American debate about where, when, and how to invade the Continent. The successful landing in Normandy quickly revealed that German land forces in the last year of the war were still quite lethal and formidable. The *Wehrmacht* fought a tenacious series of defensive battles so effectively that American officers would study them for decades, well into the Cold War years of the 1980s.[4]

Chapter 9 elaborates on the Battle of the Rhine to show the enormous scale of operations as Allied armies closed on Germany. It offers a rebuttal to the popular perception that the invasion of Europe was a mopping-up operation after the D-Day success and the breakout from the Normandy beachhead. A brutal war of attrition ensued after the Normandy breakout and the failure of the airborne assault in Holland to outflank German defenses and then drive into the Ruhr. Success was measured in small territorial increments. The "ninety-division gamble" the army of the United States undertook between 1942 and 1945 limited the margin of combat effectiveness.[5] American divisions had to learn or relearn new combat skills in the field in the midst of continual military operations.

Chapter 10 explains how the invasion of Okinawa in the spring of 1945 and the costly attrition battles that followed influenced the decision to use the atomic bomb to destroy two Japanese cities. In this case, the atomic bomb was a decisive discriminator.

A coherent understanding of the emergence of the international system from the mid-twentieth to the early twenty-first century is impossible without reference to World War II. The Allied victory in 1945 created the conditions for the international system that benefits the world to the present day. That geopolitical success came at a steep price for all combatants. The war raged for six years across the states and territories of the world where Germany, Italy, and Japan were nation wreckers. As Churchill noted in the second of his early famous speeches, "many old and famous States" fell to the grip of the Gestapo. He could have added the Italian OVRA[6] and the Japanese *Kempeitai*, because the list of nations and territories that the Axis sought to wipe out during the 1930s and 1940s was a lengthy one: Ethiopia, Poland, Latvia, Lithuania, Estonia, Ukraine, Byelorussia, Crimea, China, Indochina, the Malay Peninsula, the Philippines, and the Dutch East Indies were among the victims. All still bear scars and vivid memories from the war. More than fifty million people lost their lives.

The United States created the peace that followed the Axis surrenders with well-led, well-planned, and well-financed programs of military occupation and nation building. These initiatives lasted longer than the war itself, and they required expenditures that approached the cost of winning the war. Winning World War II left the United States with its highest historical level of public debt, which approached 120 percent of GDP.[7]

That is why the nation-building successes the Western Allies achieved are so important to remember. These accomplishments are part of the World War II benchmark, too. Many of the states of Western Europe recovered levels of prewar prosperity as early as 1947–1948. Seventy years later, most of the nations of Europe and the Pacific Rim have become participants in the most politically and economically successful international system in history, with levels of prosperity for billions unimaginable in 1939. Today, the stability of this international system is again under direct attack by enemies who are back in the odious business of wrecking nations. Islamic jihadists are bulldozing national borders, executing nonbelievers, and subjecting whole populations to their authoritarian yoke. The term *failed state* is part of the world's geopolitical vocabulary.

There is a mass of historical evidence available to deploy about World War II and the three postwar conflicts that illuminates these recurring thematics.[8] How wars end is more important than how they begin. Nation building until a generation ago had a respectable place within foreign-policy discourse. Wars cannot end in victory without long, well-thought-out end-games to guarantee the peace. Successful strategic architectures depend upon leaders who can see into the void and master the substance of aligning policy, strategy, and operations.

1

BATTLE OF BRITAIN

Winning by Not Losing

On May 10, 1940, Winston Churchill became the prime minister of the United Kingdom. On the very day he succeeded Neville Chamberlain, Hitler unleashed the *Wehrmacht* on Western Europe. The Battle of France had begun and would soon end in disaster on the beaches of Dunkirk. Less than a month later, the Battle of Britain would begin.

Freedman's definition of *strategy* includes making the best of a bad situation. That was precisely the front-to-back challenge the prime minister had to confront—Churchill's task was national survival. He needed to define a policy and strategy by which he could win by not losing. Britain possessed two critical discriminators. The historical record in this chapter shows that a well-designed, operationally prepared air force and a large navy in home waters made the difference.

POLICY

On May 13, 1940, Churchill stated Britain's war policy in the first of three famous speeches to the House of Commons:

> I would say to the House, as I said to those who have joined this government: "I have nothing to offer but blood, toil, tears and sweat." . . . You ask, what is our policy? I can say: It is to wage war, by sea, land and air, with all our might and with all the strength that God can give us; to wage war against a monstrous tyranny, never surpassed in the dark, lamentable catalogue of human crime. That is our

policy. You ask, what is our aim? I can answer in one word: It is victory . . . for without victory, there is no survival.[1]

When Churchill spoke these words, he didn't know that the military collapse of the French army was imminent. Two weeks later, on June 4, 1940, as the German invasion on the Continent was about to overwhelm France, Churchill delivered his second major speech.

> Even though large tracts of Europe and many old and famous States have fallen or may fall into the grip of the Gestapo and all the odious apparatus of Nazi rule, we shall not flag or fail. We shall go on to the end, we shall fight in France, we shall fight on the seas and oceans, we shall fight with growing confidence and growing strength in the air, we shall defend our Island, whatever the cost may be, we shall fight on the beaches, we shall fight on the landing grounds, we shall fight in the fields and in the streets, we shall fight in the hills; we shall never surrender.[2]

These eloquent words were the language of defiance. They did not define a strategic architecture to win the war. But Churchill did passionately establish that he was the man in charge, and he would eventually create one.

On June 18, 1940, Churchill delivered a third speech before a packed House, where he spoke the words that would give the battle its name: "What General Weygand[3] called the Battle of France is over. I expect the Battle of Britain is about to begin. . . . The whole fury and might of the enemy must very soon be turned upon us. Hitler knows he will have to break us in this island or lose the war."[4]

Churchill reasoned that Hitler had to establish air superiority over southeast England and the Channel as a precondition to a successful German invasion. He argued that if Britain could hold out during the summer, adverse weather in the Dover Strait would make it almost impossible for Germany to execute a large-scale amphibious assault across the English Channel by fall.

During the battle, the combatants made a chain of decisions that would broadly determine the future course of the war. Germany, in a position of military triumph after overrunning six countries on the Continent within the space of a few weeks, squandered its military initiative during the summer of 1940.[5]

During the interwar years, Britain had developed the two discriminators that favored the balance of forces in the pending conflict. RAF Fighter Command was prepared to fight precisely the kind of battle Britain faced in the summer of 1940. The Royal Navy's Home Fleet outnumbered the *Kriegsmarine* by a factor of ten to one in capital ships and destroyers.

Churchill knew something else. He understood the need to mobilize his countrymen in the summer of 1940 rather than allow the appeasement constituencies time to brood and the broader population to contemplate Britain's dark realities. He knew that his government faced a choice between two alternatives: a compromise peace with Hitler or an all-out drive for total war. Churchill chose the latter. He convinced the nation that winning the coming battle was necessary. No other British leader at the time had the willpower, the personality, or the set of talents to achieve what he did.[6]

STRATEGY

Most of the strategic decisions had been made by both sides years before the battle began. In 1940 the German air force was incapable of projecting air-power across the English Channel for decisive attacks on industrial or urban targets. German airpower in Poland and later the Low Countries operated ahead of rapidly advancing ground columns to inflict devastating damage on Allied armies, but it never occurred to German air leaders that it might need an air force of heavy bombers, protected by fighters, to break an entire country. As chapter 6 will show in greater detail, Germany in the prewar years never developed a four-engine bomber that could match the British Halifax or Lancaster or the American B-17. In 1940, German two-engine bombers were generally no match for the RAF.[7]

Fighter Command under the leadership of Air Chief Marshal Sir Hugh C. T. Dowding was the best-prepared fighter force in the world by a considerable margin. In June 1940, Fighter Command was ready to fight the battle it had planned and trained for since Dowding assumed command in 1936. By 1938, two state-of-the-art fighters were entering RAF service, the Hurricane and the Spitfire, which proved to be a match for the German Me-109.[8] These fighters were the first truly modern monoplane fighters of the era, with such features as robust airframes; powerful engines; well-engineered airfoils, enabling high-speed, high-altitude maneuverability; enclosed canopies; retractable landing gear; HF and/or VHF[9] radios; and wing-mounted armaments (cannons and/or machine guns).[10] By May 1936, the Air Ministry had placed an order for 600 Hurricanes, and shortly thereafter it placed another order for 310 Spitfires. The men with the strategic foresight to make these critical decisions served in the government of Prime Minister Stanley Baldwin.[11]

British Spitfire and Hurricane pilots had three advantages. They flew over their own territory, they could fly quick-reaction interception missions, and they could operate in the air longer. The Me-109 carried only enough fuel to remain airborne for about an hour, which meant that after spending twenty minutes flying across the Channel and back, German fighter pilots had at most forty minutes for aerial combat.[12]

Both sides possessed cadres of experienced combat pilots when the war started, but Fighter Command had lost 435 pilots between mid-May and early June in the Battle of France and during the Dunkirk evacuation. As a result, many fresh British pilots were fed into the battle with almost no preparation for aerial combat. At the height of fighting, Dowding had to agree to cut the operational training period to two weeks between learning to fly and entering combat. However, any advantage the Germans enjoyed in the air was soon neutralized because RAF pilots quickly learned their deadly business.

For the young men who climbed into Hurricane and Spitfire cockpits, it was a brave feat simply to land such a high-speed airplane, let alone do battle in one. Possessing flying skills, keen eyesight, quick reflexes, and the ability to "aim off" for the correct deflection after pressing the fire button on the control stick was not enough to shoot down enemy planes. Some pilots found the courage to fly "very, very close to the enemy," at distances between 75 and 175 yards—often on course for collision—to achieve results. In the limit, two fighters, such as a Spitfire and an Me-109, flying directly at each other on a collision course were closing at a combined speed of over six hundred miles per hour, nearly three hundred yards per second. To fly that close to the enemy, remember to fire only a short burst (the planes had only enough ammunition to fire for less than fifteen seconds), and judge whether to break left or right at the last instant in order to avoid a midair collision required extraordinary sangfroid and instant reflexes. At such close ranges, the eight machine guns on Spitfires and Hurricanes could be devastating to an enemy aircraft.[13]

The pilots were directed by one of the first real-time command-and-control systems ever developed for air defense. Known as the Dowding System, it consisted of two types of coastally deployed ground-based radars, which could detect aircraft flying at either higher (Chain Home) or lower (Chain Home Low) altitudes over the sea from the Continent. A widely deployed Observer Corps could track enemy aircraft as they flew inland because radar coverage deployed on the coastline faced seaward.[14] Years before the war, these elements had already been integrated into a fighter command, control, and communications network in which roles and functions were clearly defined.

The Dowding System emerged as the result of prewar strategic thinking and concerted preparation. A historical reckoning of the Battle of Britain can be reduced to a few individuals within "the Few," who together created the discriminator for the outcome. Stephen Bungay identified ten men whose initiative and actions in the years before the battle made the difference: Churchill, who got the battle fought; Dowding, who transformed Fighter Command into a weapons system; Air Vice Marshal Keith R. Park, who tactically wielded the weapon that Dowding strategically created; Major General Edward B. Ashmore, who commanded London's air defenses during World War I and laid down the principles for the Observer Corps; Sir Henry T. Tizard, who led the scientific team responsible for putting the RAF at the forefront of radar technology; Sir Robert A. Watson-Watt, who developed and refined Tizard's radar work until it worked well enough to be used in war;[15] Sir Sydney Camm, who in 1934 led the team that designed and produced the Hurricane fighter;[16] Reginald J. Mitchell, who designed the Spitfire; Ernest W. Hives, who developed the Rolls-Royce Merlin engine that powered both the Hurricane and the Spitfire; and Sir Ralph S. Sorley (later air marshal), who ensured that the RAF in 1940 was the only air force in the world with eight-gun fighters.[17]

Without "the Ten," there likely would have been a very different outcome.[18] The RAF pilots, of course, had by far the most dangerous and visible job. The Germans could not field an air force as knowledgeable or innovative.

Equally significant, there was a British intelligence coup early in the war. By 1940, the British Government Code and Cipher School at Bletchley Park outside London was decrypting high-grade German cipher traffic. This success derived from Polish mathematicians who in 1939 had provided Britain with German encryption sets known as Enigma and a mathematical depiction of how the Enigma electromechanical rotor cipher encryption system worked by enciphering individual letters or digits. Both the Chamberlain and Churchill governments backed the code-breaking operation that provided a reliable stream of intelligence about the *Luftwaffe*. When these sources were coupled with radar, Fighter Command was able to intercept almost every bombing raid.[19]

OPERATIONS

The map of the battle illustrates the geometry of the confined airspace, the proximity of the deployments of the air groups on both sides, and the ranges of the radars (map 1.1). Reasonably accurate data and information about enemy air formations (i.e., position, number, altitude, and direction) could be collected and processed in multiple command centers, shared widely in near real time, and passed simultaneously among multiple levels of command from headquarters at Bentley Priory outside of London to groups, sectors, and fighter stations located on forward airfields. Bungay described this system as "in effect an analogue intranet. Whilst it was used to transmit orders down the chain of command, it was also designed to allow anybody in the system to find out what they wanted when they wanted from anybody else. It was a network organization based on telephone lines rather than e-mail."[20]

Then there was the second discriminator. The Germans had to defeat an island where the naval balance of forces overwhelmingly favored Britain.[21] German *Grossadmiral* Erich J. A. Raeder doubted the feasibility of a cross-Channel invasion on the scale required. Operation *Sea Lion* planners in the *Kriegsmarine* judged the naval risks to be daunting (map 1.2).

Orchestrating the sailing of an invasion fleet and landing men and matériel on a defended, blacked-out English shore across one of the most meteorologically

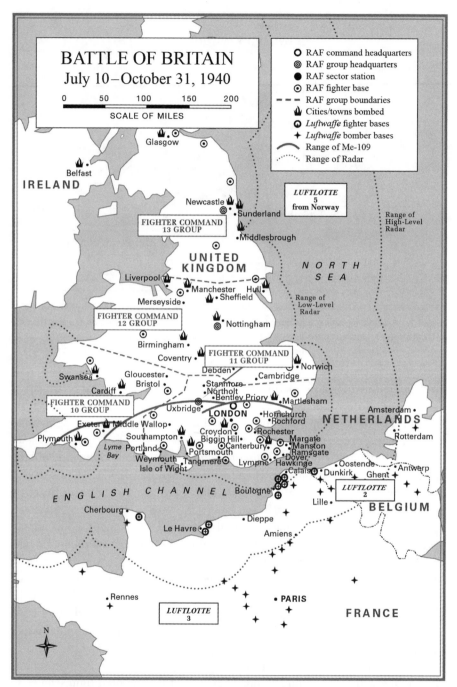

BATTLE OF BRITAIN
July 10–October 31, 1940

0   50   100   150   200
SCALE OF MILES

○ RAF command headquarters
◎ RAF group headquarters
● RAF sector station
⊙ RAF fighter base
‐ ‐ ‐ RAF group boundaries
🔥 Cities/towns bombed
Ⓐ *Luftwaffe* fighter bases
✦ *Luftwaffe* bomber bases
⌒ Range of Me-109
⋯ Range of Radar

**LUFTLOTTE
5
from Norway**

Range of
High-Level
Radar

Glasgow

Belfast
IRELAND

Newcastle
Sunderland
**FIGHTER COMMAND
13 GROUP**
Middlesbrough

**UNITED
KINGDOM**

*N O R T H
S E A*

Liverpool
Manchester   Hull
Merseyside   Sheffield

**FIGHTER COMMAND
12 GROUP**

Nottingham

Range of
Low-Level
Radar

Birmingham
Coventry
**FIGHTER COMMAND
11 GROUP**
Debden   Norwich
Gloucester   Cambridge
Swansea   Bristol   Stanmore
Cardiff   Northolt
**FIGHTER COMMAND
10 GROUP**   Bentley Priory   Martlesham
Uxbridge   **LONDON**   **NETHERLANDS**
Amsterdam
Exeter   Middle Wallop   Hornchurch
Rochford   Rotterdam
Plymouth   Southampton   Croydon   Rochester
Biggin Hill   Margate
Lyme Portland   Canterbury   Manston
Bay   Portsmouth   Dover   Ramsgate
Weymouth   Tangmere   Hawkinge
Isle of Wight   Lympne   Oostende   Antwerp
Calais   Dunkirk   Ghent

E N G L I S H   C H A N N E L   Boulogne
**LUFTLOTTE
2**
Lille   **BELGIUM**

Cherbourg
Dieppe
Le Havre   Amiens

Rennes
• PARIS
**LUFTLOTTE
3**
FRANCE

N

Map 1.1. The geometry of the confined airspace favored the RAF because British fighters flew over home territory, whereas *Luftwaffe* aircraft had to fly from the Continent, allowing shorter periods over targets.

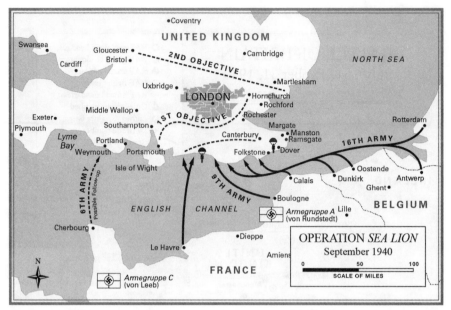

Map 1.2. Assembling, sailing, and timing the arrival of multiple German invasion fleets across the meteorologically unpredictable English Channel was a daunting enterprise.

Source: "German Invasion Plans for the British Isles 1940" (Berlin: Military High Command, Department for War Maps and Communications, 1940), English translation, archived in the Bodleian Library, Oxford University.

volatile bodies of water in the world required assembling large transport fleets from Rotterdam to Cherbourg, then launching them at night from Ostend, Dunkirk, Calais, Boulogne, and Le Havre. Maintaining tight time-tables for multiple convoys of ships in column on different compass head-ings, navigating without aid of buoys through alternately flooding and ebbing tides, sailing into fast-moving currents, and avoiding banks, shoals, rocks, and enemy minefields in the Dover–Calais Narrows did not constitute an inviting mission for the German navy.

Execution required landing an initial force of 90,000 men, 4,500 horses, and 650 tanks simultaneously on beaches along a stretch of southeast English coast spanning 225 miles, from Ramsgate in the east to Lyme Bay west of Weymouth. This landing was to be followed by a second wave of 160,000 men and 50,000 horses,[22] thirty-one divisions with eight in reserve.[23] Whether the Royal Navy would have to attack an invasion fleet became a second-order issue as the flow of events ensued. The air battle emerged as the foreground issue.

Air Vice Marshal Park under Dowding commanded Fighter Command 11 Group, the one of the four groups that occupied the central role of protecting the southeast sectors around London. For all of the vaunted omniscience of a totalitarian state, none of the German intelligence services ever bothered to acquire a staff college paper that Park had written in 1922 specifying effective fighter tactics in World War I. They were stated as four lessons learned: (1) wide dispersal of squadrons; (2) ground-strafing attacks on enemy airfields by small, fast, agile aircraft; (3) offensive patrols or fighter sweeps rather than close (bomber) escorts to establish control over airspace; and (4) ongoing, thorough appraisal of tactics on the ground instead of improvisation in the air.[24] These four points underlay the defensive air tactics that Dowding and Park developed together to fight the battle.

Park and Dowding assumed that the Germans would give up if they discovered that they were getting nowhere, even if their losses remained moderate. Park was at the center of tactical preparation insofar as it was he who decided how many aircraft to deploy against each attack and where to send his squadrons into action. The tactics were straightforward: pilots received orders over the command network to scramble, flew straight for the enemy directed by radio transmissions from sector controllers, attacked the enemy formations, and then returned to base. Squadrons deployed as single flights or small groups of flights were harder to detect than a large wing that took time to assemble and vector.[25] They attacked from different directions, easily confusing the enemy as to their numbers and overall strength.

If German Me-109s flying high cover for the bombers dove on the interceptors en masse, they abandoned the "high ground" and left their own bombers vulnerable to subsequent interceptions by Hurricanes and Spitfires. German bomber streams could be subjected in this manner to continual risk of attack. These very selective deployments meant that each Fighter Command squadron that successfully located the enemy would inevitably find a target-rich environment. Attacking the *Luftwaffe* with smaller formations reduced the risks of Dowding's entire force being decimated, especially if favorable kill ratios could be maintained. The name of the game was always to balance force commitments so that an attrition battle could be fought until the enemy realized that it was achieving small returns for such large losses of its own.

Neither side defeated the other in the traditional sense of victory. Nevertheless, Bungay's appraisal is crisp: "Fighter Command's victory was decisive." His and Richard Overy's analysis of kill ratios were the same—Bungay's ratio is 1.8:1, with Fighter Command destroying 1,887 German aircraft against British losses of 1,023; Overy's is 1.9:1.[26]

The German fighter commander, *Generalmajor* Theodore "Theo" Osterkamp, knew from the start of the battle that he faced a fundamental dilemma. He needed a very high kill ratio (on the order of five to one) in a short period of time to succeed in achieving air superiority. That had been the *Luftwaffe's* experience since Poland, when it had succeeded in destroying large numbers of enemy aircraft parked on the ground. Dowding's and Park's tactics of flying very selective interceptions into dense enemy formations prevented that.

Osterkamp had roughly two months to succeed before Channel weather worsened. This time pressure meant he needed to sustain a high kill ratio, which also meant the *Luftwaffe* had to fly every day when weather permitted.

Park was more cunning. He never rose to the bait of a big battle where he tried to intercept every German formation. As a result, Fighter Command pilots accomplished two things: on days when the Germans flew large formations, RAF pilots could rip into large enemy formations and generally achieve kill ratios exceeding their overall average of 1.8:1; on days when the Germans flew smaller formations, the *Luftwaffe* did better, but because of fewer sorties flown, the absolute numbers of downed RAF aircraft and pilots were not large enough. In other words, Osterkamp could not get both good results and big battles consistently. The overall attrition favoring Fighter Command took its toll on *Luftwaffe* strength. By October, it was a spent force.

The received wisdom about the outcome derives from Churchill's mythologization of "the Few": the perception that a few thousand British fighter pilots were a superior breed to their German counterparts. Bungay and others argue that they were not. Operationally, Fighter Command's leadership outsmarted Osterkamp and the air commanders over him. *Reichsmarschall* Hermann Göring and his three *Luftflotte* commanders, Albert Kesselring, Hugo Sperrle, and Hans-Jürgen Stumpff, were "out-generaled."[27] Bungay, Overy, and Len Deighton assembled a convincing body of evidence that the German failure over England in 1940 was a failure of leadership.

As the battle intensified, German air commanders saw neither the lethal threat Fighter Command presented nor the need for the same degree of close teamwork and hands-on command intensity that their British counterparts displayed. They failed to develop advance insights into how Dowding and Park would fight the battle. They had not read the staff paper Park had written in 1922, for example, which might have pointed them in the right direction.

Ironically, the *Luftwaffe* had created a special unit, called *Erprobungsgruppe* 210, translated by Bungay as "Operational Trials Wing." Widespread adoption of *Erprobungsgruppe* 210's techniques might have made a difference. Its specialty was accurately bombing critical targets such as the radar antennas on the English coast and Fighter Command's most important forward airfields. Had the *Luftwaffe* at the height of the battle concentrated on these kinds of critical targets and kept the pressure on by repeated attacks on them, the RAF time to recover and make good their losses of vital combat support systems, particularly when blinded by destroyed radar equipment, could have been decisively reduced, and the outcome might have been different. *Erprobungsgruppe* 210's mission results indicated that the tactics were proven, but senior *Luftwaffe* commanders did not see that this unit's combat performance was showing the *Luftwaffe* the way to break Fighter Command's ground organization. Instead, the German command vacillated among choices of target systems, wasted valuable squadrons bombing London,[28] and failed to concentrate on breaking Fighter Command's backbone of mission-critical support: the radar antennas (which were difficult to repair) and command-and-control nodes, without which early-warning radar detection information and its translation into interception orders would have been impossible.

Hitler's decision to attack Britain with airpower failed because Germany before the war began had not created the right kind of air force. Reich prewar industrial policy had failed to design and produce an air force that could successfully project airpower decisively with four-engine heavy bombers. Germany had no heavy bombers. On paper, the *Luftwaffe* presented overwhelming airpower mass, but it was the wrong kind of mass with the wrong kind of leadership at the top. *Reichsmarschall* Göring was totally unprepared to lead and command a modern air force. Hitler's 1935 appointment of Göring to command the *Luftwaffe* omitted valuable years of professional experience where he would have received a thorough grounding in command, strategy, tactics, and staff work.[29]

Neither Göring nor his key command subordinates analyzed Fighter Command as a weapons system. They could have "reverse engineered" the way Park generated fighter sorties to discover critical vulnerabilities.[30] Kesselring experimented with trial-and-error methods during the initial phases of the battle. His *Luftflotte* 2 tried large and small bomber formations, large waves of aircraft that then divided into smaller streams, surprise attacks, strafing runs, feints, and saturation targeting, including the low-altitude attacks by *Erprobungsgruppe* 210. But he failed to learn what had to be done to win. The *Luftwaffe* did not concentrate attacks on the single-point failure nodes first, such as the radar sites, then the command-and-control centers at all levels, followed by the airfields, and then the aircraft and pilots. What mattered in destroying this kind of target hierarchy was bombing accuracy. This was the strategy Park feared most: if the attacks had been pressed aggressively and frequently enough, the outcome in the air might have been different.[31]

The strategic architecture of the Battle of Britain succeeded because Winston Churchill's policy to wage war on land, sea, and air against Germany became credible as a result of Fighter Command having precisely the leaders, pilots, and aircraft it needed to fight the *Luftwaffe* to a stalemate. The two British air marshals who won the battle outthought, outled, and outfought the *Luftwaffe*.

CONCLUSIONS

Hitler's policies before the war created an air force that was not designed to project airpower across the English Channel "to break us in this island" as Churchill put it. This failure enabled Churchill to play the long game, allowing Britain to survive long enough for favorable conditions to emerge where the balance of forces could change. Neither combatant air force knew what sustained aerial combat would look like until the battle was fought. The British discovered that they had in Fighter Command a weapons system that was decisive enough. They were able to confirm this conclusion because the Enigma code-breaking efforts verified it.

Fighter Command prevailed because it was still an undefeated force of demonstrable lethality. Integrating the Dowding System and Fighter Command into an effective weapons system in the five years leading up to 1940 was a back-to-front achievement.

This strategic result enabled Britain to continue to fight as the only belligerent against the Axis until Hitler attacked the Soviet Union. By the time the full force of the *Wehrmacht* fell upon western Russia in June 1941, the *Luftwaffe* had been significantly weakened through loss of experienced pilots.

After the battle, voids opened up for both sides. For German strategists, after airpower failed to break England, Hitler and his staff were undecided about what to do next. During the summer and fall, Hitler had been considering a plan, named Operation *Felix*, for a German seizure of Gibraltar. German capture of this Royal Navy base and centuries-old fortress would have threatened British supply routes across the Mediterranean, potentially rendering the British position in the Middle East untenable. Hitler's October 23, 1940, meeting with Generalissimo Francisco Franco at Hendaye on the Franco-Spanish border failed either to gain Franco's commitment of Spain to enter the war on the Axis side or to allow the *Wehrmacht* safe passage across Spain to attack Gibraltar.[32] If there was no easy way to crack British resolution to continue fighting, Hitler, drawing on his implacable hostilities and hatreds expressed in *Mein Kampf*, began to conclude that an attack on the Soviet Union was the solution. He told his commanders that attacking Russia would remove Britain's last hope of being able to continue the war.

British strategists had to answer the same question. Where could they strike the Axis next, now that Germany had overrun Western Europe? They were busy reacting to multiple threats where any action had to confront continuing uncertainty and mortal risk. Britain had to combat Axis threats in the Middle East and in the deep waters of the Atlantic. It would take four more years before a strategy would eventually emerge for an Allied coalition to execute *Sea Lion* in reverse and invade the Continent at Normandy.

At the end of the war, *Feldmarschall* Gerd von Rundstedt was asked which battle of the war he regarded as most decisive. What he said was the Battle of Britain.[33] Upon first reading, this might seem a strange judgment to offer, given von Rundstedt's multiple high-command assignments throughout the war. As Sir Basil H. Liddell Hart commented in a postwar interview with von Rundstedt,

It seems evident that the generals had no heart in the attempted invasion, and that the admirals were even more disinclined to make the venture. They took the gloomiest view of what the British Navy might do. Göring and the heads of the air force were the only people who were keen on the plan. They were allowed to test the British strength in the air, but when they failed to drive the RAF out of the sky the generals and the admirals were quick to renew their objections to the venture—and Hitler was surprisingly ready to accept their excuses for a postponement. It was a permanent postponement.[34]

For Germany, fighting the battle was a political, strategic, and operational failure. England had made better prewar policy decisions, developed and used superior technology, and begun enough operational preparations to win the battle by not losing. Britain's success soon enabled the Royal Navy to shift destroyers less critical to the Home Fleet to convoy duty to fight the growing threat of U-boats in the Battle of the Atlantic.

Battle of Britain

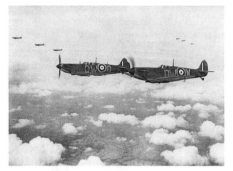

(1) Spitfires (Mark 1) in "vic" formation and (2) Hurricanes (Mark 1) in loose echelon formation with wing markings showing deployment to Air Expeditionary Force to France well before Battle of Britain. IWM photos

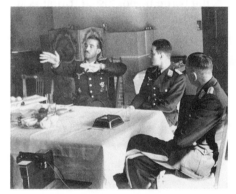

(3) German Me-109 fighter flying over English Channel with White Cliffs of Dover in background. LOC photo (4) *Oberstleutnant* (later *Generalleutnant*) Adolf Galland (left), *Major* Werner Mölders (center), and *Generalmajor* Theodor Osterkamp (right) on occasion of Osterkamp's birthday at Le Touquet on the French coast, April 15, 1941. Galland and Mölders flew in the battle and both became decorated aces. BArch photo

(5) Chain Home Low Radar Sta. at Hopton-on-Sea. The station deployed two CHL aerial arrays, one on top of the 185-ft. steel tower, and the other on a 20-ft. wooden gantry by the operations block at lower right. (6) RAF 10 Group Control Room at RAF Wiltshire. IWM photos

2

BATTLE OF THE ATLANTIC
Protecting the Maritime Lifeline

The Allies had to prevail during the Battle of the Atlantic because ensuring the safe arrival of merchant convoys meant Britain's survival as a viable belligerent. By the middle years of the war, German U-boats had sunk thousands of Allied merchant ships, threatening the transatlantic lifeline that supplied the United Kingdom. Losing this battle meant strangulation of Britain and a failure to build up the forces needed to invade the Continent from British ports in 1944.

Against the strategic architecture framework, the outcome of the Battle of the Atlantic resulted from a German failure at the levels of policy, strategy, and operations. It turned into a victory for the Allies because of their superior policy choices, strategic clarity, technological and tactical innovations, and operational perseverance.

POLICY

When the war began, both sides were inadequately prepared to fight a long tonnage war. Both the Royal Navy and the *Kriegsmarine* ignored the lessons of submarine warfare that emerged from World War I.[1]

The German submarine service (*U-bootswaffe*) began hostilities in 1939 with only fifty-seven submarines.[2] German U-boats were small, "and a general technological backwardness placed the U-boat effort in a doubtful position for the conduct of a long-term campaign."[3] The standard German World War II

Mark VII U-boat had a displacement half that of an American fleet submarine (roughly 750 vs. 1,500 tons). The U-boat was not much more technically advanced than it had been in World War I. Hitler started the war before his navy was ready. *Grossadmiral* Raeder's diary notation on the first day of the war was gloomy:

> Today [September 3, 1940] the war against England and France broke out. . . .
> It is self-evident that the navy is in no manner sufficiently equipped in the fall of
> 1939 to embark on a great struggle with England. . . . Surface forces . . . are still
> so few in numbers and strength compared to the English fleet that they . . . can
> only show that they know how to die with honor.[4]

Despite the overall increase in German U-boat numbers throughout the war, from 57 in 1939 to 1,153 built by May 1945, the German U-boat service never produced and deployed enough operational boats in the decisive waters of the Atlantic.[5] Hitler's U-boat program called for the production of twenty-five submarines per month. Such a rate might have achieved a decisive margin of three hundred U-boats in a year,[6] but the number of U-boats available for operations in the Atlantic only rose to eighty-five in May 1942 and to two hundred the following year.[7]

By 1942, *Vizeadmiral* Karl Dönitz, who commanded the *U-Bootswaffe*, had more operational U-boats on his rostered strength than ever before, nearly 250. However, only ninety-one U-boats were deployed against Allied convoys, and only twenty-three were available for Atlantic service at any given time. The rest of the submarine fleet was undergoing training and trials, was in for dockyard repairs, or was assigned to the Mediterranean or Norway.[8] Of the twenty-three boats in the Atlantic, half of them were on passage to or from operational areas. That left only ten to twelve boats simultaneously attacking American shipping off the eastern seaboard during the "Happy Time" in early 1942 when a dozen U-boats sank more than six hundred ships.[9]

Britain's policy of effective antisubmarine warfare (ASW) against the growing U-boat threat depended on top political and naval leaders assembling the necessary resources to win. The strategic ASW effort required building more ships and naval escorts than the U-boats could sink. British production of escort vessels was negligible from September 1939 through May 1940, when the U-boat menace was growing by the month. British shipyards launched only fourteen destroyers during the first eight months of the war.[10] To get all of these elements in place for an effective ASW strategic architecture required central direction from Churchill and the War Cabinet. It took four years—until 1943.

STRATEGY

The Battle of the Atlantic was unlike all the other battles fought at sea during World War II. The scale of the battle was enormous. Britain in the last years of peace imported fifty to sixty million tons per year of foodstuffs, raw materials, and fuel.[11] Imports by 1942 had dropped 62 percent to twenty-three million tons. As a maritime nation, Britain maintained the largest merchant fleet in the world at the time: three thousand oceangoing merchantmen and one thousand coastal ships. Churchill confessed in his memoirs after the war, "The only thing that ever really frightened me during the war was the U-boat peril. . . . I was even more anxious about this battle than I had been about the glorious air fight called the Battle of Britain."[12]

The range and complexity of the forces in this battle space required operations over nine million square miles of the Atlantic.[13] Not until 1943 would it be possible to take the offensive against the U-boats in a way that would achieve dominance over the Atlantic lifeline routes.[14]

Success in the tonnage war depended on the appointment of naval and air commanders who could learn to work together and overcome interservice rivalries. It required continual political oversight over the Allied industrial base to produce merchantmen in mass quantities, hundreds of escort ships, and thousands of aircraft, equipped with advanced sensor technologies and better ASW weapons. None of this could have worked without implementation of increasingly sophisticated systems of accountability by collegial wartime institutions created specifically to win the Battle of the Atlantic. Winning required a strategic architecture for a long game.

Winston Churchill gave the battle its name in a directive in March 1941 in which he outlined specific steps for taking the offensive against the U-boats. In August 1942, he established the cabinet-level Anti–U-boat Warfare Committee consisting of appropriate service chiefs that met weekly to direct the ASW campaign.

One of the committee's first tasks was to address the requirement of covering the six-hundred-mile air gap in the mid-Atlantic, south of Cape Farewell, Greenland, where there were insufficient numbers of air squadrons assigned to ASW duty (map 2.1).[15] The prime minister never relinquished his strategic oversight of Britain's maritime lifeline: "The Battle of the Atlantic was the dominating factor all through the war. Never for one moment could we forget that everything happening elsewhere, on land, at sea, or in the air, depended ultimately on its outcome, and amid all other cares we viewed its changing fortunes day by day with hope or apprehension."[16] It took Allied leaders until April and May of 1943 to develop and execute a maritime air strategy to defeat the U-boats.[17]

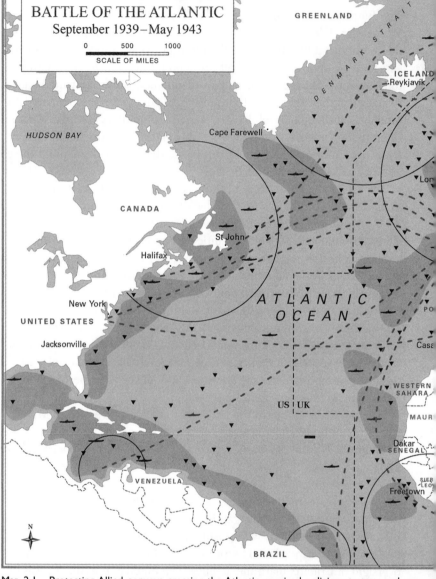

Map 2.1. Protecting Allied convoys crossing the Atlantic required policies, strategy, and operational execution to build merchantmen in mass quantities, launch hundreds of escort ships, and deploy thousands of aircraft.

Sources: Map of the Battle of the Atlantic in the War in Western Europe (June to December 1942, Map No. 1, West Point, Department of Military Art and Engineering, US Military Academy, 1952); and map of the Battle of the North Atlantic, 1940–1943, in Murray and Millett, *War to Be Won*, 237.

SWEDEN

FINLAND

NORWAY

Scapa Flow

NORTH SEA

IRELAND
Londonderry

UK
• Liverpool
LONDON
Bristol

USSR

GERMANY   POLAND

AUSTRIA

FRANCE

HUNGARY

ROMANIA

ITALY

BAY OF BISCAY

BLACK SEA

SPAIN

GREECE   TURKEY

CASPIAN SEA

Gibraltar

MEDITERREANEAN SEA   SYRIA

IRAQ

IRAN

Casablanca
MOROCCO

ALGERIA   LIBYA   EGYPT   SAUDI ARABIA   OMAN

RN
RA

AURITANIA

MALI

NIGER   CHAD

- - - Allied shipping routes

——— Limit of allied air patrols 1945

▼ General location of Allied merchant ships sunk by German U-boats between September 1939 and May 1943

Major area of U-boat activity

SIERRA LEONE   CÔTE D'IVOIRE   GOLD COAST

BURKINA

NIGERIA

ARABIAN SEA

From November 1942, Western Approaches was under the command of Admiral Sir Max K. Horton, an experienced and decorated submariner who took charge of his headquarters in Liverpool and controlled the Battle of the Atlantic from the European side "with an extraordinary singleness of purpose."[18]

At the heart of the Allied command system was the Operational Intelligence Center (OIC) located in a bombproof, underground headquarters nearby the London Admiralty, divided into four sections of which the U-boat Tracking Room was dominant. It was commanded from 1941 onward by Commander Roger N. Winn, who quickly established a close working relationship with the naval team at Bletchley Park and proved an inspired interpreter of Enigma decrypts.

Commander Winn crossed the Atlantic in April 1942 and convinced his American counterparts to emulate British convoy routing and submarine tracking plots.[19] Allied headquarters on both sides of the Atlantic developed a coordinated system for mid-ocean handing off of operational control of convoys and their escorts, a process that became known as the CHOP (change of operational control).[20]

Henry J. Kaiser's American shipyards built 2,710 Liberty ships during the war. Peter Padfield concluded,

> When the output of the Kaiser shipyards is set against U-boat sinkings in the North Atlantic, 1,006 ships in 1942 but only thirty-one in 1944, it becomes clear that Dönitz's hope of winning a tonnage war was quite misplaced. . . . However hard Dönitz drove his captains, statistics, by mid-1943, had turned decisively against them.[21]

What had begun in 1939–1940 as a losing struggle swelled during the course of the war into a major ASW campaign. It was prosecuted by an ever-larger armada of Allied destroyers, sloops, frigates, corvettes, and, critically, escort aircraft carriers. Allied convoys by 1943 were increasingly guarded by more squadrons of land-based, long-range patrol aircraft.

Between 1939 and 1945, the Allies introduced a succession of increasingly efficient detection sensors and underwater weapons of greater lethality. This hardware included sonar sets able to register depth as well as bearing; centimetric radar and high-frequency direction-finding devices (HF/DF) capable of geolocating a submarine sailing on the surface by using intercepted bearings from German HF radio transmissions; a wide variety of depth charges; advanced models of forward-firing contact weapons like the Hedgehog; and the Leigh light, a radar-directed searchlight mounted on long-range aircraft for night attacks on U-boats.[22] Once an aircraft could drop the acoustic Mark 24 torpedo, known as "Fido," on a U-boat, the Allied ASW war became much more sophisticated. Targets acquired by HF/DF sets and radar could be attacked by a first-generation, fire-and-forget weapons system. Fully integrated, state-of-the-art ASW had dawned.

By mid-1943, the panoply of purpose-built ASW ships, aircraft, radar and sonar sets, and more accurate weapons, manned by better-trained crews employing smarter tactics, put the U-boats into increasing peril. The steady addition of escort aircraft carriers, eleven built by American shipyards for the US Navy and thirty-four more for the Royal Navy, would make it increasingly difficult for Dönitz's wolfpacks to operate close to convoys. The Germans fell behind in the relentless industrial competition of the Battle of the Atlantic.

The German countermeasure to radar, Metox,[23] was a crude radar-detection device that came to be distrusted by the Germans. "As a result," observed John Keegan, "U-boat captains, like those of Nelson's frigates, depended through-out the war on line of sight, enhanced only by forming patrol lines in exactly the same way as Nelson had done." Radio extended their range a little by providing a captain who got a sighting with means to summon others, but the risk of breaking radio silence was immense. Unknown to the Germans, Allied HF/DF interception became increasingly lethal to U-boats. Thus, U-boat patrol lines were relatively short. Allied naval headquarters could steer convoys away from identified U-boat traps.[24]

Dönitz's small staff of six or seven veteran U-boat commanders directed the Battle of the Atlantic. They lacked the necessary training and background to function as an effective command staff. Their heavy workload, fatigue, and National Socialist training undermined a disinterested examination of the conflict supported by relevant statistical analysis and operations research. Their work products were no match against those produced by Commander Winn's OIC. German naval staffs tended to address operational parameters superficially.[25]

OPERATIONS

During the first months of the war, the U-boats proved to be a deadly nuisance, but not yet a strategic threat. At the end of 1939, out of 5,756 Allied vessels sailing in convoys, U-boats sank only five. The early U-boat successes were counterproductive because they alerted the British to the threat to national survival and to the need to build up merchant shipping.[26]

Because of Raeder's concentration on his surface fleet, the number of new U-boats entering operational service in 1940 barely matched U-boat losses. Nevertheless, a small number of U-boats inflicted heavy losses on shipping during 1940. After the fall of France, the geographic framework of the Battle of the Atlantic changed in Germany's favor because U-boats soon had direct and easier access from French ports along the Bay of Biscay to the sea-lanes of British lines of communication (LOCs). By 1942, with U-boat production ramped up to a strength over two hundred boats, German submarines could return to hardened, bombproof pens in French ports for maintenance and crew rest before setting out again. By eliminating the long outward and return voyage, German U-boats increased the time of their predatory deployments at sea.

From July to September 1940, with British Home Fleet destroyers preoccupied with deterring the launch of Operation *Sea Lion*, Dönitz's small fleet of U-boats sank nearly 250,000 tons per month, at a cost of less than two boats per month. When the *Sea Lion* threat ended, the Royal Navy could devote greater resources to ASW. As they encountered stronger convoy escorts in British waters, Dönitz moved his U-boats out into the Central Atlantic. But there they found it more difficult to locate convoys and to concentrate U-boats in wolfpacks. The Germans were paying for their failure to increase submarine construction significantly in the first year of the war.

Both sides were slow to exploit their airborne assets. The Allied air and naval forces took time to close the gap in air cover over the Central Atlantic and the Bay of Biscay where reconnaissance flights could detect U-boats sailing to and from the convoy areas of the Atlantic. Once U-boats reached the mid-Atlantic gap, they were much less vulnerable to air interception. Air commanders, preoccupied with missions of their own, were not fully committed to the fight until politicians forced their hand in 1942–1943 and made them commit the necessary squadrons to cover the mid-Atlantic gap. When that happened, German U-boat captains knew no rest in either the Bay of Biscay or the deep waters of the Central Atlantic.

The signals intelligence (SIGINT) battle was two sided and dynamic. Both sides built up huge code-breaking establishments. The German *Beobachtungs und Entzifferungs Dienst* (or *B-dienst*) employed over six thousand linguists and cryptanalysts at its peak, intercepting Allied naval messages from over sixty monitoring stations from Scandinavia to the Mediterranean and decrypting many of them.[27] The British SIGINT service at Bletchley Park employed ten thousand. Against the substantial and effective German code-breaking establishment, Allied SIGINT gained the upper hand by mid-1943.

Dönitz, like Admiral Horton and Commander Winn, had a great wall chart of the Atlantic showing Allied and German naval dispositions, initially in a commandeered château at Kerneval near Lorient. However, his intelligent guesswork was not as shrewd as Horton's and Winn's, even with the help of *B-dienst* decrypts.[28] Often Winn's last-minute evasive routing, practiced by the Trade Division of the Admiralty in response to Winn's OIC plots and guesses about U-boat tracks, canceled out German SIGINT advantages.

By 1942, British use of operations research began to have an effect. The Royal Navy's Operational Intelligence Center integrated intelligence from all sources—radio direction finding from U-boat transmissions, Enigma decrypts from Bletchley, sightings by aircraft and surface ships, prisoner interrogation reports, and a growing body of information about U-boat captains and their tactics. It was a constantly updated database of U-boat movements and dispositions in relation to convoy locations. The OIC had authority to forward their findings directly to commanders in charge of convoy routing and ASW operations. Over the next two years, a series of studies provided valuable tactical insights into convoy size and configuration, the number of escort ships required, and timely Bletchley Park SIGINT to produce "force multipliers." One study showed that dispatching a very-long-range aircraft to intercept a convoy known to be shadowed by a U-boat dramatically increased the probability of a U-boat sighting by forty times.[29] The prime minister took an active interest in some of these studies, as did his scientific advisor, Professor Frederick A. Lindemann.[30]

Like the Battle of Britain, the Battle of the Atlantic was an attrition battle for equally high stakes. Churchill remarked, "How willingly would I have exchanged a full-scale attempt at invasion for this shapeless, measureless peril, expressed in charts, curves, and statistics."[31]

The Americans soon established their own operations research group, the Anti-Submarine Warfare Operations Research Group (ASWORG), that produced equally useful studies as those pioneered by the British. By the following year, air attacks in the spring of 1943 destroyed thirty-three of fifty-six U-boats sunk.[32]

The overall operational metrics began to show decisive results. Curve plots showing the numbers of Allied ships sunk and built overlaid by another curve identifying the available operational U-boat strength in Atlantic waters illustrate that it took the Allies nearly four years to tip the scales in their favor. The crossover point (more ships built than sunk) occurred in late 1942. There is debate among military historians with respect to precisely when the tipping point occurred. Some argue that the Allies had grounds for optimism as early as late 1941; others contend that the battle was not won decisively until 1943.[33] Isolating the turning point is less important than understanding the factors that established Allied dominance. The changing slopes of the curves in figure 2.1 indicate that the Allies in 1941–1942 were beginning to succeed in reversing the effects of the U-boat threat.

The histogram plot of new Allied shipping construction and losses by month from September 1939 to May 1945 shows the massive scale of the Allied ship construction program (figure 2.2). By January 1943, British cryptanalysts at Bletchley Park succeeded for the second time in the SIGINT struggle by decrypting Dönitz's Enigma[34] signals traffic to and from his U-boat wolfpacks. The SIGINT struggle became a double-edged sword in 1942–1943. Although Bletchley Park's SIGINT successes in 1939–1941 enabled diversion of convoys out of harm's way in the Atlantic, this advantage abruptly stopped in February

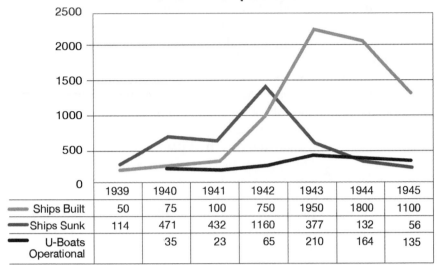

Number of Ships/Boats

	1939	1940	1941	1942	1943	1944	1945
Ships Built	50	75	100	750	1950	1800	1100
Ships Sunk	114	471	432	1160	377	132	56
U-Boats Operational		35	23	65	210	164	135

Figure 2.1. The crossover point in 1942 is the result of more ships built than could be sunk.

Source: US Merchant Marine (www.usmm.org) for Allied ships built by the United States and Allied ships sunk; and Ireland, *Battle of the Atlantic,* 226. Average number of operational U-boat data by month interpolated and then annualized by year from curve plot on diagram 4.

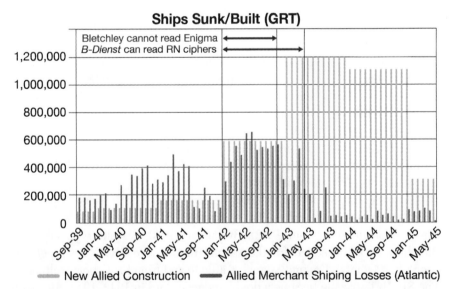

Ships Sunk/Built (GRT)

Figure 2.2. Allied ship construction ramped up dramatically by January 1943 measured in gross registered tonnage (GRT).

Source: Keegan, *Second World War,* 118–19; data are interpolated and rounded.

1942 when the *Kriegsmarine* introduced a fourth rotor to Enigma machines on all operational U-boats. When that happened, Bletchley Park was shut out of Enigma for nearly a year.[35] At roughly the same time, the *Kriegsmarine's B-dienst* was reading the Royal Navy's signals traffic directing convoys. The Admiralty did not secure its communications until the successful introduction of changes to Naval Cipher No. 3 in June 1943. The *B-dienst* by December 1942 was extraordinarily effective. Dönitz's operations staff directing the U-boats knew nearly as much as Allied Atlantic convoy planners did themselves.[36]

The period of the most intense convoy battles was 1943 when Dönitz had more than four hundred U-boats in commission and was deploying wolfpacks with as many as forty to eighty boats, an increase from the twenty-three at sea during 1941–1942.[37] Keegan acknowledges that Clay Blair, "the most meticulous historian of the U-boat war," concluded in his analysis of the statistics that Churchill's fears were exaggerated and that Dönitz, even when he acquired three hundred boats, neither threatened Britain with starvation nor "even came close to inflicting defeat on the Allied anti-submarine forces."[38] Nevertheless, it required almost four years of war before the balance shifted.

The balance of forces shifted dramatically in the late winter of 1943. After the appalling losses sustained by two large eastbound convoys,[39] Admiral Horton pressed Churchill for more naval and air assets to cover the vulnerable air gap. Fifteen more destroyers from the Home Fleet were rushed to Horton. That is how narrow the margins were in terms of his estimate of what it would take to regain the naval initiative to break the U-boat threat. Effective air coverage to fill the air gap over convoys did not occur until June 1943 with additional deliveries of VLR (very long range) B-24 Liberator patrol bombers retrofitted with extra fuel tanks, ASW ordnance, and electronic equipment for U-boat interception missions.[40]

The prime minister was able to boast in the House of Commons on September 21, 1943, that during the four-month period leading up to September 18, 1943, no Allied ships had been sunk by U-boats anywhere in the world.[41] The dramatic shift in the balance of forces in the spring months of 1943 did not mean that the battle was over. It would last until virtually the last day of the war.

The hard fact remains that the combatants had to fight it out over nearly six years to the finish. Allied convoy crews had to perform the stolid, dogged tasks of tight station keeping under the discipline of wartime convoys. They had to accept the continual zigzagging; fight back when attacked; endure appalling losses of ships and sailors, often in terrible sea conditions; and create the skilled hunter-killer teams that eventually did the U-boats in. The losses on both sides were appalling: 2,742 Allied ships with tonnage losses of 14,687,231 and 30,248 men and 784 U-boats sunk with 32,491 men, including 5,000 prisoners.[42] Dönitz wrote after the war that he knew the outcome by the spring of 1943:

Wolfpack operations against convoys in the North Atlantic, the main theater of operations and at the same time the theater in which air cover was the strongest, were no longer possible. They could only be resumed if we succeeded in radically increasing the fighting power of the U-boats. . . . I accordingly withdrew the boats from the North Atlantic. On 24 May [1943] I ordered them to proceed, using the utmost caution, to the area southwest of the Azores. We had lost the Battle of the Atlantic.[43]

CONCLUSIONS

The competing strategic architectures between the Allied ASW navies and the *U-bootswaffe* played out over six years of war. The Anglo-American navies reinvented the whole concept of effective ASW. It took until mid-1943 before policy, strategy, technology, production, and tactics created the Allied capability to force Admiral Dönitz to withdraw his U-boat fleet from the Central Atlantic. British and American leaders created ASW command organizations on both sides of the Atlantic that could operate together effectively. They formulated policies that led to effective interservice cooperation, particularly in recognizing the force-multiplier effects of using aircraft. They appointed effective naval and military commanders with large, capable staffs. They mobilized their stronger industrial and technological bases to produce enough purpose-built ships and aircraft. They installed upgraded electronic systems and weapons in them and trained their crews to use them effectively. They exploited their SIGINT systems more decisively. They used operations research results much more effectively than the *U-bootswaffe* did. These concentrated efforts resulted in a strategy that eventually provided sufficient ASW coverage over the critical operational waters of the Atlantic. The Allies won the Battle of the Atlantic because they performed these critical tasks much better than the Germans did.

By August 1945, the Allied navies grew overwhelmingly to operate as a global force. They not only defeated the German U-boat threat in the Atlantic, but the US Navy also simultaneously launched an offensive submarine campaign in the Pacific against Japanese warships and merchant shipping that, when combined with overall American naval power, wreaked peril on Japan that came close to the horrific metrics in the Battle of the Atlantic, sinking 3,032 ships displacing eleven million tons, compared to the Battle of the Atlantic losses of fifteen million tons.

Battle of the Atlantic

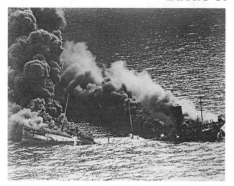

(1) US tanker burning after being torpedoed by German submarine U-71 off North Carolina, March 26, 1942. Axis submarines during the "Happy Time" sank more than 623 vessels along the eastern sea frontier of the United States between January and August 1942. NARA photo (2) Allied tanker burning off Norfolk, Virginia, in summer 1942. USN photo

(3) Antisubmarine weapons: Hedgehog, a twenty-four-barreled antisubmarine mortar mounted on the forecastle of HMS *Westcott*, a Royal Navy W-class destroyer. (4) Leigh light used for spotting U-boats on the surface at night, mounted under the wing of a B-24 Liberator bomber of RAF Coastal Command, February 1944. IWM photos

(5) View from the bridge of HMS *Viscount* illustrating often appalling weather conditions while escorting a convoy during the Battle of the Atlantic. (6) Sailors use steam hoses to clear ice from anchor chains and winches on board HMS *Scylla*, a Dido-class antiaircraft cruiser, during a cold spell on patrol in the Atlantic, February 1943. IWM photos

INVASION OF RUSSIA

Hitler's Strategic Mistake

Germany's Operation *Barbarossa* invasion of the Soviet Union on June 22, 1941, marked the first major shift in the wartime balance of forces. Hitler's surprise attack yielded astonishing victories initially. In the first four months of *Barbarossa*, the *Wehrmacht* killed or captured over four million Soviet soldiers. German generals reasoned that since they had annihilated the Red Army, the Russians had to surrender. Except they didn't because they fielded another four million soldiers.

The United Kingdom soon had a powerful ally fighting the *Wehrmacht* on a vast Eastern Front. Stalin's response to Operation *Barbarossa* was grinding attrition without regard for the enormous casualties. Stalin knew he could rely on the scale of Russian geography, the size of the Soviet population, and a rigid top-down alignment of policy, strategy, and operations by the world's largest communist totalitarian state.

POLICY

Hitler's search for an easy war-winning campaign after the *Luftwaffe*'s failure the previous summer to break England soon expanded the war into a far larger conflict in the east. Hitler's policy for *Barbarossa*'s conquered territories specified a broad, brutal program of racial rearrangement and genocide, already underway for months in conquered Poland. Enthusiastic National Socialist implementation of *Generalplan Ost* soon accelerated to an industrial scale where whole populations faced forced resettlement, subjugation, or outright liquidation. Andrew Roberts's last sentence in *The Storm of War* is very apt: "The real reason why Hitler lost the Second World War was exactly the same one that caused him to unleash it in the first place: he was a Nazi."[1]

The political-military dimensions of *Barbarossa* represented "the last great example of a medium-sized European state to impose its murderous will on a supposedly less-developed people of vastly greater number."[2] The *Ostplan* was tantamount to the complete Germanization of usable, arable lands in the east; the wholesale relocation and reallocation of national populations according to German criteria of population density; and the genocide of Jewish populations everywhere in Europe. German policy under *Generalplan Ost* proposed removal of between 60 and 85 percent of the Poles, 64 percent of the Ukrainians, and 75 percent of the Byelorussians by expelling them farther east or by allowing them to perish from disease and malnutrition.[3]

German promulgation of the infamous Commissar Order,[4] which specified the indiscriminate execution of all Soviet political leaders and administrators of the Soviet state by German army or rear-area special-operations groups (*Einsatzgruppen*), did little to win Russian hearts and minds. This order concentrated the minds of Soviet officers and commissars to fight without quarter.[5] The Germans were invading an enemy who knew the fatal consequences of losing.

For Stalin, the first year of *Barbarossa* was a military disaster. Germany's surprise attack destroyed the world's largest army and overran the richest portions of the world's largest country.[6] The Soviets fought back by doing four things well: (1) mobilizing and sacrificing more manpower by the tens of millions than the invading Axis armies could,[7] (2) trading territory for time to recover and reorganize, (3) relocating most of the country's surviving industrial base west of Moscow to sites farther east and rebuilding production capacity,[8] and (4) leading with the ruthless direction and discipline exercised by a communist dictator whose authority and competence were questioned by no one.

STRATEGY

Barbarossa initiated a chain of events that led to three of the most decisive land battles of the war: the Battles of Moscow, Stalingrad, and Kursk, fought between September 1941 and July 1943. The scale and carnage of these battles were enormous. The Battle of Moscow was the largest, ranging over a territory the size of France and lasting for six months. It involved more than seven million men on both sides, with combined losses of 2.5 million.[9] The Soviet Union by a factor of two lost more people in this one battle than British and American military forces lost throughout the war in all theaters.[10] By the end of the war, the Soviets had sustained 95 percent of the combat casualties. Fighting on this scale was never matched by Allied fighting in the Mediterranean or Western Europe.

Allied leaders soon understood two basic concepts. First, Churchill and Roosevelt knew the value of the Soviet Union bleeding German forces white. Both leaders understood "the terrible arithmetic of war."[11] Between 1941 and 1945, the Soviets killed four million German soldiers on the Eastern Front.[12] They wounded or took prisoner an estimated 5.5 million more German and Axis soldiers.[13] They did so at terrible cost to themselves. Nearly thirty million Soviet soldiers and civilians died.[14] Second, Stalin understood that he had a discriminator no other combatant had, an unlimited manpower pool of thirty-four million men of military age,[15] whom he could sacrifice in prodigious numbers.

Barbarossa's military planning was strategically flawed from its inception. The German high command, *das Oberkommando der Wehrmacht* (OKW) and *das Oberkommando der Herres* (OKH),[16] planned the Russian campaign for a force designed, configured, and trained for a highly mobile, offensive war of movement and quick victory. Popularly known as blitzkrieg, but more accurately defined as *Bewegungskrieg* (war of movement), Robert M. Citino describes the German army as one that "liked its campaigns front-loaded, meticulously planned, and designed for maximum impact."[17] Clausewitz in *On War* had formalized *Bewegungskrieg* into a strategic doctrine in 1832.[18] *Bewegungskrieg* evolved from seventeenth- and eighteenth-century Prussian battlefield experience where speed and maneuver could deliver victory after a fast, overwhelming military storm.[19] Hitler, like the OKW staff, had read Clausewitz, too.[20]

Bewegungskrieg created its own unique vocabulary and doctrinal principles: *Schwerpunkt* (point of main impact), *Kesselschlacht* (cauldron battle), *Vernichtungsschlacht* (battle of annihilation), and *Auftragstaktik* (mission command). Attack an enemy at a point of weakness, strike hammer blows against unprotected flanks, encircle the defending force, and destroy it totally. This operational focus required a flexible command-and-control system that allowed subordinate commanders to assess a situation quickly and act aggressively on their own. *Auftragstaktik* vested initiative in lower-ranking commanders who were trained to act on the spot and seize tactical opportunities.

In his first *Barbarossa* directive, Hitler ordered that "the bulk of the Russian army stationed in western Russia will be destroyed by daring operations led by deeply penetrating armored spearheads. Russian forces still capable of giving battle will be prevented from withdrawing into the depths of Russia."[21] The objective was to surround and destroy the major fighting units before they could retreat. Hitler confidently told General Alfred Jodl, chief of the OKW operations staff, "We only have to kick in the door and the whole rotten structure will come crashing down." Reich propaganda minister Josef Goebbels happily predicted, "Russia will collapse like a house of cards."[22]

The military planning professionals were much less confident of *Barbarossa's* likelihood of success because the logistics were sobering. Their analyses showed that there were insufficient trains, trucks, fuel, and ammunition for the proposed five-month campaign that would be needed to destroy the Red Army. Despite the popular legend of blitzkrieg's speed and mobility, 80 percent of the German army's transport was horse-drawn. Day-to-day logistics required an average of one million horses throughout the war. Of the 322 German divisions deployed by the middle of the war (1943), only fifty-two were armored or motorized.[23] Nevertheless, the Axis string of multiple victories on multiple continents between 1939 and 1941 left many doubting that the Allies would win the war. Indeed, many believed that German forces would be in Moscow before Christmas.[24]

Barbarossa depended on mass and speed to succeed. The *Wehrmacht* could not achieve both on the Eastern Front. The German army in the east (*Ostheer*) depended on rail transport for its long-distance offensive deployments. German staff officers who studied the maps recognized that the theater's funnel-shaped geography did not favor the *Ostheer* if the retreating Red Army could escape destruction (map 3.1). The *Ostheer* would be spreading out over an ever-broadening front as it surrounded and destroyed the Soviet armies. As its leading

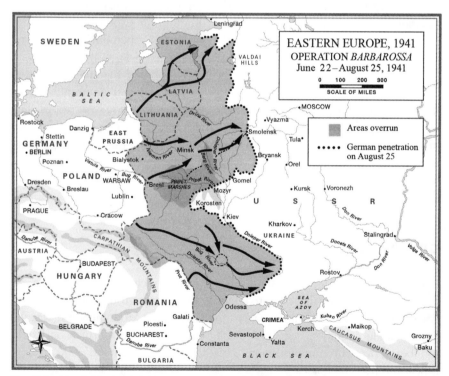

Map 3.1. The fanlike battlefield geometry meant that German armies as they advanced were farther from their bases and each other, while Red Army lines of communication became shorter.

Source: West Point Military Atlases, courtesy of the Department of History, US Military Academy, hereafter USMA Atlases.

troop units advanced ever farther from their bases, each other, and their supply lines, distance and time were parameters that favored the Red Army.

Deighton summarizes his critique of *Barbarossa's* planning in a single sentence: "In a remarkable feat of self-deception the general staff simply changed their estimates to persuade themselves that they could win in four, perhaps even one month."[25] The plan failed to take account of the realities of supporting three huge army groups over long distances with the rail and road networks available. German and Russian rail gauges were incompatible. Replacing rail with road transport would have required ten times more vehicles than the *Wehrmacht* possessed in 1941.[26] There was no alternative to using Russia's inadequate railway network.[27]

Months before *Barbarossa* was launched, the OKH's chief logistics officer calculated that the *Wehrmacht's* supply services could support the invading forces only to a depth of three hundred miles east of the frontier, a distance well short of Moscow, Leningrad, and the Donets basin. OKH logistical experts warned that advances of 180–250 miles would require a lengthy pause for resupply of forward units. The plan could not guarantee a German victory where the *Ostheer* could envelop and destroy the Red Army. Planners optimistically calculated that ammunition expenditures for the campaign would not exceed those of the battles in France during May–June 1940.[28] They were wildly off the mark.

Hence, the *Barbarossa* plan that the OKW cobbled together for Hitler, which optimistically cut back on estimates for fuel and ammunition, demanded unrealistic performance from the German army's railway troops. The fast operational tempo for the German armies required them to leap forward in a series of pincer movements for nearly four hundred miles, bringing them to Smolensk. Here a pause would be called while new rail track was laid and large supply depots built.[29] This flaw was just one of the many constraints in the *Barbarossa* plan.[30]

OPERATIONS

Operation *Barbarossa* unleashed 116 divisions, including twenty-nine armored and motorized divisions, to attack in three army groups along a front of 750 miles between the Baltic Sea and the Carpathian Mountains.[31] It was the largest single operation in recorded military history. This German onslaught numbered over three million men, 3,550 tanks, 2,779 aircraft, 7,000 artillery tubes, and 625,000 horses.

During the initial phases of *Barbarossa*, the *Wehrmacht* pounded the Red Army senseless. As the early weeks of the invasion unfolded, the *Wehrmacht* completely outfought the Red Army. As Hitler told his generals, the Russians "will think a hurricane has hit them."[32]

In the first month, German divisions advanced 470 miles in some areas of the front.[33] German mobile forces methodically encircled and destroyed large Soviet forces at Bialystok, Minsk, and numerous smaller pockets. They surrounded Smolensk, 230 miles from Moscow. The *Ostheer* was almost to Leningrad. German military power soon controlled the Ukraine west of the Dnieper. In these initial onslaughts, Citino wrote that "the Germans fought . . . to perfection . . . overrunning a huge swath of territory as large as Great Britain." The *Wehrmacht* had mastered *Bewegungskrieg* as if it were a "well-practiced drill."[34] Then he dropped the other shoe:

> And yet it was this very moment—with Soviet Russia seemingly on the ropes and the Red Army having apparently dissolved—that *Barbarossa* began to fall apart. As always, the *Wehrmacht's* maneuver scheme had been a thing of beauty, completely baffling Soviet attempts to counter it. Cooperation between the ground forces and the *Luftwaffe*, likewise, had been as good as two years of highly successful practice could make it. Virtually every other aspect of *Barbarossa* was a mess.[35]

The fanlike battlefield geography weighed in the scales. The distances were daunting: over six hundred miles to Moscow and almost five hundred miles to Leningrad. Operations in Russia were nothing like what the *Wehrmacht* had experienced in the drive across northern France to the Channel coast—a distance of 150 miles. Battlefield intelligence was even more telling. Hitler and the *Wehrmacht* thought they were on the brink of a decisive, war-winning victory. What they had not anticipated was that the Soviet Union by the end of June had called up five million reservists.

Two entries in the war diary of General Franz Halder, the chief of the OKH General Staff, reveal the contradictory impressions growing in the German high command about *Barbarossa's* prospects.[36] The first entry on July 3, 1941, was euphoric:

> On the whole, then, it may be said even now that the objective to shatter the bulk of the Russian army this side of the Dvina and Dnieper has been accomplished. I do not doubt the statement of the captured Russian corps commanding general that east of the Dvina and Dnieper we would encounter nothing more than partial forces, not strong enough to hinder realization of German operational plans. It is thus probably no overstatement to say that the Russian Campaign has been won in the space of two weeks.

Six weeks later, Halder's second entry on 11 August 1941 describes a completely different war:

> The whole situation makes it increasingly plain that we have underestimated the Russian colossus, who consistently prepared for war with that utterly ruthless determination so characteristic of totalitarian states. . . . At the outset of war, we

reckoned with about 200 enemy divisions. Now we have already counted 360. These divisions indeed are not armed and equipped according to our standards, and their tactical leadership is often poor. But there they are, and if we smash a dozen of them, the Russians simply put up another dozen. The time factor favors them, as they are near their own resources, while we are moving farther and farther away from ours. And so our troops, sprawled over an immense front line, without any depth, are subjected to the incessant attacks of the enemy.[37]

Stalin was slow to react to *Barbarossa*. In a state of shock and denial that Hitler had broken the Russo-German nonaggression pact of 1939, he retreated for days to his dacha outside Moscow, causing Politburo members to wonder whether he was still in charge. He relied on trusted subordinates to make public statements during the first twelve days. He finally broadcast a statement on July 3, 1941, and ordered the Red Army to fight back hard even when units were surrounded or deployed in hopeless positions.[38] Stalin's purges of the late 1930s had taken their toll in military competence. On the eve of *Barbarossa*, 75 percent of the field officers and 70 percent of the political commissars in the Red Army lacked vital command experience; they had held their posts for less than a year.[39]

The *Wehrmacht*'s advance on Moscow (Operation *Typhoon*) began at least a month later than the OKW and OKH planners desired. This delay resulted from Hitler's August decision to divert *Panzer* divisions from Army Group Center to overrun Kiev and Ukraine; the *Ostheer* destroyed four more Soviet armies and captured 750,000 Soviet soldiers. "But at the end of it, in September, there was no sign of Germany's final victory and the last month of mild weather was drawing to a close."[40]

In October, *Typhoon* ripped open the front line from Bryansk to Vyazma and encircled two more enormous groups of Soviet armies. The Germans claimed another six hundred thousand prisoners. However, *Typhoon* slowed because of the supply crisis and the early arrival of the fall rains in mid-October, which transformed the road net into a sea of mud.[41] November frosts enabled the German advance to resume over frozen ground. While the fifty-eight divisions of Army Group Center continued to advance toward Moscow, there was not enough strength to repeat the *Kesselschlacht* tactics of the earlier encirclements.[42] In early December, temperatures dropped to below 0°F, resulting in six hundred thousand more German casualties.[43] In the same week, fresh Soviet Siberian troops, prepared for winter warfare, counterattacked German forces on the outskirts of Moscow. By January 1942, the Soviets had blunted the German offensive even as German officers the previous month had sighted Moscow's taller buildings through their binoculars.

Stalin rushed Marshal Zhukov back from his assignment to defend Leningrad to orchestrate the defense of Moscow. Zhukov scraped together enough reserves from other Soviet frontiers, including the arrival of sixty-five Red Army divisions from Siberia, which had excellent winter clothing and weatherized equipment.[44]

Zhukov's counteroffensive was like nothing the German army had encountered in Western Europe. So ferocious were tactical counterattacks against the *Ostheer* that one German soldier described his shock at discovering that Soviet human-wave assaults were made by masses of troops where it was rumored that the commissars worked out the number of machine guns the Germans had, multiplied that number by the number of rounds per minute that they could fire, calculated how many minutes it would take a body of soldiers to cross the area, and added to the final total a couple of thousand men. Thus some men would break through the German lines.[45] No other Allied European army performed such cold-blooded attrition calculations or believed it could motivate men to execute such suicidal counterattacks. By January 1942, the Red Army had driven the *Ostheer* back 60 to 150 miles, ending the immediate threat to Moscow.

Even in the darkest hour, with the *Wehrmacht* at the gates of Moscow, none of the military debacles in the first six months of 1941 deflected Stalin from his predatory ambitions to expand the USSR's postwar boundaries. He was already probing to define the postwar political environment at a time when most Allied wartime leaders were preoccupied with ensuring national survival. British foreign minister Anthony Eden described his initial conversation with Stalin on his first visit to Moscow during the second week of December 1941.

> Stalin indicated that Poland should be given a good chunk of eastern Germany. . . . He also called for the restoration of a separate Austrian state, depriving Germany of the Rhineland. . . . As for the Baltic states, they were to be swallowed up once again by the Soviet state, and the Soviet borders with Finland and Romania would revert to what they had been before the Germans attacked. In short, he was proposing many of the terms that would eventually figure in the discussions of the great powers in Tehran in 1943 and Yalta in 1945.[46]

During the first eighteen months of *Barbarossa*, the Red Army went through four iterations of defeat and recovery. It had been virtually annihilated in the first two summer months of 1941 by the *Wehrmacht*, losing more than three million killed and missing. Stalin and the *Stavka*, the supreme military command, *Stavka Verkhovnogo Komandovaniya*, raised and fielded what amounted to another army by August of the same year, which itself was destroyed and had to be rebuilt in December 1941 to defend Moscow. Still a fourth Red Army was formed later in the winter of 1941–1942, having completed sufficient training by the fall of 1942 to stop the Germans at Stalingrad.[47]

Soviet equipment quality also began to wear down the Germans. Even in 1941, the Germans were astonished to discover the quality of Soviet armor, especially the medium T-34 tank. Period accounts of German soldiers on the

Eastern Front remarked on their first encounters with the T-34: its speed, the distinctive sloped armor, the shock of having their antitank shells bounce off.[48] This tank began to appear on battlefields in ever-increasing numbers as the Soviet industrial base recovered from the shocks of 1941.

The resilience of the Red Army in stopping the German armies from attacking Moscow in 1941, successfully defending Stalingrad in 1942, and then creating the combat power to win the tank battle at Kursk in 1943 oversimplifies the strategic significance of many "forgotten battles" that were fought in a bewildering number of campaigns between the *Ostheer* and the Red Army between 1941 and 1945. David Glantz lifts "the veil of obscurity that has cloaked the war by addressing major flaws in the historical record. . . . One of these flaws relates to the 'forgotten war,' the fully forty percent of wartime operations that, for various reasons, historians have deliberately forgotten, ignored, or simply covered up."[49]

In the spring of 1942, the *Wehrmacht* tried to win by smashing Soviet armies at Kharkov and in the Crimea in still more *Kesselschlachten*. German armies then drove toward the Volga River, Stalingrad, and the Caucasus Mountains and beyond to the petroleum fields at Baku and Maikop. The *Ostheer* came tantalizingly close to fulfilling Hitler's dream of capturing the oil the Reich desperately needed.[50]

Hitler contributed to the *Wehrmacht's* strategic difficulties by directing offensives in two different directions, breaking one of Clausewitz's fundamental principles about division of forces. He had set in motion the massive summer campaign of 1942 to seize Soviet oil fields to fuel his own armies and deprive the Red Army of its own major sources of oil. He coupled this offensive with another requirement—the capture of Stalingrad on the Volga, hundreds of miles in a different direction. The *Ostheer* lacked the combat power to do both.

How did the Soviets virtually in the course of a single year reverse the balance of forces? Three factors explain Soviet resilience in the face of what seemed in 1941 an overwhelming German juggernaut. The USSR's mobilization was cumbersome and initially slow to react, but once set in motion, it produced wave after wave of new armies to confront the German threat.[51] Second, the Soviets reorganized and rebuilt their infantry, armored, and air forces to engage the *Wehrmacht* with tactics and command-and-control systems that eventually broke Germany's offensive capabilities in the east. Third, they rebuilt their industrial base to reequip these forces. Between July and November 1941, the Soviets transported 1,360 arms and munitions factories eastward, using 1.5 million carriages of railway rolling stock.[52]

A statistical profile of individual combatant munitions figures indicates the prodigious feats of production accomplished by the Soviet Union (figure 3.1). The vertical bars on the chart illustrate that quantity mattered. *Wehrmacht* commanders and intelligence officers found themselves repeatedly surprised when they became convinced that the Soviets were down to their last

Comparative Weapons Production

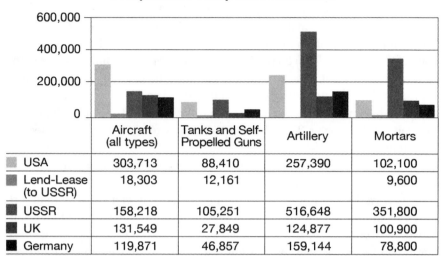

	Aircraft (all types)	Tanks and Self-Propelled Guns	Artillery	Mortars
USA	303,713	88,410	257,390	102,100
Lend-Lease (to USSR)	18,303	12,161		9,600
USSR	158,218	105,251	516,648	351,800
UK	131,549	27,849	124,877	100,900
Germany	119,871	46,857	159,144	78,800

Figure 3.1. The Soviets outproduced Germany in all major categories of weapons: aircraft, armor, artillery, and mortars.

Source: Production data sources for the United States, USSR, United Kingdom, and Germany: Margaret E. Wagner et al., eds., The Library of Congress World War II Companion (New York: Simon & Schuster, 2007), 202–4; and Glantz, "Myths and Realities" paper, 106.

battalions and reserves, only to discover that new armies were confronting them. The Soviet Union in World War II produced twice as many artillery tubes as the United States, over three times as many mortars, one-fifth more tanks and self-propelled guns, and over half as many aircraft. It was what Overy termed a "War of Engines."[53] The Lend-Lease contributions in figure 3.1 appear to be negligible. In actuality, Lend-Lease provided over 400,000 trucks and jeeps, 11,000 locomotives and rail cars, 422,000 field telephones,[54] over 4 million tons of foodstuffs, nearly 3 million tons of oil,[55] and 15 million pairs of boots. Despite these prodigious quantities, the Lend-Lease contribution to the Soviet war effort represented only 5 percent of Soviet production. Stalin's factories and farms produced the remaining 95 percent of munitions and food that his armies needed.[56]

Two and a half years later, after the Battle of Stalingrad, the Red Army on June 22, 1944, initiated Operation *Bagration* on the third anniversary of the German launch of *Barbarossa*. It was timed to help the Allied opening of the Second Front. Sixteen days earlier, on D-Day, the Allies had landed in Normandy. During the summer of 1944, with 228 *Ostheer* divisions in the east compared to fifty-eight *Westheer* divisions deployed in the west,[57] it was obvious to Hitler and the OKW where the most serious threat lay. There was no major movement of manpower westward to combat the Allied invasion of France. Soviet execution of Operation *Bagration* cleared German forces from Belorussia and eastern Poland between June 22 and August 19, 1944. By then, the Red Army was at the gates of Warsaw. *Bagration* accomplished the near destruction of the German Army Group Center. It effectively eliminated any serious prospect of Germany regaining the military initiative anywhere.

Bagration became *Barbarossa* in reverse.[58] The Russians during the middle years of the war tied down 80 percent of the *Wehrmacht's* combat power in the east. By June 1944, it was still a high percentage: 62 percent. The Red Army's offensive relieved potential pressure on the Allied coalition to land forty-seven divisions, beginning with eight on D-day, June 6, 1944, against diminished German combat power. The Allied expeditionary force, had it confronted the full strength of the *Wehrmacht*, including many of the 228 *Ostheer* divisions fighting on the Eastern Front,[59] would have encountered even more formidable resistance in Normandy.

Barbarossa by 1943–1944 was a military disaster. Soviet capacity to absorb such violent shocks of 1941–1942, rebuild its armies, regain the military initiative, recapture Eastern Europe, and by 1945 invade Germany and capture Berlin shortened the war. As a result, the Soviet Union recaptured an even bigger landscape of *Mitteleuropa*.

No other nation in the world could sustain the loss of one-third of its population, as well as most of its prewar standing army, replacing it four times, while simultaneously fighting the most highly trained and combat-hardened army in Europe.[60] The more recent *Barbarossa* literature reveals that this achievement resulted from a Soviet strategic architecture of iron-willed political determination at the top, increasingly skilled military planning and command staffing, total industrial mobilization, and obedient execution of orders by frontline commanders.

CONCLUSIONS

Operation *Barbarossa* was a major change in the balance of power favorable to the Allies less than a year after the Battle of Britain was fought. Hitler invaded the Soviet Union with a strategic architecture flawed at its inception. He defined murderous geopolitical objectives in *Generalplan Ost* that only hardened the resolve of his enemies.

Professional and aggressive as his army group commanders were, Hitler simply could not deliver a decisive victory on the endless Russian steppes. Germany had not prepared for this kind of long war. Hitler discovered that the Soviet Union was determined to survive, recover, rebuild, and retaliate with a vengeance back into the heart of the Reich. Stalin's ruthless alignment of policy, strategy, and operations helped the Allies win the war sooner because Stalin was ready to sacrifice men and matériel in quantities that no other combatant could.

Barbarossa

(1) A German sentry keeps watch in the recently captured city of Kiev in September 1941 (upper left). (2) Column of Soviet POWs captured by *Wehrmacht* at Bialystok in summer of 1941 (upper right). (3) German soldiers struggling to free vehicle from Russian mud, *rasputitsa,* on *Ostfront* in November 1941 (bottom left). (4) A column of *Sturmgeschütz* IIIs (German assault guns) roaring past soldier riding lead horse of additional animals hitched to a supply-train wagon passing in massive cloud of dust that looks like snow in the photo but photo was taken by a German propaganda company assigned to the *Ostfront* in June–July 1941 (lower right). BArch photos

(5) Stalingrad ruins with three German soldiers in foreground in September 1942. Except for their weapons, they almost look like tourists. LOC photo (6) Soldiers of SS Division, *Das Reich,* in front of *Panzer Tiger* at Battle of Kursk, June–July 1943. BArch photo

4

BATTLE OF EL ALAMEIN AND OPERATION *TORCH*

Cracking German Invincibility

As the third year of the war began in 1942, both combatant coalitions faced serious challenges with their strategic architectures that forced them to react to changing battlefield conditions. In mid-1941, German strategy had staked everything on the early success of Operation *Barbarossa*. The grinding attrition that ensued in the winter of 1941–1942 after the *Wehrmacht*'s failure to capture Moscow, the Japanese surprise attack on Pearl Harbor, and Hitler's declaration of war against the United States meant that Germany confronted a worldwide military coalition. The war had acquired truly global dimensions as its twenty-ninth month began in 1942. Hitler's problem was that the German *Barbarossa* offensive had failed to deliver a quick victory in Russia where he had committed the vast bulk of the *Wehrmacht*.

POLICY

The challenge for Reich war policy in 1942, after the terrible losses of *Barbarossa*'s first winter, was whether it could muster sufficient war-fighting power to finish the war before the Allies could mobilize their economies to equip and field armies to prevail over the Axis. What makes 1942 such an intriguing year of military opportunity for Germany was the rapid sequence of far-flung victories in Russia and North Africa where the *Wehrmacht* had achieved four of its greatest operational victories at Kerch[1] and Kharkov[2] in Russia and Gazala and Tobruk in North Africa.[3] All of them took place within weeks of one another. In the fall, German armies had advanced another one thousand miles, penetrated into the Caucasus Mountains, threatened Soviet oil supplies, and were poised to take Stalingrad.

For Allied policy, German power posed an equally menacing threat in North Africa. *Generalleutnant* Erwin Rommel had advanced comparable distances along the North African littoral. Hitler had dispatched Rommel to North Africa in February 1941 with two German divisions, initially designated the *Deutsches Afrikakorps*,[4] to bolster the Italians who were being driven out of Cyrenaica in Libya by the British 8th Army in 1941.[5] A German defeat of the British desert army in Egypt would render the British position in the Middle East untenable and sever lines of communication across the Mediterranean. In Churchill's mind, Egypt and Suez represented the center of gravity of the British Empire. It was central to the prime minister's preferred maritime strategy of attacking the "soft underbelly" of Europe from a strong base in the Mediterranean.

It was the two-pronged configuration of the German threat in mid-1942 against the Soviet Union and the British position in Egypt, after Rommel's Gazala victory, that presented the tantalizing opportunity for a deep German penetration into the Middle East, a pincer offensive by two German armies. One was poised to drive into the Middle East from the north through the Caucasus toward Iran, and the other was Rommel's *Afrikakorps* to attack east from Libya through Egypt, Palestine, Transjordan, and Iraq to the Persian Gulf.

STRATEGY

Germany by 1942 was struggling to assemble enough combat power for its armies to win in the Soviet Union and North Africa. As events unfolded, the Germans sustained two of their most decisive defeats of the war in less than three months: El Alamein in November 1942 and Stalingrad in January 1943. *Bewegungskrieg* was about to come to another dead end in the desert.

Britain's victory at El Alamein did not happen easily. The military vicissitudes during this period of the desert war, written about so extensively in British and American military histories, continue to capture the popular imagination. Two combatant commanders are the source of continuing fascination and debate: Rommel and the British general who defeated him, Lieutenant General Bernard Law Montgomery (later field marshal, the Viscount of Alamein).

After Rommel arrived in Libya in February 1941, it was not long before he made an impression not only on his enemies but also the world. Liddell Hart was among the early postwar admirers of Rommel's accomplishments:

> The impact that Rommel made on the world with the sword will be deepened by his power with the pen. No commander in history has written an account

of his campaigns to match the vividness and value of Rommel's. . . . No other commander has provided such a graphic picture of his operations and method of command. No one else has so strikingly conveyed in writing the dynamism of blitzkrieg and the pace of *Panzer* forces.[6]

A glance at a map of the Mediterranean basin (map 4.1) illustrates the strategic possibilities Rommel had in mind. Rommel wrote that the Suez Canal had "less strategic importance in this war than is generally supposed, owing to the fact that the Italians were able to bar the Mediterranean at Sicily."[7] He was looking at the oil fields in the Persian Gulf, Mesopotamia, and Iran. If Axis forces controlled the whole of the Mediterranean coastline and Mesopotamia, he reasoned, they would have an excellent base for an offensive against the southern Russian front. He understood that the principal flow of American arms and material aid to Russia passed through the Persian Gulf where tens of thousands of vehicles and thousands of tanks were unloaded on their way to the Russians.[8] Axis possession of this area would have forced the rerouting of American shipping to Murmansk, a route on which the British and American convoys were exposed to great danger from German submarines.[9]

Map 4.1. Rommel's strategic vision for the North African campaign was not about the ports at each end of the Mediterranean but, beyond Egypt, access to the oil in the Middle East.
Source: USMA Atlases.

Rommel outlined a chain of events that few German commanders were seeing as an enormous opportunity in 1942. A British defeat in North Africa would have enabled a German buildup in Mesopotamia for a major offensive against the southern Russian front. "This would have struck the Russians in a vital spot. . . . Thus the strategic conditions would have been created for us to close in from all sides and shatter the Russian colossus."[10]

Like Rommel, Montgomery endures as one of the most memorable and, between Americans and Britons, controversial commanders of World War II. Unlike Rommel's task to protect Libya, maintain Italian prestige, and keep British forces preoccupied, Montgomery was sent out to defeat German and Italian forces where a succession of British commanders had failed. Consecutively, they were General (later field marshal) Sir Archibald P. Wavell (1939–1941), General Sir Richard N. O'Connor (1940–1941), General Sir Philip Neame (1941), General (later field marshal) Sir Claude J. E. Auchinleck (1941–1942), General Sir Alan G. Cunningham (1941), and General Sir Neil M. Ritchie (1941–1942).

OPERATIONS

The Italians, under *Generalità Maresciallo* Rodolfo Graziani, had invaded Egypt in September 1940 and driven east unopposed into the Western Desert. Instead of pushing ahead to at least the railhead at Mersa Matruh, only 145 miles from Alexandria, Graziani abruptly stopped and set up a series of poorly organized fortified camps south of Sidi Barrani and west of Matruh (map 4.2a). He seemed not to know what to do next.

In January 1941, General Wavell, commander in chief (CINC) in the Middle East, ordered the Western Desert Force (WDF) to conduct a brief raid against the Italians that quickly evolved into Operation *Compass* in which the WDF captured Bardia and then Tobruk before completing the destruction of the Italian 10th Army at Beda Fomm in February. The British forces captured 110,000 prisoners including twenty-two generals.[11]

Rommel wasted no time in getting his small two-division force of the *Afrikakorps* deployed to attack British forces. Within six weeks of his arrival at Tripoli, he commenced a lightning strike on March 31, 1941, against General Neame's Cyrenaica Command, scattered the British armored division, captured Generals Neame and O'Connor, drove British forces from Cyrenaica, and besieged Tobruk, into which the Australian division had retired (map 4.2b).

What transpired between February 1941 and June 1942 were indecisive fights for ground in Cyrenaica (maps 4.2 and 4.3). The whole point of the North African campaign for both sides was the Suez Canal and the oil beyond. On one side was Rommel's relentless aggression and, on the other, the British

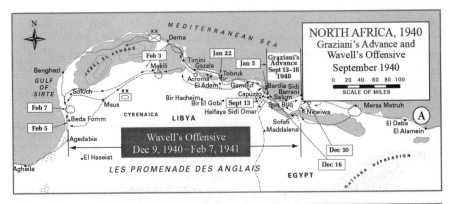

Map 4.2. The military initiative during early desert battles passed from the Italians to the British to the Germans.

Source: USMA Atlases.

struggling to find the strategic and tactical leadership to devise a winning military formula to defeat the Axis forces in North Africa. At Whitehall's instigation, General Wavell changed places with General Auchinleck, commander in chief, India, who took over as CINC Middle East; Wavell moved to the CINC India post.

After Rommel retired back to his start line at El Agheila toward the end of 1941, the British recaptured all of the territory in Cyrenaica, which Wavell's 1940–1941 *Compass* offensive against the Italians had overrun the previous winter (map 4.3a). The British in North Africa were starting to demonstrate a credible operational capability to defeat Axis land forces in the desert. Rommel, before he could renew his advance across Cyrenaica into Egypt, knew he had to solve his logistical problems.[12]

Auchinleck meanwhile put General Ritchie in command of 8th Army consisting of roughly one hundred thousand men and 850 tanks. Ritchie quickly found himself overtaken by Rommel. In February 1942, Rommel resumed the offensive, and Ritchie retreated back into prepared defensive positions at Gazala (map 4.3b).

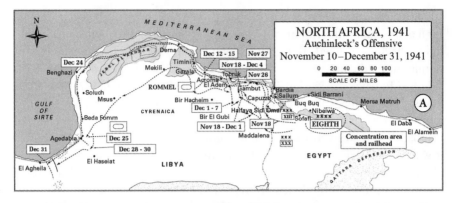

Map 4.3.   Between 1941 and 1942, the military initiative returned briefly to the British and then passed to the Germans until the Alamein battle was fought.
Source: USMA Atlases.

The construction of the Gazala Line constituted a massive defensive barrier designed to protect British forces. It consisted of huge minefields. One extended for forty-three miles inland from the coast, and a series of inland "boxes" were created, inside of which generally was a brigade. The most important boxes were at Bir Hacheim, which housed a Free French force, and at "Knightsbridge," which housed a British brigade. On an operations map, the Gazala Line appeared to be a formidable defensive barrier. However, it had serious weaknesses. British planners assumed that Rommel would attack along the coastal road. Therefore, a disproportionate amount of men and equipment was held in the coastal region at the expense of inland positions. The southern boxes had less artillery ammunition than they wanted. Rommel's intelligence suggested quite clearly that British strength in the southern part of the Gazala Line was not as strong as the British wanted to portray. Rommel's forces numbered 90,000 men, 560 tanks, and 500 serviceable planes.

The battle space at this stage was one thousand miles long and fifty miles wide along the North African littoral, and most of it was empty desert. It was ideal for maneuver warfare. There were no civilians to worry about becoming collateral damage. There was no urban property to protect. It was seductive for a commander like Rommel. Given enough supplies, the *Afrikakorps* could fight anywhere it liked. But getting enough supplies—fuel, water, food, ammunition, medicine, spares—that was a huge problem. By April 1942, each side had to truck its supplies five hundred to six hundred miles from its main bases. The challenge was harder for the Germans. Jon Latimer's metaphor of a bungee rope is apt. The farther the *Afrikakorps* advanced from its base in Tripoli, the greater was the restraining effect of that distance, and the easier it was for the defender to resist "the increasingly feeble stretch for the final objective," especially after Rommel's Gazala victory had enabled a farther eastward advance as the British retreated to El Alamein.[13]

The logistical issues in the North African theater underscored how Hitler's strategic architecture on two continents was becoming unsustainable. Every ton of ammunition, fuel, and food that the Germans consumed first had to be laboriously crated in Italy, then shipped across the Mediterranean to a port of sufficient capacity, principally Tripoli, and then trucked over hundreds of miles to the fighting front. Even water had to be transported this way. There were no railroads except the British line that ran 145 miles west from Alexandria to the railhead at Mersa Matruh. The vast empty spaces had to be entirely covered by road. Martin van Creveld's logistical metrics are illuminating. Rommel at the beginning of 1942 "demanded another 8,000 trucks for his supply columns. OKW denied the request out of hand because all German armored groups operating in Russia could only muster 14,000 trucks between them."[14] The military reality was that Rommel had advanced 750 miles from his base in Tripoli. Already, he was stretching his logistical bungee rope.

Between May 26 and June 21, 1942, Rommel resumed the offensive, initially attacking the Gazala Line with strengthened Italian units. Then, in a classic desert maneuver, he led an armored attack around the British southern flank. This initiative faltered as British tanks and guns slowed his forward movement. Ritchie now thought he had Rommel trapped as Rommel regrouped his forces for another attack and moved his armor into an area called "the Cauldron" (map 4.4). With the German force virtually surrounded by 8th Army, Ritchie believed he could destroy the *Afrikakorps*, but his attack lacked strength at the decisive point (*Schwerpunkt*) and was repulsed by the Germans. Rommel held the line in the center, broke out of the Cauldron, scattered three British armored brigades, and recaptured Tobruk in June, which changed hands for the third time.[15] The British 8th Army was in general retreat toward El Alamein.

By July 1942, Churchill was desperate for a British victory in North Africa. On July 1, 1942, his government was confronted with a vote of confidence resulting from a motion put before the House of Commons after the fall of Tobruk.[16] The prime minister won the vote of confidence handily, but the fact that such a motion went to a vote underscored the pressure under which

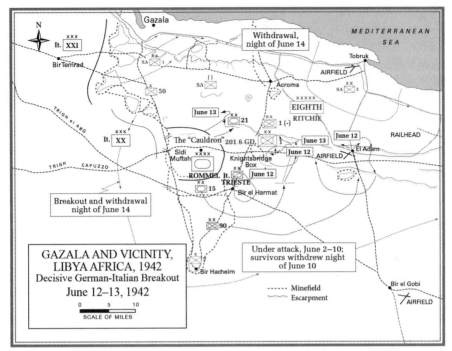

Map 4.4. British General Ritchie thought he had Rommel trapped at Gazala, but the Desert Fox broke out of "the Cauldron," attacked British and French boxes, and recaptured Tobruk.
Source: USMA Atlases.

Auchinleck served. Churchill badgered Auchinleck to go on the offensive after 8th Army had all but exhausted itself after the first battle of El Alamein. Auchinleck had succeeded in early July in stopping the German advance at Ruweisat Ridge. In Latimer's judgment, at this juncture, "one could say the tide of war turned against the Axis in North Africa,"[17] because Rommel advanced no further.

During July, Churchill hectored Auchinleck to attack Rommel, but Auchinleck argued that he needed time to prepare for a counteroffensive. It became obvious that the prime minister had lost confidence in Auchinleck, who was replaced as CINC Middle East Command by General Sir Harold Alexander (later field marshal, the Earl Alexander of Tunis). There were other changes. Lieutenant General William Gott was appointed general officer commanding 8th Army. On a transport flight returning to Cairo from the battle area, the *Luftwaffe* shot down his plane; after a crash-landing, Gott was among the passengers who died. On Gott's death, Lieutenant General Montgomery was appointed commander of 8th Army.

General Montgomery's assumption of command in North Africa on August 13, 1942, signaled a different method for the British in waging war. Montgomery had long been a believer in the well-planned, methodical, set-piece battle.

Despite his gaunt appearance and high-pitched voice, he radiated confidence. Latimer points out that "Monty," as he was soon to become known worldwide, had learned two things during his career that were to serve him well in the desert. One was the meticulously planned battle, a lesson from having served most of World War I as a staff officer. Montgomery was convinced that well-trained troops, given limited and identifiable objectives, supported by the full weight of artillery intelligently used, could force an enemy to withdraw. The other was his knowledge of the mood of the British public during the two years he spent in England between Dunkirk and his posting to Egypt. He understood that British soldiers "want to know what is going on and decide in their own minds what sort of person [their commanding general] is."[18] Montgomery wasted no time in enlightening them. The same day he assumed command in the desert, he said this to his staff:

> I want first of all to introduce myself to you. You do not know me. I do not know you. But we have to work together; therefore we must understand each other and we must have confidence in each other. I have only been here a few hours. But from what I have seen and heard since I arrived . . . I do not like the general atmosphere I find here. It is an atmosphere of doubt, of looking to select the next place to which to withdraw, of loss of confidence in our ability to defeat Rommel, of desperate defence measures by reserves in preparing positions in Cairo and the Delta. All that must cease! Let us have a new atmosphere. . . . What is the use of digging trenches in the Delta? It is quite useless; if we must lose this position we lose Egypt. . . . We will stand and fight here. *If we can't stay here, then let us stay here dead* [italics in original].[19]

At El Alamein, a British Commonwealth force of 195,000 men deployed in eleven divisions, four of them armored, defeated an Axis force of 104,000, four weak German and eight Italian divisions.[20] Montgomery's post-Alamein reputation tends to emphasize his cautious and systematic nature. He planned a methodical battle of attrition that he expected to be a "dogfight" lasting ten to twelve days. Numerous military historians have criticized Montgomery for his plodding concept of fighting the Alamein battle, disappointing those who prefer the dash and daring of aggressive maneuver. As Citino points out, "the fact remains that the terrain—the sea to the north, the Qattara Depression to the south, and wall-to-wall Axis divisions in between—hardly permitted any other approach, at least in the opening stages of the battle" (map 4.5).[21] In an account written months after the battle, the Desert Fox himself agreed because of the bottleneck terrain both armies confronted.

> The Alamein line lay between the sea and the Qattara Depression, which our reconnaissance had finally established as being impassable for major vehicle columns. Thus it was the only front in North Africa, apart from the Akarit position, which could not be turned at its southern end. All other positions could be collapsed by tying them down frontally and outflanking them to the south. Every-

where else it was possible to make a surprise sweep with motorized forces around the southern end of the line in order to seek a decision in mobile warfare in the enemy's rear. This fact of the open flank had led repeatedly to completely novel situations. But at Alamein it was different. This line, if solidly held by infantry throughout its length, completely ruled out any chance of a surprise enemy appearance in one's rear. The enemy had first to force a breakthrough.[22]

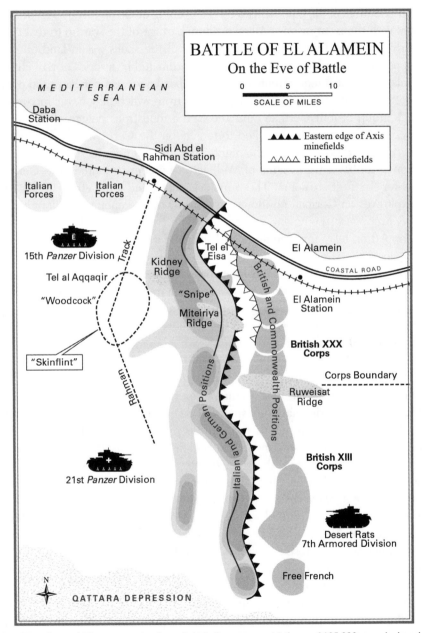

Map 4.5.   General Montgomery, leading a British Commonwealth force of 195,000 men deployed in eleven divisions, four of them armored, defeated Rommel's four German and eight Italian divisions.

Rommel had already tried to maneuver twice in this tactical area, and if the *Panzerarmee* had failed to find a solution in this terrain, 8th Army was equally likely to fail. Montgomery's plan for the operation sounded simple enough: punch a hole in the German positions, pass an armored corps with mobile, motorized infantry through the hole into enemy territory, and develop operations to destroy the Axis forces.

The Alamein battle commenced on the evening of October 23, 1942, at 2240 hours with the most massive Allied artillery barrage of the war up to that time. Nearly a thousand guns opened up so that all the shells would land on German positions simultaneously, the timing coordinated by a series of BBC timed signals. The first fifteen minutes of the bombardment was concentrated counterbattery fire on German artillery positions from which they never recovered. "Each group of four German guns received a monstrous deluge of 100 shells apiece."[23] The guns then switched to targets on the German front line where they remained for the rest of the night. Then the intensity increased as British airpower followed with flights of Wellington bombers pounding the German guns for the next six hours. The principal "shock and awe" effect of this rain of explosives on German positions was not just on the enemy's artillery but on the *Panzerarmee*'s command and control. The continuous shelling and bombing ripped up telephone landlines and smashed radio sets. RAF aircraft, fitted with electronic jamming equipment, compounded the confusion by jamming Axis radio frequency (RF) tactical networks. Two hours into the bombardment, Montgomery crammed four divisions into a narrow sector of the northern front six miles wide. By the next day, large sections of the German front in the north were in British hands. German and Italian units manning their positions along this portion of the front found themselves hammered by air and artillery and bulldozed by what seemed an overwhelming ground force.

The Axis logistical bungee was at full stretch now. Hitler was preoccupied with the stalled assault against Stalingrad on the Eastern Front. There was no manpower or matériel margin to spare. The *Panzerarmee* was forced to deploy in a line at Alamein, in defensive positions prepared in depth in front of an ocean of five hundred thousand mines, and fight a defensive battle of position. Defensive *Stellungskrieg* at this stage of the war was not yet a *Wehrmacht* specialty. Behind this line lay the mobile formations of two Italian divisions in the north and the *Afrikakorps* in the south, their armor to be used to launch what Rommel and his staff hoped to be pincer counterattacks. But few of these units had adequate fuel stocks.

Rommel was not present when the battle began, having departed for Germany the previous month to recover his physical and emotional health after eighteen months in the desert. He immediately flew back to North Africa. Rommel made his one significant operational decision of the battle. He ordered the crack 21st *Panzer* Division from its positions behind the southern portion of the line to the north.

He knew at the time he issued the command that it would be a one-way journey because the division barely had enough fuel to get there, let alone do much maneuvering and fighting once it engaged the British northern flank. Many accounts focus on the close-in combat around various positions such as "Kidney Ridge" and British strongpoints such as "Snipe" and "Woodcock," but at the operational level, at least for the Axis, "the issue was never in doubt."[24] By the first week in November 1942, Rommel was down to thirty serviceable tanks against British forces arrayed in a semicircle in front of *Afrikakorps*.[25] Rommel recognized that his army was on the brink of destruction, and he began to pull parts of it out of the line to begin a retreat.

He had no sooner issued fallback orders than Hitler shocked Rommel, promoted to *Feldmarschall* after the Gazala victory, by issuing his stand-fast order:

> It is with trusting confidence in your leadership and the courage of the German-Italian troops under your command that the German people and I are following the heroic struggle in Egypt. In the situation in which you find yourself there can be no other thought than to stand fast, yield not a yard of ground and throw every gun and every man into the battle. . . . Your enemy, despite his superiority, must also be at the end of his strength. It would not be the first time in history that a strong will has triumphed over the bigger battalions. As to your troops, you can show them no other road than to victory or death.[26]

These kinds of no-retreat orders were soon to become almost routine military communications elsewhere at places like Stalingrad. Rommel then stopped his retreat in midstream, and at that juncture the *Panzerarmee* began to fall apart. The Battle of El Alamein was over.

OPERATION *TORCH*

The war, of course, was not. As Churchill famously remarked, it was only "the end of the beginning."[27] Simultaneous with the British Alamein victory, Allied forces invaded North Africa (Operation *Torch*) on November 8, 1942. Rommel in retreat from Alamein now faced grave Allied threats in his rear. However, as 8th Army already knew, and as American forces were to discover three months later at Kasserine Pass in Tunisia, even a German army in defeat could still be extremely dangerous.

POLICY

Eleven months earlier, as 1942 opened, the Allies, like the Axis, faced their own set of strategic problems. At the *Arcadia* Conference in Washington, between December 22, 1941, and January 14, 1942, Churchill and Roosevelt had agreed upon a "Europe First" strategy. A military allocation in the 70/30 range, favoring Europe over the Pacific, appears well established among authoritative sources.[28] However, neither the president nor the prime minister nor their senior military staffs were in full agreement about the operational details for beginning a series of effective war-winning campaigns.

President Roosevelt's decision to invade North Africa emerged from the American desire to see American ground forces engaged in combat against Axis troops somewhere in the European theater of operations (ETO) before the end of 1942. Operation *Torch* grew out of Churchill's strong desire to attack the soft underbelly of the Axis as an alternative to the British reluctance to support a cross-Channel invasion of the Continent before 1943 at the earliest. *Torch* became the compromise between British hesitation to invade Europe directly until there was further attrition of the *Wehrmacht* on the Eastern Front and American eagerness to attack German ground forces somewhere because otherwise political pressure might divert more military assets to fight the Japanese in the Pacific.[29]

STRATEGY

The American chief of staff, General George C. Marshall, preferred a direct, full-scale, cross-Channel assault on the Continent that held Roosevelt's sympathy. Once it became clear that neither sufficient numbers of trained men nor matériel could be mobilized in 1942 for a cross-Channel assault, a series of proposals followed early Allied councils of war and were the source of continual Anglo-American disagreements over strategy for the next two and a half years. Four strategic proposals were under Allied debate: a British proposal to fight the Axis in North Africa in 1942 (*Gymnast*); or to build up forces in England in 1942, 5,800 combat aircraft and forty-eight divisions (*Bolero*), for an invasion of the Continent in 1943 (*Roundup*); or in the case of the imminent collapse of the Red Army to divert Allied resources to gain a small foothold in Europe in 1942 (*Sledgehammer*).[30] The back-and-forth negotiations among the Allies over *Gymnast, Bolero, Roundup*, and *Sledgehammer* a year later produced a consensus at the Casablanca Conference in January 1943 on the timing of the Germany-first strategy agreed to at the 1942 *Arcadia* Conference in Washington. American commanders would learn as a result of *Torch* that their war-fighting power and combat skills had to improve before they could assault the Continent across the Channel.

In February 1942, Marshall appointed Dwight D. Eisenhower, then a recently promoted temporary brigadier general, as head of the War Plans Division of the War Department. Eisenhower's appointment was characteristic of

Marshall's institutional approach to military staffing: identify and promote smart, aggressive, younger officers to key planning and command positions, and reassign or retire the deadwood. Marshall cashiered seven hundred officers in 1940, including most of the generals commanding divisions in the Louisiana maneuvers of 1940–1941, very quietly so he could promote more capable officers.[31]

As the war started, Eisenhower had been a lieutenant colonel. There were many others whose names soon became familiar to the American wartime public: In 1940, Terry de la Mesa Allen was a lieutenant colonel; Omar N. Bradley, a lieutenant colonel; Mark W. Clark, a lieutenant colonel; J. Lawton Collins, a lieutenant colonel; James "Jimmy" H. Doolittle, a major; Leslie R. Groves, a major; Courtney H. Hodges, a colonel; Curtis E. LeMay, a captain; George S. Patton Jr., a colonel; Matthew B. Ridgway, a lieutenant colonel; Walter Bedell Smith, a major; Maxwell D. Taylor, a major; Lucien K. Truscott Jr., a major; James A. Van Fleet, a major; and Walton H. Walker, a lieutenant colonel. The promotions of these officers and many like them were a shrewd combination from Brian A. Linn's three traditions of Managers, Heroes, and Guardians.[32] To pave the way for these younger men, most of the forty-two division, corps, and army commanders who took part in 1941 US Army GHQ maneuvers were either relieved or reassigned to new commands during 1942. The weeding-out process was ruthless and relentless throughout the war.

Thomas E. Ricks's comprehensive work on American military leadership points out that under "the Marshall system," senior American commanders during World War II "generally were given a few months in which to succeed, be killed or wounded, or be replaced. Sixteen Army division commanders were relieved for cause, out of a total of 155 officers who commanded Army divisions in combat during the war. At least five corps commanders also were removed for cause."[33] General Marshall had spent his prewar career, as had Eisenhower, thinking deeply and thoroughly about how the army would have to function as part of a coalition in any future conflict. By the mid-1930s he had started implementing personnel policies that enabled the army's cadre to be ready in 1940–1941.

The overall command of *Torch* was placed in the hands of General Eisenhower. Execution of *Torch* on the heels of Montgomery's Alamein victory meant that Rommel now found his *Panzerarmee* caught in a vice with jaws closing from both ends of the North African littoral, pursued by the British 8th Army from the east and threatened from the west by Anglo-American ground forces that landed divisions in November 1942 in Morocco and Algeria at three locations: Casablanca, Oran, and Algiers (map 4.6).

A total of 125,000 Allied soldiers, sailors, and airmen initially participated in *Torch*, 82,600 of them US Army personnel. Initial Allied casualties were relatively light. By the end of the campaign seven months later, manpower had grown to over half a million, and casualties exceeded seventy thousand.[34]

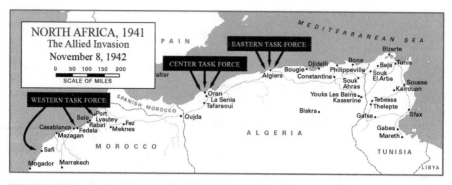

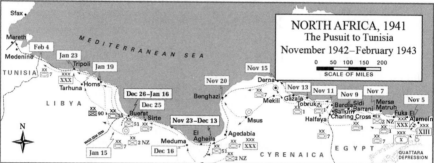

Map 4.6. The invasion of North Africa saved Allied forces from catastrophe had they invaded France in 1943 because Operation *Torch* uncovered serious operational deficiencies in the US Army, including the debacle at Kasserine Pass.
Source: USMA Atlases.

OPERATIONS

In Peter R. Mansoor's assessment, the decision to invade North Africa in late 1942 "probably saved Allied forces from catastrophe had they invaded France in 1943. Operation *Torch* uncovered serious weaknesses in joint and combined operations, combined-arms training, and small-unit leadership."[35] The Americans discovered that they had deployed an army by and large not fully prepared to fight and win its first battles, unsure of its military skills, but determined and innovative enough to win.[36]

The tactical failure at Kasserine Pass resulted in thirty thousand Americans confronting eleven thousand Germans but sustaining losses of 183 tanks, 194 half-tracks, 208 artillery pieces, 512 trucks, and "more supplies than existed in all the depots in Algeria and Morocco and . . . 6,300 troops" against 989 German casualties.[37] The debacle motivated the US Army to study and document lessons learned after the army's first introduction to land combat against German forces. The lessons included use of fire and maneuver to advance against enemy positions; the importance of careful study of terrain and the enemy; the value of detailed development and communication of comprehensive battle plans; the meticulous attention to tactical command, control, and communications, particularly to the waterproofing of radio sets and attention to their maintenance; the importance of combined-arms coordination, including close air ground support (still in its infancy); the need to train and fight at night; the use of smoke to obscure movement; the importance of small-unit training and practice; and the criticality of a well-organized logistical supply chain at the divisional level and below.[38] In mastering the basics, the US Army learned that *Bewegungskrieg* could be defeated.

Rommel later expressed high praise for the American performance in North Africa and Europe:

> In Tunisia the Americans had to pay a stiff price for their experience [inexperience], but it brought rich dividends. Even at that time, the American generals showed themselves to be very advanced in the tactical handling of their forces, although we had to wait until the Patton Army in France [Patton's 3rd Army was activated on August 1, 1944, to exploit the breakthrough during the execution of Operation *Cobra*] to see the most astonishing achievements in mobile warfare. The Americans, it is fair to say, profited far more than the British from their experience in Africa, thus confirming the axiom that education is easier than re-education.[39]

The substantial Anglo-American literature on the British victory at Alamein and the American introduction to land combat in North Africa enabled the US Army to gain early experience in how to defeat Axis armies, take back Axis territory, and hold it.

CONCLUSIONS

The outcome in North Africa can be explained by a comparison of the flawed German strategic architecture and the robust capacity of the Anglo-American architecture to adapt. The Germans failed to win in the desert because of their overreach in both the Soviet Union and the Middle East. Even though Hitler dispatched Rommel to North Africa as one of his most aggressive commanders, German strategic overreach became unmanageable. Eighty percent of the *Wehrmacht*'s deployed armies (more than 230 divisions) were fighting in Russia. Rommel had been fighting with four German divisions in Africa with insufficient combat power and logistics to win. Germany simply lacked the resources to win in either theater. Defeat in North Africa marked the beginning of a German downward slide. The Germans lost as many soldiers in Tunisia as they did at Stalingrad.

In North Africa, the Allies did not yet have all of the elements of a strategic architecture to win the war, but they aligned political leadership, selected new commanders, developed campaign plans, improved military skills, and rapidly expanded production so they could confidently proceed to the next stage of the war: continue to exploit success in the Mediterranean theater until they assembled the strength to liberate the Continent.

Battle of El Alamein and Operation *Torch*

(1) General Rommel with the 15th *Panzer* Division between Tobruk and Sidi Omar, in Libya, in 1941 (left). NARA photo (2) General Montgomery watching battle in Egypt's Western Desert from the turret of a Grant tank in 1942. IWM photo

(3) German soldiers in North Africa getting water and fuel in desert; note "jerry cans" in foreground. (4) Rommel (second from right) raising his baton in greeting to Lieutenant Colonel (*Oberstleutnant*) Fritz Beyerlein, standing in captured American M-3 half-track, in Tunisia, 1942–1943 (bottom left). (5) *Afrikakorps* soldiers on a military vehicle, one with megaphone, in March 1941 (right). BArch photos

BATTLES OF MIDWAY AND GUADALCANAL

Regaining Initiative in the Pacific

On June 4, 1942, two small US Navy carrier task forces surprised and defeated Admiral Yamamoto Isoroku's Imperial Japanese Combined Fleet during its attempt to capture Midway atoll in the Central Pacific. Exactly 180 days after December 7, 1941, a handful of American dive-bombers achieved this dynamic shift in the naval balance of power, sinking four of the six Japanese carriers that had attacked the US Pacific Fleet at Pearl Harbor.

The American victory at Midway was strategic because the US Navy recaptured the naval initiative in the Pacific after winning an attrition battle where the balance of forces favored the Japanese. Two months after Midway, the US Navy and Marine Corps seized Guadalcanal in the Lower Solomon Islands. Guadalcanal was the first offensive amphibious operation that signaled Allied intent to recapture the Western Pacific from Japan. Midway and Guadalcanal required opportunistic, front-to-back strategic architectures where American policy, strategy, and operations were designed to make the best out of what had been a very adverse situation six months earlier.

POLICY

The geopolitical goal of Japanese policy was to cripple the US Pacific Fleet at Pearl Harbor and through subsequent conquests force the United States to negotiate a peace treaty or an armistice granting Japan dominance in the

Pacific. However, Yamamoto failed to resolve the strategic menace of Nimitz's Pacific Fleet because the Pearl Harbor attack failed to catch any of the Pacific Fleet carriers in port. Pearl Harbor did not immediately enable Yamamoto to fulfill his promise to "run wild" for a year or two.[1] Events soon forced Yamamoto to react by luring Nimitz to come out and fight with his fleet carriers to defend Midway, thus provoking what Japan hoped would be the "decisive battle" of the Pacific war (map 5.1).[2] The Imperial Japanese Navy (IJN) during its prewar buildup had been optimized to fight a massive fleet engagement where the IJN would destroy American naval power in the Pacific.[3] None of the early naval battles in 1942 and 1943 were massive fleet engagements, and none were decisive for the IJN.

Japan's policy was predicated on a misperception of American weakness and a flawed Japanese assumption of American rationality. Americans were seen as businessmen, not samurai. Japan's *bushidō* ethos was an aristocrat's military creed from the samurai tradition that by the late 1930s had been transformed into a doctrine perfectly suited to suicidal total war and total defeat.[4] Japan expected that American priorities in Europe and the Atlantic would force the United States to come to terms with the fait accompli created by Japanese arms.[5] Instead, Pearl Harbor produced American fury.

President Roosevelt used the eleven fireside chats he broadcast during the war to lay out his policies for fighting a global war. In his second fireside chat of February 23, 1942, the president invited his listeners to have a map handy. He spoke candidly and comprehensively about the global situation.

> This war is a new kind of war. It is different from all other wars of the past, not only in its methods and weapons but also in its geography. It is warfare in terms of every continent, every island, every sea, every air lane in the world. That is the reason why I have asked you to take out and spread before you a map of the whole earth, and to follow with me the references which I shall make to the world-encircling battle lines of this war.[6]

In another four thousand words, theater by theater, the president discussed enemy threats and logistics issues facing the United States and the Allies. He accurately reported the damage to the Pacific Fleet at Pearl Harbor. He outlined the issues of production and the "prodigious effort" required to defeat the Axis. "Never before have we had so little time in which to do so much." It was a masterful performance.

President Roosevelt's public-opinion polling numbers validated his skills in communicating convincingly to the American people. The polling data showed high public approval ratings throughout the war. They oscillated between the 70 and 80 percent ranges from 1941 to 1943 and hovered around 70 percent for the rest of the war. Churchill's polling numbers were comparable.[7]

STRATEGY

Midway reinforces the view that the war at sea, at least for Britain and America, dominated Allied planning and strategy until the middle years of the global conflict. Overy posits that "for most of the Second World War Britain and the United States fought a predominantly naval conflict, and relied more heavily on naval power than anything else."[8]

Roosevelt directed Secretary of the Navy Frank Knox, "Tell Nimitz to get the hell out to Pearl and stay there till the war is won." Admiral Chester W. Nimitz was appointed CINCPAC after Pearl Harbor.[9] Roosevelt believed that in the wake of the shock and anger following Pearl Harbor the American public needed an early offensive act to demonstrate that the United States was capable of striking back at the enemy. He pressed War Department planners for an air strike against Tokyo. He knew such a raid would have little military effect, but he pushed the military staffs to find a way to impress the world with American resolve. The Doolittle Raid was the result.[10] On April 18, 1942, Lieutenant Colonel James "Jimmy" H. Doolittle led the raid that consisted of sixteen B-25B Mitchell bombers launched from the carriers *Enterprise* and *Hornet* deep within enemy waters in the Central Pacific. The bombers struck military and industrial targets in Tokyo, Yokohama, Yokosuka, Nagoya, Kobe, and Osaka. The raid produced a worldwide sensation.

In executing the Doolittle Raid, Admiral Nimitz directed Vice Admiral William F. Halsey Jr. to do something that had never been tried before: launching two-engine medium bombers off an aircraft carrier. American leaders were prepared to take risks for relatively high gains if improbable missions could be successful. President Roosevelt and Admiral Nimitz aligned American policy and strategy to get the best out of America's weak situation in the Pacific early in the war. Roosevelt did it with the Doolittle Raid. Nimitz later did it with his order to Rear Admirals Raymond A. Spruance and Frank J. Fletcher to attack Yamamoto's Combined Fleet at Midway.

Midway was won by the narrowest of margins—"ten bombs in ten minutes."[11] It was an extraordinary performance given the historical view that American pilots were considerably less prepared than their Japanese counterparts.[12]

The US Navy's victory soon led to the violent combat that ensued two months later in the Solomon Islands. Even with the loss of four carriers, the Japanese forced the US Navy and Marine Corps to fight a grim seven-month battle before securing Guadalcanal. Fighting in the Solomons demonstrated which combatant was in the best position to hold the military initiative given the naval balance of forces.[13] After Midway, the IJN's loss of nearly a quarter of its elite pool of aviators was irreplaceable.[14] Jonathan Parshall and Anthony Tully underscore the scale of Japanese naval air corps losses after Midway; these losses paled against the casualties in the Solomons:

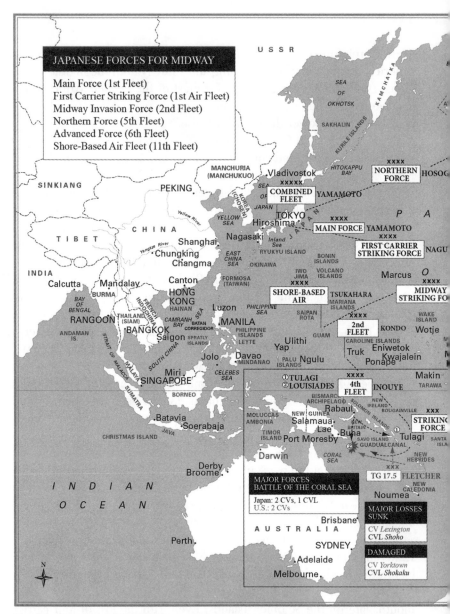

Map 5.1. Yamamoto's Midway plan was to fight and win the "decisive battle" of the Pacific war by forcing Nimitz to come out and fight with his fleet carriers to defend Midway.

Source: USMA Atlases.

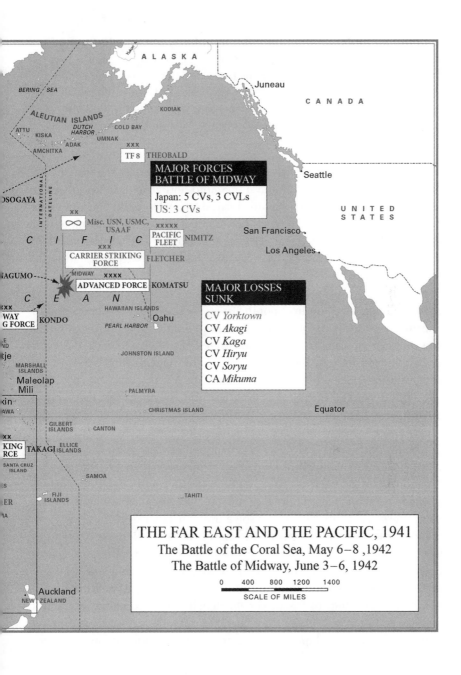

ALASKA

Juneau

CANADA

BERING SEA

ALEUTIAN ISLANDS

ATTU KISKA DUTCH HARBOR COLD BAY
AMCHITKA ADAK UMNAK

KODIAK

Seattle

UNITED
STATES

XXX
TF 8 THEOBALD

OSOGAYA

XX
∞ Misc. USN, USMC,
USAAF

XXXXX
PACIFIC NIMITZ
FLEET

San Francisco

Los Angeles

**MAJOR FORCES
BATTLE OF MIDWAY**

Japan: 5 CVs, 3 CVLs
US: 3 CVs

XXX
CARRIER STRIKING FLETCHER
FORCE

NAGUMO

MIDWAY XXXX

XXX
ADVANCED FORCE KOMATSU

C   E   A   N

HAWAIIAN ISLANDS

XXX
WAY
G FORCE KONDO

Oahu

PEARL HARBOR

JOHNSTON ISLAND

MARSHALL
ISLANDS
Maleolap
Mili

PALMYRA

CHRISTMAS ISLAND

Equator

GILBERT
ISLANDS CANTON

XX
KING TAKAGI ELLICE
RCE ISLANDS

SANTA CRUZ
ISLAND

SAMOA

FIJI
ISLANDS

TAHITI

**MAJOR LOSSES
SUNK**

CV *Yorktown*
CV *Akagi*
CV *Kaga*
CV *Hiryu*
CV *Soryu*
CA *Mikuma*

THE FAR EAST AND THE PACIFIC, 1941
The Battle of the Coral Sea, May 6–8 ,1942
The Battle of Midway, June 3–6, 1942

0   400   800   1200   1400

SCALE OF MILES

Auckland
NEW ZEALAND

Any assessment of the scale of Midway's human losses must also be measured against the backdrop of the grim combat in the South Pacific. . . . It was here, in the daily patrols, skirmishes, and raids that lasted until 1944 that the crème of Japan's naval air forces would be destroyed—some 2,817 naval aircraft alone between April 1942 and April 1943. Callous as it may seem, the existence or nonexistence of roughly one hundred carrier aircrew meant relatively little when set against this aerial meat grinder.[15]

The Japanese failed to establish an early consensus on how the war should develop after Pearl Harbor. Admiral Yamamoto and army military planners wasted five months debating what to do next. The Doolittle Raid was the clincher that broke the debate. The embarrassment persuaded Yamamoto that Midway should be the next target. He wanted to draw the US Pacific Fleet into a decisive battle around Midway because he knew that Japan had to be triumphant in 1942 or lose the war.

Japan's delay gave Admiral Nimitz and the US Navy time to recover and reorganize. Nimitz used the five months to assess senior naval officers and to make astute appointments of offense-minded admirals. The Midway battle and the invasion of Guadalcanal demonstrated his ability to pick the right people at the right time in the right place for the right mission. And he did not hesitate to replace commanders who failed to win or were not aggressive enough. Nimitz worked tirelessly at his CINCPAC headquarters to mobilize resources for his fighting admirals. For Midway, Nimitz had only two battle-ready carriers, *Enterprise* and *Lexington*. A third carrier, *Yorktown*, was in need of major dockyard repair after receiving major damage in the Battle of the Coral Sea. He convinced his repair yard manager at Pearl Harbor that *Yorktown* had to stand back out to sea in three days even though the manager thought the job required a ninety-day refit. Nimitz knew what needed to be done and pressed his subordinates to solve problems quickly.[16]

For Japan, the value of occupying Midway lay in its location. At 1,300 miles northwest of Oahu, Midway could serve as a base for future operations against the center of gravity of American naval power, Pearl Harbor and its large infrastructure. Japanese plans never included invasion of Hawaii or the US West Coast in its strategy of Pacific dominance; it possessed neither the naval nor military power to undertake such far-flung operations. However, holding Midway would enable the Japanese to intercept American naval forces operating in the north and west of the Hawaiian Islands.[17] Control of Midway would certainly make air strikes like the Doolittle Raid much harder to mount from the Hawaiian waters of the Pacific.

OPERATIONS

Yamamoto divided the naval forces into five fleets. He commanded the Main Force of battleships and cruisers of the IJN's 1st Fleet, flying his flag on the battleship *Yamato*. This body stayed three hundred miles west of the Fast Carrier Striking Force of four carriers and supporting vessels under 1st Air Fleet commander Admiral Nagumo Chūichi, who had commanded the carrier force that attacked Pearl Harbor (map 5.1). With 225 operational aircraft, Nagumo's main mission was the destruction of the American carriers. Yamamoto's staff anticipated having six fleet carriers available for the Midway operation, but the Coral Sea battle damage to *Shōkaku* and *Zuikaku* eliminated their combat service at Midway.

An advance force of IJN 6th Fleet cruisers and destroyers was tasked with covering the invasion force scheduled to land on Midway Island in operations preceding arrival of the Midway Invasion Force composed of IJN 2nd Fleet units. An IJN 5th Fleet Northern Force, including the Second Carrier Strike Force, consisting of the newly commissioned fleet carrier *Junyō* and the light carrier *Ryūjō*, steamed northeast to attack the Aleutian Islands as a diversion. Twenty-six submarines picketed the waters between Hawaii and Midway to detect American ships departing Pearl Harbor.

The code-breaking success of the top-secret "Station Hypo," commanded by Lieutenant Commander Joseph J. Rochefort, in identifying the Japanese intention to strike Midway by decrypting the Japanese Naval Code—JN 25— has become a central part of the battle's narrative. By skillful SIGINT deception, American radio intelligence persuaded the Japanese that two of the three carriers of the American Pacific Fleet were operating in the Southwest Pacific to protect Australia, too distant to affect IJN plans for Midway.[18]

Rochefort's strategic intelligence presented to Admiral Nimitz on May 14, 1942, proved remarkably accurate, identifying the time, direction, and order of battle of the Japanese attack. After the battle, Nimitz remarked, "Rochefort was one degree and one hour off in his prediction."[19] Rochefort's analysis did not pinpoint the location of the Japanese ships in a wide ocean. Locating them remained a daunting task. However, knowing Midway was the focus of the Japanese fleet enabled Nimitz to position his ships two hundred miles northeast, where they could engage the Japanese when they attacked Midway.

American land-based aircraft from Midway were in the air by 0400 on June 4, 1942. Nagumo launched his carrier aircraft to attack Midway at 0445. At 0710, US Navy and US Army Air Force planes from Midway attacked Nagumo's carrier strike force. For over an hour, Nagumo's ships successfully avoided bombs and torpedoes. At 0700, the Japanese air strike commander radioed that a second strike on Midway would be required to assure a successful invasion. At 0715, Nagumo ordered remaining aircraft to rearm for a second attack. Rearmament required a time-consuming process of replacing antiship ordinance with land bombs. At 0728, a scout plane launched from the cruiser *Tone* sighted the American task force but only reported finding cruisers and destroyers. Precisely when Nagumo learned that American carriers were present remains disputed.[20] In any event, the admiral dithered.[21] By 0805 (Overy's account indicates 0820), he countermanded the rearming order when he learned that there might be at least one American carrier present. Rather than attack the enemy at once, he decided to land his aircraft now arriving back from the Midway strike and rearm them with antiship ordnance and then reorganize for an attack on the American fleet later in the morning. This decision was a fatal mistake. For the next hour, the carriers of the *Kido Butai* (the Fast Carrier Striking Force) were at their most vulnerable, full of refueling and rearming aircraft, with only light fighter cover above the fleet, their position known to the Americans. Admirals Spruance and Fletcher shrewdly held back their own carrier attack aircraft so they could hit the Japanese ships during this crucial changeover.

Between 0800 and 0900, the size of the enemy combat air patrol (CAP) grew from nine to thirty-nine Mitsubishi Zero fighters protecting the *Kido Butai*. At 0837 the Japanese carriers began the process of recovering the Midway strike aircraft. The strike force was aboard by around 0915 and struck below to be refueled and rearmed.

According to Dallas W. Isom's analysis of Nagumo's decision, the admiral believed he had time to develop a coordinated and escorted strike package on the assumption that the American force was over two hundred miles away, too far away to launch an escorted attack because the Wildcat fighter had only a 175-mile operational range.[22]

At 0918 the *Kido Butai* spotted Torpedo Squadron 8 (VT-8) flying Douglas TBD-1 "Devastator" torpedo bombers launched from the *Hornet*. The TBDs' slow speed rendered them easy targets, and their torpedoes were defective. The planes had separated from their fighter protection and approached the Japanese fleet unescorted.[23] Nagumo turned his fleet west, and the CAP annihilated all fifteen aircraft during a fifteen-minute period.

By 0940, Torpedo Squadron VT-6 from the *Enterprise* began their attack run.[24] The second torpedo attack was equally unsuccessful, and ten of the aircraft were shot down. At 1010, *Yorktown*'s VT-3 was spotted approaching the *Kido Butai*. *Yorktown*'s bombers were protected by VF-3 commanded by Lieutenant Commander John S. Thatch.[25] The six Wildcat fighters engaged the Zeros, destroying four while losing one Wildcat. At 1015, VT-3 attacked *Hiryū* and drew the attention of the high-level CAP Zeros. The low-flying Japanese CAP had already been in extended aerial combat, had exhausted their 20 mm ammunition, and had started to land on the carriers to rearm and refuel.[26]

At 1022, Lieutenant Commander Clarence W. McClusky's thirty-three SBD "Dauntless" dive-bombers[27] from the *Enterprise* attacked the two closest carriers, *Kaga* and *Akagi*. Dive-bombers from VB-6[28] and VS-6[29] scored three hits on *Kaga* and four hits on *Akagi*.[30] As McClusky's formation was completing its attack, seventeen SBD dive-bombers, VB-3 from *Yorktown* commanded by Lieutenant Commander Maxwell F. Leslie, dived on the *Sōryū* and scored three hits down the centerline of the ship. *Sōryū*, too, was finished. By 1028, three of Nagumo's fleet carriers were crippled and burning.

The bomb damage was magnified because the torpedoes and land bombs removed from Japanese strike aircraft during fueling and rearming on the hanger deck were not returned to the ammunition lockers. The bombs penetrating the flight decks of Nagumo's carriers set off secondary fuel and ordnance explosions and raging fires that proved impossible to contain.

Thirty minutes later, Rear Admiral Yamaguchi Tamon aboard the surviving *Hiryū* launched twenty-four aircraft to counterattack the American task forces. The *Hiryū*'s strike force found Task Force 17 just before noon. *Yorktown*'s radar picked up the incoming "bogies" and directed *Yorktown*'s Wildcats to intercept. The *Enterprise* directed eight aircraft from Task Force 16 to assist. Seven Asahi carrier-based dive-bombers survived combat with the defending American CAP aircraft and severely damaged the *Yorktown* with three of the seven bombs they dropped. *Yorktown*'s speed was reduced to six knots.

Admiral Yamaguchi launched a second strike against US carriers early in the afternoon after confirmation of the successful attack on *Yorktown*. This force consisted of ten "Kate" torpedo bombers and an escort of six Zero fighters. It was instructed to attack an undamaged carrier. The Kates sighted *Yorktown*, which appeared undamaged.[31] Fighting through defending Wildcats from all three carriers, four Kates attacked *Yorktown* with their deadly Type 91 torpedoes. The torpedoes ripped open *Yorktown*'s hull, bringing it to a halt, and the ship began to list. By mid-afternoon on June 4, the order was given to abandon ship.

Admirals Spruance and Fletcher were aware that the fourth Japanese carrier, *Hiryū*, was intact and operating. By 1445, a patrol plane sighted *Hiryū* in company with two battleships, three cruisers, and four destroyers about 110 miles from *Yorktown*. Admiral Spruance immediately launched fourteen SBD dive-bombers from *Enterprise*. They hit *Hiryū* around 1700 and scored four direct hits. The resulting fires could not be controlled. One bomb had blown the forward elevator plant into the island, destroying all power lines and communications. *Hiryū*, like *Akagi*, *Kaga*, and *Sōryū*, became a flaming, inoperable wreck. The carrier was abandoned early the following morning and finally sank.

At this point in the battle, the naval calculus still favored Yamamoto. Or so he thought. Measured in terms of guns, the Japanese retained superiority. He ordered the screening group from the Aleutian Force and Midway

Invasion Force to join his Main Force the next day. However, after learning of the magnitude of his carrier losses, he decided to retire west. The battle was over.

The initial six months of wartime combat reinforced the basic soundness of the prewar preparation by Allied and Japanese combatants with regard to their respective doctrines, carrier designs, aircraft, and pilot training.[32] However, there were significant differences. At the outset of hostilities, the IJN arguably had better-performing aircraft and better-trained and more combat-experienced pilots than those in Task Forces 16 and 17, but the American dive-bombers and the aviators' flying skills and determination were sufficient to ensure that their combat performance exceeded even their admirals' wildest expectations of a major upset in the naval balance.[33] The result was a turning point. The IJN until Midway was at the peak of its war-fighting strength; the US Navy, up until Midway, was at its weakest. Midway was the first strategic milestone on Japan's path to defeat.

BATTLE OF GUADALCANAL

After the Midway victory, Admiral Ernest J. King urged his admirals to seize the initiative and invade the Lower Solomons. Guadalcanal was the first concrete opportunity. King wrote after the war,

> I sent an order to Admiral Nimitz saying that despite all other orders, large or small, the basic orders are that the Pacific Fleet must, first, keep all means of communications with the West Coast and, second, but close to the first order, keep all areas between Hawaii and Samoa clear of the Japanese and then as fast as it could expand that area toward Australia.[34]

King reasoned that although Japanese expansion had been blunted at the Battle of the Coral Sea and dealt a major defeat at Midway, Japan's expansion to the Solomon Islands threatened the Allied lifeline from the West Coast and Hawaii to Australia. King was determined to protect this route at all costs by launching a counteroffensive in the Lower Solomons. He wanted to draw in Japanese military and naval resources to divert enemy attention from other areas of the Pacific.

POLICY

After Midway, King and Nimitz seized the naval and military initiative in the South Pacific.[35] Between June 1942 and February 1943, the war in the Pacific was dominated by the Guadalcanal campaign in the lower Solomon Islands. In this campaign, the Japanese sustained a comprehensive defeat inflicted by American naval and military power. In August 1942, the US Navy landed the 1st Marine Division and a regiment of the 2nd Marine Division on Guadalcanal, a total of sixteen thousand men, under the command of Major General Alexander Archer Vandegrift.

STRATEGY

In response to the Guadalcanal landing, Yamamoto moved his headquarters to Rabaul, 650 miles north of Guadalcanal (map 5.2). He reinforced naval units at Rabaul from the IJN's major fleet anchorage at Truk. He and his staff wanted to avenge his humiliation at Midway and still sought another decisive battle. Operations demonstrated that he failed to concentrate his fleet forces, a Clausewitzian principle he ignored at Midway. He never sent sufficient IJN forces into the waters around Guadalcanal to defeat weaker American screening forces and neutralize naval protection of the beachhead.

Nimitz meanwhile directed that the Solomons campaign be conducted by his Midway concept of calculated risk: "'Having inferior forces' he wrote

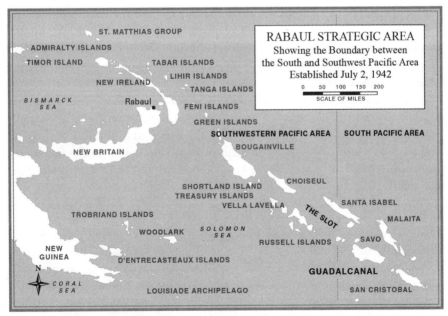

Map 5.2. Warships attacking or defending Guadalcanal had to pass through the narrow waters of "the Slot," perilous for the navies of both sides.

Source: USMC map of Southwest Pacific area, 1942, http://www.ibiblio.org/hyperwar/USMC/USMC-C-CSol/index .html.

early in the Solomons campaign, 'we must count heavily on attrition, but losing no chance to come to grips with the enemy under the principle of calculated risk.'[36] Task Forces 16 and 17 were committed to support the marines on Guadalcanal.

OPERATIONS

After landing on Guadalcanal, the marines seized the Japanese base and airfield that were under construction, moved their own combat aircraft onto the field, and named it Henderson Field after one of the marine aviators who died defending Midway. In and around Guadalcanal over the next four months, navy fleet units fought seven major actions: the Battles of Savo Island (August 9, 1942), the Eastern Solomons (August 22–25), Cape Esperance (October 11–12), Santa Cruz (October 26–27), the first and second battles of Guadalcanal (November 12–13 and 14–15), and Tassafaronga (November 30). The result of these engagements was the loss of one of the Japanese Empire's key military outposts by the IJN Combined Fleet. Some fifty smaller naval actions were fought on the waters off Guadalcanal between August 1942 and February 1943.

The eventual American victory resulted from three crucial initiatives: (1) mastering the capacity for expeditionary war where the navy could sustain and the marines could protect the air squadrons on Henderson Field, forcing the Japanese to fight the air battle from Rabaul, 650 miles away; (2) the US Navy's examination of itself, and (3) the effectiveness of the marine doctrine of amphibious warfare.

American possession of Henderson Field was essential to victory because marine airpower could attack Japanese warships and transports continually without having to fly long distances.[37] But the navy had to support the ground and air forces on Guadalcanal. To achieve naval dominance in the Solomons, navy officers had to master a new kind of warfare. James D. Hornfischer explained the learning curve on Guadalcanal:

> Expeditionary war was a new kind of enterprise, and its scale at Guadalcanal was surpassed only by its combatants' thoroughgoing deficits in matériel, preparation, and understanding of their enemy. It was the most critical major military operation America would ever run on such a threadbare shoestring. As its principal players would admit afterward, the puzzle of victory was solved on the fly and on the cheap, in terms of resources if not lives. The campaign featured tight interdependence among warriors of the air, land, and sea. For a fleet to control the sea, the pilots had to fly from [Henderson Field]. For the pilots to fly from the airfield, the [marines and later the army] had to hold the island. That tripod stood only by the strength of all three legs.[38]

Guadalcanal was the navy's battle to win. Despite the putative lesson from Midway that the aircraft carrier was now king of the seas, the battleships, cruisers, and destroyers had to fight and win control of the waters controlling the approaches to Guadalcanal. Of the seven major naval battles fought in the Solomons, five of them were principally ship-to-ship actions fought at night; only aircraft decided two, and these during daylight. The US Navy forces committed to the Solomons engaged from positions of quantitative parity because Yamamoto committed his fleet units piecemeal. Nevertheless, the IJN initially had a qualitative edge in terms of ship-handling skills, combat readiness discipline, and gunnery accuracy in the dark. For months, the final outcome was in doubt.

In the first major night action, the Battle of Savo Island in early August 1942, an IJN striking force of seven cruisers and a destroyer entered New Georgia Sound, known as "the Slot" (map 5.2), to attack the Allied screening forces and the amphibious fleet off Guadalcanal. The Japanese force surprised the screening force of eight cruisers and fifteen destroyers. Four cruisers (three American, one Australian) were sunk and others heavily damaged. It was a rout. Admiral King called it the "blackest day of the whole war."[39] The Japanese won because of superior alertness at spotting enemy ships at night (despite the Allied technological advantage of shipborne search radars), skilled ship handling, crisp signaling, devastatingly accurate gunnery, and aggressive torpedo launching by destroyers of the improved Type 93 "Long Lance" torpedo, a better weapon. The navy's reaction was to learn how to beat the IJN at its own game.

That was the second initiative. These "Gun Club" surface officers, who initially, and incorrectly, believed that decisive naval battles would involve a grand, daylight fleet engagement that would be dominated by large-caliber gunfire, started the process of rewriting the navy's surface warfare doctrine. That meant a rigorous return to the fundamentals of learning how to fight at night, how to maneuver, how to communicate with other forces, how to optimize use of the weaponry they had, and how to win.[40] They changed the management of shipboard operating routines to maximize combat readiness.[41] They learned how to use their radar sets more effectively. They practiced night operations relentlessly. They continually drilled in gunnery speed and accuracy so that American ship rapid-fire salvos and the throw weight of heavy-caliber projectiles wreaked havoc on the enemy.

Two months later, on October 13, 1942, Rear Admiral Norman Scott, commanding a cruiser task force (four cruisers and five destroyers) intercepted a Japanese bombardment group (three cruisers and two destroyers) off Cape Esperance west of Savo Island. The navy sank two Japanese cruisers, losing a destroyer. Scott and his captains won this victory at the Battle of Cape Esperance because they trained hard in preparation.

To command the navy at Guadalcanal, Nimitz had appointed Vice Admiral Robert L. Ghormley as commander, South Pacific Forces (COMSOPAC). Ghormley was not Nimitz's first choice. He was not a combat-tested admiral. His last seagoing assignment was as captain of the battleship *Nevada* in 1936. After receiving orders to the Pacific, Ghormley hurriedly left London in April 1942, scrambling to assemble a staff and assess the new terrain of his command with its huge expanses of the Pacific. He had not served in the Pacific for thirty-five years.[42] Less than three months into the campaign, Nimitz was worried about COMSOPAC. After a personal visit to Ghormley's Nouméa headquarters in early October, he knew he had to find a battle-oriented replacement driven by one guiding principle: "that war is the craft of putting ordnance on target decisively, and it is really nothing else."[43] Many fighting ashore had been asking, where is the navy?[44] Ghormley was overwhelmed with operational minutiae, and Nimitz did not have time for a commander to undergo on-the-job training in a combat zone. He needed a fast-thinking, quick-acting commander who could confront the menacing threats the IJN presented in the Solomons.

In mid-October, Nimitz sent Admirals Spruance and Halsey out to Nouméa. Halsey most certainly would have commanded the principal task force at Midway if a case of shingles had not confined him to a naval hospital at Pearl Harbor. Halsey was a fighting admiral. He had commanded the January 1942 raids on the Marshall and Gilbert Islands and the Doolittle Raid in April that set in motion the chain of events leading the IJN to attack Midway. When Halsey arrived on Nouméa, he was handed a message from Nimitz: "You will take command of the South Pacific Area and the South Pacific Forces immediately."[45]

His legendary aggressiveness prompted Evan Thomas's book on the naval campaigns in the Pacific to open with explicit reference to a billboard that Halsey had ordered constructed at the entrance to the harbor at Tulagi, which was the anchorage at a small island in the Solomon Islands, captured as a forward base because of its proximity to the Slot. Thomas included a photograph of the billboard that read, "Admiral Halsey says 'Kill japs, kill japs, kill more japs. You will help kill the yellow bastards if you do your job well.'"[46] Although crude to twenty-first-century eyes, Halsey's sailors and marines regarded it as "refreshingly blunt in 1943." So did most Americans; Japanese attitudes were reciprocal.

Halsey committed Task Forces 16 and 17 under Admiral Thomas C. Kinkaid to support the marines on Guadalcanal. This was Halsey's answer to the question, where is the navy? He promised General Vandegrift at a council of war on October 24 at Nouméa, "All right. Go on back [to Guadalcanal]. I'll promise you everything I've got."[47] He ordered the carriers *Enterprise* and *Hornet* to venture farther north than they had since August and to seek battle. Doubling down on his willingness to take risks, he sent Rear Admiral Willis

A. Lee north into Iron Bottom Sound and up the Slot with a surface striking force of the battleship *Washington*, three cruisers, and ten destroyers to sweep the area off Cape Esperance and around Savo Island. Yamamoto had been reinforcing the IJN on Rabaul to support the 17th Army's counteroffensive to recapture Henderson Field. That led to the Battle of Santa Cruz.

It was another battle of attrition. The US Navy lost the *Hornet* and a destroyer and sustained damage to the *Enterprise*, the battleship *South Dakota*, two cruisers, and three destroyers. The Japanese sustained damage to the carriers *Shōkaku* and *Zuiho*, a cruiser, and four destroyers. In the air war, the IJN lost eighty-one aircraft, the USN ninety-seven. Although the losses were similar, the 148 Japanese pilots and aircrew killed in the battle were a third more than at Midway (110).[48] The losses were another down payment on Parshall's and Tully's deadly math of the "aerial meat grinder" that began in the Solomons. After Santa Cruz, the US Navy did not have an operable carrier task force in the South Pacific until the *Enterprise* was back in service the following month.[49] That reduced the battle afloat to whichever naval force could control the waters around Guadalcanal at night. Neither could operate carriers in the Slot because of their vulnerability within a confined sea space.

The third crucial American initiative of the Guadalcanal victory was a clear discriminator in the land battle ashore. The outcome was the result of a proven marine doctrine and resources for amphibious operations against enemy-held islands developed by the USMC during the prewar period.[50] Eventually, in January 1943, the marines, reinforced by the US Army, overran the IJA's 17th Army headquarters at Kokumbona, nine miles west of the airfield. The marines and army inflicted such heavy losses on the 17th Army that the IJA eventually had to abandon Guadalcanal.

The Battle of Guadalcanal (August 1942 to February 1943) was a searing experience that forced the US Navy in the Pacific to rewrite its doctrine for how surface warships fought battles. The naval experience was particularly difficult after the carrier victory at Midway because the US Navy had to fight fifty engagements continually in the shark-infested and blood-steeped waters around Guadalcanal, mostly with the surface warships it had available. The admirals and ship captains in command of COMSOPAC fleet units learned new operational skills to break the IJN in the Solomons during months of attrition combat.

Each side lost twenty-four warships at Guadalcanal[51] and comparable tonnage: 126,240 tons for the Allies and 134,839 tons for the Japanese. The navy's combat fatalities exceeded those of the marines: over 5,000 killed at sea[52] versus 1,592 marines and army soldiers killed ashore.[53] Japanese losses were far higher: 20,800 IJA soldiers on the island and probably 4,000 IJN sailors at sea.[54]

Japanese casualties included Admiral Yamamoto himself. American SIGINT and code breakers intercepted a routine message about his planned visit to

Bougainville in the northern Solomons in mid-August 1943. A squadron of US Amy Air Force (USAAF) P-38 Lightnings from Henderson Field waited in ambush on April 18, 1943, and shot down his aircraft.[55]

Examining the Midway and Guadalcanal literature together shows how the strategic architecture for the United States in the Pacific evolved from weakness to recapture the naval and military initiative six months after Pearl Harbor. The literature also clearly reveals the emptiness of Japan's strategic architecture to launch an offensive war it could never win.

CONCLUSIONS

The Americans exploited their strengths more effectively than the Japanese did. Although the US Pacific Fleet had suffered grievous damage just six months earlier at Pearl Harbor, and the US Armed Forces were generally unprepared for global war, the outcomes at Midway and Guadalcanal resulted from a president's determination to be aggressive in the face of what appeared to be overwhelming Japanese power, particularly after one looked at a map of the Pacific in 1942 showing Japanese conquests. It also resulted from the abilities of American admirals and generals to design and improvise a campaign that exploited the success of a small group of aggressive naval aviators who won the Battle of Midway. This was war fought on a shoestring, but it worked to take the military initiative from the Japanese. They never recovered it.

Battles of Midway and Guadalcanal

(1) A USAAF B-25B Mitchell medium bomber, one of sixteen in the Doolittle Raid, takes off from the flight deck of the carrier *Hornet*, April 18, 1942. (2) Carrier *Yorktown*'s flight deck after being hit by three IJN bombs on June 4, 1942. USN photos

(3) Douglas SBD-3 Dauntless scout bomber parked on board carrier *Yorktown* (CV-5) after landing to refuel and rearm. Plane's damage visible from attack on IJN carrier *Kaga* earlier on morning of June 4, 1942. (4) Burning Japanese aircraft carrier *Hiryū*, shortly after sunrise on June 5, 1942, sank a few hours later. USN photos

(5) US troops from 160th infantry regiment landing on Guadalcanal in March 1943. US Army photo (6) Japanese soldiers killed while manning a mortar on the beach are shown partially buried in the sand at Guadalcanal in August 1942. LOC photo

6

STRATEGIC BOMBING OFFENSIVE

Breaking German Airpower

The Anglo-American strategic bombing offensive attacked and destroyed scores of German urban and industrial centers. It was a massive and expensive airpower campaign designed to break Germany's industrial capacity to wage war.

POLICY

During the early years of the war, the Anglo-American Allies were faced with a dilemma. What could they do militarily against their Axis enemies that would constitute a strategic initiative until they built up their land forces in sufficient strength to invade the Continent—the Second Front that Stalin had been pressing his allies to open since 1942? The solution they proposed to Stalin was the strategic bombing campaign that became the equivalent of the Second Front as German armaments minister Albert Speer acknowledged after the war.[1]

By the Casablanca Conference in the winter of 1943, the Allies had begun to issue a series of directives to their air forces. There were at least six strategic directives issued between February 1943 and April 1945. Two of the most important related to the sequential execution of Operation *Pointblank*, targeting the German military, industrial, and economic system, followed by the *Transportation Plan* to bomb the French rail and road networks that led to Normandy. The objective was to limit German mobility on D-Day, June 6, 1944, and during the weeks following.

By 1944, the German Air Ministry estimated that five thousand planes a month would have to be produced to neutralize the growing Allied air threat.

Allied bombers destroyed both aircraft factories and vital oil refineries and fuel production facilities, which left the *Luftwaffe* dependent on stockpiled fuel by June 1944.[2] The relentless attacks on fighter bases, troop depots, storage dumps, and, most important, the rail infrastructure in France in the weeks before D-Day broke the *Luftwaffe*, leaving the skies open to even more destructive bombing missions against German targets.[3]

Overy poses the question whether area or precision bombing helped the Allies win the war. He concludes that the direct effects of bombing were substantial but difficult to quantify conclusively.[4] When Overy turns to the evidence of the indirect effects—the attrition of the *Luftwaffe*'s fighter squadrons; the diversion of military and civilian manpower for air defense and war plant repair; and the diversion of guns, ammunition, electro-optical components, and radar and communications equipment needed for air defense—he concludes that the combined effects of direct destruction and diversion of resources denied "German forces approximately half their battle-front weapons and equipment in 1944. It is difficult not to regard this margin as decisive."[5] Randall Hansen reviewed much of the same evidence and reached the same conclusion: "There can be no doubt . . . that the task of defending Germany required massive amounts of resources that could not by definition be used elsewhere."[6]

Between 1940 and 1945, the United States and Great Britain produced more than 130,000 bombers and dropped nearly two million tons of bombs on Europe.[7] Figures 6.1 and 6.2 show that Allied production of bombers exceeded German production by a factor greater than seven. The total bomb tonnages delivered by the American and British air forces exceeded those Germany dropped on Great Britain by a factor greater than twenty-five.[8]

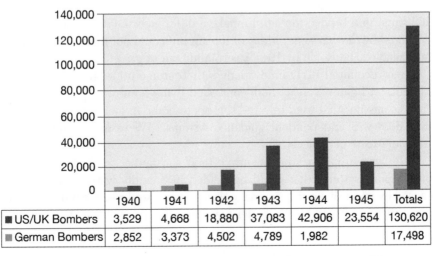

Comparative Bomber Production

	1940	1941	1942	1943	1944	1945	Totals
■ US/UK Bombers	3,529	4,668	18,880	37,083	42,906	23,554	130,620
■ German Bombers	2,852	3,373	4,502	4,789	1,982		17,498

Figure 6.1. The Allies built more than seven times as many bombers as Germany did.
Source: USAAF, *Statistical Digest of the War* (London: HMSO, 1951).

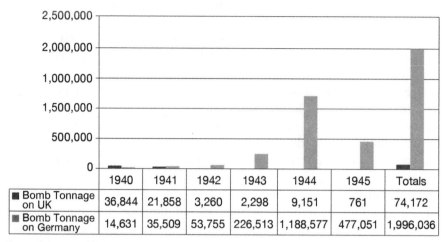

Comparative Bomb Tonnage Delivery

	1940	1941	1942	1943	1944	1945	Totals
■ Bomb Tonnage on UK	36,844	21,858	3,260	2,298	9,151	761	74,172
■ Bomb Tonnage on Germany	14,631	35,509	53,755	226,513	1,188,577	477,051	1,996,036

Figure 6.2. The Allies dropped twenty-five times as many bombs on Germany as Germany dropped on Great Britain.
Source: Overy, Air War.

The German aircraft industry, poorly led by Third Reich leaders, failed to overcome critical deficiencies in the way it chose to design and build combat aircraft. German decision makers failed to appreciate the long timelines required to transform promising prototypes into field-effective aircraft designs in time to make a difference. Too many new designs (there were eighty-six) and poor standardization caused inefficiencies that reduced aircraft production numbers and degraded quality.[9] In contrast, the Allies built more than seven times as many bombers as Germany did.[10]

The Me-262 was an example of a lost technological opportunity.[11] Although it was the first operational jet fighter fielded by any of the combatants, the Me-262 came into service too late to make a difference; 1,430 aircraft had been delivered by the war's end. Many of the aircraft could not fly because fuel was unavailable. The Reich by 1944 was running out of gas.

Speer recounted R&D innovations with Teutonic pride. In addition to the Me-262 jet fighter were remote-controlled flying bombs, a "rocket plane," a "rocket missile" that used infrared sensors to home in on enemy aircraft, and torpedoes with independent guidance systems. "We were literally suffering from an excess of projects."[12]

The German failure to concentrate their substantial productive resources on weapons systems that could be fielded in quantity was a serious deficit caused by impulsive war industrial policies that wasted resources on terrifying but ultimately ineffective "wonder weapons" like the V-1 and V-2 rockets.[13]

The R&D search for war-winning technologies diverted engineering and scientific talent, a skilled labor force, and resources and infrastructure to many
fruitless pursuits. These decisions skewed the German industrial base away
from producing more warplanes that could have made a strategic difference.

Allied aircraft industries were much better organized. The Americans and
British chose designs that balanced performance and capabilities against pro-
ducibility, quality, and quantity. The Americans and British understood the
long timelines and resources required to field new aircraft. Both countries had
already decided in the late 1930s that heavy bombers were the strategic air
weapons of the future. Most of the airplanes with which they fought the war
were modified versions of prewar designs.

The American Boeing B-17 heavy bomber emerged from an established
prewar pedigree, a design introduced in 1935. The B-17 dropped more bombs
on Germany than any other airplane. American aircraft production marshaled
industrial resources to produce truly prodigious numbers of large, complex
aircraft. The B-24 factory at Willow Run in Michigan represented a triumph
of industrial innovation, efficiency, and practical, factory-floor-level expertise.
This war plant at its peak ramped up to produce fully half of the eighteen
thousand B-24s produced by war's end. Willow Run's semiautomated line enabled the high-volume manufacture of the bomber where components, subas-
semblies, and assemblies were continuously fed into a moving assembly line.[14]

The USAAF's primary long-range fighter escort, the P-51, entered service
in late 1943, derived from an aircraft designed and built for the RAF in 1940
by an American manufacturer. "Beginning in 1942, Allied engineers mated the
excellent P-51 airframe with a derivative of the equally excellent Merlin 61 engine that powered the Spitfire. The result was a spectacular success. The P-51
with two 108-gallon tanks could escort the bombers out to 850 miles, which
meant they could protect the bombers when attacking any target in Germany
and beyond." Ultimately, 14,819 P-51s were built; USAAF pilots, who flew the
P-51, destroyed 4,950 enemy aircraft in Europe to make it the highest-scoring
fighter in the European theater.[15]

The principal combatants in the European theater thus fought the war with
two very different kinds of air forces. Germany had created its air force essentially as an adjunct to support its ground forces. The *Luftwaffe* had no heavy
bombers, and this would remain the case throughout the war.

The Allies began the war with more balanced air forces capable of flying
effective state-of-the-art fighters as well as twin-engine medium bombers and
four-engine heavy bombers. All of their operational aircraft were based on
proven designs, which they could ramp up into mass production. The Allies
outproduced Germany by a factor of five in all types of aircraft (figure 3.1).

STRATEGY

During the early years of the war, the top echelons of Allied political and military leadership were divided about the purpose and efficacy of the offensive air campaign. Air Chief Marshal Arthur T. Harris was a stubborn advocate of area bombing by RAF Bomber Command in the early years of the war, believing that airpower by itself could win the war. He had company among American air commanders eager to prove their own strategies.

For Allied air strategists, precision bombing of military targets remained an idealized, theoretical construct throughout the war. For example, a B-17, equipped with the well-known but classified Norden bombsight, reputedly could drop a bomb in a "pickle barrel." In operational practice, it was far from accurate. The late Ralph H. Nutter, the lead navigator who survived more than twenty-five missions with Brigadier General Curtis E. LeMay's 305th Bombardment Group, recalled that crew training in the United States prepared them poorly for the missions they later flew over Germany:

> Our bombing practice was limited to a few practice runs on chalk circles drawn in the desert sand [a Mojave Desert bombing training range in California]. The sky was almost always clear in the desert, visibility almost perfect. Those practice bomb runs in the desert with our new Norden bombsight gave us a false sense of optimism about bombing accuracy. We believed the press releases that boasted we could place our bombs in a pickle barrel from high altitude. No one explained to us the contrast between making an unimpeded, peaceful bomb run in the cloudless desert skies and bombing . . . a heavily fortified, cloud-covered, camouflaged German city defended by hordes of fighter planes and a blanket of flak.[16]

In January 1943, LeMay after deployment to England wrote a brutally honest memorandum to the USAAF Training Command emphasizing the kind of methods, training, and techniques that were required to bomb targets accurately and with lower losses. LeMay's memo identified the following successful mission attributes: tight-formation flying, intensive navigation training (map reading using English aeronautical charts, coupled with dead reckoning, to find camouflaged targets), bombing accuracy, gunnery, and maintenance.[17]

British nighttime carpet bombing of German cities was a direct response to heavy losses during daylight missions and the known limitations of the RAF in accurately locating industrial targets in Germany. In 1942, Professor Lindemann, Churchill's scientific advisor, "the Prof," wrote his famous "dehousing" paper that presented a statistical analysis that the explosive tonnages theoretically deliverable on the housing stock of Germany's fifty-eight largest cities offered the most effective use of Bomber Command.[18] Air Chief Marshall Harris made a plausible case that killing German workers in large numbers by bombing them in their cities would hasten the war's end; however, such lethal operational results were never achieved.[19]

In direct contrast, American air planners were pressing for a different approach. They believed that attacks against key economic systems, such as transportation networks, electrical power generation plants, munitions factories, chemical plants, and later petroleum, oil, and lubricants (POL) complexes would so demoralize the population that the same effects could be achieved without resorting to indiscriminate carpet bombing of civilians.

The uncertainties and risks of airpower were compounded by the fact that until late 1943, American bomber formations flew without fighter escorts during daylight missions when they penetrated deep into Germany. Their losses by the summer of 1943 had become unsustainable. Map 6.1 is of Western Europe at the time of the D-Day invasion on June 6, 1944, showing three arcs (dashed, dotted, and solid) demarcating the easternmost limits of daylight bomber operations from British bases between July 1943 and June 1944. By the summer of 1944, Allied bombers could fly missions against urban or industrial targets anywhere over the Reich with the introduction of the P-51 Mustang. The bombers could only fly these long-range missions without sustaining unacceptable loss rates when P-51 fighters escorted them all the way to and from their targets and intercepted German fighters attacking the bombers.

They still sustained heavy losses from both *Luftwaffe* air defense squadrons and antiaircraft artillery or flak (*Flugzeug Abwehr Kanonen*). By 1944, two million German soldiers were engaged in air defense. Speer estimated that 30 percent of total gun output, 20 percent of heavy ammunition, and 33 percent of the electro-optical equipment needed for radars and communications equipment were required for flak installations, starving the fighting fronts of essential resources. Overy points out that by the end of 1943 two-thirds of *Luftwaffe* fighters were diverted to the west to defend German cities against Allied bombers. At the end of the same year, there were fifty-five thousand flak guns, including 75 percent of the excellent 88 mm antiaircraft guns, diverted to air defense of German cities.[20] The *Wehrmacht* knew that the "88" doubled as an effective antitank weapon. *Ostheer* combat units would have welcomed many more 88s to attack Russian armor during the Battle of Kursk.

OPERATIONS

RAF Bomber Command and the USAAF 8th Air Force by mid-1942 had built up bomber fleets to become truly destructive. Harris, after he built up his bomber groups into a capacity to execute one-thousand-plane raids, set about

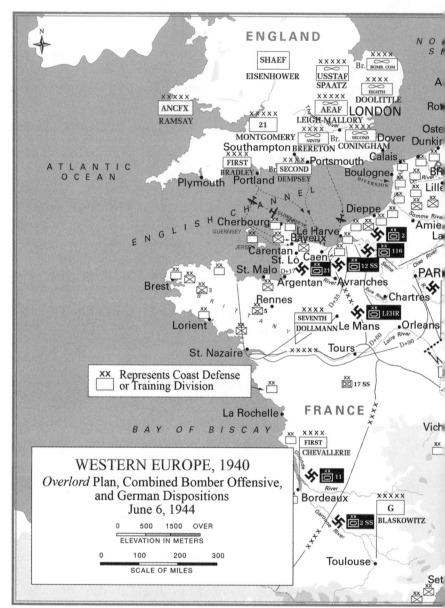

Map 6.1. The three, time-phased arcs on this map of Western Europe show the increasing ranges Allied bombers could fly over Germany after long-range fighters entered service to protect them all the way to and from their targets.

Source: USMA Atlases.

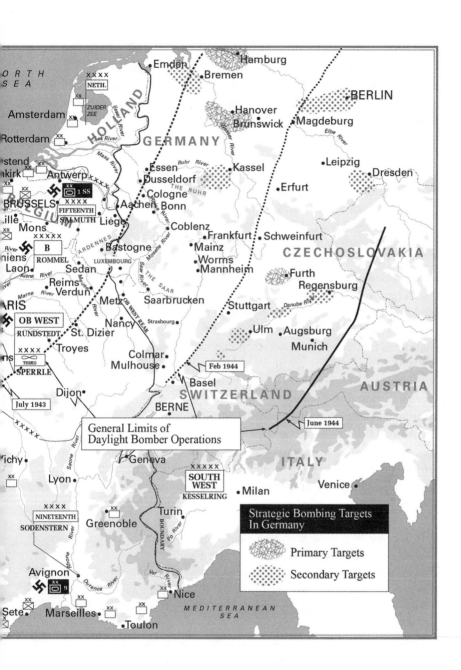

NORTH SEA

Amsterdam

Rotterdam

stend
kirk

BELGIUM

BRUSSELS

ille

Mons

niens

Laon

ARIS

ns

July 1943

ichy

Emden

Bremen

Hamburg

NETH.

ZUIDER ZEE

HOLLAND

Ijsek River

Maas River

Hanover

Brunswick

BERLIN

Magdeburg

Elbe River

Weser River

GERMANY

Antwerp

1 SS

FIFTEENTH SALMUTH

Liège

Aachen

Cologne

Bonn

Essen

Ruhr River

Düsseldorf

THE RUHR

Kassel

Leipzig

Erfurt

Dresden

ARDENNES

B

ROMMEL

LUXEMBOURG

Bastogne

Coblenz

Rhine River

Frankfurt

Schweinfurt

Mainz

Worms

Mannheim

CZECHOSLOVAKIA

Furth

Regensburg

Sedan

Reims

Verdun

Aisne River

Marne River

Meuse River

Moselle River

Saar River

THE SAAR

OB WEST REAR

Metz

Saarbrucken

Stuttgart

Danube River

Nancy

Strasbourg

Ulm

Augsburg

Munich

OB WEST

RUNDSTEDT

St. Dizier

Troyes

THIRD

SPERRLE

Colmar

Mulhouse

Feb 1944

Basel

SWITZERLAND

AUSTRIA

Dijon

BERNE

June 1944

General Limits of Daylight Bomber Operations

Geneva

ITALY

Lyon

Saone River

SOUTH WEST

KESSELRING

Milan

Venice

NINETEENTH

SODENSTERN

Greenoble

Turin

Rhone River

BOUNDARY

Po River

Strategic Bombing Targets In Germany

Primary Targets

Secondary Targets

Avignon

9

Durance River

Var River

Nice

Sete

Marseilles

Toulon

MEDITERRANEAN SEA

demolishing German cities. The most well-known attack was on Hamburg in July–August 1943. Harris ordered a series of four raids that initiated a conflagration in a concentrated residential area in the southeast of the city that developed into a firestorm that swept into the city's center. The destruction was widespread. The city's shipyards were pulverized, including twenty-five U-boats under construction. The railway stations were destroyed; rivers and canals were blocked; the harbor and rivers were clogged by sunken ships; and gas, water, and electricity supplies were all cut off. In addition, over ten thousand factories and businesses, eighty military installations, twenty-four hospitals, and 122 National Socialist offices were destroyed.[21] In total, 56 percent of Hamburg's dwellings (about 256,000) were destroyed, and nine hundred thousand people were rendered homeless. Some forty thousand more were killed, and a further 125,000 required medical treatment, many for severe burns.

The devastation of Hamburg was an enormous shock to the Germans. Goebbels had a hard time believing the first reports in July 1943. He recorded in his diary, "Kaufmann gave me a first report on the effect of the British air raid. He spoke of a catastrophe that simply staggers the imagination. A city of a million inhabitants had been destroyed in a manner unparalleled in history. We are faced with problems that are impossible of solution."[22] Within five months, however, Hamburg regained 80 percent of its former productivity due to Speer's organizational and management skills. Speer undoubtedly contributed to the war lasting longer, perhaps by as much as a year.

As the Allied bombing program expanded, the whole structure of the *Luftwaffe* became distorted. Demands for electronics for the V-1 and V-2 rocket programs skewed critical resource allocations. The furious expansion of flak batteries represented an enormous expenditure of resources diverted from the production of weapons needed at the fighting fronts. Flak batteries consumed ammunition at a prodigious rate. The 88 mm flak gun required an average expenditure of more than sixteen thousand shells to hit, not necessarily shoot down, an Allied bomber on a mission over the Reich.[23]

By the summer of 1943, "the German air threat at the Battle of Kursk and in the long retreat that followed visibly melted."[24] The Reich had to allocate its increasingly unbalanced air assets among multiple fronts. These distortions and deficits became irreversible.

Allied loss rates were high, too, but the Allies were better prepared for such attrition. They had planned and provisioned for training enormous numbers of pilots. The Americans alone produced nearly two hundred thousand pilots, whereas the Germans trained only fifty thousand, of which fifteen thousand were badly needed fighter pilots.[25]

By the late spring of 1944, "the *Luftwaffe* cracked; its exhausted pilots could take no more. 'Monthly losses, which included most of the experienced German fighter pilots, averaged 450 in the first five months of 1944; by the end of May, 2,262 had been killed.'"[26] The attrition was relentless. Between June and October 1944, thirteen thousand German aircrew had been shot down, principally by P-51 Mustangs.

These USAAF accomplishments stand in contrast to the determined efforts of RAF Bomber Command to smash Germany's urban centers of war production. In fact, there was an inverse effect. German war production increased in response to bombing, as analysts of the US Strategic Bombing Survey later concluded.[27] Overy's assessment is that "between 1941 and 1944, in step with the escalating bombardment, German military output trebled."[28] In short, the Prof's dehousing strategy was not working as predicted.

Recently published histories indicate a more balanced explanation of the bombing campaign's effects between British and American strategies. Adam Tooze draws stark conclusions about the Harris-directed Battle of the Ruhr during April–July 1943:

> Reading contemporary sources, there can be no doubt that the Battle of the Ruhr marked a turning point in the history of the German war economy, which has been grossly underestimated by postwar accounts. As Speer himself acknowledged, *the RAF was hitting the right target* [italics in original]. . . . Allied bombing had negated all plans for a further increase in production. Bomber Command had stopped Speer's armaments miracle in its tracks.[29]

Richard Evans's explanation is not substantially different from Tooze's: "The more the fabric of Germany's cities was destroyed, the more the fabric of German society began to fall apart."[30] Michael Burleigh's assessment concludes that "the German war economy gradually fragmented into regionally discrete units, which in turn made extended transportation routes highly vulnerable to aerial interdiction. . . . Those in charge of Germany's war economy concurred, by highlighting the disruption of freight transport as being most responsible for hampering Germany's ability to wage war."[31]

While no consensus emerged that a bombing offensive by itself could produce a war-winning outcome, the Allies, had they known by the spring of 1944 how effective their bombing had been, might have been able to defeat Germany's wartime economy more quickly. For example, after the two 1943 Schweinfurt raids on the ball-bearing factories,[32] they came tantalizingly close. A few days after the first raid on August 17, 1943, Speer wrote that "we barely escaped a further catastrophic blow."[33] He made that entry after production had fallen by 38 percent.[34] What he told the *Luftwaffe* Procurement Office had ominous specificity: "We are approaching the point of total collapse . . . in our supply industry. Soon we will have airplanes, tanks, or trucks lacking certain key parts."[35]

The second raid against Schweinfurt on October 14, 1943, resulted in a 67 percent drop in ball-bearing production. A direct hit shattered machinery, lit the oil baths, and sent fires racing through the complex of one ball-bearing factory. Speer quickly adapted to this crisis by importing small quantities of ball bearings from Sweden and Switzerland, drawing down reserve stores, and ordering factories to produce slide bearings rather than ball bearings.[36] With these desperate measures, Speer restored production, but at sharply reduced levels.

In his memoirs, Speer admitted, "In those days, we anxiously asked ourselves how soon the enemy would realize that he could paralyze the production of thousands of armaments plants merely by destroying five or six relatively small targets." The Allies at the time did not adequately appreciate that Schweinfurt was in effect a single-point failure node. When raids against the ball-bearing plants at Schweinfurt, Erkner, and Steyr were mounted six months later, Speer recorded with alarm, "After only six weeks our production of bearings had been reduced to twenty-nine percent of what it had been before the raids. At the beginning of April 1944, however, the attacks on the ball-bearings industry ceased abruptly. Thus, the Allies threw away success when it was already in their hands."[37]

The American 8th Air Force sustained catastrophic loss rates on the two 1943 Schweinfurt missions: 19 percent of the attacking force, 60 B-17s with over 100 aircraft damaged out of a force of 376 bombers in the first raid, and 60 planes lost and 138 damaged out of nearly 300 bombers, of which 220 reached the target, in the second raid.[38] Losses at these appalling levels were unsustainable, despite the heavy damage to German industry. An additional one hundred bombers were permanently lost as a result of battle damage, a total loss of approximately 40 percent of the attacking forces. Repeated attacks against Schweinfurt would have been suicidal.[39] Daylight precision bombing at this point was at an impasse because of the heavy losses. Indeed, after Schweinfurt, American bombers never flew unescorted again.[40] It was not until 1944 with the entry of P-51 fighter squadrons in sufficient numbers to escort B-17 and B-24 bombers that the USAAF resumed bombing missions deep into Germany.

Once the USAAF introduced the long-range P-51 in large numbers, German airpower went into a death spiral. By December 1943, nearly a quarter of the strength of the German fighter fleets was lost. German production could not keep pace with this attrition. By 1944, Overy indicates that the losses had become much worse: "During 1944 losses of fighter aircraft rose to seventy-three percent of strength per month." *Luftwaffe* loss rates on the Eastern Front grew from 615 per month before June 1941 to 1,167 per month between June 1941 and December 1943, and 1,755 per month in 1944.[41]

Speer wrote to Hitler during this period, "The enemy has succeeded in increasing our losses of aviation gasoline up to ninety percent by 22 June. Only through speedy recovery of damaged plants has it been possible to regain partly some of the terrible losses."[42] Speer told postwar interrogators that he viewed these losses as catastrophic. The synthetic oil plans were large industrial complexes and could not be easily rebuilt much less broken up and dispersed, although the Germans spared no effort in postattack recovery.

Achieving air supremacy over Europe was bought at a huge price for both Allied air forces. Like the Battle of the Atlantic, Allied losses were very heavy. Over six years, 158,546 USAAF and RAF aircrew lost their lives: 79,265 (USAAF) and 79,281 (RAF). When computed against total Anglo-American military fatalities during World War II, this figure represents one-fifth of the total. These statistics fail to reveal how dangerous flying bombers over Europe was. It is one thing to compute losses against the rostered strength of the USAAF and RAF personnel assigned to air combat units as the US Strategic Bombing Survey did in its statistical appendix to its overall report about the European bombing campaign: 13 percent for the USAAF and 11 percent for the RAF.[43] However, a look at the table of organization and equipment (TOE) of a heavy bomber group assigned to the ETO in 1943 reveals that only about one-third were assigned to fly. From this perspective, one gets a more realistic picture of an individual airman's chances of survival. The casualty statistics compute as 38 percent for the USAAF and 33 percent for the RAF. For many courageous airmen in the USAAF and RAF, the math did not work.[44] Flying bombers and surviving the required minimum of twenty-five missions was dangerous, debilitating, and lethal for American and British aircrew.

The popular postwar view of bombing has oversimplified the survey's narrow focus on how much German production was diminished by bombing. A closer reading of the survey indicates that quite a lot of damage to German war-fighting capacity resulted from bombing. For example, if the USAAF had kept on pounding the ball-bearing factories, Speer's remarks about Schweinfurt suggest that Germany's war production might have been brought to a halt.

The airpower histories of World War II establish the vital contribution the bombing offensive made to the Allied strategic architecture by diverting critical German manpower and resources to air defense of the Reich. Execution of Operation *Pointblank* and the *Transportation Plan* made possible the Anglo-American invasion on D-Day, June 6, 1944.

CONCLUSIONS

Churchill and Roosevelt worked tirelessly to persuade Stalin that the Anglo-American bombing offensive was a serious down payment on the "Second Front" until they could build up sufficient forces to invade the Continent in 1944. The bombing offensive never became a war-winning strategy through airpower, but it did enable invasion of the Continent by mid-1944 by establishing air superiority over Normandy. Simultaneously, it supported the USSR by drawing two-thirds of the *Luftwaffe* fighter strength to the west. Roosevelt and Churchill, in issuing directives to air commanders, communicated a clear vision of the necessity of air superiority.

The Allies harnessed their political leadership and modernity to outlead, outproduce, and outfight the *Luftwaffe*. As Speer put it, the strategic bombing campaign was "the greatest lost battle on the German side."[45]

Allied strategic airpower caused a major shift in the balance of forces between the Allies and the Axis. The *Luftwaffe* became an increasingly distorted air force compelled to react to the increasing destruction of Germany's industrial base by Allied airpower. The strategic architecture in the European theater of operations that achieved air supremacy was the result of clear political direction, the selection of resolute military leaders, courageous execution, superior industrial organization, and effective communication among Allied combatants on multiple levels.

Strategic Bombing Offensive

(1) B-17s over Schweinfurt on August 17, 1943, as city and ball-bearing factories burn after the raid; visible behind the B-17 in upper right corner of the photo is an arc of smoke trails from smoke generators in an effort to camouflage the grass airfield and *Flugplatz* west of the city used for training Stuka Ju-87 pilots. USAAF photo

(2) Schweinfurt *VereinigeKugellagerfabriken* AG (VKF) ball-bearing plant in ruins; VKF was a subsidiary of the Swedish firm *SvenskaKullagerfabriken* (SKF). USSBS photo taken in April 1945 (3) Willow Run assembly line of B-24 Liberator bombers, a Ford Motor Company purpose-built factory sprawling over nine hundred acres in Ypsilanti, Michigan. US Office of War Information photo

7

INVASION OF ITALY

Deciding to Fight Somewhere in Europe in 1943

The United States' acceptance of the North African commitment in 1942 had been reluctant because of its follow-on implications in the Mediterranean. The Americans suspected that Churchill's soft-underbelly strategy was the thin edge of the wedge to widen the Mediterranean into a primary theater as a possible alternative to the cross-Channel invasion of the Continent. The Allied defeat of *Heeresgruppe Afrika* in Tunisia in May 1943 intensified Anglo-American strategic policy differences about what to do next. Policy differences came to a boil between the Americans and British that had been simmering for more than a year since the *Arcadia* Conference and the acrimonious debates over *Bolero* (the buildup of forty-eight divisions in the UK and nearly six thousand combat aircraft) and *Roundup* (an invasion of the Continent in 1943).

POLICY

The Casablanca and Washington Conferences in January and May 1943 resolved some but not all of the Allied disagreements. In particular, they failed to produce a clear answer to General Marshall's "anxiety to learn the British concept as to how Germany is to be defeated."[1] As the American conferees reluctantly recognized that there would be no cross-Channel invasion in 1943, the Washington Conference produced a compromise. The Combined Chiefs of Staff had been at loggerheads for three days. Rather than conceding strategic planning to the president and prime minister, a prospect anathema to every military man in the room, General Marshall proposed that the room be cleared except for the chiefs. Ninety minutes later, they had negotiated an agreement. A cross-Channel attack, soon code-named *Overlord*, would be mounted on May 1, 1944, "to secure a lodgment on the Continent from which further offensive operations can be carried out." It was later agreed at the Quebec Conference in August 1943 that four American and three British divisions would be transferred from the Mediterranean to staging bases in Britain after an invasion of Sicily.[2]

Operation *Husky*, the liberation of Sicily, had been in the planning stages since the Casablanca Conference to secure maritime lines of communication across the Mediterranean. General Eisenhower was instructed to plan whatever operations following the capture of Sicily seemed "best calculated to eliminate Italy from the war and to contain the maximum number of German Forces."[3] The compromise was that the Americans got a hard date set for *Overlord* in exchange for the British getting latitude to pursue Churchill's soft-underbelly strategy at least as far as Sicily and later, perhaps, onto the Italian mainland. It also reflected realistic military arithmetic that both parties to the compromise thoroughly understood. President Roosevelt four months earlier had pointed out the metrics to the Joint Chiefs of Staff during a pre-Casablanca planning conference at the White House. The minutes of the meeting reflected the obvious:

> The President pointed out that we now have 800,000 or 900,000 men in North Africa. . . . The question then arose what to do with the additional 500,000 [after 100,000 allocated for the protection of Syria and 200,000 for the occupation of Algiers, Morocco, and Tunisia after the Axis had been expelled] that might be built up in the United Kingdom.[4]

That left Eisenhower, as Allied commander in chief in the Mediterranean, with twenty-seven divisions and 3,600 aircraft "to continue the war against the soft underbelly, although a direct invasion of Italy was not specified."[5]

STRATEGY

At the heart of the Anglo-American deliberations were quantitative questions of how much of a strategic military burden a concerted effort in the Mediterranean would impose on Germany and Italy. As Allied armies approached Rome in late May 1944, "no fewer than fifty-five German divisions were deployed in Italy" and four related countries, southern France, Yugoslavia, Albania, and Greece, according to Willmott.[6]

OPERATIONS

Willmott divides the military chronology of the Italian campaign between July 1943 and June 1944 into four parts: (1) the conquest of Sicily, (2) the Allied amphibious landings in southern Italy in September that led the US 5th Army and British 8th Army to the stalemate on the German Winter Line by the end of November, (3) the Anzio landing in January 1944 to outflank the Winter Line, and (4) Operation *Diadem* in May 1944 that led to the capture of Rome early the following month.[7]

On July 10, 1943, Operation *Husky*, the invasion of Sicily, began with the landing of seven Allied divisions, four British and three American (map 7.1). *Husky* was designed to open the shipping lanes in the Mediterranean, eliminate the island as an Axis base, and encourage the fall of Mussolini's government. General Eisenhower was appointed overall commander and British General Alexander as ground commander. Alexander's forces for the assault consisted of the US 7th Army under General Patton and the British 8th Army under

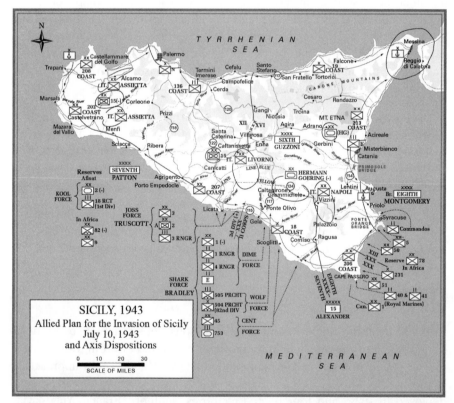

Map 7.1. The first phase of the Italian campaign began with the Allied conquest of Sicily, Operation *Husky*.
Source: USMA Atlases.

General Montgomery. Facing an Allied strength of five hundred thousand were roughly three hundred thousand Italians under General Alfredo Guzzoni and thirty thousand German troops deployed to Sicily by *Feldmarschall* Kesselring's Army Group C in Italy. *Husky* was notable for the fact that it constituted the largest amphibious operation of World War II in terms of size of the landing zone and number of divisions put ashore on the first day, more than were landed in Normandy on June 6, 1944.[8] Guzzoni and Kesselring fought a defensive battle for thirty-eight days, reinforced by three German divisions, and then withdrew their surviving forces, one hundred thousand German and Italian troops and ten thousand vehicles,[9] intact across the Strait of Messina to Italy despite Allied air and naval superiority. Liberation of Sicily achieved the goals specified initially at Casablanca. Axis air and naval forces were driven from Sicily and the Mediterranean shipping lanes, eliminating the threat to the chokepoint between Sicily and Tunisia's Cap Bon Peninsula.

As Operation *Husky* developed, Mussolini was toppled from power on July 25, 1943, succeeded by the government of Marshal Pietro Bagdolio. Sicily's close proximity to the mainland and German occupation of Italy after Bagdolio's surrender in early September rendered expansion of the mission irresistible. The Allies landed on the Italian mainland during the first week of September.

Code-named Operation *Avalanche*, the Allies invaded southern Italy in three widely separated places by executing landings at Reggio di Calabria by two British divisions on September 3, 1943, at Taranto by one British division on September 9, and simultaneously at Salerno by one American and two British divisions south of Naples (map 7.2). The geography and hydrography of southern Italy forced the Allies to accept the Gulf of Salerno as one of the few places south of Naples where a major landing could be attempted. Two German divisions of the 14th *Panzerkorps* were already in the south as a result of their being used to disarm Italian formations after Badoglio's surrender. Kesselring ordered them to oppose the US 5th Army landing at Salerno under the command of Lieutenant General Mark W. Clark.

Kesselring's best opportunity to break the Allied offensive was during the nine-day battle around the Salerno beachhead. Although Salerno offered excellent landing opportunities to the Allies with twenty-two miles of beaches, a sheltered bay, and negligible tides, it was hemmed in by mountains that encircled an alluvial plain, exposing the beachhead to observation, artillery fire, and attack from higher ground. As the campaign developed, Italy as a strategic battleground was a bad choice for the Allies. It was a peninsula eight hundred miles long, "the most vertebrate of countries, with a mountainous spine and bony ribs," confirming a maxim of Napoleon: Italy should be invaded only from the top.[10] For nearly two more years, Allied armies would have to fight for mountain after mountain, hill after hill, mounting

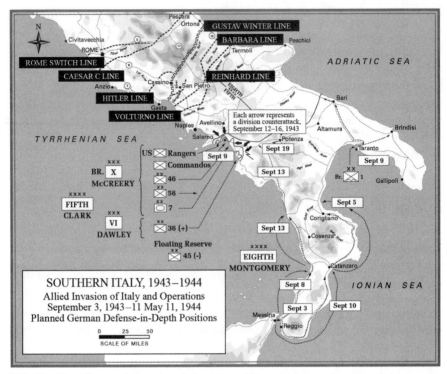

Map 7.2. The Allies invaded southern Italy with amphibious landings at three separate points; the Germans responded by building a powerful defense in depth with multiple fortified lines across Italy.
Source: USMA Atlases.

offensive operations over a terrain that perfectly suited Kesselring's plan to fight a defensive war of attrition. The Salerno landing was an inauspicious beginning with much worse to come.

The crisis of the Salerno battle erupted on September 13, 1943, when the 16th *Panzer* Division fought its way to within two miles of the sea along the boundary separating 10th British Corps and 6th US Corps. This counterattack was one of several mounted by the German 10th Army, commanded by *Generaloberst* Heinrich Gottfried von Vietinghoff, as it moved six divisions, three of which were *Panzers*, against the Allied beachhead within five days of the landings. This reinforcement altered the tactical military balance against Clark; by this time, 5th Army only had four divisions ashore.

However, Vietinghoff's concentration of forces around the Salerno beachhead created the conditions for his own defeat. The divisions he had gathered around Salerno, including two *Panzergrenadier* divisions, had been withdrawn from Montgomery's front at Calabria and therefore could not oppose his northward advance from the south. The British 8th Army advanced three hundred miles in just over two weeks to link up with the US 5th Army at the southeastern end of the beachhead on September 16.[11] With massive naval gunfire, artillery, and air support, German attempts failed to find a weak spot in the Allied lines around the beachhead. German losses, particularly in tanks, were heavy.

By September 16, Vietinghoff reported to Kesselring that the Allied air and naval superiority was decisive and that he lacked the combat strength to neutralize this magnitude of firepower. "Vietinghoff had shot his bolt."[12] Kesselring authorized a general retreat that included the proviso that Vietinghoff hold the Volturno River twenty miles north of Naples at least until October 15 to allow time for three fortified defensive lines to be prepared that together constituted the Winter Line (map 7.2).[13]

Clark's 5th Army reached the Volturno River on October 5, and Montgomery's 8th Army reached the Volturno Line two days later. Both Allied armies were drawn into the steep mountainous slopes of the Apennines to fight a series of sanguinary, inconclusive battles against Kesselring's defense in depth along the Winter Line during the fall and winter of 1943–1944.[14]

Clark and Montgomery had to break Kesselring's Winter Line, which lay across the Apennines from the Gulf of Gaeta on the Tyrrhenian Sea to the Adriatic just south of Ortona (map 7.2). They fought one grinding battle after another, taking casualties numbering in the tens of thousands. On the western Tyrrhenian side, Clark's forces encountered the miseries of fighting in places like Mignano Gap, Monte Camino, San Pietro, Camino, La Difensa, Monte Sammucro, and Monte Lungo, and on into the Rapido-Garigliano floodplain through Sant' Ambrogio and Sant' Angelo, the principal destination being the most fortified town in Italy, Monte Cassino, with the high, ten-foot-thick walls of the sixth-century Benedictine Abbey dominating the landscape. Cassino stood athwart the approaches to the Liri valley and Rome.

On the eastern Adriatic side, Montgomery's forces faced similar hardships and large casualties at Bari, Orsogna, and Ortona. Alexander ignored the advice Montgomery confided in his diary on October 31, 1943: "If I remember, Caesar used to go into winter quarters—a very sound thing to do." Alexander gloomily did not share Montgomery's attitude about winter operations. "'We'll just have to punch, punch, punch, and keep Jerry on the run until we reach Rome,' he told reporters. Privately, he saw 'no reason why we should ever get to Rome.'"[15]

The strategic views in both Washington and London failed to recognize that the Allied armies in Italy might not be strong enough to achieve a decisive result. What began with Churchill's belief in Europe's soft underbelly soon became something else, the prime minister's default justification: "The fact that the enemy have diverted such powerful forces to this theater vindicates our strategy."[16]

Allied commanders urged their troops to cross the overflowing rivers and to endure the cold, sleet, mud, and continual shelling by the Germans from the heights they occupied everywhere. This was a stalemate waiting for still another irresistible strategy.[17]

What happened between January and May 1944 is a story of bitter, costly fighting between the combatant armies. The tactical prize for the Allies of getting forces across the Gari, Garigliano, and Rapido Rivers and of taking Monte Cassino was the Liri valley, a flat, wide route than ran northwest to Rome, along which Allied armor could advance at speed. Once Cassino eventually fell in May, Clark and 5th Army were in Rome within three weeks.

In January 1944, the Allied plan to break the stalemate at the Gustav Line was an amphibious one-hundred-mile hop up the coast to land at Anzio and then to outflank and get behind the fifteen divisions of the German 10th Army. Meanwhile, 5th Army would try to break through the Winter Line anchored at Monte Cassino.[18]

The amphibious landing at Anzio, code-named Operation *Shingle*, offered Clark and Alexander what they thought was an outflanking opportunity. The plan proposed a triple offensive. First, 8th Army would attack the Winter Line on the Adriatic side to draw German reserves over to the east coast. Second, 5th Army would attack the Winter Line on the Tyrrhenian side with Cassino as the objective and the Liri valley as the pathway to Rome. And third, the *Shingle* amphibious landing at Anzio by a two-division corps (US 6th Corps) would cut Kesselring's supply lines between Rome and 10th Army. There were three vulnerable German land routes, the railway and Routes 6 and 7 (map 7.3).

The US Army officer selected by Clark to command 6th Corps to execute *Shingle* was Major General John P. Lucas. He was to land two infantry divisions at Anzio (one American, one British) approximately one hundred miles up the coast from Naples and cut the German LOCs south of Rome. Successful execution of *Shingle* was intended to enable Clark's 5th Army to push Vietinghoff's 10th Army north of Rome to the Pisa–Rimini line.

Lucas was an avuncular, corncob-pipe-smoking, fifty-three-year-old with a milquetoast demeanor. Lucas's command presence was the antithesis of Patton's aggressive image. Patton, in bidding farewell to his friend on the eve of the operation, morbidly remarked to Lucas, "John, there is no one in the Army I hate to see killed as much as you, but you can't get out of this alive. Of course you might be only badly wounded. No one ever blames a wounded general for anything." Patton advised Lucas to read the Bible, and to one of his aides he added, "If things get too bad, shoot the old man in the back side."[19]

Lucas's nonmilitary bearing and appearance concealed a shrewd tactical brain. He recognized, as Patton undoubtedly did, that the means allocated to the *Shingle* mission were insufficient. The initial allocation of two divisions to the landing force lacked the combat power to secure the beachhead and cut German LOCs simultaneously.

During the early morning hours of January 22, 1944, troops of 6th Corps swarmed ashore on a fifteen-mile stretch of Italian beach near the prewar resort towns of Anzio and Nettuno and surprised Kesselring. Initial German

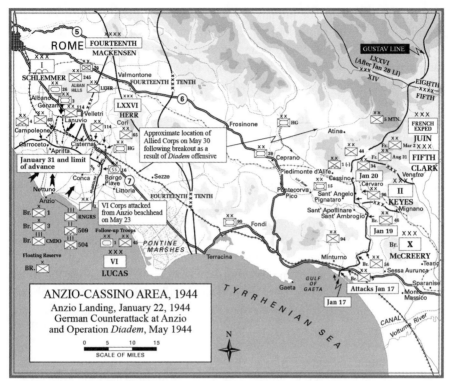

Map 7.3. The Allied amphibious landing at Anzio, designed to outflank German defenses, failed to break the stalemate along the Winter Line until the breakout from the Anzio beachhead and Operation *Diadem* opened the path to Rome, proving that there was no soft underbelly in the Mediterranean.
Source: USMA Atlases.

resistance was light so that British and American units gained their first day's objectives by noon, moving three to four miles inland by nightfall. Kesselring immediately understood the threat to his rear. Within twenty-four hours, he flooded the beachhead perimeter with forty thousand troops.

Lucas's failure to exploit 6th Corps' tactical surprise has been the subject of critical analysis ever since, most recently by Roberts. Within two days of the landing, fifty thousand Allied troops and 5,200 vehicles were ashore. Roberts argues that had Lucas pushed inland to seize and hold the towns of Aprilia, Campoleone, and Cisterna, he would have cut both the railway and Route 7. He might have succeeded in putting pressure on Kesselring's supply lines and been better prepared for Kesselring's counterattacks that Ultra SIGINT intelligence advised him were imminent.[20]

As a strategic maneuver designed to produce a rapid break in the Winter Line stalemate, *Shingle* had already failed. Churchill, who had been its most enthusiastic proponent, admitted when the operation was little more than a week old at the end of January 1944, "I had hoped that we were hurling a wild cat on to the shore, but all we have got was a stranded whale."[21] For weeks during 1943–1944, the prime minister had championed *Shingle* as a campaign-winning stroke.[22] What it produced was another grinding battle of attrition where the Allies were forced to reinforce the Anzio beachhead with more manpower and matériel.[23]

Kesselring directed 14th Army under *Generaloberst* Eberhard von Mackensen to contain Anzio while leaving the Gustav Winter Line defense to Vietinghoff's 10th Army. Kesselring deftly juggled his available troops between the Gustav Line and Anzio. He did this so skillfully that the Allies were forced to ship reinforcements to the Anzio beachhead from units previously allocated to attacks on Cassino and the Gustav Line.[24]

A week after 6th Corps had landed, the Germans outnumbered the Allies around the beachhead, an estimated seventy-two thousand to sixty-one thousand. Mackensen continued to add more German reinforcements and executed a determined counterattack in mid-February 1944 intended to throw the Allies back into the sea. The Germans opened the battle with a 452-gun bombardment and committed even more troops (125,000) into the battle against by then the Allies' one hundred thousand. Mackensen drove a wedge one mile deep and two miles wide into the middle of the 45th Division. However, the Allied "weight of metal" prevailed. Allied artillery and naval guns fired sixty-five thousand rounds on the first day alone.[25] The Mediterranean Allied Air Force committed eight hundred planes, which dropped one thousand tons of explosives along the 6th Corps front line, the heaviest tactical payload on any single day of close air support in the war thus far. In the month since the landing, both the Allied and Axis armies at Anzio had sustained forty thousand battle and nonbattle casualties, "a double decimation that would impose a temporary stalemate at the beachhead." Anzio quickly took on a new name "the Bitchhead."

After the German counterattack, Clark relieved Lucas and replaced him with Major General Lucian K. Truscott Jr., a highly respected, energetic presence at the beachhead, who was already serving as Lucas's deputy. Upon taking command, he told reporters the truth: "We're going to have a tough time here for months to come. But, gentlemen, we're going to hold this beachhead, come what may."[26] February 1944 was a sobering month for the Allies in Italy. Their combat losses were the highest in the theater to date. There would be no quick, decisive success either at the Anzio beachhead or for Clark's 5th Army seventy miles to the south attacking Cassino. Alexander candidly commented on Allied weakness and German strength: "He is quicker than we are, quicker at regrouping his forces, quicker at thinning out a defensive front to provide troops to close gaps at decisive points . . . quicker at reaching decisions on the battlefield. By comparison, our methods are often slow and cumbersome."[27]

The renewal of the Allied offensive to the south after four battles to overcome Monte Cassino, including the bombing of the abbey to rubble, the breakout from the Anzio beachhead, and the subsequent execution of Operation *Diadem* to take Rome, cost 312,000 Allied casualties, 40 percent of the Allied losses suffered in northwest Europe. The fighting revealed to the Allies that there was no soft underbelly in the Mediterranean.

Any responsible critique of the Italian campaign should answer the following question: If not Italy, where? Martin Blumenson addressed the strategic case on the merits:

> Of the whole campaign in southern Italy from the Allied point of view, the question has often been asked: was the expenditure of lives in the dreadful conditions of terrain and weather justified? The alternative was to concentrate Allied forces elsewhere. But within the context of the strategic thinking of the time, it is difficult to see where else Allied forces, practically and realistically, could have fought the Germans. . . . To have moved all or most of the resources to the United Kingdom for *Overlord* would have showed the Axis categorically where the next Allied blow would be struck. . . . The Allied strategy was largely predetermined by what had gone before, and the successive campaigns of North Africa, Sicily, and Italy reflected the influence that events impose on the will of man.[28]

Blumenson explained how and why the Italian campaign fit into the broader strategic architecture that began to unfold in mid-1944. Historians continue to debate the strategic value of the campaign.

CONCLUSIONS

The Allied strategic architecture of an early invasion to liberate the overrun countries of northwest Europe was not viable in 1943. The series of Allied conferences were ambiguous about a hard date to invade the Continent until General Marshall forced the result in May 1943 at the Washington Conference. With the *Overlord* date finally settled, Churchill had his opening to push for Italy over the course of the next year.

Italy did not present any opportunities for the combatants on either side to create a war-winning strategic advantage. It took the Allies nine months of hard fighting to capture Rome, at which point they could rightly lay claim to have taken the first major Axis capital. Within two days of Rome's capture on June 4, 1944, D-Day in Normandy had eclipsed the Italian campaign. Blumenson makes the most persuasive case for the campaign. Given the limited strategic options available, the Allies invaded Italy in 1943 because they could.

One historian and Italian veteran, Sir Michael E. Howard, himself a Coldstream Guards officer who received a Military Cross for his service in Italy, wrote sixty-five years later, "If I can speak as one of the dwindling number of those who took part in the campaign, although Italy was a perfectly bloody place to fight, it never occurred to any of us that we should not be fighting there at all."[29]

Invasion of Italy

(1) Patton instructing troops on Sicily, July 11, 1943. LOC photo (2) Japanese-American soldiers of the 442nd Regiment running for cover from German artillery shell about to hit outside building. NARA photo

(3) *Feldmarschall* Albert Kesselring (left) and *Generaloberst* Heinrich von Vietinghoff (right) photographed somewhere in Italy around the time of the Salerno landing between August and September 1943. BArch photo (4) RAF Baltimore light bomber drops bombs during an attack on a railway station at a strategic point on the east–west route across Italy in February 1944. IWM photo

(5) Moving up through Prato, infantry column of the 370th Infantry Regiment has yet to climb the mountain that lies ahead. (6) US soldier of 30th Infantry standing in reverence before an altar in a damaged Catholic Church in Acerno; the pews at left appear undamaged, while debris from bomb-shattered roof is strewn about the chancel. NARA photos

8

D-DAY AND THE BATTLE FOR NORMANDY

Retaking the Continent

Between 1939 and 1944, the Anglo-American Allies built their air forces, navies, and ground forces to levels of overwhelming strength so that they could cross the English Channel to liberate the Continent.[1]

To some historians, D-Day represents the full integration of the Allied strategic architecture to defeat Germany first. By June 6, 1944, the Allies were united behind a comprehensive planning organization, the Supreme Headquarters Allied Expeditionary Force (SHAEF) under one commander, General Eisenhower. The years of acrimonious debates were behind them. The Allies had sufficiently coordinated their plans so that Anglo-American execution of Operations *Neptune* and *Overlord** preceded Soviet execution of Operation *Bagration* by only sixteen days.[2]

D-Day in the popular mind supports "the weight of myth"[3] because it magnifies the importance of this monumental day on the beaches of Normandy while relegating to professional accounts of military historians the harsh realities of the remainder of the European war. Execution of *Overlord* required eleven more months of hard fighting and heavy casualties.

This chapter and the next show that the plan for *Overlord* was essentially a logistical document to get Allied armies ashore, establish a beachhead lodgment, and break out of it. It did not offer a strategy for what to do next except to plot

---

*The code name *Overlord* refers to the planning and execution of the whole of the campaign in northwest Europe and the operations that ended in May 1945 with the surrender of Germany. The assault landings on June 6, 1944, were part of Operation *Neptune* subsumed under *Overlord*. *Neptune* officially ended on June 30, 1944, after completion of the preliminary buildup of Allied forces in the Normandy beachhead.

a series of "phase lines" on a map, demarcating expansion of the entire lodgment to the Seine River by D+90. Events happened so rapidly after the August
breakout that the Allies had liberated Paris by D+80.[4]

Overlord lacked an overall plan for maneuver and operations to destroy the
Westheer, the German army in the west. For the Allied strategic architecture
to succeed, it would require adaptation and operational learning by commanders and soldiers in the field. Frontline soldiers who survived the first shocks
and horrors of combat learned that survival depended on their ability to adapt
and learn because the only honorable exit from the fighting was a wound severe enough to get sent home (the "million-dollar wound"), death, or winning
the war. The epic of D-Day has masked the relentless violence, destruction,
and death that followed. For Allied soldiers deployed in frontline units, the
continuing combat was brutal and lethal for hundreds of thousands.

POLICY

By the summer of 1944, the Allies were in solid alignment for the invasion
of the Continent and its political purpose, the unconditional surrender of the
Axis powers. Roosevelt and Churchill made good on their promise to Stalin of
a Second Front. Six Allied conferences between 1942 and 1943 established a
sequence of strategic decisions that led to the decision to invade Normandy.
The first conference in Washington from December 1941 to January 1942
established the "Germany First" consensus. The second conference in Washington in June 1942 resulted in the decision to invade North Africa. The third
conference at Casablanca in January 1943 expanded the Mediterranean strategy and the direction of the strategic bombing offensive. The fourth conference in Washington in May 1943 broadened the Mediterranean strategy to include the Italian campaign and, most important, confirmed General Marshall's
insistence on a firm date for the invasion of the Continent, May 1944 (latter
slipped to June 1944). The fifth conference in Quebec in August 1943 resulted
in further direction for the Italian campaign and planning for *Overlord*. The
sixth conference in Tehran in November–December 1943 included Stalin for
the first time, who pressed relentlessly for the Second Front.

The United States and Great Britain established innumerable joint chains of
command and committees to oversee every military and industrial aspect of D-
Day. Experienced, proven commanders had been assigned to *Overlord*. General
Eisenhower presided over a coalition populated by strong-willed, and in some
cases politically connected, personalities of American, British, Canadian, and
French commanders, where tact, diplomacy, and above all the willingness to
make decisions under pressure were essential to hold the coalition together.

Unlike the Germans' amateurish plan to launch Operation *Sea Lion* in
1940 by towing barges across the difficult waters of the Dover Strait, the Al-

lies designed and built thousands of purpose-built landing craft for an array of specialized applications. The comprehensiveness of Allied R&D to create amphibious technology led the British at Churchill's continual prodding to develop specialized antimine and assault vehicles under the direction of a leading tank expert, Major General Sir Percy C. S. Hobart.[5] The specialized armored vehicles Hobart developed and produced were given the title AVRE (armored vehicle, Royal Engineers), also known as "Hobart's Funnies." Seven of his designs saw action in Normandy, including a floating tank and a tank modified to clear minefields.

The British, also at Churchill's instigation, developed artificial harbors known as "Mulberries." After the great storm in the English Channel and along the coast of the invasion beaches on June 19–21, 1944, naval and shore parties restored the British Mulberry, but the American one was destroyed.[6] The Americans then transshipped all their supplies directly over the beaches. A pipeline laid under the ocean (PLUTO) on August 12, 1944, between Britain and Cherbourg supplied fuel for the Allied fully mechanized force.[7]

The German policy for defending Western Europe against the Allied assault depended first of all on the construction of the Atlantic Wall. The German *Organisation Todt* began constructing the *Atlantikwall* on Hitler's orders in December 1941. The 3,600 miles of Atlantic coastline, running from Norway to the Franco-Spanish frontier, had been decreed as early as December 1941 to become an impregnable line of defense. Work was accelerated and broadened to cover areas between the maritime port fortresses at Dunkirk, Cap Griz Nez, Boulogne, Le Havre, Cherbourg, Brest, Lorient, St. Nazaire, and La Rochelle. Hitler had appointed *Feldmarschall* Rommel in late 1943 as inspector of the *Atlantikwall*. *Organization Todt* by May 1943 had nearly three hundred thousand French and foreign workers from twenty nationalities constructing fifteen thousand concrete bunkers to shelter three hundred thousand troops permanently and deployed fifty thousand beach obstacles.[8]

However, behind these formidable coastal fortifications, the *Westheer* lacked both a clear defensive strategy and a coherent chain of command that could make tactical decisions quickly. Hitler and the commanders assigned to defend the Pas de Calais and Normandy squabbled continually over command arrangements, deployments, placement and control of reserves, and where the Allied threat would strike.

STRATEGY

Overlord was the largest deployment of Allied land, sea, and air power ever assembled. The *Westheer* theoretically had the military advantage of interior supply lines buttressed by the *Atlantikwall*. *Feldmarschall* von Rundstedt, as *Oberbefehlshaber West* (OB West), exercised control over two army groups,

Armeegruppe B, consisting of the 7th and 15th *Armees* east and west of the
Seine with the bulk of the *Panzer* and infantry divisions, and *Armeegruppe* G
south of the Loire, to defend against an attack from the Mediterranean. Rundstedt had tasked *Feldmarschall* Rommel in command of 7th Army to defend
Normandy and the Cotentin Peninsula.

As pre–D-Day operations developed, the Allies created two discriminators: Allied air superiority and the success of their deception campaign. Air
supremacy over Europe seriously reduced German capacity to move forces
quickly into Normandy and continued to degrade the Reich's industrial capacity. Allied disinformation initiatives ensured dispersal of German dispositions
at the time of the greatest Allied vulnerability at the Normandy beachhead.

At the heart of the *Neptune* plan was a complex package of deception
measures that turned out to be more effective than the Allies' most optimistic
expectations. They were intended to convince Hitler, OKW, and OB West
that the main effort would invade the Pas de Calais directly across the Dover
Strait, deceiving the Germans into concentrating substantial German air and
ground forces there for at least fourteen days. In England, Operation *Fortitude* created a phantom US 1st Army Group (FUSAG) in East Anglia under
the command of General Patton, who was respected and feared by German officers. Deception measures included elaborate bogus bases, training grounds,
communications networks, fabricated communications traffic, fake orders
of battle, and a false target, the French coast between Calais and Boulogne.
Fortitude worked so well that by August after the breakout, there were still
Germans, including Hitler, who believed that the main Allied thrust was yet to
happen and that when it did it would be in the Pas de Calais.[9]

It is on the larger canvas of both the German *Westfront* and *Ostfront* that
a comprehensive, strategic picture of the final year of the war in Europe
should be reconstructed. During the first three weeks of June 1944, the
Allies unleashed two massive offensives. The simultaneous execution of Operations *Neptune* and *Overlord* to assault the *Westheer* in Western Europe
and Operation *Bagration* to break the *Ostheer* on the Eastern Front stunned
the Germans. Operations *Overlord* and *Bagration* forced Hitler into balanc-
ing combat power among his armies on four weakening fronts: in France,
where Rundstedt and Rommel had to prevent the Allied breakout from the
Normandy beachhead and later in August to resist Operation *Dragoon*, the
invasion of southern France;[10] the Eastern Front, where over two hundred
Ostheer divisions were fighting the Red Army; in Italy, where Kesselring's
twenty-five divisions were defending the territory north of Rome; and over
the Reich, where decimated *Luftwaffe* fighter squadrons were defending
key industrial centers after resumption of the around-the-clock strategic
bombing offensive.

The strategic challenge for the Anglo-American Allies was daunting because an expeditionary campaign on this scale required the vertical integration of three levels of war planning and execution—strategic, operational, and tactical.[11]

At the strategic level, SHAEF planners assumed full responsibility for air, sea, and land forces in an entire theater. By mid-1944, the industrial bases of the United States and Great Britain were sufficiently mobilized to equip, train, and deploy the required air, naval, and ground assets necessary for a cross-Channel assault to attack the *Wehrmacht* in northwest Europe.

For Roosevelt, Churchill, Marshall, Brooke, and Eisenhower, *Overlord* meant achieving militarily the unconditional surrender of Germany.[12] Planning for this outcome had been underway for over a year at SHAEF headquarters in London. General Montgomery, who had been reassigned from Italy to return to England to assume overall planning and command of the land battle, took over from Lieutenant General Sir Frederick E. Morgan, who with his staff had undertaken the preliminary planning beginning in March 1943 and had served as chief of staff to the supreme Allied commander (COSSAC).[13] On May 15, 1944, after months of planning, Generals Eisenhower and Montgomery conducted at St. Paul's School in London a grand briefing before a glittering assemblage of senior Allied political and military leaders. Eisenhower opened the proceedings by emphasizing the collaborative aspects of the Allied planning effort and turned over the podium to Montgomery.

At the operational level, the Allied plan of attack, as Montgomery briefed it, took the form of an eight-division assault across a seventy-mile front of five beaches, including three airborne divisions committed to flank protection. He indicated that British and Canadian forces would land on *Sword*, *Gold*, and *Juno* Beaches on the eastern flank and push generally south and southeast from the beachhead and capture Caen on D-Day. US forces would land on *Omaha* and *Utah* Beaches on the western flank and would also attack south with the exception of pushing northwest toward Cherbourg to capture the port (maps 8.1–8.3).

At the tactical level, Normandy was the only part of the north French coast that satisfied three fundamental requirements simultaneously: a full moon to aid navigation of thousands of ships and assault craft in the approach to the invasion area; an early-morning low tide that permitted assault craft to stay clear of obstacles sited just below the high-water mark and warships and aircraft during daylight to perform missions in direct support of the landing; and a second low tide during the hours of daylight of the assault for landing second- and third-echelon formations ashore. The battle space geography precluded any serious consideration of the Pas de Calais area because of the relative ease with which OB West and OKW could move reinforcements into this part of France where the German 15th Army was already deployed behind substantial *Atlantikwall* fortifications.

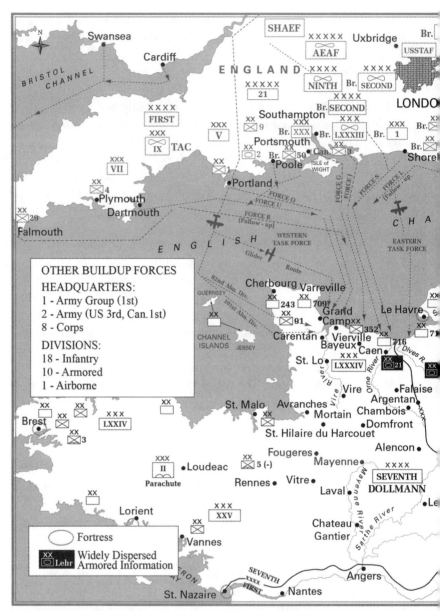

Map 8.1. The Allied plan to invade Normandy proposed a five-division amphibious assault on five beaches across a seventy-mile front supported by three airborne divisions dropped to provide flank protection.
Source: USMA Atlases.

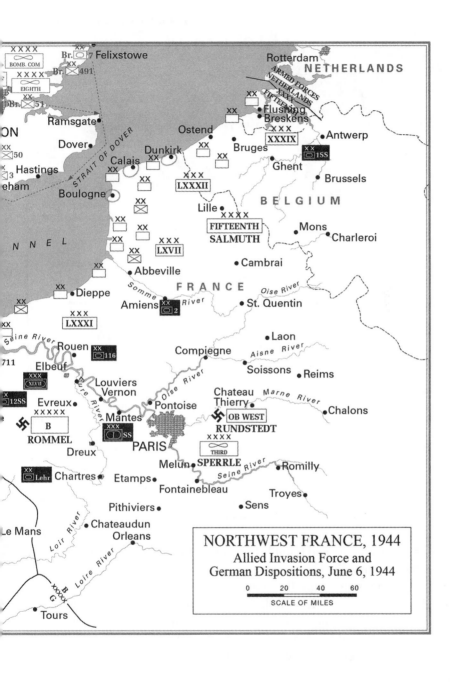

Felixstowe
Br. 7
Br. 491
XXXX BOMB. COM
XXXX EIGHTH
Br. 51
ON
XX 50
X 3
eham
Hastings
Ramsgate
Dover
STRAIT OF DOVER
Boulogne
N N E L

Rotterdam
NETHERLANDS
ARMED FORCES NETHERLANDS
FIFTEENTH
Flushing
Breskens
XXX XXXIX
XX 1SS
Antwerp
Ostend
Bruges
Ghent
Brussels
Dunkirk
Calais
XXX LXXXII
Lille
BELGIUM
Mons
Charleroi
XXXX FIFTEENTH SALMUTH
XXX LXVII
Abbeville
Cambrai
Dieppe
Somme River
FRANCE
Oise River
Amiens
XX 2
St. Quentin
XXX LXXXI
Seine River
Rouen
Laon
Compiegne
Aisne River
Soissons
Reims
711
XX 116
Elbeuf
XXX XLVII
Louviers
Vernon
Eure River
Oise River
Chateau Thierry
Marne River
Chalons
X 12SS
Evreux
XXXXX B ROMMEL
Mantes
XXX SS
Pontoise
OB WEST RUNDSTEDT
Dreux
PARIS
XXXX THIRD
Melun
SPERRLE
Romilly
XX Lehr
Chartres
Etamps
Fontainebleau
Seine River
Troyes
Pithiviers
Sens
Le Mans
Loir River
Chateaudun
Orleans
Loire River
XXXX B G
Tours

NORTHWEST FRANCE, 1944
Allied Invasion Force and
German Dispositions, June 6, 1944

0   20   40   60
SCALE OF MILES

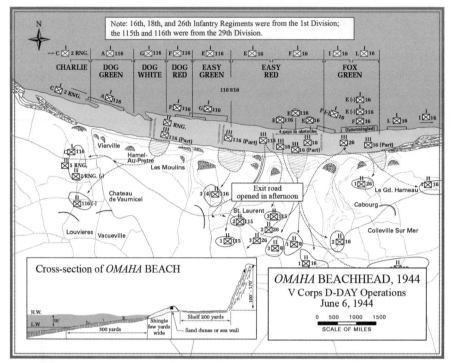

Map 8.2. Invading American soldiers leaving their assault boats on *Dog Green* Beach had to wade three hundred yards in the water, avoid mined beach obstacles, and then cross two hundred yards of shingle and sand (see inset) where German defenders on higher ground caught them in a cross-fire of machine guns and mortars.
Source: USMA Atlases.

Execution of *Neptune* encourages the historical impression that the outcome was foreordained because of Allied numerical superiority. The list of Allied advantages is indeed formidable. The sheer size of the invasion force had never been seen before and is unlikely ever to be replicated again: five infantry and three airborne divisions, supported by a fleet of almost seven thousand ships—5,700 transport ships, including 4,266 landing ships and landing craft, and 1,200 warships, including battleships, cruisers, and destroyers—for shore bombardment of German defensive positions during and after the initial landings. Matching this scale, there were thirteen thousand aircraft committed to *Neptune*.[14] The relentless execution of the air interdiction campaign under Operation *Pointblank* and the *Transportation Plan* isolated the battlefield.[15]

The notion of the inevitability of Allied victory over the *Westheer* in France in the summer of 1944, with its focus on Anglo-American commanders and the vast logistical infrastructure they had at their disposal, tends in Anglo-American narratives to discount the equally menacing, concurrent threat to the *Ostheer* on the Eastern Front. During 1944, the Soviets launched a series of ten offensives that resulted in fourteen major encirclements of Axis forces and the destruction of ninety-six divisions and thirty-four brigades.[16] As Roberts noted, "German defeat simply became a matter of blood and time."[17]

Operation *Bagration* was the fifth in the succession of ten Soviet offensives between 1944 and 1945 that Stalin timed with the Normandy landings. He launched *Bagration* on June 22, 1944, the third anniversary of Hitler's attack on the USSR. *Bagration* destroyed twenty-eight Axis divisions in the first twelve days and resulted in advances of 360 miles to the gates of Warsaw by August. Its offensive metrics rival *Overlord*'s: nearly a two-to-one Soviet manpower superiority, 4,000 tanks, 24,000 guns, and 5,300 aircraft.[18] This was the offensive power the Red Army had arrayed against the German *Armeegruppe Centre*, which had deployed forty-three *Ostheer* frontline divisions and eight security divisions, the largest *Wehrmacht* command on the *Ostfront*.[19] Operations *Overlord* and *Bagration* were creating devastating synergistic effects, imposing losses on the *Wehrmacht* it had not experienced during the war up to that time. Whole army groups were starting to disappear off OKW and OKH operations maps in military headquarters on both fronts.

Soviet deception tactics during *Bagration* rivaled Operation *Fortitude* deceits. They were so successful that local force-superiority ratios of ten to one were achieved along selected axes of attack. Indeed, the reserve units allocated by the *Stavka* to *Bagration* were so substantial that the Soviets could double their forces at will along local zones of the front.[20] The Red Army destroyed 106 *Ostheer* divisions on the *Ostfront* in 1944.[21] That loss approached by a factor of two the total number of roughly sixty *Westheer* divisions deployed on the *Westfront* on D-Day under *Feldmarschall* von Rundstedt.

By mid-1944 the Allies had achieved air and naval supremacy against the Axis everywhere in Europe. The bombing campaign throughout the winter and spring months of 1944 had not only pounded the *Westheer*'s transportation infrastructure in northern France but also had broken the back of the *Luftwaffe*. Allied air forces had reversed the natural balance of advantage between combatants' maritime and overland lines of communications to such an extent that by June 5, 1944, all but two bridges over the Seine below Paris had been destroyed. By D-Day, 75 percent of the railroad system within 150 miles of the assault beaches had been rendered unserviceable.[22] Williamson Murray quotes from a *Luftwaffe* intelligence report dated June 3, 1944, that underscores the damage inflicted on the French rail network by Allied air forces.

> The systematic destruction that has been carried out since March of all important junctions of the entire network . . . has most seriously crippled the whole transport system. . . . Similarly Paris has been cut off from long distance traffic, and the most important bridges over the lower Seine have been destroyed. . . . The rail network is . . . completely wrecked.[23]

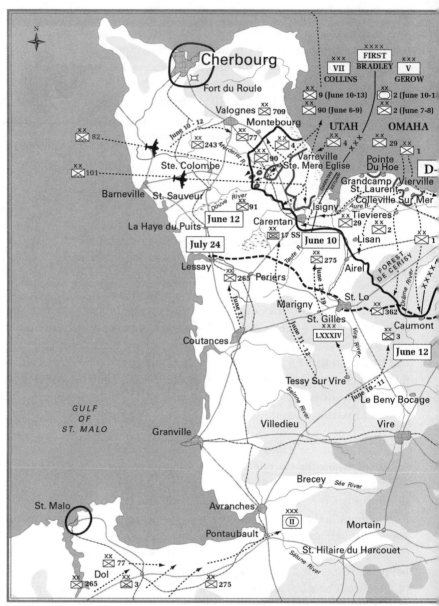

Map 8.3. General Montgomery's plan called for the capture of Caen on D-Day; he still had not done so by D+30. The Germans massed forces around Caen because they, too, needed the communications network around Caen if their counterattacks were to succeed.
Source: USMA Atlases.

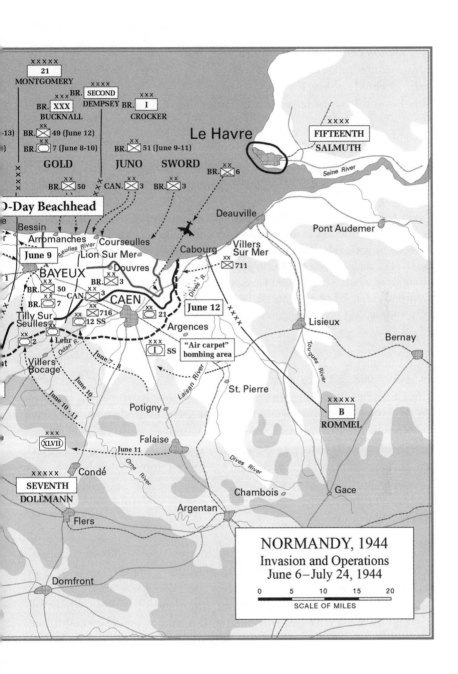

NORMANDY, 1944
Invasion and Operations
June 6–July 24, 1944

0   5   10   15   20
SCALE OF MILES

This degradation of the German capacity to move reinforcements quickly to concentrate counterattack forces against the Allied beachhead ensured that the *Westheer* could not win the buildup race.

Rommel sent this saturnine report to Hitler nine days after D-Day in mid-June:

> The situation on the Normandy front is growing worse every day and is now approaching a grave crisis. Due to the severity of the fighting, the enemy's enormous use of matériel—above all, artillery and tanks—and the effect of his unrestricted command of the air over the battle area, our casualties are so high that the fighting power of our divisions is rapidly diminishing. Replacements from home are few in number and, with the difficult transport situation, take weeks to get to the front. As against 97,000 casualties (including 2,360 officers)—i.e., an average of 2,500 to 3,000 a day—replacements to date number 10,000, of whom about 6,000 have actually arrived at the front. Matériel losses are also huge and have so far been replaced on a very small scale; in tanks, for example, only seventeen replacements have arrived to date as compared with 225 losses.[24]

Against Rommel and Rundstedt, the Allies landed 2,052,299 men, 438,471 vehicles, and 3,098,259 tons of supplies in the first eighty-seven days after D-Day.[25] The Allies won the reinforcement race, mostly over open beaches because they were prepared for contingencies, even unpredictable ones like weather. No fully capable port was open to them until Antwerp became operational in November 1944, despite the earlier capture of Cherbourg (destroyed by German demolition) and Le Havre (not captured until September).[26]

OPERATIONS

The Normandy beachhead confronted an interior laced with one impenetrable hedgerow after another, topographical features that the *Overlord* plan had not addressed adequately in advance. The beachhead was a confined lodgment area where the Allies took almost two months to develop their full offensive combat power. The infantrymen in the landing craft heading to the beaches did not know the depth of this military challenge. They first had to land ashore, then survive to overcome the beach defenses, and then take the fight inland. The Allied armies discovered that they had to find a tactical solution to dislodge the *Westheer* from the hedgerows.

Willmott argues that the *Westheer* in Normandy, offered as the principal example of a German army skillfully fighting a costly attrition battle against an adversary, blessed with a military cornucopia of men and equipment, is a "pernicious myth."[27] Willmott's historical perspective is a comparison of the

German army in 1940 and 1944. Nevertheless, the German army in Normandy in 1944 resisted the Allies with tenacity, causing 425,000 casualties to all combatants.[28]

It was on *Omaha* Beach that the worst setbacks on D-Day took place. Problems had arisen long before the first wave landed. The troops had been transferred to their landing craft while they were still eleven miles offshore. Their run to the beach was twice the distance the British had to run to their beaches. It took three to four hours in a rough sea. Many were seasick multiple times, having been fed a steak-and-eggs breakfast aboard the troopships in the small hours of the morning. Every man was carrying a heavy combat load, almost seventy pounds of ammunition, water, and rations. Able Company's landing was not that unusual for the first wave on *Dog Green* of *Omaha* Beach:

> When the company was still 5,000 yards out, the men saw the barrage from the rocket boats striking the water about 1,000 yards to their right front. They saw nothing hit on their beach or anywhere near it. A [company] came on in six assault boats. . . . The men recognized that they were coming straight into the designated landing point. They were at the sides looking toward the enemy shore. What they saw was an absolutely unblemished beach, [without craters from artillery] or bomb fire and wholly barren of shingle or any other cover. The first ramps were dropped at 0636 in water that was waist-deep to over a man's head.

Map 8.2 presents an inset cross-section of the elevation of *Omaha* Beach. Once the assault troops went into the water, some had to wade through hundreds of yards of waves and surf; avoid beach obstacles, some of them mined tetrahedrons that the Germans had prepositioned; traverse a few yards of shingle; and then cross two hundred yards of sand dunes to the base of the bluff, all the while caught in preregistered German automatic weapons fire and a barrage of mortar rounds. The Able Company narrative that was reconstructed decades later by seven survivors continues:

> As if this had been the signal for which the enemy waited, the ramps were instantly enveloped in a crossing of automatic fire which was accurate and in a great volume. It came at the boats from both ends of the beach. "A" had planned to move in three files from each boat, center file going first, then flank files peeling off to right and left. The first men tried it. They crumpled as they sprang from the ship, forward into the water. Then order was lost. It seemed to the men then that the only way to get ashore with a chance for safety was to dive head first into the water. . . . In one of the boats, a third of the men had become engaged in this struggle to save themselves from a quick drowning. That many were lost before they had a chance to face the enemy. . . . In those first confused minutes when the men were fighting the water, dropping their arms and even their helmets to save themselves from drowning, and learning by what they saw that the landing

had deteriorated into a struggle for personal survival, every sergeant was either killed or wounded. It seemed to the others that enemy snipers had spotted their leaders and had directed their fire so as to exterminate them. . . . Within twenty minutes of striking the beach, "A" had ceased to be an assault company and had become a forlorn little rescue party bent on survival and the saving of lives. Orders were no longer being given by anyone; each man who remained sound moved or not as he saw fit.[29]

Brigadier General Norman H. Cota, deputy commander of the 29th Infantry Division (ID), landed on *Omaha's Dog White* Beach under heavy fire right next to *Dog Green* roughly an hour after A Company. Three soldiers were instantly killed when the ramp was lowered. Although the leading elements like A Company had been on the beach for about an hour, none had advanced farther than the seawall at the base of the dune shelf.[30] By 0800, Cota's command group with the 116th Regiment was searching for a point to break through the German wire toward the Les Moulins draw. Colonel Charles D. Canham had gone to the left to find an exit from the beach. Cota carried out a reconnaissance to the right. Anthony Beevor offers vivid detail with respect to what senior officers said and did that morning on *Omaha* Beach:

Canham, "tall and thin, with wire-rim glasses and a pencil thin mustache," was a southerner who had warned his men that two-thirds of them would be killed. He was shouting for officers to get their men off the beach. "Get these men the hell off this beach! Go kill some goddamned Krauts!" A lieutenant colonel sheltering from the mortar barrage shouted back, "Colonel, you'd better take cover or you're going to get killed." "Get your ass out of there!" Canham screamed back. "And get these men off this goddamned beach."[31]

Other senior officers were acting and shouting in the same manner. Colonel George A. Taylor, commander of the 1st Division's 16th Infantry Regiment on *Omaha's Easy Green* Beach, east on Cota's left, also moved from one officer to another, shouting, "We've got to get off the beach before they put the 88s on us. If we've got to get killed, we might as well kill some Germans. . . . The only people on this beach are the dead and those that are going to die—now let's get the hell out of here!"[32]

Cota and men from the 116th by midday were moving toward Vierville. Cota during the morning had ordered Lieutenant Colonel Robert R. Ploger to assemble enough engineers and explosives to blow a gap in the bluff to create a beach exit toward Vierville. Ploger was among the first wave on *Dog White* in command of an engineering combat battalion. Ploger had been wounded in an ankle immediately upon landing, but he hobbled around the beach at General Cota's behest.[33] By the end of D-Day, American forces on Omaha held positions as deep as two miles inland along a six-mile front.

On the British and Canadian beaches, Montgomery's plan to secure Caen on D-Day had become a major flaw (map 8.3). By D+30, the British on the left had mounted four costly and inconclusive operations to capture Caen. Initially, it was the failure to push hard enough to take the crossroads town of Villers-Bocage when the Germans were still relatively weak. Then there were three more failures: the *Epsom* offensive east of the Orne River to strike at Caen,[34] followed by *Charnwood*[35] and *Goodwood*.[36] In the wake of the failure to capture Villers-Bocage southwest of Caen, Montgomery launched *Epsom* to attack on a narrow front toward the Odon River, west of Caen, to surround the city from the south. The operation was abandoned after less than a week after British divisions lost over five thousand men.

Charnwood was a "head on" attack to capture Caen in response to the pressure on Montgomery from Whitehall to capture the city. A massive bombing by 467 Lancasters and Halifaxes of RAF Bomber Command to soften the northern fringe preceded it. It failed to destroy the German positions that had been targeted and resulted in reducing much of the city to rubble, still with fifteen thousand French civilians inhabiting it. The rubble, Stalingrad-style, created excellent defensive terrain for the Germans. Beevor judges *Charnwood* "a very partial success" insofar as British forces took the northern part of the city. However, the operation failed to capture enough ground to permit the buildup of a force adequate to break through the German hard crust.

Operation *Goodwood*, like *Epsom*, named after the English racecourse, was Montgomery's third plan of attack to take Caen. It was to be executed simultaneously with Bradley's Operation *Cobra*, but once *Cobra* was postponed, *Goodwood* became an independent military enterprise. Like *Charnwood*, it began with a massive air bombardment by two thousand aircraft, followed by a strong artillery preparation. British armor was massed to penetrate the German defensives, but the presence of mines the Allies themselves had previously laid to protect their supply lines slowed the armored advance, allowing the Germans time to reorganize their defenses. The offensive was abandoned three days after it began.

Operation *Neptune* by its end in June had evolved into an attempt to grind the German army to dust by the application of Allied air and naval firepower and the commitment of military manpower capable of fighting hard battles of attrition along a broadening front.[37] From the plan that Montgomery had presented to the St. Paul's School audience on May 15, 1944—that is, get ashore, penetrate inland to gain space for the buildup, capture Caen, and then develop operations on a broad front toward the Seine—he had only accomplished the first task by D+30.[38]

Carlo D'Este tellingly quotes from Blumenson to explain why Montgomery's plan as briefed did not result in the early capture of Caen:

The Germans massed their forces [around Caen] . . . not because Montgomery drew them there but because they were trying to fulfill a purpose of their own. Traditional German military stressed the attainment of victory by a decisive act rather than by strategy of gradual and cumulative attrition. As a consequence, throughout the month of June, the Germans sought to launch a bold and massive counterattack that would destroy the Allied beachhead and drive the Allies back into the sea. They concentrated their forces and their efforts for that decisive action in the terrain around Caen, for that was the only place they could do so—not only because as Montgomery had calculated, the communications network converged toward that point, but also because the ground itself favored that deployment.[39]

Operation *Cobra*, launched by the US 1st Army, represented General Bradley's third attempt to break out of his beachhead. The first, begun on July 3, 1944, had been checked by hard fighting along the Douve River flood line. The second, begun on July 13, resulted in the capture of St. Lô after five days but at the cost of eleven thousand casualties. *Cobra* promised to be better because the weight of forces was in the Americans' favor, fifteen divisions against seven German divisions (only three of them armored). *Cobra* offered an element of surprise because the Germans did not expect an offensive on such unfavorable terrain. By *Cobra*, the Americans had learned to improve their tactics in the hedgerows. In mid-August, Bradley's execution of *Cobra*, aided by Montgomery's continuing pressure on the left flank, led to the cracking of the German defensive crust and the breakout.[40] Patton's 3rd Army exploitation of the breakthrough succeeded in breaking the Western Front wide open to Paris (map 8.4).

Cobra, planned and executed by Bradley on the right and exploited by Patton's 3rd Army, finally broke what some were starting to think was a stalemate. The conduct of the Allied battle for Normandy, and the fall and winter operations that followed after the breakout, has been the subject of debate about the performance of individual commanders. These debates are eclipsed by the doctrinal differences between the combatants. The one episode of the Normandy campaign that provokes endless debate to the present day is the Falaise battle (map 8.4). Analyses by military historians have picked apart the Allies' failure to complete the encirclement of the forces of *Armeegruppe* B when they had the chance.[41]

What has long been obvious to Willmott[42] is that neither the British nor the American armies had developed a war-fighting strategy or a doctrinal base underpinning it for the conduct of such a battle of encirclement and annihilation. Mansoor observed, "History had cast the American army in a different mold." Ulysses S. Grant launched the Army of the Potomac directly at the Army of Northern Virginia. This strategy resulted in both high casualties and decisive victory. The American Expeditionary Forces attacking "directly into the teeth of German defenses" in the Argonne-Meuse offensive of World War I, again with high casualties, repeated the same strategy. "In spirit if not in body, the American army of World War II landed in Normandy alongside its Civil War and Great War brethren."[43] Maneuver and encirclement simply were not part of the Anglo-American military DNA the way they were for the officers and soldiers of the *Wehrmacht*. Patton may have understood their potential in his aggressive pursuit of the Germans across Brittany; but he was not operating with clear direction from his superiors, and his 3rd Army was moving along divergent axes of advance, not convergent ones, toward Falaise until it was too late. The reality is more fundamental. Up until this point in the war, neither the British nor the Americans had ever encountered such a large opportunity to destroy an entire army in one stroke.

Mansoor is less generous about professionalism at the strategic level: "American generals . . . demonstrated their tactical competence, although their ability to craft tactical engagements into a larger operational strategy to close with and destroy the enemy remained questionable."[44] Here, of course, Mansoor is referring to the failure to close the jaws of the Falaise trap. But even at this stage, the Germans could no longer come close to matching American organizational and combat capacity, not without careful husbanding and marshaling of resources deep in their rear.[45]

What compensated for the US Army's strategic shortcomings were the capable officers assigned to the armies from all three of the army's martial traditions, Managers, Heroes, and Guardians. Linn categorizes Marshall and Eisenhower as Managers, who at their best created the massive army for World War II, equipped with modern weapons, trained in large-unit operations, and controlled by educated professionals. But Heroes and Guardians were not absent in the European theater.[46] They played important roles in the strategic architecture, too. Guardians, who believe that war is best understood as an engineering project in which the outcome is determined by the correct application of technical principles, were the problem solvers who helped greatly in devising tactics and improvising equipment in the field to overcome the Germans dug into the hedgerows. Lieutenant Colonel Ploger recovered from his D-Day wounds and went back to the front to work with combat teams to weld six-inch, iron-pipe retrofits to tanks to break through the hedgerows.[47] Patton, the archetype in the heroic mold ("wars are fought with men, not weapons"[48]), led the breakout even if his bosses failed to see the opportunity he saw at Falaise.

Rommel, while convalescing in Germany after being seriously wounded in Normandy while traveling from the front in his Horch staff car, recognized how the three martial traditions came together in Normandy:

> Technically and strategically the landing in Normandy was a brilliant achievement of the first magnitude. It showed that the Americans had the courage,

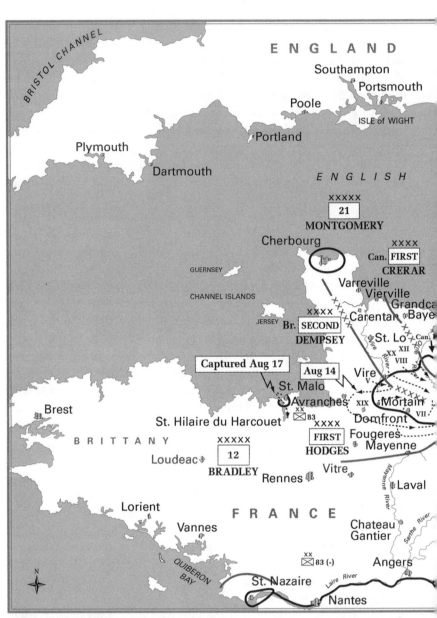

Map 8.4. General Bradley's third attempt with 1st Army to break out of the beachhead succeeded with Operation *Cobra* in late July. General Patton's 3rd Army exploitation of the breakthrough succeeded in opening up the Western Front to Paris.
Source: USMA Atlases.

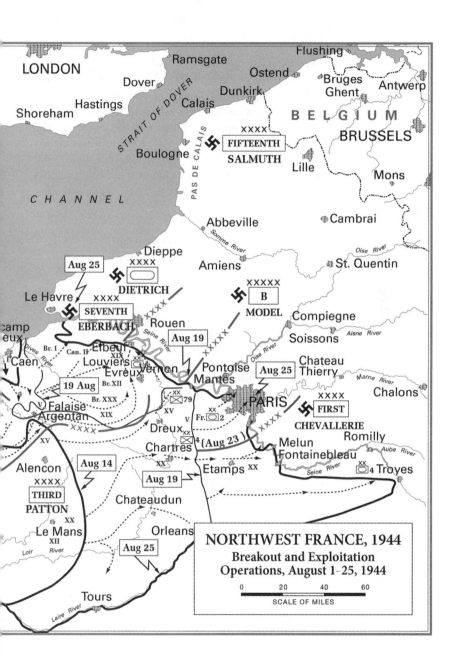

NORTHWEST FRANCE, 1944
Breakout and Exploitation
Operations, August 1–25, 1944

0   20   40   60
SCALE OF MILES

at any rate in the technical field, to employ a multitude of devices hitherto untried in action. European generals of the old school could certainly have executed the invasion from the forces available, but they never could have prepared it—neither technically, organizationally, nor in the field of training. The functioning of the Allied fighting machine, with all its complexity, surprised even me, and I already had a fairly high opinion of their powers. [In Rommel's paragraph that follows, he adds this clause that threads back to Tunisia and forward to Normandy:] the American generals showed themselves to be very advanced in the tactical handling of their forces, although we had to wait until the Patton Army [US 3rd Army] in France to see the most astonishing achievements in modern warfare.[49]

Mansoor's assessment of D-Day and the Normandy campaign dampens Rommel's characterization of "astonishing achievements." He cites Blumenson's revisionist account that castigates Bradley, along with Eisenhower and Montgomery, for missing the opportunity presented at Falaise. There, the Allied armies came close to trapping the bulk of German forces in the west but allowed most of them to escape. He points out that "by any accounting, Allied operational performance was sorely lacking," insofar as 50,000 German soldiers escaped the jaws of the trap at Falaise and 240,000 Germans escaped the potential trap across the Seine. The *Overlord* plan only defined where on the Continent the armies should fight, what beaches they were to land on, what corps and divisions were assigned to each, and what phase lines were to be reached when, modeled as much by logistics as by arbitrary military staff forecasts.[50]

Tactically, however, Mansoor assigns high marks to individual American divisions in Normandy. Most of these divisions quickly learned the methods of hedgerow fighting. The *Overlord* plan provided no information about how to attack hedgerows or a coherent plan for maneuver once the armies had broken free of the *bocage*, the mass of fields surrounded by the tangled vegetation of hedgerows that made maneuver very difficult.[51] The US Army in Normandy was forced to become a learning army in the field. As in North Africa and Italy, a lessons-learning system developed on the initiative of local commanders at the divisional level.

> The ability of division commanders to adapt to the situation on the ground in Normandy was the key difference that allowed some divisions to succeed in hedgerow fighting while others initially failed. All divisions sooner or later overcame the disadvantages of the terrain, but the slow learners paid a higher price in casualties and time lost. Often division commanders or operations officers would append a list of "lessons learned" to their monthly after-action report. The 1st, 3rd, 9th, and 29th Infantry Divisions, among others, began this practice early and continued throughout the war. More important, successful divisions ensured that subordinate units understood and used these lessons in combat.[52]

By the commencement of *Cobra*, the divisions in Bradley's 1st Army had largely solved the problem of attacking through hedgerows. Small, combined-arms units learned to operate effectively with infantry, armor, and engineer units by training during lulls in combat. Through hard trial and error, units discovered that tanks were critical to infantry success in penetrating through the *bocage*.

Tactical innovations to break through the *bocage* happened in the field because the kind of army the United States deployed to retake the Continent contained enough combat leaders in the mix from its culture of Guardians, Heroes, and Managers to enable tactical success. There were combat engineers in addition to capable infantry leaders, leaders who knew how to improvise and make technical improvements in the field. The ingenuity of their tactical contributions helped make the strategic architecture work as envisioned by higher-level *Overlord* commanders (the Managers). Without all three types of officers, who had been trained to work together, Allied land forces might have found themselves bogged down in the Normandy lodgment much longer.

Allied tactical air superiority over the battle space in Normandy was a discriminator that enabled the strategic architecture to succeed. Major General Elwood R. "Pete" Quesada's 9th Tactical Air Command accelerated ground spearheads during *Cobra*. A flight of four fighter-bombers flew ahead of each column. A pilot was assigned to ride with the column in a Sherman tank modified with the correct radios for real-time ground–air communications. In clear weather, the aircraft provided excellent reconnaissance information and could deliver immediate fire missions on call. By the fall of 1944, the 9th's tactical air squadrons could deliver air support almost as quickly as artillery fire.

Russell A. Hart argues that the *Cobra* defeat of German forces in the west was not only the result of better Allied combat performance but also fundamentally a logistical defeat, "for the *Westheer* proved unable to reinforce and resupply a field force of sufficient size to contain the Allies in their lodgment." The *Westheer* had to impose a stringent rationing system to preserve its dwindling supplies as the Allied armies approached the German border (map 8.5).[53]

CONCLUSIONS

By late August 1944, the Allies had won a strategic victory in Normandy months ahead of the original *Overlord* schedule and phase lines. Hitler's heavy investments in the *Atlantikwall* had been wasted because the coastal defenses were overcome in a matter of hours. Hitler and the OKW had failed to agree on a defensive strategy that could push the Allies back into the sea as they had in 1940. The Reich was starting to crack.

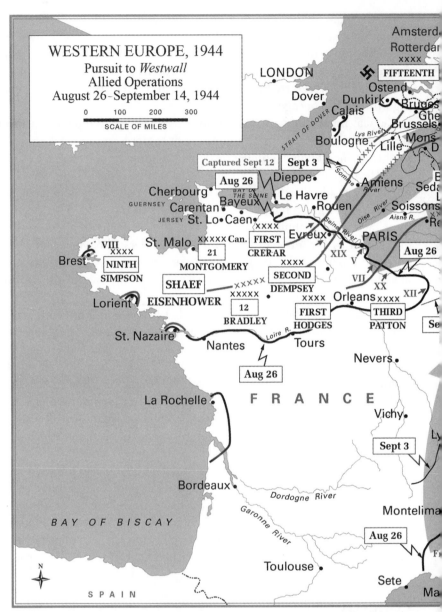

WESTERN EUROPE, 1944
Pursuit to *Westwall*
Allied Operations
August 26–September 14, 1944

SCALE OF MILES
0   100   200   300

Amsterd.
Rotterdar
xxxx
FIFTEENTH
LONDON
Dover
Ostend
Dunkirk
Calais
Bruges
Ghe
Brussels
Boulogne
Lys River
Lille
Mons
D
Captured Sept 12
Sept 3
Dieppe
Amiens
Sed
Aug 26
Somme
River
Cherbourg
Le Havre
Rouen
Soissons
BAY OF THE SEINE
GUERNSEY
Carentan
Bayeux
Oise River
Aisne R.
R
JERSEY
St. Lo
Caen
Evreux
Seine River
PARIS
xxxx Can.
FIRST
St. Malo
21
CRERAR
XIX
V
Aug 26
VIII
xxxx
xxxx
Brest
NINTH
MONTGOMERY
SECOND
VII
SIMPSON
xxxxx
DEMPSEY
XX
XII
SHAEF
xxxxx
xxxx
Orleans xxxx
Lorient
EISENHOWER
12
FIRST
THIRD
Se
BRADLEY
HODGES
PATTON
St. Nazaire
Loire R.
Tours
Nantes
Nevers
Aug 26
La Rochelle
F   R   A   N   C   E
Vichy
Ly
Sept 3
Bordeaux
Dordogne River
Montelima
Garonne River
BAY   OF   BISCAY
Aug 26
N
F
Toulouse
Sete
Ma
SPAIN

Map 8.5. By late August 1944, the Allies had won a strategic victory in Normandy, months
ahead of the original *Overlord* schedule and phase lines.
Source: USMA Atlases.

By the early fall of 1944, the Allied liberation of France, Belgium, Luxembourg, and part of the Netherlands meant more than staggering losses for Hitler and the *Westheer*. In Keegan's words, "a whole OKW theater had been obliterated in a single campaign." The military and economic consequences of these territorial losses were enormous. The position of OB West may have remained a major military appointment in the German chain of command, but its boundaries had shrunk to little more than those of the Reich itself as opposed to what it had been in June, stretching south past the Pas de Calais to Cape Finisterre. The loss of France and Belgium was much more than symbolic to the Reich. France had been "the Golden Goose" of German occupation policy. France had consistently contributed as much food to German tables as the whole of the occupied *Ostfront* between 1941 and 1944 and provided five hundred thousand of the 2.7 million horses requisitioned to draw the *Wehrmacht's* transport and artillery. France was compelled to export 75 percent of its iron ore, 50 percent of its bauxite, and 15 percent of its coal production, to which 85 percent of rail movements in France were dedicated in 1944. As Keegan summarizes these metrics, "the total value of goods and services extracted in the last full year of occupation, 1943, equaled a quarter of Germany's whole national product in the last full year of June 1938." The strategic results of D-Day and the battle for Normandy represented the greatest military disaster Hitler had suffered in the field thus far.[54]

Yet, as events were to play out in the succeeding months, Hitler's Reich was in no danger of imminent collapse.[55] Despite Allied optimism in the west that the door was now open into Germany and the industrial heart of the Reich, the war was not to end by Christmas 1944 as many officers and soldiers on the Western Front in September 1944 were hoping. Germany was still capable of frantic measures of rearmament, recruitment, and resistance.[56] The Allies were soon to discover that they faced problems and constraints, too. The strategic architecture to win the war in Europe was not yet complete.

D-Day and the Battle for Normandy

(1) American troops landing in Normandy shown just as they left the ramp of a landing craft on June 6, 1944. NARA photo

(2) General Eisenhower speaking to paratroopers of the 101st Airborne Division before takeoff on eve of D-Day. NARA photo (3) Allied troops unload equipment and supplies on *Omaha* Beach in early June 1944. LOC photo

9

BATTLE FOR THE RHINE

Attacking Germany's Vitals

The pursuit of the German armies across France created an increasingly broader front. By early September, the front ran more than six hundred miles from Ostend east to Maastricht, south to the Swiss border, and then south again to Nice. In the south of France, Operation *Dragoon*, launched August 15, 1944, presented a new threat to the *Westheer*. General Jacob Devers's 6th Army Group, consisting of the US 7th and French 1st Armies, had advanced three hundred miles, north of Grenoble, in the Rhône-Alpes region (map 8.5).

Allied operations had been the most spectacular of the war to that point. Having crossed the Seine on August 20, Patton's 3rd Army advanced another two hundred miles in the next twelve days until it stopped in front of Metz. General Courtney H. Hodges's 1st Army, to Patton's north, had gone even farther, reaching the Albert Canal in eastern Belgium on September 6. Montgomery's 21st Army Group had marked a slower rate of progress since the *Cobra* breakout but surged forward across northern France and Belgium, capturing Antwerp and its port intact on September 5, although not the Scheldt estuary approaches. Montgomery came to a halt on the Meuse–Escaut Canal on September 9 (map 9.1).

POLICY

The configuration of Allied forces quickly brought to a head the issue of what to do next. The issue reduced to whether the Allies should execute a broad-front strategy, with all armies advancing simultaneously, or a narrow-front one, with only one or two armies given logistical preference. All armies by September were outrunning their supply lines.

Eisenhower at a SHAEF staff meeting on August 20, 1944, modified his strategic policy. Instead of following his May directive along the twin axes to the Ruhr, Bradley's 12th Army Group was to advance toward Metz and the Saar and link up with Devers's 6th Army Group as it came up the Rhône valley. This decision shifted the weight of the Allied strategy to the east, and it left Montgomery's 21st Army Group with no clear strategic role, other than to clear the Channel ports, eliminate the V-1 flying bomb and V-2 rocket sites in the Pas de Calais, and capture the Scheldt that so Antwerp, with its large unloading capacity, could be a port usable to the Allies.[1] It was shortly after this SHAEF meeting that Montgomery sent Eisenhower a message. It was brief, blunt, and to the point.

1. I consider that we have now reached a stage where one really powerful and full-blooded thrust towards Berlin is likely to get there and thus end the German war.
2. We have not enough maintenance resources for two full-blooded thrusts.
3. The selected thrust must have all the maintenance resources it needs without any qualification and any other operation must do the best it can with what is left over.
4. There are only two possible thrusts: one via the Ruhr and the other via the Saar.
5. In my opinion the thrust likely to give the best and quickest result is the northern one via the Ruhr.[2]

Debate over the strategic feasibility and logistical viability of this proposal has been the subject of historical controversy ever since. Did the Allies miss a once-in-a-lifetime opportunity to end the war in 1944 by failing to concentrate their forces in a single "full-blooded" assault to overwhelm the Ruhr, as Montgomery was recommending?[3] There was a political element introduced into this controversy by the first V-2 hitting London on September 8, 1944. The V-2 attacks caused the British government to demand that 21st Army Group overrun the launching sites in Holland. This development led Montgomery to modify his Ruhr narrow-front thrust plan by proposing to move north to the Zuider Zee.

Montgomery's proposal segued to the rapid planning and failed execution of Operation *Market Garden* on September 17, 1944 (map 9.1). *Market Garden* was the unsuccessful airborne operation to seize the bridge at Arnhem across the Rhine and force an entry into the Reich and the industrial Ruhr. *Market Garden*'s defeat rendered moot the broad- versus narrow-front debate.

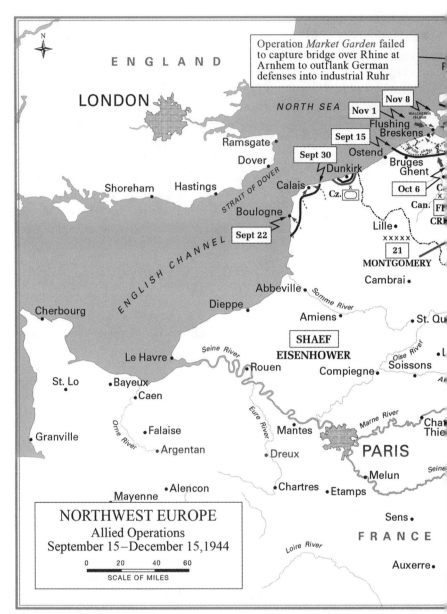

Map 9.1. After *Market Garden* failed, Allied armies on the Western Front were outrunning their supplies by the fall of 1944.

Source: USMA Atlases.

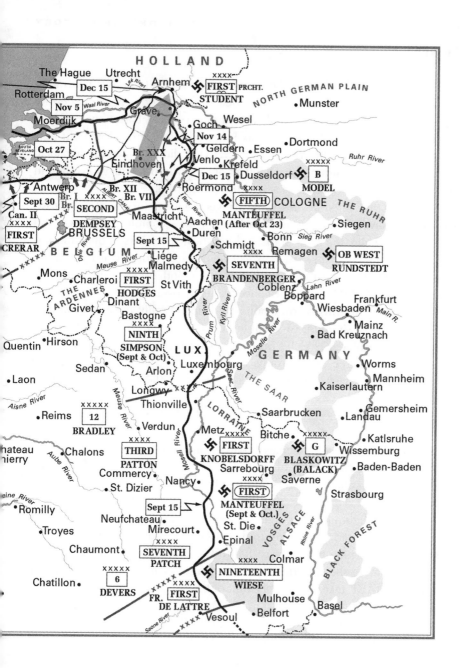

STRATEGY

Until *Market Garden's* failure, Allied armies were trying to do two contradictory things at the same time: (1) pursue a beaten foe relentlessly and penetrate deep into Germany's industrial vitals (Montgomery's and Patton's views) and (2) maintain an offensive force along six hundred miles of front without outrunning its supply lines (SHAEF's view). SHAEF did not have the logistical networks in place to continue supplying all of the forty-three divisions then in the ETO for offensive operations across the entire front.[4]

By the time the Allied armies were arrayed against Rundstedt's reconstituted forces, they had to learn new hard lessons to accomplish their assigned missions. Meanwhile, the army staffs and logistical specialists in the Communications Zone (COM Z) forward logistical headquarters for northwest Europe had to determine how to sustain this large force. "Both efforts were crucial to ultimate victory."[5] COM Z's performance was controversial.[6]

Resumption of the broad-front policy did not literally mean that all the armies would close "shoulder-to-shoulder and track-to-track" on the German frontier and the Rhine. SHAEF's broad-front strategy entailed simultaneous offensives by the three army groups on their respective fronts where discrete, coordinated attacks could be made with the available logistical support spread out evenly.

This military policy accorded with long-held US military doctrine dating back to Ulysses S. Grant and the Civil War. Every army should be in action all the time attacking the enemy armies in battles of attrition. This view coincided with Eisenhower's philosophy of war, developed over decades of reading, thought, and discussion with peers and mentors.[7]

Eisenhower believed that the broad-front policy required a strong logistical base close to the fighting fronts. The solution was Antwerp, a port that could handle eighty thousand to one hundred thousand tons of cargo per day.[8] The military task of opening up Antwerp fell to the Canadians. Many of the difficulties confronting the Canadian 1st Army on the Scheldt might have been avoided had SHAEF taken earlier account of the logistical importance of Antwerp and the problems of opening it up to shipping traffic after the Normandy breakout. It was not until October 9, 1944, that Eisenhower appreciated the importance of Antwerp as a logistics hub.[9] He sent Montgomery a message on that date: "I consider Antwerp of first importance in all our endeavors on entire front from Switzerland to Channel."[10] The mission of clearing the Scheldt was a hard, costly operation for the Canadian 1st Army, something often overlooked in historical accounts. This army had to fight its way north from the Seine, first dealing with German garrisons left behind at Le Havre, Dieppe, Boulogne, Calais, Ostend, and Dunkirk before turning to the Scheldt. The Canadian campaign bore "the hallmarks of an epic."[11]

Supply shortages before Antwerp became operational as a port in the first week of November, along with the deteriorating fall weather, meant that the Allies were locked in a campaign of attrition on the periphery of Germany in the fall of 1944 without two things on which they relied heavily: their prodigious ammunition stores to support their ample artillery firepower and tactical air support on demand, weather permitting. Flyable days were limited.[12]

Meanwhile, *Feldmarschall* von Rundstedt and his commanders of *Armeegruppen* B and G implemented crisis management measures. They included the improvisational formation of scores of *Kampfgruppen* (combat groups) out of the remnants of broken divisions and the arrival of rapidly recruited and trained *Volksgrenadier* units. These efforts restored order to the *Westheer*'s front lines.[13] The Germans called this period of respite "the Miracle of the West."[14]

The Germans since D-Day had lost 500,000 men, 1,800 tanks, 3,500 guns, and 20,000 vehicles of all kinds.[15] Von Rundstedt's OB West order of battle was nevertheless a formidable force. It consisted of forty-five infantry divisions and fifteen *Panzer* divisions, plus several *Panzer* brigades, at least on paper. Many of these units were severely worn down and short of everything needed to remain in combat, including men, guns, tanks, and ammunition. A more realistic appraisal of the forces available to OB West amounted to about twenty-five divisions of various types, many of them *Kampfgruppen*.[16] Rundstedt realized that he needed time as much as men and munitions. If he could gain enough time, fresh military assets could be put into the German defensive line along the fortified *Westwall*.

With the failure of *Market Garden* to outflank the *Westwall* in the north, thereby denying the Allies an open path east into Germany, the Allies now had to tackle the *Westwall* head-on and batter a way east toward the Rhine, regardless of the axis of attack. Since the pursuit of the *Westheer* across the Seine, there had been three major Allied offensives in progress by the time *Market Garden* was mounted. The British 2nd Army was heading north toward the Rhine and the Ruhr. Hodges's 1st Army was also heading in the same direction, north of the Ardennes, heading via the Aachen Gap to the Rhine, Cologne, and the Ruhr. And Patton, south of the Ardennes and east of Paris, was heading to the Rhine via Metz and the Saar. By the end of September, all of them were stalled.

OPERATIONS

Eisenhower soon had fifty-four divisions he could employ along the broad front, twenty-three of them American infantry divisions. The American divisions in the line were to find themselves embroiled in bitter, ugly, high-casualty battles for Aachen; the Hürtgen Forest; Alsace, including the city of

Colmar; and Lorraine, with its capital city of Metz. Even Patton's 3rd Army, after its spectacular advances after the Normandy breakout, was now bogged down in attempting to penetrate the *Westwall* fortifications.

In Mansoor's judgment, "the combat effectiveness of American divisions was equal to or superior to that of their German adversaries."[17] He argued that American generals had demonstrated their tactical competence in the battle for Normandy, although he faults their operational ability to craft these tactical engagements into a larger operational strategy to close with and destroy the enemy (the missed opportunity at Falaise). He pointed to the determination and skill with which American infantry, armored, and combat engineering units learned to work together to succeed in the hedgerow terrain of Normandy. He identified improved combined-arms methods and the integration of tanks, infantry, field artillery, combat engineers, and tactical airpower in overpowering German forces. He documented how American use of superior command, control, communications, and intelligence (C^3I) systems enabled different units and services to operate together.

The most persuasive evidence of American combat capability is an *Armeegruppe* B intelligence report dated October 23, 1944:

> Strong use of equipment, preservation of manpower. Attacks begin on a narrow front. Exceptionally strong massing of artillery, lavish expenditures of munitions. Before attacks begin, systematic, lengthy artillery preparations. Infantry and tanks advance behind a heavy curtain of mortar and machine gun fire. The artillery is divided into three groups. The first supports the attack with a rolling barrage; the second fires in support of individual calls-for-fire from the infantry in the main battle area; the third conducts counterbattery fire (with effective use of aerial observers). Multiple smoke screens obscure the attack zone. . . . Little massing of infantry. . . . Units broken down into small assault groups to exploit the terrain. . . . The infantry advances only after the strongpoints have been neutralized. The enemy immediately prepares captured terrain against counterattacks. The attack goes according to a well-timed and organized plan. . . . If the attack plan is disturbed, the attack is broken off and renewed only after reinforcement by greater material assets.[18]

As it did in Normandy, the US Army was drawing upon all of its martial traditions. Its leadership included enough officers from each of Linn's three traditions of Managers, Heroes, and Guardians for the strategic architecture in the European theater to succeed. General Marshall and the SHAEF commanders poured in more manpower and matériel to replace losses. There were enough capable and aggressive Guardians and Heroes in the frontline units, who learned in the field. In the midst of tactical operations, they read enough of the lessons-learned reports or experimented with tactical methods to break German defensive tenacity by executing better-planned small-unit operations, where infantry-tank teams and combat engineers became increasingly skilled in the grim business of reducing *Westwall* fortifications.

For the soldiers ordered to assault the fortifications—there were over fourteen thousand pillboxes on the *Westwall* stretching along the front for three hundred miles—casualties were heavy.[19] As they increased, so did the need for replacements. One of the most difficult and costly lessons learned was the reception, in-theater training, and integration of individual new replacements into combat units. While the US Army since the Civil War had used a system of replacing combat-worn regiments with fresh ones, the policy had changed in World Wars I and II. The War Department chose to maintain its deployed divisions at full strength or near full strength by providing enough individual replacements to restore losses without withdrawing one division or regiment for a whole-unit replacement. Infantry divisions, once they were committed to the front, tended to remain engaged for extended periods without relief. They had to integrate thousands of replacements from replacement depots (known to GIs as "repple depples") on or near the front line as combat veterans were wounded.

As time progressed, veterans became an endangered breed. Van Creveld's observation is stark: "The sheer size of the problem may be gauged from the fact that, on the average, three months of intensive combat in World War II cost an American infantry regiment a hundred percent of its personnel in casualties."[20] Mansoor's high-to-low tabulation of total battle and nonbattle casualties of the forty-two American infantry divisions in the European theater between 1944 and 1945 is equally stark. Casualty losses ranged from 252 percent for the 4th ID at the top of the list to 9 percent for the 86th ID at the bottom. In the top twenty divisions, the percentages ranged from 252 to 95 percent.[21] These appalling casualty figures meant that divisions at the top of the list had a total personnel turnover approaching a factor of three.

Effective divisions developed better, smarter approaches to respond to the problem of integrating replacements from the repple depples into combat units during extended operations. Major General Charles H. Gerhardt of the 29th ID, which had assaulted *Omaha* Beach on D-Day, formed a training center using combat-experienced officers and NCOs to train combat replacements. Gerhardt also used his training center to rehabilitate soldiers who performed poorly in combat, committed criminal acts, or were exhaustion (battle fatigue) cases.[22]

The battles along the borders of the Reich in the fall of 1944 revealed the strengths and weaknesses of the US Army. By being forced to learn new methods, American assaults produced eventual victories at Aachen and Metz and in the Vosges. They also produced costly, brutal assaults that doomed multiple divisions in the Hürtgen Forest. Backed by superior artillery and airpower on flyable days of clear weather, American infantry soldiers rarely lost a tactical engagement in the fall of 1944, according to Mansoor's comprehensive study of the performance of American infantry divisions. He argued that the quality of units was more important than their quantity. He concluded that one of the most important components of combat effectiveness was the force's ability to sustain and regenerate combat power. The principal strength of the Allied armies in Normandy had been their ability to win a battle of attrition. That would remain true until the war was won.[23]

Mansoor further argued that Marshall's decision to cap the US Army at eighty-nine divisions for deployment worldwide in all theaters of World War II (the "ninety-division gamble") was a flawed decision insofar as by 1944 it constrained the number of replacements and additional divisions available in the European theater, not to mention elsewhere. The US Army did not fight in Europe with an overwhelming manpower advantage, particularly after the heavy casualties incurred by many of the divisions that landed in Normandy. "As the weeks and months passed, the combat effectiveness of American divisions rose and fell as they lost men to enemy fire, disease, cold weather, injuries, and exhaustion, and had then to integrate thousands of [individual] replacements into their ranks."[24] The War Department's ninety-division gamble was a decision that cost the lives of thousands of servicemen and limited the margins of combat effectiveness.[25]

Between the beginning of October and mid-December 1944, the three Allied army groups executed a series of limited but difficult offensives. The 21st Army Group's British 2nd Army cleared the approaches to Antwerp. By November 8, 1944, the Canadian 1st Army had swept the Scheldt estuary of the enemy. With Antwerp operational, the supply distance to Allied divisions at the front had been reduced from four hundred to seventy miles.[26] Bradley's 12th Army Group, in addition to taking Aachen, also captured most of Luxembourg and Lorraine. Devers's 6th Army Group secured northern Alsace but was unable to clear the Germans from the Colmar pocket until February 1945.

Hitler had been planning his own operational gamble since mid-August. He had begun preparing a major counterattack in the west and had gradually assembled a strong force of twenty-five divisions, including ten *Panzer* divisions. His reasoning was that he lacked the forces and the fuel to undertake anything decisive after the destruction of Army Group Center on the Eastern Front. Indeed, he recognized the probability of a general defeat of the Reich. He was convinced that without such a counterattack, Germany was certain to lose the war. He therefore proposed splitting the forces of Eisenhower's army groups in two, inflicting heavy losses, and capturing Antwerp, the main Allied supply base. It was front-to-back desperation: attack a weak area of the Allied front with a heavily armored *Schwerpunkt* and then hope for the best. Spearhead German units did not even have enough fuel to reach critical objectives if they failed to capture Allied fuel dumps. It was hardly a war-winning plan. It became famous as the Battle of the Bulge.

Hitler's plan envisaged a strike northwest out of the Ardennes across Belgium and Luxembourg to capture Antwerp. Under strict security, the Germans assembled a force of 250,000 men.[27] Hitler assigned *Feldmarschall* Walter Model's *Armeegruppe* B to command the attack under Rundstedt's nominal supervision as OB West. Model had three armies positioned north to south in the Ardennes, two of them *Panzer* armies tasked with capturing Antwerp and Brussels.[28]

The main effort was a double-pronged counteroffensive by the 5th and 6th *Panzerarmees* to crack open the weakly defended American front in the Ardennes. Then these forces were to pivot north to cross the Meuse River and converge on Antwerp. The 6th *Panzerarmee* was to maneuver along an inner arc past Liege with 5th *Panzerarmee* on an outer arc past Namur (map 9.2). The German 15th *Armee* was to help 6th *Panzerarmee* with a flanking thrust north of Liege, while the 7th *Armee* was to provide flank cover for 5th *Panzerarmee* as both armies wheeled north toward Antwerp. The boldness of the scythe-like sweep of the German plan was the objective of cutting off Montgomery's 21st Army Group from its bases and Bradley's 12th Army Group to the south—posing the threat of a "Dutch Dunkirk."[29] The plan was risky given the limited resources available to the Reich, especially fuel. The German plan only allowed Model seven days to split the Allied front in two before he ran out of gas.

Under the broad-front deployment policy, the fifty-four divisions Eisenhower had at his disposal amounted to little more than one division per twelve miles of front. Ironically, after the Allied debate between the broad- and narrow-front strategies, it was Hitler who chose concentration of force in one last thrust of *Bewegungskrieg*. In the Ardennes-Schnee-Eifel[30] area, perceived as a quiet sector of the front, some American divisions had to defend thirty miles of front.[31] The German attack breached the Allied line across a forty-mile front on December 16, 1944. Hodges's 1st Army had just two infantry divisions, one armored regiment, and various minor detachments in the Ardennes sector that the Germans had selected as the main point of attack by no fewer than five *Panzer* and eight *Volksgrenadier* divisions.

The Germans surprised the Allies because of a SHAEF intelligence failure to uncover the presence of the 5th and 6th *Panzerarmees* in the Eifel. Allied generals discounted a reprise of the strategic surprise of the wildly successful German offensive through the Ardennes into Belgium and France in 1940. General Patton was the exception. He and his 3rd Army staff anticipated what was about to happen and prepared plans to react quickly.[32] A period of bad winter weather grounded Allied airpower for a week after the German counteroffensive began.[33] However, the German onslaught was only partially successful even in its initial stages.

Scores of books have been written about the Battle of the Bulge; there is no space here to do more than sketch the main events and their relevance to

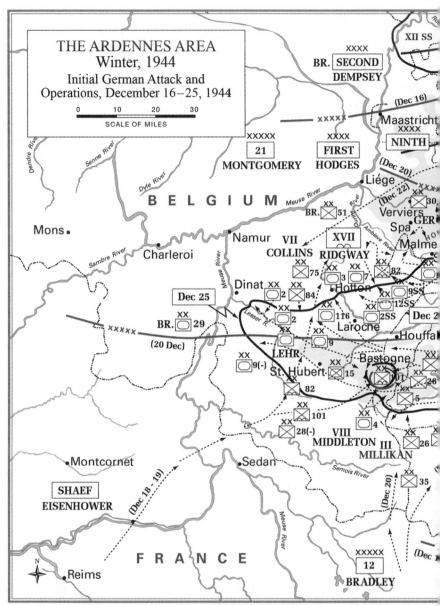

Map 9.2. Hitler's counteroffensive plan was to strike out of the Ardennes across Belgium and Luxembourg to capture Antwerp and split the Allied armies in two.
Source: USMA Atlases.

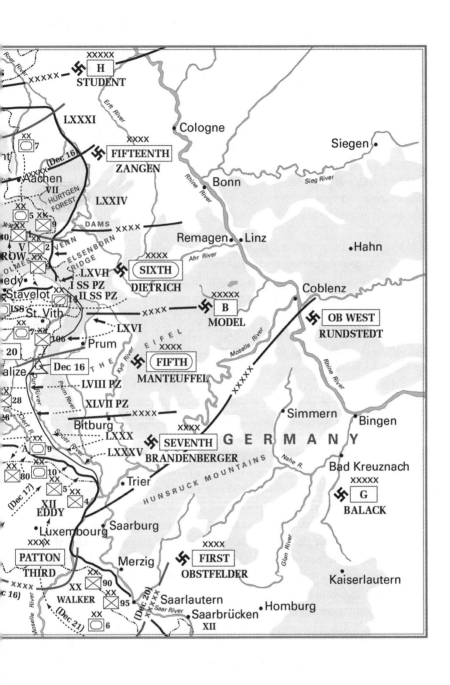

the overall strategic situation. The German offensive caused deep concern in Washington. Stanley Weintraub points out that President Roosevelt held a press conference on December 22, 1944, one week into the battle:

> The president refused any comment other than that "The end was not yet in sight." Afterward he summoned Secretary Stimson and Major General Leslie R. Groves of the supersecret Manhattan Project, and asked whether the atomic bomb could be rushed into readiness if urgently needed to close the salient. (Even had the Bomb been completed, it would have been useless as a tactical weapon.) Groves advised that no trigger mechanism yet existed, but he hoped that the device would be ready by summer—perhaps by August [1945].[34]

That is how gravely Roosevelt regarded the military situation in private.

The 5th *Panzerarmee* penetrated the American front with ease on the first day of the offensive. However, it was only able to defeat a small part of the forces that the Allies quickly moved into the Ardennes. The 6th *Panzerarmee* to the north failed to clear the Americans off the Elsenborn Ridge so that the offensive, instead of breaking through northwest toward Antwerp as it was directed to do, made only minor progress toward the west. The ferocious fighting around Elsenborn on the northern shoulder of the Bulge is not as celebrated as the heroic combat around Bastogne because no war correspondents were present to report it as they were for the heroic fighting farther south.

The Germans, operating on a poor road net and hampered by deep snow, plummeting temperatures, American-laid minefields, and short hours of daylight, found their advanced units bogged down in the narrow valleys of the Ardennes. American resistance was stubborn in the areas around St. Vith in the north and Bastogne in the south, two key communications centers for both sides. By December 21, 5th *Panzerarmee* had overrun St. Vith and surrounded Bastogne. Model's *Armeegruppe* B was trying to widen the frontage of the offensive and by December 23 had reached Celles, four miles from the Meuse River. However, on the same date, the weather cleared and Allied airpower entered the battle in strength. It remained that way for the next five days.[35] The impetus of the German offensive was spent.

D'Este colorfully recounts the Allied council of war four days earlier on December 19, 1944.[36] Allied generals had converged on Verdun to determine the Allied response. The meeting took place in a dismal, cold, second-floor room of a French stone barracks in a tense atmosphere. The generals quickly agreed to stop all offensive action along the Allied front and to concentrate on blunting the German drive. Eisenhower's plan was to draw a stop line at the Meuse River, beyond which there could be no further retreat. Once the German attacks had been contained, the Allied armies would counterattack. Then he turned to Patton: "George, I want you to command this move—under Brad's supervision, of course—making a strong counterattack with at least six divisions. . . . When can you attack?" "The morning of December 21, with three divisions," was Patton's instant reply. That was forty-eight hours hence. Eisenhower retorted, "Don't be fatuous, George." Patton was not being fatuous. A lifelong student of war, he had already devised three plans, each tailored to meet any contingency he thought either Eisenhower or Bradley might specify.

Blumenson, an authority on Patton, one of his biographers, and a military historian of seventeen works on World War II who served in 3rd Army, observed, "This was the sublime moment of his career." After thirty-four years in the army, it was as if destiny had groomed Patton for this single defining moment in that dingy room, in which the future of Allied fortunes depended on the right decisions being made and executed by the right men. Patton had been prepared. While near panic existed elsewhere, Patton believed that the Battle of the Bulge was an excellent opportunity to strike a killing blow. Unlike the other commanders at Verdun, Patton had quickly grasped the problem facing the Allied armies, and he had created a plan to counterattack Rundstedt's forces and to reinforce the defense of Bastogne, which, while not yet surrounded, would be so the following day. "Pointing to a map and the obvious 'bulge' in the St. Vith–Bastogne sector [map 9.3] and speaking directly to Bradley, he said, 'Brad, the Kraut's stuck his head in a meatgrinder.' Turning his fist in a grinding motion, he continued, '[a]nd this time I've got hold of the handle.'"[37] He then proceeded to answer a lot of skeptical questions with spe-

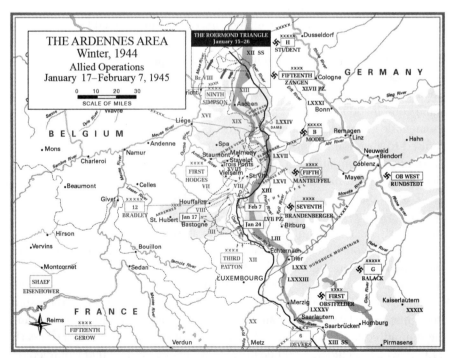

Map 9.3.   German forces were pushed back to their start lines where they had begun their offensive one month earlier.
Source: USMA Atlases.

cific, well-rehearsed answers. Within an hour, details had been worked out, the divisions to be employed, objectives to be met, and new army boundaries to be defined. Patton was offering in the middle of a winter storm to disengage multiple divisions of 3rd Army against German forces on his own front, turn them ninety degrees, and advance north one hundred miles. Patton extricated two of his three corps for the counterattack into the Ardennes. Lieutenant General Alexander M. Patch's 7th Army took control of most of the 3rd Army sector in the Saar. It was the most remarkable hour of Patton's military career.

Eisenhower had already ordered the two airborne divisions, the 82nd and 101st, resting in the Allied rear after *Market Garden*, into the Ardennes by truck. He had also summoned Major General Ridgway's 18th Airborne Corps headquarters from England. The 101st Airborne Division arrived in Bastogne just in time to join an element of the US 10th Armored Division and several other units as German forces began entering the town. Bastogne was then surrounded and under siege. In the days that followed, the 101st would fight one of the bitterest battles in its distinguished history. The acting commander of the 101st, Brigadier General Anthony C. McAuliffe, soon achieved martial immortality when he uttered a single word rejecting a German demand to surrender: "Nuts." Bastogne would become one of the historical icons of the war in the European theater. Patton lived up to his commitment at Verdun. His army attacked three days later and relieved Bastogne on December 26, 1944.[38]

On Christmas Day, the German 2nd *Panzer* Division, stalled for lack of fuel at Celles just a few miles short of the Meuse, was shattered by the American 2nd Armored Division and pounded by American fighter-bombers, while the 116th and 2nd SS (*Schutzstaffel*) *Panzer* Divisions, farther to the east, deployed on either side of the Ourthe River, were "severely handled" by the same combination of air and ground attacks. The northern flank was for the moment deadlocked.[39] Around Bastogne, battle continued to be joined. Hitler refused to abandon the offensive and wanted Bastogne captured so that 5th *Panzerarmee*'s communications westward would be open. Six American divisions were drawn into a series of battles around Bastogne until January 3–4, 1945, when the last German attempt to take Bastogne was defeated.

What was the turning point? The German offensive went out of control within forty-eight hours of the start of the attack, and the German armored mass failed to come forward as planned.[40] The German defeat on the southern Bastogne flank coincided with the start of Hodges's 1st Army counteroffensive on the northern flank. On January 8, 1945, Hitler acknowledged defeat, and by January 16, 1945, German formations had been pushed back to their start lines (map 9.3). They had lost an estimated one hundred thousand troops and eight hundred tanks.[41] American losses were substantial, too: a total of nearly 77,000, which included 8,600 dead, 21,000 missing, and 47,000 wounded, to which should be added about 20,000 nonbattle casualties.[42]

Hitler's Ardennes offensive had made another gamble. He had judged that there would be no Soviet offensive in Poland for the *Ostheer* to resist, even though the path west from Poland led directly into the Reich. That gamble turned out to be correct but for the wrong reason. He assumed that the summer offensives had mauled the Red Army so badly that they could not undertake further offensive operations until they built up their strength.

By January 1945, there were eight Soviet armies deployed along the Eastern Front from the Baltic to Belgrade. Any two of these armies were as large as the Anglo-American forces in the west. This overwhelming military capability was to affect the negotiations at the most important wartime conference at Yalta.

The Yalta Conference was the meeting between February 4 and 11, 1945, that defined the final actions and goals of World War II. Convened by the "Big Three," Roosevelt, Churchill, and Stalin, Yalta, in addition to defining the military requirements of Allied cooperation for concluding the war, was intended to achieve two other purposes: the implicit if not explicit delineation of spheres of influence, particularly for the Soviet Union, and laying the groundwork for a peace conference that might occur in 1946. Three recent studies establish that Roosevelt and Churchill came to Yalta with a weak military hand.[43] American forces in February 1945 were still recovering from the setbacks during the Battle of the Bulge and were only beginning to enter Germany.

Serhii M. Plokhy points to these military realities on both fronts:

> In the game of wartime diplomacy, the player with the most troops had the loudest voice. Stalin was in a particularly strong position at Yalta because of the swift advance of the Red Army. While the Western Allies were recovering from the Ardennes debacle and still planning their crossing of the Rhine, approximately 600 kilometers [~360 miles] from Berlin, Soviet forces had launched an impressive winter offensive that brought them within striking distance of the Nazi capital. Since 12 January [1945], when the offensive began, the Red Army had broken through German defenses and advanced up to 500 kilometers in some sectors. It had established bridgeheads on the west bank of the Oder, a mere seventy kilometers [less than forty-five miles] from Berlin.[44]

The Soviets already were in control of much of Eastern Europe. They could not be evicted anywhere except by force.[45]

The traditional historical literature of the final year of the European war tends to focus on the comparison between German and Anglo-American tactical proficiency, the Bulge surprise and recovery, and the military-political decision not to drive for Berlin. More recent works reveal the enormous military scale and political significance of the Soviet offensives on the *Ostfront*, which weighed greatly in the balance of forces. From the wartime tripartite perspective of the Allied strategic architecture, Soviet operations demonstrated the value of an ally that was prepared to fight the bulk of *Wehrmacht* land forces for four years, sustain 95 percent of the casualties, survive, win, and gain geo-political dominance of *Mitteleuropa*.

CONCLUSIONS

The United States and Great Britain were the only two powers with the requisite industrial bases, trained military manpower, and naval and air assets capable of fielding and sustaining a large expeditionary force on the Continent across oceans. The Anglo-American strategic architecture in the ETO required the alignment of industrial policies, military strategy, and strategic and tactical execution by enough resourceful officers at the tactical level.

The military power of the Red Army in 1944–1945 directly helped the Allies succeed in the west. The Eastern Front tied down many more Axis divisions and denied reinforcements to von Rundstedt's *Westheer*. The immense combat power of the Red Army favored the USSR with respect to the post-Yalta political configuration of Eastern Europe. Churchill and Roosevelt realistically had allied themselves with a totalitarian regime because the Red Army killed more Germans than the rest of the Allied armies combined. By February 1945 on the eve of the Yalta Conference, Stalin had the military upper hand. He had mobilized over seven hundred divisions by this stage of the war.

The land war in Europe was decided largely on the Eastern Front. Between June 1941 and June 1944, 93 percent of Germany's combat losses were inflicted by the Red Army. In the terrible arithmetic of war up to June 6, 1944, the Red Army inflicted 4.2 million German casualties (dead, wounded, or missing) on the Eastern Front, against the Allies inflicting 329,000 Axis casualties in North Africa and Italy, a USSR/US-UK carnage ratio greater than twelve to one by D-Day.[46]

The military balance of forces among the Allies determined the postwar political reality in the ETO. Within weeks after Yalta, Soviet political undermining and suppression of democratic forces in Eastern Europe introduced new tensions into the wartime alliance. Shortly after Roosevelt's death in April 1945, ambassador to Moscow W. Averell Harriman was warning President Harry S. Truman about the Soviet consolidation of power in Eastern Europe. Deputy Chief of Mission George F. Kennan a year later, on February 22, 1946, sent a long cable from Moscow to the secretary of state outlining what came to be known as the "containment strategy."[47] In Fulton, Missouri, Churchill, on March 5, 1946, was to deliver his famous "Iron Curtain" speech. A year after that, on March 12, 1947, a thoroughly disillusioned President Truman would proclaim the Truman Doctrine, providing military and economic aid to Greece and Turkey to prevent their falling within the domain of Soviet hegemony in Eastern Europe.[48] The Cold War had begun.

Battle of the Rhine

(1) Allied paratroops land in Holland during Operation *Market Garden* in September 1944. (2) Men of 8th Infantry Regiment seek cover in outskirts of Belgium town of Libin on September 7, 1944. NARA photos

(3) US infantry of 60th Infantry Regiment of the 9th Infantry Division advance into a Belgian town under the protection of a tank on September 9, 1944. (4) US infantry antitank unit fires on Germans who machine-gunned their vehicle, somewhere in Holland on November 4, 1944. NARA photos

(5) Men and equipment of 1st US Army pour across the Remagen Bridge, the first bridge captured over the Rhine—two knocked-out jeeps in foreground—on March 11, 1945. NARA photo

10

BATTLE OF OKINAWA AND THE BOMBING OF JAPAN

Ending the War

In the spring of 1945 the end of the war was in sight in the European theater but not in the Pacific. Between 1942 and 1945, execution of American strategy in the Pacific consisted of two drives across the Pacific north and south of the equator. Admiral Nimitz's island-hopping campaigns had advanced steadily west across the Central Pacific to retake the Gilbert, Marshall, and Mariana Islands, including Saipan, Guam, and Tinian, which were needed for basing B-29 bombers to attack Japan. Capture of the Marianas and the destruction of Japanese carrier airpower after the Battle of the Philippine Sea (the Marianas "turkey shoot") in June 1944 were final and irreversible blows to Japan's power in the Pacific. General MacArthur's Southwest Pacific campaigns had captured New Georgia, Rabaul, Bougainville, the Admiralty Islands, and New Guinea, and in the fall of 1944 had begun the liberation of the Philippines. MacArthur in 1945 was still completing the recapture of the Philippines; the fighting to liberate Manila ended on March 3, 1945.

POLICY

The final phases of the Pacific war had been planned but not yet executed. The invasion of Iwo Jima commenced on February 19, 1945; the island was secured in late March. Okinawa was next in April (map 10.1).

The invasion of the Japanese home islands was planned for October 1945, with casualty estimates ranging from five hundred thousand to one million.[1] Okinawa became the most reliable benchmark for estimating the high Allied casualties required for the invasion of the home islands, which was to be executed in two phases as Operations *Coronet* and *Olympic*.

Japan lacked any plausible strategic architecture for ending the war, much less winning it. It was obvious that American power had become overwhelming in the Pacific and would grow much stronger. Policy demanded implacable resistance, but the only strategy left to Japan amounted to national suicide.

Roosevelt and Churchill at Yalta hoped that the secret Manhattan Project to develop the atomic bomb would be successful as a war-winning weapon. But in February 1945 it was not ready for use. For security reasons, they did not risk telling Stalin about the bomb's development, although he had already known about it for years through his own very efficient espionage programs.[2] At both the Yalta and Potsdam Conferences in 1945, America and Britain were eager for the Soviet Union to help defeat Japan because Stalin had remained neutral toward Japan since December 1941. So telling Stalin about the bomb would have weakened their case for cobelligerence.

General Marshall and Admiral Nimitz both assumed that the strategic architecture in the Pacific could require years to complete, even with the transfer of Anglo-American forces from Europe to the Pacific. The Imperial Japanese Army (IJA) had 2,350,000 regular troops based on the home islands, and the Japanese government had prepared plans to impress thirty million more into a "citizen militia" and had trained eight thousand pilots to fly kamikaze missions.[3]

STRATEGY

In April 1945, the Allies were ready to invade Okinawa, which represented the last in the long sequence of offensives to recapture the Pacific island chains and bring the war directly to the Japanese home islands. Okinawa was 325 miles from Kyushu, the southernmost of the home islands, where the majority of the surviving kamikaze squadrons were based.[4]

On Okinawa, Lieutenant General Mitsuru Ushijima, commander of the 32nd Army of nearly one hundred thousand troops, evacuated the waist of the island by withdrawing almost all of his infantry battalions and approximately ninety tanks, most of the artillery, and heavy weapons to the southern third of the island. His repositioning was designed to lure most of the American troops into costly attrition battles in the south, which had been divided into hundreds of defensive compartments. Ushijima had written a slogan for his troops: "One Plane for One Warship; One Boat for One Ship; One Man for Ten of the Enemy or One Tank."[5] The Japanese planned for kamikaze air and small-boat squadrons to attack the Allied naval fleet to sink or damage enough ships to force the fleet to withdraw.

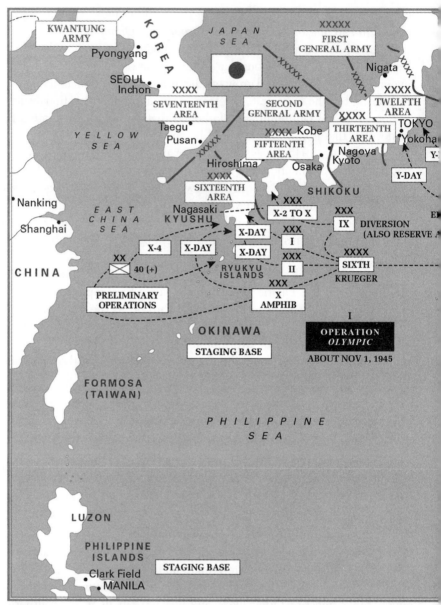

Map 10.1. After capturing Okinawa, Operations *Coronet* and *Olympic* were the Allied plans for the invasion of Japan.

Source: USMA Atlases.

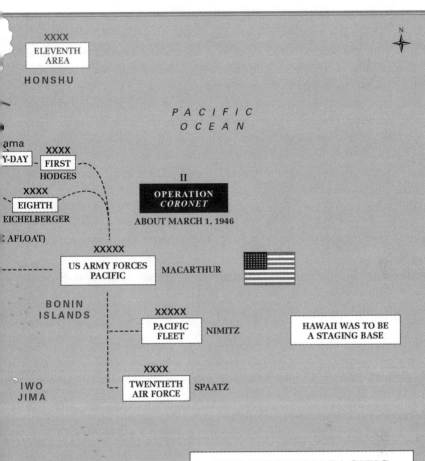

XXXX
ELEVENTH AREA

HONSHU

PACIFIC OCEAN

ama
Y-DAY — XXXX FIRST
HODGES

XXXX EIGHTH
EICHELBERGER

(AFLOAT)

II
OPERATION *CORONET*

ABOUT MARCH 1, 1946

XXXXX
US ARMY FORCES PACIFIC — MACARTHUR

BONIN ISLANDS

XXXXX
PACIFIC FLEET — NIMITZ

HAWAII WAS TO BE A STAGING BASE

XXXX
TWENTIETH AIR FORCE — SPAATZ

IWO JIMA

MARIANA ISLANDS

STAGING BASE

SAIPAN
ROTA
GUAM

THE WESTERN PACIFIC
Japanese Homeland Dispositions
August 1945
and Allied Plans for the
Invasion of Japan
(Operations *Coronet* and *Olympic*)

0   10   200   300   400
SCALE OF MILES

Defending Okinawa by sacrificing every last man, woman, and child might persuade the United State that attacking the home islands would be a bloodbath. From this military perspective, Okinawa offered an excellent killing ground to test suicidal tactics with its small area (450 square miles), irregular shape, and mountainous, jungle-covered topography.

The two most senior members of Ushijima's staff were divided about the tactics for defeating the American forces. Lieutenant General Isamu Cho, Ushijima's chief of staff and a veteran of the long war against China, advocated the traditional mixture of small-group infiltration, concentrated artillery fire, and timely banzai-charge counterattacks. Colonel Hiromichi Yahara, operations officer of the 32nd Army, favored "sleeping tactics," where IJA forces remained hidden and passive behind strongly fortified and camouflaged defensive positions until American troops maneuvered into killing zones, where 32nd Army soldiers could ambush and massacre them in large numbers. He reasoned that many more Americans would die trying to root out each Japanese soldier from his underground fighting position than from all-out counterattacks.[6] Ushijima vacillated. He refused to commit his army entirely to one plan until the battle reached the point where he no longer had a choice.

Ushijima transformed the southern third of the island into a fortified zone, where his men created a chain of fortresses, the so-called Shuri Line. The centerpiece was Shuri Castle, a medieval strongpoint that enabled unhindered observation of the surrounding terrain and offshore waters. Ushijima's tactics conformed to the precepts of skilled fortress design, where outer works were not so much barriers as killing zones. "The job of Japanese defenders [on Okinawa], after all, was not to keep the Americans at arm's length but to kill them."[7]

OPERATIONS (OKINAWA)

The US invasion of Okinawa was the largest amphibious operation of the war in the Pacific. An invasion fleet of more than 1,600 vessels, under the command of Vice Admiral Richmond K. Turner, who had commanded the Guadalcanal landing, included forty aircraft carriers of various types (sixteen of them fleet carriers), eighteen battleships, twenty-two cruisers, almost two hundred destroyers, and hundreds of assault ships. The fleet transported over 250,000 soldiers and marines of the US 10th Army to Okinawa, commanded by General Simon Bolivar Buckner Jr.[8] Over twelve thousand combat aircraft were dedicated to the operation.[9]

On April 1, 1945, an unopposed landing took place southwest of the narrow waist of the island on relatively flat land that separated the jungle-covered mountains of northern Okinawa from the densely inhabited hills of the south where the bulk of the island's population of 475,000 lived. The invasion area offered eight miles of landing beaches, the only place where four American divisions could land abreast and where two of the island's four airfields were within rifle shot of the beaches (map 10.2).[10]

US forces landed fifty thousand men on the first day, losing only twenty-eight killed, and had taken the first four days' planned objectives by nightfall. Two airfields were captured within hours. General Buckner's senior marine commander, General Roy S. Geiger, remarked on the initial rapid penetrations and light casualties, "Don't ask me why we haven't had more opposition. I don't understand it. But now we're in a position to work over the Jap forces at our leisure at the least possible loss to ourselves." Admiral Turner reported to Nimitz's headquarters, "I may be crazy, but it looks like the Japanese have quit the war, at least in this sector."[11] Events soon demonstrated how wrong they were.

The early actions of Buckner's invasion force confirmed the benefit of Colonel Yahara's "sleeping tactics." Instead of trying to stop the invasion at the beaches, as Rommel had advocated at Normandy, Ushijima planned a defense in depth where he lured Americans into killing-ground ambushes supported by bunkers, tunnels, and fortifications. The combat was more intense than US forces had encountered anywhere else in the Pacific.[12] Ushijima's multiple defensive lines sited observation points on high ground, located machine guns and mortars with mutually supportive fields of fire, buried mines along every avenue of approach, and positioned artillery to deliver preplanned concentrated fire once American troops entered a killing zone. The 32nd Army possessed ammunition in abundance.

Japanese antitank rounds suddenly destroyed tanks. Snipers killed officers. Withering cross fires caught whole squads or platoons as they entered ravines. The American "steel typhoon"[13] and three-to-one manpower advantage was not a tactical discriminator when the Japanese could concentrate their forces to defend a narrow front (map 10.2). This was casualty-intensive warfare a few brutal yards at a time.

In General Buckner's mind, there was no alternative but to launch repeated frontal assaults against Japanese positions, precisely what Ushijima and Yahara wanted him to do. The only way to outflank this kind of defense was to launch an amphibious assault where Japanese defenses were weaker. This was marine advice that Buckner ignored.

It was small-unit cohesion, practiced teamwork, and savvy junior officer and experienced NCO leadership that overcame the 32nd Army, one objective at a time. Those who survived the lethal first encounters learned realistic combat survival skills.[14]

General Cho ordered multiple suicidal banzai charges. Some were multibattalion counterattacks. The large enemy losses resulting from these mass charges opened seams along the front. Once American units discovered them, they started unraveling the defense. Overcoming strongpoints and caves

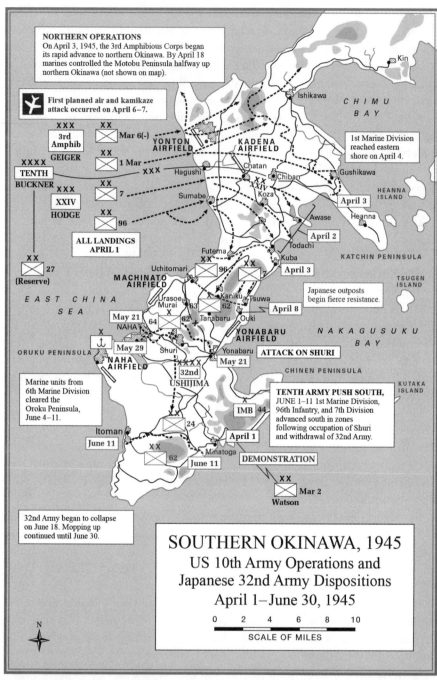

NORTHERN OPERATIONS
On April 3, 1945, the 3rd Amphibious Corps began its rapid advance to northern Okinawa. By April 18 marines controlled the Motobu Peninsula halfway up northern Okinawa (not shown on map).

First planned air and kamikaze attack occurred on April 6–7.

XXX **3rd Amphib** GEIGER
XX Mar 6(-) YONTON AIRFIELD
XX 1 Mar
XXXX **TENTH** BUCKNER
XXX Hagushi
XXX **XXIV** HODGE
XX 7 Sumabe
XX 96

ALL LANDINGS APRIL 1

XX 27 (Reserve)

KADENA AIRFIELD
Chatan
Chiban
Koza
Gushikawa

1st Marine Division reached eastern shore on April 4.

HEANNA ISLAND
April 3
Awase
Heanna
April 2
Todachi

KATCHIN PENINSULA

EAST CHINA SEA

MACHINATO AIRFIELD
Uchitomari
Urasoe Murai 63
64 62
Tanabaru
Ouki

Futema
XX 96
Kaniku 62 Tsuwa

Kuba
April 3

April 8

Japanese outposts begin fierce resistance.

TSUGEN ISLAND

May 21
NAHA
May 29
Shuri
Yonabaru
May 21

CHINEN PENINSULA

YONABARU AIRFIELD
N A K A G U S U K U B A Y

ATTACK ON SHURI

ORUKU PENINSULA
NAHA AIRFIELD
XXXXX 32nd
USHIJIMA

Marine units from 6th Marine Division cleared the Oruku Peninsula, June 4–11.

KUTAKA ISLAND

TENTH ARMY PUSH SOUTH,
JUNE 1–11 1st Marine Division, 96th Infantry, and 7th Division advanced south in zones following occupation of Shuri and withdrawal of 32nd Army.

IMB 44
24
April 1

Itoman
June 11

XX
Minatoga
XX 62
June 11

DEMONSTRATION

XX Mar 2
Watson

32nd Army began to collapse on June 18. Mopping up continued until June 30.

SOUTHERN OKINAWA, 1945
US 10th Army Operations and
Japanese 32nd Army Dispositions
April 1–June 30, 1945

0   2   4   6   8   10
SCALE OF MILES

N

C H I M U B A Y
Kin
Ishikawa

Map 10.2. The three-to-one American manpower ratio required high-casualty tactics against a narrow, fortified Japanese front.

Source: USMA Atlases.

became a process of combining soldiering with different weapons mixes. The extensive use of flamethrowers, satchel charges, hand grenades, and, in some cases, bulldozers became a grim but predictable process. Once the mutual support among Japanese defensive positions was undermined, it "was no longer a matter of tactics but of engineering."[15]

The last of the major Japanese counterattacks was launched on May 4, 1945. In the weeks that followed, 32nd Army units either retired to more defensible ground or held out to the end.

Ushijima's premise that the rapid defeat of the Allied naval fleet by kamikaze attacks and suicide boats would isolate the American invasion force turned out to be wrong. Despite the US Navy's appalling losses of one-quarter of its fleet of 1,600 vessels, nearly 36 warships sunk and more than 368 damaged during the campaign, the fleet remained.[16]

The Japanese had initially prepared four thousand planes for suicide attacks, to commence immediately after the landings.[17] During each week of the Okinawa invasion, four ships were hit every day for the duration of the naval deployment off Okinawa. Many warships of all classes were damaged, some severely, but no aircraft carriers, battleships, or cruisers were sunk by kamikazes off Okinawa.[18] Most of the ships sunk were destroyers or smaller vessels, especially those on picket duty, a total of fifty-nine ships.[19]

Victor Davis Hanson describes that the ferocity of the repeated kamikaze attacks well into June became a cause for serious worry:

> The Americans appeared to be tiring from the daily barrage. On 11 May [1945] the Japanese hit Admiral Mitscher's flagship itself, the carrier *Bunker Hill*, and left it a burning wreck,[20] and also hit again the battleship *New Mexico*. American officers by the end of May calculated that if the *kamikazes* continued to score at the present rates, the entire fleet would have to withdraw by the middle of June.[21]

But by mid-June, the campaign to capture Okinawa was close to succeeding, and by June 18, the 32nd Army was starting to collapse. Okinawa was declared secure on July 2, 1945.[22] It came at a steep price for both sides. US military and naval personnel casualties exceeded ninety thousand; a Japanese shell killed General Buckner.[23] For the Japanese defenders, military losses were estimated to be between 70,000 and 110,000 soldiers.[24]

OPERATIONS (BOMBING OF JAPAN)

In 1945, airpower was already becoming decisive in the Pacific war. Major General Curtis LeMay on January 20 assumed command of 21st Bomber Command, the principal air combat echelon that was later expanded to become the 20th Air Force. By March, he was ready, with multiple wings of the new four-engine B-29 long-range bomber, to begin a series of incendiary attacks against urban areas of Japan. These attacks were dramatically more effective than those of the European bombing campaign. The first attack, against Tokyo, flown by 279 B-29s on March 9, 1945, proved to be enormously destructive.[25] The raid burned sixteen square miles of the city, killed 83,793 people, injured 40,918, and destroyed 267,000 buildings.[26]

In rapid succession over the course of the next ten days, LeMay's bombers concentrated on the "Big Five," the cities of Kobe, Osaka, Nagoya, Tokyo, and Yokohama, where much of Japan's war industry was concentrated. Tokyo was singled out for particular intensity. As an Air Staff document published shortly after the war in 1945 noted, "Tokyo, in addition to being the Empire's administrative and political nerve-center, teemed with thousands of shack-like workshops, too numerous to be selected as individual targets."[27]

Firebombing was a major departure from the American strategy of bombing only military targets in Europe and completely abandoned the myth of daylight precision bombing. LeMay's plan was tantamount to acceptance that everything was a target. Everything included the "thousands of shack-like workshops" that the Air Staff report indicated were interspersed throughout the industrial-residential areas of Tokyo. And the wood construction of most structures rendered them highly flammable. The USAAF was not capable of bombing such discrete targets accurately from any altitude day or night. Neither the Norden bombsight nor radar could isolate discrete targets so they could be bombed with precision.[28] LeMay proposed low-altitude attacks at five thousand to six thousand feet, with the B-29s stripped of their defensive equipment to accommodate bigger bomb loads. Initially, everyone but LeMay considered these tactics too risky.

LeMay called in all of his flak experts from the wings along with selected airplane commanders with experience over both Europe and Tokyo. To a man, they told him he would lose 70 percent of his airplanes over Tokyo if he sent them in at five thousand to six thousand feet. They spoke with conviction of the effectiveness of flak at twenty-five thousand or thirty thousand feet. LeMay remarked mildly, "If you are right, we won't have many airplanes left if we go in low." He wanted to know how many aircraft had been lost to enemy flak at high altitude. The command's "Statistical Control" said the figures were not impressive. What did the aircraft commanders think? He heard them out, too. Some thought he could succeed. LeMay decided on the low-altitude approach. He believed the Japanese defenders would be flummoxed by the B-29 Superfortresses flying their bomb runs at such a low altitude. His decision ran against every design element of this most state-of-the-art bomber. "He decided that it was probably not a gamble, that if it was a gamble, he was going to take it anyway."[29]

This tactic proved to be extraordinarily successful. When the first strike reports came into General LeMay's Guam headquarters on March 9–10, 1945, they initially indicated that ten square miles of one of Tokyo's two great industrial districts was the scene of a conflagration that later spread to nearly sixteen square miles, more than two-thirds of the land area of Manhattan burned out in a single strike. Only two B-29s were lost. On the next two missions, none were lost. As LeMay explained to Lieutenant Colonel St. Clair McKelway, his chief public-relations officer, over a Coca-Cola in the middle of the night on March 9, 1945, while the two officers were awaiting the first radio messages at their base in the Marianas,

> A war is a very tough kind of proposition. If you don't get the enemy, he gets you. I think we've figured out a punch he's not expecting this time. I don't think he's got the right kind of flak to combat this kind of raid and I don't think he can keep his cities from being burned down—wiped right off the map. He hasn't moved his industries to Manchuria yet, although he's starting to move them, and if we can destroy them before he can move them, we've got him. I never think anything is going to work until I've seen the pictures after the raid, but if this one works we will shorten this damned war out here.[30]

The strike photos amply confirmed the initial reports.

From mid-May into June, B-29 bomber formations of 21st Bomber Command dropped 44 percent of their total tonnage on the Big Five. Serious industrial damage ranged from 25 percent in Osaka to 43 percent in Nagoya. Aircraft plants in those cities sustained 50 percent damage. The Air Staff report stated that "so thoroughly gutted were most sections of the 'Big Five' (their burned areas total 103 square miles) that they were no longer considered essential targets except for occasional pinpoint 'policing' tactics."[31]

Target selection criteria by 20th Air Force proceeded largely on the basis that bombing war plants offered an immediate rather than a long-term effect on Japan's ability to resist. The focus was on aircraft factories, oil refineries, arsenals, fuel stations, engineering works, chemical plants, and coal liquefaction facilities. After the Big Five, the B-29s relentlessly attacked medium-sized cities, the equivalents in Japan of Toledo and Bridgeport. A total of sixty-nine cities were subjected to "burn jobs," as the Air Staff report callously phrased these incendiary missions, creating up to ten million refugees.

The bomb damage assessment of these raids, based on poststrike photoreconnaissance flights, established that 175 square miles of industrial urban area were wiped out. The same Air Staff document reported that housing for 10,548,000 was destroyed. "This is 50.3 percent of the 1940 population in the 69 cities."[32]

LeMay's B-29 raids came at a price, but not as steep as what 8th Air Force in the ETO sustained. Michael S. Sherry reported that the 20th Air Force, "the most devastating of all the wartime air forces, took only 2.8 percent of all losses by American air forces during the war . . . some 3,415 casualties, of whom, 576 were killed and 2,406 missing—while [the USAAF] in Europe and the Mediterranean endured 94,565 casualties."[33] David A. Anderson puts total B-29 losses in the Pacific at 450 aircraft, a loss rate of 1.38 percent out of a total of thirty-three thousand sorties flown.[34] LeMay believed that by driving his crews he could force surrender before the invasion had to be launched.[35]

President Truman's decision to use the atomic bomb intervened. Many military leaders, when they first learned of the atomic bomb's devastating effects, considered this new weapon as simply a more powerful version of conventional ordnance. As Conrad C. Crane pointed out at the conclusion of *Bombs, Cities, and Civilians*, "Once the fire raids became accepted policy any form of warfare against Japan seemed permissible." He observed, "The [nuclear] 'knockout blow,' in all its horror and inhumanity, finally proved its point."[36]

Debate about whether the nuclear bombings of Hiroshima and Nagasaki on August 6 and 9, 1945, induced the Japanese to surrender, or whether the Soviet invasion of Manchuria was more decisive, has been the subject of scholarly controversy for the last two decades. In the wake of the acrimonious controversy over the display of the B-29 *Enola Gay*[37] at the Smithsonian in the 1990s,[38] serious historians have been engaged in a historical debate over just what the decisive tipping point was in convincing the "Big Six" of Japan's Supreme War Council for the Direction of the War[39] and Emperor Hirohito of the necessity of unconditional surrender, without any exceptions constraining implementation of the Potsdam Declaration.[40]

Tsuyoshi Hasegawa builds a persuasive case that the Russian invasion of Manchuria on August 9, 1945, confronted Japan with a war on two fronts, abrogated the Soviet-Japanese nonaggression pact, eliminated any role the Soviet Union might play as a mediator with the Allies, rendered the collapse of the IJA's Kwantung Army in Manchukuo inevitable against the Soviet invasion of Manchuria by three overwhelming front armies, weakened the defense of the home islands (Operation *Ketsu-Gō*), and implicitly threatened the imperial house with a potential Russian occupation and thus the high probability of consigning Hirohito and his family to the same fate as the Romanovs.[41] Hasegawa's analysis of the documentary evidence concludes that Soviet entry into the war was the clincher.[42]

Richard B. Frank presents a more convincing case that the shock effect of the two atomic bombs compelled the three war hawks among the divided Big Six to begin defining terms under which Japan might capitulate. After Nagasaki, the emperor intervened the next day. He gave three reasons: fear of domestic upheaval, inadequate preparation for homeland defense to resist the expected Allied invasion, and the vast destructiveness of the atomic bomb.[43] Hirohito did not refer to Soviet intervention either then or in the imperial rescript broadcasting of the capitulation five days later on August 15, 1945.[44]

The real weight in Frank's analysis shows that continuation of the war would have caused immense additional loss of life—well in excess of the Hiroshima and Nagasaki casualties. He describes the planned strategic attack on Japan's railroad systems "as the crescendo of the overall blockade-and-bombardment strategy."[45]

Frank's conclusion challenges the standard postwar canon that the use of the atomic bombs was both unnecessary and immoral. He grounds his case in an empirical counterfactual about the predictable effects of Japanese mass starvation in the fall of 1945 that would have resulted from intensification of conventional USAAF bombing attacks against Japan's vulnerable food-delivery network in the home islands. Japanese starvation deaths would have been far greater in number than the deaths that resulted from the atomic bombs that destroyed Hiroshima and Nagasaki. In August 1945, no one could have predicted confidently that atomic weapons would end the war. Indeed, senior American military leaders were sharply divided. For example, Generals Eisenhower, LeMay, and MacArthur and Admirals Halsey, Leahy, and Nimitz all expressed opposition to using atomic weapons.[46] Only with historical hindsight and the evidence Frank marshals so convincingly can we see that he presents a rigorously constructed case that the two atomic bombs ended the war.

On August 11, 1945, General Carl A. Spaatz, as commander of the US Strategic Air Forces in the Pacific, had ordered a major reorientation of the strategic air war against Japan, away from the massive urban incendiary bombing campaign. This decision stemmed from the findings of the US Strategic Bombing Survey with respect to bombing effects on Germany. The principal finding of interest to Spaatz and his staff was that concentration on two target systems, oil and transportation, "contributed in decisive measure to the early and complete victory which followed."[47] In an operational directive to 20th Air Force, Spaatz listed primary objectives as Japan's transportation system, including railroad yards, facilities, and bridges; the aircraft industry; munitions storage; and urban industrial areas. A total of 210 targets were allocated between the 20th and 8th Air Force, elements of the latter now having been redeployed to the Pacific theater from the ETO. By August 1945, the 20th Air Force at bases in the Marianas numbered 1,002 B-29s and 76,539 personnel.

Spaatz's air directive, had it been implemented, would have caused far more loss of life by starvation than the atomic bombs caused. Japan in the summer of 1945 was facing the prospect of a mass famine brought on by the destruction of its transportation system. Three out of four Japanese inhabited the island of Honshu, half in the southwestern part of the island. Japan harvested the great bulk of its food supply on Hokkaido, parts of Kyushu, and northern Honshu. Tokyo required delivery of 97 percent of its rice supply from the other home islands. Food consumption had dropped to alarming levels by 1945.[48] Japan's food-distribution system depended on combined sea and rail transportation networks. By August 1945, US Navy blockade ships and submarines had virtually destroyed the IJN's warships and most of Japan's merchantmen. Japanese shipping losses had been staggering, totaling 3,032 ships displacing eleven million tons, which approached the fifteen million tons lost in the Battle of the Atlantic.[49]

It is not difficult to imagine what the months of the fall would have been like had 20th Air Force been unleashed to bomb the transportation system except to observe that an already severe mass-malnutrition situation was likely to become a mass-famine one. The death toll could have run into the millions. As it was, over the course of the next year after the surrender, the United States shipped eight hundred thousand tons of food to Japan, six times the rice tonnage the government had on hand on November 1, 1945 (133,000 tons), to stave off malnutrition if not starvation.

The terrible arithmetic of war suggests that the use of the atomic bombs, however horrific the immediate effects or the longer-term death toll caused by radioactive poisoning, reduced the Japanese death toll by probably millions, this without even considering what Allied invasion casualty figures would have been, estimated at between five hundred thousand and one million.

CONCLUSIONS

The American strategic architecture for the final phase of the war in the Pacific theater required Japan's unconditional surrender, formalized by the Potsdam Declaration. General Buckner and Admiral Turner both believed, based on previous Pacific combat experience, that they would have to fight a costly attrition battle to overrun Okinawa. The Americans had ample reserves and logistical resources to make good on their losses. Admiral Turner's resolve to support the invasion with his fleet, despite the kamikaze damage to a quarter of it, enabled Buckner to break Ushijima's defense.

Critics argued that Buckner should have fought a smarter campaign using amphibious assets to outflank Japanese defensive positions as marine officers recommended. American small-unit determination to execute orders in the field, learn survival lessons, and experiment with trial-and-error methods to overcome Japanese defensive positions eventually assured the victory.

General Ushijima's defensive plan of fighting a defensive battle behind well-prepared fortifications and defensive lines ensured that General LeMay by early August 1945 was preparing to execute General Spaatz's operational directive to destroy Japan's transportation system prior to invasion of the home islands. If that directive had been carried out, the destruction would have stopped food deliveries to Japan's most populated cities, precipitating mass starvation. Airpower became a discriminator whether its attacks were conventional or nuclear. The atomic destruction of two Japanese cities proved to be more decisive in forcing the Japanese to surrender sooner.

The success of the Manhattan Project traces not simply to the physicists who designed and engineered the atomic bomb. It also traces to Major General Groves and the engineering officers who came from the army's Guardian tradition capable of managing such a complex program.[50] The United States had the industrial and R&D strength to undertake multiple projects on the scale of the atomic bomb. American GDP values in 1941 exceeded Japan's by a factor of six and Germany's by a factor of three; by 1945, the overall American/ Axis GDP ratio was in excess of three to one.[51]

On September 2, 1945, in Tokyo Bay, a Japanese delegation signed the "Instrument of Surrender" during a ceremony held aboard the battleship *Missouri*. To paraphrase Frank's last sentence in *Downfall*, had American wartime leaders been able to foresee the American-Japanese future of peace and tranquility that has transpired between the two countries since that sanguinary summer of 1945, a future still without any prospect of serious conflict, they would have felt that their hard choices to use atomic weapons had been vindicated—and so should we.

Paul Fussell, a twenty-one-year-old second lieutenant commanding a rifle platoon in the ETO in 1945, agreed instantly and enthusiastically. He wrote this passage in 1988:

> When the atom bombs were dropped and news began to circulate that "Operation *Olympic*" would not, after all, be necessary, when we learned to our astonishment that we would not be obliged in a few months to rush up the beaches near Tokyo assault-firing while being machine-gunned, mortared, and shelled, for all the practiced phlegm of our tough facades we broke down and cried with relief and joy. We were going to live. We were going to grow into adulthood after all.[52]

One eyewitness aboard the battleship *Missouri* had a "bird's-eye view," Lieutenant William B. Hussey (later captain, USNR), flag lieutenant to Rear Admiral John F. Shafroth, commander of Battleship Division 8:

> During the ceremony, held on the veranda deck near Number Two Turret, starboard side, General MacArthur was more impressive than ever before, lending dignity, simplicity, purposefulness, and even the spirit of hope to the assemblage. Afterwards, many remarked how flawless his manner had been, how perfect the tone of his voice, which was free of hatred, accusation and yet filled with absolute finality—a no-meddling tone, if you will. The officers of different nations, newspapermen, broadcasters, and photographers all had quickly gathered from around the world, some with barely an hour's notice to record the moment. At the end of the ceremony B-29s roared overhead in tight formation. They were followed by countless other [USAAF] planes, and navy fighters and bombers. The Japanese looked up in complete astonishment at the vast armada. Their government propaganda had led them to believe we had few planes left.[53]

No such display of overwhelming power was to occur after any of the conflicts involving the armed forces of the United States after 1945.

Battle of Okinawa and Bombing of Japan

(1) Marine draws a bead on a Japanese sniper with his tommy gun as his companion ducks for cover before the town of Shuri on Okinawa. (2) Carrier *Bunker Hill* after being struck by kamikaze off Okinawa on May 11, 1945. NARA photos

(3) Squadrons of warplanes fly in formation over the battleship *Missouri* on September 2, 1945, after the Instrument of Surrender was signed. NARA photo

⬤
THE STRATEGIC ARCHITECTURES
OF WORLD WAR II

The last ten chapters have been a comparative examination of the evolving strategic architectures of the principal World War II combatants as they fought critical battles and campaigns. In analyzing the architectures of Germany and Japan, neither aggressor succeeded in aligning policy and strategy with the operations they executed. The Allies, however, reacted by developing a superior strategic architecture that delivered victory because they aligned policy and strategy with realistic operations they could execute victoriously.

GERMAN STRATEGIC ARCHITECTURE

Aggressive statesmen, who initiate a conflict without completely thinking through the feasibility of achieving their defined geopolitical outcomes and thoroughly addressing the risks, court peril. This Clausewitzian caveat is so obvious that it seems axiomatic that any rational statesman, even a dictator, would accept it.

The German strategic architecture failed in the rational definition of its war objectives. The Reich's war aims, which of course meant Hitler's war aims, were impossible to achieve because National Socialist policies of genocide and subjugation under *Generalplan Ost* proposed to kill or starve whole populations. Hitler clearly had defined in *Mein Kampf* the policy foundations for his strategic architecture in the east.[1] German implementation of the *Ostplan* undermined any rational strategic architecture in the east and destroyed human capital and resources the regime could have used to advantage. One need only think of Germany's failure to advance its nuclear technology because of Nazi elimination of Jewish scientific talent through genocide and the forced emigration to the Allies of those Jews and Eastern European refugees who were able to escape from the Third Reich.[2]

By the end of the summer of 1940, German leaders after the stunning victories in Poland and the Low Countries appeared uncertain about where to attack next. When the *Luftwaffe* lost the Battle of Britain, Hitler the next year turned his aggressive energies east. Operation *Barbarossa* resulted in the execution of military plans that were fundamentally flawed. The German "win-quick" doctrine of *Bewegungskrieg* was very high risk because German OKW and OKH planning staffs did not account for potential reverses as a result of the Soviet Union and the Allies eventually mobilizing overwhelming war-fighting power. Germany failed to plan for a long war of attrition that led to war-losing deficits. It underestimated the strength of the Soviet and American industrial bases and the speed with which both could react.

During the middle years of the war, the Allied strategic bombing offensive deprived German frontline units of half of the weapons and munitions they needed and drew two thirds of the *Luftwaffe*'s fighter wings to the west to defend German cities. The Reich failed to mobilize its industrial infrastructure and focus it on producing weapons systems in quantity. Hitler's distraction with advanced weapons like the V-1 and V-2 rockets and the Me-262 jet fighter diverted critical technical resources from producing the armaments the *Wehrmacht* needed on every front.

Hitler lived with his own version of the OKW staff and surrounded himself with state-of-the-art C³I paraphernalia, including operational maps, banks of Enigma encryption sets, secure teleprinters, radio and telephone networks, and so on. Despite spending a majority of his time during the war in purpose-built command centers in places like Rastenburg (in East Prussia, now Poland), Vinnitsa (Ukraine), and later underground Berlin, he avoided the largest and best-equipped center at Zossen south of Berlin.[3] Indeed, he spent eight hundred days at his Rastenburg *Führerhauptquartier*, code-named *Wolfsschanze* (Wolf's Lair). That represented two-thirds of his time between June 1941 and November 1944. Hitler's deliberate isolation from larger *Wehrmacht* and OKH professional staffs and experts and the administrative establishment of the Third Reich reinforced his inclination to avoid collegial leadership. He was most comfortable with party and staff loyalists. He rarely sought out the best economic or military counsel before making decisions or monitoring the implementation of economic or industrial plans; he simply demanded results.

Ian Kershaw explains that Hitler, even at the zenith of his power in 1941, never designed an effective system for administration of the National Socialist state. The very nature of the authoritarian regime he created had built into it the erosion and undermining of regular patterns of government and, at the same time, the inability to keep in view all aspects of rule of an increasingly expanding and complex Reich. . . . Hitler was for lengthy stretches away from Berlin and overwhelmingly preoccupied with military events. . . . In a modern state, necessarily resting on bureaucracy and dependent upon system and regularized procedure, centering all spheres of power in the hands of one man—whose leadership style was utterly unbureaucratic and whose approach to rule was completely unsystematic . . . could only produce administrative chaos amid a morass of competing authorities . . . [because] every strand of authority was dependent on him. Changing the "system" without changing its focal point was impossible.[4]

Hitler's governance of the Third Reich can be most realistically viewed as a series of competing power centers. Göring commanded the *Luftwaffe* and controlled a number of ministries and industries. Himmler controlled most of the security agencies including the police, SS, Gestapo, concentration camps, and, after the July 20, 1944, plot to kill Hitler, the Reserve Army. There were the German armed forces, but the *Wehrmacht* was scattered across multiple theaters and much less powerful after the plot. Bormann was Hitler's gatekeeper who ran the National Socialist Party apparatus throughout the Reich. There were other power centers: Speer's Armaments Ministry, with six million workers and slave laborers; Goebbels's Propaganda Ministry, which controlled the media; Admiral Canaris's *Abwehr* (intelligence); and the diplomatic corps. In this pseudo-Darwinian world that kept all potential rivals busy defending their own turf, Hitler's divide-and-rule competition became increasingly inefficient as the war evolved into attrition battles in every theater that the *Wehrmacht* could not win.[5]

JAPANESE STRATEGIC ARCHITECTURE

Japan's attack on the US Pacific Fleet at Pearl Harbor was based on a strategic architecture with two false premises. First, Japanese leaders believed that the United States would yield to a peace accommodation that conceded Japanese hegemony in the Central and Western Pacific areas. Second, they believed they could fight and win a "decisive battle" against the US Navy.

With the Roosevelt administration demanding Japan's withdrawal from mainland Asia after months of negotiations as a condition for lifting crippling economic sanctions, the militarists in Hideki Tojo's government believed that their only option was to inflict so much damage on the US Navy that it would be unable to retaliate, and simultaneously to launch a naval and military campaign to seize the oil and strategic raw materials of Southeast Asia.[6]

As the IJN began rehearsing for the Pearl Harbor surprise attack, some Japanese leaders wondered how a country with less than one-fifth the GDP of the United States could expect to prevail. Even if the attack were success-ful, Japan could not win the war in one stroke. To assume that Americans would behave like businessmen and perform a cost-benefit analysis of their weak position in the Pacific and accept a hegemonic demarche could only make sense to people who knew little of American history or culture. Ameri-cans may not have fit the behavioral template of samurai, but only twenty years earlier they had joined the World War I Entente coalition against the Central powers—at a cost of more than one hundred thousand combat deaths and two hundred thousand wounded. Less than two generations earlier, Americans had fought savagely against each other in the Civil War, which resulted in 750,000 combat deaths according to the latest historical estimates.[7] It was a fatal mistake to believe that Americans would not react with implacable fury after the surprise attack on Hawaii.

Japanese military and naval leaders after Pearl Harbor wasted six valuable months debating what to do next. After the defeat at Midway, Japanese power, particularly after one looked at a map of Japanese conquests in the Pacific in mid-1942, seemed formidable, but it was no longer the menacing threat to the West Coast it seemed to be in December 1941.

ALLIED STRATEGIC ARCHITECTURE

The Allies did not define their strategic architecture in a single process. In-stead, Roosevelt and Churchill after Pearl Harbor set about creating a politi-cal-military architecture to build a huge war machine in early 1942 involving large numbers of political leaders, staff officers, and civil servants supporting many high-level military and industrial committees, which eventually included General Eisenhower's SHAEF organization numbering twenty thousand mul-tinational personnel.[8]

Presidents, prime ministers, and dictators who closely question military commanders, not to mention fire them when they fail to win, do better than those that do not. Lincoln learned this early and relieved seven commanders of the Army of the Potomac.[9] Unlike Lincoln, Roosevelt had found his generals because he had already promoted General Marshall, who promoted hundreds of younger, more innovative officers over the heads of more senior incumbents.

Allied military staffing succeeded because American, British, and Soviet leaders did not hesitate to sack ineffective commanders. In the American case, General Marshall very quietly but ruthlessly cashiered seven hundred officers in 1940, including most of the generals commanding divisions in the Louisiana maneuvers of 1940–1941, so he could promote more capable officers. One of them was Eisenhower, whom Marshall promoted over hundreds of officers to put into the War Plans division of the War Department as the army's chief planner as World War II began. John L. Gaddis assessed the wisdom of Marshall's choice this way:

> Eisenhower's skills were not those required to command armies on battlefields: in this respect, he lacked the talents of his World War II contemporaries Bradley, Patton, and Montgomery. But in his ability to weigh costs against benefits, to delegate authority, to communicate clearly, to cooperate with allies, to maintain morale and especially to see how all the parts of the picture related to the whole (it was not just for fun that he later took up painting), Eisenhower's preparation for leadership proved invaluable. . . . Roosevelt found in Eisenhower, with Marshall's help, the only general he needed to run the European war.[10]

Effective war plans emerged through the iteration of policy, strategy, and operations over years as Allied statesmen, generals, and admirals reacted initially to adversity and later to opportunities presented by their enemies. The Allies won because they realized from the outbreak of war that they would have to fight and win a long series of attrition battles. There was no "decisive battle" that won the war, no win-quick military solution that either side could impose on the other. It was a long war requiring massive mobilization of resources. Early in the war, they created integrated organizations that could operate together. They organized their industrial bases to produce weapons, ships, and aircraft to equip large armies, navies, and air forces. They possessed superior economies that developed and fielded innovative technologies. By 1945, Americans were convinced that firepower and technology were a war-winning combination.

Throughout the war, American and British intelligence and code-breaking organizations were sources of strategic insights not only into battlefield opportunities but also into enemy plans, logistical states, technology developments, and deception operations. Anglo-American code breaking enabled victories in the war's early years—during the Battle of Britain, the U-boat war in the Atlantic, defeating Rommel in North Africa, and sinking Yamamoto's carriers at Midway—and later in Italy, at D-Day and the subsequent validation of *Fortitude* deceptions during the summer of 1944 in Normandy, and in 1945 breaking Japanese power after Potsdam.[11] Intelligence by itself could not win the war. Large well-led armies, navies, and air forces had to do that during all six years of mortal combat against the Axis powers.

At no point did Allied leaders believe that an armistice accommodation with the Axis was feasible or morally desirable. They regarded Nazi Germany and Japan as mortal threats to the international system that required total defeat. Even in the early years of the war, they began to think specifically about what they would do after they had won the war. They knew they had to prepare thoroughly for well-planned, well-directed occupations of the defeated enemy states so that their enemies could eventually rejoin the postwar international system with dramatic economic recoveries.

ENDING WORLD WAR II

For the Axis states, the final outcome of World War II was not simply defeat—it was surrender. Defeat is a military fact, the point at which a combatant is no longer capable of winning a war. Surrender is a political decision that recognizes the fact of defeat and accepts the will of the victors.[12]

The occupations of Germany and Japan were massive, diverse undertakings, lasting longer than the war itself. They spanned eleven years in Germany and seven in Japan. Military civil affairs planning began one month after the war started on January 6, 1942. General Marshall authorized the creation of a school to train officers in military government functions, building on the politico-military courses on military government already underway at Cambridge University.[13] A field manual followed, specifying the creation of a civil affairs section in corps and higher staff headquarters operating outside the United States. Planning continued with the creation of COSSAC, which by the end of 1943 had laid the foundations for civil affairs in northwest Europe and for military government in Germany.

The Allied occupation was a major event in German history and in the history of the postwar world. Tony Judt's sweeping narrative describes the European recovery as only one element involving two halves of a continent. In three sentences, he opens up the mythology to a more complex, layered story: "Europe's recovery was a 'miracle.' 'Post-national' Europe had learned the bitter lessons of recent history. An irenic, pacific continent had risen, 'Phoenix-like,' from the ashes of its murderous—suicidal—past."[14]

In 1947, the United States initiated the Marshall Plan, officially known as the European Recovery Program (ERP), to rebuild a stronger economic foundation for the countries of Europe. The initiative was popularly named after General Marshall, who by then was serving as secretary of state. For the US government it was a mission second only in scope and significance to the war itself. Postwar historians of the German occupation adopted an easy shorthand as a way of describing the goals and policies for the occupation of Germany, the "four Ds": disarmament, demilitarization, denazification, and democratization.[15] The American occupation continued until 1955 at significant cost and commitment of military and civil resources.[16]

Marshall spoke of the urgent need to help the European recovery in his address at Harvard University in June 1947. The Marshall Plan was in operation for four years beginning in April 1948. During the four-year period (1948–1951), $13 billion in economic and technical assistance was given to help the recovery of seventeen European countries.[17] This $13 billion (in present-value dollars more than $129 billion accounting for inflation)[18] was in the context of a US GDP of $275 billion in 1948.[19] The Marshall Plan dramatically added $12 billion, making a total of $25 billion in American aid to Europe between the end of the war and the completion of the Marshall Plan. Computing the present value of the total of $25 billion in occupation and recovery expenditures approaches $330 billion.[20] The most recent history puts the value much higher at $846 billion.[21] Seventy years later, the postwar occupations continue to be judged as huge successes.[22]

While not as large in scale, there was a similarly comprehensive occupation of Japan by the US Armed Forces.[23] President Truman empowered General MacArthur as supreme commander, Allied powers (SCAP), to exercise his authority through Japanese governmental machinery and agencies, including the emperor. The SCAP organization functioned exclusively as a headquarters structure and used Japanese officials from top to bottom. MacArthur's enlightened administration of Japan was quite unlike that of Germany or Italy. Ruth Benedict assessed its boldness this way:

> Probably among no other peoples would a policy of good faith have paid off as well as it did in Japan. In Japanese eyes it removed from the stark fact of defeat the symbols of humiliation and challenged them to put into effect a new national policy, acceptance of which was possible precisely because of the culturally conditioned character of the Japanese.[24]

By 1952, the American occupation had introduced a newly rewritten constitution and a new democratic political order that enacted basic and fundamental political reforms guaranteeing human rights.

The Allied occupations lasted longer than the war itself. The Allied leaders of the international system that emerged after 1945 assumed that Germany and Japan would resume their places in the system as peaceful, democratic, and prosperous participants. By 1952, with help from the Marshall Plan, the economy of every European state in World War II had surpassed its prewar levels. The United States since 1945 has had the largest GDP and maintained the most powerful armed forces establishment in the world. Its economic, diplomatic, and security interests have expanded exponentially to every major region of the world.

If World War II may be considered the benchmark for a victorious national commitment, parts III, IV, and V examine how and why Korea, Vietnam, and Iraq became so unsatisfying and controversial for the American people.

PART III

THE KOREAN WAR

Hasty arrangements in the Far East at the end of World War II left Korea divided into two states, a communist-dominated North Korea and a nationalist South Korea, both vying for political control of the peninsula. The Korean War began in June 1950 with a surprise attack by the North Korean army across the 38th parallel into South Korea. The United States entered the war as the North Koreans rapidly moved south and overran most of the peninsula. General MacArthur regained much of this lost ground after a stunning military success at Inchon that cut off the North Korean army below the 38th parallel.

The Truman administration and MacArthur failed to define a realistic strategic architecture at the post-Inchon conference on Wake Island for terminating the war. Despite intelligence warnings of intervention by communist forces of the People's Republic of China (PRC), President Truman accepted MacArthur's confident assurance that he could march victoriously into Pyongyang and north to the Yalu River virtually unopposed. Instead, PRC forces poured across the border into Korea to reinforce the North Korean army. A bloody attrition war lasted another two and a half years and ended where it began, along the 38th parallel (map III.1). The United States never succeeded in designing a strategic architecture in Korea that led to an outcome Americans wanted to celebrate.

The idea that the United States could deter conflict because it had evolved into the only nuclear superpower would prove illusory, as was the decision to demobilize and reduce the size of the US Armed Forces, given the global scope of the international policies of the Truman administration. The US

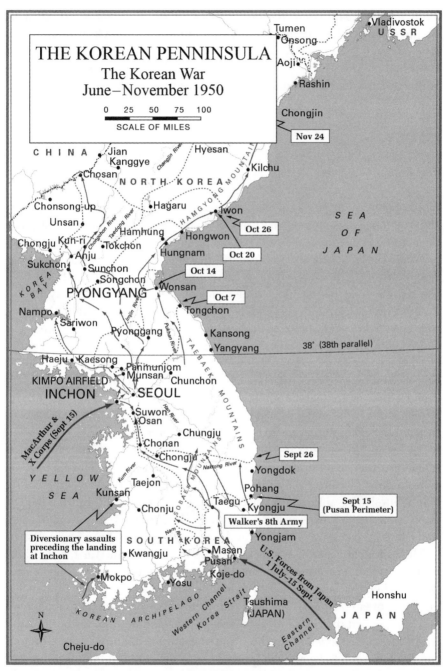

THE KOREAN PENNINSULA
The Korean War
June–November 1950

0   25   50   75   100
SCALE OF MILES

Map III.1. North Korea's invasion of South Korea forced the UN Command into a retreat to defend the pocket around Pusan until General MacArthur's Inchon counteroffensive changed the balance of forces—temporarily.

Source: USMA Atlases.

Army in May 1945 was at the peak of its wartime strength: 8,290,000 men. By the summer of 1950, massive demobilization after the German and Japanese surrenders reduced its rostered strength to 7 percent, or 592,000.[1] As described by Max Hastings, "The nation's armed forces had not merely been reduced—they had been allowed to crumble to the brink of collapse."[2]

POLICY

The Korean War presented a new strategic context for warfare after 1945.[3] No longer could major combatant states define their war aims as the total defeat of an opponent. American possession of atomic weapons and Russian acquisition of nuclear status in 1949 made comprehensive warfare prohibitively dangerous. The Korean War was the first example of a limited war after 1945.

When the war erupted, no American leader was considering reunification of North and South Korea as the geopolitical goal. Indeed, throughout the summer and fall of 1950, American policy makers and military leaders in Washington were indecisive about whether the purpose of the war was to unify the North and South or to preserve the integrity of South Korea. The Truman administration did not explicitly answer this question for six months. Battlefield events forced the answer in December 1950 when the United States abandoned its goal of achieving a total military victory and accepted the reality of having to fight a limited war. In the summer of 1950, President Truman tentatively defined it as a "police action," but the military response lacked a clear policy definition on what a police action entailed.

American involvement in another shooting conflict so soon after winning a global war was an enormous shock to the American public. The Truman administration, mindful of the appeasement policies of the 1930s, reacted swiftly. The White House authorized MacArthur to commit units drawn from the Occupation Army in Japan, ordered a naval blockade of the entire Korean coast, and committed the US Air Force in the Far East against the communists.

The historical chain of events leading up to the Korean War reached back more than half a century. Korea had been part of the Empire of Japan since 1910.[4] When the Japanese surrendered in 1945, Japanese power in Manchuria and Korea collapsed. The Red Army's invasion of Manchuria on August 9, 1945, opened the door for Soviet troops to penetrate into northern Korea. The path was also open in southern Korea to American forces, whose original mission had been to invade the Japanese home islands. The Allied occupation of the Korean Peninsula after World War II was more by circumstance than by any strategic design. The Yalta and Potsdam Conferences in 1945 only briefly addressed Korea. The Allies at the end of World War II were improvising in real time. Don Oberdorfer describes how two American army officers during an all-night meeting late on August 10, 1945, in the Executive Office Building next to the White House hurriedly established the 38th parallel as the division between North and South Korea.

> Around midnight, two young officers were sent into an adjoining room to carve out a U.S. occupation zone in Korea, lest the Soviets occupy the entire peninsula and move quickly toward Japan. Lieutenant Colonel Dean Rusk . . . and [Colonel] Charles Bonesteel . . . had little preparation for the task. Working in haste and under great pressure, and using a *National Geographic* map for reference, they proposed that U.S. troops occupy the area south of the 38th parallel . . . and that Soviet troops occupy the area north of the parallel.[5]

Bruce Cumings's account of the Korean War usefully pointed out much history unknown to Americans in 1950, indeed even to the present day, about Korea and what he calls "the unknown war."[6] American historical and cultural ignorance of Korea in 1945 as troops were landed for the postwar occupation in the South reverberated adversely for the next five years.

Japanese ambitions to colonize Korea coincided with Japan's rise as the first modern Asian power. Japan instigated a war with Qing China in 1894 and defeated it a year later. A decade of imperial rivalry over Korea ensued, culminating with the Japanese defeat of tsarist Russia. In 1904 the Japanese moved a large army into Korea, historically not for the first time.

Centuries before, Japan had invaded Korea in the late sixteenth century. Shogun Toyotomi Hideyoshi, a samurai warrior and dictator, attempted twice to conquer Korea and China. In 1592, he led an invasion force of 150,000 men that landed at the southern ports of Pusan and Tadaejin. The operational profile of the conflict has striking historical parallels to 1950. Two Japanese divisions quickly overran the defending Korean forces and captured Seoul and then Pyongyang, driving the remnants of the Korean army north across the Yalu River into China. In 1593, regular and guerrilla Korean and Chinese forces recrossed the Yalu, retook Pyongyang, and drove the Japanese south to Pusan. In 1597, after a five-year truce, Hideyoshi invaded again with a force of 140,000. This time the Koreans and Chinese stopped his advance south of Seoul. Both conflicts were fought over the same rugged terrain and battlegrounds that General MacArthur's UN forces would encounter almost 360 years later.[7]

Korea became a Japanese protectorate in 1905 and a colony in 1910. Although Japanese education, language, roads, railways, and sanitation were introduced, none of these improvements gained the slightest gratitude from the fiercely nationalistic Koreans. Korean independence was dead for thirty-five years. Despite indigenous resistance, the Japanese maintained their rule in Korea until 1945, leaving a deep Japanese-Korean enmity that lasts to the present day.

The Americans were pragmatic in their own policies as occupiers of Korea in 1945. They could rely on only one local stabilizing force, the Japanese, who skillfully made themselves indispensable to the American military governor, Lieutenant General John R. Hodge, and his men. One of Hodge's first acts was to confirm Japanese colonial officials in their positions. Japanese remained the principal language of communication. Japanese soldiers and police retained responsibility for the maintenance of law and order. Although General MacArthur directed Hodge to remove Japanese from office, many held on to their influence for weeks as unofficial advisors. These acts of cooperation, even camaraderie, between Japanese and American officers were not lost on the Koreans. According to Hastings, "the senior officers of 24th Corps possessed no training or expertise of any kind for exercising civilian government—they were merely professional military men, obliged to improvise as they went along."[8]

General Hodge shipped seventy thousand Japanese colonial civil servants and six hundred thousand Japanese soldiers back to Japan. But the damage to American relations with the Koreans was already done. Many of the replacements chosen for the former Japanese positions were Korean collaborators detested by their fellow countrymen. In the political competition that developed, Syngman Rhee became the principal beneficiary.

Syngman Rhee, seventy-five years old in 1950, was the first among his Korean countrymen to receive Ivy League advanced degrees (a Harvard MA and a Princeton PhD). He had been imprisoned early in the century for political activities (1899–1904); then, except for a brief return visit in 1910, he spent thirty-five years living in the United States, where he lobbied relentlessly for American support for Korean independence, financed by Korean compatriots. He possessed one great advantage from his long absence abroad. He was untainted by collaboration with the Japanese who had colonized Korea in 1910.

To the Americans, "Rhee was a comfortingly comprehensible figure: fluent in the small talk of democracy, able to converse about America and American institutions with easy familiarity, and above all, at home in the English language." This "acerbic, prickly, uncompromising . . . obsessive, ruthless nationalist and anti-communist seemed a plausible father figure for the new Korea."[9] Bony, venerable, and elderly, Rhee had returned to Seoul in 1945 with the assistance of General MacArthur and General Hodge. Rhee positioned himself to dominate the political process. Rhee's right-wing, anticommunist party gained popularity and with three other groups gained an effective majority in South Korea's new constitutional assembly in the 1948 elections. Rhee and his supporters instituted a presidential system of government, and he was inaugurated president in July 1948.

Korean War historians frequently cite Secretary of State Dean G. Acheson's speech to the National Press Club on January 12, 1950, as one of the proximate causative actions in the chain of events that precipitated the Korean War. In the speech, Acheson left South Korea out of the defensive perimeter that defined American vital interests in the Far East. Robert Leckie calls it Acheson's "famous speech excluding Korea—and Formosa—from the American defense line in the Far East."[10]

Hastings held Acheson "largely to blame for sending misleading signals to Pyongyang and Moscow which made the communists believe they could attack with impunity."[11] David Halberstam in the second sentence of his book referred to Acheson's "colossal gaffe" because he "neglected to include South Korea in America's Asian defensive perimeter."[12] Cumings challenged this historical consensus:

> Acheson's Press Club speech was the opposite of an ill-considered gaffe: instead it unlocks key aspects of U.S. policy toward Korea before the war. Why did he not include Korea in his perimeter? The best answer is that Acheson "wanted to keep secret the American commitment to Korea's defense." Acheson implied that should an attack come there, the United States would take the problem to the U.N. Security Council—which is what Dean Rusk [assistant secretary of state for Far Eastern affairs] had secretly recommended to him nearly a year before the war, in July 1949, and exactly what Acheson did when the war erupted. In the many drafts leading up to this speech, South Korea was consistently seen as a direct American responsibility, along with Japan. But Acheson did not want to say this publicly, lest Syngman Rhee be emboldened to start a war; that is also why he blocked tanks and an air force for the ROK.[13]

Cumings pointed out that "Stalin, thanks to Kim Philby[14] and other spies . . . was reading Acheson's secrets with his breakfast and had no reason to pay attention to speeches for public consumption."[15] Cumings's views are regarded as revisionist, but on the issue of Acheson's speech being one of the proximate causes of the Korean War, his historical homework is thorough and illuminating.

Kim Il Sung had been installed as the communist leader of North Korea by the Soviets in 1945. For the next five years, he repeatedly asked Stalin for permission to attack the South. His entreaties intensified in 1949 and early 1950 after Mao Tse Tung's success in China. Kim made a number of secret trips to Moscow to push for permission. John L. Gaddis described Stalin's "green light" to Kim as part of a larger strategy for seizing opportunities in East Asia and Southeast Asia, building on the momentum of Mao's 1949 victory over Chiang Kai Shek's Kuomintang (Nationalist Party) in China, Chiang's retreat to Formosa, Mao's creation of the PRC, and Ho Chi Minh's revolutionary Viet Minh initiatives in Indochina.[16]

Cumings explained Kim's motives for launching the invasion in 1950. Kim Il Sung had an "impeccable pedigree in the resistance" against the Japanese occupation. So did his family. His father, middle brother, and an uncle were jailed during the 1920s and 1930s for anti-Japanese activities; the father and brother died as a result. Kim took an early leading role in the Sino-Korean guerrilla campaign to resist the Japanese occupation. He organized the first Korean guerrilla unit in 1932, made a name for himself at the Battle of Dongning in 1933, and later assumed a leading role in forging Sino-Korean cooperation in the Manchurian guerrilla struggle. He was fluent in Chinese. Cumings characterized him as "the Manchurian candidate."[17]

Cumings's history identified how much has been left out of the American geopolitical narrative. There had been a civil struggle going on since the Japanese colonization. In all but name, it became a civil war by 1932 and has never ended. The Americans' demarcation of the 38th parallel and their pragmatic occupation methods infuriated Kim. He always thought he had been on the right side of history—a capable Marxist guerrilla leader of peasant revolts, a fervent anticolonialist, and an ardent enemy of the Japanese. He had paid his ideological dues and wanted a unified Korean communist state. The Americans had denied him this lifelong goal and conspired against him by installing Rhee in the South. All of these events and frustrations were conflated in Kim's mind as outrages. By 1950 he really wanted to get even, but he needed, and finally got, Stalin's green light.

STRATEGY

President Truman had appointed General MacArthur on V-J Day, August 15, 1945, as the supreme commander of the Allied powers (SCAP), responsible for the postwar occupation of Japan.[18] Five years later he became "triple hatted" as commander in chief of the United Nations Command (CINCUNC) in addition to already being commander of the US Army Forces, Far East (USAFFE).

American order-of-battle data in June 1950 showed that the two combatant armies were at equivalent strength. However, the numbers did not account for the superior training and battle experience of the Korean People's Army (KPA), particularly among those large contingents that were veterans of the Chinese civil war fought before, during, and after World War II.[19] North Korea also had Soviet T-34 tanks, arguably the best medium tank in World War II for its weight, survivability, maneuverability, speed, and armament. The North also had a small but useful air force of fighters and light bombers.[20] The Americans provided World War II surplus equipment to the South Koreans but denied them armor, antitank weapons, and artillery heavier than 105 mm.

Early on the morning of June 25, 1950, North Korea, the Democratic People's Republic of Korea (DPRK), invaded South Korea, the Republic of Korea (ROK), sweeping aside the poorly equipped South Korean army. The invasion began at 0400 with a devastating artillery and mortar barrage. A skillfully prepared deception plan so masked the North's attack that it achieved complete strategic and tactical surprise. The Korean War had begun and would run for more than three years.

General MacArthur flew to Korea on June 29, 1950, to personally evaluate the situation. Hastings describes MacArthur's visit as "characteristic." His Lockheed Constellation, christened the *Bataan*, was bounced by a North Korean fighter that was driven off by escorting P-51 Mustangs and landed safety. For eight hours MacArthur toured the rear areas of the battlefields. He saw the long columns of terror-stricken refugees pouring south with large numbers of ROK soldiers among them. He saw artillery and mortar smoke and gazed upon the distant buildings of Seoul already in KPA hands. "He later declared that it was there, at that moment, that he conceived the notion of a great amphibious landing [at Inchon] behind the enemy flank."[21] Then he drove back to the *Bataan* and flew back to his Dai Ichi headquarters in Tokyo.[22]

MacArthur immediately reported to the army chief of staff, General J. Lawton Collins, that South Korea could only be restored by the commitment of US Armed Forces, including ground units. He urged the Truman administration to make a military commitment on the most powerful possible scale.

> I have today inspected the South Korea battle area from Suwon to the Han River. My purpose was to reconnoiter at first hand the conditions as they exist and to determine the most effective way to further support our mission. . . . Organized and equipped as a light force for maintenance of interior order [the South Korean Army was] unprepared for attack by armor and air. Conversely, they are incapable of gaining the initiative over such a force as that embodied in the North Korean Army. . . .
>
> If authorized, it is my intention to immediately move a United States Regimental Combat Team to the reinforcement of the vital area discussed and to provide for a possible build-up to a two-division strength from the troops in Japan for an early counteroffensive. Unless provision is made for the full utilization of the Army-Navy-Air team in this shattered area, our mission will be needlessly costly in life, money and prestige. At worst it might even be doomed to failure.[23]

Secretary of State Acheson moved even faster than MacArthur. On the night of the invasion, he took the issue of North Korean aggression to the United Nations. Over the next forty-eight hours, Acheson drove American decision making. At White House emergency meetings, he argued for an immediate increase in military aid to the ROK, US Air Force cover for the evacuation of American civilians in South Korea, and the interposition of the US Navy's 7th Fleet between Taiwan and the PRC mainland. Cumings flatly asserts that the decision to intervene militarily was Acheson's decision, supported by President Truman, but taken before UN, Pentagon, or congressional approval. Acheson's geopolitical reasoning focused on American prestige and credibility and had little to do directly with any perception of Korea's intrinsic strategic value.

Within two days, the UN Security Council passed two resolutions condemning North Korea's aggression, Resolution 82 on June 25, passed by a vote of 9–0, and Resolution 83 on June 27 calling for an immediate cessation of hostilities and recommending that the UN members "furnish such assistance to the Republic of Korea as may be necessary to repel the armed attack and to restore international peace and security in the area."[24] The vote on Resolution 83 was unanimous in favor. Ironically, the USSR was not present to veto either of these resolutions, as the Soviet ambassador to the United Nations, Yakov A. Malik, had been ordered by Stalin to boycott the Security Council because the United Nations refused to admit the PRC to its membership in January 1950. This accident of history, the Soviet boycott of the Security Council, enabled the UN vote to send troops to Korea. Korea was the first conflict where an international organization voted to intervene between two warring parties, not just with peacekeeping resolutions and token forces, but also with unequivocal military support. General MacArthur was appointed commander in chief of the United Nations Command on July 10, 1950.

The Truman administration during the first year of the war conducted an energetic diplomatic campaign to broaden the participation of UN member military forces. If the concept of the Korean War was to be perceived as a credible act of collective security rather than as a narrow pursuit of American national interest, the member states of the UN had to be seen as contributors on the battlefield. Twenty-two countries dispatched forces to the Korean War, with the United States and the ROK providing the most.[25]

OPERATIONS

The North Koreans launched the invasion with a coordinated plan that ran coast to coast. The KPA had assembled seven infantry divisions supported by an armored brigade equipped with the T-34 because the ROK lacked antitank weaponry and armor. Half of the enemy assault forces were arrayed in a forty-mile arc around the Uijongbu Corridor, an ancient invasion route that led directly to Seoul fifteen miles to the south.[26] Terrain and natural obstacles hindered the advance more than the ROK forces. Four ROK divisions defended the area north of Seoul, but the surprise of the attack and the shock of enemy armor overwhelmed their defenses. The front just north of Seoul began collapsing at once. Battalions and companies retreated in broken, undisciplined streams and abandoned their equipment, desperate to keep ahead of the advancing KPA units. The KPA was clearly superior to the ROK Army in several critical dimensions. The KPA possessed 150 Russian

T-34 tanks; the South Koreans had no tanks. The KPA had superior artillery outclassing the South Koreans by a ratio of three to one. The North Koreans had a small tactical air force; the South Koreans had none. One-third of the KPA attacking force consisted of Korean veterans of the Chinese communist forces that "gave it a combat-hardened quality and efficiency that it would not otherwise have had."[27]

Kim's KPA divisions were threatening Seoul within two days. The failure of the four ROK divisions to hold the key line of communication along the Uijongbu Corridor north of Seoul ensured the quick loss of the capital. South Korean units panicked, mutinied, or fled before the oncoming KPA forces. The capital fell two days later, with the KPA destroying 60 percent of the ROK Army in the process. Rhee left the city the following day, June 27, 1950. That left the surviving ROK units north of Seoul engaging a well-equipped, well-trained enemy without communications or organized logistical support. ROK soldiers simply melted into the general population of South Korean refugees streaming south. The KPA's capture of Seoul by the next day caused the Han River bridges to be prematurely destroyed on June 28,[28] killing hundreds of soldiers and civilians who were crossing them at the time.[29] Retreating ROK divisions were trapped north of the Han and lost a large number of fighting personnel and all of their equipment and supplies.[30] Thus began a steady retreat of the ROK Army south, ending with American intervention in force and the desperate defense of the Pusan Perimeter.

American forces conducted a fighting retreat from Seoul down the peninsula; then they consolidated with the ROK Army and fought to defend the Pusan Perimeter. MacArthur's successful landing at Inchon in the fall changed the balance of forces until his overconfidence in rushing north to the Yalu led to the entry of the PRC into the conflict by the winter of 1950.

After Inchon, as subsequent chapters will show, the UN Command had an opportunity to restore the territorial integrity of South Korea and end the war without trying to gain complete political control of all of Korea. Western capitals were receiving diplomatic signals indicating that the PRC would intervene if the UN Command attacked into North Korea. MacArthur and his military and political bosses in Washington were so confident of total victory that Secretary Acheson dismissed these signals out of hand as "mere vaporings."[31] MacArthur's decision to push north had all the earmarks of a front-to-back plan. Because the Truman administration was ambivalent about the political objective of the war, unification versus protection of the integrity of the South, MacArthur's post-Inchon strategy to cross the 38th parallel lacked clear political or military supervision.

If the Truman administration had prudently defined its strategic architecture for fighting in Korea and fully evaluated the available intelligence at the meeting on Wake Island, it could have clarified what ultimately became the geopolitical goal of the war, the restoration of South Korean sovereignty. Instead, Truman and his national security advisors accepted General MacArthur's wildly optimistic assessment of the low risk of PRC intervention. As a result, the Korean War evolved into an ugly, nasty war of attrition that ended nearly three years later after much more loss of life by both sides. For many Americans, the outcome did not merit the large sacrifice in lives and consumption of war-fighting matériel. It would take another half century before Americans realized that the "forgotten" or "unknown" war enabled the emergence of a democratic, sovereign state on the Pacific Rim that now enjoys the respect of the world.

General Matthew B. Ridgway, MacArthur's successor in the UN Command, had a more realistic view of the strategic challenges of limited war. He retrospectively explained that the UN Command lacked the manpower and matériel to attack and hold a permanent military position in North Korea.[32]

Chapters 12 through 16 reveal why the strategic architecture for a limited war had to be different from the strategic architecture of victory in World War II. They reveal the interactions between policy makers in Washington and commanders in the field and the difficulty of aligning strategy with operations.

The Korean War was a direct conventional confrontation involving American soldiers in combat against hundreds of thousands of communist Chinese, as well as small numbers of Russians.[33] It bore many of the characteristics of a World War II theater involving millions of soldiers arrayed along front lines. Allied operations over the fall and winter of 1950–1951 stabilized the fighting along what soon was called the Main Line of Resistance (MLR). The fighting continued for thirty more months, and the war ended when both sides realized that victory was improbable. The MLR in July 1953 metastasized into the demilitarized zone (DMZ) and remains a permanent territorial scar.[34]

12

BATTLE OF THE PUSAN PERIMETER

Getting the Most Out of a Bad Situation

During July 1950, the KPA imposed one humiliating tactical defeat after another on American and ROK forces. The US Army thought that its deployment would send the North Koreans scurrying back across the 38th parallel.[1] The Americans thought the KPA was a hastily assembled peasant rabble, ill equipped, poorly trained, and incapable of overwhelming the soldiers of the country that was the undisputed victor of World War II.

Hastings in 1985 interviewed Colonel Jonathan F. Ladd, who in 1950 served as a captain under General Edward M. "Ned" Almond, MacArthur's chief of staff. Ladd, looking back on the events at MacArthur's Dai Ichi headquarters thirty-five years later, saw the seeds being sown for later disappointments and frustrations during his service as a soldier and advisor in Vietnam:

> All those officers, those generals: they really thought that they were going to go over there and "stop the gooks"—just the same as in Vietnam. Just who "the gooks" were, they didn't know, and didn't want to know. You could have asked any American senior officer in Korea: "Who commands the Korean 42nd Division— ROK or communist—and what's his background?" He wouldn't have known what you were talking about. A gook is a gook. But if the Germans had been the enemy, he'd have known.[2]

The first American unit to encounter the KPA juggernaut was the ill-fated Task Force Smith, and it was a shock; the action lasted no more than a few hours. Lieutenant Colonel Charles B. "Brad" Smith's scratch battalion,[3] committed from the 24th ID, had been quickly assembled in Japan, hastily and poorly equipped, and flown to South Korea. Deployed between Suwon and Osan on July 5, 1950, Task Force Smith was ordered to confront the enemy.[4] This rapidly deployed unit, consisting of inexperienced garrison troops from the Occupation Army, with no coordinated artillery, no tanks, and no antitank weapons that could stop a T-34, and primarily equipped with small arms, only served as a speed bump against the enemy's advance. The story of Task Force Smith is a staple in virtually every history of the Korean War.[5]

The summer of 1950 was not an abject military disaster. American and South Korean forces in seeming disarray had inflicted fifty-eight thousand casualties on the KPA between June 25 and early August. By the end of July, American and ROK forces outnumbered the KPA along a collapsing front, ninety-two thousand (forty-seven thousand of whom were Americans) against seventy thousand KPA soldiers.[6]

In early August, the 1st Marine Division landed at Pusan and halted the KPA advance. The front stabilized around the Pusan Perimeter, a sixty-by-one-hundred-mile rectangle on the southeast coast of the Korean Peninsula, a 160-mile line anchored along its longer western flank by the Naktong River and on its northern flank by the coastal city of Pohang (map 12.1). The Naktong River provided a natural defensive obstacle but was shallow enough to be forded by the enemy in places. Steep hills overlooked the river on both banks, an advantage for the defenders. Taegu, a major city, remained under US/ROK control in the center of the defensive line.

On July 13, 1950, General Walton H. "Johnnie" Walker, a corps commander who had served in Patton's 3rd Army in Europe during World War II,[7] established his 8th Army headquarters in South Korea, with operational responsibility for UN forces under MacArthur's overall command. MacArthur's messages to the JCS started to produce delivery of the military resources he wanted, a multidivision army that could resist and defeat North Korea's aggression.

The Battle of the Pusan Perimeter, beginning on July 29, 1950, could be called "Walker's War." Hastings quotes from Walker's "ringing order of the day" on July 29, 1950, as the battle for Chinju developed and as the last of Walker's retreating army crossed the Naktong River to defensive positions on its eastern banks.

> There will be no more retreating, withdrawal, readjustment of lines or whatever you call it. . . . There are no lines behind which we can retreat. This is not going to be a Dunkirk or Bataan. A retreat to Pusan would result in one of the greatest butcheries in history. We must fight to the end. We must fight as a team. If some of us die, we will die fighting together.[8]

On the battlefields around the Pusan Perimeter, American and UN power slowly began to reclaim the military initiative. In early September, the KPA committed thirteen infantry divisions and an armored division,[9] 98,000 men

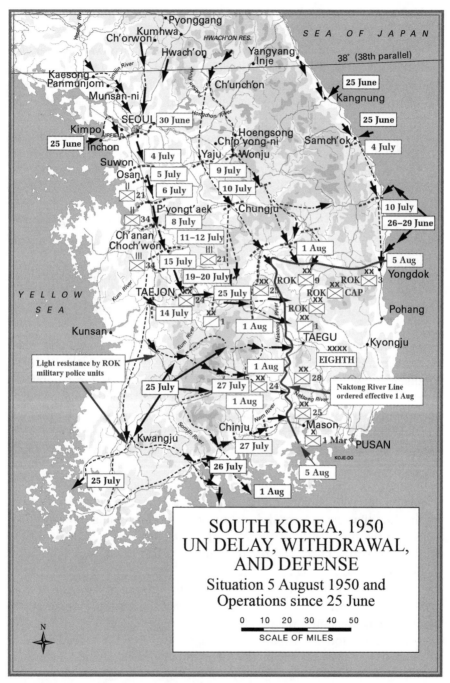

Map 12.1. General Walker's Pusan Perimeter formed a sixty-by-one-hundred-mile defensive rectangle in South Korea.

Source: USMA Atlases.

against Walker's 180,000. The KPA sustained casualties estimated as high as sixty thousand.[10]

In addition to superior manpower, firepower, and airpower, Walker had two other advantages: shortened interior lines and tactical intelligence. The Armed Forces Security Agency (AFSA) achieved what Matthew M. Aid calls the "thirty-day miracle" of breaking all of North Korea's tactical codes and ciphers. By the end of July 1950, AFSA was cracking and translating over one-third of all North Korean enciphered messages that were being intercepted by SIGINT stations all over the world.[11] The output was limited only by the shortage of Korean translators. As Aid recounted, "The net result was that AFSA's spectacular codebreaking successes gave [General] Walker what every military commander around the world secretly dreams about—near complete and real-time access to the plans and intentions of the enemy forces he faced."[12] The SIGINT intercepts showed that the KPA's supply system under the relentless air attacks almost stopped functioning. Ammunition shortages in enemy units around the Pusan Perimeter severely degraded the combat capabilities of frontline enemy units.

Walker was an energetic, effective commander. He worked to patch units together when he needed to reinforce one part of the line. He would borrow a battalion from one regiment to lend it to another. He frequently relied on the marines and the 27th Wolfhounds infantry regiment of the 25th ID, commanded by the effective Colonel John H. Michaelis (later general), to serve as mobile fire brigades to stanch potential KPA breakthroughs. Walker knew the enemy positions in detail, and with the AFSA SIGINT products, he could anticipate KPA attacks. He also knew the combat terrain intimately because he flew over the battle space in a small reconnaissance plane throughout the battle.[13]

In August, despite their heavy losses and the logistical pressures from UN air attacks, the KPA launched their last major offensive against the perimeter, making "startling gains" over the next two weeks. Kim Il Sung threw his divisions into the final battle of the Naktong River. Walker's perimeter on the northern flank defended by three ROK divisions had to fall back south after the KPA captured Pohang in mid-August.[14] The perimeter was close to breaking at multiple points, with North Korean units pressing on Kyongju, Masan, and Taegu. American commanders reported that the frontline situation was the most dangerous since the perimeter had been set up. American casualties were mounting, totaling twenty thousand, with nearly 4,300 dead by mid-September. However, the plight of Walker's 8th Army was about to change.

13

INCHON—OPERATION *CHROMITE*

MacArthur's Masterstroke

In mid-September, General MacArthur executed the most brilliant operation of his long career. His amphibious landing at Inchon was the first strategic turning point of the Korean War. After his first visit in late June, he started planning the counteroffensive at Inchon, over 150 miles northwest of Pusan on Korea's western coast on the Yellow Sea, roughly twenty miles southwest of Seoul. For weeks, the Far East Command had been building up its forces, which MacArthur preempted with a first call on the arriving units sent to Japan.[1]

MacArthur reasoned that an amphibious landing would break the KPA's stranglehold on the Pusan Perimeter by attacking far enough north along the Yellow Sea coast to (1) cut off the KPA's long logistical tail, (2) liberate Seoul, (3) force Kim Il Sung into fighting a war on two fronts, and (4) trap virtually all KPA divisions south of the 38th parallel. He convinced himself that the only way out of the impasse of the Pusan attrition was an amphibious landing behind enemy lines. The risks were obvious and substantial. Failure would mean instant and probably irreparable damage to the UN Command.

Code-named Operation *Chromite*, the plan on briefing charts looked brilliant. As a sequence of objectives, it was straightforward. First, capture the poorly defended island of Wolmi-do at the entrance to the port of Inchon. Second, use the island as a springboard for the invasion of the mainland. Third, capture Inchon. Fourth, immediately attack northeast to capture Seoul's major airport, Kimpo, to prevent the North Koreans from flying in reinforcements. And fifth, maintain the offensive momentum to capture Seoul and deliver the capital back to Syngman Rhee. MacArthur fervently believed that the KPA divisions deployed around the Pusan Perimeter would be forced to retreat. The enemy divisions heading north would be trapped between General Walker's pursuing 8th Army and MacArthur's *Chromite* forces positioned to interdict them in the center of the Korean Peninsula.

The strategic implications of such a triumphant outcome were as bold as the risks. The KPA could be annihilated—a classic Clausewitzian outcome of getting into the rear of one's enemy and wreaking havoc and destruction. MacArthur knew the strategic and tactical mechanics of such an operation because he had learned them in World Wars I and II.

World War I had taught him the dangers of frontal assaults because the Western Front attacks for both sides consistently deteriorated into set-piece, casualty-intensive battles of attrition. World War II had taught him that a deft amphibious campaign of long island-hopping distances, maneuvering around Japanese strongpoints, attacking where the Imperial Japanese Army could be isolated, and leveraging naval and airpower against weaker garrisons was a battle-winning military recipe. MacArthur wanted a military solution where audacity and surprise were at the heart of the plan.

In July, he sent this message to Washington:

> I am firmly convinced that an early and strong effort behind [the KPA] front will sever his main line of communication and enable us to deliver a decisive and crushing blow. Any material delay in such an operation may lose this opportunity. The alternative is a frontal attack which can only result in a protracted and expensive campaign to slowly drive the enemy north of the 38th parallel.[2]

Much has been written about the deliberations between senior officers in Tokyo and their superiors in Washington, but MacArthur had supreme confidence in his plan. There was a major command assemblage for a briefing on August 23, 1950, on the sixth floor of the Dai Ichi war room between MacArthur and many of America's senior commanders. MacArthur, after listening carefully to the navy's skepticism and assessment of the risks of the Inchon plan, spoke for forty-five minutes. His peroration carried the room.

> "It is plainly apparent that here in Asia is where the communist conspirators have elected to make their play for global conquest. The test is not in Berlin or Vienna, in London, Paris, or Washington. It is here and now—it is along the Naktong River in South Korea. . . . I can almost hear the ticking of the second hand of destiny. We must act now or we will die. . . . We shall land at Inchon, and I shall crush them." The deep voice fell away to a whisper. . . . The Chief of Naval Operations [Admiral Forrest P. Sherman] stood up and declared emotionally, "General, the Navy will get you to Inchon."[3]

Captain Ladd, General Almond's aide, was present for the briefing and MacArthur's theatrics. Halberstam reports that Ladd smiled to himself as MacArthur concluded his final pitch—"he's got them now." Washington approved the operation five days later.

Historically, *Chromite* would become MacArthur's brilliant military triumph and his alone. The assault on Inchon was set for September 15, 1950 (map 13.1). The Inchon amphibious force included the 1st Marine Division, the army's 7th ID, and some ROK Army units, a total of seventy thousand men, virtually every available amphibious ship, and dozens of other navy warships. The invasion fleet totaled 260 ships sailing from Yokohama under the command of Vice Admiral Arthur D. Struble, one of the navy's most experienced amphibious commanders. It was not a large fleet by World War II Pacific theater standards.[4] Most of the Inchon-bound marines had recently arrived from US bases, while the 1st Provisional Marine Brigade had just been withdrawn from the Pusan Perimeter a few days before.

The memory of Anzio hovered over the Inchon landing, a beachhead that Kim Il Sung was capable of potentially pinching off and strangling. But Kim was no *Feldmarschall* Kesselring, capable of quickly sizing up the situation and reacting with fire-brigade speed and ferocity as the German commander had at Anzio.

Another factor favored the UN Command. Kim Il Sung had been careless. Normally in an amphibious landing, surprise is crucial. In the case of Inchon, from Tokyo's Press Club to Yokohama to Pusan, *Chromite* could have been dubbed "Operation *Common Knowledge*." Any intelligence picked up by the KPA about *Chromite* preparations or MacArthur's thinking was ignored by Kim. Mao Tse Tung, however, was not so easily taken in. Mao had assigned one of the ablest analysts working with the People's Liberation Army general staff, Lei Yingfu, Chou En Lai's military secretary, to divine what MacArthur might be up to and predict where he might strike. Certain OPSEC signatures were obvious to Chinese intelligence: Japan's harbors, especially Yokohama, were filled with amphibious shipping. There was MacArthur's long history of World War II amphibious landings. Lei studied all the available intelligence and MacArthur's military record and concluded that the Americans were preparing a trap for the North Koreans and that they were going to execute a surprise landing far behind the KPA's lines around Pusan. Lei examined six candidate ports and, given MacArthur's aggressive personality, put Inchon at the top of his list. Lei, on the day of MacArthur's council of war in Dai Ichi, passed his findings to Chou, who passed them to Mao. A three-page memorandum was prepared and immediately passed to Kim. It made no serious impression on Kim. Even Kim's Soviet advisors suggested that he heed the warning, recommending

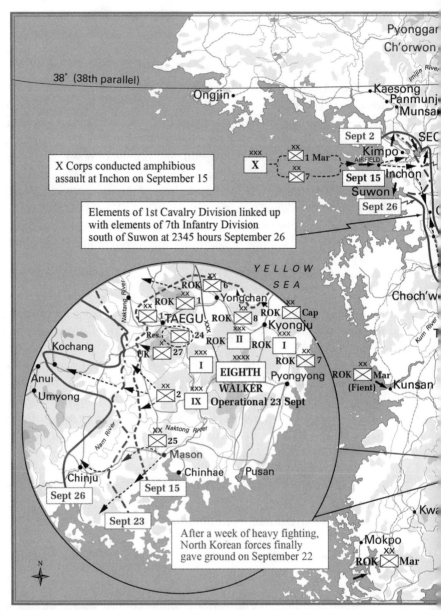

Map 13.1. General MacArthur's brilliant amphibious counterstroke at Inchon cut off the KPA in South Korea and enabled General Walker's 8th Army to go on the offensive.
Source: USMA Atlases.

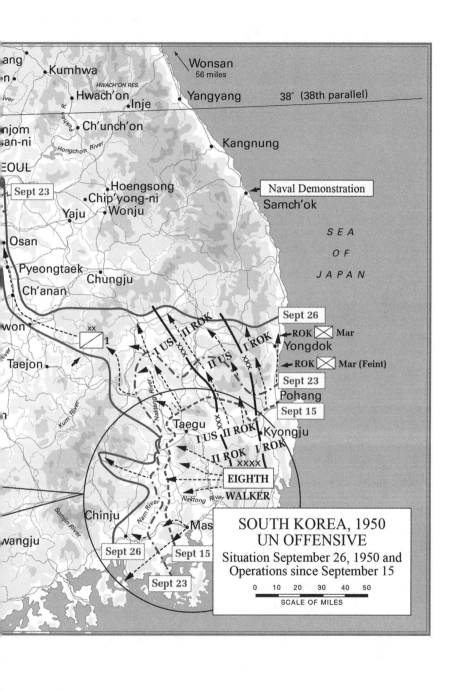

ang
n

Kumhwa

HWACH'ON RES.

Hwach'on • Inje

Ch'unch'on

njom
an-ni

Hongchon River

EOUL

Sept 23

Yaju

Osan

Pyeongtaek

Ch'anan

won

Taejon

Kum River

Naktong River

Taegu

Chinju

Nam River

Somjin River

wangju

Wonsan
56 miles

Yangyang   38° (38th parallel)

Kangnung

Naval Demonstration
Samch'ok

SEA

OF

JAPAN

Hoengsong
Chip'yong-ni
Wonju

Chungju

1

Sept 26

I US   II ROK

II US   I ROK

ROK ⊠ Mar
Yongdok

← ROK ⊠ Mar (Feint)

Sept 23
Pohang
Sept 15

I US   II ROK Kyongju

II ROK   I ROK

EIGHTH
WALKER

Naktong River

Mas

SOUTH KOREA, 1950
UN OFFENSIVE
Situation September 26, 1950 and
Operations since September 15

Sept 26   Sept 15

Sept 23

0   10   20   30   40   50

SCALE OF MILES

that Kim direct the KPA to consider retreating from Pusan, shortening his logistical tail, and strengthening North Korean defenses at vulnerable ports. A senior Soviet advisor, Pavel Yudin, even pointed to a map and specifically mentioned Inchon as the most likely target. Still, Kim ordered no defensive preparations. He did not even mine Inchon harbor.[5]

Meanwhile in Tokyo, as Halberstam and Hastings describe the milieu of MacArthur's military staff, no officer was allowed to make an independent name for himself.[6] Indeed, when officers arrived at their new postings in Mac-Arthur's headquarters in Tokyo, any who had served in Europe during World War II, or worse had worked under Eisenhower or Marshall, was judged to have fought in the wrong theater, served under the wrong commanders, and had the wrong mentors and friends, and thus could expect never to fit in or be accepted.[7] General Walker, a Patton man, bore this baggage. There were a few exceptions, like General Ridgway, who would succeed Walker and subsequently MacArthur, but they were very few in number.

MacArthur's staffing biases, fed by his resentments about the 70/30 allocation of support in the Pacific theater during World War II, are only one dimension of how a theater commander's egotism can undermine a strategic architecture. Another even more critical dimension is the tone and substance that govern effective civilian-military relations. Generals Eisenhower and Marshall were the archetypes of effective "Managers" who could work effectively and collaboratively with presidents and prime ministers. They worked well in the corporate and collegial politico-military environment that characterized the institutional structures of World War II.

That was not the case in the postwar Far East with the way MacArthur's "Hero" personality and "the Bataan Gang," as MacArthur's inner circle was called, viewed presidential authority. Their views reflected a kind of loyalty test to MacArthur first because most of them had been there at the low point in MacArthur's career on Corregidor in 1942, where they believed they were abandoned by Roosevelt's failure to send reinforcements to the Philippines. MacArthur's long years abroad after the mid-1930s and his highly opinionated views about American politics, often expressed in the form of his own presidential ambitions, harbored a deep-seated problem with presidential authority.[8] His egocentric posturing undermined the respect and trust needed for a serious, substantive exchange of views on the Korean War at his meeting with President Truman a few weeks later.

Chromite's execution went smoothly. Despite the seeming improvisation, the landing went like clockwork, better than MacArthur could have dreamed. Sea conditions proved better than expected. Initial resistance was comparatively light, despite tactical surprise having been given away by the five-day bombardment on the island of Wolmi-do. The navy's planning had been skillful and detailed, and Admiral Struble's execution was flawless. The marines quickly captured Wolmi-do Island, which opened up the harbor. The main landings, even though the window of daylight for an amphibious operation was limited by the tides to two or three early-evening hours, were successful, with only twenty Americans killed on the first day.

Recently declassified documents reveal that the AFSA-generated SIGINT was indispensable at Inchon. SIGINT products provided MacArthur and his intelligence staff with a clear understanding of the KPA order of battle, including the locations, strengths, and equipment levels of all thirteen KPA infantry divisions deployed around Pusan as well as the fact that there were no large North Korean units in the Inchon area. In mid-August, SIGINT decrypts indicated that the North Koreans were pulling frontline combat units from the Pusan Perimeter and moving them to defensive positions along the east and west coasts of South Korea, suggesting to analysts that the North was concerned about the possibility of a UN amphibious landing behind KPA lines. By early September, decrypted communications traffic showed that North Korean senior commanders believed US forces might attempt a landing on the Yellow Sea coast, but they incorrectly guessed it would likely occur south of Inchon at Mokpo or Kunsan. Aid's research implies that Kim might have taken seriously some of what Lei Yingfu wrote in his intelligence memorandum, but not the threat to Inchon. The result was that the KPA was caught unprepared. Their counterattack against the Inchon beachhead was picked up by SIGINT well before it began and was mauled by US air strikes. In a matter of hours, the North Korean force was destroyed.[9]

MacArthur, who had selected General Almond to command the Inchon landing force, designated 10th Corps, gave Almond ten days to capture Seoul. He wanted to make a grand entrance and a gesture by turning the capital back over to Rhee precisely ninety days after North Korea's attack on June 25, 1950. So Almond felt pressure to meet an arbitrary, political schedule as soon as the Inchon force was ashore. General O. P. Smith, commander of the 1st Marine Division assigned to 10th Corps, had explicitly warned Almond that the ease of capturing Inchon was deceptive because they had surprised and overwhelmed small garrisons of rear-echelon troops. Taking Seoul was a very different military proposition.[10] Marine preliminary reconnaissance missions indicated a well-defended city protected by thousands of elite KPA troops. Smith's estimates turned out to be true.

Ambitious to establish a successful military record after his mediocre World War II performance, Almond's aggressive command style reflected his World War II experience of maneuver and firepower in Europe.[11] The marines and the army in the Pacific theater fought a different kind of grinding war, attacking one island after another. They took few Japanese prisoners because few ever surrendered. When the Japanese gave ground, they did so grudgingly, often measuring tactical success by how many Americans they killed. Gains were measured in yards, not miles. These different war-fighting perspectives were at the heart of the Almond-Smith tension.

As marine, army, and ROK forces moved toward Seoul, North Korean resistance stiffened. As the KPA lines hardened, friction developed between Generals Almond and Smith. It was almost as if these two officers came from different war-fighting cultures, what Linn would describe as the Manager versus the Hero. Almond, who had come late to join the Bataan Gang, had quickly earned MacArthur's confidence and become a protégé. MacArthur's ego did not permit being surrounded by talent that might overshadow his own reputation. Unlike Marshall and Eisenhower, who had mentored and promoted field and staff officers alike into important command positions, the MacArthur staff in the Pacific displayed none of these dynamics. MacArthur's rewarding loyalty over war-fighting competence in giving Almond command of 10th Corps would later introduce even bigger military risks when MacArthur decided to attack north across the 38th parallel with his forces divided.

The fighting for Seoul became a costly, block-by-block urban battle. Kim after Inchon had rushed twenty thousand additional troops, one full division and three separate regiments, into the Seoul area. Upward of thirty-five to forty thousand KPA soldiers defended Seoul. The North Koreans fought hard and fanatically, and they had the advantage of being embedded in "urban terrain" ruins to fight such a brutal, defensive military operation in a built-up area (MOBA).[12] American combat power eventually decided the outcome, but the city was devastated in the process. Amid the destruction, Seoul changed hands for the second time.

The damage to Seoul became an issue of lasting historical controversy. MacArthur had told Almond that he wanted Seoul recaptured quickly. In 10th Corps' path stood forty thousand still-resolute communist troops.[13] David Rees's history of the Korean War reiterates the fundamentals of the military thought process, which had its origins in World Wars I and II: "the belief that machines must be used to save men's lives; Korea would progressively become a horrific illustration of the effects of a limited war where one [side] possessed the firepower and the other the manpower."[14]

The tension between Generals Almond and Smith intensified.[15] Almond took to flying over the battle space in a small reconnaissance spotter plane, as Walker did over the Pusan Perimeter, giving orders directly to Smith's marine regimental, battalion, and even company commanders without going through Smith's 1st Marine Division headquarters. Almond "was sure that he was a brilliant tactical officer" as he flew over Smith's units, "radioing instructions to whatever unit he spotted below him." Smith protested angrily against this breach of military protocol and finally ordered his chief of operations to refuse to accept any more orders without confirmation from his own headquarters.[16]

Two factors made this antagonism worse. One was Smith's belief that the pressure was falsely driven, that it did not reflect the tactical need for quicker battle-space dominance but instead reflected MacArthur's deadline to capture Seoul by September 25. The other was the confusion and coordination problem within 10th Corps that would last well beyond Inchon. According to one of the official military histories, 10th Corps was a "hasty throwing together of a provisional Corps headquarters" and was "at best only a half-baked affair."[17] The 1st Marine Division did most of the planning for and execution of the Inchon landings because 10th Corps was neither fully formed nor experienced enough in amphibious operations to operate as a functional headquarters. This deficiency was one that would leave serious command deficits after MacArthur ordered the UN Command to cross the 38th parallel and drive north to the Yalu.

A week after the Inchon landing, Walker's 8th Army broke through KPA lines on September 22, scattering enemy forces into the hills where many units would later regroup to form guerrilla bands. On September 27, Almond's 10th Corps linked up with the 8th Army near Osan, South Korea. Two days later, MacArthur flew to Kimpo to preside over the solemn ceremony in the shattered Capitol Building in Seoul. He spoke in a flood of rhetoric—"By the grace of merciful providence, our forces fighting under the standard of that greatest hope and inspiration of mankind, the United Nations, have liberated this ancient capital city of Korea." The ceremony concluded with MacArthur solemnly turning to Rhee: "Mr. President, my officers and I will now resume our military duties and leave you and your government to the discharge of the civil responsibility." He flew back to Tokyo, "imbued with an aura of invincibility that awed even his nation's leaders. He was confident that the war for Korea had been won, and that his armies were victorious. Now it was just a matter of cleaning up."[18]

MacArthur, with the consent of his superiors in Washington, now planned to complete the destruction of KPA forces in Korea, cross the 38th parallel, and reunify the country under Rhee. MacArthur's masters discounted warnings that PRC diplomats were expressing in "neutral" capitals and to selected statesmen around the world: it would not tolerate the movement of UN forces across the 38th parallel. Secretary of Defense George Marshall in late September sent him this instruction: "We want you to feel unhampered tactically and strategically to proceed north of the 38th parallel." President Truman himself approved the message.[19] This guidance underscored the Truman administration's ambivalence with respect to the strategic architecture of the Korean War. The absence of a clear policy for ending the war, based on a front-to-back strategy of waiting to see how far MacArthur, 8th Army, and 10th Corps could drive north, led to operational failure when Chinese attacks slammed into UN forces two months later.

14

CROSSING THE 38TH PARALLEL AND DRIVING NORTH TO THE YALU

The Risks of Overreaching

By the end of September, UN forces began to prepare for a push north to the Yalu River and the Chinese border (map 14.1). MacArthur's original decision to give 10th Corps to Almond had disturbed many in Tokyo and Washington, but it had been viewed as a temporary move.[1] Walker's 8th Army had been busy defending the Pusan Perimeter, and as Halberstam put it, "MacArthur's headquarters was hardly rich in talent."[2] However, Almond was to be placed permanently in charge of 10th Corps and would not report to Walker at all.

Under this divided command structure, Walker would have to compete with Almond's corps in the race north. An amphibious landing was planned for 10th Corps at Wonsan, north of the 38th parallel on the east coast. This plan necessitated Inchon being used to take men and equipment out rather than flooding supplies in to support 10th Corps and 8th Army. The two forces linked up at Osan to maneuver east from Seoul and create giant pincers, trapping KPA divisions retreating from Pusan. As North Korean troops were trying to flee north pursued by Walker, Almond's 10th Corps was driving south through Inchon to embark on navy transports for the sea voyage to Wonsan. That included General Smith's 1st Marine Division and the army's 7th ID, which had been assigned road priority heading south for embarkation to Wonsan. On the narrow main supply route, convoys moving north to support Walker's 8th Army gave way to convoys moving south, violating a basic military canon that pursuing forces should never lose contact with the enemy.[3]

Wonsan was a mishap waiting to happen. Vice Admiral C. Turner Joy, commanding the naval forces in the Far East, was appalled by the idea. Joy feared,

rightly, that Wonsan harbor would likely be filled with mines. He tried to see
MacArthur in Tokyo but was never allowed near CINCUNC. The push to
Wonsan could have been accomplished more quickly and practicably simply
by letting the 10th Corps units drive north. Instead, the planning became a
SNAFU. The planners were behind schedule; delay followed delay. In fact,
ROK troops from the 3rd and Capitol Divisions were the first to reach Wonsan
via overland routes, arriving on October 10 virtually unopposed.

Walker flew in the next day with Major General Earle E. Partridge, the
theater commander of the 5th Air Force. Partridge immediately started
ferrying in supplies for the South Koreans. On October 19, troopships carrying the marines arrived off Wonsan harbor. The marines remained aboard
ship while navy minesweepers slowly cleared the harbor of mines. The split
command was a real danger to success at Inchon. If one unspoken canon of
American doctrine was to never lose contact with the enemy, another was
even more sacrosanct: never divide your forces. Yet MacArthur was dispatching forces under a divided command into difficult, hostile terrain, with
the fall weather already starting to drop toward winter temperatures.[4] Worst
of all, invasion planning reflected MacArthur's contempt for the enemy,
especially the Chinese. The phrase "Chinese laundrymen" would permeate
many order-of-battle briefings and threat assessments of the enemy for the
next three months.[5] Intelligence failed to grasp the reality that UN forces
faced two fundamentally different kinds of armies.

The KPA was a conventionally equipped force. It was road bound like US,
ROK, and UN forces. Over the next weeks, however, 8th Army and 10th
Corps would discover that China's PLA was not simply an inferior version of
the KPA but a different army altogether—with unique strengths, weaknesses,
tactics, and operational preferences. The light Chinese divisions could hide in
and infiltrate through forests and villages; employ excellent camouflage skills,
similar to Soviet *maskirovka*; and subsist on provisions requisitioned from local peasants or carried by their own troops. The PLA frontline units did not
depend on large motorized supply columns that clogged the limited road nets
of North Korea. They attacked mainly at night, used large quantities of hand
grenades because they were easily portable, used light machine guns and mortar fire at very close ranges, and deployed limited artillery and few if any tanks.
The Chinese would try to approach an enemy from the rear, having already
infiltrated UN lines, frequently distracting the UN forces' fire by sniping or
playing bugle or pipe music.[6]

Operationally, the Chinese PLA military leadership had a more subtle approach than the North Koreans. Mao Tse Tung wrote his own version of the
art of war, referring explicitly to Sun Tzu's war-fighting principles. Know the
enemy and know yourself. Use feints and probes because successful warfare
is based on deception. Pretend inferiority and encourage enemy arrogance.

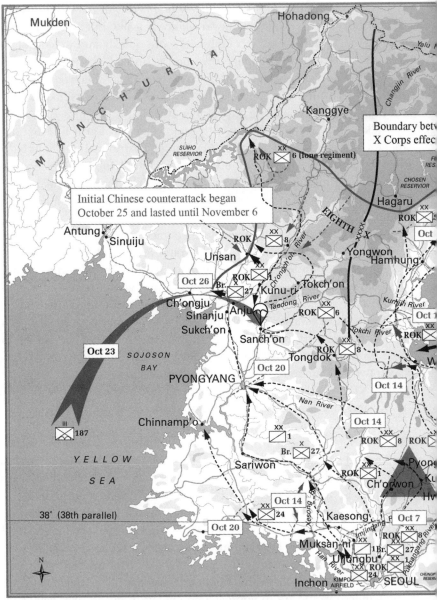

Map 14.1. General MacArthur told President Truman on Wake Island that the risk of PRC intervention was "very little" given his intention to attack north toward the Yalu River along North Korea's border with the PRC.

Source: USMA Atlases.

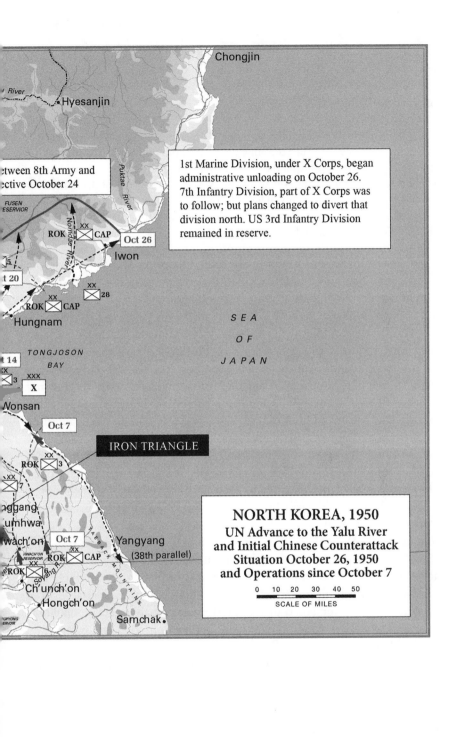

Chongjin

Hyesanjin

River

etween 8th Army and
ective October 24

FUSEN
ESERVIOR

ROK ⊠ CAP   Oct 26

Puktae River

Namdae River

Iwon

XX
⊠ 28

ROK ⊠ CAP

Hungnam

t 20

TONGJOSON
BAY

SEA

OF

JAPAN

14
X
⊠ 3   XXX
X

Wonsan

Oct 7

IRON TRIANGLE

ROK ⊠ 3
XX
⊠ 7

ggang
umhwa
wach'on   Oct 7
HWACHON
RESERVOR   ROK ⊠ CAP
ROK ⊠ 6
Soyang R.

Yangyang
(38th parallel)

TAEBAEK MOUNTAINS

Ch'unch'on
Hongch'on

Samchak

NGPYONG
ERVOR

1st Marine Division, under X Corps, began
administrative unloading on October 26.
7th Infantry Division, part of X Corps was
to follow; but plans changed to divert that
division north. US 3rd Infantry Division
remained in reserve.

NORTH KOREA, 1950
UN Advance to the Yalu River
and Initial Chinese Counterattack
Situation October 26, 1950
and Operations since October 7

0   10   20   30   40   50
SCALE OF MILES

Attack where he is unprepared. Attack weakness, not strength.[7] Mao believed in these concepts on a tactical level, but he also understood Clausewitz's strategic formulation of war. In 1938, he was explicit about what Clausewitz meant by "other means": bloodshed.

> "War is the continuation of politics by other . . . means." When politics develops to a certain stage beyond which it cannot proceed by the usual means, war breaks out to sweep the obstacles from the way. . . . When the obstacle is removed and our political aim attained the war will stop. Nevertheless, if the obstacle is not completely swept away, the war will have to continue until the aim is fully accomplished. . . . It can therefore be said that politics is war without bloodshed while war is politics with bloodshed.[8]

Mao had the manpower in Korea to shed the blood. As 8th Army and 10th Corps advanced deeper into North Korea toward the Yalu, the Chinese military threat was not yet manifest on military situation maps.

On October 15, 1950, President Truman met with General MacArthur at Wake Island in the middle of the Pacific. MacArthur had ducked Truman's two previous requests to meet following President Roosevelt's death. In the wake of the Inchon victory, which appeared to be a war-winning masterstroke, the White House believed that a meeting was desirable, but not everyone in the administration thought it a good idea. Acheson thought that a trip to Wake that mixed politics and policy was a bad idea.[9] He wanted no part of it because Truman had faced a considerable volume of criticism early in the war when the repeated defeats and retreats dominated the headlines and underscored the inadequacy of the nation's military readiness. To try now to share some of the glory that redounded to MacArthur, in the guise of a council of war, could easily be construed as blatant and obvious. MacArthur, of course, knew this.

Truman flew to Wake without a formal agenda for discussing and exchanging views with his theater commander about where the war was headed or about the strategic architecture for winning or terminating the conflict. Truman had called it a "police action,"[10] not a war. On the presidential level of grand strategy, there remained unanswered questions about the geopolitical scope, international purpose, military risks, enemy definition and intent, and UN capability to resolve the conflict.

MacArthur on the flight to Wake was in a foul mood about having to make the trip because he viewed it, correctly, as a political summons and an opportunity to create favorable publicity for the president. He "flew to Wake . . . entirely unreceptive to open discussion of serious issues."[11]

The meeting began auspiciously enough, with MacArthur warmly greeting the president, although reporters were quick to note that the general did not salute the president, a breach of military protocol.[12] Two meetings occurred on Wake within the interval of a morning: a private one first between Truman and MacArthur that lasted about an hour and a second longer meeting of about ninety minutes where staffs were present. No official record was kept of the first meeting except what the two principals later reported.[13]

General Bradley, chairman of the Joint Chiefs of Staff, prepared an official, top-secret, published record of the second meeting.[14] Bradley's eight-page report, redacted for security reasons by Congress in 1951, presents MacArthur's military summary of the situation in Korea this way:

I believe that formal resistance will end throughout North and South Korea by Thanksgiving. There is little resistance left in South Korea—only about 15,000 men—and those that we do not destroy, the winter will. We now have about 60,000 prisoners in compounds. In North Korea, unfortunately, they are pursuing a forlorn hope. They have about 100,000 men who were trained as replacements. They are poorly trained, led, and equipped, but they are obstinate and it goes against my grain to have to destroy them. They are only fighting to save face. Orientals prefer to die rather than to lose face. I am now driving with the 1st Cavalry Division up the line to Pyongyang. I am thinking of making a tank and truck column and sending it up the road to take Pyongyang directly. It depends on the intelligence we get in the next forty-eight hours. We have already taken Wonsan. I am landing the 10th Corps, which will take Pyongyang in one week. The North Koreans are making the same mistake they have made before. They have not deployed in depth. When the gap is closed the same thing will happen in the north as happened in the south. It is my hope to be able to withdraw the 8th Army to Japan by Christmas.[15]

The next three pages indicate conferee exchanges about the planned Korean elections and budgetary estimates for Korea's "rehabilitation." Then President Truman asked, "What are the chances of Soviet or Chinese intervention?" MacArthur replied,

Very little. Had they interfered in the first or second months it would have been decisive. We are no longer fearful of intervention. We no longer stand hat in hand. The Chinese have 300,000 men in Manchuria. Of these probably not more than 100,000 to 125,000 are distributed along the Yalu River. Only 50,000 to 60,000 could be gotten across the Yalu River. They have no Air Force. Now that we have bases for our Air Force in Korea, if the Chinese tried to get down to Pyongyang there would be the greatest slaughter.[16] With the Russians it is a little different. They have an air force in Siberia and a fairly good one, with excellent pilots equipped with some jets and [bombers].[17] They are probably no match for our Air Force. They would have difficulty putting troops in the field. [MacArthur elaborates for a bit on a Chinese ground–Russian air combination.] I believe it just wouldn't work with Chinese communist ground and Russian air. We are the best.[18]

MacArthur's predictions could not have been more wrong. Roy E. Appleman's CMH history indicates that on the day MacArthur answered President Truman's question, 120,000 PLA soldiers had already crossed the Yalu into Korea, and by the end of October two PLA armies had completed their crossing into North Korea.[19]

At the Wake Island meeting, no probing questions were asked about the evidentiary basis for any of MacArthur's assertions. No one asked whether or why North and South Korea should be reunited, whether such a proposal would be politically or militarily feasible, or how such an outcome might occur. MacArthur's forces had been across the 38th parallel for barely a fortnight.

The Truman administration had provided contradictory direction for a strategic architecture to end the war. On September 27, 1950, MacArthur received the top-secret National Security Council Memorandum 81/1 from Truman reminding him that operations north of the 38th parallel were authorized only if "at the time of such operation there has been no entry into North Korea by major Soviet or Chinese communist forces, no announcements of intended entry, nor a threat to counter our operations militarily."[20] However, three days later, he received Marshall's JCS message indicating that he should feel unhampered to cross it. The definition of a successful outcome of the fighting was ambiguous, whether the action was called a war, a police action, a limited war, or, as a later generation would describe such a situation, a low-intensity conflict. This ambiguity was not simply grappling with semantics but ran to the fundamental geopolitical purpose of deploying armed force. NSC 81/1 and Marshall's JSC message were sending MacArthur mixed signals: destroy the KPA, attack north across the 38th parallel, but only if China and Russia do not intervene. NSC 81/1 failed to define a clear geopolitical or military outcome to the Korean conflict. Paragraph 7 of NSC 81/1 left open the option that a negotiated settlement was desirable: "In view of the importance of avoiding a general war, we should be prepared to negotiate a settlement favorable to us. Such a settlement should not leave the aggressor [North Korea] in an advantageous position that would invite a repeat of the aggression."[21] These kinds of options to end the Korean War were not explored at the Wake Island conference.

No one at Wake thought to ask a what-if question after MacArthur indicated that he planned to capture Pyongyang—what if UN forces were deployed to hold defensible positions just north of Pyongyang, across Korea's "narrow waist" to Wonsan? South of this line was North Korea's industrial "Iron Triangle," bounded by Ch'orwon, Kumhwa, and Pyonggang (not to be confused with the capital, Pyongyang) (map 14.1). The UN Command at this stage would have held strong bargaining leverage in a negotiated armistice. Alternatively, the UN Command would have to occupy the entire Korean Peninsula, make political provision for unification of the country as a noncommunist state, and judge whether this would be construed as threatening to either the

PRC or the USSR. As General Matthew Ridgway who succeeded MacArthur wrote years later in his own book about the war,

> At the end of the campaign, our battle line would have been stretched . . . to 420 miles [across North Korea's border with the PRC, map 14.2], and the major responsibility for holding it would have been ours, for it would have been beyond the capability of the ROK army. The questions then would have been: Will the American people support an army of the size required to hold this line? Will they underwrite the bloody cost of a Manchurian campaign? Will they commit themselves to an endless war in the bottomless pit of the Asian mainland? I thought then and I think now [1967] that the answer to these questions was "No."[22]

Had American leadership been dealing with a *Wehrmacht*-style European enemy rather than an Asian enemy, as Colonel Ladd's remarks scathingly imply, would more probing questions have been asked based on an all-source picture?[23] MacArthur was right in his contemptuous misgivings about the meeting on Wake as time wasting and pointless, but for the wrong reasons. Nobody on Wake Island learned anything new about the flawed strategic architecture for ending the war, including CINCUNC himself.

As MacArthur had confidently predicted, Pyongyang fell on October 19. UN forces continued to advance north, although slowed by logistical problems and steady if weakening KPA resistance. On October 26, units of Almond's 10th Corps began landing at Wonsan while US and ROK divisions of 8th Army to the west advanced north to Unsan (map 14.1), one of the few access points into the hilly terrain of the Yalu River Sino-Korean border.

In early November, UN forces were spread east to west across Korea along a thinly held front. There was a fifteen-mile gap between the US 24th ID and the ROK 1st ID, with the 24th on its left and another ROK division on its right. The PLA launched a pincer movement at Unsan against the South Koreans, what the Chinese called their First Phase Offensive. Chinese forces struck suddenly from the hills around Unsan and then withdrew after inflicting heavy casualties on several ROK divisions, the ROK 1st, 6th, and 8th IDs, and mauling at least two battalions of the 8th Cavalry Regiment of the US 1st Cavalry Division.

When the Unsan operation ended, the 8th Cav had eight hundred casualties among the estimated 2,400 men in the regiment. It was the worst defeat of the Korean War up to that point, made more frustrating because it had taken place after four months of battle when it seemed the tide had turned.[24] Suddenly, as if out of nowhere, the PLA had shattered a veteran regiment from an elite division. And then the Chinese disappeared. No one knew where. They had withdrawn to hidden positions farther north to wait for 8th Army and 10th Corps to advance into an even bigger trap farther away from their logistical

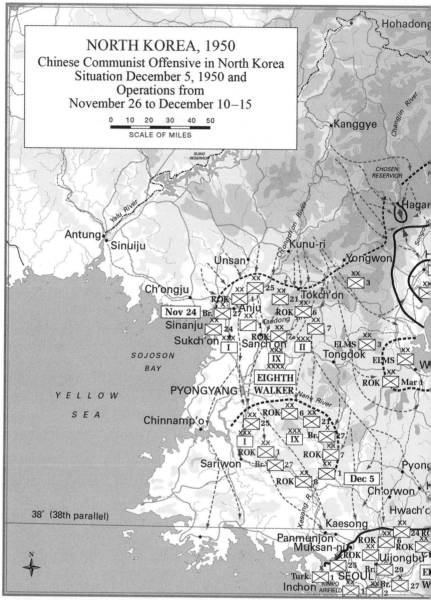

Map 14.2. PRC intervention destroyed MacArthur's boast of returning the troops home by Christmas of 1950; shortly after Thanksgiving, he cabled Washington that "we face an entirely new war."

Source: USMA Atlases.

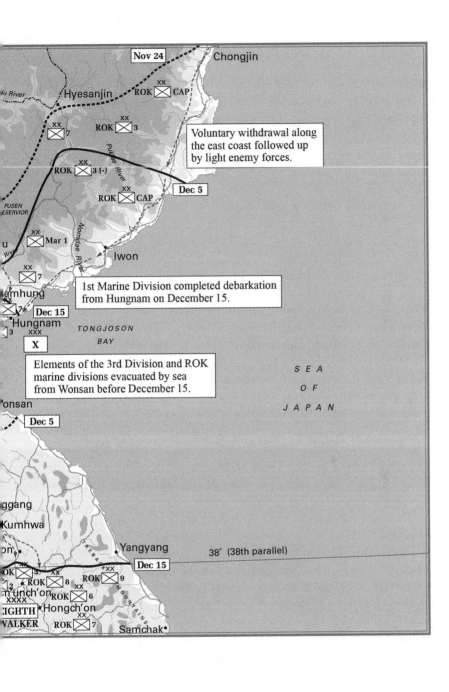

Nov 24

Chongjin

Hyesanjin ROK XX CAP

lu River

XX 7   ROK XX 3

Voluntary withdrawal along
the east coast followed up
by light enemy forces.

ROK XX 3 (-)

Pukgee River

ROK XX CAP   Dec 5

FUSEN
ESERVIOR

u   XX Mar 1

River

XX 7

amhung

XX 7   Dec 15

Hungnam   TONGJOSON
3   XXX   BAY
X

1st Marine Division completed debarkation
from Hungnam on December 15.

Elements of the 3rd Division and ROK
marine divisions evacuated by sea
from Wonsan before December 15.

SEA

O F

J A P A N

onsan

Dec 5

ggang

Kumhwa

on   Yangyang   38° (38th parallel)

OK XX 3   +XX   Dec 15
2   ROK XX 8   ROK XX 9
runch'on ROK XX 6
XXXX
IGHTH   Hongch'on
VALKER   ROK XX 7
Samchak

bases. The Battle of Unsan was only a taste of worse to come farther north in even colder weather about three weeks later.

Over the next month, UN forces paused and then began their final push north to the Yalu. By mid-November, ROK Army headquarters issued an optimistic communiqué asserting, "Our army is continuing its exterminating drive against the enemy, who are taking refuge in the mountains." Over 135,000 communist POWs were in UN hands, more than double the prisoner count MacArthur reported a month earlier at Wake Island, and total North Korean casualties were estimated at 335,000.[25]

In the mountains were multiple PLA corps, but this fact was not showing up on any UN force situation maps. The men of 8th Army in the front lines were served a traditional Thanksgiving turkey meal on November 24 despite the intense cold, at the expense of displaced shipments of essential winter clothing and ammunition. Indeed, many 8th Army units were crating up their equipment and gear for shipment to Japan or the CONUS because most were still confident in MacArthur's claim that the troops would be home by Christmas. That confidence lasted for about another day or two. On the night of November 26, the PLA slammed into 8th Army and 10th Corps. Two days later MacArthur cabled the JCS that "we face an entirely new war."[26]

ROK divisions disappeared from situation maps. "For the first time since the Battle of the Bulge, official reports referred to whole American divisions as 'combat ineffective.'"[27] Chinese units surrounded the 1st Marine Division and parts of the 7th ID in the east. US and ROK units began to retreat under appalling winter conditions, which for Walker's 8th Army in the west were rendered worse by the sudden onset of Siberian winter. The memory of this debacle in late November and December 1950 is persistent and vivid. At the time, it was a shock.

After Unsan, PLA senior commanders studied how easily conventional American and ROK units disintegrated when attacked. The performance of the US 1st Cavalry Division was examined in considerable detail by Chinese commanders.[28] The PLA had adapted Sun Tzu's tactics and operational preferences, transforming weaknesses into strengths and the converse, turning enemy strengths into weaknesses, such as the fact that both US and ROK ground units were road bound. The Chinese victory at Unsan was as much a surprise to the Chinese leadership as it was to the UN forces and eased the fear of the Chinese leadership about intervening in Korea.

The second PLA offensive, beginning on November 26–27, 1950, committed three hundred thousand Chinese troops, organized into eighteen lightly armored divisions against the 8th Army front and twelve divisions against 10th Corps. Opposing them were seventeen 8th Army and 10th Corps divisions, seven of them American, plus British, Commonwealth, and Turkish combat units equivalent to another division. Including surviving KPA forces, the combatants were roughly equivalent in manpower at about four hundred thousand men each.[29]

Eliot Cohen and John Gooch have meticulously reconstructed this military disaster, concluding that it was a double failure: a failure to anticipate the probable behavior of the enemy and a failure of operational learning. The first failure, which involved not just MacArthur but the entire US government, flowed from a misjudgment of Chinese willingness to fight a large war to prevent unification of Korea. Regardless of where one may try to isolate culpability, it clearly concerned all who participated in the Wake Island meeting and the decision, almost taken by default, to allow UN forces north of the 38th parallel without a clearly thought-out strategic architecture.

The Truman administration's strategic architecture had failed to delineate clear boundaries around what MacArthur was authorized to undertake militarily north of the parallel. Two months earlier, NSC 81/1 had specified that operations north of the 38th parallel were authorized only if neither the Chinese nor the Soviets intervened in North Korea or announced their intention to do so, but Marshall undermined this direction three days later by telling MacArthur that he should feel unencumbered.[30] This was therefore a failure by Washington to design a coherent strategic architecture for fighting the Korean War in a way that would produce an acceptable geopolitical outcome. It made the second failure even more costly on the battlefield.

The second failure is the operational question: Why did US forces suffer so badly at the hands of the Chinese? Specifically, why did the 1st Marine Division fight so much better than 8th Army or the army units in Almond's 10th Corps? The marines who found themselves surrounded at the Chosin Reservoir retreated in good order, bringing out their dead and wounded and all of their equipment when they withdrew by sea from Hungnam (map 14.2).[31] They inflicted heavy casualties on the Chinese. "By dint of stout fighting, a force of some 25,000 strong, or barely a sixth of U.S. forces in Korea (a 20th of all U.N. forces), had disabled between approximately a quarter and a third [100,000–133,000] of all Chinese forces in Korea."[32]

Cohen and Gooch trace the roots of 8th Army's operational failure in November–December 1950 to ignorance of the intelligence about the Chinese threat and to the army's downsizing of 8th Army's combat strength.[33] They created a "failure matrix" to pinpoint 8th Army's shortcomings at multiple levels of command, from the national command authority (NCA) level down to the tactical levels of battalion and company unit command, along five descriptive dimensions: resources, communications and monitoring, doctrine, understanding the enemy, and data on the enemy. They linked the shortcomings into clusters for purposes of analysis.

The first failure cluster was unquestioning faith in the airpower of Far East Command and a failure to understand accurately the nature of the enemy and the war they were fighting.[34] The Cohen-Gooch analysis traces the failure at the operational level to the flawed strategic architecture that the Truman administration allowed to persist after the Wake Island meeting. It was the failure to follow the classic Clausewitzian canon in the first chapter of *On War*, the answer to the most fundamental strategic question: What is the nature of the conflict one is fighting?[35] It was a failure at all levels of command, threading top down from the theater level, where inaccurate intelligence was linked to operational reliance on air, penetrating down to the small-unit command level where the PLA was perceived as an inferior version of the KPA.

The PLA, which did not depend on a large, road-bound logistical tail and was adept at concealing itself, was not as vulnerable to air attack and interdiction as were the Axis armies in Europe.[36] The fact that 8th Army units were themselves road bound made them acutely vulnerable when confronted with the unexpected shock tactics of the PLA's light divisions. This vulnerability was the converse of what MacArthur had confidently predicted at Wake Island: that the Chinese would be vulnerable to the "greatest slaughter" from the air.

A second cluster showed that a failure to keep a tight grip on the locations of frontline units led to confusion at multiple levels of command, particularly as poor information was filtered up the chain of command to army and theater levels. Field headquarters were out of touch with one another at multiple levels of command and failed to construct an accurate picture of the enemy. The only exception was the marines on their fighting retreat from the Chosin Reservoir. They knew that airpower would only work if there were obvious targets to bomb. An elusive enemy could neutralize much of the lethality unleashed from the air. The marines' mastery of the basics of ground warfare enabled them to perform much better and inflict heavier losses on the enemy.

In this sense, 8th Army and the marines in 10th Corps were operating under the "incubi" of two different wars. Many of the army's commanders in Korea were armor or infantry officers who fought in the European theater in World War II, including Generals Walker, Almond, Ridgway, Van Fleet, Clark, and Taylor. The marines fought their war in the Pacific, where from the inception they had trained in basic infantry tasks and had fought in close combat repeatedly in Nimitz's island-hopping campaign across the Pacific. Their war-fighting skills would again prove essential and effective in their retreat from Chosin. MacArthur's Pacific experience was somewhat different because he had relied heavily on the air forces in his South Pacific campaigns. He emerged from World War II dedicated to the integration of land, naval, and air forces— "triphibious" warfare.[37] The marines had an advantage deriving from their prewar and wartime organizational and professional experience. Many had experience as garrison troops in the last chaotic days of the Chinese Civil War in the 1930s; some were also observers with Chinese forces. These men learned and pioneered the important tactical organizational concept of dividing an infantry squad of a dozen men into three fire teams. This tactical innovation came from marine observers attached to Mao Tse Tung's 8th Route Army.[38] Cohen and Gooch explain part of the marines' better performance under the arduous conditions at Chosin because they were far more likely, from their military professional and historical experience, to assess the Korean War accurately.

Unlike the infantry battalions and companies of 8th Army, marine units at Chosin did not break under the pressure of enemy attacks. Cohen and Gooch quote from one of the official marine histories:

> The Marines established a tactical principle . . . that to nullify Chinese night attacks, regardless of large-scale penetrations and infiltration, defending units had only to maintain position until daybreak. With observation restored, Marine firepower [including naval gunfire as well as combat air support as they withdrew to Hungnam on the coast] would melt down the Chinese mass to impotency.[39]

What has received less attention in the historical literature is the recovery of Almond's 10th Corps from the disasters of the last days of November and early December 1950. In the face of possible destruction, the 10th Corps staff planned and executed a series of complex operations beginning in early December: the successful withdrawal of the 1st Marine Division from the Chosin Reservoir (the "breakout to the coast"), the consolidation of the corps in the Hungnam port area, and the deliberate, progressive withdrawal from Hungnam by December 23, 1950.[40] While not flawless, the withdrawal of 105,000 men, 17,500 vehicles, and 350,000 tons of supplies in three weeks under enemy pressure was successful.[41]

The marines' combat performance during the Chosin retreat became clearer once General Ridgway took command of 8th Army after General Walker was killed in a road accident on December 23, 1950. A veteran World War II airborne commander, Ridgway quickly assessed 8th Army's inadequacies and imposed a return to infantry fundamentals. He was thoroughly versed in the requirements of effective infantry combat. In the field, he wore his signature field dressing and a grenade on his chest. Almost twenty years later, he explained himself this way, as quoted approvingly by Cohen and Gooch:

> What I told the field commanders in essence was that their infantry ancestors would roll over in their graves could they see how roadbound this army was, how often it forgot to seize the high ground along its route, how it failed to seek and maintain contact in its front, how little it knew of the terrain and how seldom took advantage of it, how reluctant it was to get off its bloody wheels and put shoe leather to the earth, to get into the hills and among the scrub and meet the enemy where he lived. As for communications, I told them to go back to grandfather's day if they had to—to use runners if the radio and phones were out, or smoke signals if they could devise no better way.[42]

Ridgway over his first three months in command relieved one of his corps commanders, five of his six division commanders, and fourteen regimental commanders.[43] And he corrected basic infantry training weaknesses. He took a similarly ruthless attitude toward tightening up 8th Army's logistical systems, imposing discipline everywhere. With these kinds of remedial measures and without an infusion of more military forces except for replacements, Ridgway turned the situation around. He stabilized the lines, although not without first having to fall back to the Han River and letting Seoul be recaptured (the capital changing hands for the third time). Then, during the winter and spring of 1951, Ridgway began pushing north again, executing Operations *Ripper* and *Killer*.

15

OPERATIONS *RIPPER* AND *KILLER*

Recovery and Frustration

In a few months, Ridgway's dynamic command actions had turned the Korean War around. Strong, determined leadership went a long way.[1] Colonel Michaelis of the 27th Wolfhounds described Ridgway's assumption of command as "magic, the way Ridgway took that defeated army and turned it around. He was a breath of fresh air, a showman, what the army desperately needed."[2] Ridgway demanded that tactical commanders pay attention to terrain, assess key features of topography that could be defended, get off the roads, and take and hold the high ground. Ridgway and MacArthur both perceived the advantage of shortening UN supply lines after the retreat south of Seoul. The military initiative was about to change hands again.

As Ridgway was stabilizing the front, MacArthur pressed to extend the war across the border into China. In a long series of letters and cables to the JCS, CINCUNC argued for bombing the Yalu bridges and beyond. However, on December 29, 1950, the JCS issued a new directive that he could expect no further major reinforcements and that Korea was the wrong place to precipitate a major war. MacArthur was told to maintain the front as best he could with "successive positions." If the UN Command was forced back to the Kum River (map 15.1), then US forces might need to consider an evacuation of the Korean Peninsula, although Ridgway, more confident, was having none of this.

MacArthur continued to disagree with Washington, demanding a blockade of the Chinese coast, an air and naval bombardment of China's industrial capacity, reinforcement of UN forces with Chiang Kai Shek's Nationalist Chinese forces, and removal of all restrictions on Chiang to launch direct attacks against

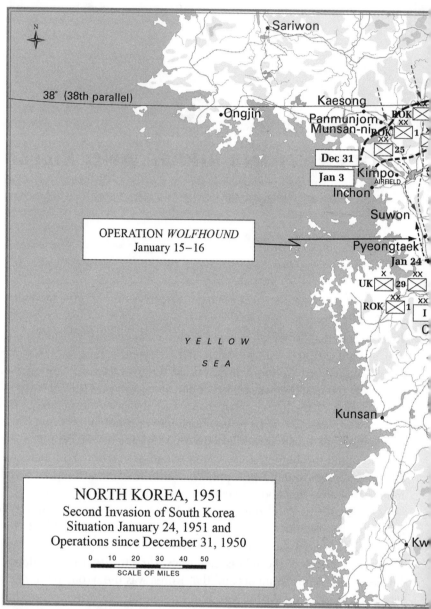

Map 15.1. The communist Chinese counteroffensive crossed the 38th parallel, and Seoul changed hands for the third time.
Source: USMA Atlases.

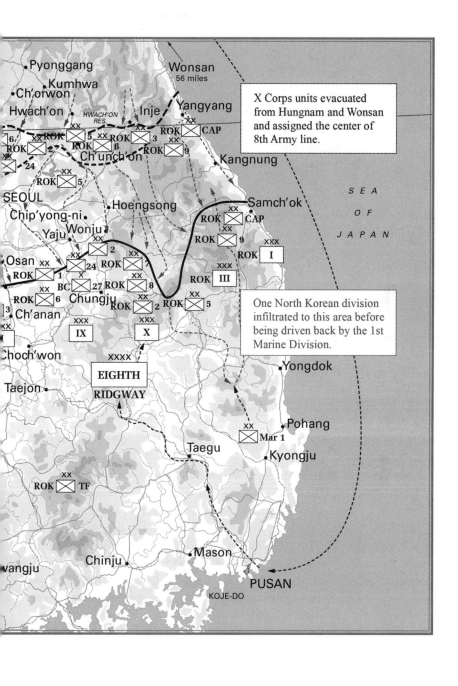

X Corps units evacuated
from Hungnam and Wonsan
and assigned the center of
8th Army line.

One North Korean division
infiltrated to this area before
being driven back by the 1st
Marine Division.

the Chinese mainland. The Joint Chiefs were getting two different impressions at this stage: MacArthur's pessimism and Ridgway's growing optimism. MacArthur was accurate in one assessment: there was no longer any realistic expectation of achieving a unified noncommunist Korea. Washington was basing its hopes on gaining sufficient military leverage at an acceptable level of casualties to 8th Army to force Peking and Pyongyang to negotiate a return to the prewar division of Korea. The UN remained focused on that objective from the winter of 1952 to the end of the war in 1953. Ridgway accepted this concept of a limited war to secure peace.

MacArthur did not accept this view of the war. He persisted for weeks in his steady stream of messages, eventually forcing to a head the crisis in civil-military relations that left President Truman with no choice but to respond decisively. MacArthur's letter to Speaker of the House Joseph W. Martin Jr., publicly disclosed on the floor of the House on April 5, 1951, with the famous phrase, "There is no substitute for victory," became an issue that no president could overlook.[3] The confrontation between Washington and Tokyo had become too public, and within a week Truman relieved MacArthur of all his commands. At the Senate hearing following MacArthur's relief from command, General Bradley testified that to have followed MacArthur's plan would involve the country "in the wrong war at the wrong place at the wrong time, and with the wrong enemy."[4]

This confrontation was public, but another was hidden. Aid's SIGINT research shows that AFSA code breakers were intercepting and decrypting political telegrams between General MacArthur and his chief of staff, Major General Charles Willoughby, and the ambassadors to the United States from Spain, Portugal, and Brazil. MacArthur and Willoughby candidly disclosed their extreme views on the USSR and the PRC. "Among the comments that MacArthur made was that he hoped the Soviets would intervene militarily in Korea, which he believed would give the United States the excuse to destroy once and for all Mao Tse Tung's regime. . . . MacArthur also told the foreign ambassadors that he thought war with Russia was inevitable."[5] These intercepts convinced President Truman that his commander in the Far East was not only ignoring orders from Washington but was also actively communicating with foreign diplomats without administration authorization or approval.

These acts of direct military insubordination would require any president to take action. MacArthur's public utterances were undermining the chain of command and therefore the strategic architecture for fighting a limited war. The relief of MacArthur stunned the American public, and the president's poll numbers "sank like a stone in the months that followed. By mid-1951, his approval ratings had plummeted to twenty-three percent, the lowest ever recorded by the Gallup Poll for a sitting American president."[6]

Ridgway's leadership in the winter of 1951 stiffened the UN lines south of Seoul. By January he had led UN forces back northward toward the Han River opposite the capital. In late February, he launched a series of colorfully named limited-objective attacks, including Operations *Killer* and *Ripper*. *Killer* closed up UN lines south of the Han by March, enabling Ridgway to recapture territory to secure stronger defensive positions.[7] On March 7, *Ripper* succeeded *Killer* with a measured advance that forced enemy evacuation of the capital. Seoul changed hands for the fourth time on March 14. *Ripper* forces advanced to a series of tactical phase lines. Another landmark was passed when ROK forces crossed the 38th parallel on March 27.

This time, however, there would not be another race to the Yalu. Ridgway's objective was merely to reach the Iron Triangle south of Pyongyang, the heart of the communist supply and communications network. By early April, UN forces had passed through more phase lines. Later the same month, the last major PLA offensive was turned back. By the late spring of 1951, the fighting stabilized along lines similar to those that mark the Korean DMZ today, with UN forces occupying north of the parallel on the eastern side and KPA-PLA forces occupying territory south of the parallel on the western side. This demarcation would be about where the war ended after frustrating negotiations and another two years of bloody fighting. Mostly it consisted of positional battles of attrition that remind many historians of World War I trench warfare.

The Korean War resulted in a military stalemate, ending near where it began. Was the war a loss for the UN and the United States? Many public figures viewed it as such, even while the fighting continued. MacArthur had argued for a complete victory and advocated attacking bases inside Manchuria that were supporting the KPA and PLA forces in the south. Truman, Acheson, most members of the Joint Chiefs, and certainly most governments that had dispatched forces and matériel to the UN Command feared that attacking the PRC would lead to a larger conflict that might trigger World War III.

As Bevin Alexander summarized the war, it was "exceeded in violence, death, destruction, and despair only by the First and Second World Wars." He concluded that

the United States—with the aid of South Korea and the support of some United Nations members—won one war against the North Koreans, and lost another war against the Red Chinese. The causes of these two wars were essentially and totally different. The North Koreans were bent on overt aggression and were thwarted. The Red Chinese were trying to protect their homeland from the potential threat of invasion and were successful.[8]

16

THE STRATEGIC ARCHITECTURES
OF THE KOREAN WAR

Accepting the constraints of a limited war was the reality for the combatant coalitions fighting the Korean War. Their strategic architectures required them to prevent a regional war from engulfing the whole international system. Indeed, Gallup polling between July 1950 and September 1951 revealed that half of the American population believed that the fighting in Korea was the beginning of the next world war.[1] No longer could the combatants view war as total in the sense that one side could comprehensively defeat the other—not with both sides possessing nuclear weapons. No one in 1950 understood what nuclear warfare might be like. Indeed, no one adequately knows to the present day how devastating a nuclear war would be except the inhabitants of Hiroshima and Nagasaki.

The preceding chapters on the Korean War show that the combatants had to draw clear boundaries around their policy, strategic, and operational choices during the conflict. The underlying reasoning of their policies for engagement, their choice of military strategies as the war became prolonged, and their execution of military operations show that the United States and the UN Command created a more realistic and effective strategic architecture, but at the terrible cost that by war's end no one was prepared to call a triumph.

NORTH KOREAN AND CHINESE (PRC)
STRATEGIC ARCHITECTURE

Kim Il Sung's aggression in June 1950 turned out to be a colossal misjudgment insofar as the expected geopolitical result of a Korea under a communist regime failed to appear. Like Hitler, he ignored Clausewitz's axiom that no sane statesman starts a war without first being clear as to its political viability and military feasibility. He wildly underestimated Truman's determination to resist. He equally failed to see that the United States would organize the resistance under the collective-security resolutions of an international organization. What had been at stake militarily between the combatants was the capacity to bear heavy costs in human lives and the ability of an Asian nation to match the technological superiority of the US Armed Forces. Mao, of course, knew the manpower demographics thoroughly. What distinguished Mao from his enemies was his willingness, like Stalin, to accept the calculus cold-bloodedly.

The Korean War was a war of miscalculation. Kim, Mao, and Stalin did not expect or plan for the speed, vehemence, and military effectiveness of the American reaction. Kim Il Sung underestimated the risks of invasion because he misconstrued Acheson's initial omission of South Korea inside the US Asian defensive perimeter in the Far East. It remains unclear whether he ever became privy to the insights of Philby's espionage. Stalin viewed Kim's invasion of the South as low risk for drawing in direct Soviet participation or strategic vulnerability to American nuclear weapons. Stalin had two Asian communist proxies to undertake the fighting and the dying. The war became a contest of prolonged attrition until Stalin's death in 1953.

The PLA successfully intervened after the first six months of the conflict in support of the routed KPA. They effectively combined Mao Tse Tung's guerrilla warfare with main-force attritional combat and capitalized on Sun Tzu's military concept of turning strengths into weaknesses. These tactics worked until Ridgway took over, restored defensive skills by focusing on infantry fundamentals, and regained the offensive initiative in early 1951.

US-UN COMMAND STRATEGIC ARCHITECTURE

The Truman administration, after the June 1950 surprise attack, failed to think through what the geopolitical reality of a reunified Korea would require with respect to military resources and risks. The administration had reacted immediately to the North Korean aggression, quickly mobilized UN support, secured resolutions for the UN Command during the Soviet self-imposed boycott of the Security Council, and conducted a diplomatic campaign that obtained military support from twenty-two countries. US and ROK forces were the principal allied combatants. The president, senior diplomats, military commanders, and intelligence officers failed to anticipate the PRC's reaction to a UN advance to the Yalu River.

Neither side had adequate intelligence of the other's strategic geopolitical intentions, although Stalin, with superior HUMINT assets, understood and exploited Acheson's reasons for not including Korea in the US Asian "defensive perimeter." He accepted Kim's assurances of a quick victory and was willing to take the risk and sustain communist combat losses if required. The United States never had clear insight into Stalin's or Mao's initial reluctance to enter the war or their early willingness to cut losses. Americans failed to read PRC diplomatic warnings correctly after Inchon. Lower-level SIGINT and COMINT military products were second-order effects, although they were tactically valuable to General Walker's defensive deployments around Pusan and MacArthur's execution of Inchon. The problem was that American military success after Inchon lacked a design for ending the war.

MacArthur's dominance of the meeting at Wake Island preempted such strategic discussion. No one really addressed how the communist leaders might react.[2] Mao was prepared to support Kim in a prolonged war of attrition.

Although many nations contributed manpower and matériel to the defense of South Korea, the United States and the ROK bore the brunt of the casualties and costs. Allied presence was not decisive because the Americans possessed technological advantages and, with the ROK Army, adequate combat manpower. However, the PLA's entry into the conflict, with the continued support of the USSR, meant that the PLA and Kim could commit to a strategy of continual attrition using China's large reserves of manpower.

General Walker's tenacious defensive battle at Pusan enabled MacArthur's Inchon success. General MacArthur planned and executed a military masterstroke at Inchon and then suffered a humiliating defeat after his overconfident advance to the Yalu. The JCS failed to get a firm grip on MacArthur's command autonomy and eventual confrontation with President Truman. The Truman administration failed to develop a coherent theory of bringing the Korean War to a satisfactory geopolitical conclusion except to restore the status quo, resulting in more than three years of costly fighting.

At the Wake Island meeting, Truman had an opportunity to review the strategic architecture in Korea and determine how to end the war. However, no one in a senior position was asking the right what-if questions and evaluating alternative outcome scenarios, particularly if the PRC intervened. Everyone accepted, however uneasily, MacArthur's commanding, post-Inchon confidence that the war was over except for mopping-up operations in the North. No one focused on bringing the war to an early resolution. US decision makers assumed that the UN Command held the military advantage and could impose a settlement based on MacArthur's seemingly total defeat of the KPA after the Inchon landing. Kim Il Sung and his PRC allies were not prepared to accept a US-ROK-reunified Korean Peninsula.

Initially, President Truman's dispatch of US forces to Korea drew high public approval because the administration appeared to occupy the high moral ground bolstered by UN resolutions grounded in collective-security principles. The heroic defense of the Pusan Perimeter and the Inchon counterstroke happened within a four-month period, and opinion polling reflected high confidence in a victorious outcome. That was the kind of expectation to which Americans only five years before had grown accustomed. When the war became protracted and casualties mounted, the Truman administration's strategic architecture of an attrition war was no longer sustainable. It had not prepared the American people for a long, limited conflict because, after Inchon, it did not expect one. That was a strategic mistake. A war without clearly defined military and political benchmarks, directed toward a nebulous outcome for an independent South Korea, is a difficult case to argue compellingly in the language of a police action. By 1953 as the Eisenhower administration was about to assume office, only 36 percent of the American public supported an unpopular war. This would be the first but not the last time Americans would grow weary of postwar conflicts.

By the spring of 1951, the Korean War was a military stalemate. General Van Fleet had by this time taken over command of 8th Army from Ridgway. General Van Fleet had created a reserve position north of Seoul, the "No-Name Line," after the British 29th Infantry Brigade had fought a heroic stand along the Imjin River until they had to withdraw in April.[3] The Chinese offensive momentum in the wake of Operations *Ripper* and *Killer* had been spent. Yet the PLA continued to reinforce failure. In April and May of 1951, Marshal Peng Te' Huai launched a new offensive known as the Fifth Phase Offensive with a plan for two converging thrusts to break through the UN line and encircle the 8th Army divisions one by one. Mao and Marshal Peng were intent on winning more victories on the battlefield before serious cease-fire negotiations began. Carter Malkasian's history points out that the communist willingness to enter into negotiations and fight a limited war marked their abandonment of Kim Il Sung's goal of reunifying Korea. General Van Fleet's success in stopping Peng's Fifth Phase Offensive "laid the basis for a negotiated settlement to the conflict."[4] Along this front, with minor tactical changes at various locations limited to a few miles, the UN Command would hold the line for the remaining two years of the war.

Both sides had to acknowledge the changed military and geopolitical realities in Korea. Americans discovered a painful new lesson that would repeat itself a generation later: war can be waged doggedly and determinedly at a negotiating table while carnage continues to pile up on the battlefields of a country neither side regarded as strategic for national survival. Mao and Peng realized that the losses they had incurred since January 1951 meant that the UN Command could not be decisively defeated.

Given the strategy and tactics both sides were using, neither side could prevail militarily. The debacle of the 8th Army in driving north to the Yalu resulted from a failure to anticipate the probable behavior of the enemy and a failure of operational learning. After Ridgway stabilized the defensive line, the ensuing battles of attrition during the drawn-out armistice negotiations left both parties essentially with the same territorial domains with which the conflict began.

In July 1951, talks began at the communist-proposed site of Kaesong; by August 22, the talks had gotten nowhere, having been "dragged down into a morass of ideological rhetoric and empty irrationality."[5] The talks lasted five weeks, as both sides dug into defensive positions. The Chinese dug trenches and tunnels into the hillsides, over 155 miles from coast to coast across Korea, creating a front of fortified positions, manned by 855,000 men, that were nearly impregnable to artillery fire and assaults. Successive lines were constructed in some places between fifteen to twenty-five miles in depth. Talks began a second time at Panmunjom in a no-man's land between the combatant forces. Van Fleet was ordered to desist from major offensive action and limit UN forces to defense of the MLR. Local attacks were permissible, but operations of more than one battalion required authorization from Ridgway.

The Chinese contented themselves with a correct perception of war weariness among the United States and its UN allies. The negotiations ground on interminably through wrangling over each side's treatment and return of prisoners, with embarrassing revelations of communist brainwashing of American POWs. General Van Fleet handed over command of 8th Army to General Taylor. Both generals were distinguished World War II veterans. To them, defeat and victory had been absolutes in their previous combat experience. Van Fleet expressed particular frustration because he believed that 8th Army had the combat power to breach the MLR and eventually roll it up. Between the summers of 1951 and 1953, under the strategic architecture of a limited war, that outcome was remote. Neither Washington nor the UN member capitals would entertain such a plan.

The PLA undertook a series of local attacks to test the UN Command's will along the MLR as the Panmunjom negotiations reached the final phase. These attacks resulted in some of the war's bitterest fighting, connected to names like "Old Baldy" and "Pork Chop Hill," the former a hilltop in the middle of the Korean Peninsula that possessed no particular strategic significance during the summer and fall of 1952. A company-size position established in 1952, this outpost's nickname came from its shape on a map. Pork Chop became emblematic of the combat actions fought during the war's final eighteen months. The Chinese launched three major attacks in 1953 to take the outpost, and the third attack in early July was the heaviest. The 7th ID rotated five infantry battalions in five days through the position to hold it, with the assistance of tremendous amounts of artillery fire. With the Chinese apparently determined to take the outpost at whatever cost and the Korean War armistice imminent, General Taylor concluded that the cost of holding Pork Chop was not worth the price in small-unit casualties. He ordered the position abandoned two weeks before the armistice was signed.[6]

World War II veterans dominated the military leadership on both sides of the Korean War. General MacArthur was the dominant figure among them, but those who served under him or succeeded in senior positions had mainly served in Europe: Walker, Almond, Ridgway, Van Fleet, Clark, and Taylor. Senior marine officers, of course, had served mostly in the Pacific. Hastings quoted one unnamed senior officer, a veteran of both the Korean and Vietnam Wars, this way: "We went into Korea with a very poor army, and came out with a pretty good one. We went into Vietnam with a pretty good army, and came out with a terrible one."[7]

The post–World War II downsizing produced deep deficits in manpower, combat readiness, training, leadership, and equipment. The recovery of the military initiative inside the Pusan Perimeter and at Inchon was a short-lived recovery from disaster. What happened to the 8th Army advancing to the Yalu and then retreating south of Seoul in less than three months set the stage for a second recovery by General Ridgway, who possessed the hardened experience of a World War II combat infantryman. As an airborne commander, he brought with him an obsession for better tactical intelligence. He peppered his staff with questions about the Chinese enemy: How many miles can they move at night? How flexible are their tactical plans once a battle begins? How much ammunition and food do PLA soldiers require per day? How long can they sustain an offensive? What he really wanted to know was how UN forces could shape the battle space to their advantage.[8]

Like Walker, Ridgway flew over the battle areas after Unsan in a small reconnaissance plane looking for the enemy. His discovery that they were invisible only increased his respect for them. He built a profile of how the Chinese operated and fought and how he intended to fight them. The PLA operated with significant logistical and communications deficits. The bugles, flutes, and loudspeakers in the middle of the night might be terrifying to inexperienced UN troops, but the fact that the PLA fought with the ammunition and food it could carry and was using musical instruments to communicate meant that they could not exploit sudden, unexpected changes in a tactical situation. The US Army could resupply its frontline units in a way impossible for the Chinese, who lacked an air force that could impose air superiority and who had few tanks and artillery. Equally advantageous, the UN forces could communicate in real time with radios and telephones that were interconnected to company, battalion, regiment, and division headquarters; airborne ground support squadrons; and offshore fleet bombardment units in ways inconceivable to the Chinese.

The 8th Army's recovery, refusing to retreat when surrounded, ensuring that its flanks were covered, and paying attention to the details of coordinated moving, shooting, and communicating was the essence of a lethal World War II combat division in Europe. In these respects, according to

Hastings, Halberstam, and Cumings, Korea was a dress rehearsal for Vietnam less than a quarter century later.

The combatants fielded different kinds of armies during the Korean War. The North Koreans sent a Russian-trained-and-equipped conventional force into the South across the 38th parallel. The Chinese People's Liberation Army that entered the conflict six months later bore striking similarities to the kind of army Sun Tzu imagined. Ridgway's 8th Army had to relearn the World War II infantry fundamentals. It was not the same army that had triumphed in 1945. It was a downsized, peacetime, garrison army that had to relearn the lessons that its predecessors had learned the hard way in Europe and the Pacific. Know the enemy and the weaknesses of his tactics. Study the terrain of the battle space. Walk; don't ride near or on a battlefield. Take and hold the high ground. Dig in everywhere. Leverage combined-arms assets and practice the orchestration of moving, shooting, and communicating.

Diplomacy was a weak contributor to the development of a coherent American Korean War strategy. Early UN Security Council resolutions were ambiguous on specific war aims. Resolutions 82 and 83 condemned the DPRK's aggression, called for an immediate cessation of hostilities, and proposed that UN members "repel the armed attack and restore international peace and security in the area." Joseph C. Goulden points out that in the early days the Truman administration in both its public and private declarations displayed no desire to take the war beyond South Korea. Truman told the National Security Council (NSC) on June 29, 1950, that he "wanted it clearly understood that our operations in Korea were designed to restore peace there and to restore the border." As the American military commitment deepened, debate developed about whether the United States could use defeat of the KPA as an opportunity to enforce postwar UN resolutions on Korean unification. The State Department was divided on this issue. This debate was never subjected to focused discussion and argument to force resolution. A State memorandum of July 25 asserted, "It is unlikely that the Kremlin at present would accept the establishment of a regime which it could not dominate and control." It further warned that UN military action north of the parallel might "result in conflict with the USSR or Communist China" and foresaw a reluctance of UN member states to attempt unification. After identifying these downsides, the memo muddied the issue by recommending that no unification decision be made until the military and political situations clarified.[9]

When President Truman dispatched US forces to Korea in June 1950, 78 percent of Americans said they approved of the decision, and 15 percent disapproved. By February 1951, with the 8th Army pushed back south of Seoul, public support had eroded. When Americans were first asked about the Korean War in August 1950, 65 percent supported the war. By January 1951, public opinion had shifted dramatically: nearly half thought the war was a mistake, only 38 percent said it was not, and 13 percent had no opinion. A data plot of eight opinion polls thereafter indicated considerable fluctuation, with the "it was a mistake" percentage ranging from 37 percent (April 14, 1951) to 50 percent (February 26, 1952) and dropping to 36 percent (January 9, 1953) as President Eisenhower was about to assume office.[10]

The protracted nature of the attrition warfare after the spring of 1951, the frustrations of the truce talks, and the resulting military stalemate created limited opportunities for the Truman administration to design a winning strategic architecture for fighting a limited war. Truman's police-action phraseology was not the basis for a compelling architecture. MacArthur's "there is no substitute for victory" declaration became for many an emotional leitmotif that persists to the present day.

ENDING THE KOREAN WAR

The Korean War finally ended in July 1953. Left in its wake were four million Korean casualties, 10 percent of the population. Five million more became refugees. Korea's industrial base was wiped out. North Korea's armed forces lost six hundred thousand men in the fighting, in addition to two million casualties. The Chinese suffered one million casualties. Losses to the ROK armed forces are estimated at 70,000 killed, 150,000 wounded, and 80,000 captured, the majority of whom died from starvation or mistreatment. One million South Korean civilians were killed or injured. The armed forces of the United States lost 33,600 Americans, 103,200 wounded.[11] Several historians, including Hastings, Halberstam, and Leckie, described it as the "forgotten war"; Cumings described it as the "unknown war." Whatever the description, it was a limited war, fought for limited purposes, and it resulted in a limited outcome. Given the high casualties on both sides, it was difficult for many to assert flatly for many years after the armistice that the conflict was worth even a small fraction of those lives.

In the decades after the Vietnam War, the pessimistic view of the deficits of the Korean War began to change profoundly. The communist regime that survived in the North is now regarded almost universally as an international pariah with an impoverished, undernourished population. South Korea has evolved into one of the most successful democratic, capitalist nations in the world, with a population of nearly fifty million free and prosperous citizens, a record of constitutional and peaceable changes of government, and a $1.85 trillion GDP in 2015,[12] exporting products that are household names globally. For those who fought and died there, these geopolitical facts must now weigh in the historical scales. Fighting to a stalemate in the Korean War yielded a geopolitical success. The Republic of Korea nearly seventy years later is a sovereign, prosperous "tiger" on the Pacific Rim. South Korea's security is still dependent on the presence of the armed forces of the United States deployed there.

Korean War

(1) South Koreans fleeing from the battle zone as American soldiers march to the front early in the Korean War in August 1950. LOC photo (2) Sixteen-inch salvo from the battleship *Missouri* at Chong Jin, Korea, in effort to cut North Korean communications near the PRC border on October 21, 1950. NARA photo

(3) General MacArthur watches the attack on Inchon from the USS *Mount McKinley* on September 15, 1950. US Army photo

Korean War

(4) Marines landing at Inchon on September 15, 1950. USMC photo (5) Wreckage of bridge and enemy tank south of Suwon after air strike, US Army photo on October 7, 1950. (6) Marine at the crest of a ridge near Chosin Reservoir in Korean winter of 1950. NARA photos

(7) UN forces retreat from Pyongyang, recrossing the 38th parallel having earlier crossed it on the offensive north. (8) F-86 Sabre jets searching for communist MiG-15s over mountains of North Korea on October 19, 1950. NARA photos

PART IV

THE VIETNAM WAR

The enduring question of the Vietnam War is explaining how a revolutionary movement was victorious over a thirty-year period between 1945 and 1975 despite the considerable efforts of two Western powers, first France and then the United States, to defeat it. For more than a decade, the American military, naval, and air forces executed combat missions in support of the armed forces of South Vietnam, which numbered over one million men under arms by 1971. How and why did this massive effort fail? That is the persisting conundrum. It dominates the growing number of titles that have been published since the late 1960s about this controversial conflict.[1]

As it did in Korea, the Cold War left Vietnam divided. After Ho Chi Minh[2] defeated the French in 1954[3] with General Vo Nguyen Giap's victory at Dien Bien Phu, the Geneva Accords partitioned the country with a DMZ at the 17th parallel (map IV.1).[4] Ho then established a communist state in the north, while the Americans sought to find an anticommunist alternative in the south. The United States finally settled in 1954 on Ngo Dinh Diem. Diem was an exile, like Syngman Rhee, untainted by cooperation with the French colonial power. Diem, also like Rhee and Chiang Kai Shek, was an authoritarian. By the early 1960s, Diem's Government of (South) Vietnam (GVN) had become vulnerable. The GVN was the target for renewed action by the southern National Liberation Front (NLF), a revolutionary movement, popularly known as the Viet Cong (an abbreviation of *Cong San Viet Nam*, which means Vietnamese Communist). Diem, aware that US credibility was on the line, emulated the examples of Rhee and Chiang and warned that his regime

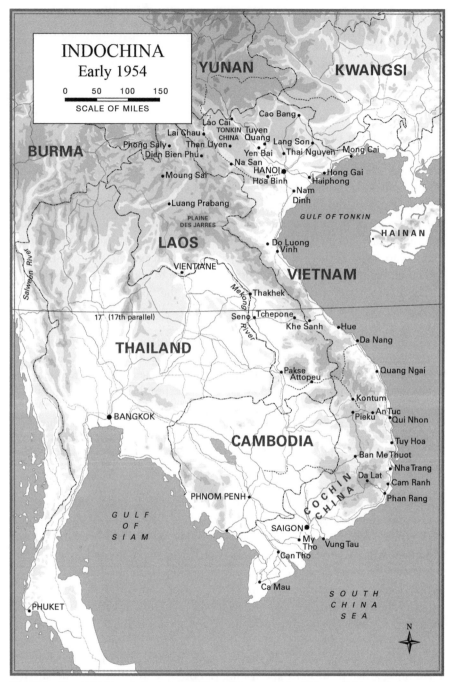

might fail without increased American support. The strategic architecture that the United States designed and implemented at enormous cost between 1955 and 1975 ended in failure.

POLICY

Five consecutive presidencies designed and executed failed policies in response to Diem's warning that the GVN would fail without American political, economic, and military support. What the Eisenhower, Kennedy, Johnson, Nixon, and Ford administrations all shared was the policy illusion that the United States "could reshape Vietnamese politics through persuasion and the commitment of resources [including the massive deployment by President Johnson of land, air, and sea forces], when, in fact, it was the South Vietnamese client who wielded the influence over its American patron who had invested too much blood, treasure and political credibility to allow the GVN to fail."[5]

The Eisenhower administration introduced the "falling domino" thesis in April 1954 at a press conference:

> Finally, you have broader considerations that might follow what you would call the "falling domino" principle. You have a row of dominoes set up, you knock over the first one, and what will happen to the last one is the certainty that it will go over very quickly . . . when we come to the possible sequence of events, the loss of Indochina [would lead to the fall] of Burma, of Thailand, of the [Malay] Peninsula, and Indonesia. . . . Finally, the geographical position achieved thereby does many things. It turns the so-called island defensive chain of Japan, Formosa, of the Philippines and to the southward; it moves in to threaten Australia and New Zealand.[6]

When John F. Kennedy succeeded Eisenhower in January 1961, he inherited a deteriorating situation in Southeast Asia. The Army of the Republic of Vietnam (ARVN) numbered 150,000 troops, which had been raised and equipped with American aid since 1950 and had been advised by a Military Assistance Advisory Group (MAAG). Despite American assistance, the ARVN had seriously underperformed when the Central Committee of the Vietnamese Communist Party formed the National Liberation Front in 1959 and launched a campaign to overthrow the Diem government. President John F. Kennedy's inaugural speech offered ringing rhetoric: "Let every nation know, whether it wishes us well or ill, that we shall pay any price, bear any burden, meet any hardship, support any friend, oppose any foe to assure the survival and the success of liberty."[7] The Kennedy administration developed the concept of "flexible response" to counter communist aggression on any level of conflict, including operations that would soon be labeled counterinsurgency (COIN).[8] The keys to combating communist insurgency were sufficient political will, winning "the battle for hearts and minds" through good governance and creating a national identity, psychological operations, and the application of force by police and indigenous forces. Victory would flow from the centralized coordination of resources by the client state on all fronts to win over the population with a comprehensive civil-military program of nation building.[9] President Kennedy, in a CBS interview with Walter Cronkite on September 3, 1963, underscored that COIN success depended on the efficacy of Vietnam as an American client state:

> In the final analysis, it is their war. They are the ones who have to win it or lose it. We can help them, we can give them equipment, we can send our men out there as advisers, but they have to win it—the people of Vietnam—against the communists.[10]

Two months after this interview, Diem, despite his many accomplishments as South Vietnam's first president—including winning the Battle of Saigon in April 1954 and defeating the Binh Xuyen organized crime syndicate,[11] passing a land reform statute, and implementing the Strategic Hamlet Program—was deposed and executed by a military coup d'état on November 2, 1963.[12]

The succeeding administration of Lyndon B. Johnson soon decided on a policy of not only direct military support of the GVN but also a massive deployment of American combat forces. It was a military commitment that at its peak in 1968 consisted of the deployment of more than twelve divisions,[13] major fleet carrier and surface units of the US Navy's 7th Fleet,[14] and US Air Force fighter and bomber wings from three separate numbered air forces.[15] This military commitment also included massive, direct participation by American construction contractors in Vietnam. The US government in 1962 engaged a joint venture, RMK-BRJ, to provide construction services under the auspices of the US Naval Facilities Engineering Command. From 1962 to 1972, RMK-BRJ[16] employed more than two hundred thousand Vietnamese to construct bridges, highways, jet airfields, hospitals, deepwater ports, communications facilities, water supply systems, power plants, supply depots, and other logistical facilities and infrastructure. The venture worked on projects totaling $1.9 billion,[17] equivalent to $14 billion in 2016 buying power.[18]

This decision for direct military intervention was made in the mid-1960s after numerous visits and reports prepared by military and civilian leaders in the Defense and State Departments.[19] The coup that overthrew Diem had been undertaken with American approval under the expectation that Diem's removal would strengthen the South Vietnamese government.[20] That was not the result, however. By 1964 the revolutionary movement had established bases and sanctuaries from the northernmost tier of provinces near the 17th parallel, south through the Central Highlands of the Annamite Cordillera, and into the Mekong River delta. "The Viet Cong had obtained 200,000 US weapons by mid-1964. Meanwhile, Viet Cong terrorism [had grown] steadily."[21]

A decade after President Eisenhower posited the domino theory, President Johnson continued to use it to buttress his own policy statements. However, when he posed an intelligence question to the CIA in 1964 about the validity of the domino thesis, the agency's response was inconclusive.[22] The domino thesis was irrelevant to the issue of whether the GVN could create effective governance sufficient to defeat the revolutionary movement. Johnson's policies, backed by the largest overseas military deployment of the armed forces of the United States since World War II, failed in the judgment of the American public in early 1968 after the communists launched the Tet Offensive.

The succeeding administration of Richard M. Nixon implemented a policy of Vietnamization that was designed in response to the reduced domestic support for the war and the need to find a more effective strategy for reducing levels of military commitment. Vietnamization, too, would fail. In April 1975, the GVN collapsed in the face of a North Vietnamese invasion, after more than two decades of massive American military and economic support and the sacrifice of more than fifty-eight thousand American lives.

STRATEGY

The Vietnam War was a policy failure; it was also a strategic failure because policy makers and military decision makers failed to achieve a sufficiently pragmatic and realistic understanding of their enemy.

During the first Indochina War that ended in 1954, Dien Bien Phu became the decisive battle. General Giap was able to shift from a Phase 2 guerrilla insurgency to a Phase 3 conventional-type conflict in a matter of a few months in the winter and spring of 1954. American students of military history who studied this battle readily understood why the Viet Minh won it because its elements were intelligible within the framework of conventional warfare.[23] After Dien Bien Phu fell, popular support in the French Fourth Republic collapsed for holding on to Indochina as a colonial possession. The Geneva Accords, instead of resolving the conflict, triggered a new one that devolved back to a Phase 1 revolutionary conflict, where the Viet Minh survivors in South Vietnam began rebuilding the movement in 1955. The revolutionary movement succeeded twenty years later with a conventional invasion of the South employing twenty North Vietnamese Army (NVA) divisions.[24] How did they win?

Recent scholarship challenges the roles played by Ho and Giap in the final victory in 1975. Lien-Hang T. Nguyen's careful examination of North Vietnam

National Archives reveals a heretofore obscure figure, Le Duan, as the "architect, main strategist, and commander in chief" of North Vietnam's victory.[25] Le Duan emerges from the historical shadows, along with his right-hand man, Le Duc Tho (later chief negotiator at the Paris Peace Talks), as the dominant player in Vietnam War leadership. Le Duan was a Vietnamese communist politician and a founding member of the Indochina Communist Party in 1930. By 1969, he had risen to the dominant leadership position of the North Vietnam Worker's Party (*Dang Lao Dong Viet Nam*) as general secretary of the Central Committee of the Communist Party of Vietnam. He never held a formal position in the government of North Vietnam. Le Duan was a bland figure; he knew he lacked the grandfatherly charisma of Ho or the military prowess of Giap. After Ho's death in 1969, it was Le Duan who outmaneuvered rivals and manipulated the Sino-Soviet split to advantage during the 1972 Sino-American rapprochement and American-Soviet détente. He remained resolute that North and South would be united under a communist military victory and succeeded in defeating both the United States and the Republic of Vietnam.

Le Duan wrote one of the leading tracts about revolution in South Vietnam. He was a firm believer that "defeat of the enemy militarily is indispensable for the victory of the resistance and the revolution."[26] He would play key leadership roles in the initiation of the 1968 Tet Offensive, the 1972 Easter Offensive, and the victorious 1975 offensive drive south that ended at the Presidential Palace in Saigon.[27] Le Duan and Le Duc Tho both knew that signing the Paris Accords in 1973 meant nothing. For them, the end of the Vietnam War was North Vietnam's military victory in 1975.

Mao Tse Tung, Ho Chi Minh, and Vo Nguyen Giap had written extensively about the strategy, stages, and tactics of revolution and the political and military requirements for success. The writings of Mao and Giap provided the conceptual framework of a people's war.[28] As theoreticians and dogmatists, they knew Sun Tzu's emphasis on the asymmetry of strength and weakness. They presented revolutionary conflict as a social process that develops in three phases: initially an organizational phase, then a period of sustained guerrilla warfare, and finally overt military confrontation once the balance of forces between the revolutionary movement and government forces permits open and successful conventional warfare.

What Americans could not learn from these writings was the behavioral dynamics of the revolutionary social process itself. Very few possessed the linguistic skills and historical knowledge to learn why and how the revolutionary movement succeeded in making deep inroads into Vietnamese rural society during the early phases. Few grasped how a communist movement operated and succeeded in its own game of winning hearts and minds. The communist tracts about revolution and people's war did not translate revolutionary theory into operational practice.

What policies did the movement create to motivate a sufficient number of rural Vietnamese to risk death in combat? One American junior officer who had learned Vietnamese as he was shipping out in 1965 started to find answers to this question simply because he was observant and intensely curious. A newly minted ROTC army lieutenant from the Harvard class of 1965, Jeffrey Race, who served two combat tours in Vietnam, explained the behavioral dynamics of the revolutionary movement in a seminal book published in 1972.

Race was the first to offer a comprehensive, coherent explanation "of the victory in a single province of Vietnam of a revolutionary social movement, led by a communist party, using the techniques of people's war."[29] Race's work deserves close attention because it uniquely reveals how both sides viewed revolutionary conflict in Vietnam. Examining Race's explanation of how both sides developed concepts for fighting the Vietnam War reveals how and why the American strategic architecture was doomed to failure.

The province to which Race refers in his title, *War Comes to Long An*, is in the Mekong River delta, located southwest of Saigon, with a population at the time of 350,000 in a country with a population of approximately sixteen million. Long An reaches across South Vietnam at one of its narrowest geographical points, from the Rung Sat (Jungle of Death) on the east coast to the Plain of Reeds where it meets the Cambodian border in the west (map IV.2). Studying the map reveals that the Americans and Vietnamese divided South Vietnam into four Corps Tactical Zones (CTZs) numbered I through IV.[30]

Race explained that he selected Long An because it was strategically important to both sides in the conflict. Historically, the province was a source of Viet Minh strength. GVN control of the Rung Sat was necessary to prevent enemy forces from attacking lines of communications into Saigon, or the capital itself, from their bases in the Rung Sat and the Plain of Reeds. All international shipping had to pass through the Rung Sat to reach the port of Saigon. Cutting completely across the country, from Cambodia to the South China Sea, Long An sits athwart the fertile rice-producing provinces of the Mekong delta, separating those provinces from the rest of the country. An enemy capable of interdicting the water and land routes between the heart of the Mekong delta and the rest of the country possesses two advantages. It can separate the country from its richest food-producing areas and everything farther north and also be in a "commanding position either to attack the capital or to starve it, or both."[31]

When Race's *War Comes to Long An* first appeared, his concepts elicited hostility from many in officialdom. He encountered resistance to his conclusions. Indeed, during the 1970s, he argues it was willful.[32] This state of affairs would persist for another generation.[33] However, his work has withstood the test of time and is now part of the curriculum of US military service schools. Evidence for the continuing credibility of *War Comes to Long An* is its listing in the US Army's Command and General Staff College "Military Classics"

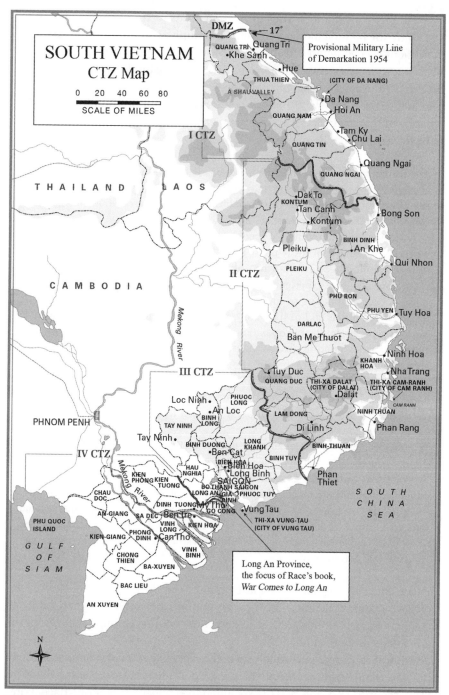

SOUTH VIETNAM
CTZ Map

0 20 40 60 80
SCALE OF MILES

DMZ — 17°

Provisional Military Line
of Demarkation 1954

QUANG TRI Quang Tri
• Khe Sanh
• Hue
THUA THIEN   (CITY OF DA NANG)
A SHAU VALLEY
                              • Da Nang
QUANG NAM   • Hoi An
                              • Tam Ky
I CTZ   QUANG TIN • Chu Lai
                              • Quang Ngai
                              QUANG NGAI

THAILAND   LAOS
                              Dak To
                              KONTUM
                              • Tan Canh   • Bong Son
                              • Kontum
                                        BINH DINH
                              Pleiku • • An Khe
CAMBODIA   PLEIKU
                   II CTZ   • Qui Nhon
                              PHU BON
                                        PHU YEN • Tuy Hoa
                              DARLAC
                              Ban Me Thuot
                                                 • Ninh Hoa
                                        KHANH
III CTZ   HOA   • Nha Trang
                   • Tuy Duc   THI-XA DALAT   THI-XA CAM-RANH
                   QUANG DUC (CITY OF DALAT) (CITY OF CAM RANH)
Loc Ninh •   PHUOC   • Dalat
        • An Loc LONG   LAM DONG CAM RANH
PHNOM PENH BINH   • Di Linh NINH THUAN
         TAY NINH LONG   • Phan Rang
   Tay Ninh • BINH DUONG LONG   BINH-THUAN
IV CTZ   • Ben Cat KHANH
            HAU BIEN HOA BINH TUY
            NGHIA • Bien Hoa
        KIEN   • Long Binh • Phan
        PHONG KIEN SAIGON   Thiet
        TUONG BO-THANH SAIGON
   CHAU   LONG AN GIA- PHUOC TUY   SOUTH
   DOC   DINH   • Vung Tau CHINA
   AN-GIANG DINH TUONG My Tho   SEA
PHU QUOC SA DEC • Ben Tre GO CONG
ISLAND   VINH KIEN HOA THI-XA VUNG-TAU
   KIEN-GIANG PHONG LONG (CITY OF VUNG TAU)
GULF   DINH • Can Tho
OF   CHONG   VINH
SIAM   THIEN   BINH
        BA-XUYEN   Long An Province,
                         the focus of Race's book,
        BAC LIEU   War Comes to Long An

   AN XUYEN

N

Map IV.2. The Americans divided South Vietnam into four Corps Tactical Zones (CTZs) numbered I–IV.
Source: USMA Atlases.

bibliography with the following annotation on its website: "This is an instructive study for understanding why the Communist-guided revolutionary social movement succeeded in a Vietnamese province and why the American-South Vietnamese counterrevolutionary initiative consistently failed. Race uses firsthand information, but his perspective is balanced; he lets his extensive research speak for itself."[34] Race's book is also listed as a "classic" in the bibliography of the army's latest COIN manual.[35]

In Race's preface, he observed,

> The reader will find few evil or incompetent characters in this book, but rather an account of how such a revolutionary movement was able to gain victory despite the efforts of a considerable number of honest and conscientious men, acting according to their best understanding.
>
> The desirability of [writing] a [book] such as this occurred to me during 1967, while I was serving in the United States Army as an adviser to a Vietnamese district chief in Phuoc Tuy province, about sixty miles southeast of Saigon. It was clear from my army experience that my fellow officers and I frequently had to make decisions affecting people's lives with an insufficient understanding both of actual conditions and of the nature of the conflict itself of which we were a part. The models implicit in operational doctrines seemed inadequate to account for the events around us, just as the programs we were charged with executing seemed an inadequate response to these events.[36]

In chapter 4, "Lessons from Long An," Race assesses the competing strategies between the revolutionary movement and the GVN:

> If a single factor could explain the victory of the revolutionary movement in Long An, it could be stated as the communist leadership's *comprehensive view of revolution as a stage-by-stage social process* [italics in original]. The sophistication of communist strategic thought was never matched on the government side. Instead, the government's one-dimensional conception of a multidimensional process ensured its defeat, regardless of its resources. Its strategy—to the extent it could be said to have had one—was simply a strategy of defeat. The communist strategy was a strategy of victory.[37]

Race came to this conclusion after tracing the development of the revolutionary movement in Long An through hundreds of interviews and captured documents in a bottom-up effort to depict the conflict through the eyes of the participants on both sides.

Race walks his reader through several concepts central to communist revolutionary thought: the concepts of class, contradiction, force and balance of forces, security, and victory.[38] In explaining the concept of security, Race writes one particularly helpful passage that distinguishes conventional war concepts from revolutionary ones:

In a tactical sense, any terrain, any installation, or any group of people can be secured by a sufficient concentration of military forces. While this foundation of security may be valid for a limited number of pieces of terrain, installations, or groups of people, it obviously cannot be valid when applied to a whole theater or national unit. There is a logical contradiction in "concentrating one's forces everywhere," because concentrating means centralizing dispersed forces in a limited number of locations. Thus security as it applies to a theater or national unit must have a different foundation.

And then Race gets to the heart of the matter:

> The foundation of security in a strategic sense is a *sympathetic environment* [italics in original], that is, an environment (the population) composed of sympathetic elements, from which the hostile elements have been removed. It can be seen that a sympathetic environment throughout the theater of operations leads to the same result as would the concentration of forces "everywhere," but at much lower cost, because the network of sympathizers [the villagers] reveals the location of enemy forces. By doing so it makes possible [for the revolutionary movement] a flexible use of forces that can disperse to avoid attack or concentrate to defend against, or to conduct, an attack.[39]

This description fits Mao's metaphor of the revolutionary fish swimming in the sea. The sea was the rural population; most of them were rice farmers by and large indifferent to the communists, except where incentives altered such indifference, and some (probably well under 10 percent) who were sympathetic to the movement's policies.

Race wrote that the communist leadership's acts of assassination, execution, threat, kidnapping, and military violence were generally epiphenomena (second-order, not first-order, effects) of a larger program of social change. The communists, whether South Vietnamese, NLF, Viet Cong, or North Vietnamese, used violence selectively and strategically to create popular sympathies favoring one side over the other. The communist leadership's use of "preemptive" policies such as land redistribution, progressive taxation, and decentralization of political authority appealed to the majority of villagers. All of Race's respondents involved with the movement, and some of the GVN officials he interviewed, identified these policies as reasons for the revolutionary movement's popular appeal. Of particular focus was the movement's success at motivating participants it succeeded in recruiting.

To explain motivation, Race developed the concept of a "contingent incentive," which he defined as an incentive that is contingent both on certain kinds of behavior by the target individual and on the continued existence of the sponsoring organization, the revolutionary movement.[40] For example, if a villager wanted to receive land, he had to support the revolutionary movement. If a young man wanted to avoid the government's national draft, he would receive protection from the NLF (removal to a hidden safe haven when government recruiters were about to enter the countryside) so long as he was willing to fight for the movement when called.

The GVN had its own land redistribution policies for the villagers of Long An, but Diem's land reform was rigidly administered under an inflexible law promulgated in Saigon, resulting in landholding and tenancy patterns that benefited far fewer villagers.[41] The NLF devolved its redistributive authority down to the village level, where policies directly affected rural taxation, the administration of justice, and military recruitment. The communist land redistribution policy offered an incentive to the individual villager that was contingent on his behavior: he got land only as long as he assisted the movement in required, specified ways, such as by not serving as a government spy, paying rural taxes to the movement (lower than GVN taxes), and allowing a male son to serve in the NLF when called. Failure to meet these requirements resulted in land forfeiture. Moreover, the incentive was contingent on the movement's retaining control of the rural village. If the GVN pushed the movement out, the land was also forfeit. So villager retention of newly redistributed land was closely tied to the NLF's success in maintaining its political influence and control of the rural area.

The movement implemented similar preemptive policies with respect to promotion and status within its political and military organizations. GVN village and hamlet officials were already at the peak of their career paths. Above the village chief were the district chief and province chief and their staffs appointed by the central government. By the late 1960s, military officers and civil servants mostly populated these key administrative positions in GVN provinces. Advancement above the village level required either the requisite civil service rank or entry into the military officer corps. Acquisition of such rank was conditional upon holding the equivalent of a French baccalaureate. Entry into either the civil service or officer ranks was effectively limited to the urban middle and upper classes and the rural landlord and rich peasant classes. "That meant that the overwhelming majority of the rural population was simply excluded from power over the decisions affecting their own lives. Instead, power was exercised by those social elements who were least capable of empathizing with the rural population, and whose personal interests were in conflict with those they ruled."[42]

By contrast, the communist revolutionary movement created a vertical, meritocratic career structure both for its military and for political cadres. Promotions, often frequent given attrition in the ranks, were awarded as the result of demonstrated performance. The positive perception of the movement's promotional policies effectively exploited this fundamental government vulnerability. Race documented other policies exploiting government vulnerabilities arising from the movement's rural "redistribution of values": policies

of localized "assimilation of forces" (local recruitment, deployment, and logistics versus GVN recruitment and posting of military recruits away from their
home districts) and policies of "provocation and protection" (provoking the
government into repressive and violent actions in response to the revolutionary movement's deliberate, calculated acts of selective violence).

The GVN presence in Long An never clearly identified the distributive
conflicts in rural Vietnamese society. The revolutionary movement drove
wedges between those holding administrative power and the subject population, between landowners and the vast majority who were landless tenants,
and between all who were taxed by both the GVN and the movement's cadres.
The GVN responded to the movement's operations with weakly motivated and
poorly assimilated forces to resist the movement's penetration into the structures of Long An's rural society. The government failed to create a leadership
that understood the processes that were relentlessly undermining its legitimacy and authority in the countryside. No GVN official formulated a clear
conceptual basis for designing an effective response.

Andrew R. Finlayson offers a similarly compelling analysis of how communist cadres at the village level in Quang Nam Province in I Corps penetrated
and "organized the rural population using mass-based social organizations and
skillful propaganda," often with a minimum of coercion and violence.[43]

Had either the GVN administration in Long An or the Diem regime in
Saigon analyzed the situation in Long An as a revolutionary conflict where
there were obvious tradeoffs between a purely preemptive or reinforcement
strategy, they might have been able to identify the important factors that
drove the conflict's dynamics. For example, had the GVN recognized with its
American sponsors that the situation in Long An in 1959 represented a state of
low mobilization of military strength by the revolutionary movement, it could
have chosen to analyze conflict escalation in terms of the same variables the
movement was using: (1) the depth of the social conflicts that each side was
capable of manipulating to generate forces, (2) the effectiveness of the opposing forces, and (3) the conflict-aggravating consequences of mobilization and
their relative effects on each side.[44]

Choosing a purely preemptive strategy would have focused on measures
that tried to redirect villagers' attitudes toward favoring the GVN by eliminating the motives for revolution, such as a more effective and equitable land
redistribution policy, redesigning local tax policies with more progressive
scales, simplifying licensing procedures for small businesses, and including
rural groups in political decision making.

The revolutionary movement's program of selective coercion understood
how rural villagers analyzed their own self-interests. The movement skillfully
and subtly combined coercive measures such as killing village headmen with
its preemptive strategy. Fredrik Logevall's most recent work on Vietnam

cites a study undertaken in 1957 by Bernard B. Fall in which he determined that 452 village officials had died within a year in the rural villages around Saigon where there were clear links between the movement's guerrilla activities and the deaths.

> These killings were not random; they conformed to a pattern. The victims were village chiefs who had been landlords and were not much loved by the villagers. The insurgents got the double benefit of being Robin Hoods to the local population and putting other village notables on notice they could be next. When Saigon appointed a new acting village chief, chances were he too would soon be found with a machete in his back or a bullet in his head. How would number three on the list respond? Simple, Fall surmised: Unless he wanted to die a martyr's death, he'd quietly declare his fidelity to the revolution. And just like that, another village would have gone communist. The change would be invisible to the outsider; everyday life would go on as before. ARVN [Army of Vietnam] units coming through the village would be greeted courteously, but the insurgents who came through later would get the intelligence and the rice and the use of the U.S.-supplied radio set. The ARVN hadn't been outfought per se, but it had been "outadministered," which in the end would matter even more.[45]

Alternatively, choosing a purely reinforcement strategy would have focused on actions that strengthened existing security measures, such as building barbed-wire perimeters, constructing fortified strongpoints, guarding local offices and headquarters, recruiting paramilitary forces and arming them, and rounding up movement sympathizers and incarcerating or killing them. In short, a reinforcement strategy reduced to the question of whether the existing system could be defended at affordable levels of mobilization and attrition, given the economic and political status quo. Race indicated that the government in Long An made no such explicit analysis of its choices and trade-offs and took no conscious decision to adopt a purely reinforcement strategy because it was either ignorant of or insensitive to the social bases of the situation it confronted. "In this the thinking in Long An completely reflected the thinking in Saigon."[46] It simply drifted toward a reinforcement strategy.

On a nationwide basis, the American and South Vietnamese governments in the decade between 1965 and 1975 created and implemented by default a reinforcement strategy of open-ended escalation based on American conventional-force doctrines. The doctrinal tenets consisted of finding, fixing, fighting, and finishing the enemy[47] with firepower, technology, and deployment of ground forces in multiple-division strength. That was the kind of conflict the army knew how to fight and had been trained to fight because these doctrines had proven effective during World War II and Korea.

Race offers a "retrospective view" of the self-serving nature of these concepts: insufficient security (physically protecting villages), terrorism (the movement was forcing people to support it), infiltration (cadres from North Vietnam), insufficient propaganda (the GVN did not advertise or explain itself adequately), underdevelopment (reducing poverty by offering new increments of help and modernization such as building health clinics and schools, digging wells, installing modern irrigation systems, etc.), corruption (preventing elites from enriching themselves), no ideology (the GVN lacked an ideology, a "magic formula"), poor administration (incompetence fixed by efficiency), and lack of national consciousness (the need for duty and loyalty to the state).[48]

For any of the corrective actions on this list to work, there first had to be physical security of the population; that was at the top of the list. A reinforcement strategy was therefore the logical solution to inadequate security. The GVN, with inexorable American logic, had created its own self-defining tautology. It was not necessary to explore how the enemy thought and acted in terms of competing social policies. All one needed to know was the threat: the enemy's order of battle, weapons, command structure, guerrilla fieldcraft, and tactics. The Americans would supply ample combat power to engage and destroy the enemy's battalions. Meanwhile, the ARVN and its paramilitary forces would deploy to strengthen rural institutions at the village level. The programs designed to achieve a secure rural countryside would go through several nomenclature iterations between 1960 and 1975: strategic hamlets, pacification, and Vietnamization.

The late Colonel Harry G. Summers, a decade after Race published *War Comes to Long An*, published a best-selling critical analysis of the war. Summers was a serving colonel on the staff of the Strategic Studies Institute of the US Army War College at the time he wrote *On Strategy* in 1982. He had served as a corps operations officer in Vietnam. *On Strategy* argued that a lack of appreciation of military theory and strategy, based on Clausewitz's fundamental concepts, resulted in a faulty definition of the nature of the war.[49] He opened his book by asking "how we could have done so well in tactics but failed so miserably in strategy." He critiqued the strategy this way:

> Our new "strategy" of counterinsurgency blinded us to the fact that the guerrilla war was tactical and not strategic. It was a kind of economy of force operation on the part of North Vietnam to buy time and wear down superior U.S. military forces. . . . In other words, we took the *political* [italics in original] task (nation building/counterinsurgency) as our primary mission and relegated the *military* task (defeating external aggression) to a secondary consideration . . . the effect was a failure to isolate the battlefield. . . . Just as the North Koreans and their Chinese allies were the "root of the trouble" in the Korean war, so the root in the Vietnam war was North Vietnam (*not* the Viet Cong). In Vietnam as in Korea our political objectives dictated a strategic defensive posture. While this prevented us from destroying the "root" at the source through the strategic offensive, Korea proved that it was possible to achieve a favorable decision with the strategic

defensive. It restored the status quo ante, prevented the enemy from achieving his goals with military means, and provided the foundation for a negotiated settlement. All of this was within our means in Vietnam.[50]

Colonel Summers's case for "isolating the battlefield" later found persuasive support by Finlayson, a retired marine colonel who, like Summers, was a Vietnam combat veteran who served two tours as a junior officer in Vietnam:

> Of all the possible strategies proposed for an American victory in Vietnam, the strategy of cutting the Ho Chi Minh Trail in southern Laos offered the best chance for success. . . . The use of U.S. ground troops along the Dong Ha-Savannakhet axis [map IV.3] would cut the Ho Chi Minh Trail, making it impossible for North Vietnamese troops and equipment to move into South Vietnam. U.S. and ARVN forces would no longer need to protect a border with North Vietnam, Laos and Cambodia that stretched for over 1,200 miles, but could concentrate their forces along a frontage of only 225 miles, the distance from the East China Sea to Savannakhet. In order for North Vietnamese supply columns to move south, the North Vietnamese would need to breach this barrier using large numbers of conventional forces fighting in terrain that heavily favors the defense. Even if they broke free, they would have to maintain the breach continuously or face isolation of their forces moving south through mountainous terrain. . . . It is hard to imagine that the North Vietnamese would be able to maintain their monthly infiltration figures of 8,000 men and 500 tons of equipment and ammunition per month if U.S. forces were occupying defensive positions from Dong Ha to Savannakhet. . . . By 1969 the U.S. employed eleven divisions in South Vietnam with over 500,000 troops. The plan to establish the Dong Ha-Savannakhet defensive barrier would require only two U.S. Marine divisions in Quang Tri Province, South Vietnam, and four U.S. Army divisions in southern Laos, with an additional U.S. Army division positioned in the vicinity of Paksane, Laos, where it could screen the Mekong River north of Savannakhet and threaten the right flank of any North Vietnamese force moving against the barrier to the south.[51]

Execution of such a proposal would have played to the army's proven strengths in combat engineering, effective artillery firepower, and conventional combat tactics.

Summers's and Finlayson's assessments need to be juxtaposed with Race's analysis of the US reinforcement response against the revolutionary movement. Summers's classical Clausewitzian analysis of going for the "root" cause and Finlayson's concept of interdicting the Ho Chi Minh Trail raise the question of what would have been a war-winning strategy. Summers, writing in the early 1980s, omitted any mention of Race's *War Comes to Long An* and did not include it in his *On Strategy* bibliography, perhaps because he was unaware of it or disagreed with it. Finlayson, on the other hand, had studied *War Comes to Long An* thoroughly; joined Race in teaching courses decades

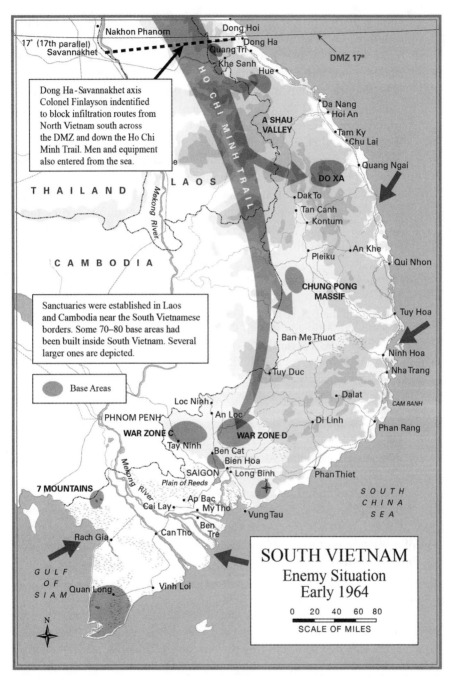

**Dong Ha-Savannakhet axis
Colonel Finlayson indentified
to block infiltration routes from
North Vietnam south across
the DMZ and down the Ho Chi
Minh Trail. Men and equipment
also entered from the sea.**

**Sanctuaries were established in Laos
and Cambodia near the South Vietnamese
borders. Some 70–80 base areas had
been built inside South Vietnam. Several
larger ones are depicted.**

Base Areas

17° (17th parallel)
Savannakhet

Nakhon Phanom

Dong Hoi

Dong Ha
Quang Tri

Khe Sanh

Hue

DMZ 17°

HO CHI MINH TRAIL

Da Nang
Hoi An

A SHAU
VALLEY

Tam Ky
Chu Lai

Quang Ngai

THAILAND

LAOS

DO XA

Dak To

Tan Canh

Kontum

Mekong River

CAMBODIA

Pleiku

An Khe

Qui Nhon

CHUNG PONG
MASSIF

Tuy Hoa

Ban Me Thuot

Tuy Duc

Ninh Hoa

Nha Trang

Dalat

CAM RANH

Loc Ninh

PHNOM PENH

An Loc

Di Linh

Phan Rang

WAR ZONE C

Tay Ninh

Ben Cat

Bien Hoa

WAR ZONE D

7 MOUNTAINS

Mekong River

SAIGON

Plain of Reeds

Long Binh

Phan Thiet

SOUTH
CHINA
SEA

Cai Lay

Ap Bac

My Tho

Vung Tau

Rach Gia

Can Tho

Ben
Tre

GULF
OF
SIAM

Quan Long

Vinh Loi

N

SOUTH VIETNAM
Enemy Situation
Early 1964

0   20   40   60   80

SCALE OF MILES

Map IV.3. The Ho Chi Minh Trail stretched for over 1,200 miles from North Vietnam south
through Laos and Cambodia; the most promising region where it could be interdicted on the
ground was across the Dong Ha-Savannakhet axis.
Source: USMA Atlases.

later to junior marine officers at the Marine Corps War College at Quantico, Virginia; and readily acknowledges that successful interdiction of the Ho Chi Minh Trail could not by itself have won the Vietnam War without an effective, simultaneous counterinsurgency and nation-building program.

What the Johnson administration decided to do in 1965 renders counterfactual speculation moot. At the time of President Johnson's decision to commit combat forces, official army doctrine had been written on the premise that US Armed Forces should be prepared to fight a "mid-intensity" (nonnuclear) war against the Soviet Union. The kind of combat for which the army was preparing emphasized heavy weapons; direct confrontation of an enemy in set-piece battles; high expenditures of ammunition (especially artillery), bombs, and missiles; and offensive sweeps through (but not occupation of) enemy territory.[52] American military commanders assigned to Vietnam wanted to carry out main-force missions fully consistent with the military doctrine of finding, fixing, and destroying the enemy.

John A. Nagl offered this evaluation of the army's doctrine:

> An assessment of the U.S. Army's success in developing doctrine and techniques to accomplish the twin objectives in South Vietnam [SVN] from 1965 through 1972—creating an ARVN capable of defeating insurgency in SVN and assisting in the defeat of the insurgency and of the NVA units in SVN through the directed application of U.S. combat power—reveals very limited success, little of which could be described as a result of the U.S. Army's own initiatives. The overall American goal remained the creation of a non-communist SVN free to choose its own form of government.[53]

As commander, US Military Assistance Command Vietnam (COMUSMACV), General William C. Westmoreland's implementation of the main-force strategy used the considerable military assets deployed at his disposal. Between 1965 and 1968, Nagl assesses the policy as "counterproductive." He approvingly cites, as Westmoreland's successor, General Creighton W. Abrams's interruption of a briefing on the combined campaign plan for fiscal year 1969: after the briefer stated that the mission was to "'seek out and destroy the enemy' Abrams wrote out on an easel: 'The mission is not to seek out and destroy the enemy. The mission is to provide protection for the people of Vietnam.'"

This confusion over combat policy and doctrine reflected the view that the army's objectives in South Vietnam were not being achieved. Nagl quotes from an official study sponsored by the Advanced Research Projects Agency (ARPA) in 1968:[54] "At present there is no effective hamlet security in most of South Vietnam. Current strategy is directed toward protecting the autonomous cities, province and district capitals, and the lines of communications which connect them."[55] Regardless of the differences between Westmoreland

and Abrams in their approach to combat and security, both were following what Race would categorize as a reinforcement, not a preemptive, strategy.

This point is hardly surprising. Westmoreland and Abrams were veterans of World War II, where firepower against a sophisticated, industrialized enemy was a tactical differentiator. Westmoreland, an artillery officer, fought in Tunisia, Sicily, France, and Germany, emerging from the war a colonel. As a lieutenant colonel in command of an artillery battalion in the 9th ID at Kasserine Pass, Westmoreland maneuvered his battalion just in time to open fire and blunt a German counterattack. On Sicily, Westmoreland's artillery battalion was attached to General Terry de la Mesa Allen's 1st ID, where the division was engaged in intensive combat resisting twenty-four German counterattacks. In one of these engagements, he was thrown into the air and nearly killed when his jeep ran over a German Teller mine.[56] In Korea, he commanded an airborne regimental combat team. Westmoreland's knowledge of the capabilities and effects of firepower was acquired the hard way—up close. Abrams commanded one of the tank spearheads in Patton's 3rd Army that relieved Bastogne during the Battle of the Bulge. General Patton highly valued Abrams: "I'm supposed to be the best tank commander in the Army, but I have one peer—Abe Abrams. He's the world champion."[57]

For MACV forces, whether under Westmoreland or Abrams, Andrew J. Birtle argues that

> defeating the enemy [main-force units] remained "the single best way of achieving security." The means employed differed somewhat, only because the situation differed. The gradual evolution of American operations from major offensives to a more balanced, area control and pacification approach represented little more than the natural progression envisioned by Westmoreland and Army doctrine. That this transformation remained incomplete had more to do with the ultimate failure of the Army to win the main-force war and isolate the battlefield than a dogmatic adherence to large-unit operations.[58]

Nagl's critique of Westmoreland's application of army doctrine and his approval of Abrams's security approach needs to be balanced against Birtle's recognition that insurgencies required a "multifaceted" response. "At no time did Westmoreland or any of his senior lieutenants ever advocate the exclusive use of either large-unit or small-unit operations. Both had their place. In fact from the beginning of Westmoreland's tenure, small-unit operations vastly outnumbered large-unit operations."[59]

Westmoreland created three broad categories of military operations, each designed to satisfy a particular mission. There were "search-and-destroy" operations to attack the enemy's main-force units and base areas. The second category were "clearing" operations to break up the enemy's guerrilla forces in areas identified for pacification. The third category were "securing" operations, which represented the final stage in the solidification of government control over an area, where US Army and ARVN units would break down into progressively smaller units, and continuous patrolling would enable security to be maintained by paramilitary and police forces.

That was the doctrinal theory. In practice it failed to work because "more often than not, [large-unit] sweeps uncovered communist supplies and killed enemy troops, but rarely generated decisive battles." Whether a decisive battle was sought or the objective was clearing or securing a specific rural area, both required considerable manpower. As Birtle explains, "When one considers that a battalion was generally needed to surround a single village and that two battalions were required to effect the average encirclement, the necessity of using large units during pacification operations becomes apparent."[60]

Military scholars continue to debate whether Westmoreland and Abrams were pursuing the same "one war" strategy.[61] Issues include whether COIN principles were in conflict with large-unit sweeps, or whether pacification programs were a radical departure from the one-war strategy. They also debate whether a more direct strategy of isolating the battlefield (Summers's and Finlayson's concepts) by sealing the border with North Vietnam and severing the Ho Chi Minh Trail, thus freeing the ARVN to deal with the guerrillas, could have succeeded.[62] None of what the armed forces of the United States undertook in Vietnam could overcome the greater will of the Vietnamese communists to win, as the succeeding chapters demonstrate.[63]

Douglas Porch considered the critiques of the army's operational solutions in Vietnam (by Summers and Andrew F. Krepinevich Jr.) and concluded "that there is no evidence that Washington could have won in Vietnam with a more-COIN-based strategy from the beginning, not least because the GVN was slow to embrace the political and economic reforms required to translate counterinsurgency tactics into positive political results."[64] Indeed, shifting to a conventional offensive is precisely what North Vietnam did in 1975 to overrun South Vietnam.

Porch concurs with two other scholars, James H. Lebovic and Eric M. Bergerud

> that the population in the Mekong Delta evinced no enthusiasm for the GVN; American-forced political reforms only vindicated communist accusations of a "puppet" GVN; that more people were willing to die for the communists than for the GVN; and finally that attrition was the only viable strategy Westmoreland could employ because winning hearts and minds was dead on arrival because an outside power like the United States could not create the political conditions that allowed COIN to succeed.[65]

OPERATIONS

Chapters 17 through 23 discuss in operational detail the failure of the US government to design a strategic architecture that delivered a successful outcome to the war. In each case, the attempt to align policy and strategy with operations in the field failed to produce victory or a successful outcome where the GVN survived as a viable governing authority in South Vietnam. The nonlinear nature of the conflict in Vietnam does not render it easily divisible into discrete battles or campaigns. There was no front line behind which the GVN with American help could protect the civilian population in rural areas as the US and ROK armies did in Korea.

Chapter 17 opens with the Battle of the Ia Drang Valley in 1965–1966 as an early battle where General Westmoreland's application of his main-force strategy, with the advantages of air mobility and overwhelming firepower, failed to produce a strategic result. Ia Drang was the first of many operations intended to break the enemy through attrition of large NVA/VC military units.

Chapter 18 outlines the escalation of the ground war to the major bombing campaign with the implementation of Operation *Rolling Thunder* and later its high-tech complement, Operation *Igloo White*, to sever the revolutionary movement's supply chains. Airpower delivered four times the total ordnance dropped in Europe in World War II, eight million tons, but failed to break a third-world adversary. Operation *Igloo White*, representing the engineering ingenuity and resources of the world's most sophisticated technology society, could not defeat the revolutionary peasant society.

Chapter 19 analyzes the pacification and Civil Operations and Revolutionary Development Support (CORDS) program initiated in 1967. The creation of CORDS demonstrates how a theater headquarters created an innovative staff organization to manage a multiagency COIN effort to secure and pacify the Vietnamese countryside, a failed initiative that Race would classify as another reinforcement rather than preemptive strategy.

Chapter 20 identifies the Tet Offensive in 1968 as the turning point with respect to the collapse of domestic political support for the Johnson administration's strategic leadership of the Vietnam War. The Tet Offensive undermined the credibility of the Johnson administration's pacification claims of "light at the end of the tunnel."

Chapter 21 describes President Nixon's Vietnamization policy of turning over the fighting of the war to the ARVN and paramilitary forces through increased training, logistics, and support for pacification simultaneous with deep troop withdrawals. Vietnamization produced a brief, flawed peace that did not last because NVA combat capability remained deployed in the South. Recent scholarship shows that the Nixon administration's diplomacy during this period was a serious attempt to bring the war to an end, "peace with honor." However, it was another instance of a failure to align policy, strategy, and operations where success depended on reforming a flawed regime.

Chapter 22 examines the final years between 1969 and 1975 and shows why the GVN failed to create either political or administrative institutions and policies that enjoyed sufficient popular support or to lead its armed forces to defend the regime and the society underpinning it.

Chapter 23 explains why the American strategic architecture led to a self-inflicted defeat.

17

BATTLE OF THE IA DRANG VALLEY

Not Fighting the Decisive Battle

The chain of events running up to the Battle of the Ia Drang Valley began in the fall of 1965 in the Central Highlands with an NVA attack on a special forces camp at Plei Me, which the Green Berets repulsed. To pursue the enemy, General Westmoreland committed the 1st Cavalry Division (Airmobile) to combat less than a month after it had arrived in-country. The result was the Battle of the Ia Drang Valley, named for a small river that flowed through the tactical area of operational responsibility (TAOR). For thirty-five days the division pursued and fought the 32nd, 33rd, and 6th North Vietnamese Regiments, until the enemy, suffering heavy casualties, returned to its bases in Cambodia. One of the army's CMH titles describes it as "a costly and problematic victory."[1]

The official NVA history describes the communist strategy of luring the Americans into combat. "In the Central Highlands, in order to study the fighting methods of the Americans in actual combat, the Front Command launched the Plei Me Campaign in [Pleiku] province, carrying out a plan to besiege a position and annihilate the relief force." First Secretary Le Duan's fingerprints are all over this strategy insofar as he had appointed a new commander in the South "to prove [to his Central Committee party colleagues] they could win." General Nguyen Chi Thanh was Hanoi's new commander in the South, "a charismatic military leader with a fervent belief in the Maoist doctrine that spirit could overcome superior firepower." The initial operations in 1965 that unfolded in the Central Highlands and the Battle of the Ia Drang Valley were learning experiences for both sides.

The 1st Air Cav's operations demonstrated the mobile and flexible capability army divisions had achieved by the early 1960s. The integration of large numbers of helicopters into the 1st Air Cav's combat capability enabled mobility operations over a large area. During the Ia Drang operation, artillery batteries, for example, were moved sixty-seven times by helicopter. Intelligence, medical, and extensive logistical support benefited as well from the speed and flexibility provided by helicopters.[2]

Helicopters provided military advantages in Vietnam, but their use was also costly in terms of aircrew and equipment losses. Van Creveld indicates that the total number of military helicopters that saw service in Vietnam was about twelve thousand, of which 5,086 (43 percent) were lost in combat or accidents. Almost all these losses were sustained in an airspace dominated by US airpower. Despite this dominance, helicopters were hit by hostile fire twenty-two thousand times.

With the rapid changes in tactical situations, airmobile command-and-control procedures enabled the division to move and keep track of its units over a large area and to accommodate the frequent and rapid changes in command arrangements as units were moved from one headquarters to another.[3] That was the concept of air mobility. In practice, it became something else. What began as an offensive operation rapidly turned into a defensive one.

As described by Van Creveld, the mobility advantages achieved by helicopters did not necessarily translate into a military advantage on the ground. "Linked by an intricate set of electronic communications, helicopters provided the U.S. and South Vietnamese ground forces with an entirely new kind of mobility. . . . Initially the promise of the new units appeared very great." Once troops were inserted into an area where the enemy was believed to be located, the military advantage diminished.

> Once all the troops were safely on the ground, they would move toward the tree line in search of the enemy. Provided the [enemy] simply did not choose to melt away, the outcome was almost certainly an encounter, in which the American and their South Vietnamese allies were at no particular advantage; furthermore, owing to the close quarters at which such combat took place, they were unable to use their superior firepower.[4]

The enemy had planned to develop Vietnam's Central Highlands into a major base area from which to mount operations in other areas. A communist-dominated highlands would be a strategic pivot point, enabling the NVA to shift the weight of its operations to any part of South Vietnam. In American planners' minds, the Central Highlands formed a "killing zone" where communist forces could mass, and where Westmoreland's main-force tactics could be exploited to devastating effect.

The 1st Air Cav moved with its 435 helicopters into this "hornet's nest" in September 1965, establishing its main base at An Khe, a government stronghold on Route 19, halfway between the coastal port of Qui Nhon and the highland city of Pleiku (maps IV.2 and 17.1). At An Khe, the division could help keep open the vital east–west road from the coast to the highlands and could pivot, like the enemy, between the highlands and the coastal districts, where the Viet Cong had made deep inroads. With scout platoons of its air cavalry squadron covering its front and flanks, each battalion of the division's 1st Brigade established company bases from which patrols searched for enemy forces.

The search for the main body of the enemy continued as airmobile units concentrated their efforts in the vicinity of the Chung Pong Massif, a mountain near the Cambodian border believed to be an enemy base. As 1st Air Cav units established bases and landing zones at the base of the mountain, Landing Zone (LZ) *X-Ray* became one of several American positions vulnerable to attack by the enemy forces that occupied the surrounding high ground. On November 14, 1965, near this LZ, the fighting began that pitted three American battalions against elements of two of the NVA regiments.

Withstanding repeated mortar attacks and infantry assaults, the Americans used every means of firepower available to them, including the division's helicopter gunships, massive artillery bombardment, hundreds of strafing and bombing attacks by tactical aircraft, and bombs dropped by B-52 bombers flying *Arc Light* missions from Guam to turn back a determined enemy.[5] The communists lost more than one thousand dead, the Americans seventy-nine.[6]

General Westmoreland could take only partial satisfaction that the 1st Air Cav penetration into the Ia Drang valley was a tactical success. He had scored attrition points in the body count, but he had not leveraged the firepower he possessed into strategic success. One of his battalion commanders whose unit bore the brunt later agreed with him.

Lieutenant Colonel Harold G. "Hal" Moore (later lieutenant general) commanded the 1st Battalion, 7th US Cavalry (then in the 3rd Brigade Combat Team of the 1st Air Cav), in this operation. With his battalion encircled by enemy soldiers, and with no LZ clear from enemy fire that would enable him to withdraw, Moore persevered despite a sister battalion only two and a half miles away being massacred the next day. Moore's spirited defense led to a high ratio between North Vietnamese and US casualties in the first major engagement of the war. Moore himself later considered the battle a draw because US forces left the area, allowing the North Vietnamese to reassert control.

After the battle, Westmoreland asked for more forces by requesting more rapid deployment of the army's 25th ID, based in Hawaii and scheduled to deploy to South Vietnam in the spring of 1966. By the end of 1965, the division's 3rd Brigade had been airlifted to the highlands and, within a month

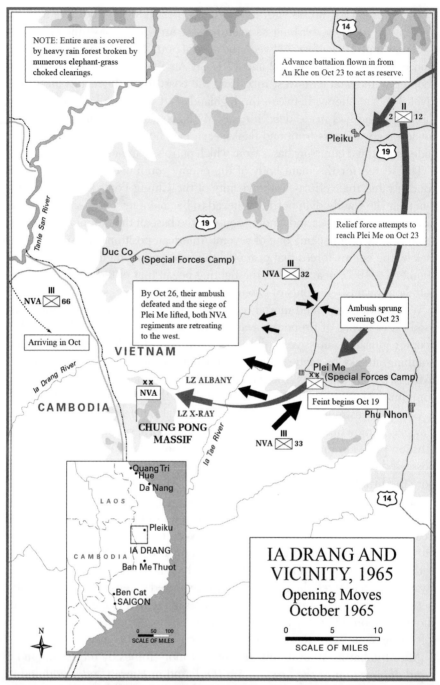

NOTE: Entire area is covered by heavy rain forest broken by numerous elephant-grass choked clearings.

Advance battalion flown in from An Khe on Oct 23 to act as reserve.

2 ⊠ 12

Pleiku

19

Tanle San River

19

Duc Co (Special Forces Camp)

NVA III ⊠ 32

Relief force attempts to reach Plei Me on Oct 23

NVA III ⊠ 66

By Oct 26, their ambush defeated and the siege of Plei Me lifted, both NVA regiments are retreating to the west.

Ambush sprung evening Oct 23

Arriving in Oct

VIETNAM

Ia Drang River

XX NVA

LZ ALBANY

Plei Me XX (Special Forces Camp)

CAMBODIA

LZ X-RAY

Feint begins Oct 19

Phu Nhon

CHUNG PONG MASSIF

Ia Tae River

NVA III ⊠ 33

Quang Tri
Hue
Da Nang

LAOS

Pleiku

CAMBODIA

IA DRANG

Ban Me Thuot

Ben Cat
SAIGON

N

0 50 100
SCALE OF MILES

IA DRANG AND VICINITY, 1965
Opening Moves October 1965

0   5   10
SCALE OF MILES

Map 17.1. The Ia Drang valley in the Central Highlands became the focus of both sides for the first major engagement between American and North Vietnamese forces.

Source: Cartographic data drawn from CMH, *American Military History*, vol. 2, 308, http://www.history.army.mil/books/AMH-V2/AMH%20V2/chapter10.htm and USMA Atlases.

of its arrival, had joined elements of the 1st Air Cav to launch a series of operations to screen the border. Army units did not detect any major enemy forces trying to cross from Cambodia into South Vietnam. Each operation, however, killed hundreds of enemy soldiers and refined airmobile techniques as army units learned to cope with the vast territorial expanse and difficult terrain of the highlands.[7]

Despite high casualties, the NVA did not leave the Ia Drang valley. One of the army's official histories states that elements of the 66th North Vietnamese Regiment moving east toward Plei Me engaged an American battalion on November 17, 1965, a few miles north of *X-Ray* at LZ *Albany* (map 17.1). The fight that resulted was a sanguinary reminder of the North Vietnamese mastery of the ambush. The NVA regiment pinned down three US companies. The official history described what happened.

> As the trapped American units struggled for survival, nearly all semblance of organized combat disappeared in the confusion and mayhem. Neither reinforcements nor effective firepower could be brought in. At times combat was reduced to valiant efforts by individuals and small units to avert annihilation. When the fighting ended that night, seventy percent of the Americans were casualties, and almost one of every three soldiers in the battalion had been killed.[8]

After Ia Drang, the NVA left the US Army operating in II Corps in little doubt that it would continue to infiltrate and attack American forces in the Central Highlands. The NVA official history, first published in Hanoi in 1988 almost a quarter century after the battle, concurs and provides its own version of the attrition metrics:

> To rescue the 3rd Air Cavalry Brigade the U.S. Command was forced to use B-52 strategic bombers in support of ground combat operations. . . . The 1st Air Cavalry Battalion had been almost completely annihilated, and the 2nd Air Cavalry Battalion had suffered heavy casualties. Fifty-nine helicopters had been shot down and eighty-nine enemy vehicles and many artillery pieces had been destroyed. . . . The Air Cavalry Division, the first helicopter-transported air mobile division in history to engage in combat, a unit the Americans believed would be able to react quickly and conduct rapid envelopment operations, the unit that was "the greatest hope of the American army," together with its combat method of conducting "relief operations to break sieges" and its "leapfrog" tactics, had been defeated in the mountains of Vietnam.[9]

Both sides were trying to convince themselves during and after the battles in the Central Highlands that they possessed winning formulas. Their histories, written decades later, reflect the early confidence both sides had that their respective forces would win, but as combat operations continued in I and II Corps, it would be the Americans who began to harbor doubts, not the North Vietnamese.

The 1st Air Cavalry Division discovered that the use of helicopters for its main-force operations did not necessarily provide the kind of tactical leverage it needed to win decisively. Even if the NVA regiments could be kept at bay in II Corps by airmobile reinforcement, there was still the problem of implementing preemptive social and economic reforms, and that required the full cooperation of the GVN.

Hundreds of military operations were undertaken over the next eight years (1965–1973) to help the GVN regain control of the rural countryside.[10] US Army units in battalion or larger strength engaged in search-and-destroy or cordon-and-search operations, often coordinated with locally deployed ARVN and paramilitary Regional Force (RF) and Popular Force (PF) units to support local pacification effort by the GVN's rural administration. These operations represented an explicit military reinforcement strategy to defeat the NVA and Viet Cong.

However innovative the 1st Air Cav's tactics—COIN or main-force/search-and-destroy—in the Ia Drang valley and Binh Dinh Province, they made no difference to the outcome in Vietnam. In Porch's judgment, the real problem was understanding the political and strategic context in which the war was fought. Neither tactical adjustments nor operational innovations "were going to buck up a corrupt and illegitimate South Vietnamese government and its morale-challenged military in the face of an enemy who enjoyed an inviolate sanctuary, nationalist legitimacy, solid political and military leadership, a motivated and adaptable military force, a command economy, and two powerful communist allies [the PRC and USSR] who supplied diplomatic cover and virtually unlimited matériel."[11]

After these frustrations with its strategic architecture to defeat the revolutionary movement on the ground, the Johnson administration escalated the war to an increasingly counterproductive air campaign.

18

BOMBING CAMPAIGN AND HIGH-TECH INITIATIVES

Operations *Rolling Thunder* and *Igloo White*—
Airpower and Technology Indecisive

In 1965, in addition to the first large increase in troop levels, a massively ramped-up air campaign began. President Johnson and his advisors turned to airpower in 1965 out of frustration that the war was not producing decisive strategic results. Operation *Rolling Thunder*, lasting between March 2, 1965, and October 31, 1968, became the longest bombing campaign ever conducted by the US Armed Forces up to that time. Air force, navy, and marine airmen flew 3.4 million sorties and dropped eight million tons of munitions on targets in Southeast Asia.[1]

The bombing destroyed 65 percent of North Vietnam's oil storage capacity, 60 percent of its power-generating capability, and most of its industrial infrastructure, including the three factories in the north "worthy of the name," the Thai Nguyen Steel Works, an ammunition plant, and the country's only cement plant. Other targets included ammunition depots, highways and bridges, petroleum facilities, airfields, and army barracks. The target list grew from the original ninety-four devised by the JCS in 1964 to over four hundred targets by late 1967.[2] "At one time or another, half of [North Vietnam's] major bridges were down. Nearly 10,000 trucks, 2,000 railroad cars, and a score of locomotives were destroyed."[3] The bombing's intensification in 1967 had no apparent effect on the battlefields of South Vietnam. As indicated by Earl H. Tilford, an Army War College historian who wrote the *Rolling Thunder* entry in Spencer C. Tucker's Vietnam encyclopedia,

According to MACV's own estimates, the flow of troops and supplies moving from North Vietnam into South Vietnam doubled [during] each year of *Rolling Thunder*. The North responded to the bombing by building redundancy into its transportation system so that by 1968 it was capable of handling three times as much traffic through the panhandle as it could in 1965.[4]

Rolling Thunder's failure to achieve a decisive, war-winning result derives from four flawed assumptions. The first was a failure to recognize that the Vietnam War was not a repetition of either World War II or the Korean War from an airpower perspective. Crane observed that the operations research and systems analysis (ORSA) approach to strategic bombing that the USAAF had pioneered during World War II "had become almost a religion in the Department of Defense headed by Secretary Robert S. McNamara. . . . The process proved useful to structure [airpower] forces for a war but not to fight it. Human and political factors and the inconsistencies of actual war were incompatible with ORSA, and plans and strategies developed through the process were too inflexible to deal with alternatives"[5]

The second flaw was that neither Johnson's objectives nor McNamara's quantifications were readily amenable to what American strategic or tactical airpower had been designed to accomplish in a conflict—namely, decisive victory through intensive offensive action. *Rolling Thunder* became a convoluted campaign, executed through incremental phases, often micromanaged by civilians in Washington.[6]

The third flaw was interservice rivalry that blocked the creation of a single-point command for *Rolling Thunder*. Each service preferred to direct and control its own air assets and personnel. This parochialism led to a complex organizational structure with command-and-control chains running back to Washington. James C. Thompson suggests that resolution of interservice "Route Package" conflicts might have enhanced the effectiveness of the *Rolling Thunder* campaign, but Van Creveld indicates that they were too pervasive.[7]

The fourth and fatal flaw relates to North Vietnam as a target:

Vietnam could hardly be considered an industrial area. North Vietnam was an agricultural country with a primitive transportation system and almost no industry. Furthermore, the North Vietnamese Army did not follow conventional Western organizational forms, using large amounts of supplies. That army did not need to be supported with a large logistics tail involving massive supply convoys and large supply bases.[8]

Tilford, writing in Tucker's encyclopedia, drives the point home:

[North Vietnam] was not vulnerable to the kind of bombing that played a role in defeating industrial powers such as Nazi Germany and Imperial Japan. North

Vietnam had no war-making industries. Its primitive economy could not be held hostage to an emerging industrial base. Besides, its leadership held that reunification was more important than industrialization.[9]

Tilford concludes that the air force generals and navy admirals who planned and executed the bombing campaign were "victims of their own historical experience." Their World War II and Korean War experience had created a conviction that strategic bombing was effective.

As *Rolling Thunder* escalated, so did the resources committed by both sides. As the bombing campaign got underway, North Vietnam was defended by 1,500 antiaircraft guns. Within a year, these numbers had tripled. North Vietnam's air defenses eventually became quite sophisticated, with radar-controlled antiaircraft batteries that rivaled the density around Berlin at the height of World War II. The North Vietnamese air defense forces also possessed state-of-the-art Soviet surface-to-air missiles (SAMs) that triggered an escalation in electronic warfare.[10] The North Vietnamese shot down nearly one thousand aircraft, captured hundreds of aircrew as POWs, and killed hundreds more airmen or left them missing in action.

The bombing of North Vietnam by *Rolling Thunder* was proving ineffective by 1966. The Office of the Secretary of Defense and ARPA began a major program to exploit technology to create a barrier across Vietnam. The barrier was equipped with state-of-the-art electronic and physical barrier devices. The physical barrier, known as the McNamara Line, was never completed. However, the electronic barrier, the airborne sensor insertion program, classified top secret and code-named *Igloo White*,[11] became quite large. At least $2 billion was spent on the program.[12] It represented an attempt to transform the Ho Chi Minh Trail into an electronic battlefield instrumented with high-tech sensors. Some described its scale and sophistication as the Vietnam equivalent of the Manhattan Project during World War II.

Igloo White's concept of operation utilized the airborne sowing of electronic sensors over chokepoints of the Ho Chi Minh Trail. The sensors broadcast remote sensor data to airborne communications aircraft, which then transmitted the data to a remote secret base in northeastern Thailand. There, the data were analyzed by computers in an attempt to produce automated intelligence products that could support precise targeting of enemy logistic concentrations on the Ho Chi Minh Trail. The principal targets were trucks.[13] The system was designed to vector strike aircraft to their targets. Some electronic sensors detected motion; others could detect and discriminate among seismic signatures made by trucks, animals, or people. Dropped from aircraft, these battery-powered sensors, designed and built by Sandia Corporation in Albuquerque and camouflaged to disguise their insertion, either hung in the canopies of dense jungle foliage or embedded themselves in the ground depending on their underlying sensor technology (seismic to detect vibration, infrared to detect heat, etc.).[14] Each sensor contained an RF transmitter so that sensor data could be sent to ground or airborne receivers and relayed to the northeastern Thailand central processing base at Nakhon Phanom (NKP) Air Base. The team of air force technical experts and analysts, known as Task Force Alpha,[15] manned the Infiltration Surveillance Center at NKP. They used state-of-the-art mainframe computers to process and analyze the sensor data to produce air tasking orders that resulted in air strikes directed against specific infiltration targets identified by the sensors. *Igloo White* operated from 1968 until the end of 1972. US Air Force figures claim that the air interdiction campaign destroyed thirty-five thousand trucks between 1968 and 1971, the last full year of *Igloo White* operation.[16] These loss numbers may sound substantial. However, for all of the effort and expenditure, an ARPA evaluation indicated that *Igloo White* was not decisive in interdicting the flow of enemy matériel down the Ho Chi Minh Trail:

> U.S. analysts, though they could not chart the Ho Chi Minh Trail complex and had little more than tabulations of explosions to verify the damage done, nevertheless tried to evaluate aerial interdiction on the basis of the information available. Thomas C. Thayer, for three years the chief of the Operations Analysis Division of ARPA's field unit in Saigon that analyzed the Vietnam War for the Office of the Secretary of Defense, stated the obvious: "the more than 1.5 million sorties flown in the out-of-country interdiction campaign did not choke off VC/NVA activity in the South."[17]

Van Creveld explains one of the interdiction difficulties by pointing to the loose links in the "kill chain": between the *Igloo White* sensors on the ground, the communications relays to Task Force Alpha at NKP, and then interpreting the intelligence to create accurate air tasking orders for the airborne shooters. The expenditure of aircraft and ordnance was not only wasteful but also ineffective. Where the Ho Chi Minh Trail had to cross into Laos to avoid the targeted chokepoints of North Vietnam's southern panhandle, "[Laos] became the second most heavily bombed country in history after South Vietnam."[18]

The escalation in the air failed to isolate NVA units operating in the South or to interdict their supply lines down the Ho Chi Minh Trail. The airpower campaign failed to stop the flow of supplies from the North to the NVA in the South.

19

THE PACIFICATION PROGRAM (1967–1968)

Failing to Change Behavior

While MACV's main-force strategy and *Rolling Thunder* missions gained momentum between 1965 and 1968, until 1967 less emphasis was placed on counterinsurgency efforts to defeat the revolutionary movement in the countryside. There was a reason for this lack of attention: a COIN strategy had already failed in Vietnam in the early 1960s.

The US-supported GVN in the early 1960s had implemented the Strategic Hamlet Program, modeled after the British success in defeating the Malayan insurgency. Between 1948 and 1960, the British had fought a successful counterinsurgency campaign in Malaya against the Malayan Communist Party. Nagl describes the organizational and operational learning by the British army over the decade of the 1950s.[1] Britain was able to employ all the elements of counterinsurgency—diplomacy, information operations, intelligence, financial control, and military power—"remarkably well in Malaya" to achieve the political objectives of establishing a stable national government by 1957 that could secure itself against internal and external threats.

The man selected to defeat the Malayan insurgency was General Sir Gerald W. R. Templer, a World War II veteran who had commanded a division and had served as the director of the military government in Italy and as the director of military government in the British zone of occupied Germany after the war. Templer understood the principles of the indirect approach and accepted the "Five Principles of Counterinsurgency" prescribed by Sir Robert G. K. Thompson, serving as secretary of defense for Malaya.

- The government must have a clear political aim: to establish and maintain a free independent and united country which is politically and economically stable and viable.
- The government must function in accordance with law.
- The government must have an overall plan.
- The government must give priority to defeating the political subversion, not the guerrillas.
- In the guerrilla phase of an insurgency, a government must secure its base area first.

Thompson (at the time a British lieutenant colonel) and Templer worked closely together in developing and implementing successful counterinsurgency plans. Their success led Americans into a "blithe sense" that defeating communist insurgencies was feasible.[2]

Nagl paints a fairly rosy picture of British Malayan COIN policy and execution. He argues that the British in Malaya took the approach of separating villagers from the guerrillas. The Malayan version of "New Villages" evolved as

> settlements for the Chinese squatters, estate workers, and villagers that protected them behind chain link and barbed wire fences, lit with floodlights and patrolled by Chinese Auxiliary Police Forces. More than concentration camps, the New Villages would include schools, medical aid stations, community centers, village cooperatives, and even Boy Scout troops. As the locals gained confidence in the determination of the government to protect them, they would progress from serving in an unarmed Home Guard through to keeping shotguns in their homes, ready for instant action. . . . By the end of 1951 some 400,000 squatters had been resettled in over 400 "New Villages."[3]

Porch's recent scholarship indicates that the British COIN goal of "resettling" half a million Chinese squatters into New Villages did little to earn the locals' confidence; what happened was coercion.[4] The British prevailed in the Malayan Emergency with a force that had been doubled to twenty-one battalions, "more men than the British had seen fit to deploy to defend Malaya and Singapore against the Japanese in 1941."[5]

Birtle, in his own equally researched work on the evolution of COIN doctrine, made this observation about early American enthusiasm for British practices in Malaya:

> All too often Americans saw only what they wanted to see in [COIN] episodes. They tended to overestimate the ease and extent to which resettlement programs and political reforms had won the hearts and minds of the people while ignoring contradictory evidence and minimizing the role that coercion had contributed to the success of [the campaign].[6]

David French's recent scholarship indicates that reusing the elements of a seemingly effective COIN strategy from a successful colonial power's template, no matter how well intentioned, risks failure and frustration.[7] During the early 1960s, the Americans designed their own version of the Malayan New Villages program and rebranded it the Strategic Hamlet Program without thinking through all the elements of the Templer-Thompson indirect strategy.

Nevertheless, during 1962, the Diem regime was reporting major progress with the Strategic Hamlet Program, which was expanding rapidly in almost every province. In the Mekong River delta by the end of 1962, the GVN had built four thousand strategic hamlets out of a program goal of sixteen thousand. The Diem regime and its American sponsors were claiming that the program had enabled the GVN "to gain effective control over one-third of the rural population in the Mekong delta and two-thirds of the people living between Saigon and the 17th parallel." General Paul D. Harkins, the first commander of MACV and General Westmoreland's predecessor, predicted in early 1963 that South Vietnam would enjoy a "white Christmas" in 1963 because insurgent activity would be reduced to the point that the ARVN's color-coded maps would show all provinces as white (the color that designated an area under firm government control).[8]

One might conclude that the American and South Vietnamese optimism in 1962–1963 was grounds for believing that the Diem regime was winning the war, but the North Vietnamese reacted to the Strategic Hamlet Program with a strategy of their own. The official NVA history acknowledges the scope, scale, and effectiveness of the Strategic Hamlet Program. The strategic hamlet number in the Pribbenow translation of the NVA official history is 3,250 and concurs with the GVN conclusion that it controlled two-thirds of the rural population. At this stage, the North Vietnamese politburo decided to send major NVA reinforcements to South Vietnam, forty thousand cadres and soldiers by the end of 1963.[9]

The Strategic Hamlet Program was an early instance of how the American and Vietnamese governments viewed their respective concepts of nation building. Edward Miller's recent research shows that although the GVN with American help had built thousands of strategic hamlets,

> there was precious little evidence that hamlet residents had embraced the self-sufficient outlook that [Ngo Dinh Diem and his close adviser brother, Ngo Dinh Nhu[10]] had defined as the *raison d'etre* of the program. Indeed, Nhu frequently complained to his subordinates, the government's own officials had largely failed to understand the ideological goals behind the program. In lieu of such understanding, these officials concentrated on the construction of hamlet fortifications and on the physical control of the population via coercive and even brutal methods. . . . Most retrospective studies of the Strategic Hamlet Program at the

provincial and local levels in South Vietnam have underlined the program's coercive character, as well as the gulf that separated the theories formulated in Saigon from the regime's actual practices in the countryside.[11]

One of the sources Miller cited is Race, who described the program's collapse in Long An:

The strategic hamlet concept exemplifies in clearest form the government's reinforcement strategy. It might be said that the program gathered into one effort all the government strategic errors: the incentives for living in the strategic hamlet were not relevant to the reasons for assistance to the revolutionary movement (and in fact these incentives, irrelevant as they were, never materialized in any case); the program devoted its resources to a physical reinforcement of the existing social system and of those who held power under it; the form of physical reinforcement adopted was founded on an explicit conception of security as the physical prevention of movement; security was explicitly intended to apply to the population in general, although the population was not the object of attack; and the thinking which led to the adoption of the strategic hamlet program was based on a severe miscalculation of its conflict aggravating consequences. . . . The strategic hamlets . . . represented no positive value to the majority of their inhabitants—on the contrary, as the testimony of even government officials showed, they were a terrific annoyance, through controls on movement which interfered with making a living, through demands for guard duty which interfered with sleep, through the destruction of homes and fields.[12]

The recognition was growing within the US government and among some officers in MACV that South Vietnam could not ultimately sustain itself as an independent state unless it undertook serious "political reform and true self governance prevailed at the top while also working its way up from the bottom."[13] This recognition failed to identify the differences between preemptive policies that might have motivated the rural population to turn away from the revolutionary movement and reinforcement policies that focused on providing physical security for a rural population that neither sought it nor needed it.

This dichotomy did not diminish official American enthusiasm for a comprehensive program. President Johnson in May 1967 assigned one of his senior and most vigorous White House aides, Robert W. Komer,[14] to pull together government-wide resources into a new pacification organization, Civil Operations and Revolutionary Development Support (CORDS), with the rank of ambassador.

Known as the "Blowtorch," Komer's "hyperkinetic" bureaucratic style was regarded as effective among some Americans, but much less so with the Vietnamese.[15] Having been handpicked for the job by President Johnson, he was extremely confident in his position, unused to being challenged, and very powerful as long as he lasted. His deputy, Ambassador William E. Colby, a veteran intelligence officer whose career dated back to the World War II Office of

Strategic Services and who had served in Saigon as CIA chief of station in the early 1960s and who also ran the Phoenix Program, succeeded Komer in November 1968. Phoenix was designed to identify the civilian cadres supporting the National Liberation Front of South Vietnam, often and more commonly referred to as the Viet Cong Infrastructure (VCI), and to neutralize it by capturing Viet Cong operatives and persuading them to defect to the GVN side or killing them. Colby directed the Phoenix Program under CIA funding.[16]

The creation of CORDS was "perhaps the most remarkable example of American institutional innovation during the Vietnam War" because it incorporated personnel from the CIA, US Information Agency (USIA), US Agency for International Development (USAID), State Department, White House, MACV, and all of the military services into one theater-level organization numbering at its peak eight thousand staff and advisors.[17] The effectiveness of CORDS is a continuing point of debate among a number of Vietnam War scholars.[18]

Ambassador Komer's tenure as Westmoreland's (later Abrams's) civilian commander of "the other war" lasted eighteen months (May 1967 to October 1968). Komer's record as President Johnson's director of the CORDS pacification program has until recently been relegated among the group of "second-echelon" officials largely ignored because of their association with an unpopular war under Johnson and, no doubt in Komer's case, because of his aggressive, overbearing personality. He clashed with both American and Vietnamese leaders and military commanders, eventually clashing directly and publicly with General Abrams. Komer thus became a transitional figure in Vietnam. But his organizational skills, leadership, and understanding of the criticality of the GVN's responsibility for pacification enabled him to hand off to his deputy, Ambassador Colby, a functioning organization that continued to operate. The CORDS organization that Komer created not only imposed horizontal integration of the civil and military components of pacification but also ensured vertical integration through the establishment of lines of control and communication from the embassy in Saigon to the districts in the countryside. Komer also tried to impact the GVN bureaucracy by increasing the authority, responsibility, and competence of Vietnam's forty-four provincial governments.

Komer in 1972 wrote a Rand monograph about his and CORDS performance in Vietnam, *Bureaucracy Does Its Thing: Institutional Constraints on U.S.-GVN Performance in Vietnam*.[19] It is a remarkably candid and insightful document both for what its author believes was the war's flawed strategy and for what he ignores. The phrases "institutional constraints" or "bureaucratic inertia" and their variants are mentioned sixteen times in the nine-page summary (of a much longer report) as a way of explaining the US "lack of unified management" in Vietnam. Indeed, Komer spends four out of nine chapters on this subject.[20] *Bureaucracy* reads like a primer on the frustrations of public administration for US agencies operating abroad, but not on how to align policy,

strategy, and operations to win a war. Race's incisive analysis of the revolutionary movement's theory of victory made no impression on Komer. It was as if
he were reading something by someone from another empirical universe.[21]

Among the many programs brought under CORDS management and control, Komer viewed one of his principal jobs as that of measuring the effects
between pacification efforts in the countryside and what the military was
accomplishing in the field. One of CORDS' key measurement systems was
the Hamlet Evaluation System (HES). No one during the Vietnam War was
more involved in quantification and measurement than Secretary McNamara.
McNamara's focus on statistics to evaluate progress during the Vietnam War
included number of operations, number of enemy killed, number of captured
weapons, and, in the case of HES, scoring the effectiveness of pacification
progress. Komer's CORDS evaluation systems emulated McNamara's quantification. The Hamlet Evaluation System placed Vietnam's thousands of rural
hamlets in one of six categories: A, B, C, D, E, or V. The A–C categories de-
noted degrees of hamlets being relatively secure, while D and E meant they
were contested. Those designated V, for "under VC control," were considered
to be under enemy control. The HES, launched in January 1967, involved
some 250 MACV or MACCORDS district advisors completing monthly evaluation worksheets for 12,700 of South Vietnam's hamlets using a worksheet of
eighteen equally weighted indicators: nine relating to physical security and
nine relating to development.[22] Despite its data-gathering problems, HES
was considered more accurate than the subjective system it replaced.[23] The
HES designers believed they could identify and measure major pacification
trends and problems.[24] At the end of 1967, HES indicated that two-thirds of
the population were living in "relatively secure" areas, though that figure was
open to interpretation and debate.

By 1968, HES reports also included a countrywide map (map 19.1) indicating that 67 percent of Vietnam's population lived in secure hamlets, towns, or
cities. The January 31, 1968, HES map plotted 5,300 color-coded letters in
blue for A, B, and C (secure), green for D and E (contested), and red for V
(under VC control), representing 12,700 hamlets.

It was CORDS work products like the HES map plot that prompted General Westmoreland to express optimism about the war's progress in a November 1967 speech to the National Press Club in Washington and a press conference at the Pentagon. While he never publicly used the phrase "light at the
end of the tunnel" to characterize the progress, others in the administration
did. In fact, Westmoreland used it in a military cable to his deputy, General
Abrams.[25] This phrase lingered in the public mind long after the war ended
as an expression of the perceived bankruptcy of the Johnson administration's
military and pacification strategy. If HES was intended as a way to measure
the effectiveness of the administration's strategic architecture in Vietnam, by

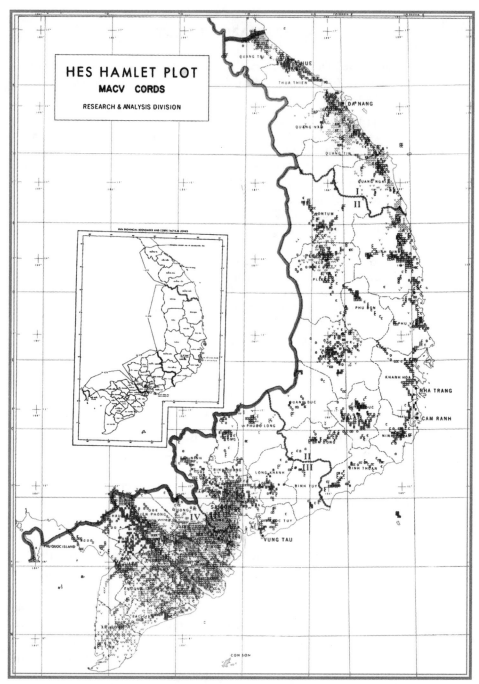

Map 19.1. The CORDS Hamlet Evaluation System map plot for January 1968 showed that 67 percent of Vietnam's population lived in secure hamlets, towns, or cities.

Source: Map acquired by author from MACV headquarters, Ton Son Nhut Air Base, Saigon, in March 1968. Shown is a black-and-white electronic scan of the original color-coded computer-generated output of 22.5 × 29 in. plot; darker data points are V-scored (under VC control) hamlets.

HES HAMLET PLOT

The January 1968 HES data, plotted as 5,300 data points representing 12,700 hamlets on a 1:1,000,000 map, indicated that 67 percent of the population lived in "secure" (A+B+C) hamlets.

A   Adequate security forces, infrastructure, public projects underway, economic picture improving. About 18 percent of total hamlets are A and contain about 5 percent of the total hamlet population.
B   Not immune to VC threat but security is organized and partially effective, infrastructure partially neutralized, self-help programs underway and economic programs started.
C   Subject to infrequent VC harassment, infrastructure identified, some participation in self-help programs.
D   VC activities reduced but still an internal threat. Some VC taxation and terrorism. Some local participation in local hamlet government and economic programs. Contested but leaning toward GVN.
E   VC are effective although some GVN control is evident. VC infrastructure intact. GVN programs are non-existent or just beginning.
V   Under VC control. No GVN or advisors except on military operations. Populace willingly or unwillingly support VC.

Note: Population is a far better measure of GVN control than hamlets. Countrywide, approximately 67 percent of population (including urban) is in A+B+C categories, i.e., secure. Yet only about 40 percent of hamlets are secure. "A" hamlets average 3,000 people each; VC hamlets average 710.

Source: Printed by the 66th Engr Co (TOPO) (CORPS)

implying that its quantitative scores were the basis for claiming a light at the end of the tunnel, it had failed.

The Tet Offensive, which the NVA and VC launched on February 1, 1968, initially appeared to make the HES plot irrelevant for accurate measurement of the security situation. Nevertheless, there was a frenetic rush to get district advisors back into the field in the following weeks to produce a new map plot. The classification of countrywide HES reports and map plots went from pre-Tet "For Official Use Only" to post-Tet "Top Secret," limited to a small group of senior MACV and CORDS personnel under very strict "need-to-know" criteria among those cleared for TS, signifying to many informed sources in Saigon that the administration's credibility would be further damaged if the HES reports were released to a wider distribution.

Ironically, the pre-Tet ratings had put 67 percent of the population in the relatively secure categories. The post-Tet measurements indicated that the figure was knocked down to 60 percent during the offensive but rebounded back to 66 percent by August 1968.[26] So release of the HES work products might have helped bolster the administration's and MACV's positions on the merits, but its top-secret classification rendered public release moot.

In the late fall of 1968, Colby succeeded Komer. His service as CORDS deputy under Komer had already established a strong working relationship with General Abrams as COMUSMACV, who had succeeded General West-moreland in July 1968, and Ambassador Ellsworth Bunker, who had suc-ceeded Henry Cabot Lodge in 1967. Three recent Vietnam War historians re-gard Abrams, Bunker, and Colby as an effective triumvirate that dramatically reversed a deteriorating situation between 1968 and 1972.[27]

Although designed to operate in a series of advisory and support roles, CORDS began to assume the form of a parallel structure to the GVN itself. While CORDS officials in the field served as advisors and enablers of paci-fication, they were never intended to assume governance roles in the society hosting them, although many of them probably wanted to.

Colby initiated an "accelerated pacification program" to increase security in all hamlets. In December 1969, HES scores were showing that 90 percent of hamlets merited C ratings or better, half of them in the A and B categories. By late 1972, this figure reached 97 percent. As John W. Root observes,

> Unquestionably, much of this "progress" was due to a drop in the intensity of the war, increasing the Regional and Popular Forces, and the success of the Phoenix Program. Retrospective studies show that HES figures suffered from inflation caused principally by command pressure and undervaluing security. Surveys of former district advisers revealed the existence of "gut HES" parallel reports that were more realistic and pessimistic, but these never got into the computer.[28]

Another possible explanation for inflated HES scores is that they were an im-portant factor in American military advisors' Officer Efficiency Reports (OERs). Having good OERs in one's service jacket was essential to promotion. So there was an inherent conflict of interest built into the HES insofar as the scorers could influence their OER evaluations by fudging HES scores in a positive di-rection. There is no evidence that this happened on a systematic basis, but the opportunity to manipulate scores to one's advantage was built into the system.

David W. P. Elliott is a Vietnam War scholar who has studied the utility of HES data products in some detail. While he acknowledges that HES "became a symbol of both the technocratic-managerial mentality of McNamara and his 'whiz kids' and their failure to understand the underlying complexities of revo-lution and social transformation," he points out that HES gave an indication of the "'security situation' in a hamlet, and provided a reasonable indication of the likelihood of a GVN force getting shot at if it operated in the hamlet." He is equally balanced on what HES did not reveal:

What does HES not tell us? Political loyalties, as opposed to observable behavior are beyond the reach of HES, both in principle and by design. As the HES evolved, it was aimed increasingly at eliminating subjective judgment and concentrating only on verifiable facts. Did the hamlet chief sleep in the hamlet or not? Was a bridge being built or wasn't it? Both the binary logic of the computer and the desire to standardize local responses so some meaningful national data could be generated dictated this approach. One of the paradoxes of the HES is that as its designers sought less subjectivity, they also increasingly attempted to measure more subtle indicators of "progress" in the complex struggle. When the early versions of the HES merely attempted to reflect the security situation, its rough indicators were suitable to the task, but as it addressed the more abstract questions of socioeconomic development, the rating process seems to have bogged down in the task of measuring the unmeasurable.[29]

In 1968, thirty-five years before Elliott's publication, the late Lieutenant Colonel William R. Corson, who commanded the Marine Combined Action Platoon program in I Corps and who was intimately familiar with HES, had published scathing remarks about "measuring the unmeasurable." His book was withering in its critique of HES and the purposes for which it was used:

Although the HES appears thorough and elaborate, it is accurate only to the extent that those who are using it in the field are accurate. And herein lies another very definite weakness in the system. Each district in which we have advisory teams has between fifty and 100 hamlets. On the average, due to the activity conditions and other demands on the adviser's time, he cannot visit in a month more than one out of four hamlets, yet he must "grade" each one (except for Viet Cong–controlled hamlets) every month. In addition, the time spent in the hamlets actually visited is about thirty minutes to an hour. As a final straw, the adviser possesses no special skills such as fluency in Vietnamese, experience in development economics, in knowledge of anthropology, sociology, or political science to help him carry out the complex grading task. As a result, the rating assigned to each hamlet is based on the grossest of measurements. In spite of these weaknesses, HES would not lack some utility if it were used to reveal problems rather than trumpet paper progress for political reasons.[30]

Corson analyzed the ambiguity of the HES grading criteria under the A–E and VC categories. He then drove home his point by illustrating the meaninglessness of the A and B scores by pointing out that a hamlet near the provincial capital of Quang Nam Province in I Corps, Cam An, oscillated between an A and B score throughout 1967. Cam An was used as a pacification showcase for a personal fact-finding visit by Senator Clifford P. Case, briefed by Ambassador Henry L. T. Koren, the deputy for CORDS in the I Corps area. Corson pointedly observed,

In point of fact there had been *no* [italics in original] overt military incidents for several months against Cam An, but the hamlet's residents were being taxed regularly by the Viet Cong. Each of the peasants who traveled the four miles to the [provincial] capital to market his fish and rice carried with him a Viet Cong tax receipt to insure his safe conduct through the "enemy lines." This is the reality of the GVN's pacification situation—the incidents of terrorism, attacks, and sabotage are only the visible portion of the iceberg. The ubiquitous and pervasive presence of the Viet Cong is evident in the entire fabric of Vietnamese society.[31]

While these issues of measurement were debated between Saigon and Washington, McNamara's and Komer's "war by the numbers" was never reconciled with the visible violence the public was seeing in news reports and telecasts during and after the Tet Offensive. A month into the Tet Offensive, CBS news anchor Walter Cronkite said the following in an unusual and unprecedented "editorial opinion" at the end of the evening news broadcast on February 27, 1968: "For it seems now more certain than ever that the bloody experience of Vietnam is to end in a stalemate."

President Johnson said after watching this broadcast, "That's it. If I've lost Cronkite, I've lost middle America."[32] The Pentagon's and MACV's confidence in the CORDS measurement systems and the optimistic outputs they were producing in late 1967 and early 1968 had been fatally undermined, no matter what the numbers were showing. The Tet Offensive had shattered the American public's confidence in the war, and with it the Johnson administration's strategic architecture.

20

THE TET OFFENSIVE (1968)

Strategic Disaster

The Tet Offensive commenced on January 31, 1968, the last day of the Lunar New Year and the most important holiday in the Vietnamese year in both the North and the South. The NVA planned it as a one-two punch consisting of a "General Offensive" and a "General Uprising," resulting in the overthrow of the GVN. Its outcome was a double-edged irony for both sides.

Recent scholarship indicates that Le Duan and his "War Politburo" planned the Tet Offensive. After years of indecisive warfare, Le Duan wanted to find the American breaking point. While Ho Chi Minh and Giap were urging caution, "Le Duan and his hawks in the Politburo strove for total victory through an ambitious and risky large-scale offensive aimed at the cities and towns of South Vietnam." Le Duan found a more compliant general to implement his risky military strategy in Senior General Van Tien Dung. Dung had shrewdly positioned himself to replace General Nguyen Chi Thanh, who had commanded NVA forces in the South during the Ia Drang battle and who later died from a heart attack on July 6, 1967, under murky circumstances. It was Le Duan and General Dung who unveiled their plans at a high-level meeting in Hanoi on July 18–19, 1967. They proposed that while NVA main-force units tied down American troops away from urban centers, the VC would mount large-scale attacks on the cities and towns throughout Vietnam to incite a mass insurrection that would topple the GVN regime in Saigon.[1]

The success of the plan depended on three assumptions: (1) the ARVN would collapse under the weight of the countrywide general offensive (map 20.1), (2) the people of South Vietnam would follow through with a general

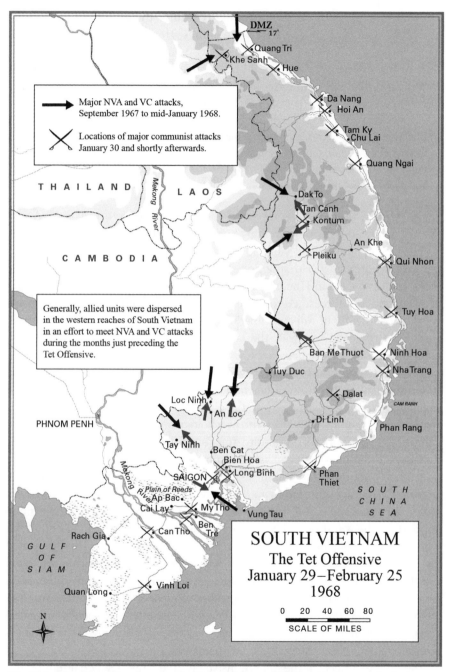

Map 20.1. The plan of First Secretary Le Duan and General Van Tien Dung to attack all major cities and towns in South Vietnam failed to deliver a military victory, but it undermined the American public's confidence in the war.

Source: USMA Atlases.

uprising, and (3) American political will to continue the war would crack in the face of the overwhelming assault. None of these things happened as predicted. Neither the NVA nor the revolutionary movement achieved the military objectives of the offensive or the political objective of the uprising. However, the American public did undergo a major shock. As NVA brigadier general Tran Do, who was one of the Tet planners, retrospectively remarked,

> In all honesty, we didn't achieve our main objective, which was to spur uprisings throughout the south. Still, we inflicted heavy casualties on the Americans and their puppets, and this was a big gain for us. As for making an impact on the United States, it had not been our intention—but it turned out to be a fortunate result.[2]

For MACV, the outcome appeared to be a tactical victory. The NVA and the VC achieved significant military surprise, but they were unable to exploit it. The NVA planners had violated Clausewitz's principle of mass. By attacking everywhere, they had superior strength nowhere. The general uprising failed to occur, even in Hue, where General Tran Do took personal command of NVA and VC forces.[3] Across the country, as Tet unfolded, the offensive was launched without full coordination of enemy units, north and south, with respect to timing. Even with the advantage of surprise, the NVA offensive achieved few military gains.

The Viet Cong's efforts in Saigon were piecemeal, uncoordinated operations. A nineteen-man VC platoon breached the wall of the US embassy compound in Saigon. It never penetrated into the chancery. This force was wiped out in a matter of a few hours. However, the psychological effect was devastating to the Johnson administration's credibility. Images of the American symbol of power in Saigon under enemy siege flashed around the world, out of all proportion to its military importance. When these images were coupled with reports that the presidential palace, the radio station, and numerous other targets in Saigon had been attacked as well, President Johnson's credibility evaporated. Public support for the war dropped twelve points between the "light at the end of the tunnel" public-relations campaign of the previous fall and the Tet Offensive.[4] By late March, another poll revealed that 78 percent of Americans surveyed felt that the United States was not making any progress in the war, and only 26 percent of the American public approved of Johnson's handling of the war. On March 31, 1968, President Johnson in a nationally televised speech indicated that he would not seek election to a second term. The enemy plan's third assumption about American will had been correct.

The military effects of the Tet Offensive deserve more detailed attention because Americans in their opinion responses, and the increasingly acrimonious antiwar protests, never allowed either the Johnson or Nixon administrations to recover a wide base of popular support for the war. A historical understanding of events as they unfolded reveals a more complex narrative that became increasingly irrelevant to public opinion.

Reconstruction of the North Vietnamese plan for the Tet Offensive reveals that it was a classical deception plan borrowed from Chinese communist doctrine and the principles of Sun Tzu. One key element in the plan was a peripheral campaign designed to draw American and Vietnamese combat units out of the urban areas toward the borders of the country. On January 21, 1968, several NVA divisions converged on the isolated marine outpost at Khe Sanh in northern I Corps near the DMZ (maps 20.1 and 20.2). The NVA in attacking Khe Sanh was relying on the Americans to misread history and see the developing battle as another Dien Bien Phu in the making. This part of the deception worked—for a short time—until the Tet Offensive was launched nine days later. Khe Sanh drew the attention of most of the military and political leadership from Saigon to Washington. President Johnson's attention was riveted on Khe Sanh. It became an obsession for him. He had a scale terrain model of the marine base built for the Situation Room in the White House.[5]

Colonel Finlayson offers a more intriguing explanation for why the NVA attacked the marine base at Khe Sanh. During 1968, as a marine captain assigned to the Provincial Reconnaissance Unit in Tay Ninh Province, Finlayson worked closely with the CIA case officer for the "Tay Ninh Source," who served as the highest-level US/GVN HUMINT penetration of the Central Office of South Vietnam (COSVN), the revolutionary movement's headquarters in the South. The Tay Ninh Source had reported to the CIA that the North Vietnamese fear of an invasion of southern Laos was the main cause for their decision to attack the marine base at Khe Sanh and launch the Tet Offensive. An invasion of the Laotian panhandle, as Finlayson noted earlier, was the North Vietnamese leadership's deepest strategic fear that the Americans might successfully block the Ho Chi Minh Trail by inserting sufficient forces into Laos.[6]

On January 2, 1968, a marine reconnaissance patrol spotted shadowy figures on the slope near the base's outer defensive perimeter. The marines opened fire and killed six NVA officers. This incident convinced Westmoreland that several thousand enemy soldiers were near Khe Sanh and that they wanted to repeat their Dien Bien Phu victory at Khe Sanh against the marines. Westmoreland, who clearly was using the marines as bait to draw out the NVA units, saw this as an opportunity to fight a decisive engagement.

With this enemy buildup, the communists had cut Route 9, the only east–west line of communication to the coast. Westmoreland poured in supplies and reinforcements by air. Included on the flights into Khe Sanh were reporters eager for a big combat story. Their reporting elevated the Khe Sanh story out of all proportion to its strategic significance, as subsequent events showed. By mid-January, six thousand marines defended the main plateau and four surrounding

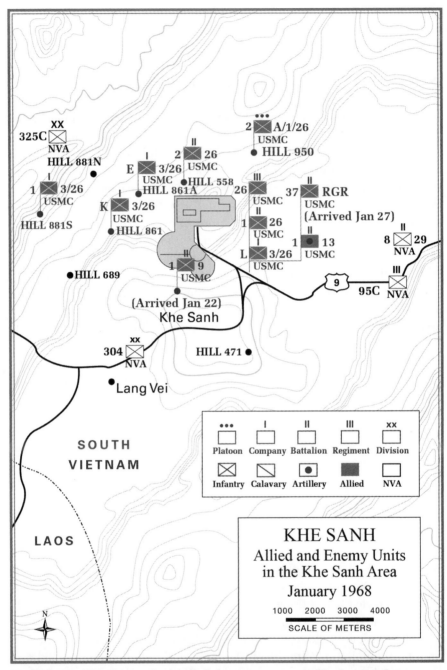

Map 20.2. The NVA divisions that attacked the marine outpost at Khe Sanh in I Corps were a response to the enemy's strategic fear that the Khe Sanh position might be the start of a MACV strategy to block the Ho Chi Minh Trail.

Source: Based on USMC map and military unit data, dated 1968, hosted by Wikipedia Commons, http://en.wikipedia .org/wiki/File:KhSh9colkey.png.

hills named for their elevations—Hills 950, 881, 861, and 558 (map 20.2). Approximately half of the marine force defended the Khe Sanh base itself, and the remainder was deployed among the hill positions. Infantry at each garrison were supported by 105 mm howitzers, and the garrison could call on the prodigious airpower of 7th Air Force headquartered at Ton Son Nhut Air Base outside Saigon and the SAC B-52 wings based on Guam and in Thailand.

As brutal as the fighting at Khe Sanh became, the engagements fought over the next four months constituted neither the decisive battle that Johnson and Westmoreland expected nor a set-piece repetition of Dien Bien Phu in 1954. The battle commenced a week before Tet with the NVA 325thC Division launching an unsuccessful three-battalion assault on marine defensive positions outside the main firebase. Then, for the next three weeks, there was a seeming hiatus while the Tet Offensive raged throughout South Vietnam.

The marines at Khe Sanh effectively neutralized repeated NVA ground attacks, often after intense hand-to-hand fighting. Aid indicates that the SIGINT evidence shows that the NVA had to strip units from the front lines around Khe Sanh and send them south to support communist units mauled in fighting elsewhere. Aid judges Khe Sanh to be a SIGINT tactical success story rather than the decisive, strategic battle that General Westmoreland wanted and President Johnson needed to restore war policy credibility.[7]

Meanwhile, the communists had been using the Christmas 1967 cease-fire to move and mass their forces into position.[8] At the same time, American SIGINT assets in late 1967 and early 1968 were intercepting increased radio traffic between NVA headquarters and subordinate combat formations, indicating that the enemy was preparing to attack cities in the Central Highlands (II Corps) and increase the pressure on Khe Sanh. None of these SIGINT reports were indicating any plans to mount a general offensive operation south of II Corps. At the same time that the National Security Agency (NSA)[9] was reporting these intelligence developments in the north, a SIGINT station outside Saigon, the 303rd Radio Research Battalion at Long Binh, was reporting increased RF traffic much closer to Saigon. By mid-January, intelligence analysts were concluding that three NVA and VC divisions were now deployed in an arc around Saigon, within easy striking distance of the capital. Radio traffic between January 15 and 25, 1968, increased to an "almost unprecedented volume of urgent messages passing among major [enemy] commands."[10]

NSA intercept sites in Southeast Asia continued to pick up further "hard" indicators that the North Vietnamese were about to be unleashed. One on January 28 revealed that "N-day" to launch the offensive was going to be January 30 at 0300. This message went straight to President Johnson. The Defense Intelligence Agency (DIA) discounted the imminence of these messages, believing that the Viet Cong would wait until the end of the Tet lunar holiday before commencing offensive operations. Then, a day later, on the night of

January 29–30, 1968, as one radio-direction-finding post at Bien Hoa Air Base outside Saigon reported, every VC/NVA radio in the country went silent. As one army SIGINT specialist later recounted, "We could not raise a ditty bop for love nor money. It was the damnedest thing I never *didn't* [*sic*, italics in original] hear. Complete radio silence."[11]

Three hours later, one hundred thousand NVA and VC troops launched the massive and seemingly coordinated offensive against over one hundred cities, towns, and major military bases throughout South Vietnam, attacking thirty-eight of the country's forty-four provincial capitals and seventy (of 250) district capitals, capturing Hue and seizing significant portions of Saigon. Although the communist plan included objectives nationwide, Saigon and the major US and ARVN bases in nearby Long Binh and Bien Hoa were important strategic objectives. This area, formed by a thirty-mile radius around the capital and known as the Capital Military Zone or Saigon Circle, was indeed strategic, but its symbolic significance was even larger in the collective mind of the American public. If Saigon was not secure, how could any place in the country be secure?

Fortuitously, Lieutenant General Frederick C. Weyand, commander of US II Field Force headquartered at Long Binh, had read the same NSA reports as MACV and did not like the pattern of increased enemy RF traffic reported in the Saigon area. In November 1967, troopers of the 101st Airborne Division had captured a communist document calling for a general offensive/uprising.[12] While US intelligence analysts dismissed this along with the SIGINT reports on the grounds that it was beyond the capabilities of the enemy to launch a countrywide offensive, as most on the MACV staff believed, General Weyand convinced Westmoreland to let him pull more US combat maneuver battalions back in around Saigon. As a result, when the Tet Offensive broke, there were twenty-seven battalions instead of the planned fourteen in the Capital Military Zone to fight when the attack came. Weyand's foresight significantly mitigated the damage caused by Tet in the Saigon area. Indeed, by mid-March, the number of US maneuver battalions around Saigon had increased to 152.[13]

Militarily, the Tet Offensive was a tactical disaster for the communists. By the end of March 1968, North Vietnam had not achieved its two principal military objectives, only to achieve something else, what proved to be the most crucial, the collapse of American public opinion about the war. However, on a hard-numbers reckoning, more than fifty-eight thousand NVA and VC troops died in the offensive. US military losses were 3,895 dead, with ARVN losses at 4,954. Non-US allies lost 214. More than 14,300 South Vietnamese civilians died. Most of the VC infrastructure that surfaced in many provinces was cut down or captured because VC guerrilla forces in the south in III and IV Corps led the major attacks and suffered the heaviest casualties. David T. Zabecki's Tet entry in Tucker's encyclopedia asserts flatly that "the guerrilla infrastructure developed over so many years was wiped out."[14] Lewis A. Sorley and others challenge Zabecki's sweeping conclusion:

> The fact that the Viet Cong infrastructure had remained largely intact after Tet 1968 was confirmed by continuation of the enemy's ruthless campaigns of terrorism and assassination. More than a year later, the newly installed Nixon administration's comprehensive survey of the situation in Vietnam[15] also reached that conclusion.[16]

Elsewhere in the country, the Tet Offensive's effects in the countryside weakened the GVN's standing. Nearly five hundred of the five thousand paramilitary Regional Forces (RFs) and Popular Forces (PFs) outposts were abandoned or overrun. The government had to withdraw RF/PF units from rural hamlets into besieged cities and towns in many cases to provide additional defensive and blocking forces. More than 6,500 territorial forces soldiers were killed, were missing, or had deserted. The VC had attacked a number of Revolutionary Development Cadre (RDC) teams, and as a result the GVN had reassigned roughly half of the RDC teams, half of the ARVN battalions supporting them in pacification, and Vietnamese National Police and National Police Field Force units to help defend the cities. Most ARVN battalions resumed pacification duties at the end of February, but this relatively rapid resumption of the pacification mission was lost on any observer outside of MACV and its subordinate units.

Equally serious in the overall American perception was the malfeasance of some National Police and ARVN personnel. The most emblematic episode was the execution by Nguyen Ngoc Loan, director general of the National Police, of a handcuffed Viet Cong soldier on February 1, 1968, on a Saigon street in front of two witnesses, a Vietnamese cameraman working for NBC and an Associated Press photographer. The Pulitzer Prize–winning photograph would become one of the most recognized images of the war. Loan quickly became a one-man target for antiwar demonstrators, and more generally a representation of everything Americans at home feared about the Saigon regime: the impression of out-of-control violence, autocracy, corruption, and lawlessness.[17]

By the spring of 1968, it had become clear to the Johnson administration that the American people were no longer willing to accept the high casualty rates and open-ended commitment incurred by the armed forces of the United States in the Vietnam War. They averaged over three hundred Americans killed in action per week during 1968.[18] No amount of nation building, it seemed to many critics dragging President Johnson down in the polls, could turn the situation around. The American strategic architecture to fight the Vietnam War had been broken by the nationwide violence of the Tet Offensive. Policy, strategy, and operations were perceived by the American public as wildly out of rational alignment. If American policy was to defend South Vietnam against a communist takeover by North Vietnam, and if the strategy was a combination of main-force military attacks against the NVA (by MACV and the ARVN) and COIN pacification in the countryside (by the GVN with CORDS), and if HES was showing light at the end of the tunnel, how could the Johnson administration explain the fighting countrywide that went on for months after Tet, especially when General Westmoreland had just requested 250,000 more troops?[19]

21

VIETNAMIZATION

Never a Winning Strategy

In January 1969, Dr. Henry A. Kissinger, about to become President Richard M. Nixon's national security advisor, criticized General Westmoreland's main-force attrition strategy in a January 1969 *Foreign Affairs* article:

We fought a military war; our opponents fought a political one. We sought physical attrition; our opponents aimed for our psychological exhaustion. In the process, we lost sight of one of the cardinal maxims of guerrilla war: the guerrilla wins if he does not lose; the conventional army loses if it does not win. The North Vietnamese used their main forces the way a bullfighter uses his cape—to keep us lunging into areas of marginal political importance.[1]

Kissinger thought it was time for the army "to adopt a strategy which is plausible because it reduces casualties. It should concentrate on the protection of the population, thereby undermining communist political assets. We should continue to strengthen the Vietnamese army to permit a gradual withdrawal of some American forces."[2] By summer, this strategy had a name: "Vietnamization."

Three years later, with Vietnamization failing to produce the results the Nixon administration wanted—extrication from Vietnam and "peace with honor"—Nixon and Kissinger were blunt to each other about defining the war's outcome. During an August 3, 1972, Oval Office meeting, the president and Kissinger had this exchange:

NIXON. Let's be perfectly cold-blooded about it. . . . I look at the tide of history out there, South Vietnam probably is never gonna survive anyway. I'm just being perfectly candid. . . . [C]an we have a viable foreign policy if a year from now or two years from now, North Vietnam gobbles up South Vietnam? That's the real question.

KISSINGER. If a year or two years from now North Vietnam gobbles up South Vietnam, we can have a viable foreign policy if it looks as if it's the result of South Vietnamese incompetence. If we now sell out in such a way that, say, in a three-to-four-month period, we have pushed President Thieu over the brink . . . it will worry everybody.

NIXON. I know.

KISSINGER. So we've got to find some formula that holds the thing together a year or two, after which—after a year, Mr. President, Vietnam will be a backwater. If we settle it, say, this October [1972], by January '74, no one will give a damn.[3]

This cynical Oval Office conversation suggests that implementation of the Nixon Vietnamization policy never seriously contemplated an end state in which the GVN could be bolstered to survive on its own. According to Jeffrey Kimball's research, the documentary record shows that, from 1969 to 1972, Nixon and Kissinger both clung to the goal of an independent, noncommunist South Vietnam until "political, economic, and military circumstances" forced them to accept the "decent-interval" settlement.[4] Indeed, their acquiescence in having to accept this solution can be construed as evidence of the flaws in the strategic architecture of Vietnamization they pursued.

Insisting on an independent South Vietnam was never realistic given the Vietnamization strategy that was pursued. Vietnamization never created, nor was it intended to create, a sufficiently robust GVN that could defend itself, not without the in-country presence of American power or a different, more intrusive, whole-of-government approach by CORDS.

Melvin Small, a scholar of the Nixon presidency, reminds his readers of the strength of the antiwar movement and its dissatisfaction with the pace of American troop withdrawals and the failure of the Paris Talks because of the intransigence of both sides. As one example, in October 1969 the Vietnam Moratorium Committee, consisting of "antiwar moderates," turned out "the most successful antiwar demonstration in history, involving over two million people in over 200 cities." Between 1969 and 1972, there were twelve mass antiwar demonstrations in Washington, DC; six of them involved large crowds: 250,000 (October 1969), 600,000 (November 1969), 50,000 (April 1970), 100,000 (May 1970), 500,000 (April 1971), and 35,000 (May 1971).[5]

The Nixon administration, like the Johnson administration, had to pay close attention to the public mood and to compete aggressively to rally public support for the war. The president's "Silent Majority" speech in November 1969 and White House strategies to neutralize the media, which Nixon believed favored antiwar doves, were intended to counter the antiwar movement. Ironically, the appeal to a silent majority and the assault on what it perceived to be the eastern seaboard liberal media came from a president who had promised to bring the nation together, not divide it. The administration was relying "on a polarizing strategy to regain the upper hand in the battle for the hearts and minds of the American people."[6]

Eventually the middle-class and university student origins of the protest movement began to cross social and class boundaries. Early participants included civil rights, black power, nationalist, and self-determination activists; antiwar elements of the labor movement; and later thousands of active-duty soldiers. Working-class conservatism began to break down.[7] In short, the administration's position on the war never remained secure for very long.

Penny Lewis indicates that the battle to influence public opinion on the war affected broad segments of the population. Her research indicates that "working class people were never more likely than their middle-class counterparts to support the war, and in many instances, they were more likely to oppose it. . . . Johnson and Nixon found their most consistent support among more affluent and educated groups. Working-class people formed opinions of the war that showed they were increasingly skeptical of their leaders, even when they were willing to give them more chances." It was a complex public-opinion profile crossing multiple social and class boundaries. Overall, however, Gallup polling numbers indicated that "by the end of 1968, a majority of Americans wanted out [of Vietnam], and by September 1970, a majority of Americans wanted *immediate* [italics in original] withdrawal, regardless of outcome."[8]

The foregoing sketches the political background leading up to the August 1972 Oval Office conversation. The administration was under increasing domestic political pressure to end the war. Nixon and Kissinger were frustrated by the war because they had bigger Cold War geopolitical designs on their minds. They had been working since 1969 to establish a new relationship with the PRC. The Vietnam War, therefore, was seen as a constraint on establishing what a year later was the beginning of a rapprochement with the PRC. At the same time, they were also seeking détente with the Soviet Union. Negotiations with the Soviets began in Helsinki in November 1969, eventually leading to the signing of the first Strategic Arms Limitation Treaty (SALT I) in May 1972.

President Nixon visited China in February 1972 ending twenty-five years of Cold War separation between the two powers. This initiative had been in the planning stages for years.[9] The success of the Kissinger-China initiative, secret until it was revealed in 1972, required at least the appearance of US resolve in Vietnam. Therefore, MACV, CORDS, and the combat units worked hard to make Vietnamization viable. And thousands continued to die in performance of their duties.

The 1969 campaign plan General Abrams had approved as COMUSMACV early that year recognized that public support for the war had diminished. The "One War: MACV Command Overview, 1969–1972" specified that

> the key strategic thrust is to provide meaningful, continuing security for the Vietnamese people in expanding areas of increasingly effective civil authority. . . . It is important that the command move away from the over-emphasized and often irrelevant "body count" preoccupation. . . . In order to provide security for the population our operations must succeed in neutralizing the VCI [Viet Cong Infrastructure] and separating the enemy from the population. The enemy main forces and NVA are blind without the VCI. They cannot obtain intelligence, cannot obtain food, cannot prepare the battlefield, and cannot move "unseen."[10]

In July 1969, the Nixon administration formalized its policy of turning over the fighting responsibilities to the South Vietnamese while MACV and MACCORDS continued to supply matériel and financial assistance. Incoming secretary of defense Melvin R. Laird created the term *Vietnamization* to describe the transformation. In principle, Vietnamization sounded like a return to words spoken six years before by President Kennedy in the CBS interview with Walter Cronkite: "In the final analysis, it is their war. They are the ones who have to win it or lose it."[11]

The Abrams-Bunker-Colby triumvirate pursued Vietnamization tirelessly. An official CMH narrative describes the intensity of the effort. It implicitly acknowledges an irony in Vietnamization:

> By 1967 the Vietnamese Army was devoted almost entirely to pacification security missions and, in the minds of many, had been relegated to a secondary role in the conduct of the war. Vietnamese Army units often reflected this attitude in their overall lack of enthusiasm and in their willingness to leave most of the fighting to the Americans.[12]

A Southeast Asian army that had never succeeded in its pacification mission was now returning to conventional training for war fighting against NVA main-force units while Colby and MACCORDS tried to build up the RF/PF and RDC personnel in the countryside to improve hamlet HES scores. Simultaneously, American troop strength was drastically diminished from 542,000 in January 1969 and a monthly casualty count of 795 KIA, to 45,600 by July 1972 and a monthly casualty count of 36 KIA.[13]

Ambassador Colby defined Vietnamization broadly as the "practical consequences of the Nixon Doctrine, that is, withdrawal of American troops and reinforcement of South Vietnamese forces to withstand North Vietnamese."[14] What were those "practical consequences"? They included improving and modernizing the ARVN, providing pacification in the countryside, strengthening the country's political institutions, delivering essential governmental services, building a viable economy, and, most important of all, ensuring security for the population. These goals were expressed in the vocabulary of nation building, a commonplace term in the late 1960s but one that would be virtually banished from the country's foreign-policy terminology after the Vietnam War; indeed, nation building is still eschewed, particularly when it is stated as "armed nation building."

MACCORDS undertook a broad range of tasks to accomplish nation building: expanding and improving the police and paramilitary RF/PF forces, land reform, economic control of inflation (to minimize the effects of infusions of USAID dollars into South Vietnam's economy), conducting local elections at the rural level, and ferreting out the Viet Cong Infrastructure. All of these goals and tasks under Vietnamization amounted to another version of a reinforcement strategy as opposed to a preemptive one. They failed to define the core issue of the motivation problem: how does a foreign power inject resources into a Southeast Asian society where most of the population either distrusts the government and its institutions or is indifferent to it? There was no civic culture in South Vietnam inclining and preparing the rural population to accept the physical and security risks of supporting the government. Reinforcement did not reach down to the behavioral fundamentals of enough people being prepared to risk death on behalf of the regime. The North Vietnamese knew that the Nixon administration was trying to negotiate from a position of strength, but what leverage did it have if it was withdrawing troops, curtailing bombing north of the 17th parallel, and energetically trying to strengthen a regime that had never established the kind of civic, patriotic loyalty that Western democratic societies enjoyed as a matter of course?

General Abrams's "one war" strategy clashed head-on with the organizational cultures of both armies, American and Vietnamese. Douglas S. Blaufarb explained that under Westmoreland's main-force strategy, with American units attacking main-force NVA combat units, the pacification mission was much less glamorous:

> In fact, the pacification support mission was not popular with ARVN commanders who, naturally, derived their values from their American mentors. It seemed demeaning compared with the main-force war. It also called for tedious, very basic, small-unit operations with little opportunity for dramatic battles using the full panoply of weapons at their command. Success in pacification did not bring glory and promotions. It brought hard, tedious work, nighttime operations, and casualties.[15]

And there was powerful opposition within the US Army's senior leadership. The Westmoreland-Abrams main-force operations continued. Nagl quotes one anonymous officer who was vociferous: "I'll be damned if I permit the United States Army, its institutions, its doctrines, and its traditions to be destroyed just to win this lousy war." Lieutenant General Julian J. Ewell, who first commanded the 9th ID and later II Field Force, "continued to demonstrate a preoccupation with body counts rather than pacification." In his debriefing report of September 1969, he wrote, "I guess I basically feel that the 'hearts and minds' approach can be overdone. In the delta the only way to overcome VC control and terror is by brute force applied against the VC." A combat historian serving in II Field Force recalled that the "policy was to bring in all available firepower—air strikes and all the artillery in II FFV—and then go in and sweep after the firepower had done the killing." Operation *Speedy Express*, executed in the Upper Mekong delta under Ewell's command between December 1968 and June 1969, killed 10,883 of the enemy at a cost of 267 Americans killed. CORDS observers reported, "The high body counts achieved by the 9th ID were not composed exclusively of active VC. The normal ratio of three or four enemy KIA for every weapon captured was raised at times to fifty to one; this leads to the suspicion that many VC supporters, willing or unwilling, and innocent bystanders were also eliminated."[16]

As Krepinevich summarized the two years following the Tet Offensive, 1968–1970,

> Army main-force units continued to operate much as they always had. While there were cases of units breaking down into smaller elements and providing population security over an extended period of time, they were the exception. Following one last great search-and-destroy operation into Cambodia in April–May 1970, the withdrawal of U.S. ground forces proceeded apace, and questions of strategy became academic. The Army was going home.[17]

Krepinevich is referring to the invasion of Cambodia, ordered by the Nixon administration in the spring of 1970. Known at the time as the "Cambodian Incursion," it involved fifty thousand ARVN and thirty thousand US troops to relieve pressure on Cambodian armed forces after Prince Norodom Sihanouk had been overthrown and succeeded by General Lon Nol.[18] Lon Nol had sent his small army against the sixty thousand VC troops entrenched in three border provinces. NVA and VC forces counterattacked, occupying two more Cambodian provinces and threatening the capital, Phnom Penh. Although very controversial, Nixon and Kissinger believed the Cambodian Incursion dealt a stunning blow to the communists, drove mainforce units away from the border, and damaged their morale. ARVN and US units captured more than ten times the amount of supplies captured inside Vietnam in the previous year.

Sadly for South Vietnam, the results of Vietnamization were not sufficient to prevent the GVN's collapse five years later.

22

THE FINAL YEARS (1969–1975)

The Losing Path

Until 1969, Viet Cong units in South Vietnam operated almost exclusively as a Phase 2 guerrilla insurgency. With US force levels drawing down rapidly under the Nixon Doctrine, the revolutionary movement gradually switched to Phase 3 warfare over the next three years at Le Duan's urging. The balance of forces was starting to shift in favor of the communists. The Viet Cong, joined by NVA units, gradually became capable between 1969 and 1972 of conducting open conventional warfare.

After 1969, the policy of the ARVN to transform itself, organizationally and doctrinally, from pacification to conventional warfare, meant that it could perform neither mission well. Its American mentor and sponsor, while excelling at conventional warfare and the relentless application of large-scale, combined-arms firepower when it could find appropriate targets, had not prepared the ARVN for either its pacification or its conventional mission. It failed in the former because the US Army establishment never aligned as a war-fighting institution behind counterinsurgency doctrine. And it failed in the latter because South Vietnam's politicians, most of whom were military officers themselves, never staffed the ARVN with leaders in an accountable chain of command where military skills, competence, and winning results dominated strategic and tactical decisions top to bottom. There were numerous division, brigade, regimental, and battalion commanders, small-unit company and platoon commanders, and NCOs who excelled in their jobs, but they never coalesced into an integrated army determined to prevail. They had become dependent on American combat and logistical support to operate in the field. Under Vietnamization, they never prepared for the eventuality that they might have to fight and survive on their own.

By 1972, to supply and reinforce NVA and VC combat units, the North Vietnamese had increased the length of all-weather roads down the Ho Chi Minh Trail from 1,070 miles in 1965 to eight times that figure, running from North Vietnam through southern Laos and eastern Cambodia into South Vietnam. That accomplishment was a clear indication that the *Rolling Thunder* interdiction campaign had failed.[1] Entire divisions, replete with artillery and tanks, started taking up positions in South Vietnam. By March 1972, Le Duan felt strong enough to order a major invasion of South Vietnam.

This was the largest military operation mounted by a communist enemy since the Korean War. By this time, the number of in-country US Air Force aircraft had fallen to seventy-six, 75 percent of which consisted of F-4 Phantom fighter-bombers. About one hundred other jet fighters operated from Thailand, and B-52s were still based on Guam. As Van Creveld points out, "Thanks to Nixon's policy of Vietnamization, the South Vietnamese Air Force (RVNAF) had considerably more combat aircraft and helicopters than remaining U.S. forces did; however, it was still afflicted by lack of technical capability as well as fighting morale."[2]

On March 29, 1972, the NVA launched the Easter Offensive, a coordinated, three-front attack designed to strike a decisive blow against the GVN and its armed forces. In I Corps (MR-I in map 22.1*) on March 30, 1972, NVA divisions attacked across the DMZ into Quang Tri Province toward Hue and Da Nang, with other forces pressing east from the A Shau valley. The NVA wanted to force the GVN to commit reserves to protect the northern tier of provinces so that it could launch a second attack against the Central Highlands and a third attack from Cambodia to threaten Saigon. The overall objective of these attacks was to split South Vietnam in two, possibly leading to the regime's collapse or, at the very least, a peace agreement on Hanoi's terms.[3] After a month of fierce fighting, ARVN forces were driven out of Quang Tri City. The ARVN, backed by US airpower, successfully defended Hue before recapturing Quang Tri City on September 15, 1972.

In II Corps (MR-II in map 22.1), NVA divisions pushed into the Central Highlands from northern Cambodia on April 12, 1972, with the objective of capturing Kontum City. After coming close to splitting South Vietnam in two, the NVA attack was driven back two months later on June 9 by a combination of ARVN counterattacks and US airpower.

In III Corps (MR-III in map 22.1) on April 7, 1972, North Vietnamese forces launched a series of attacks into Binh Long Province from Cambodia and began an assault on An Loc, sixty-five miles northwest of Saigon. An

---

Military Region was now the designation for a Corps Tactical Zone (Corps or CTZ).

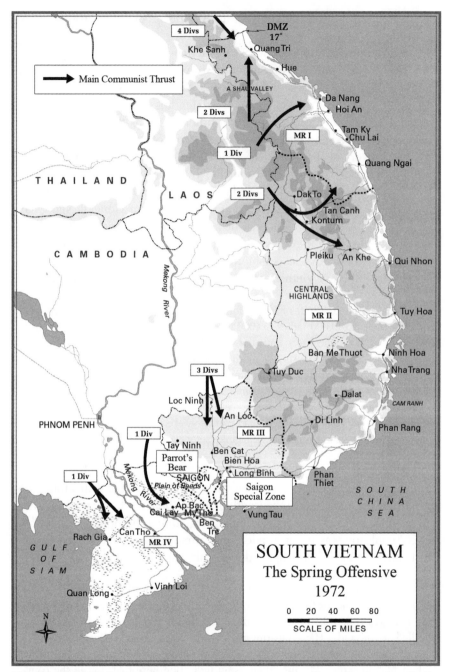

Map 22.1. The 1972 Easter Offensive was the largest communist military offensive since the Korean War; Le Duan and his NVA commanders wanted to win the Vietnam War militarily.
Source: USMA Atlases.

The following labels appear on the map:

4 Divs
DMZ 17°
Khe Sanh
Quang Tri
Hue

Main Communist Thrust

A SHAU VALLEY
Da Nang
Hoi An
2 Divs
Tam Ky
Chu Lai
MR I
1 Div
Quang Ngai

THAILAND
LAOS
2 Divs
Dak To
Tan Canh
Kontum

CAMBODIA
Mekong River
Pleiku
An Khe
Qui Nhon
CENTRAL HIGHLANDS
MR II
Tuy Hoa

Ban Me Thuot
Ninh Hoa
3 Divs
Tuy Duc
Nha Trang
Dalat
CAM RANH
Loc Ninh
An Loc
Di Linh
Phan Rang
PHNOM PENH
1 Div
MR III
Tay Ninh
Parrot's Bear
Ben Cat
Bien Hoa
Long Binh
Phan Thiet
1 Div
Mekong River
SAIGON
Plain of Reeds
Saigon Special Zone
SOUTH CHINA SEA
Ap Bac
Cai Lay
My Tho
Vung Tau
Ben Tre
Rach Gia
Can Tho
MR IV
GULF OF SIAM
Quan Long
Vinh Loi
N

SOUTH VIETNAM
The Spring Offensive
1972

0   20   40   60   80
SCALE OF MILES

ARVN counteroffensive, combined with American bombing, drove the NVA out of the city by June 18.

As the fighting continued, the North Vietnamese reinforced the offensive until they reached fourteen divisions and six hundred tanks deployed in South Vietnam; this order of battle did not include Viet Cong units.[4] In resisting this onslaught, some ARVN units, like those defending Quang Tri, including the crack 1st ARVN Division, fought well;[5] others, such as the 3rd ARVN Division (newly created and manned by castoffs from other units), broke in disarray.[6] The bravery of the individual ARVN soldier generally was not the main problem; instead, it was poor leadership by politically appointed generals. President Nguyen Van Thieu relieved the commander of I Corps and replaced him with one of the ablest ARVN generals, Lieutenant General Ngo Quang Truong, who steadfastly defended Hue and the northern region. The issue, as always, was whether the ARVN had adequately staffed itself with sufficiently competent and effective leadership to stand on its own. Dale Andradé summarized the effects of Vietnamization on the ARVN and its officer corps:

> By 1972, the United States had provided 640,000 M-16 rifles, 54,000 M-79 grenade launchers, 40,000 radios, 20,000 trucks, . . . more than 500 state-of-the-art M-48 tanks, 500 helicopters, and almost 1,000 fixed-wing aircraft. . . . [However], by June 1972, there was such a shortage of field-grade officers that out of 104 [ARVN] maneuver battalions, only four were commanded by lieutenant colonels [the rank generally appointed to command a battalion in most armies]. The rest were commanded by majors, captains—even lieutenants. . . . In the end, therefore, guns and tanks—of which Saigon had plenty—were not as crucial to South Vietnamese military effectiveness as intangible factors such as leadership and morale.[7]

By this stage of the war under the Nixon Doctrine, the United States hardly had any combat ground forces left in South Vietnam, with a total troop strength of fewer than fifty thousand, many of them staff, advisory, logistical, and combat support system personnel, not combat-hardened infantry.[8] All MACV could do was bring in additional aircraft, which it did. Van Creveld caustically narrates what happened in the air war:

> Yet in the face of this magnificent target, old habits proved hard to break; when the air force generals first presented Nixon with plans for Operation *Linebacker I*, as it was called, he considered them too timid. To address the problem he called on Alexander Haig,[9] an army general who was then serving as deputy assistant for national security, for advice. The latter came up with what the president thought he needed. Possibly, there is an indication here that, for all the complaints about McNamara's gradualism and its ill effects, the air force commanders themselves were not always as ready to put their money where their mouths were as they later claimed.[10]

Despite initial hesitancy, execution of *Linebacker I* resulted in sustained bombing of North Vietnam's military installations, storage facilities, transportation networks, and conventional combat units.

Between March 31 and October 23, 1972, 155,548 tons of bombs fell on the North. Tilford's entry in Tucker argues that *Linebacker I* succeeded where *Rolling Thunder* had failed because President Nixon was prepared to use airpower more decisively than President Johnson had, directing the air force to attack targets in the North with more destructive and comprehensive strike packages. Geopolitical developments helped to facilitate escalation in the air. Kissinger's diplomacy had exploited the Sino-Soviet split to the point where the air campaign was no longer the dominant political constraint that it had been for Johnson.

The nature of the conflict had also changed. The fourteen NVA divisions and the hundreds of tanks and trucks, requiring substantial quantities of ammunition and fuel, presented a rich set of targets for the air force. The introduction of the first generation of precision-guided munitions (PGMs), laser-guided bombs (LGBs), electro-optically guided bombs (EOGBs), and long-range navigation (LORAN) bombing techniques made such precision strikes feasible and much more accurate, with reduced collateral damage. Tilford concludes that "these factors combined to make *Linebacker I* the most effective use of airpower in the Vietnam War. It remains [for its time] the classic air interdiction campaign."[11] By May 1972, *Linebacker I* had successfully destroyed the North's ability to sustain its Easter Offensive by severing supply routes into North Vietnam and by preventing NVA reinforcements from entering the South.[12]

Execution of *Linebacker I* increased the number of B-52s based on Guam to 210, which represented the largest assembly of aircraft of that kind at one base. These bombers alone could deliver almost three times as many bombs as General LeMay had used to devastate Japan twenty-seven years earlier. The introduction of PGM ordnance into the strike packages meant that aircraft, especially the F-4s, could fly at much higher altitudes to deliver bombs, thus avoiding the risk of getting hit by North Vietnamese antiaircraft fire. That included the much-dreaded SA-7 "Strella" shoulder-launched, heat-seeking, surface-to-air missile that American pilots were encountering for the first time. In addition, the scope of *Linebacker I* included the mining of Haiphong harbor to close it to Soviet supply vessels.

By the time *Linebacker I* ended in October, it had broken Hanoi's maximum effort to switch from guerrilla (Phase 2) to large-scale conventional (Phase 3) warfare and end the war. However, hostilities in the south did not cease. NVA troops simply melted back into the countryside as they had so often done before. The air campaign did not compel the North Vietnamese leadership to sign a peace agreement that had been under discussion in Paris

since August 1969. However, the North Vietnamese made a major conces-
sion at the talks, offering for the first time to accept a cease-fire without
insisting on the removal of President Thieu or the creation of a coalition
government. North Vietnam's Easter Offensive failed to achieve anything
like the decisive blow it was aiming to inflict. The NVA and VC sustained an
estimated one hundred thousand casualties.

The Nixon administration, aware that time was not on its side, increased the
stakes three months later by ordering *Linebacker II*, which commenced on
December 18, 1972, and ran for eleven days. Often referred to as the "Christmas Bombing," targets again consisted of Haiphong harbor, mined for the second time, airfields, warehouses around Hanoi, and railway marshaling yards.
By Christmas 1972, the air campaign displayed no sign of having the intended
effect of military intimidation. So the 7th Air Force and Navy Task Force 77
switched tactics and started attacking the missile batteries. Using the new
tactics and strike packages with precision laser-guided and electro-optically
guided bombs, F-111, F-4, and navy A-6 Intruders all hit these antiaircraft
targets, including SAM sites, radar sites, and, equally important, an antiaircraft
missile-assembly plant. For the first time during the war, North Vietnam ran
out of SAMs. The B-52s, with their thirty-ton ordnance payloads, were free
"pretty much [to] do what they pleased, including [threatening] the destruction of the dams [the "Red River dykes" flood-control system] on which North
Vietnam depended for feeding its population."[13]

On January 9, 1973, Henry Kissinger, by then secretary of state, and North
Vietnam's chief negotiator Le Duc Tho resolved their remaining differences
in the Paris Accords. The final American air campaign of Operations *Linebacker I* and *II* succeeded in taking down very capable antiaircraft defenses
and hitting whatever targets were considered relevant to North Vietnam's war-
fighting capability. The PGMs, many of which had been used for the first time
in warfare, played a key role in the effort. Operationally, *Linebacker I* and *II*
produced two results: they undermined North Vietnam's plan to end the war
through a conventional Phase 3 offensive, and they validated an axiom since
1939 that no large-scale conventional campaign is viable in the teeth of an
enemy's domination of the airspace above the battlefields.[14]

North Vietnam could not challenge US air operations over the South because
their antiaircraft batteries were stationary, not mobile with the field units. The
enemy had misjudged the risks of escalating to Phase 3 from Phase 2 guerrilla
operations (i.e., what its forces could accomplish without neutralizing American
air superiority). What North Vietnam's leaders did not know was how subsequent events would unfold after the War Powers Act of 1973—restricting the
exercise of presidential war power without congressional assent in any future
conflict—became law on November 7, 1973, after a vote overriding President

Nixon's veto. The Watergate scandal, after its details became known in 1973, fatally weakened the political legitimacy of the Nixon presidency.[15]

The Paris Accords, formally the "Agreement on Ending the War and Restoring Peace in Vietnam," signed on January 27, 1973, provided for a cease-fire where Vietnamese forces on both sides would remain in place. Resupply of weapons, munitions, and matériel was permitted, but only to replace items destroyed or consumed during the truce. Some 23,000 American troops, the last of a force that at its peak numbered approximately 550,000 military personnel, left South Vietnam in the sixty days following the truce. The practical effect of this cease-fire provision meant that the NVA had 220,000 troops in South Vietnam.[16] There was no provision for establishing, even in rough terms, where the forces of each side belonged. Fighting immediately resumed as if the agreement was irrelevant. Both sides took the position that military operations were justified because of the jockeying for advantage in the hours leading up to the signing of the agreement, thus altering the deployments and unit locations that the true battle lines were intended to freeze in place. President Thieu ordered ARVN forces to recapture what had been lost in the final hours before the cease-fire and reoccupied the lost territory. But the fighting did not stop. It continued in an endless cycle of cease-fire violations and retaliations so that peace gradually disappeared; fifty-one thousand South Vietnamese soldiers were killed during 1973–1974, the highest two-year toll of the entire war.[17] Two years after the agreement was signed, the Paris Accords had been forgotten by both sides.

When the North Vietnamese attacked again in 1975, they barely had to modify their battle plan and attack axes of 1972. The result, however, was tragically different. Sorley writes that General Abrams had often said that "the Vietnamese could do anything they *thought* [italics in original] they could do." Quoting Douglas Pike's observation, "The army that had fought so well against such a strong force in 1972 didn't fight at all against a lesser force in 1975."[18] Sorley's narrative features this dismaying passage:

> They [the ARVN] had run out of that conviction, no doubt helped by the realization that their sometime ally the United States had abandoned them, and by the impending depletion of the means to carry on the fight. And, it must be admitted, they ran out of leadership. Concluded South Vietnam's best field general, [Lieutenant General] Ngo Quang Truong, in the final month of an insightful and scrupulously honest analysis, "Good leadership and motivation were definitely not developed to an adequate extent and . . . this failure had a disastrous effect on the eventual outcome of the war."[19]

The chain of events that triggered the GVN's doom was the Battle of Ban Me Thuot where three NVA divisions attacked this large city in the Central

Highlands. The 1,200-man ARVN garrison was defeated within days, and the result unhinged Military Region 2 defenses farther north at Pleiku and Kontum (map 22.2). The loss of Ban Me Thuot precipitated a disastrous attempt to withdraw forces from the highlands and reposition them farther to the south and east. Originally conceived by North Vietnam's military leadership as Campaign 275, executed by NVA Senior General Dung, the fighting in the Central Highlands was to prepare the way for a decisive general offensive the following year in 1976.[20] President Thieu's order on March 14, 1975, for regular ARVN units to withdraw en masse to bolster defenses around Saigon and along the coast precipitated a general military collapse in MR-II. When ARVN units began pulling out of Pleiku, trying to escape along secondary roads toward An Khe and the coast, panic resulted in civilian and military forces alike.

The limited road net was soon jammed with fleeing refugees and disorderly retreating ARVN units. The enemy accelerated Campaign 275 into what became the final Ho Chi Minh campaign of 1975.[21]

As MR-II was collapsing in the Central Highlands, comparable panic ensued in MR-I to the north. Thieu had withdrawn critical units there as well for deployment closer to Saigon, and what was left could not hold their positions.[22]

Quang Tri, Quang Nam, Hue, and Da Nang fell in rapid succession, along with the collapse of four retreating ARVN divisions. As in the highlands, the roads were flooded with panicked civilians adding to the military chaos and disintegration. The NVA capture of the coastal cities of MR-II followed: Qui Nhon, Tuy Hoa, and Nha Trang. Eventually Saigon was overrun as well. It was only a matter of time: fifty-five days start to finish.

Nguyen Cao Ky, commander of the air force in the 1960s, before becoming prime minister in the military junta from 1965 to 1967 and then vice president until his retirement from politics in 1971, offers a biting critique of the ARVN's poor military leadership under Thieu in 1975. Ky had long recognized the strategic importance of the Central Highlands and the threat to Ban Me Thuot. In his memoirs, Ky's version of events is not in serious conflict with other narratives already described. What enhances Ky's credibility about the failure of ARVN leadership is his description of how American military advisors had functioned over the years leading up to the withdrawal of American combat forces after the Paris Accords of 1973. He explains how American military advisors were caught in a conflict of interest between offering candid, honest military judgments about the ARVN officers they were advising and knowledge that such candor, if negative, would be reflected in their own officer efficiency reports and likely limit their promotional prospects.

> I believe that nearly every American adviser came with honest and pure intentions to advise their Vietnamese counterparts. But over the years a few dozen advisers grew to become tens of thousands, and as the American commitment became

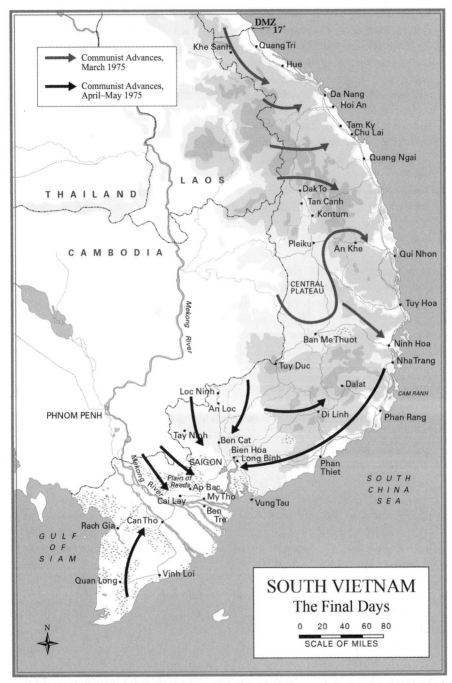

Map 22.2. The North Vietnamese Army won the Vietnam War with a conventional military offensive that defeated the ARVN and overran Saigon in less than two months.

Source: USMA Atlases.

bigger and bigger, their own chain of command put pressure on them to show results. Each adviser prepared regular reports on his activities and sent them up his chain of command. American captains and majors learned that if the colonels and generals whom they advised were described as intelligent, cooperative, and eager to fight, these qualities would reflect, in part, their own performance as advisers. Advisers whose Vietnamese counterparts were brave tigers got medals and career advancement. If the commander they advised was stupid, corrupt, and cowardly, however, an adviser risked a poor efficiency report and being passed over for promotion. Even so, I think that most U.S. advisers had the integrity to resist these pressures. At the highest levels, however, where the U.S. adviser was a colonel or general, the pressures were greater and he had more to gain or lose. When advisers went home, they usually received the highest decoration, a medal that only their Vietnamese counterpart was in a position to recommend. Such decorations were important to careers, so many American advisers promoted their own interests by reporting that an ARVN general was terrific, and ran a crack unit. Ninety percent of senior Vietnamese commanders were repeatedly lauded by their American advisers. These were the officers that presided over the debacle that started with Ban Me Thuot and ended with enemy tanks crashing into the grounds of the Presidential Palace less than two months later.

Ky also believed that there was another Vietnamese military deficiency leading to the defeat in 1975, the years of ARVN acquiescence in letting American forces assume the primary role in main-force combat because of their superior training, proficiency in preparation for combat, and rigorous professionalism:

Americans come from a wealthy and confident army. We Vietnamese regarded them as big brothers who had come to help us. There was a language barrier; few Vietnamese spoke good English, and far fewer Americans spoke understandable Vietnamese. . . . The Americans were well schooled in such matters [as fire support planning, maintenance, facility construction, and combined-arms operations], had trained for years in the small details that are crucial to success. It was mostly new to us Vietnamese. But if you have a big brother who knows how to do everything and is impatient to put into practice what he has learned in training—let him do it! . . . So we let our big brother, who was capable and eager, do as much of the fighting as he cared to.[23]

Ky's remarks ring true. Marvin J. Wolf recently corroborated Ky's memoirs.[24]

The Ky excerpts illustrate the different military value systems of the two armies. The US Army's officer corps demanded performance. The chain of command down to the junior officers and NCOs at the company and platoon levels reflected this demand for results. Small units were led aggressively by leaders who knew that their commanders expected high performance. Fighting proficiency and effectiveness may have varied from unit to unit, but the US Army could never be remotely characterized as one where promotion depended on the kind of venal transactions Ky described for the ARVN. Ky's characterization of his military experience shows how the practice and tolerance of quid pro quo arrangements, independent of fighting ability, could readily undermine the integrity and meritocratic values that an army in combat absolutely has to have to win and to motivate its soldiers to risk death on a daily basis.

Lewis Sorley traced the political-military failure in 1975 to three factors. His first was the termination of political and matériel support as the result of congressional action. The Foreign Assistance Act of 1973 forbade any American combat activity "in, over or from off the shores of North and South Vietnam, Laos, or Cambodia."[25] The second was leadership. He amplifies General Truong's assessment, asserting that the task was never adequately accomplished of providing effective leadership for a military establishment that "rapidly and hugely expanded over a relatively short time." He buttresses this assertion by pointing to a postwar interview of a senior enemy officer, NVA Colonel Bui Tin, who served on the general staff:

> Bui Tin, speaking from the enemy's perspective, said that a key step for the allies to win the war would have been to "train South Vietnam's generals. The junior South Vietnamese officers were good, competent and courageous, but the commanding officers were inept." Despite some very significant exceptions, that judgment was hard to argue with, and in fact it was one that responsible South Vietnamese themselves made after the war.[26]

Sorley's assertion is debatable. Even Bui Tin acknowledged that the ARVN produced generals who were outstanding battlefield commanders and identified nine as educated, uncorrupted, and courageous. He balances his praise with these two sentences: "On the other hand, there were also many ARVN generals who engaged in business deals and extracurricular activities—on a much wider scale than in the north—so it is no wonder that their prestige suffered in society . . . and that there was a general drop in public morality." He then adds, "The mid-level and lower-level officers of ARVN were, generally speaking, better trained in standard formations than those of [the NVA] and, of course, far better than those belonging to the NLF forces."[27]

Sorley's third factor was the "the failure to isolate the battlefield, to cut enemy infiltration and resupply," again pointing to Colonel Bui Tin, who argued that to succeed the allies needed to "cut the Ho Chi Minh Trail inside Laos."[28]

Sorley's threefold explanation of the GVN/ARVN failure in 1975 is plausible. It is true that federal law precluded direct American combat support after 1973 without congressional consent, but not all aid was cut off.[29] It is equally true that the senior GVN and ARVN leadership echelons were weak and performed poorly at the senior command level in 1975, starting with

President Thieu's issuance of orders to withdraw from MR-II and MR-I to protect Saigon. And it is also true that American airpower had been withdrawn and would not return. The explanations invite the possibility of what-if counterfactuals, such as the ARVN performing better had matériel and airpower support been provided earlier, or if better leadership had been provided by more training and advisory support in the field before Vietnamization.[30] Would such an approach have produced better military performance? Sorley sets up the argument by writing, "Some historians argue against such speculation, denigrating it as 'counterfactual analysis.'" He knocks over his own straw man, suggesting that smart military leaders, and perhaps historians as well, should not be so dismissive.[31] Sorley insists that officers with sound military training are taught "to make what is called an 'estimate of the situation,' the heart of which is consideration of what enemy courses of action might be provoked by various friendly courses of action."[32]

What would Sorley's own "estimate of the situation" have been? He marches through a long list of "missed opportunities" during the early years of the war: selecting General Westmoreland as COMUSMACV, President Johnson's failure to call up reserve forces in 1968 or "to effectively mobilize public support for the war," and failure to cut the Ho Chi Minh Trail. He identifies two more failures—insufficient development of South Vietnamese forces during the period of American domination of the war and the year's delay in Abrams's succession to top command. For the later years of the war, he continues with a list of requirements: better diplomats, field generals, and political leadership; population security versus body count as the relevant "measure of merit"; and "concentration on 'one war' involving pacification, combat operations, and improvement of South Vietnamese armed forces rather than fixation primarily on American combat operations."[33]

The text reads like a laundry list. It is neither an estimate of the situation nor a systematic analysis of policies, strategies, or operations that might have produced victory. Indeed, Sorley ends *A Better War* by quoting from a monograph written a decade after the war by ARVN General Cao Van Vien who served as chairman of the South Vietnamese Joint General Staff: "[His] unflinchingly honest and insightful monograph admitted that though South Vietnam's senior leadership had done its best, 'it still proved inadequate for this most difficult episode of our national history.'"[34]

Sorley ends up, like Ky, pointing to the South Vietnamese themselves. His quoting ARVN General Vien is a mirror image of NVA Colonel Bui Tin's evaluation of the ARVN senior leadership, whom he also quotes in *A Better War*. Tin's assessment comes from the perspective of an informed adversary. He concluded that the ARVN senior leadership was not organized and aligned top to bottom sufficiently to prevail in the face of the enemy offensives after 1972. Sorley offers no systematic evidence that either the leadership or the motivation was in place to fight and win.

In 1975, the ARVN collapsed with shocking speed, mentored as it had been by Americans who had trained and equipped it to fight precisely against the kind of conventionally organized enemy the NVA had become by 1975. Why did the ARVN fail in 1975?

When the Americans packed up and went home, the NVA was positioned to win. The NVA had been opposed by a superpower foe whose leadership could be characterized by irresolution through loss of public support, often institutionally at cross purposes with itself, with its constitutional division of powers and agencies competing with one another for bureaucratic advantage. The North Vietnamese won the final test in 1975 because they had the sheer willpower to stay in the arena of conflict. When the Americans intervened in force a decade earlier, North Vietnamese leaders were forced to restructure the planning and operational execution of their revolutionary strategy. They had to determine how to bypass the military advantages that MACV possessed: well-equipped, highly mobile conventional divisions, massive firepower, and prodigious airpower. The revolutionaries grasped what MACV and ARVN did not. The insurgent force can lose in a direct, armed confrontation and still not lose the war. The revolutionary movement had to fall back into temporary stalemate, as it did after 1954 for nearly a decade, after the Tet Offensive in 1968, and after the Easter Offensive in 1972, but it could rebuild, regroup, and prepare for new offensives. For the Americans, they had won all of their battles; not once did they sustain a significant military defeat in the field, but they did not win the war.

Pike, who spent many years in Vietnam during the war as a recognized expert on the Viet Cong, published his comprehensive study of the NVA in 1986.[35] He traces the long evolution of the NVA as a unique, "improbable" military organization that was the result of "a peculiar alchemy: a messianic leadership of extraordinary insight acting as catalyst on a singular, centuries-old martial spirit. The combination of personality and culture made possible, inevitable even, the People's Army of Vietnam (PAVN)."[36] His first chapter describes the historical foundations of the NVA as "the Prussians of Asia." He presents an "idealized profile of the cadre[37] cum PAVN officer" who can motivate, energize, communicate, and, above all, organize because he integrates the competencies of five people: (1) a skilled master of the "technique of mobilization" and organization, someone who can get things done, who is endowed with an "innate ability plus experience" that is not principally the product of education or ideological training; (2) a zealous ideologue who is highly class conscious and proletarian oriented, "red in that he maintains close, even mystic relations with the masses, and has not simply memorized Marxist-Leninist text," someone whose "ideological state is more intuitive than intellectual"; (3) a self-disciplined ascetic who is not tempted by material lures, "idealistic even to the point of naiveté"; (4) a loyal and obedient cadreman/ officer who does not question the philosophic underpinnings of his society, who responds to orders, and "who does not innovate widely in carrying them out"; and (5) an expert substantively or professionally trained "who is technically proficient in some area."[38]

While Pike acknowledges that this ideal often diverged from reality, a military organization populated with a large number of leaders manifesting just enough of these characteristics in the right combination is a formidable adversary and one that is very difficult to beat, especially if the top leaders like Ho Chi Minh, Giap, and Le Duan were prepared, as they were, to play a long waiting game with the Americans. All they had to do was not lose and to remain a force in being.

Race's compelling thesis in *War Comes to Long An* is that the NVA, VC, and NLF had an integrated theory of victory that implemented preemptive social and economic policies, with just enough contingent incentives to motivate urban and rural Vietnamese to join the revolutionary movement. The GVN, lacking adequate preemptive policies to undermine the movement, formed a reliance on American ground forces and airpower, which eventually produced a downward spiral for Saigon authorities ending in their final collapse.[39]

The movement was convinced that time and history were on its side. It helped that the movement's key cadres were NVA officers who dominated the leadership from top to bottom. It also helped that the American and South Vietnamese response was to use overwhelming firepower wherever it could. Arrayed against the revolutionary movement and its ruthless leadership was a GVN regime that never realized that it always had been their war to fight and win. The Americans could not win it for them.

23

THE STRATEGIC ARCHITECTURES
OF THE VIETNAM WAR

After World War II and the Korean War, the Vietnam War represented a new kind of warfare. In the traditional sense, it was impossible to classify it simply as a war of combatant states and armies engaged in conventional battles. It was hardly a war in this old-fashioned sense of what American or European soldiers regarded war to be. One could not find or define a front until the last weeks of the war.

Vietnam presented for the first time a different set of problems for an American army that had a long history of operational learning. How does an army find, fix, and finish an enemy that it cannot find and engage at times and on terrain to its own strategic advantage, not the enemy's? And how does it operate in the middle of a war surrounded by people whose language it cannot speak? Neither firepower nor technology was a war-winning discriminator if the target was so difficult to find. Success in the combat environment of Vietnam meant finding leaders who were capable of adapting and learning. It meant, in the best case, understanding the difference between Race's preemptive and reinforcement policies, how they might affect Vietnamese behavior and motivation, and what policies created contingent incentives that could motivate military behavior to resist the NLF and Viet Cong.

Another difference was how this new kind of war was supported. In conventional conflicts, combatants are generally supplied from outside the locus of conflict. In a revolutionary conflict, the movement gets much of what it needs from the people it is trying to draw to its cause and seizes matériel and usable assets from the government it is trying to overthrow. That was one of the insights gained from the Malayan Emergency—isolate the insurgents from their source of supply. Malaya is a peninsula of some fifty thousand square miles with a narrow land border with Thailand[1] and much of its territory, like Vietnam, uncultivated jungle. The insurgents could not benefit from an outside, geographically contiguous power to supply them. However, Vietnam offered no such advantage to COIN operators because geography worked against them. Vietnam had a porous, 1,200-mile border contiguous with North Vietnam, Laos, and Cambodia, all countries providing routes for men and matériel to reinforce the revolutionary movement in South Vietnam. The Ho Chi Minh Trail proved impossible to interdict from the air, and serious proposals to block it with ground forces were rejected.

NORTH VIETNAMESE STRATEGIC ARCHITECTURE

If the Vietnam War was not a traditional war fought by conventional combatants, there was general agreement among American and Vietnamese military leaders that the NVA and the NLF/VC cadres in the south were trying to impose their will on the South Vietnamese population through a unique strategy that blended military, political, and psychological elements of coercion and persuasion.

The revolutionary movement's theory of victory was a simple one: Overthrow South Vietnam as a corrupt, reactionary, neocolonialist, capitalist society and replace it with another, fairer, redistributive, classless, Marxist-Leninist society. Use violence wherever, whenever, and against whomever it is advantageous to do so. Negotiate when you have to, but never abandon the vision of overthrowing the enemy society.

The revolutionary war was exactly what the communists had said it was. The conflict was partly military and displayed at certain moments the undeniable features of war recognizable to any World War II or Korean War veteran. But it was also a nonmilitary conflict, waged by an implacably hostile, politically sophisticated revolutionary movement determined not only to overrun South Vietnam's government but to overthrow the entire society underpinning it and impose a new communist-designed social order. On the military level, the counterstrategy under which the GVN, ARVN, and MACV fought had proven just barely adequate over the long years of warfare up until 1972. However, the political, nonmilitary strategy under which South Vietnam and the United States operated was never a match for the comprehensive struggle that the revolutionary movement designed and executed. The GVN, with its powerful American ally, never went through the thought process of designing an effective counterrevolutionary or counterinsurgency strategy.

Le Duan's leadership adhered to the concept of sustaining Phase 2 guerrilla operations while carefully preparing for the ultimate Phase 3 military offensive. As one of the early revolutionary leaders in the South and as head of COSVN until 1957, Le Duan never lost sight of his vision of a total military victory, however long it took: "Defeat of the enemy militarily is indispensable for the victory of the resistance and the revolution."[2] His leadership dominated the 1968 Tet Offensive, the 1972 Easter Offensive, and the victorious 1975 offensive drive south that ended at the Presidential Palace in Saigon. Le Duan constantly probed for the US/GVN breaking point, even if it meant gambling with tens of thousands of lives. For him, the end state of the Vietnam War was not the Paris Accords in 1973. It was North Vietnam's military victory in 1975.

US/GVN STRATEGIC ARCHITECTURE

A successful strategic architecture required American–South Vietnamese agreement on aligning four things: (1) a clearly stated policy that made a compelling case to the American and South Vietnamese people for why the GVN deserved such a massive American national commitment to nation building resulting in the sacrifice of nearly sixty thousand American lives; (2) a political strategy that undermined the revolutionary movement's preemptive social and economic policies with GVN policies that were at least equally preemptive and compelling in the areas of land reform, taxes, military recruitment, and administrative staffing; (3) a military strategy in which MACV, CORDS, ARVN, and GVN agencies integrated their officers, troops, and personnel into organizations where they could truly plan and interoperate together; and (4) operations that balanced conventional and COIN operations because, as events showed, the ARVN had to be capable of both.

North Vietnam succeeded in its own efforts at nation building. If ever there was a case of effective "armed nation building," it was the NLF/NVA operating in South Vietnam over thirty years. Race has made their playbook intelligible to any COIN student for forty years.

For the US government, a strategic architecture of nation building would have required more intrusive policies affecting GVN political elites at the national level. Policy implementation would have required painstaking negotiations with GVN leaders resulting in bilateral agreements or memoranda of understanding about how South Vietnamese ministries operated both internally and locally at the provincial and district levels. It would have addressed criteria of accountability, such as how the rural administration was staffed and how the ARVN officer corps was staffed, and so on. Execution of such agreements would have required diplomatic, MACV, and CORDS personnel who spoke Vietnamese, displayed deep knowledge about Vietnamese public administration and cultural protocols, and were effective in building relationships of trust with their counterparts. The US Country Team never thought comprehensively in these terms; neither did Washington, which had to provide the authority and funding.

Action in the field would have meant creating the necessary leverage to influence the GVN's administrative apparatus to appoint honest, effective ministers; create new, preemptive policies that drew in the rural population; and impose rigorous methods of accountability inside Vietnamese ministries. The United States and the Allies of course did precisely these things after World War II in the cases of defeated Axis states such as Germany and Japan, but they never imagined that they would or should intrude into the affairs of a sovereign client state like the Republic of Vietnam. It would have meant that the GVN, CORDS, and AID budgets needed to be broader in scope, reaching down into Vietnamese governmental layers where American expenditures would be contingent on effective administrative and military performance and accountability.

Instead, MACV, CORDS, and USAID tried to work with the government as they found it—as an anointed client. Working with the GVN, the US government discovered that South Vietnamese leaders would not change their administrative infrastructure, personnel, or governing modus operandi in any fundamental way, reinforced as they often were by the ARVN, police, paramilitary forces, and Phoenix operatives. The revolutionary movement's armed, coercive, ideologically motivated echelons had the strategic edge. They were shrewder and wilier because, despite their appalling losses, they were always prepared to outwait the Americans. Patience turned out to be a strategic discriminator.

The Johnson administration's decision to intervene failed to address the essential nature of the war it was getting the armed forces of the United States into. It was a cognitive meltdown involving endless skirmishes among political and military policy makers about whether it was a war at all. *Victory* was a term looming in the background. What did it mean? In the Vietnam War, victory went to the side that was the best organized for the conflict it planned and was prepared to fight, remained the best organized for the long haul, and best understood how to wear down and outwait the enemy.

In a broad geopolitical sense, the fighting during the Vietnam War never threatened the stability of the international system the way the Third Reich represented a menacing threat to the world in 1939.[3] Vietnam did not produce strategic resources essential to the survival of the "Free World" in the same way a Rommel victory at El Alamein, for example, would have threatened Middle East oil supplies. Indeed, no one in Embassy Saigon could find a policy statement on file about what the US strategic interest was in Vietnam in 1968.[4]

At a conference thirty-five years after the war ended, the late Ambassador Richard C. Holbrooke[5] could not articulate one. Neither could former secretary of state Henry Kissinger[6] whose address preceded Holbrooke's. Kissinger outlined the requirements for a strategy without defining one for Vietnam. "When we consider going to war, we need a global strategic analysis that explains to us what the significance of this is. The purpose of a war is some definition of victory; stalemate is not a strategy, and victory needs to be defined as an outcome that is achievable in a period sustainable by American public opinion."

Holbrooke opined more expansively on American Vietnam policy and military strategy:

And so we failed the first test [presumably a strategy that could have worked]. Our beloved nation sent into battle soldiers without a clear determination of what they could accomplish and they misjudged the stakes. And then we couldn't get out, as Henry [Kissinger] spoke already to that point. We fought bravely under very difficult conditions. But success was not achievable. . . . I cannot escape the feeling that in the end, whatever we did, the long-term outcome would have been the same. And ironically, that outcome is precisely the one that Secretary [Hillary R.] Clinton outlined to you earlier this morning as she talked about the remarkable state today of U.S.-Vietnamese relations.[7]

Holbrooke's reference to Clinton was her remarks in the opening address at the conference. She put substance to the irony:

The progress between Vietnam and the United States has been breathtaking. . . . An entire generation of young people has grown up knowing only peace between Vietnam and America, and the relationships that they are forming through educational and cultural exchanges, through new businesses and social networks are drawing us even closer together.[8]

Neither the Johnson nor Nixon administrations formulated an effective policy to enable an authoritarian regime like the GVN to combat the implacable hostility of the revolutionary movement in its midst. The GVN was by and large powerless to eliminate the terrorist explosions against vulnerable urban targets of opportunity, the daily kidnappings and assassinations of its officials in the countryside, or the never-ending ambushes of its police, paramilitary personnel, and soldiers. These epiphenomena occurred year after year in a never-ending cycle of bloodletting and social trauma throughout the society. The revolutionary movement was a force that clearly intended to continue such bloodshed. It accepted the mounting casualties until the South Vietnamese social fabric began inexorably to unravel.

When this process accelerated after the NVA invasion in 1975, individuals' allegiance to law and order, or right and wrong, had become irrelevant. The GVN was doomed because there was no civic culture to sustain it. Individual not collective survival would emerge as the dominant choice; it was every man for himself. The revolutionary movement understood the social pathologies it was creating, and it was skilled in provoking the GVN and the Americans to overreact, often with massive firepower. The revolutionary movement was prepared, as it did, to fight a thirty-year war. Few democratic societies, much less a South Vietnamese authoritarian one, possess the fortitude to fight and win such a long war, not without first offering its population a compelling vision for why victory would be worth the sacrifice.

US losses were staggering for a "limited-intensity conflict": 58,177[9] American servicemen dead, 153,303[10] wounded. A total of more than 8.7 million American men and women served in the Vietnam War.[11] South Vietnamese casualties were much higher: 260,000 for all services[12] and two million civilian casualties. North Vietnamese official reports of casualties are even higher: 1.1 million North Vietnamese military killed and 600,000 wounded. In addition, there were two million North Vietnamese civilian casualties in the north and another two million in the south.[13]

The armed forces of the United States deployed to Vietnam with services that organized themselves as if they were still fighting World War II or the Korean War, with war-fighting strategies and doctrines that were much better suited to fighting in conflicts where conventional militaries functioned in the same way they always had, where civilian populations could be protected behind an expanding front, and where military government was essentially a postwar activity. The same was true of the diplomatic and intelligence establishments. They, too, functioned as they had traditionally operated, without intensive area training or insistence on language skills. Some Vietnam War historians have addressed the issue of MACV's size and cumbersome structure and inability to learn in the middle of a shooting war. Nagl points out that General Westmoreland resisted a recommendation that he establish an intermediate headquarters between himself and his field commanders so that he could have freed himself and part of his MACV staff from their day-to-day operational responsibilities and devoted more time to defining and analyzing the larger issues of the war.[14]

Undertaking such questioning and innovation was not how the World War II and Korean War veterans had been trained to assume high command. They came from a professional "can-do" military culture where confidence in firepower produced decisive results. They did not view their command jobs as theoretical exercises in questioning what they believed were proven strategies or doctrines. They had seen these doctrines validated when they had served as junior officers in combat assignments. The innovative ideas that were percolating up from the Vietnam junior officers in the field, some of whom displayed a sophisticated understanding of the war's issues, never gained any solid institutional footing upon which to base a reexamination of fundamental assumptions about the nature of the war.

President Johnson himself was hesitant to engage in such questioning.[15] Indeed, Johnson once complained to his wife, "I can't get out [of Vietnam], and I can't finish it with what I have got. And I don't know what the hell to do!" He moaned, "I'm not temperamentally equipped to be commander in chief."[16] Johnson never systematically questioned his top military commanders on whether their war-fighting strategies would succeed. "If I left that war and let the communists take over South Vietnam," President Johnson reflected years later to his biographer, "then I would be seen as a coward and my nation would be seen as an appeaser, and we would both find it impossible to accomplish anything for anybody anywhere on the entire globe."[17] President Johnson reluctantly decided to intervene and dispatched US forces to Vietnam incrementally. He did so in response to worry that he would be perceived as weak by his political opponents. That is not a sound rationale for a policy to escalate a military-assistance mission into an expeditionary, interventionist war.

> Despite his recognition that his advisers had "no plan for victory militarily or diplomatically," Lyndon Johnson remained resolved to do only what was necessary to avoid defeat in Vietnam. Fixated on short-term expedients and lacking a comprehensive estimate of what the war might cost the United States in the long term, the president focused on the more easily discernible price of withdrawal. Pulling out [once the incremental buildup was underway], Johnson confided to one of his most trusted advisers [in a telephone conversation with Secretary McNamara], made him "shudder to think what all of 'em would say."[18]

Presidents who do not probe deeply into the substance of interventionist policies where large military forces are deployed in combat risk failure. Neither President Johnson nor his first national security advisor, the late McGeorge Bundy, was particularly interested in Vietnamese history or culture, the origins of Vietnamese nationalism, or the NLF as a revolutionary movement. Johnson in 1966 complained to his director of the CIA about the lack of intelligence about North Vietnamese intentions. Why couldn't the CIA penetrate the interior of the government in Hanoi, he remonstrated?

> I thought you guys had people everywhere, that you knew everything, and now you don't even know anything about a raggedy-ass little fourth-rate country. All you have to do is get some Chinese coolies from a San Francisco laundry shop and drop them over there and use them. Get them to drop their answers in a bottle and put the bottle in the Pacific.[19]

That remark may have been a president in a private moment of frustration, but it did reveal the virulent lack of curiosity about the adversary he and MACV were up against. Bundy, even forty years later, still exhibited the same total lack of interest in the Vietnamese:

It was clear from the beginning that Bundy was distinctly uninterested in the topics of Vietnamese nationalism and the origins of the communist insurgency [speaking to a collaborator, Gordon M. Goldstein, with whom he was proposing to write a retrospective analysis of the Vietnam War]. . . . Bundy had no enthusiasm for examining the Vietnamese calculus of interests that contributed to war with the United States. The decision to Americanize the Vietnam War in 1965, Bundy told me, was a decision made in Washington, and not in Hanoi. It was inherently a *presidential* [italics in original] decision, he argued, and thus had to be studied through the prism of the two men he served who held ultimate authority for questions of war and peace—President Kennedy and President Johnson.[20]

How Bundy—one of the premier national security authorities of his generation, a scion of two Boston Brahmin families on his maternal side, a Yale Skull and Bones alumnus, a noted professor of government at Harvard in the early 1950s, dean of the faculty at Harvard at the age of thirty-four, in short, exhibit A of Halberstam's "the best and the brightest"[21]—could retrospectively make a statement forcefully claiming such incuriosity about the Vietnamese revolutionary movement is astonishing.

Equally astonishing are Robert McNamara's regrets for not having confronted President Johnson with his views during 1967 and 1968, which indicated that the American military in Vietnam could neither succeed nor prevent the continued erosion of popular support for the war. Bob Woodward in 2009 interviewed both Bundy and McNamara late in their lives. Both were thinking about how posterity would view their actions. Bundy said, "I had a part in a great failure. I made mistakes of perception, recommendation, and execution. If I have learned anything, I should share it."[22] He certainly did not think such sharing included any knowledge about the Vietnamese; he never was interested in them.

The late James C. Thompson Jr., a junior Harvard professor, had a firsthand opportunity to observe the decision-making milieu in Washington where Bundy and McNamara occupied central positions. He was in a position "to watch the slide down the slippery slope during five years (1961–1966) of service in the White House and Department of State." He published an account of his experience in the April 1968 issue of *The Atlantic*. Written nearly fifty years ago, its relevance persists because it reads like a national security policy primer, useful today in assessing the Iraqi and Afghan Wars. Thompson asked, "Where were the experts, the doubters, and the dissenters? The answer is complex but instructive." He made telling points about expertise and effectiveness.

"In the first place, the American government was sorely *lacking in real Vietnam or Indochina expertise*" (italics above and below are in original). He pointed out that the State Department treated Vietnam until 1954 as an adjunct of Embassy Paris. French-speaking Foreign Service personnel of narrow European experience largely staffed Embassy Saigon and the Vietnam Desk at

State from 1954 onward. "A recurrent and increasingly important factor in the decision-making process was *the banishment of real expertise*."

Thompson assessed the Vietnam policy process this way:

> Even among the "architects" of our Vietnam commitment, there has been persistent confusion as to what type of war we were fighting and, as a direct consequence, confusion as to how to end that war. . . . Was it, for instance, a civil war, in which case counterinsurgency might suffice? Or was it a war of international aggression? . . . Who was the aggressor—and the real enemy? The Viet Cong? Hanoi? Peking? . . . And confused throughout, in like fashion, was the question of American objectives; your objectives depended on whom you were fighting and why.[23]

President Johnson had surrounded himself with many of the most able people from the Kennedy administration, yet he never found a substantive voice with which to explain either to himself or to the American people why deploying twelve divisions, scores of warships, thousands of aircraft, and over half a million men, who sustained tens of thousands of deaths and casualties, was done in pursuit of a core national security interest of the United States. Once he ordered those deployments, he did not as commander in chief compel the right questions to be asked about what those forces should accomplish for a client state he so poorly understood. The end state was never clear. Such a state of strategic affairs within the highest councils of government is not a basis for convincing a skeptical American public.

Given the high casualties on both sides, it is a serious challenge for anyone on either side to assert that fighting the Vietnam War was worth even a small fraction of those lives. The historical, what-if counterfactuals of the Vietnam War continue to engage American politicians as well as historians to the present day. Two works by Fredrik Logevall and Mark Moyar about the decision to escalate offer new and fundamentally differing insights and documentary evidence into how the war could have been avoided[24] or conducted without the intervention of ground forces.[25] Two other writers about Vietnamization, Lewis Sorley and Rufus Phillips, among the most recent and responsible, draw attention to some of the lessons of the war. All of these writers would do well to consider Race's incisive analysis of the effectiveness of the revolutionary movement or Elliott's magisterial two-volume work. Their works drive to deeper insights, not simply because both were there as participants and observers, but because they became Vietnamese speakers, interviewed Vietnamese at length, cross-checked what they learned against documentary sources, and let the Vietnamese on both sides speak for themselves.

Elliott, perhaps, anticipating these revisionist writers by almost a decade, preempts some of the alluring "if-only" speculations. For example, he offers the counterfactual that had the United States been in Vietnam with five hundred thousand troops at the end of World War II, or had the GVN existed in 1945 as it had in 1972 with more than one million armed troops, it probably could have easily defeated the Viet Minh guerrillas of that period. But he quickly dismisses his own straw man as pointless speculation. The second counterfactual is closer to the events: whether the belated land reform of the Thieu government after 1968 had taken place earlier or whether a change in US military strategy and tactics in 1965 rather than 1968 would have enabled the GVN to defeat the revolutionary movement.[26] Again, it is tempting to think so. However, the movement had repeatedly demonstrated how aggressively it could recover from any military setback inflicted on it by MACV or the ARVN. Elliott points to Kissinger's clause in his *Foreign Affairs* article in 1969: "the guerrilla wins if he does not lose."

In his final chapter of *Misalliance* addressing what happened between the governments of Ngo Dinh Diem and the United States, ending in the military coup and the execution of the Ngo brothers in 1963, Miller concluded, "From its formation to its dissolution, the alliance between Ngo Dinh Diem and the United States was defined by the politics of nation-building."[27] As the Vietnam War intensified over the next twelve years, American leaders conceived of nation building through the historical lenses of World War II. Nation building occurred after the fighting ended. After the Axis surrenders, nation building followed the constitutional templates and public administration dictates of the Allied victors occupying West Germany and Japan. By the mid-1960s, nation building had become a staple in the graduate syllabi of top American university political science departments.[28]

In Vietnam, nation building was something that was ancillary to the main business of war fighting. CORDS and COIN operations were the "other war," even while these operations were undertaken simultaneously with main-force combat and the Operation *Rolling Thunder* air campaign. As Miller explains, nation building was conceived by the Americans and South Vietnamese in the early 1960s under Diem to be

> a field of competition and contestation in which both Americans and Vietnamese advanced diverse ideas and agendas. . . . It soon became clear, however, that the conceptual and cultural divide between the two [governments] was wider than it had first appeared. The problems did not derive merely from the Ngo brothers' abstruse and confusing pronouncement about the merits of [the Diem government's policies]. They were also rooted in specific, practical disagreements between the Ngos and the Americans over the meaning of key concepts such as democracy, community, security, and social change. Such disagreements did not mean that every [American–South Vietnamese] nation-building initiative was doomed from the beginning. The two sides' respective visions of development were not so dissimilar as to make collaboration impossible. Nevertheless the

differences between them were real and substantial and were a key cause of the strains that were evident even in the alliance's earliest days.[29]

How were the two sides going to collaborate if they were functioning inside two very different cognitive universes? The American universe saw nation building with a client state to be a challenge in the intricacies of effective public administration: the bedrock of a constitution underlying rule of law, rigorous standards of accountability expected inside any competent civil service, and the ability to throw a lot of money at a problem.

The Vietnamese universe saw nation building in completely different cultural terms. The Ngo brothers, to gain power, had to strike political accommodations among diverse and competing power constituencies and therefore potential rivals simply to gain power in 1954. There were power bases within the army, many with close ties to French military officers and colonial administrators, and diverse religious sects such as the Cao Dai (combining the three teachings of Buddhism, Confucianism, and Taoism with beliefs and practices borrowed from Catholicism and European spiritualism), with a stronghold in Tay Ninh Province west of Saigon. There was another nationalist religious group with broad popular appeal in the Mekong River delta known as the Hoa Hao, whose leaders during the 1940s used Japanese-supplied aid to establish armed militias that allied themselves with the Viet Minh at one point and later with the GVN. By June 1954, Hoa Hao warlords controlled several provinces in the delta and controlled thousands of fighters. There were other groups: the Binh Xuyen criminal cartel that controlled Saigon's underworld and the Dai Viet Party, which had been a key player in anticommunist politics in Indochina since its founding in 1939. Miller's early chapters sketch "this daunting collection of opponents and political rivals"[30] out of which Diem and his military coup successors were trying to build an effective anticommunist, putatively democratic South Vietnam. They received billions of dollars[31] during the twenty-year period between 1955 and 1975, and yet all of that aid failed. K. W. Taylor in his recently published history of the Vietnamese makes a strong defense of Diem and explains the diversity of his responses to the legacy of French colonialism, which "disgusted" him, and his failed attempts to find a noncommunist nation-building alternative.[32]

Because serious nation building was never even formally part of the American goal in Vietnam, development became the operative term to describe what US agencies actually did in the field. Development and nation building are two fundamentally different concepts driven by different behavioral conceptions of how leaders and the governed interact. Development is providing inputs with little regard for their behavioral outputs: how many VC or NVA the Americans or South Vietnamese killed or neutralized, how many wells they drilled in villages, or how many medical dispensaries they constructed. Such American reinforcement inputs failed to change Vietnamese behavior. Only contingent incentives motivating decisions by individual Vietnamese to assume the risk of death could do that.

Nation building was about what a wealthy foreign benefactor did to affect GVN behavior and how it used its plentiful resources to change how a host government functions for its people. The State Department would have objected vehemently if change became too intrusive: "You can't do that with a sovereign state!" Why not? the Johnson and Nixon White House staffs could have asked. By 1968, the United States had half a million men deployed to the theater risking their lives for South Vietnam, and the American people were by then paying billions each year to fund the war (in 1968, the figure was $35 billion; today's present value would be $240 billion). Americans could have said to the South Vietnamese, "It's our blood as much as yours, and our money as well as yours, that is sustaining South Vietnamese sovereignty in the face of a mortal threat to the regime and the society underpinning it." Reading their enemies' doctrinal literature told them as much. Such a forthright negotiation would have required early and careful judgment and timing about who had leverage over whom. For example, proposing such a negotiation with GVN leaders in 1968–1969 would have been too late. The Vietnamese by 1968 knew that the Americans would not carry out a threat of withdrawal. By then, the Johnson and Nixon administrations were too deeply invested in the war to pull out without admitting defeat.

Amplification of such a back-to-front national commitment would have required diplomats and soldiers trained and empowered by rigorously aligned policies, strategies, and operations designed to defeat the revolutionary movement. The US government would have needed to recruit and train thousands of American diplomats and soldiers who would have needed specific functional and linguistic qualifications. To be effective in their jobs, they would have needed Vietnamese-language fluency (and for some, literacy, so that Americans could read Vietnamese documents), knowledge of Vietnamese culture and history, and skills and experience across a broad range of academic disciplines (public administration, economics, banking, finance, education, law, and so on). With their Vietnamese counterparts, the Americans would have had to design a set of joint institutions where Americans and Vietnamese worked together inside various ministries, agencies, and military commands. Americans assigned to these joint organizations eventually might have worked themselves out of the job if the United States and South Vietnam together had won the war. It might have taken a decade or more. That was the paradigm for the wartime occupations during and after World War II. In Vietnam, realigning policy, strategy, and operations would have been a process of reverse engineering—from a defined end state specifying a polity that could function and establish legitimacy among the Vietnamese people. It would have required commitment to a long game where the narrative was compelling to the American people. It would have had to be equally compelling to the South Vietnamese.

The negotiation would have required Americans who understood that politics was at the heart of what their Vietnamese counterparts needed to form governmental coalitions, whether they were the Ngo brothers or their post-coup successors. South Vietnamese elites saw nation building through completely different cultural lenses than Americans. Vietnamese leaders, simply to gain power, had to build an effective coalition of opposing parties. All Vietnamese leaders had to strike political accommodations among very diverse and competing power constituencies, including potential rivals inside the military and other bases of power. That the Ngo brothers had succeeded in the 1950s and early 1960s was a major accomplishment. Any Vietnamese government had to accommodate a wide range of powerful rivals, ethnic groups, political parties, criminal enterprises, and economic interests. Americans would have required deep knowledge and skill to help their Vietnamese counterparts navigate through these constituencies to form stable political coalitions.

Effective nation building never happened. The GVN's failure to create effective governmental institutions had a price. When the NVA attacked with twenty divisions in 1975, nation building was irrelevant because it was too late for the ARVN to function even as an effective conventional army to defend South Vietnam. The tragedy for the United States and its GVN client was that the American strategic architecture failed to motivate the South Vietnamese to defend their country themselves.

The failed strategic architecture of the Vietnam War left a profound and poisonous legacy within the American body politic. It left Americans with a deep loss of confidence that the nation's political and military institutions are capable of great enterprises as they had demonstrated by winning World War II. Is the United States institutionally incapable of successfully intervening with expeditionary forces where nation building is required? Is military intervention in a faraway land, in an unknown foreign culture, against a ruthless adversary worthy of the United States' fundamental values? Can Americans summon the will and the wisdom to insist that a foreign host nation undertake necessary measures for its own survival as a condition of continued American assistance, especially where its armed forces are sustaining large casualties in combat? Does the US government know how to stand up a host government to function on its own, be accountable to its people, and defend itself? Are the right strategic architectures blocked by the large institutional infrastructures in Washington? The post-Vietnam question is this: Are there certain kinds of conflicts, even for a superpower like the United States, that remain unwinnable?

Vietnam War

(1) Medic from 1st Infantry Division searches the sky for a medevac helicopter to evacuate a wounded buddy in June 1967. (2) Marines moving along rice paddy dikes search for Viet Cong in December 1965. NARA photos

(3) Soldier using flame thrower during Operation *New Castle* in March 1967. (4) Marine covering captured VC as they move toward collection point during Operation *Golden Fleece* in October 1965. NARA photos

Vietnam War

(5) President Johnson (second from left) studying model of Khe Sanh area in White House Situation Room in February 1968. NARA photo

(6) President Johnson, Vice President Hubert Humphrey, looking forlorn at General Abrams in White House Cabinet Room, while the Tet Offensive continued in March 1968. NARA photo

PART V

THE IRAQI WARS

Shortly before his death in 1933, the king of Iraq, Faisal bin Hussein bin Ali al-Hashemi, commented with bitter prophecy that there was "still no Iraqi people but only unimaginable masses of human beings, devoid of any patriotic idea, imbued with religious traditions and absurdities, connected by no common tie, giving ear to evil, prone to anarchy, and perpetually ready to rise against any government whatever."[1]

Six decades later, Faisal's prophecy about his subjects would draw the United States into five consecutive Iraqi conflicts between 1990 and the present. Hanson defined four of them in 2005.[2] There are now five spanning five American presidencies.

One might reasonably ask how it is possible to examine different strategic architectures across multiple conflicts and presidencies and still use the term *architecture*. It makes sense if a strategic architecture is thought of as continually evolving policies, strategies, and operations by which successive presidencies endeavor to define and achieve outcomes that safeguard American core interests. These are the subjects under examination with respect to the Iraqi Wars.

Steven Metz describes American "strategic culture" as a "peculiar" blend of "impatience; pragmatism; a quest for permanent solutions to strategic challenges; a propensity to seek technological . . . solutions to security problems; and a recurring lack of confidence in the exercise of power" because America has never really functioned as a colonial ruler with any enthusiasm when it deploys power into remote foreign places.[3] These cultural attributes have all been present as American administrations have tried to formulate policies, design strategies, and execute operations during the five consecutive conflicts in Iraq.

War I (August 1990–March 1991), or the "Persian Gulf War," as described in chapter 24, started with Saddam Hussein's invasion of Kuwait. The administration of George H. W. Bush quickly responded by forming an international military coalition and skillfully arranged UN resolutions to align with a principled, collective-security response. Bush defined the end state to the war as the liberation of Kuwait. The strategic architecture that the administration developed led to the first incontrovertible victory by US forces in a major conflict since 1945. However, its successful execution did not eliminate Saddam as a regional hegemon or resolve the issues among the peoples over whom Faisal had briefly reigned six decades earlier.

War II (March 1991–March 2003), as described in chapter 25, soon followed as a thirteen-year nebulous effort that involved far more direct military engagement than is generally realized because it required more than four hundred thousand air sorties to police two no-fly zones.[4] A decisive strategic architecture was difficult to construct within a policy of containment and a strategy designed to control Saddam with airpower. Iraq therefore festered as a strategic problem for the United States, but one that policy makers believed could be controlled by "keeping Saddam in his box."

War III (March 20–April 9, 2003), as described in chapter 26, was the second Bush administration's invasion of Iraq. The containment policy of War II was abandoned in 2002–2003, exacerbated by the events surrounding 9/11. The administration of George W. Bush, with a majority of the American people who supported him at the time, invaded Iraq a second time in early 2003. There was widespread belief that Saddam was still building weapons of mass destruction (WMDs) in violation of UN sanctions. The president argued that he wanted to eliminate any possibility of Saddam mounting or enabling a terrorist strike with WMDs, particularly nuclear weapons. War III began with the initial "shock and awe" air campaign and the bombing of Baghdad, coupled with an orchestrated ground drive up the Tigris-Euphrates valley to take Baghdad, which ended the rule of Saddam Hussein's government.

War IV (April 2003–December 2011), as described in chapter 27, began immediately after the end of the conventional fighting of War III and continued until December 2011, when the administration of Barack H. Obama withdrew all American military forces from Iraq. More than three years of increasing violence led to the military surge in 2007–2008 that created an opportunity to define a potentially back-to-front strategic architecture that remains elusive to the present day. War IV spanned the younger Bush and Obama presidencies.

War V (January 2012–the present), as described in chapter 28, began gradually after the end of War IV. Now, six years after the withdrawal of US combat forces from Iraq, Iraqi War V developed as al Qa'ida in Iraq began a dramatic recovery. By 2013 a new, more violent and militant enemy had emerged, the Islamic State of Iraq and Syria (ISIS). ISIS by the summer and fall of 2014 controlled a wide swath of territory in Mesopotamia running from Aleppo in Syria to Mosul in Iraq.

These five conflicts, covered in the next five chapters, cannot be adequately examined without at least a brief historical sketch of when, why, and how Iraq became a state in the heart of the Middle East. Iraq is an early 20th-century creation, historically a country in name only. Like several other states that constitute the modern Middle East, it emerged from decisions after World War I.

Before 1914, the geopolitical structure of the Middle East differed from its configuration today. Iraq, Jordan, Syria, Saudi Arabia, and Israel did not exist then. In David Fromkin's somnolent phraseology, most of the Middle East "still rested, as it had for centuries, under the drowsy and negligent sway of the Ottoman Empire, a relatively tranquil domain in which history, like everything else, moved slowly."[5]

In Arabic, *Iraq* means the fertile land on either side of a great river. The alluvial plain of the Tigris and Euphrates valley, known as Mesopotamia from the ancient Greek, denotes the land between the rivers. The populations inhabiting this "Fertile Crescent" evolved into "irrigation societies" that were eventually unified in ancient times under a succession of dynasties. Phebe Marr characterized the modern history of Iraq as drawing on three elements that have shaped its institutions and governmental practices: the civilization of ancient Mesopotamia, the Arab-Islamic heritage, and governance under the Ottoman Empire. She contended that knowledge of the ancient civilization and its rich cultural contributions, including writing, the wheel, metalworking, literature, mathematics, and science, was scant until the nineteenth century when Mesopotamia's remains were uncovered by archaeologists. She concluded that the Arab-Islamic conquest in the seventh century "has been the decisive event in shaping current Iraqi identity." Arabic became the predominant language while Islam became the religion of almost all of the country's inhabitants. The Ottoman conquest of Iraq began in the sixteenth century as an outgrowth of Ottoman-Persian religious wars where the territory in dispute constituted most of contemporary Iraq. These wars continued on and off until 1818. The Ottomans came to rely on the only element in the region that they believed would support them, urban Sunnis. "During these long wars, the seeds of Sunni dominance in government were sown."[6]

Under the Ottomans, the three Ottoman provinces of Baghdad, Mosul, and Basra were populated by Sunni and Shia Arabs and the Kurds, a separate people, not Arab but Muslim, with their own language. For the Shia, many early Islamic political struggles were fought in Iraq. Husain, the Prophet Muhammad's grandson, was killed near Karbala in 680, creating a deep, lasting schism in Islam and giving Shia Islam a martyr. From the seventh century, "Iraq acquired a reputation that it retains today of a country difficult to govern."[7]

As the Ottoman Sunnis tightened their grip on power, the Shia became alienated and strengthened their ties to Persia, especially in the holy cities of Najaf and Karbala. By the end of the nineteenth century, Persian influence in much of southern Iraq was strong. Over four centuries of rule, the Ottoman Empire's own central government became weak by the seventeenth century, and direct administration in Mesopotamia's river valleys weakened. Iraq faced a long period of stagnation and neglect. In the north, new Kurdish dynasties were established, and in the center and south, there were great tribal migrations from the Arabian Peninsula that reinforced tribalism. Competing historical "narratives" would arise among Iraqis to express their understanding of twentieth-century Iraqi politics and governance.[8] As the Ottoman Empire collapsed after World War I, and from the moment Iraq was created by the victorious Entente powers in the 1920s, Britain and France, "it was clear that there were very different [competing] ideas about [Iraq's] future."[9]

Ottoman Turkey, entering World War I on the German side, doomed the empire, and the Arab provinces fell to the British and French. Between 1914 and 1922, historians have traced the emergence of several states to a series of documents prepared by the winning powers that imposed a settlement on the overall "Middle Eastern Question." One of the most comprehensive was the secret Sykes-Picot Agreement of 1916 that defined spheres of influence between Britain and France.[10]

The agreement effectively divided the Arab provinces of the Ottoman Empire outside the Arabian Peninsula into areas of future British and French control or influence (map V.1). The terms granted France direct administrative control in a zone consisting of Greater Lebanon and along the coastal areas of Syria. Britain received similar rights within southern Mesopotamia in a zone that leapfrogged from Baghdad to a tiny coastal enclave encompassing Haifa and Acre, along with rights to a railroad linking the three cities. Palestine and its Holy Places were to be internationally administered with a smaller zone, details to be resolved after the war. In the penumbral areas between the French and British zones, the imperial signatories agreed to "protect and recognize an independent Arab state or a Confederation of Arab States" under the suzerainty of an Arab chief, occupying sizable territory that incorporated the historic inland cities of Damascus, Aleppo, and Homs, together with the province of Mosul. As Karl E. Meyer and Shareen B. Brysac described the terms, "this hypothetical Arab state was to be further divided into spheres of indirect influence, within which Britain and France would each possess the exclusive right to 'supply advisers or foreign functionaries at the request of the Arab State or Confederation.'"[11] The hypothetical Arab states that emerged were Iraq and Syria.

Iraq was a particularly difficult case for the British functionaries. Their names read like an imperial *Who's Who*. Winston Churchill, who was colonial secretary, left his mark in the wake of Sykes-Picot. As Fromkin described

BLACK SEA

USSR

GEORGIA

ARMENIA

AZERBAIJAN

Ankara •

TURKEY

CYPRUS

SYRIA
• Aleppo

Mosul
• Irbil
• Kirkuk

• TEHRAN

MEDITERRANEAN SEA

• Homs
Haifa • Beirut
• DAMASCUS

IRAN

ISRAEL
TEL AVIV
Jerusalem
• AMMAN

• BAGHDAD
IRAQ Karbala
• Najaf
Samawah
An-Nasriyah •
• Basra

CAIRO •

JORDAN

EGYPT

• Aqabak

KUWAIT CITY •
King Khalid Military City

Al-Jubayl •
Dhahran •

PERSIAN GULF

• RIYADH

SAUDI
ARABIA

	French control and occupation
	British control and occupation
	Russian control and occupation
	Zone "A" independent Arab state(s) as French protectorates
	Zone "B" independent Arab state(s) as British protectorates
	International zone of Israel and Palestine

YEMEN

SUDAN

MODERN MIDDLE EAST
1990

0   100   200   300
SCALE OF MILES

N

ETHIOPIA

Map V.1. Sykes-Picot territorial allocations, overlaid on map of Modern Middle East, divided the Arab provinces of the Ottoman Empire into British and French spheres of influence and created new states, including Iraq and Syria, a legacy from World War I that persists to the present day.
Source: Jewish Virtual Library, http://www.jewishvirtuallibrary.org/jsource/History/sykesmap1.html.

Churchill's handiwork, "there are frontier lines [including Iraq's] now running across the face of the Middle East that are scar-lines from these encounters with him."[12] Colonel T. E. Lawrence was another functionary, who left a "bewildering paper trail" and who "could be an orthodox upholder of British imperial interests or, conversely, a champion of oppressed peoples, depending upon date, whim or circumstances."[13] During the Arab revolt, Lawrence persuaded powerful colleagues to make Prince Faisal bin Hussein bin Ali al-Hashemi king of Iraq. Faisal was the third son of Sherif Hussein, the hereditary Hashemite ruler of Mecca until he was driven out by Abdul Aziz ibn Saud.[14] That Faisal was a Sunni reigning over a restless Shia majority in Iraq is something that bothered neither Lawrence nor any of the other British imperialists in the Middle East after World War I. The British under the Iraq Mandate from 1920 to 1923 oversaw the creation of a largely Sunni Arab provisional government and in 1921 proclaimed Faisal king of Iraq.[15]

Once Sykes-Picot had prescribed the broad outlines of Anglo-Franco geopolitical intent, other declarations and settlements resulted in the Palestine Mandate, the Balfour Declaration, and the Churchill White Paper that were the sources of Jordan[16] and Israel;[17] the Allenby Declaration[18] that established nominal independence for Egypt in 1922; the French Mandate for Syria and Lebanon; and the proclamation of Russia that reestablished eventual Soviet rule in Muslim Central Asia.[19]

The British became discouraged over the next decade by their failure and expense to build any sort of coherent nation-state in Iraq. In 1931, Great Britain agreed to grant Iraq independence. In short, the British left Faisal and his heirs and the Iraqis to their own devices.[20] From that time forward, Iraq became an arena for the struggle of ambitious individuals to acquire supreme political power in a country without the safeguards of political institutions of state. There was one horror after another, including massacres of tribal and Kurdish populations, expulsion of Jews, a revolt in 1941 in favor of Hitler's Germany, military coups and political assassinations (including the lynching of nineteen-year-old King Faisal II and members of his family in 1958), and the subsequent seizure of power by one strongman after another, whether nominally Ba'athist or communist.[21] Saddam Hussein Abd al-Majid al-Tikriti would emerge from this violent turbulence as the most brutish, murderous strongman of all in 1979.[22]

Americans in 1990 became the involuntary heirs to this imperial legacy. Given the political convolutions, it is difficult to remember who did what to whom, when, and why in the Middle East. It is difficult to distinguish Ba'athists from jihadists, Saudi Wahabbists from al Qa'ida or ISIS terrorists, Shiites from Sunnis, Shiites from Iranians, Kurds from all of the above, Israelis from Palestinians, Hamas in Gaza from Hezbollah in Lebanon, or tribes from one another, often scattered across national borders.

24

IRAQI WAR I, PERSIAN GULF WAR

Defeating Saddam, Losing Politically

Saddam Hussein invaded the emirate of Kuwait on August 2, 1990, as a solution to Iraq's economic problems and his need for debt relief from Arab nations, especially Kuwait. Iraq had accumulated at least $35 billion in debt as a result of the eight-year Iran-Iraq War (1980–1988), much of it in short-term, high-interest loans from Kuwait and Saudi Arabia.[1] Saddam saw seizure of Kuwait as an easy means of greatly increasing Iraq's share of the world's oil reserves and a bold demonstration that Iraq was now the dominant military power in the Middle East. Conquest of Kuwait meant the addition of approximately two million barrels (bbls) of oil per day to Iraq's production of 3.5 million bbls/day,[2] a near doubling of Iraq's total oil reserves from 113 billion bbls to 217 billion bbls[3] (constituting 16 percent of the world's total proven reserves), and a fait accompli to a fossil-fuel-dependent world.

Iraq seized the entire country in two days. Within a week, Saddam had declared that Iraq would annex Kuwait as its nineteenth province, an irredentist goal of long standing. Iraqi forces then deployed along Kuwait's southern border with Saudi Arabia well positioned to seize the kingdom's oil-rich Eastern Province.

POLICY

Saddam assumed that the world would acquiesce in his sudden and ruthless invasion of Kuwait and would fail to organize any effective military opposition.

However, Saudi Arabia and the other Gulf states immediately supported the Kuwaiti government-in-exile. The Council of the Arab League voted to condemn Iraq on August 3 and demanded that Saddam withdraw his army from Kuwait. Other Arab states, including Algeria, Egypt, and Syria, supported Kuwait, although Jordan, Libya, Mauritania, the Sudan, and the Palestine Liberation Organization (PLO) supported Iraq.

The invasion happened so fast that the Bush administration appeared to be taken by surprise. Initial international reaction outside the Middle East was cautious. There were suggestions that the invasion was an Arab problem and that it was a matter of indifference from whom the United States purchased its oil. Then President Bush left for Camp David, quietly assembling his diplomatic and military advisors.[4] He had already asked a critical question the day before at the first NSC meeting: "What happens if we do nothing?"[5]

The answer was not long in coming. As a former oilman, Bush knew the answer to his own question. He "seemed horrified that Saddam might invade Saudi Arabia. He engaged in an extended analysis of the effect on world oil availability and price. . . . With just twenty percent of the world's oil, Saddam would be able to manipulate world prices and hold the United States and its allies at his mercy. Higher oil prices would fuel inflation, worsening the already gloomy condition of the U.S. economy."[6] The following day, Sunday, August 5, 1990, after landing by helicopter on the White House lawn from Camp David, President Bush declared, "This will not stand."

Two days later, the president announced that the United States would send military forces to the Persian Gulf. Britain, France, most other European nations, the USSR, Canada, and Japan had already condemned Saddam's invasion of Kuwait. The end of the Cold War allowed the UN to take decisive action under US initiative.[7] On the day of the invasion, the Security Council within hours voted 14–0 (Resolution 660) to demand Iraq's immediate withdrawal from Kuwait. The United States, Great Britain, and Saudi Arabia led the UN in forming a coalition of thirty-eight states[8] under the command of General H. Norman Schwarzkopf Jr., commander in chief, Central Command (CINCCENT). The coalition quickly began to deploy military forces to enforce UN-imposed economic sanctions (Resolution 661) and to defend Saudi Arabia.

In 1990–1991, the United States led the UN-approved coalition in two military phases. Operation *Desert Shield* was the first phase, a defensive operation spanning six months (August 1990–January 1991), in which the United States and the coalition initially rushed to build up defensive forces necessary to protect Saudi Arabia and the rest of the Gulf states, coupled with UN-imposed economic sanctions. Operation *Desert Storm* was the second, offensive phase to liberate Kuwait. *Desert Storm* commenced on January 17, 1991, with an intensive air campaign. The land war followed five weeks later and ended victoriously after four days with negligible casualties for the coalition. This skeletal summary might suggest that victory in War I was inevitable. At the time, until it actually happened, it was not.

The legacy of the Vietnam War had left bitterness in US civilian-military relations. The post-Vietnam generation of military officers, many of them Vietnam War combat veterans, believed that failure in Vietnam had been the result of a deadly combination of political leaders failing to set a clear geopolitical goal, of military leaders failing to define an effective strategy, and of civilians micromanaging the incremental escalation, especially the bombing campaign.

In hindsight, the Vietnam diagnosis was more complex. It had been a failure of interaction between politicians and generals to test a theory of victory against the realities in the field. The civilians did not ask whether the military force that had been deployed possessed the right doctrines and structures; had been given clear, achievable objectives; and above all had the right leaders. They did not engage in systematic cross-examination of the Vietnam strategy and its results. It was not so much a failure to immerse themselves in military details. It was whether they were looking at the right details and drawing the right conclusions from them. As Cohen put it in *Supreme Command*, "It was a failure to understand [the Vietnam War's strategic] tasks, not its desire to micromanage, that constituted the fatal flaw of civilian leadership."[9]

STRATEGY

Between 1975 and 1990, the armed forces of the United States had changed profoundly. The US military had evolved into an all-volunteer, professional force. The Reagan defense buildup of the 1980s had transformed the confidence, technology, capabilities, and strategic thinking in all of the military services. Three other salutary developments transpired during this period. In November 1984, Secretary of Defense Caspar W. Weinberger postulated six principles for the use of force in a speech to the National Press Club titled "The Uses of Military Power." Reduced to their essentials they prescribed that the United States should only commit forces as a last resort in defense of a vital national interest where such commitment is to win according to clearly defined political and military objectives with the full support of the American people and Congress. The Weinberger principles were accepted as canon within the military, were widely reprinted, and appeared in the syllabi of staff colleges. The Powell Doctrine reinforced them. When he became chairman of the Joint Chiefs of Staff (CJCS), General Colin L. Powell added to the Weinberger principles the concepts of risk, cost, exhaustion of nonviolent policies, "exit strategy," and "overwhelming force." In 1986 the Goldwater-Nichols legislation had made the CJCS the primary military advisor to the president, and in Powell's politically skilled hands the chairmanship by 1990 had become an exceptionally powerful position.

In addition to strengthening the position of CJCS and the Joint Staff, the Goldwater-Nichols Department of Defense Reorganization Act of 1986 also improved joint (interservice) and combined (interallied) operations in the field by increasing the authority and influence of American commanders in chief assigned to the unified combatant commands worldwide. This augmentation enhanced the authority of General Powell as CJCS and General Schwarzkopf as CINCCENT. Both were Vietnam veterans who recognized the importance of unified command that could coordinate the actions of individual services, which no theater commander had ever formally possessed before.[10] Now, as senior officers, they were serving under a streamlined chain of command that bypassed the service chiefs, making them directly accountable to the secretary of defense and the president. These institutional developments significantly strengthened the strategic architecture of War I. Now military advice was centralized in the chairman of the JCS as opposed to the service chiefs. The CJCS was designated as the principal military advisor to the president. The Weinberger-Powell principles and the Goldwater-Nichols provisions enabled the synchronization of ground, naval, air, and space-based systems so that the evolving doctrine of AirLand Battle could be demonstrated under an integrated plan to attack and defeat an opponent in depth.

Schwarzkopf would emerge from the Gulf War as not only a winning general but also a media star. Max Boot described him as "big, colorful, outspoken, blustering, profane," and with "an unexpected flair for deadpan wit."[11] He was a skillful briefer on television.[12] So was Powell.[13]

With the end of the Cold War and the rapid withdrawal of the USSR as the main threat, Schwarzkopf, who had been CINCCENT since 1988, had been thinking proactively about a war plan to counter the aggressive ambitions of Saddam Hussein. Saddam was a known hegemon. He had attacked Iran and provoked a destructive eight-year war of attrition. In late July 1990, Schwarzkopf had already developed and tested a war plan in a staff simulation called *Internal Look*. A few days later, Schwarzkopf and US Central Command (CENTCOM) had a real threat on their hands.[14]

The most immediate concern for President Bush was that Saddam Hussein would attack Saudi Arabia. There was little military force to stop him pushing farther south into Saudi Arabia's oil fields. Saudi Arabia controlled 25 percent of the world's proven petroleum reserves.[15] Iraq built up its military forces in the Kuwait theater of operations (KTO) to 336,000 troops and a total of forty-three divisions, 3,475 tanks, and 2,475 artillery tubes. The Iraqi army was one of the best equipped in the Middle East and included state-of-the-art Soviet T-72 tanks and MiG-29 fighters. The army as a whole totaled nine hundred thousand men and was battle tested from the eight-year Iran-Iraq War. The forces that Saddam had massed to invade Kuwait could easily have kept right on going into Saudi Arabia.

A high-level American delegation, which had flown to Riyadh, quickly secured permission from Saudi king Fahd bin Abdul Aziz al Saud to send US troops to defend his kingdom. Whether Saddam had intentions to invade Saudi Arabia and seize the kingdom's eastern oil fields was the subject of intense debate in both Washington and Riyadh. The CIA in early August had concluded that Saddam had the capability to reach the Saudi capital in three days.[16] CENTCOM began airlifting units into Saudi Arabia within five days of the invasion, starting on August 7–8, 1990, with an F-15 squadron and a lightly armed brigade of the 82nd Airborne Division.[17]

By late August, to defend Saudi Arabia, Schwarzkopf and Powell had worked fast to assemble and deploy a larger force of seven army brigades, three aircraft carrier battle groups, fourteen fighter squadrons, seven thousand marines, and, at the US logistics base on Diego Garcia in the Indian Ocean, a B-52 squadron.[18]

By November, Operation *Desert Storm* had an even more formidable force deployed: 60 warships, 1,000 aircraft, 250,000 troops, and 800 tanks.[19] Schwarzkopf was now in a position to guarantee the defense of Saudi Arabia, but the White House was pressing him to plan for the expulsion of Iraqi forces from Kuwait.

The initial plan for an offensive, which Schwarzkopf and the CENTCOM staff prepared, did not receive a warm reception in Washington. When the plan, known as the one-corps plan, which envisioned an attack straight into Kuwait, was briefed in Washington for the first time on October 10–11, 1990, there was great dissatisfaction with it. The air campaign that had been briefed at the beginning of the overall presentation of the plan was accepted with few questions. Air Force Brigadier General Buster C. Glosson, who served under General Charles Horner, commander, CENTCOM Air Forces, led the air planning effort in Riyadh and briefed a three-phase Master Air Plan. The initial phase was intended to take a few days and to be followed by Phases II and III to destroy half of Iraq's tanks, armored personnel carriers, artillery, antiaircraft guns, rocket launchers, and SAMs before ground combat commenced. Such an ambitious mission was significant in the history of air warfare, although at the time it was hardly noticed.[20]

The army by 1990 had adopted the AirLand Battle Doctrine, where four tenets drove planning and offensive action: initiative (change the terms of battle through aggressive action), depth (fight deep, close, and rear battles simultaneously), agility (think and act faster than the enemy), and synchronization (arrange battlefield activities in time, space, and purpose to concentrate the greatest possible combat power at the decisive point).[21] General Glosson therefore had to plan and synchronize two simultaneous battles: the deep battle in the rear and the close battle against the forty-three Iraqi divisions deployed in and around Kuwait. The deep battle would be Phase I of *Desert Storm*.

The initial thinking was that a well-coordinated attack deep in the enemy's rear might in fact prove decisive. This marked the first recognition in American military doctrine that a conflict might not necessarily be decided along the line of contact.[22] The operational essentials of the AirLand Battle, developed as a Cold War doctrine, fit well with the strategic architecture of War I. Joint, interservice, and synchronization practices were widely understood and accepted by the US Armed Forces. AirLand had been the basis of extensive training, military planning exercises, and operational command-and-control simulations.

The Phase IV ground campaign, however, raised many questions both in the Pentagon and at the White House. General Brent Scowcroft (USAF, Ret.), the national security advisor, was very unhappy about what he saw as a straight-forward drive into the teeth of Iraqi defenses. Secretary of Defense Richard B. Cheney thought it was just "a bad plan."[23] Some NSC staffers at the White House ridiculed it as "hey diddle diddle, straight up the middle."[24] The point of the critique was that there had to be a way that American power could be harnessed in a more imaginative war plan than simply attacking straight into Kuwait. Schwarzkopf himself knew that the ground plan was a work in progress and had instructed his generals who were to present the ground plan to display a final chart at the conclusion of the briefing. It read,

> Phases I, II solid and high confidence in successful execution
> Phase III executable in preparation for Phase IV [the ground offensive]
> Phase IV offensive ground plan not solid
> We must not assume away enemy capability and willingness to fight
> Present assessment—We do not have capability to attack on the ground at this time
> Need additional heavy corps to *guarantee* [italics in original] successful outcome.

Before leaving Riyadh for Washington, Schwarzkopf admonished his senior staff,

> One of the things we have going for us is that we don't bullshit the President. You should explain our capabilities, but do not tell the President we're capable of something we're not. This is no time for a "can-do" attitude. Do not speculate when you answer questions: confine your responses strictly to what we've analyzed.[25]

Despite uniformly hostile reaction to the plan as unimaginative, Schwarzkopf and the CENTCOM staff indeed had considered a one-corps flanking attack. Schwarzkopf recognized from the outset the appeal of a grand, flanking, enveloping attack from the desert wastes west of Iraq, but he ruled it out for sound military reasons. When General Scowcroft asked, "Why straight up the middle? Why don't you go around?" Powell replied, "Logistics. We don't have enough force to go around."[26]

Solid military factors weighed against a flanking attack from the west with the forces available in October 1990. West of the Wadi al-Batin, the dry river valley that runs roughly 130 miles southwest to northeast along Kuwait's western border with Iraq and drains into the Persian Gulf, was at this stage of the planning terra incognita. Whether the desert west of the wadi was "trafficable," capable of supporting thousands of tanks, trucks, and other vehicles, was unknown. One armored division could consume hundreds of thousands of gallons of fuel per day and consume thousands of tons of ammunition. The ability to drive fuel and ammunition trucks into this western desert could be a dead end until the ground had been probed. Equally troubling, a flank attack under the one-corps concept would require virtually all of the available coalition ground forces, leaving no reserve. Iraq had displayed the capability during the Iran-Iraq War of being able to counterattack quickly, moving armored divisions sixty miles in a day.[27] Gambling on a flank attack without more combat power backed up by a robust, ground-based logistics train was judged at this stage to be too big a risk. CENTCOM intelligence later discovered that the desert was indeed trafficable after special forces teams were inserted to assess the terrain and return with soil samples for analysis.

Powell flew to Riyadh ten days later. For two days he peppered Schwarzkopf and the CENTCOM planners with questions. What emerged from discussions was the two-corps concept that amounted to a doubling of the American deployment, approved by President Bush at the end of October.[28] Powell, as Bush's principal military advisor, had encouraged the president to double the combat power in the theater. The continuing reviews and exchanges between senior civilian and military leaders, always with the president's approval of major changes, were probing and intensive. These planning iterations produced a better plan. CINCENT would receive even more forces than he had requested; he got three additional aircraft carriers, a second marine division, and, to bolster what became the proposed 18th Airborne Corps "Left Hook," the heavily armored 7th Corps from Germany, no longer needed by NATO to deter a Warsaw Pact invasion. The concept was to deploy a force so overwhelming as to seem invincible once it had massed in the Saudi desert. In Secretary Cheney's "infelicitous phrase—[this was] 'the don't-screw-around school of military strategy.'"[29] What Bush's force augmentation accomplished was tighter, more realistic alignment among policy, strategy, and operations. The order of battle grew to a total of nine US divisions deployed from west to east, in addition to five coalition divisions and brigade combat units.

Between the first October review and mid-December, the plan went through additional iterations, with arguments among planners in Riyadh over how far west the two army corps should deploy. What emerged was the flanking attack identified as the Left Hook launched from locations 250 miles to the west deep in the Arabian Desert (map 24.1). This flanking maneuver would require mobility and logistical feats of a speed never before requested.[30] It could not begin until Horner's and Glosson's air campaign had ensured that the Iraqis could not fly reconnaissance aircraft over the battle space to detect the scale of this Left Hook threat on their western flank.[31] Logistically, it would require the creation of multiple logistics bases in the west to supply the vast quantities of fuel, ammunition, water, food, and spare parts necessary to sustain more than eight divisions over sixty days of continuous combat, the time span CENTCOM planners had prescribed. The logistical calculations were daunting. For example, a single armored division needed 400,000 gallons of fuel, 213,000 gallons of water, and 2,400 tons of ammunition each day.[32] The practical consequences of so ambitious a maneuver plan meant that CENTCOM had to be ready quickly to move the entire 18th Airborne Corps and 7th Corps—more than eight divisions, 250,000 combat personnel, and 64,000 vehicles—250 miles west in a span of fourteen days. In the event, it would require considerable ingenuity.[33] Once these forces were in position and the offensive began, this large force would have to be supplied on the move.

General Schwarzkopf later characterized this maneuver in his now famous CENTCOM briefing on February 27, 1991, as the "Hail Mary play in football," using the analogy to explain the westward deployment of 18th Airborne Corps and 7th Corps. Massing such a large mobile force deep into the Saudi desert and then launching the offensive where the Iraqis had not prepared any defenses would enable 18th Airborne Corps and 7th Corps to outflank the enemy by attacking northeast along multiple parallel axes (map 24.1). Simultaneously, directly south of Kuwait's southern border with Saudi Arabia, the two marine divisions and the Arab forces would attack straight into Kuwait to fix the Iraqi defenders in place. The two corps would execute the Left Hook and swing wide around toward the east to catch the Iraqi army in a pincer and rip into its rear. It was a formula for a double envelopment leading potentially to the enemy's utter annihilation, a late twentieth-century version of the *Wehrmacht*'s legacy of *Bewegungskrieg* (war of movement) and *Vernichtungsschlacht* (battle of annihilation). Schwarzkopf was about to execute the AirLand Battle Doctrine for real, a capability for which the armed forces of the United States had been preparing and training for the preceding fifteen years.

War I provided the first demonstration of high-tech AirLand Battle where a well-trained, all-volunteer American force proved to themselves and the world how skilled and lethal they had become in their combat abilities and mastery of modern weapons and technology. The doctrinal, institutional, personnel, and

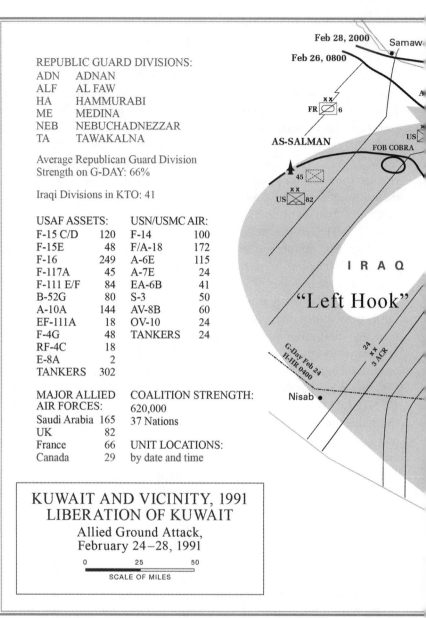

REPUBLIC GUARD DIVISIONS:
ADN ADNAN
ALF AL FAW
HA   HAMMURABI
ME   MEDINA
NEB NEBUCHADNEZZAR
TA   TAWAKALNA

Average Republican Guard Division
Strength on G-DAY: 66%

Iraqi Divisions in KTO: 41

USAF ASSETS:		USN/USMC AIR:	
F-15 C/D	120	F-14	100
F-15E	48	F/A-18	172
F-16	249	A-6E	115
F-117A	45	A-7E	24
F-111 E/F	84	EA-6B	41
B-52G	80	S-3	50
A-10A	144	AV-8B	60
EF-111A	18	OV-10	24
F-4G	48	TANKERS	24
RF-4C	18		
E-8A	2		
TANKERS	302		

MAJOR ALLIED AIR FORCES:
Saudi Arabia 165
UK   82
France   66
Canada   29

COALITION STRENGTH:
620,000
37 Nations

UNIT LOCATIONS:
by date and time

Feb 28, 2000   Samaw

Feb 26, 0800

FR 6

AS-SALMAN   US
             FOB COBRA

45

US 82

I R A Q

"Left Hook"

G-Day Feb 24
H-HR 0400

24
3 ACR

Nisab

KUWAIT AND VICINITY, 1991
LIBERATION OF KUWAIT
Allied Ground Attack,
February 24–28, 1991

0   25   50
SCALE OF MILES

Map 24.1. Execution of Schwarzkopf's "Left Hook" maneuver plan completely outflanked Iraqi defenses in Kuwait; the map depicts *Desert Storm* ground operations between February 24 and 28, 1991, by unit locations on four consecutive dates and times. *AO Eagle* refers to 101st Airborne holding positions; *FOB* refers to "forward operating base."
Source: USMA Atlases.

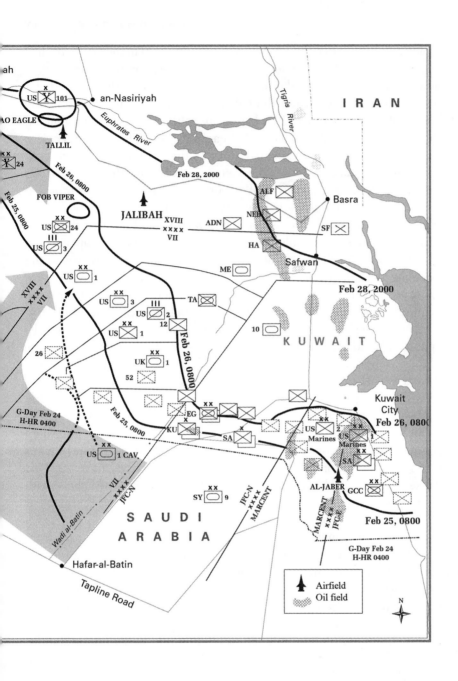

technological changes that the US Armed Forces initiated in the late 1970s had a profound effect on the execution of the War I strategic architecture.

Between 1970 and 1990, the armed services had gone through a major personnel transformation. After the failed Iranian hostage mission to rescue embassy staff in Tehran in 1979, what began as the Carter defense buildup accelerated under President Ronald W. Reagan in 1981. The military services provided the leadership and Congress provided the resources to actively seek and train higher-quality recruits. The Vietnam-era junior officers and NCOs who remained to pursue professional careers in the armed services provided much of the leadership. James Fallows, writing a critique of national defense policy midway through this twenty-year renewal, pointed out that the transformation was "most noticeable among the junior officers, the captains and majors who talk with fervor about the need to recommit themselves to the special obligations demanded of military leaders."[34]

The army and marine corps went from being perceived as organizations for high-school dropouts and drug users to being very capable armed services where young men and women could learn valuable skills, acquire self-discipline and leadership abilities, and earn respect from their countrymen. All of these developments were reinforced by better pay and a new version of the World War II GI Bill that would offer scholarships to soldiers after they left the service. By 1990, the army had been preparing to fight precisely the kind of war Schwarzkopf wanted them to fight. Most of the battalions sent to the Gulf, including all National Guard units, had practiced realistic simulated engagements in the Mojave Desert at the Army's National Training Center in Fort Irwin, California. They practiced against an opposing force (OpFor) modeled and equipped like a Soviet motorized rifle regiment. By fighting with weapons and equipment linked to the Multiple Integrated Laser Engagement System (MILES), units could hone their tactical and military skills in MILES force-on-force engagements, review the after-action reports, and learn from their mistakes. This combat training came as close to simulating what war was like as any previous training program by any army in history.[35]

The Reagan Cold War defense buildup had also led to the development and fielding of a new generation of high-tech weapons systems. This buildup had been implemented with the Soviet Union as the strategic enemy, not a regional hegemon like Saddam Hussein. But the improved capabilities easily fit within the strategic, operational, and tactical requirements of the CENTCOM mission.

The US Air Force fielded high-tech stealth attack aircraft like the F-117 "Nighthawk" fighter equipped with two-thousand-pound laser-guided bombs; two new agile fighter-bombers, the F-16 Fighting Falcon and F-15 Eagle, and the B-1 bomber;[36] the A-10 "Warthog" close air support fighter-bomber; the Airborne Warning and Control System (AWACS) aircraft; and the airborne

Joint Surveillance and Target Attack Radar System (JSTARS). AWACS, a modified Boeing 707/320 commercial airframe with a rotating radar dome, in service since 1977, could provide an accurate, real-time situational awareness picture of friendly and hostile air activity through all-altitude and all-weather surveillance of the battle space, together with command and control and battle management of air assets over a large tactical area of responsibility.[37] JSTARS, a joint air force–army development,[38] could provide comparable ground situational information through secure communications data links, with army mobile ground units and intelligence centers to complement the picture of the battle space provided by AWACS.

In addition, the air force and navy had air-launched cruise missiles (ALCMs) and Tomahawk land-attack cruise missiles (TLAMs). Both are long-range, subsonic, jet engine-powered missiles, equipped with terrain contour matching (TERCOM) guidance systems and one-thousand-pound warheads capable of accurately hitting an enemy target at distances up to 1,350–1,500 miles. The navy also had carrier-based, high-performance fighter-bombers, the F-14 Tomcat and F/A-18 Hornet, and Aegis guided-missile cruisers capable of simultaneously performing antiship, antiaircraft, antimissile, and antisubmarine missions for a fleet battle group.

The army fielded the M1/A1 Abrams state-of-the-art main battle tank, the M2/M3 Bradley Fighting Vehicle armored personnel carrier (APC), the AH-64 Apache attack helicopter, the UH-60 Black Hawk transport helicopter, the Patriot air defense system, and the M270 Multiple Launch Rocket System (MLRS). Thousands of Global Positioning System (GPS) receivers were carried by the infantry and armored units, enabling Schwarzkopf's forces to navigate accurately in a desert that was not unlike an ocean environment.[39] Ground-based weapons systems, including tanks; armored fighting vehicles; and command, control, communications, and computers/intelligence, surveillance, and reconnaissance (C⁴/ISR) systems, were interfaced to GPS to enable better interoperability among different weapons systems and war fighters in all services.

OPERATIONS

The operations order (91-001), issued on January 17, 1991, by Washington to CENTCOM through the military chain of command, was a model of clarity. It included a single thirty-four-word sentence that defined the mission completely: "Attack Iraqi political-military leadership and command and control; gain and maintain air superiority; sever Iraqi supply lines; destroy chemical, biological, and nuclear capability; destroy Republican Guard forces in the Kuwaiti Theater; liberate Kuwait."[40]

At H-hour, 0300 on the same day the order was issued, the air campaign commenced. Operation *Desert Shield* had become *Desert Storm*. Execution of General Glosson's Master Air Plan started to unfold as aircraft took off in response to hundreds of computerized air tasking orders (ATOs) matching targets to strike packages and air squadrons (map 24.2). The overlapping Phases I through III of the air campaign would last thirty-nine days—forty-three if the Phase IV ground war is included.[41] CENTCOM air forces quickly achieved air supremacy. Iraqi command-and-control systems had been paralyzed by the time the ground war began. General Horner's coalition aircraft flew nearly 110,000 sorties[42] and dropped 88,500 tons of ordnance over the forty-three days of the air campaign.[43] The Strategic Air Command (SAC) deployed seventy-four aging B-52G bombers of Vietnam *Arc Light* and *Linebacker* vintage from bases in the CONUS, Europe, Saudi Arabia, and Diego Garcia in the Indian Ocean. The B-52s flew 1,620 sorties, representing approximately 3 percent of the combat-mission sorties but accounting for 30 percent of the total bomb tonnage dropped.[44]

On February 23, the CINCCENT bomb damage assessment (BDA) indicated that air attacks had destroyed 1,688 Iraqi tanks (a 39 percent kill rate), 1,451 artillery pieces (47 percent), and 929 APCs (32 percent). General Schwarzkopf's color-coded charts showed that most of the Iraqi frontline divisions had been degraded to 50 percent effectiveness, while the divisions deployed in the rear, including the six enemy Republican Guard divisions, were still at or above the 75 percent level.[45]

Overall, the coalition air campaign was judged a great success. However, it was much less effective against dug-in equipment than against command-and-control nodes and logistical assets. This situation changed radically when ground fighting forced the hidden Iraqi equipment into movement. Then the combined-arms coordination CENTCOM achieved by employing ground and air assets simultaneously demonstrated how lethal joint, interservice synergy had become. These accomplishments were frequently cited as early demonstrations of the "revolution in military affairs."

One limit on the operational success of the air campaign was the distraction caused by Iraqi Scud missile launches against Israeli and coalition targets. This development during the first week of the war brought an urgent diversion of air assets to mollify the Israelis, who were threatening to retaliate against Iraq, complicating the politics of the coalition. The Iraqis launched eighty-eight Scuds; these relatively primitive missiles had impacts well beyond their number. After the United States deployed the Patriot surface-to-air missile defense system to Israel and Saudi Arabia, concerns eased somewhat thanks to what was perceived to be superior Patriot interception performance.[46]

The ground war began thirty-eight days after the air campaign, early on the Sunday morning of February 24, 1991, at 0400. The weather was cloudy,

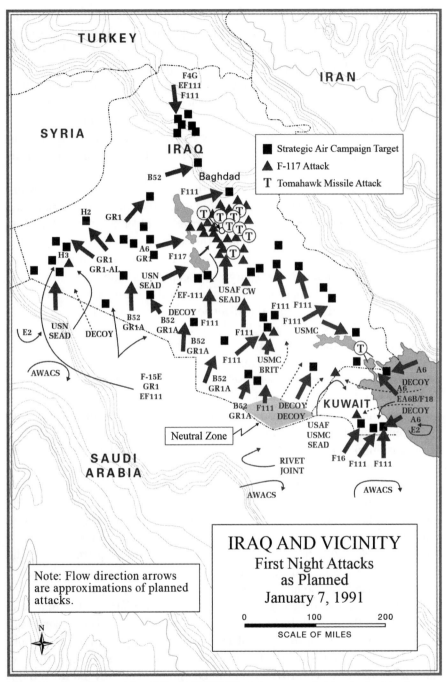

TURKEY

IRAN

SYRIA

F4G
EF111
F111

IRAQ

	Strategic Air Campaign Target
▲	F-117 Attack
T	Tomahawk Missile Attack

B52   Baghdad

F111

H2   GR1

H3   GR1   A6   F117
      GR1-AL   GR1
            USN
            SEAD

              EF-111
                        USAF CW
              DECOY   SEAD
E2   USN   B52   B52 F111   F111 F111
      SEAD DECOY GR1A GR1A   F111
                        B52   USMC
AWACS   GR1A
                        F111 USMC
      F-15E   B52   BRIT
      GR1   GR1A
      EF111
                        B52   F111 DECOY   KUWAIT
                        GR1A   DECOY
            Neutral Zone   USAF
                                    USMC
                                    SEAD
SAUDI   RIVET   F16 F111 F111
ARABIA   JOINT

              AWACS   AWACS

T (multiple Tomahawk markers near Baghdad)

T (Tomahawk marker near Kuwait)

A6
DECOY
A6
EA6B/F18
DECOY
A6
E2

IRAQ AND VICINITY
First Night Attacks
as Planned
January 7, 1991

0   100   200
SCALE OF MILES

Note: Flow direction arrows
are approximations of planned
attacks.

N

Map 24.2. On the first night of War I, CENTCOM air forces attacked hundreds of Iraqi targets in Kuwait and Iraq.

Source: USMA Atlases.

rainy, and miserable. The 1st and 2nd Marine Divisions and the army tank brigade assigned to the marines attacked straight into the Iraqi defenses along the Kuwait-Saudi border. The Iraqi defenders did not set the oil-filled ditches on fire. They did not use chemical weapons, a major CENTCOM fear. They fired some artillery, but it was quickly neutralized by counterfire supported by tactical counterbattery radars that could trace enemy shells back to the grid coordinates of their emplacements. The dozens of frontline Iraqi infantry divisions that were to decimate coalition forces as they had done to the Iranians in the Iran-Iraq War did nothing of the kind. Iraqi positions started collapsing almost immediately.

Simultaneously, hundreds of miles to the west, 18th Airborne Corps encountered even fewer obstacles as the 82nd and 101st Airborne Divisions and the French 6th Light Armored Division moved on objectives in western Iraq that could be used as bases to dominate the southern Euphrates River valley, key to cutting Iraqi supply lines into Kuwait. The 101st moved ninety-three miles into Iraq the first day, in the largest helicopter operation ever attempted, to seize their first main operating base deep on the enemy's flank. These attacks were intended to be first-day diversions.

The main CENTCOM thrust had been intended for the next day by 7th Corps, with more than 1,500 tanks and 146,000 soldiers, to rip into the Iraqi flank between the two airborne and marine assaults. With the unexpected success of the preliminary attacks, Schwarzkopf accelerated the 7th Corps assault, moving it up to the same day. At 1430 in the afternoon of February 24, 7th Corps, under the command of Lieutenant General Frederick M. Franks Jr.,[47] commenced one of the most intense artillery barrages since World War II, unleashing 155 mm howitzers and MLRS launchers with more than eleven thousand shells and rockets in a "rain of steel" lasting thirty minutes.[48]

General Franks's 7th Corps had 48,500 vehicles, including 1,587 tanks, 1,502 Bradley Fighting Vehicles and armored personnel carriers, 669 artillery pieces, and 223 attack helicopters.[49] The 1st ID (mechanized), the "Big Red One" of both World War I and II fame, led the advance as tanks, with plows and rollers, cleared paths through the minefields. Any Iraqi troops who did not surrender were buried alive in their trenches by the armored bulldozers.

Two days later, by the afternoon of Tuesday, February 26, Kuwait City was completely surrounded by coalition forces. The next morning, the first Arab units entered the capital. In the west, the 24th mechanized ID, under Major General Barry R. McCaffrey, part of 18th Airborne Corps, had reached Highway 8 in the Euphrates valley, almost 190 miles from its start line, by the evening of February 26. The 101st Airborne Division had already interdicted this key LOC between Baghdad and Basra. The Iraqis no longer had an avenue of retreat to the west. Their only possible escape route was to the north, up the Tigris River valley or into Basra.

The one element in the Op-order 91-001 that would not be completely fulfilled was the destruction of the Republican Guard divisions. They had been kept back from the front lines and were better supplied and better protected with antiaircraft batteries than the Iraqi conscript forces that had been overrun. They still had 75 percent of their armor and were able to maneuver as cohesive units. They assumed blocking positions in front of the 7th Corps advance with the intent of enabling the bulk of the Iraqi army units to escape from Kuwait.[50]

The heaviest ground fighting of the war was about to begin. Troopers of the 2nd Armored Cavalry Regiment (2ACR), a brigade-size screening force, advanced ahead of 7th Corps. E Troop of the 2nd Squadron of 2ACR, under the command of Captain H. R. McMaster, a West Point alumnus who five years later earned a PhD from the University of North Carolina after writing a dissertation about Vietnam, was a major participant in the Battle of 73 Easting.[51] The 2ACR destroyed more than an entire Iraqi brigade, two hundred vehicles, and most of an armored division, the Tawakalna Republican Guard Division, deployed about fifty miles west of the Kuwait-Iraq border.[52] The 73 Easting engagement is a micro-example of what happened to the Iraqis over the next two days when the full mass of the 7th Corps divisions attacked the remaining Republican Guard divisions that chose to put up a fight. What ensued was a rout.

Meanwhile, the Iraqis had already started evacuating Kuwait on the morning of February 26. For the better part of the next two days, a long line of traffic streamed north out of Kuwait City as Iraqi soldiers took whatever vehicles they could find, loaded them with whatever they could steal, and tried to flee from the coalition. They did not get very far. The two air force JSTARS aircraft detected and tracked their movement and directed relentless coalition air attacks on the convoys. More than 1,900 vehicles were destroyed along the six-lane Al Jahra highway running north out of Kuwait City. The photography of the destruction from the air, as far as the eye could see, yielded near real-time video images that were broadcast on television around the world.[53] This road quickly became known as the "Highway of Death." Journalist Michael T. Kelly's account was graphic in a *New Republic* column:

> For a fifty or sixty-mile stretch just north of Jahra to the Iraqi border, the road was littered with exploded and roasted vehicles, charred and blown-up bodies. . . . [It] was thick with the wreckage of tanks, armored personnel carriers, 155-mm howitzers, and supply trucks. . . . The heat of the blasts had inspired secondary explosions in the ammunition. The fires had been fierce enough in some cases to melt windshield glass. . . . Most of the destruction had been visited on clusters of ten to fifteen vehicles. But those who had driven alone, or even off the road and into the desert, had been hunted down too. Of the several hundred wrecks I saw, not one had crashed in panic; all bore the marks of having been bombed or shot.[54]

General Powell and other senior policy makers in Washington, watching these televised images, worried that the violence was excessive and might undermine international opinion and tarnish the brilliance of Schwarzkopf's victory. On February 27, Powell called Schwarzkopf in Riyadh and told him that President Bush wanted to announce a cease-fire effective at 0800 the following day, stopping the war at one hundred hours, a symmetry that appealed to Bush and the White House staff. Schwarzkopf agreed.

Difficulties emerged almost immediately because the Iraqis managed to get a large number of their tanks and APCs out of Kuwait. The marines and Arabs had advanced so rapidly toward Kuwait City that they had pushed many Iraqi units out of Kuwait before 7th Corps could trap them. Commanders in the field knew that a Cannae-style envelopment was not yet complete, but no one with sufficient authority was willing to challenge Schwarzkopf, who in turn was unwilling to challenge his chain of command. So the cease-fire became a fait accompli, even though it left the stated goal in Op-order 91-001 of destroying the Republican Guard only partially fulfilled. This error would be compounded at the cease-fire talks in Safwan on March 3, 1991, when Schwarzkopf permitted the Iraqis to fly armed helicopters, ostensibly to ferry senior officials around the country and move medical supplies.[55] Within days, dozens of Soviet-built Hind and Hip helicopters, part of the surviving fleet of hundreds, reinforced by tanks, were being used by Iraqi forces to suppress Shia and Kurd rebels who, at American instigation, had risen up against Saddam's tyranny.[56] The bloodbath that ensued in Basra and the Kurdish north would ensure that Saddam and his Ba'athist regime remained in power.

No American military decision since the Vietnam War had provoked more controversy. It took some time to develop after the initial euphoria of liberating Kuwait had faded and the magnitude of the surviving Iraqi forces became apparent. Did the decision to end the war come too soon because the CENTCOM encirclement was incomplete? Perhaps.

Atkinson, two years after War I ended, asserted that "the decision wears well with time." He judged that no substantive evidence can be elicited that the surviving Iraqi forces escaping from Kuwait proved decisive in suppressing the postwar Shia and Kurdish rebellions. It is true, as the Defense Intelligence Agency later reported, that "as many as one third of the [Republican] Guard's T-72s made it out of the KTO [Kuwait theater of operations]." Other intelligence assessments concluded that approximately 800 tanks and 1,400 APCs escaped destruction from the air as a result. However, even if this war-fighting equipment south of the Euphrates had been totally destroyed, Saddam still possessed "an enormous force north of the river which totaled more than 3,000 armored vehicles and 1,000 artillery tubes available elsewhere in the country." Indeed, Powell had come to similar conclusions. North of the Euphrates, the Iraqis also had at least twenty divisions that Powell had to assume would survive the war.[57]

Those were the near-term justifications. The strategic point to remember is that the Bush administration went to war with the liberation of Kuwait, not regime change, as its geopolitical goal. Even if it was the case, as General Schwarzkopf boasted, that the road to Baghdad was unopposed, the War I strategic architecture never contemplated a serious policy of regime change, never planned for it, and never prepared for a postwar occupation. Given the war objectives spelled out in the War I Op-order 91-001, Kuwait had been liberated, and Iraq's capability to wage war had been seriously degraded to the point that it could no longer threaten neighboring states.

At the time, the Bush administration had never been interested in undermining Iraq's buffer function between Iran's revolutionary Shia regime and the perceived threat to the Sunni states to the west (Jordan and Lebanon), the Arabian Peninsula, and the Persian Gulf states. Indeed, that buffer function was precisely behind the American decision not to remain neutral during the Iran-Iraq War. The US government quietly supported Saddam. Even though Henry Kissinger in 1985 would cynically remark about this bloody war, "I hope they kill each other. Too bad they can't both lose,"[58] the Reagan administration came to believe that strict neutrality was not in America's strategic interest and favored Saddam's regime financially and diplomatically, providing occasional tactical intelligence from national technical means not otherwise available to the Iraqis.

This political background loomed behind the Bush administration's decision-making restraint. The Bush administration had skillfully and painstakingly assembled a broad international coalition, including Arab armies; fought the war for limited objectives that ensured unity of purpose; and did not try to reach for bigger prizes such as regime change. Should it have? Such a plan could easily have undermined Sunni Arab support from Saudi Arabia, Egypt, Syria, and the Gulf states, perhaps with the exception of Kuwait. More to the point, the Bush administration neither developed a plan for regime change nor deployed the capability to implement one.

Twenty-five years ago, the military consequences of War I were perceived as profound. The quick outcome had not been foreseen, at least in the eyes of the public. The coalition, before *Desert Storm*, had lacked the canonical three-to-one force ratio advantage traditionally considered necessary for an offensive force to prevail. Schwarzkopf had mentioned this in his February 27 briefing. What accounted for the sudden victory that in retrospect became a cakewalk?

The Iraqi failure to fight effectively traces first to the lower quality of their personnel and leadership. Iraqi commanders thought they could fight an unimaginative, dogged war of attrition from their static, entrenched positions in

Kuwait, just as they had ploddingly and successfully fought many times against Iranian assaults between 1980 and 1988.

The armed forces of the United States and the coalition it led were making the Iraqis fight against a well-trained, technologically superior adversary led by professional commanders who had spent years studying and practicing the kinds of operations they executed in the Gulf. The Iraqis found themselves completely unprepared. Their historical Iran-Iraq War attrition template was irrelevant once operations began. General Schwarzkopf was forcing them to fight a war of maneuver for which their static, defensive deployments made no sense. Generals Horner and Glosson had achieved air supremacy almost immediately, leaving the Iraqis in the dark about where the main ground attack would strike.

Technologically, there was a very significant gap between the armaments fielded by both sides. The average US weapons system used in *Desert Storm* was introduced in 1973; the comparable year for the Iraqis was 1961.[59] This twelve-year gap was much wider than that between World War II and Korean War combatants. In the air, the qualitative disparities were even wider because a handful of American weapons systems, like AWACS and JSTARS, ensured that attacks on Iraqi ground forces were accurate and lethal.

In retrospect, the outcome could not have been in doubt. The way it was achieved was. It is commonplace now to regard the Persian Gulf War as easy and low risk. That was not the consensus before the ground operation was launched. CENTCOM knew that Iraqi engineers had constructed an elaborate defense in depth in southern Kuwait consisting of barbed wire; hundreds of thousands of mines; an elaborate network of bunkers and trenches, including ditches filled with flammable oil; and thousands of tank and artillery emplacements, a defensive line "worthy of Verdun." Before the war, planning experts confidently predicted that the coalition would suffer tens of thousands of casualties based on computer models of past conflicts. The DoD had stockpiled sixteen thousand body bags. In fact, the coalition lost 240 soldiers and 776 wounded out of a total force of 795,000. The United States, with 550,000 troops in the Kuwaiti theater of operations, lost 147 killed in action and 467 wounded. Boot's statistics showed that American men between the ages of twenty and thirty were actually safer on average fighting in *Desert Storm* than staying at home in the CONUS.[60] These extraordinarily low casualty figures (the fatality percentage was 0.03 percent[61]) would have far-reaching effects in conditioning the American public's initial approval of War III and their impatience with War IV.

CONCLUSIONS

The substantial technological edge held by the coalition, particularly by the US Armed Forces deployed to CENTCOM, and the superior training and leadership of the Americans and their NATO partners were discriminators. They were deployed by a president who convinced a majority of Congress and his countrymen that a vital global asset was at stake: continued access to the free flow of petroleum from the Persian Gulf. In this sense, Saddam's invasion of Kuwait and menace to Saudi Arabia was a threat to the stability and continuing prosperity of the international system. President Bush and his national security team effectively interacted with General Schwarzkopf, gave him more than the military resources he had requested, and left him free to execute his plan pursuant to a clear, succinct set of orders.

General Schwarzkopf succeeded dramatically beyond anyone's initial expectations. War I was perceived as a live demonstration of the Weinberger-Powell principles, including a quick "exit strategy." For the United States, there was a major restoration in public confidence in the armed forces of the United States and its high-tech industrial base. Gallup reported its highest post–Vietnam War rating of 85 percent confidence in February–March 1991.[62] Confidence levels this high could not be sustained, but they would oscillate between 66 and 79 percent between 1991 and 2010, significantly above the Vietnam period and its immediate aftermath. President Bush in 1991 exclaimed, "By God, we've licked the Vietnam syndrome once and for all."[63] But as successful as the United States had been by the spring of 1991, Wars II through V would demonstrate that that success was short-lived and that the Vietnam syndrome would persist.

25

IRAQI WAR II, THIRTEEN-YEAR AIR CONFLICT

The Limits of Airpower

The end of War I left the United States seemingly in a strong position in the Gulf region. Iraq's military forces had been seriously degraded so that they were no longer a threat to neighboring states. The US government signed a series of access agreements, prepositioned matériel in Kuwait, sold large quantities of arms to its Gulf allies, and arranged for the presence of significant US forces in the region on a permanent basis.

War II spanned thirteen years, 1991–2003. There were no discriminators or serious differentiators in this conflict other than the supremacy of American and coalition (British and French) airpower to police two no-fly zones (map 25.1). War II was an ongoing conflict without clearly defined goals beyond immediate satisfaction of tactical military or diplomatic objectives. It had no effect in terms of strategic conflict resolution in Iraq.

POLICY

UN resolutions, starting with No. 687, vested the United Nations Special Commission (UNSCOM) with a mandate to carry out immediate on-site inspections of Iraq's nuclear, biological, and chemical (NBC) weapons, stocks, and components. Thirteen additional resolutions provided for UNSCOM and the International Atomic Energy Agency (IAEA) to monitor Iraq's compliance with the destruction of NBC weapons, the capacity to produce them, and sales or supplies from third-party countries to Iraq of dual-use items that might have applications for weapons programs prohibited to Iraq.[1]

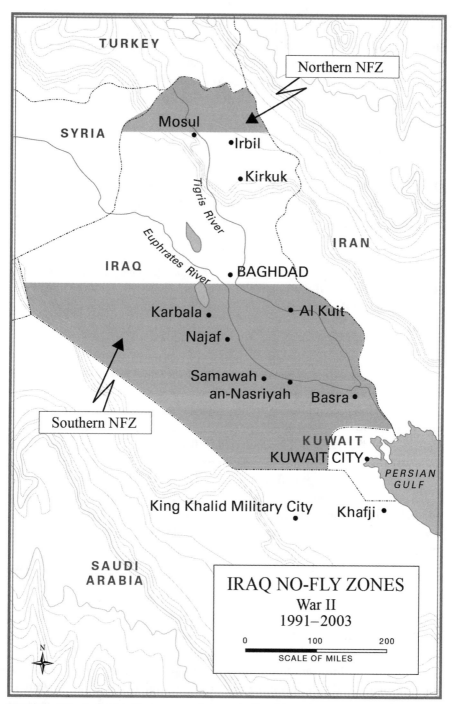

Map 25.1. War II was the thirteen-year mission to police two no-fly zones.

Source: CIA, *The World Factbook*, https://www.cia.gov/library/publications/the-world-factbook/geos/iz.html.

The UN's primary tasks were emergency relief, security intervention, and refugee resettlement. Only the second task, enforcing the security of the airspace over the Iraqi no-fly zones, was essentially a military mission. The remaining two were suitable for civilian relief agencies, assisted by UN management, but the coalition forces in Operation *Provide Comfort* were the decisive component for the successful completion of all three tasks.[2]

STRATEGY

Once UN resolutions were in place, American strategy evolved almost by default into one of military action, economic sanctions, and containment. Saddam had initially accepted UNSCOM provisions under the fourteen UN Security Council Resolutions passed between April 1991 and December 1999. He accepted intrusive UNSCOM inspections for the next seven years after War I, the creation of a de facto protectorate over the Kurdish-populated areas of northern Iraq in 1991–1992, and the imposition of two no-fly zones (NFZs). Concurrent with the UNSCOM inspections, the United States, Great Britain, and France had imposed the NFZs over Iraqi airspace to protect humanitarian operations for the Kurds and other minorities. The no-fly policy was enforced by American, British, and French aircraft patrols, although France withdrew in 1998.[3]

Concurrent with these developments in the spring and summer of 1991, the Kurds of northern Iraq had revolted against Saddam's regime, only to be brutally suppressed and forced to flee across a mountainous border into Turkey. In response to international outcry, the United States in early April 1991 spearheaded the *Provide Comfort* relief effort as a joint and multinational endeavor that involved US Army, Air Force, Navy, and Marine Corps units as well as military contingents from twelve other countries.

US Army Lieutenant General Jay M. Garner was appointed commanding general of the effort in northern Iraq. It was under his leadership that the coalition of American and European forces delivered relief assistance to the Iraqi Kurds. A decade later in 2003, the Bush administration selected General Garner to lead the Office of Reconstruction and Humanitarian Assistance (ORHA) in Iraq during the proposed postwar phase of War III.

OPERATIONS

There were over four hundred thousand air sorties flown during War II, four times as many as flown during *Desert Storm* in War I.[4] These air operations were virtually daily; occasionally there were surges, specific air operations mounted to coerce Saddam into nominal compliance with UN resolutions. The most notable was Operation *Desert Fox* ordered by the Clinton administration in December 1998 to enforce compliance with UN inspections. This air action was a four-day air and cruise missile campaign launched against Iraqi military targets involving roughly six hundred aircraft sorties and four hundred cruise missile strikes against approximately one hundred targets.[5]

Saddam routinely defied the no-fly zones and repeatedly obstructed UN inspectors. In 1994, he began a military buildup near Kuwait causing the United States to deploy forces to that country.[6] Iraq deployed two Republican Guard divisions near the Iraq-Kuwait border and made bellicose statements regarding Kuwait and threatened to expel the UN inspectors. The United States responded by rapidly deploying forces to the theater, including a Marine Corps Expeditionary Unit, an Army Mechanized Task Force, and a carrier battle group, threatening large-scale air strikes if Iraq did not withdraw. The United States and Great Britain acted under UN Security Council Resolution 949, which demanded that Iraq pull back its forces and not deploy them near the Kuwait border again. Both countries warned Saddam that they would use force to stop any Iraqi buildup south of the 32nd parallel, the demarcation for the southern no-fly zone. More standoffs ensued over UN inspections between 1999 and 2003.

Another Security Council resolution (No. 986) established the ineffective Oil-for-Food Program in 1995 to allow Iraq to sell oil on the world market in exchange for food, medicine, and other humanitarian supplies for ordinary Iraqi citizens without allowing Iraq to boost its military capabilities. An investigation of the program by the UN Independent Inquiry Committee, chaired by former US Federal Reserve chairman Paul A. Volcker, established that

> the Iraqi regime skimmed about $1.8 billion of illegal surcharge and kickback payments that it solicited from its buyers of oil and its suppliers of humanitarian goods. The U.N. responded slowly and with limited effect; little was done in response to Iraqi manipulation of the program. Meanwhile, outside of the program, the Iraqi regime smuggled about $8.4 billion in oil to neighboring countries during the life of the program and the U.N. rejected measures to bring this trade under the program, much less put a stop to it altogether.[7]

In December 1999, Security Council Resolution 1284 replaced UNSCOM with the United Nations Monitoring, Verification and Inspection Commission (UNMOVIC). Four countries, including Russia, France, and China, abstained from voting on Resolution 1284, which enabled Saddam to reject the legitimacy of the resolution because he saw it as a way for the UN to claim Iraq as a "protectorate." This development effectively ended the UN inspection regime.[8]

CONCLUSIONS

The Bush (both elder and younger) and Clinton administrations made military and diplomatic adjustments to a strategic architecture where end results were defined tactically, not strategically. A decade of economic sanctions and the application of airpower to enforce the no-fly zones did little to strengthen the UN inspection regime or to weaken Saddam's hold on power. Indeed, by 2003, Saddam's repeated defiance of the UN had led to the withdrawal of UN weapons inspectors.

In July 2000, General Tommy R. Franks became the seventh CINCCENT. With increased emphasis on force protection and combating global terrorism, CENTCOM would continue active engagement and monitoring in the region until al Qa'ida's surprise attacks on September 11, 2011 (9/11), resulted in intervention in Afghanistan in the fall of 2001. Iraqi War II had been an inconclusive period in which unresolved issues arising out of War I continued to fester until the second Bush administration decided to invade Iraq, preemptively, for a second time in 2003.

26

IRAQI WAR III, INVASION OF IRAQ

Winning without an Endgame

It is difficult to examine War III without preliminary reference to the war in Afghanistan, which began in the fall of 2001 as a direct response to al Qa'ida's 9/11 attacks on two iconic targets of American economic strength and military power: the World Trade Center's Twin Towers in New York City and the Pentagon in Washington. These were the first major foreign attacks on US mainland targets since 1814 (the opening skirmishes of the Mexican-American War of 1846 excepted) and the first successful attacks on American territory since Pearl Harbor in 1941.

POLICY

After its success in War I and the seemingly placid decade that followed, the United States appeared to emerge as the most important global power, poised to take full advantage of the simultaneous social, economic, intellectual, and political opportunities presented by the huge post–Cold War release in the international flows of money, people, trade, and energy everywhere in the world, what everyone was calling "globalization." Against this rapidly evolving phenomenon, there appeared to be no power that could hope to compete directly against the global reach of the United States.

American dominance was not welcomed everywhere, even by one former War I partner. The French would complain throughout the 1990s about the American "hyperpower." But a serious menace was festering in the Middle

East. In this region, American strength was neither welcomed nor shared by small organizations of political and religious zealots, intoxicated by Islamic extremism, who were trapped in the stagnant dictatorships that had emerged in the Middle East in the decades following Sykes-Picot. Saudi Arabia, Egypt, Jordan, Iraq, Syria, Iran, Algeria, Tunisia, Libya, Yemen, and Pakistan were all authoritarian regimes. Boot described these zealots as mostly unemployed young men or those from better economic and educational backgrounds who could manipulate the less educated: "The more astute among them came to understand that the Information Age offered new opportunities for what strategists call 'asymmetric warfare'[1]—the ability to inflict great damage on a powerful adversary by using unconventional weapons. Like commercial airliners."[2]

When al Qa'ida struck on 9/11, the administrations of Presidents William J. Clinton and George W. Bush had been tracking al Qa'ida for years. Both presidents had been briefed multiple times on the danger it posed to American interests worldwide. The government also knew that it was based in Afghanistan with close ties to the radical Islamist Taliban government that had seized power in 1994. Many Taliban had been educated in madrassas[3] in Pakistan and were largely from rural southern Pashtun backgrounds. In 1994, the Taliban developed enough strength to capture the city of Kandahar from a local warlord and proceeded to expand their control throughout Afghanistan, occupying Kabul in September 1996. By the end of 1998, the Taliban occupied about 90 percent of the country. After 9/11, Bush was determined to strike back immediately at al Qa'ida and its leader, Osama bin Laden, and to do as much damage to al Qa'ida "as rapidly and visibly as possible."

Kagan pointed out that there was little else that the Bush administration was clear about in the fall of 2001. Most senior decision makers, with the possible exception of National Security Advisor Condoleezza Rice, "were almost totally unfamiliar with Afghanistan and its history."[4] Kagan argued that "in addition to its ignorance about conditions in Afghanistan the Bush administration misread Afghanistan's history."

In 2001 CENTCOM had no contingency plan for an attack on Afghanistan. CENTCOM had been preoccupied with War II for over a decade, overseeing the policing of the no-fly zones over northern and southern Iraq, and was intimately involved with the enforcement of UN economic sanctions against Iraq and monitoring Saddam's efforts to smuggle oil out of the country and to circumvent the Oil-for-Food Program. Whether or not these military and diplomatic concerns can be construed as an excuse for not considering Afghanistan as the source of a potential threat, the reality was that CINCCENT,[5] General Franks, tried frantically to put a plan together.

Secretary of Defense Donald H. Rumsfeld was soon drawn to the CIA's proposed approach where veteran intelligence officers, familiar with the Afghan tribes, which had fought effectively against the Soviets, and fluent in the languages required, were inserted into Afghanistan with substantial quantities of cash and special forces teams prepared to direct air strikes with PGMs on al Qa'ida and Taliban forces.

On October 7, 2001, American and British forces began a bombing campaign, Operation *Enduring Freedom*, that targeted Taliban forces and al Qa'ida (map 26.1). On the ground, the Afghan Northern Alliance, supported by the CIA and special forces teams, quickly prevailed against a Taliban weakened by bombing and massive defections. The Alliance captured Mazar-e-Sharif on November 9, 2001; it was the first Afghan city (fourth largest) to fall. The Taliban's defeat in Mazar quickly turned into a rout in the rest of the north and west of Afghanistan. The Alliance rapidly gained control of most of northern Afghanistan and took control of Kabul on November 13 after the Taliban unexpectedly fled the city. The Taliban were restricted to a smaller and smaller region, with Kunduz, the last Taliban-held city in the north, captured on November 26. Most of the Taliban fled to Pakistan.

The war continued in the south of the country, where the Taliban retreated to Kandahar. After Kandahar fell in December, remnants of the Taliban and al Qa'ida continued to resist. The Battle of Tora Bora followed in December 2001 to destroy the Taliban and al Qa'ida in Afghanistan. Neither the Afghans nor Americans who penetrated into Tora Bora succeeded in capturing or killing Osama bin Laden. The CIA intelligence officer who controlled the teams believed bin Laden could have been captured after being trapped in the Tora Bora cave complex in the White Mountains if CENTCOM had committed more military assets to the operation.[6]

Kagan's analysis of the initial military planning and successes of *Enduring Freedom* concludes that the US government failed to think through a viable postwar political configuration for Afghanistan. The Bush administration was not clear about its own objectives other than to defeat al Qa'ida and the Taliban. "The failure to establish a clear objective caused serious problems for the military operation and, especially, the postwar reconstruction and stabilization effort that is limping along even today" (written in 2006).[7]

No one senior in the Bush administration realized that the Taliban during the fall of 2001 were a weak government. It did not control all of the country, and it did not have strong, consistent, popular support among the population.[8] Simply destroying the Taliban and al Qa'ida without creating a clear plan for developing a new, stable government that was able to control its own territory would accomplish little.

A strategic architecture for Afghanistan required clear policy guidance that defined a political end state for American operations in Afghanistan. If the goal were the creation of an Afghan state and a government that could function after the Taliban and al Qa'ida were defeated, then the expeditionary strategy required planning and resources that went well beyond defeating the

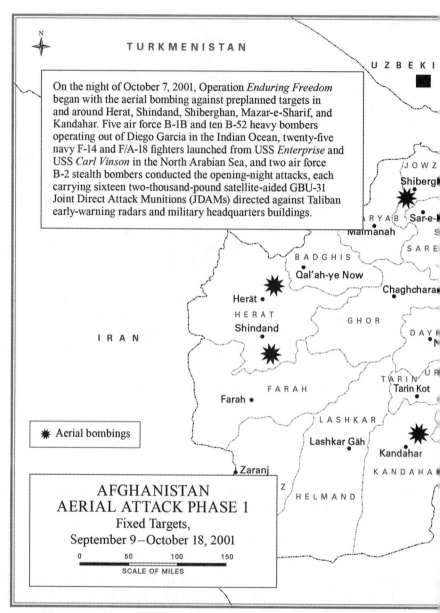

TURKMENISTAN

UZBEKI

On the night of October 7, 2001, Operation *Enduring Freedom* began with the aerial bombing against preplanned targets in and around Herat, Shindand, Shiberghan, Mazar-e-Sharif, and Kandahar. Five air force B-1B and ten B-52 heavy bombers operating out of Diego Garcia in the Indian Ocean, twenty-five navy F-14 and F/A-18 fighters launched from USS *Enterprise* and USS *Carl Vinson* in the North Arabian Sea, and two air force B-2 stealth bombers conducted the opening-night attacks, each carrying sixteen two-thousand-pound satellite-aided GBU-31 Joint Direct Attack Munitions (JDAMs) directed against Taliban early-warning radars and military headquarters buildings.

JOWZ

Shiberg

RYAB Sar-e-

Malmanah S

SARE

BADGHIS

Qal'ah-ye Now

Chaghchara

Herāt

HERĀT

Shindand

GHOR

DAY

IRAN

TARIN R

Tarin Kot

FARAH

Farah

LASHKAR

✳ Aerial bombings

Lashkar Gāh

Kandahar

Zaranj

KANDAHA

AFGHANISTAN AERIAL ATTACK PHASE 1
Fixed Targets,
September 9–October 18, 2001

Z HELMAND

| 0 | 50 | 100 | 150 |

SCALE OF MILES

Map 26.1. In early October after the 9/11 terror attacks, Operation *Enduring Freedom* began with multiple air strikes against al Qa'ida and Taliban-held targets nationwide.
Source: USMA Atlases.

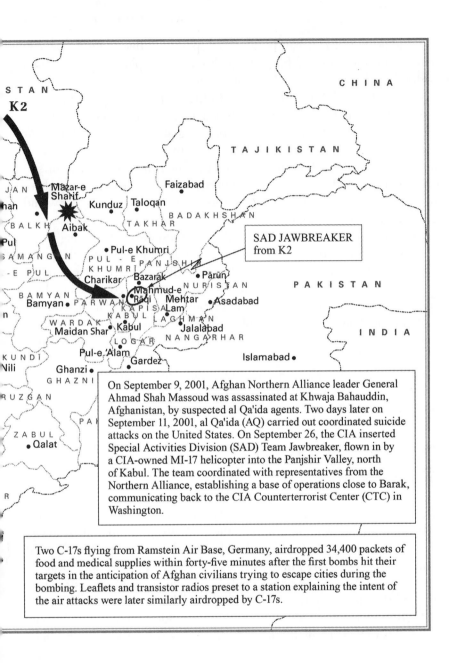

STAN

K2

CHINA

TAJIKISTAN

JAN

han

Mazar-e
Sharif

Faizabad

Kunduz   Taloqan

BALKH

Aibak

BADAKHSHAN

TAKHAR

Pul

SAMANGAN

-E PUL

• Pul-e Khumri

PUL - E
KHUMRI

PANJSHIR

SAD JAWBREAKER
from K2

BAMYAN

Bamyan •

PARWAN

Charikar   Bazarak

Mahmud-e
Raqi   Mehtar

KAPISA   Lam

• Parun

NURISTAN

• Asadabad

PAKISTAN

n

WARDAK

Maidan Shar • Kabul

KABUL   LAGHMAN

Jalalabad

NANGARHAR

LOGAR

INDIA

KUNDI

Nili

Ghazni •

GHAZNI

Pul-e Alam

Gardez

Islamabad •

RUZGAN

PA

ZABUL

• Qalat

R

On September 9, 2001, Afghan Northern Alliance leader General
Ahmad Shah Massoud was assassinated at Khwaja Bahauddin,
Afghanistan, by suspected al Qa'ida agents. Two days later on
September 11, 2001, al Qa'ida (AQ) carried out coordinated suicide
attacks on the United States. On September 26, the CIA inserted
Special Activities Division (SAD) Team Jawbreaker, flown in by
a CIA-owned MI-17 helicopter into the Panjshir Valley, north
of Kabul. The team coordinated with representatives from the
Northern Alliance, establishing a base of operations close to Barak,
communicating back to the CIA Counterterrorist Center (CTC) in
Washington.

Two C-17s flying from Ramstein Air Base, Germany, airdropped 34,400 packets of
food and medical supplies within forty-five minutes after the first bombs hit their
targets in the anticipation of Afghan civilians trying to escape cities during the
bombing. Leaflets and transistor radios preset to a station explaining the intent of
the air attacks were later similarly airdropped by C-17s.

Taliban and al Qa'ida. It meant postconflict operations that required capable personnel with the required linguistic, cultural, and diplomatic background supported by substantial nation-building resources.

This failure to think through the back-to-front aspects of a sound military and postconflict plan that fit within the broader design of a strategic architecture for Afghanistan was repeated in the planning and execution of Iraqi War III. In the case of Afghanistan, a serious back-to-front plan would have meant confronting the contradictions between, on the one hand, the CIA's efforts to arm and build up regional and tribal warlords who did not necessarily share political goals and, on the other hand, power-sharing arrangements that would be necessary for a national government that could replace the Taliban.

The Afghan constitution that emerged in 2004 established a strong presidential system under President Hamid Karzai, but it did not solve the problem of competition among warlords with their tribal interests.[9] To enable a central government to function credibly would have required substantial US ground forces to carry out a series of operations to ensure that the country did not fragment into a collection of competing tribal areas. Because the Bush administration had followed a front-to-back plan in launching *Enduring Freedom* in Afghanistan, achieving stunning success in less than three months, it failed to consider what kind of military forces and diplomatic and USAID infrastructure it would need at the decisive moment of success. The White House, CENTCOM, the CIA, and the Departments of Defense and State were not in realistic alignment about what should happen to enable Afghanistan to become a viable, independent state. This lack of a clear, detailed, back-to-front plan ensured that the Afghanistan War would continue for another sixteen years.

The Bush administration's launch of Operation *Iraqi Freedom* in March 2003 differed from the intervention in Afghanistan fifteen months earlier. War III was a preemption. Shortly after the 9/11 attacks, President Bush had pressed for serious planning to be undertaken for the invasion of Iraq. Even if Saddam bore no complicity with al Qa'ida's strikes on New York and Washington, the "Global War on Terrorism" had shifted the administration's calculus of risks and threats. There was widespread belief that Saddam was still building WMDs in violation of UN sanctions. The president wanted to eliminate any possibility of Saddam mounting a terrorist strike with WMDs, particularly nuclear weapons.

It is not necessary here to debate the validity of the intelligence about WMDs on the merits because the archival facts are not yet fully known. However, two points can be established. The first is that all of the world's major intelligence services, including the American CIA, British MI6 (Secret Intelligence Service), Russian FSB (Federal Intelligence Service), and French DGSE (*Direction générale de la sécurité extérieure*) agreed that Saddam still possessed WMDs and was probably continuing to develop a nuclear capability. This prediction turned out to be false. No significant WMDs were found in Iraq after the invasion and exhaustive searches of all known clandestine weapons caches, although there was one exception.[10] The second point is more fundamental because it might have helped the Bush administration recognize more clearly the deficiencies of its front-to-back strategy. Had the Bush administration asked itself the wrong question? Instead of asking whether Saddam constituted a threat because he possessed operationally usable WMD, could the administration have posed another question: Was regime change really the central basis for Iraqi War III? The US Congress authorized a joint resolution based on a total of twenty-three specifications, only eight of which mentioned WMDs. Fifteen other clauses referred to serious breaches of international peace and the thwarting of the implementation of fourteen UN Security Council Resolutions. Clause 17 specified that "it should be the policy of the United States to support efforts to remove from power the current Iraqi regime and promote the emergence of a democratic government to replace that regime."[11]

The president and many of his top advisors believed that replacing the repressive Ba'athist regime with a representative government could begin the transformation of the entire region. Outside the administration, a few scholarly voices were making the geopolitical case for regime change in Iraq and that American military preemption and intervention had deep historical roots dating back two centuries.[12]

The geopolitical goal was the removal of Saddam from power and the installation of a stable, representative government in place of the Ba'athist regime. It was generally understood that only a large-scale conventional military campaign would suffice to achieve this result. In that sense, War III's goals went well beyond War I and the Afghanistan campaign because it explicitly defined regime change as a goal. The Iraqi War I and Afghanistan outcomes had avoided the Vietnam shibboleth of nation building. President Bush exclaimed in October 2001 before hostilities commenced in Afghanistan, "Look, I oppose using the military for nation-building. Once the job is done, our forces are not peacekeepers. We ought to put in place a U.N. protection [force] and leave, but if fighting resumes and the Taliban come back from the hills, who has to stabilize the situation?" An answer to this prescient presidential question would have required defining a postwar set of conditions for Afghanistan that addressed how an Afghan government without the Taliban would operate.[13] No one offered an answer.

The administration's hostility to nation building would persist in War III's execution despite serious early attempts to think through postwar planning. Kagan documented the considerable planning that went into preparing for the political objective of a post-Saddam, representative Iraq and then explained the Bush administration's failure to benefit from it. Specifically, he questioned why did the US military seem so unprepared to stop the widespread violence and looting that broke out after the fall of Saddam's regime?[14]

STRATEGY

Secretary Rumsfeld and his senior staff had been so impressed with what they thought were the lessons learned from Afghanistan that they pressed for the lightest possible force and postwar footprint in Iraq. When Rumsfeld directed General Franks to present a plan in November 2001, he had nothing to offer but Desert Storm Redux, Operations Plan (Oplan) 1003-98, last updated in 1998. It called for weeks of bombing followed by an invasion by four hundred thousand soldiers, trimmed from five hundred thousand according to Woodward.[15] Franks knew that the plan was out of date. For example, it did not account for advances in PGMs, unmanned aerial vehicles, and "net-centric" C^4/ISR systems, what generally was perceived as the "revolution [or transformation] in military affairs."[16]

If there were serious lessons to be learned from Afghanistan, the most pertinent ones related to the absence of serious back-to-front planning for what the ground forces would do after they occupied Baghdad. Rumsfeld and others in the administration ignored these deficiencies. When US Army chief of staff General Eric K. Shinseki—a Vietnam combat veteran who had served during the peacekeeping mission in Bosnia—in answering a question about force size in testimony before the US Senate Armed Services Committee responded that "something on the order of several hundred thousand soldiers" would be necessary to establish order, he had made a career-ending utterance.[17] General Franks, also a Vietnam veteran but whose early career experience had been as an artilleryman and who had never been assigned to a manpower-intensive peacekeeping mission, did not insist on a force of the size Shinseki indicated. Franks knew politically that Rumsfeld would never agree to it. Deputy Secretary of Defense Paul Wolfowitz dismissed Shinseki's estimate, in words that he might later regret, as "wildly off the mark."[18] CENTCOM planners, in any case, did not see the establishment of a new regime as its responsibility. That task belonged to a planning group in the Office of Reconstruction and Humanitarian Assistance (ORHA), where retired lieutenant general Jay Garner had started to work in January 2003.

Kagan pointed out that strategic planning for a postwar Iraq did not lack in thinking about the probable postwar situation in Iraq and the transition from hostilities to a desired political objective, a free, democratic, and independent Iraq. The State Department, the CIA, CENTCOM, the Strategic Studies Institute of the US Army War College, USAID, ORHA, the Rand Corporation, and the American Enterprise Institute had all initiated postwar planning efforts on various scales and time horizons. The earliest had been the State Department's Future of Iraq program begun in 2001.[19] This initiative was not the only one to point to the importance of establishing security in the postwar environment of Iraq. As Kagan described these studies,

> Almost all of the prewar studies and projects made that point [about security], and many highlighted one or another of the various other issues, developed by the State Department's team of Iraqi exiles. The Army War College's report was particularly insightful and ominous in this regard. Whatever else is true about prewar planning for the Iraq war and post-war, therefore, it cannot be said that security, corruption, infrastructure, or governance problems that the United States encountered after the end of hostilities were unforeseen, let alone unforeseeable, or that the decision simply to disband the Iraqi army [as Ambassador L. Paul Bremer III soon did after assuming General Garner's responsibilities in May 2003] was generally accepted as the wisest course of action.[20]

Kagan's exposition of this issue of inadequate postwar planning for Iraq began with acknowledgment of the critiques that have been leveled against Secretary Rumsfeld and Deputy Secretary Wolfowitz and the suspicion and enmity between Secretary Colin Powell's State Department and the Pentagon, but his real substance is political, the awareness of the Bush team "that the war would be a hard sell domestically and internationally."[21] Rumsfeld's war planning recognized the political and diplomatic difficulties the administration faced. The administration needed a war plan that balanced preserving the president's diplomatic options with respect to his position on Saddam disarming and accepting a negotiated settlement late in the confrontation process. That meant keeping the US military footprint in the theater as small as possible. Only by proposing an invasion with a much smaller force, one-third the size of the coalition in Iraqi War I, could Rumsfeld avoid the obvious and massive buildup that would make a mockery, so he thought, of Bush's claims that he had not yet decided on war.[22] This was one of the traps the Bush administration fell into in relying on the WMD argument as the principal casus belli for Iraq rather than a fully thought-out plan for regime change and a compelling geopolitical rationale to persuade the American people of the necessity of the mission.

OPERATIONS

The air campaign began simultaneously with the ground operation to invade Iraq (map 26.2). Unlike *Desert Storm* twelve years earlier, the allied coalition that invaded Iraq in 2003 already had air superiority. American and British

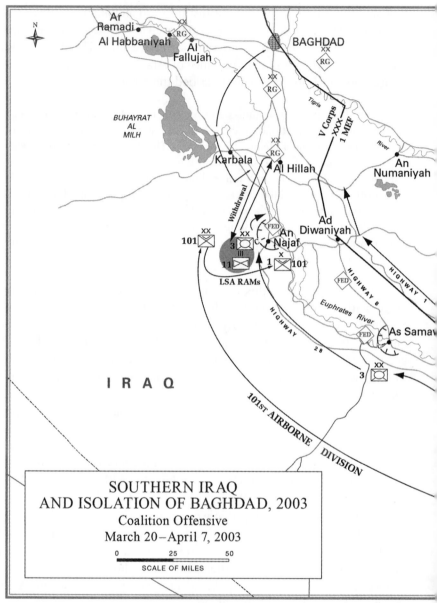

SOUTHERN IRAQ
AND ISOLATION OF BAGHDAD, 2003
Coalition Offensive
March 20–April 7, 2003

```
0          25          50
```
SCALE OF MILES

Map 26.2. A CENTCOM force one-third the size of the force in War I invaded Iraq and
entered Baghdad in less than a month.

Source: USMA Atlases.

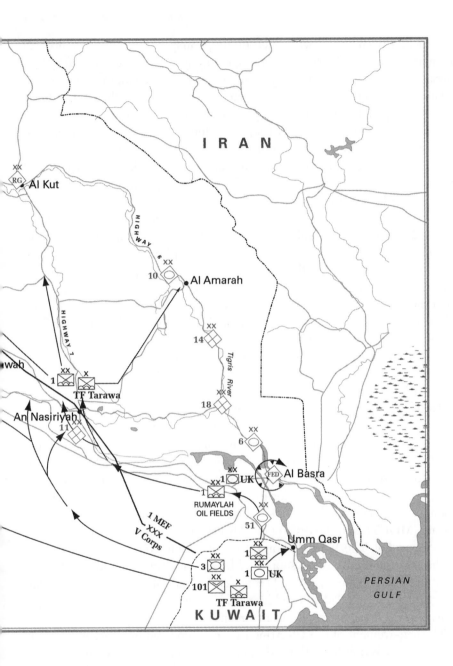

I R A N

XX
RG • Al Kut

HIGHWAY 6

10 ⬭ XX
• Al Amarah

HIGHWAY 7

XX
14 ◈

Tigris River

wah

1 XX ⬭
X
TF Tarawa

XX
18 ◈

An Nasiriyah

11 XX ◈

XX
6 ⬭

XX
⬭ 1 ⬭ UK
XX   FED ↻ • Al Basra

1 XX ◈
RUMAYLAH
OIL FIELDS

XX
51 ◈

1 MEF
XXX
V Corps

XX
1 ⬭
XX

Umm Qasr

1 ⬭ UK

XX
3 ⬭

XX
101 ◈   X
TF Tarawa

K U W A I T

PERSIAN
GULF

aircraft had been flying over much of Iraq's airspace since 1991, enforcing the northern and southern no-fly zones; regularly attacking antiaircraft radars, missile sites, and gun emplacements in those zones; and gathering "phenomenal amounts of intelligence about Saddam's air defenses and their capabilities. In the run-up to the invasion, the U.S. military launched a series of attacks that helped cripple the already weak Iraqi air defenses."[23] The number of combat aircraft required to establish air dominance was little more than half of those that had been required by Generals Horner and Glosson in 1991.[24] Described by the Pentagon as "shock and awe," the air campaign was over quickly and was superseded by ground operations.

The invasion of Iraq and the initiation of Operation *Iraqi Freedom* on March 20, 2003, can be easily outlined. The 3rd ID surged across the Kuwait border and advanced up the west bank of the Euphrates toward the Karbala Gap, where it paused briefly before maneuvering into positions in front of Baghdad. The 1st Marine Expeditionary Force simultaneously moved across the Kuwait border toward the northeast, seized the al Rumaylah oil fields, and advanced on Baghdad from the southeast. The British 1st Armored Division moved rapidly toward Basra.

As General Franks became concerned for his lengthening supply lines, he committed the 101st Airborne Division, under the command of Major General David H. Petraeus, to pacifying bypassed urban centers, particularly Najaf. He committed a brigade of the 82nd Airborne Division to securing the supply lines farther back. There were two brief pauses. The first was caused by a sandstorm, a severe *shamal* between March 24 and 26, which delayed the 3rd ID for about a week.[25] The second pause occurred after it had advanced close to Baghdad. The 3rd ID launched a series of massive armored raids, what became known as "thunder runs," into the center of the capital. These initiatives preempted a drawn-out, Stalingrad-style military operation in urban terrain (MOUT), and the 3rd ID quickly established its combat presence inside the capital. The 173rd Airborne Brigade (reinforced) positioned its units in the north around Bashur, supported by a small armored contingent flown from the 1st ID. Once the 3rd ID was clearly established in Baghdad to stay, the regime fell, and Saddam and his sons went into hiding. The major operations of *Iraqi Freedom* were over in a month.

The achievement of the US Armed Forces appeared impressive. No army had ever attacked faster with fewer losses. A CENTCOM force one-third the size of the one used in *Desert Storm* had accomplished far more, albeit against a less formidable opponent.

The sense of "mission accomplished" and military omnipotence after CENTCOM's dash to Baghdad did not last long. The collapse of Saddam's dictatorship was followed by the disintegration of law and order nationwide. Pervasive looting broke out all over the country. Government and commercial buildings were stripped of everything. Street crime became common-place. The breakdown of public order in Baghdad and other regions of the country shortly gave way to mounting resistance to the coalition (primarily American and British) occupation. How did this deteriorating state of affairs develop so rapidly?

CONCLUSIONS

In War III, the Bush administration repeated the flawed front-to-back strategic thinking that drove the early stages of the campaign in Afghanistan. The administration's launch of Operation *Iraqi Freedom* resisted a back-to-front strategic architecture for regime change that would have required a comprehensive mobilization of the necessary expertise and resources to occupy Iraq as a defeated state and transform its government the way the Allies did after World War II.

A retired diplomat, Ambassador James F. Dobbins Jr., a veteran of postwar reconstruction efforts in Haiti, Somalia, Bosnia, Kosovo, and Afghanistan, summarized the situation at the end of War III succinctly: "While the U.S. could take Iraq with three divisions, it couldn't hold it with three divisions."[26]

27

IRAQI WAR IV, THE INSURGENCY AND THE SURGE (2007–2008)

Relearning Counterinsurgency

War IV began as soon as the main-force combat of War III ended. It would take more than three years after the breakdown of law and order and the eruption of the insurgency to convince President Bush that his War III strategic architecture was failing. If the goal of War III had been regime change, policy guidance for the final phase of the war did not address in any detail the restoration of effective governance in Iraq. Policy failed because the administration's assumptions about the willingness or capability of Iraqis to replace Saddam's dictatorship with a representative, functioning government were wrong. As a result, CENTCOM in the years that followed 2003 was engaged in endless operations to respond to the escalating violence.

POLICY

The lack of an integrated, interagency plan for the postwar occupation of Iraq and the transition to national sovereignty left CENTCOM by default with many missions for which it was both poorly prepared and without the necessary civil affairs assets in place. Ambassador Dobbins quoted from one after-action report prepared by the 3rd ID in April 2003:

> There was no guidance for restoring order in Baghdad, creating an interim government, hiring government and essential services employees, and ensuring that the judicial system was operational. The result was a power/authority vacuum created by our failure to immediately replace key government institutions. . . .

The President announced that our national goal was "regime-change." Yet there was no timely plan prepared for the obvious consequences of a regime change.[1]

In 2008, Dobbins coauthored a Rand study[2] that looked at seven cases of postwar reconstruction, Germany, Japan, Somalia, Haiti, Bosnia, Kosovo, and Afghanistan. The study concluded that the debate in Washington since 2003 had been about what the appropriate model was for the reconstruction of Iraq. Dobbins asserted that "the German and Japanese occupations remain the gold standard for postwar reconstruction. . . . In both cases, U.S. occupation policy was extensively planned and skillfully executed."[3]

No subsequent nation-building effort after the World War II occupations achieved comparable success. In the case of Iraq, Dobbins pointed out that the Bush administration chose the organizational model employed in Germany and Japan a half century earlier but without a remotely comparable commitment of resources. He explained,

> DoD [the Department of Defense], not DOS [the Department of State], would oversee both democratization and economic development, including . . . the creation of a free media, the promotion of civil society, the establishment of political parties, the drafting of a constitution, and the organization of elections—all activities with which DoD had little modern experience. . . . Bush decided to put all aspects of the operation under DoD, thereby ensuring unity of command and unreserved commitment to the mission. However, DoD proved poorly equipped to assume the new responsibilities thrust upon it. The Coalition Provisional Authority, established under DoD auspices to govern Iraq, was never close to fully staffed, and most of those working in Iraq remained for only a few months; most of CPA staff were billeted in the secure "Green Zone" and some "behind the wire" of one of several large military bases in and around Baghdad.[4] Many of CPA administrator Paul Bremer's most senior advisers came from other agencies, but there were never enough, and the expertise below [the top] level dropped sharply. What institutional memory the U.S. government retained in the field of nation-building thus remained largely untapped.[5]

Dobbins amplified on this assertion in a 2003 PBS *Frontline* interview after examining the two Balkan cases, Bosnia and Kosovo:

> Now, Iraq . . . is like Yugoslavia, a state that was carved out of the Ottoman Empire at the end of World War II. Like Yugoslavia, it unites a disparate group of ethnicities, and with religious divisions, and communal divisions, and with tensions among these groups. It's Muslim, like Bosnia and Kosovo. But the one major difference is that it's ten times bigger. And so, it was always likely that the process of nation-building in Iraq was going to be ten times more difficult, more expensive. Not necessarily more time-consuming, but more resource-consuming, in manpower and money, than Bosnia or Kosovo.[6]

Dobbins concluded in the Rand monograph,

> Successful nation-building requires unity of effort across multiple agencies and, often, multiple governments. . . . While integrated political-military planning is important, so is establishing a clear and enduring division of labor for various aspects of nation-building. . . . For the past fifteen years, critical functions, such as overseeing military and police training, providing humanitarian and reconstruction aid, and promoting democratic development have been repeatedly transferred from DOS to DoD and back again. . . . Despite recent and projected future expansion, the total number of personnel in civilian agencies associated with nation-building, including USAID, the CIA, and DOS, is dwarfed by [the military personnel] number. Budgets are similarly weighted toward the military. Absent some effort to redress this imbalance and to create an operational civilian cadre for nation-building, the implementation of U.S. policy in this field is likely to remain stunted no matter how good the quality of its decision-making.[7]

Dobbins's work is a useful framework against which to examine the inadequacy of postwar planning and implementation in Iraq. Secretary Rumsfeld assigned the job of postwar planning to Undersecretary of Defense for Policy Douglas J. Feith. "Feith himself was known more as an articulate advocate and tenacious bureaucrat than as an administrator." His staff possessed "no experience and very little capacity needed to organize and run a massive operation of this sort."[8] However, DoD, once charged with overall responsibility for postwar planning, blocked several efforts to plan across agency lines. Rumsfeld rejected a number of State nominees to serve under General Garner in his Office of Reconstruction and Humanitarian Assistance (ORHA).[9] Rajiv Chandrasekaran reconstructs Garner's difficulties with Feith and Rumsfeld and the internecine conflicts with other agencies, particularly their hostility to State personnel assigned to General Garner's ORHA office. After Rumsfeld had rejected several top ORHA staffers at a Pentagon meeting with Garner shortly before he left for Kuwait to begin his ORHA assignment, he told Garner, "I'll get you new people." Garner shot back, "You don't have time to get me new people." Chandrasekaran elaborates on this exchange:

> After more back-and-forth, Rumsfeld asked Garner to look over his staff list and indicate who "you absolutely have to keep." [Garner said,] "By the way, who would DoD have that's qualified to do agriculture?" And he didn't say anything, so I said, "How about education?" And I went down [the list] and I said, "How about banking? Who could do banking?" So he said, "Look, I don't want to argue with you on this one, but I'm gonna get you better people."[10]

These kinds of exchanges indicate the nature of the last-minute, helter-skelter guidance and oversight ORHA received from the Rumsfeld Pentagon.

Among the "better people" was the staffer who was sent to the Coalition Provisional Authority (CPA) in 2003 to reopen Baghdad's stock exchange, gutted by looters. He was a twenty-four-year-old Yale alumnus, "bored with his job at a real-estate firm," who had submitted his resume to the White House. He had not studied economics or finance at Yale where he had majored in political science. "His passion was the Middle East and although he had never been there, he was intrigued enough to take Arabic classes and read histories of the region in his spare time." This kind of background, education, expertise, and experience was not untypical of the young ORHA and CPA staffers supplied under the imprimatur of Rumsfeld and Feith in DoD or the White House. They had stricken from the roster the names of senior State personnel as "too low-profile and bureaucratic."[11]

The ORHA staff encountered administrative difficulties that should have been resolved months in advance so that an up-and-running organization would have been ready for deployment to Iraq. Instead, it wasted time with a host of "administrivia": finding office space, furniture, computers, communications, getting paid, getting travel orders, and so on. Once ORHA became operational, Garner focused his planning on three major problems that turned out not to be crucial to what happened: responding to a major refugee crisis, fires in Iraq's oil fields and flooding as a result of dam destruction throughout the country, and humanitarian assistance; the latter was Garner's focus in the Kurdish areas during War II. None of these problems occurred in any significant magnitude.

In addition to focusing on the wrong problems, General Garner's planning proceeded under three flawed operational assumptions: that large numbers of Iraqi army and security forces would remain in place to support the occupation; that the rest of the international community, including the UN, would quickly deploy resources to Iraq; and that an Iraqi government would form quickly, allowing the United States to hand off responsibility for governing the country shortly after the regime change.

General Garner and ORHA staffers believed that Iraqi government ministries would continue to function between the fall of Saddam's Ba'athist regime and the establishment of a new government. He thought that the top levels of ministerial leadership and Ba'athist officials could be removed and replaced without breaking the chain of command and that civil service administrative routines would continue within the ministries. He was confident that DoD would keep the Iraqi army in place to assist with reconstruction projects and avoid unleashing a flood of unemployed young men into the general population. All of these assumptions proved to be wrong. "There was no plan B, nor any discussion within the Bush administration about what would happen if the underlying assumptions turned out to be false."[12]

Ambassador Dobbins's observation about "no Plan B" got to the heart of the flawed strategic architecture of War III. Not since the end of World War II had the United States been confronted with the issue of determining how a conflict should end and the depth of the commitment and resources required to sustain the peace. World War II ended successfully with well-planned occupations of the principal Axis enemy states that lasted longer than the war itself and transformed those states into successful, productive members of the international system. The Korean War ended in a stalemate where American military power restored the prewar status quo for an Asian client, but it also required a permanent US military presence in Korea that lasts to the present day. It was a long endgame. It took Americans nearly half a century to recognize that South Korea had become a success story and therefore worth the sacrifice in lives and money. The Vietnam War ended in defeat because the attempt at nation building by the Kennedy, Johnson, and Nixon administrations did not succeed in leaving behind a South Vietnam that on its own could defeat the revolutionary movement. Indeed, Americans concluded after Vietnam that American intervention with expeditionary armies in remote corners of the world with alien cultures should not include deep commitments to nation building.

With this historical legacy as a backdrop, General Garner's mission in Iraq confronted the difficulty of constructing a strategic architecture that could succeed. Before Garner even reached Iraq, efforts were already underway in Washington to replace him. Secretary Rumsfeld was looking for a professional envoy to Iraq who could operate as a "superadministrator or even a viceroy,"[13] but with little thought as to what such an envoy was expected to accomplish.

Rumsfeld telephoned Garner shortly after he left Washington for Iraq to tell him that after one month Ambassador L. Paul Bremer would assume the position as administrator of the CPA of Iraq and supersede him. Shortly before departing for Baghdad, Bremer met with Feith, who showed him a draft of a de-Ba'athification order that he had intended General Garner to issue. The draft order seemed to be the extent of Feith's "viceregal" guidance. Bremer demurred and asked Feith to wait until he could issue it himself once he got to Iraq.

When he arrived in Baghdad, Bremer was perceived on first impression by Stanford political science professor Larry Diamond, whom Bremer hired to join his CPA staff, as "a skillful, take-charge leader . . . a man in control." Diamond added that Bremer "was . . . impressive in his grasp of detail and yet incessantly micromanaging."[14]

Two years later, Diamond wrote about what he believed were the flaws in the planning to bring War III to a successful end. He retrospectively posed a counterfactual scenario that consisted of ten operational actions that fundamentally would have changed what Bremer and the CPA did.[15]

1. Anticipating the chaos and looting that might transpire after the war, the United States deploys an invasion force of 250,000 to 300,000 troops.

2. Immediately on taking Baghdad, coalition troops surround major public buildings, infrastructure, and cultural and historical sites with thousands of troops, armed not only with heavy weapons but also with tear gas and other means of crowd control, and with orders to protect the structures from looting and sabotage. Public order is then reestablished relatively rapidly, with only moderate damage and loss of life.

3. Tens of thousands of coalition troops and supporting aircraft are deployed to Iraq's borders to prevent the incursion of foreign fighters—and the exit of Saddam loyalists.

4. The Iraqi police are called back to duty, with promises of retention, increased pay, and professional retraining for all those who pass an extended vetting process.

5. All soldiers and officers (up to a certain level) in the Iraqi army are told to report to regional centers, where they are processed to receive continuing pay and then considered for readmission to duty.

6. A policy is announced that bans a few thousand top Ba'ath Party and government officials from public life, while subjecting the other top tiers of party membership to a vetting process that retains them in their public sector jobs, and their right to run for office, if they are not found guilty of serious abuses under the old order. The Ba'ath Party itself is allowed to emerge under a new leadership.

7. Immediately upon establishing authority in Baghdad, the United States proposes to transfer to the United Nations the primary authority for constituting, within three months, an Iraqi interim government, beginning with the selection of national conference delegates from communities around the country and ending with the conference choosing the members of an interim government.

8. In the emerging political processes, Iraqi exile groups must compete for standing with leaders and social forces that remained in the country and the resulting national conference runs the gamut of political tendencies from mainstream forces to former Ba'athists and radical Islamists (a minority presence).

9. During the first six months after the war, local elections are conducted, to the extent possible, in communities across the country.

10. The United Nations and the United States ask the interim government, in interaction with the national conference delegates, to draw up a timetable for the election of a constitutional convention, the drafting of a constitution, and the election of a permanent government.

Diamond qualified his scenario:

> There is no guarantee that [my] scenario would have been successful. But it
> might have taken the steam out of the resistance and focused Iraqis on peacefully
> reorganizing and rebuilding the country. The other cleavages—ethnic, regional,
> sectarian—would have asserted themselves as they inevitably do. Even so, the
> country might have been able to get on with the political challenges it faced.[16]

Had Secretary Rumsfeld and his staff tested their assumptions against a
scenario like Diamond's, they might very well have instructed General Franks
to consider adding more military police and civil affairs brigades[17] to the
CENTCOM force. And they might have taken General Garner's ORHA mission
much more seriously. But Rumsfeld wanted to minimize the military footprint
preparatory to launching Operation *Iraqi Freedom* to give the president room
for diplomatic maneuver. He took a big risk in doing this. As War III came to a
close, War IV had already begun. Washington had not seen it coming.

Upon arrival in Iraq, Bremer structured his organization poorly, created isolated lines of authority that prevented different groups from working together,
and chose managers poorly, although he had plenty of help in this regard
from Washington. The government failed to recruit well-qualified personnel
and never sent enough to Iraq; six hundred were sent where thousands were
needed because Bremer's first two decrees created a power vacuum.[18]

On May 16, 2003, Bremer, within days of his appointment, issued CPA Order Number 1, De-Ba'athification of Iraqi Security, which excluded the top
four levels of Ba'ath Party membership from public employment, a decision
inspired by the German model of the "four Ds," especially the denazification program begun in 1945.[19] The CPA estimated that the practical effect
of this decree would exclude approximately 1 percent of all party members,
or twenty thousand people, from Iraqi public service. A week later, Bremer
issued CPA-2, Dissolution of Entities, which dissolved all Iraqi national security ministries and military formations.[20] Although Garner's postwar plan had
been to co-opt and reform the Iraqi army, the Iraqi army did not remain a
force in being after Saddam's defeat. Iraqi army units had been expected by
CENTCOM to capitulate on a large scale; in fact, few did.[21]

After the regime's collapse, Iraqi soldiers melted into the population and
returned home with their equipment and weapons. In dissolving the Iraqi security forces, Bremer put out of work 385,000 members of the armed services
and another 335,000 who had served in the police, Saddam's security units,
and other internal security forces. The second order, which dissolved the army
and national security formations, created a large pool of discontents, most of
them young, unemployed men, all of whom had been trained to use lethal
weapons and explosives.[22]

With the CPA understaffed and concentrated in Baghdad, Lieutenant General Ricardo S. Sanchez's Combined Joint Task Force–7 (CJTF-7) assumed by default most of the responsibility for administering Iraq, rebuilding the damaged infrastructure, and resuscitating the economy, essentially running the country. American military commanders began serving as mayors, city managers, economic planners, and local governmental facilitators. Bremer frequently countermanded decisions these officers made even though no CPA staff were in the localities to determine whether they were justified. Worse, he retained tight control over budgets, especially reconstruction money, rather than delegating these decisions down through Sanchez's chain of command. Compounding this state of affairs, Sanchez, like Bremer, was a micromanager.[23]

Bremer's CPA and Sanchez's CJTF-7 never succeeded in developing a smooth working relationship. "The U.S. presence in Iraq was a 'jury-rigged command structure, in which there was no one American official, civilian or military, on the ground in Iraq in charge of the overall American effort.'"[24] Both Bremer and Sanchez reported up through separate chains to Secretary Rumsfeld, seven thousand miles away in the Pentagon.

As the CPA expanded its responsibilities, it quickly compounded its already significant staffing difficulties. As a unique, ad hoc organization built by DoD, which had no experience creating or running such an institution since World War II, much of the CPA's early effort, like Garner's ORHA, was expended on issues of internal management and start-up. When the subject of Vietnam experience was raised, Bremer quickly quashed it. For example, the Vietnam-era CORDS organization might have been a potential model, but Bremer was not interested in Vietnam. Ricks recounts that when retired marine colonel Gary Anderson, a Vietnam veteran who had gone to Iraq at Deputy Secretary of Defense Wolfowitz's personal behest as an unpaid consultant, suggested to Bremer in July 2003, "'Mr. Ambassador, here are some programs that worked in Vietnam,' Bremer exploded. 'Vietnam! I don't want to talk about Vietnam. This is not Vietnam. This is Iraq!'"[25]

Michael R. Gordon and Bernard E. Trainor have written the most authoritative, comprehensive work published so far on the machinations, convolutions, and policy incoherence inside the Bush and Obama administrations that ensued between 2003 and 2012. Their narrative reveals an immense amount of policy and operational confusion over the need for clearheaded planning and execution of Iraq's post-Saddam governance.[26]

The Bush administration found itself trapped between its public hostility to nation building and its soaring rhetoric defining its democratic ambitions for postwar Iraq. It did not grasp the depth of the ethnic, religious, and tribal realities of Iraq's lamentable twentieth-century history since Sykes-Picot. President Bush had repeatedly declared that he wanted to see democracy and freedom flourish in Iraq. His assertions implied a democratic, constitutional polity that rendered majoritarian representation inevitable. This meant that the long-suppressed Shiite population would dominate Iraqi politics if elections were held without constitutional safeguards with respect to majority rule. A constitutional framework of countervailing provisions and legal guarantees would be needed to control and restrain Shiite political dominance that would protect Sunni minority interests and ensure their political participation. It was the Sunnis who suddenly found themselves with the tables turned in 2003, not only having lost their monopoly on power under Saddam's dictatorship but also now at risk from Shiite political vengeance and exclusion from a political process that the Shia majority was empowered to design.

Before the invasion, Gordon and Trainor point out that Saddam had taken steps to prevent another insurrection like the one that occurred in 1991 after General Schwarzkopf concluded the armistice at Safwan with Saddam's generals. Saddam by 2003 had expanded paramilitary organizations like the Fedayeen Saddam and Ba'ath Party militia. He had created distributed networks of safe houses and arms caches for these tribal groups all over the country, including materials for making improvised explosives. If the Kurds or Shia mounted another rebellion, either in the north or the south, the regime's paramilitary forces were prepared to defend the Ba'athist regime against these internal enemies until the Iraqi army and air force could establish order. Or so Saddam thought until his government collapsed. The dictator in effect had developed his own counterinsurgency strategy to fight internal threats, but it had another unintended effect. With so many weapons and explosives already positioned all over the country in secure locations, these paramilitary groups could go into action with their own agendas. They were already deployed and equipped. Coalition forces had encountered them driving up the Tigris-Euphrates valley to Baghdad in 2003, and many in the US Armed Forces had dismissed their activity as the last gasps of a dying regime. Yet these groups quickly proved themselves to be astonishingly proactive, resourceful, adaptive, and, above all, increasingly violent and destructive in the years after 2003.

Colonel Derek J. Harvey led the intelligence team for General Sanchez's CJTF-7. Among Harvey's Arabist qualifications as an intelligence officer was a PhD in Islamic political thought and jurisprudence and fluency in several Middle Eastern languages. General Petraeus later recruited Harvey to join his staff as an expert advisor after his retirement in 2006. Between 2003 and 2006, Harvey and his small staff in Baghdad, the "Red Cell," prepared classified assessments on the evolving insurgency and were among the first to identify the presence of an al Qa'ida affiliate in Iraq, *Jama'at al-Tawhid wa-al Jihad*.[27] In 2003, Harvey reported that after Saddam was toppled, there were sixty-five thousand to ninety-five thousand Special Republican Guard officers, Iraqi Intelligence Service officers, Fedayeen Saddam paramilitary forces, Ba'ath

Party militias, and the like who had gone to ground in and around Baghdad.[28] These were men who clearly saw no future after Ambassador Bremer had promulgated CPA Orders 1 and 2 abolishing the Iraqi armed forces and the Ba'ath Party. Colonel Harvey's threat assessments were not widely accepted at the time. However, as the violence increased, he found himself by December 2004 in the White House Situation Room defending an updated Red Cell briefing before a skeptical President Bush and the NSC staff. Colonel Harvey presented his case to President Bush:

> The insurgency the U.S. was facing was well trained and linked by family, tribal, and professional ties. It was stronger than most other insurgencies in history because it was exploiting the remnants of a collapsed state and had both leadership and direction. . . . The insurgency, Harvey argued, was also likely to get stronger unless the U.S. changed its strategy.

Bush pressed Harvey on what qualifications or evidence he had to offer for such a disturbing assessment, one that was not consistent with what either General George W. Casey Jr. or Embassy Baghdad was reporting. Harvey cited the "troubling information and intelligence about insurgent leaders and their networks, but the president did not appear to be persuaded."[29]

Gordon and Trainor describe in detail the years of intense interactions between 2003 and 2007 among National Security Advisor Condoleezza Rice; her deputy, Stephen J. Hadley; Defense Secretary Rumsfeld; Defense Undersecretary Wolfowitz; Ambassador Bremer; Secretary of State Powell; Undersecretary of State Richard L. Armitage; Ambassador John D. Negroponte; CIA director George Tenet; and the US field commanders in Iraq, Generals Sanchez and Casey. Gordon and Trainor describe Bremer's private Oval Office meetings with Bush where initially the ambassador thought he was in the business of nation building. He even talked to former ambassador Dobbins at Rand who was a professional friend and who offered advice about nation building.[30]

Gordon and Trainor include in their historical narrative the administration's interplay with key Iraqis, including the late Ahmed Abdel Hadi Chalabi, an Iraqi exile who had returned to Baghdad in 2003 and was regarded as influential among some in the administration; Ayad Allawi, Iraq's interim prime minister appointed before Iraq's 2005 legislative elections; and Nouri Kamil Mohammed Hasan al-Maliki, who became Iraq's first elected prime minister. This historical record is too complex to relate in detail here except to point out that the administration inadequately understood the realities of the competing elements that were in play.

The administration found itself facing the same conundrum that confounded the Johnson administration in Vietnam a generation earlier: who among the welter of ambitious Iraqis should they support, who could they

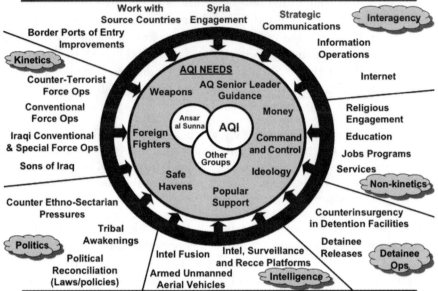

Figure 27.1. Petraeus created his "puzzle diagram" chart in PowerPoint briefings to illustrate the complexity of Iraqi tribal relationships and interactions of military and nonmilitary elements in surge operations.

Source: Chart is excerpt from congressional testimony, April 2008.

trust, who held legitimacy? The Americans wanted to empower the Iraqis to make democracy work, but the Iraqis ran circles around the administration, gaming the Americans with their endless machinations. Americans, who remained ignorant of Iraq's history and culture, who could not speak Arabic,[31] and who lacked basic knowledge about family and tribal interrelationships, were operating at a huge disadvantage. General Petraeus years later created a PowerPoint chart to describe this complexity—what he called his "puzzle diagram" (figure 27.1).[32]

By August 2003, Condoleezza Rice concluded that Rumsfeld had not been as involved with postwar Iraq planning and implementation as he had been with the war plan. Rice directed her staff to reestablish the interagency Executive Steering Group (ESG) that had been disbanded the previous May. This resumption of the ESG, while shifting oversight for Iraq postwar policy from DoD to the NSC staff, still left Bremer reporting to Rumsfeld. The result was confusion about who worked for whom. Dobbins recounts a meeting in the White House Situation Room where Rumsfeld and Rice argued over whom Bremer worked for. Rice told Rumsfeld that Bremer worked for him. Rumsfeld said, "No . . . he works for the NSC."[33]

In mid-October, the UN Security Council, acting on American urging, set a December 15, 2003, deadline for the CPA's Interim Governing Council (IGC) to submit a plan for drafting a constitution and electing a government. This CPA transition plan laid out a timetable for the IGC to draft a transitional administrative law in February 2004 and for the CPA to ratify a status-of-forces agreement (SOFA) on coalition forces in March 2004. Local caucuses in Iraq's eighteen provinces were to choose a transitional national assembly that would then elect a transitional government to assume power at the end of June 2004, simultaneous with the disestablishment of the CPA and IGC. Bremer did indeed depart from Iraq at the end of June, and the CPA ceased to exist.

President Bush in May 2004 signed National Security Presidential Directive (NSPD) 36, which terminated the CPA on June 30, 2004, creating in its place the US Mission in Baghdad that would be responsible for US activities in Iraq. NSPD 36 shifted responsibility from DoD to State, with one significant exception: the chief of mission, the ambassador, would be "responsible for the direction, coordination, and supervision of all U.S. government employees, policies, and activities in county except those under the command of an area military commander."[34] This realignment of postwar lines of authority was similar to all post–World War II occupations of the preceding half century. The practical effect of this action was that the entire CPA bureaucratic structure built up over the preceding year had to be dismantled and its functions returned to Iraqi ministries or to the new American embassy. The new ambassador, John Negroponte, who had replaced Bremer, and the new military commander, General George W. Casey Jr., who had succeeded General Sanchez as commander, Multi-National Force–Iraq (MNF-I),[35] developed a solid working relationship, but Negroponte left after only six months to become the new director of national intelligence.

Beginning during the summer of 2003, when Americans ventured outside the Green Zone in Baghdad or "beyond the wire" of a secure base, they were vulnerable to attack. The Sunni insurgents, and later al Qa'ida foreign fighters and Shia militias, started using improvised explosive devices (IEDs) and later vehicle-borne IEDs (VBIEDs, pronounced "vee beds"), accounting for more than half of all US combat casualties in War IV. The insurgents were becoming progressively more cunning at hiding explosives in roadside trash, destroyed vehicles, dead animals, and other debris, and they increasingly buried IEDs in roadbeds.

It is worth pausing for a moment to define who the insurgents were. Anthony H. Cordesman characterized them this way:

> The insurgency in Iraq has not been a national insurgency. Iraqi Kurds have never supported it, and only small numbers of Shi'ites have taken an active role. It has been driven by a relatively small part of Iraq's population concentrated in part of the country, and its most violent actions have been led by a group of foreign volunteers and extremists which did not seem likely to exceed 3,000 full-time insurgents as of September 2005.

Although there are no accurate census data, the Arab Sunni population may only be around fifteen to twenty percent of Iraq's total population. . . . Regardless of the exact ethnic and sectarian split, only about six to eight percent of Iraq's total population is located in the areas most hostile to the Coalition and the Iraqi government.

Cordesman acknowledged that estimates varied widely as to how many insurgents there actually were in Iraq:

Estimates of the size of the insurgency have varied widely ever since the struggle first became serious in August 2003. Much depends on the definition of insurgent and the level of activity and dedication involved, and virtually everyone who issues such estimates admits they are little more than sophisticated "guesstimates." U.S. officials kept repeating estimates of total insurgent strengths of 5,000 from roughly the fall of 2003 through the summer of 2004. In October, they raised their estimates to a range of 12,000 to 16,000 but have never defined how many are hard-core and full-time, and how many are part-time. . . . Estimates as divergent as 3,500 and 400,000 were being cited in the spring and early summer of 2005.[36]

Colonel Harvey's Red Cell intelligence put the upper range close to one hundred thousand.

Regardless of how the US government or think-tank community characterized the nature and scale of the insurgency, the IEDs and VBIEDs it used became increasingly lethal. Soldiers on patrol were relatively safe inside a sixty-ton M1 Abrams tank, less secure in the twenty-eight-ton Bradley Fighting Vehicle or the newer and lighter twenty-one-ton Stryker armored fighting vehicle, and vulnerable in the jeep replacement, the 2.5-ton, soft-skinned Humvee.[37] The Humvee provided no protection against IEDs, rocket-propelled grenades (RPGs), or AK-47 assault rifle rounds. Until DoD ramped up a series of programs[38] to produce armored Humvees and trucks in quantity and ship them to Iraq, soldiers on patrol in 2003 and 2004 were "sitting ducks" when targeted by a proficient insurgent enemy. Boot described the consequences:

To see what comes easily to an Information Age military and what does not, compare casualty figures for the initial invasion [War III] with those for the subsequent occupation [War IV]. Between 20 March and 9 April 2003, the United States had suffered 139 dead and 542 wounded. . . . Between 1 May 2003 and 1 May 2005, 1,510 Americans died and 11,346 were wounded. In other words, the first two years of the guerrilla phase were eighteen times more costly than the conventional combat operations which had ended on 1 May 2003.[39]

Troops commuting from main operating bases to areas of insurgency, or simply patrolling LOCs, were not well prepared either to "win hearts and minds," the mantra used over and over about Vietnam, or to gather "action-able" intelligence about the insurgents.

Some combat units, however, did much better than others because of lead-ership at lower levels of command. Indeed, some counterinsurgency activities between 2003 and 2004 appeared to be going well. Some junior officers started developing learning aids on their own by which they could exchange ideas with their peers. In 2000–2001, even before Wars III and IV had commenced, cap-tains and lieutenants had set up two websites on their own initiative.[40]

Moyar calls attention to the 1st Marine Division, under the command of Major General James N. Mattis (later general and appointed in 2010 com-mander, CENTCOM, and now secretary of defense under President Donald J. Trump). Mattis's marines had helped capture Baghdad, then occupied Tikrit (Saddam's hometown), and later redeployed to southern Iraq in the spring of 2003. Mattis had long been a student of counterinsurgency. Upon arriving in southern Iraq, he sent the division's M-1 Abrams tanks, APCs, and artillery to Kuwait to prevent his marines from using heavy firepower that might un-necessarily antagonize local Iraqis. He told his marines to avoid persecuting former Saddam supporters in revenge for friends killed or maimed by IEDs or VBIEDs. As Moyar recounted,

[Mattis told his marines] to concentrate on gaining the population's assistance in identifying and isolating miscreants. Some Marines cleaned city streets and re-stored electrical power while others conducted armed patrols, all of them build-ing relationships with local leaders and gathering information from the citizens. Marine commanders dissipated hostile crowds through carefully chosen words and force of personality. When unemployed former Iraqi soldiers demonstrated in public, Marine officers met with them, listened respectfully to what they had to say, and convinced them to desist.[41]

Major General David H. Petraeus[42] commanded the 101st Airborne Divi-sion during Operation *Iraqi Freedom*. Petraeus had already foreseen that the most challenging phase of War III would begin after the capture of Baghdad. It would seem as if his military career up to that juncture had been an express preparation for the postwar situation in Iraq, War IV. Graduating in the top 5 percent of the West Point class of 1974, Petraeus was an overachiever and learner. He had spent his early career as a junior officer in light infantry assign-ments with units such as the 24th ID (Mech), had become airborne Ranger qualified, and had kept himself in extraordinary physical condition. He had become a top student at the army's Command and General Staff College and had gone on to earn a PhD in political science at Princeton's Woodrow Wilson School of Public and International Affairs, completing a doctoral dissertation on the Vietnam War in 1987.

At the time he wrote his dissertation, Vietnam lessons were not central subjects in the army's AirLand Battle community.[43] Petraeus summarized the "conventional wisdom" as four criteria:

These criteria may be phrased as cautions to a president: "Don't commit American troops, Mr. President," they hold, "unless: (1) You really have to (in which case, presumably vital U.S. interests are at stake). (2) You have established clear-cut, attainable military objectives for American military forces (that is, more than just some fuzzy political goals). (3) You provide the military commander sufficient forces and the freedom necessary to accomplish his mission swiftly. (Remember, Mr. President, this may necessitate mobilization of the reserve components—perhaps even a declaration of war.) (4) You can ensure sufficient public support to permit carrying the commitment through to its conclusion."

Deeper in the text, he wrote this sentence: "The most serious charge leveled at the lessons of Vietnam is made by those who perceive them as promising national paralysis in the face of international provocation." He concluded: "American involvement in Vietnam should nonetheless be studied in detail; there is much in that experience that *may* [italics in original] be relevant to the use of force in other situations." He ruminated about the relevance of other historical cases in addition to Vietnam, adding that

the Vietnam analogy should be used with care. It should not, first of all, be the only case considered. . . . Vietnam should not be allowed to become such a dominant influence in the minds of decision-makers that it inhibits discussions of specific events on their own merits. It would be more profitable to address the central issues of any particular case that arises than to debate endlessly whether the situation could evolve into another Vietnam.

General Petraeus would get his own opportunity in the field to address Iraq as his "particular case" twenty years after he wrote this sentence.[44]

Focusing on Vietnam may not have been what most ambitious officers would have regarded as an obvious path to move up the army's promotional ladder. However, Petraeus by the 1990s would find himself a lieutenant colonel in command of an airborne battalion, briefly sidelined as a result of a 1991 shooting accident during training (by a trooper accidentally firing an M-16 assault rifle round into his chest). More airborne training came at Fort Bragg in the 2000 decade. Petraeus by then had been promoted to brigadier general and was posted to a peacekeeping assignment in Bosnia and Herzegovina.

The 101st assumed occupation duties in Mosul in the spring of 2003. Petraeus began the occupation of Mosul by airlifting enough soldiers into the city to stop the looting, destruction, and disorder. He and his staff met every day with Iraqi leaders and gained their cooperation through direct interaction with Iraqis and offers of reconstruction assistance. Petraeus was one of the army's leaders who was an early and effective champion of the use of the Commander's Emergency Response Program (CERP).[45] Some of the methods Petraeus used in Mosul were very different from those employed in Vietnam. For example, he facilitated reconstruction by hiring Ba'athists into middle-management jobs, in defiance of Bremer's de-Ba'athification order. Once he got money out of Bremer, convincing him to release funds captured during the invasion, he challenged his brigade, battalion, and company commanders "to outspend each other on schools, clinics, irrigation projects, and other local economic, infrastructure, and governance projects." By the end of its one-year tour in Mosul, the 101st had spent over $57 million on 5,026 projects, one-third of the total spent nationwide.[46] An empathetic leader, Petraeus insisted that his troopers respect local customs, ordering them not to barge into Iraqi houses without first knocking and waiting at the door. He improved living conditions in prisons, cracked down on interrogators who abused detainees, and invited Iraqi religious and civic leaders to visit the prisons themselves.

These kinds of methods and approaches may not appear to be significantly different than the MACV and CORDS reinforcement strategy so trenchantly analyzed by Race in Vietnam. One might rightly ask, where were the key motivating contingent incentives and preemptive policies? What Petraeus was trying out in Mosul were methods that he and his subordinates by and large devised themselves, testing to find what might work, scrounging for resources, wheedling money out of Bremer, and not relying on top-down direction. In the trial-and-error process, Petraeus also discovered the importance of matching the strengths of individual officers to specific tasks. As Moyar explained,

> All of his officers had new duties on top of those for which they had been trained. The trick was to match tasks to personalities. "One of the jobs of a leader is to employ everybody in his organization in the best way possible to get the most out of them, to help them be all they can be," said Petraeus. "In other words, the S-3 (operations officer) must do the S-3 business, but it may be that [the commander] also can use the S-3 to engage with certain leaders because he's really good at it. Or maybe not, maybe the S-5 (civil affairs officer) has to do it, or the deputy commander." [He would later observe] that "The key to many of our successes in Iraq, in fact, has been leaders—especially younger leaders—who have risen to the occasion and taken on tasks for which they'd had little or no training, and who have demonstrated enormous initiative, innovativeness, determination, and courage."[47]

Petraeus and others were recognizing that without cultivation of critical leadership attributes, commanders could not turn ideas into productive, executable actions in Iraq. Cohen's view on military staffing reinforced this recognition:

> [T]he character of individual military commanders, at the division level and often below, had large consequences for the conduct of military operations. The 101st

Airborne Division, 1st Cavalry Division [restructured and reorganized from its days in Vietnam's Central Highlands], and 1st Armored Division under Generals Petraeus, [Peter W.] Chiarelli, and [Martin E.] Dempsey adapted remarkably quickly to the counterinsurgency mission, pursuing a combination of reconstruction and focused violence which achieved notable success in restoring some semblance of normality in their areas of operation.[48]

During the 2004–2005 period, several deployed American units demonstrated that the army and marine corps were capable of the kind of initiative, innovation, and determination Petraeus spoke of—without much top-down command direction.

The most dangerous problem confronting Iraqis and Americans in the spring of 2004 was the city of Fallujah in al Anbar Province, long considered the most troublesome city in Iraq, known for its hostility to outsiders, its religious fanaticism, and its "rough-and-tumble" men. Major General Mattis's 1st Marine Division had arrived in the spring of 2004 with hopes of defusing violence through the same approach it had used successfully in the south in 2003. However, by 2004 the Sunnis in Anbar were much more hostile to Americans than were the Shiites the 1st Marine Division had been working with in the south. The benevolent approach was doomed from the start. The week after the marines assumed responsibility for Fallujah, insurgents ambushed four American contractors, butchered them and dragged their bodies through the streets, and hanged them from a trestle bridge as television images were transmitted around the world. Both General Mattis and his boss, I Marine Expeditionary Force commander Lieutenant General James T. Conway, recommended patience. They wanted to work on developing Iraqi security forces and gradually gaining support in the city, believing that the perpetrators would be apprehended in due course. But Rumsfeld, Bremer, and Sanchez believed that a powerful military response was required. President Bush decided to send the marines into the city with overwhelming force.

Mattis ordered a marine regimental combat team in early April 2004 to take control of Fallujah and remove the insurgents and heavy weapons. For five days, the marines fought their way into the city, encountering fierce resistance from hundreds of insurgents. It was a MOUT (military operation in urban terrain) battle, building by building. Before they could complete sweeping the insurgents from the city, however, President Bush ordered a halt. The marines proposed a solution to the impasse by pulling back and arming a force of two thousand Iraqis, known as the Fallujah Brigade. This force fulfilled some of its promises but did not remove heavy weapons or foreign fighters or prevent kidnappings and murders by Islamist insurgent factions dominating the city. By the end of the summer, Fallujah again had become a safe haven for the insurgents, a situation that became intolerable to the American and Iraqi governments. So nine marine and army battalions and six Iraqi battalions went back into the city and fought another destructive MOUT to eradicate the insurgents. By the time the insurgents had been cleared from the city, nearly half of the city's buildings (eighteen thousand out of a total of thirty-nine thousand) had been destroyed or damaged. Too few of the Iraqi forces, however, had the discipline and determination to prevail in the "hold" phase.

As the insurgent conflict festered in 2004, General Casey's "clear and hold" strategy was producing mixed results. In the spring of 2005, Colonel H. R. McMaster, who had distinguished himself while a troop commander as a captain in War I in the Battle of 73 Easting during Operation *Desert Storm*, had assumed command of the 3rd Armored Cavalry Regiment, which had arrived in Tal Afar in Iraq's northwestern desert. McMaster put some of his soldiers through short courses on the Arabic language and culture and issued everyone in the regiment a list of recommended counterinsurgency readings. He later explained to a *New Yorker* writer what he learned:

> "When we first got here, we made a lot of mistakes. We were like a blind man, trying to do the right thing but breaking a lot of things." Later, he said, "You gotta come in with your ears open. You can't come in and start talking. You have to really *listen* [italics in original] to people."[49]

From May to September 2005, the 3rd Armored Cavalry Regiment and two Iraqi army brigades engaged in intense block-by-block MOUT fighting, calling on helicopters and artillery when they judged the risk of civilian collateral damage to be low. In September, the regiment established twenty-nine small outposts in the city and lived in them side by side with the population they were trying to protect. His officers and men courted Tal Afar's tribal leaders, spending forty to fifty hours per week meeting with Shiite and Sunni sheikhs. Eventually they persuaded the sheikhs to recruit 1,400 men into the police. Conscious of the previous failures to hold the city, which had followed previous American withdrawals from Tal Afar, McMaster kept over 1,000 of his soldiers and 1,500 Iraqi soldiers in the city until the police force was fully trained and employed.

Similar clear-and-hold efforts also produced local results in the north in 2005. Lieutenant Colonel Michael "Erik" Kurilla (later major general) led an infantry battalion in Mosul. Kurilla's example of leading from the front and indifference to danger enabled him and his battalion to earn the respect of local Iraqis, especially the sheikhs, in helping to secure Mosul. Michael Yon, whose online blogs eventually became a best-selling book, was an independent journalist who chronicled the battalion's effective leadership and operations.[50]

> Kurilla excelled in social settings, which helped him win the cooperation of Iraqis and gain the counterinsurgents favorable coverage from the media, whom he

actively cultivated. On top of everything else, Kurilla displayed uncommon in-genuity in combating the enemy. Making extensive use of captured cell phones, he deceived and disrupted the enemy's operations and tracked down insurgents. On one occasion, he had his soldiers stage a fake IED attack on an Iraqi security force to lure insurgents, who were accustomed to preying on vehicles in distress. When insurgents tried to pounce on the seemingly disabled truck, American snipers in surrounding buildings shot them to pieces.[51]

In the west in the late summer of 2005 in al Anbar's al Qaim district, Lieu-tenant Colonel Dale Alford led a marine battalion in a building-by-building MOUT, later spreading out in November with an Iraqi battalion to control the population and increase pressure on what by then had become al Qa'ida in Iraq (AQI). Al Qaim's tribes served as the first way station in western Iraq for foreign Muslim extremists to travel from Syria to the Euphrates valley, and from there to expand into insurgent hotbeds in Iraq's interior. Al Qaim by 2005 was a logistical hub for AQI and foreign fighters. Al Qaim's tribes, which were initially hostile to the Americans, had become disenchanted with AQI's extremism and violent behavior by the spring of 2005. For these reasons, al Qaim became a matter of considerable interest to General Casey. Moyar re-counts what Alford's battalion accomplished after the close combat:

> What followed next were holding operations that the U.S. military later taught in counterinsurgency courses as models of excellence. Marines and Iraqi sol-diers established a galaxy of small outposts in [al Qaim's] towns and along its roads, which they used as living quarters and bases for combined patrolling. The sociable Alford and his Marines engaged the Iraqi population with such success that they were invited into Iraqi homes for tea or food on a daily basis. Meeting regularly with sheikhs, imams, and city councilmen, the battalion's officers convinced 1,300 local men to join the local police force [as McMaster was doing in Tal Afar].[52]

These contacts enabled the marines to collect intelligence from the local population and neutralize the insurgents. With financial support from the ma-rines, the Iraqis restored water and electrical service, brought hospitals back into operation, repaired roads, and enabled Iraqi entrepreneurs to take out small loans from American civil affairs officers to start new businesses.

While all these events were transpiring between mid-2003 and 2006, the economic, political, and social disorder that persisted in Baghdad and else-where in the country had been undergoing two mutations. The first occurred during 2003–2004 as the coalition force's significant acts database[53] was show-ing that the daily average number of attacks carried out against all targets in Iraq had quadrupled.[54] The second was the mounting resistance to the Ameri-can occupation, particularly in the wake of the Abu Ghraib scandal in 2004,[55] which increased after the transfer of sovereignty and the national elections that followed in 2005.

As the months went by, the frequency and violence of these attacks became much worse. The source of attacks shifted from Sunni resistance against the coalition occupation to the Shia-dominated government that emerged in the wake of the CPA's enabling political actions. Shia militias (and Shia-dominated police) retaliated against Sunni attacks with atrocities of their own. Al Qa'ida in Iraq exploited these internecine conflicts, attacking Shia targets precisely to exacerbate violent responses against Sunnis, thereby intending to plunge the country into further disorder.

The year 2006 would turn out to be the most important in terms of the way War IV developed. It got off to a violent and shocking start with the bombing of the golden dome of the Askariya Mosque on February 22, 2006, in Samarra, considered one of the most important Shia shrines in Iraq. That explosion became a media symbol of out-of-control violence in Iraq. The MNF-I's significant acts database had been recording steady increases in violence since March 2005. The reports of violence continued to grow after the mosque bombing until they peaked in June 2007. The mosque destruction had made US political and military leaders face reality: they could no longer claim any basis for optimism about Iraq's future. It was becoming harder to argue that there were enough military personnel in Iraq to defeat the insurgency.

Meanwhile, Petraeus, who had been promoted to lieutenant general in June 2004, completed a second tour in Iraq,[56] and in October 2005 he assumed command of the US Army Combined Arms Center at Fort Leavenworth. Over the course of the next year, he led the development and publication of the army's new *Counterinsurgency Field Manual*, No. 3-24 (hereafter FM 3-24).[57] The most revealing sentence in FM 3-24 appears on page 46: "An effective counterinsurgent force is a learning organization"—under the header "Learn and Adapt." The manual in emphasizing learning and adapting was pointing out to its military readers that all the answers to an effective COIN strategy would not be found in FM 3-24. It was not a "how-to" manual for every problem officers and NCOs would encounter in Iraq or Afghanistan.

Early in 2005, Petraeus assembled a large team,[58] under army and marine corps sponsorship, to write and publish a coherent, relevant doctrine for the US Armed Forces for the first time in a generation.[59] As the foreword noted upon publication a year later, it had been twenty years since the army had published a field manual devoted exclusively to COIN operations, and twenty-five years for the marines.[60] The army's new COIN manual was packed with a lot of unimpeachable advice about what to do and what not to do; for example, it made intelligent and cogent points about the futility of trying to kill one's way out of an insurgency,[61] and about intelligence, use of force and collateral damage, and host-nation support:

Isolate insurgents from cause and support. It is easier to separate an insurgency from its resources and let it die than to kill every insurgent . . . killing every insurgent is normally impossible.

Intelligence drives operations. Without good intelligence, counterinsurgents are like blind boxers wasting energy flailing an unseen opponent and perhaps causing unintended harm.

Use appropriate force and avoid collateral damage. An operation that kills five insurgents is counterproductive if collateral damage leads to the recruitment of fifty more insurgents.

Support the Host Nation. U.S. forces committed to a COIN effort are there to assist a HN [host nation] government. In the end, the host nation has to win on its own [echoing President Kennedy's widely quoted line about Vietnam to Walter Cronkite in 1963]. Achieving this requires development of viable local leaders and institutions. U.S. forces can help, but HN elements must accept responsibilities to achieve real victory. While it may be easier for U.S. military units to conduct operations themselves, it is better to work to strengthen local forces and institutions and then assist them. HN governments have the final responsibility to solve their own problems. Eventually all foreign armies are seen as interlopers or occupiers; the sooner the main effort can transition to HN institutions, without unacceptable degradation, the better.[62]

Any experienced MACV staff officer, CORDS development administrator, or military advisor fifty years ago reading FM 3-24 in Vietnam might very well have nodded in agreement reading such maxims. But he might have wondered how he could get a host nation "to solve [its] own problems" and "win on its own." What contingent incentives did he have if the only thing he could do was support and assist the host nation? How was he going to get host-nation military officers, policemen, government administrators, or village (or tribal) chiefs to win if such behavior meant risking death? FM 3-24 does not offer its readers any answers to these questions because they are still left with trying to design "contingent incentives" that motivate Iraqis to put their lives on the line. Another FM 3-24 deficiency is that it offers very limited guidance on how the military could leverage its superior budgetary and logistical resources to enable nonmilitary agencies in Iraq to operate as one integrated mission. That was a problem that CORDS never solved. Neither did FM 3-24 two generations later.

It was not lost on Petraeus that he might be being groomed for his next assignment, putting theory into practice. Selecting junior officers and matching their talents to the right tasks was one thing; leading by example was another. Whatever the limitations of the new playbook, there would need to be some additional top-down action necessary to get Iraqis to risk death. That was equally true for key Iraqi politicians; they would have to make decisions that they might not want to make, as Petraeus and his civilian counterpart, Ambassador Ryan C. Crocker, would discover as they returned to Iraq in 2007. Fundamentally, it would require a change in the strategic architecture of War IV.

By the summer of 2006, Baghdad was on fire. Sunni-Shia sectarian and AQI violence was growing and widespread. What was also becoming increasingly clear was that Baghdad itself was not secure.

After three more months of parliamentary deadlock and increasing sectarian violence, Ibrahim al-Jaafari, the ineffective incumbent prime minister of Iraq's transitional government between 2005 and 2006, was persuaded to step aside. Nouri Kamil al-Maliki succeeded him in May 2006.

By mid-2006, Ricks indicated that the intensity of the insurgency was becoming increasingly alarming. CENTCOM's metrics were reporting detonations of about one thousand IEDs and roadside bombs per week. During May, car bombs killed thirty people in Karbala, a Shiite Muslim city; fifty-one bodies were found in Baghdad, handcuffed, blindfolded, and shot; nine bombs were detonated in the capital, killing thirty-seven more; a truck bomb exploded in Sadr City, the huge slum on the eastern side of Baghdad, killing or wounding another ninety-nine people; and six policemen were killed in Qaim where police found forty bodies. The growing violence marked the beginning of a slide into anarchy after Maliki assumed office.[63] Violence during 2006 was increasing dramatically: "Murders, executions, mortar attacks, IEDs rose only 3 percent from March to April 2006" but were "39 percent higher in May 2006 than in March and 73 percent higher in July 2006 than in March."[64] The violence in Baghdad had grown to such an extent that in late June 2006 the new Maliki government declared a state of emergency.

STRATEGY

In Washington, there was a growing perception that War IV was intensifying to the point that the "strategic edifice" of the American policy in Iraq was collapsing.[65] After the Samarra bombing the previous winter, Secretary Rumsfeld and the Bush administration were finding that their claims that "Iraq is making steady progress in meeting the president's short-term and medium-term security goals" encountered deep skepticism if not outright disbelief and rejection. Retired senior officers were beginning to speak out against a failed strategy privately and occasionally publicly.[66]

In November 2006, the midterm congressional elections confirmed the American public's dissatisfaction with Wars III and IV. It was a turning point that transferred control of both houses of Congress to the Democrats. Bush called it a "thumping." Secretary Rumsfeld, in an unusually subdued frame of mind, expressed his own verdict the same day, asserting inarticulately that Iraq is "a little understood, unfamiliar war, the first war of the 21st century—it is not well known, it was not well understood, it is complex for people to comprehend."[67] His characteristic public confidence had abandoned him. He lost his job the next day. President Bush appointed Robert M. Gates, an intelligence officer whose twenty-six-year career had been capped by serving as director of central intelligence under the elder Bush and, in retirement, president of Texas A&M University and a member of the congressionally appointed Iraq Study Group.[68] Exuding a calm personality where Rumsfeld's was blustery, and steeped in the issues surrounding Iraq, Gates was expected to bring a fresh perspective to debate inside the Bush administration about what to do.

Concurrent with these political developments, retired general John "Jack" Keane, according to Ricks, had started to become de facto chairman of the JCS, "stepping in to redirect U.S. strategy in [the] war, to coordinate the thinking of the White House and the Pentagon, and even to pick the commanders who would lead the change in the fight."[69] Keane had been worried about Wars III and IV since his first visit to Iraq in the summer of 2003. Ricks quotes him reminiscing this way:

> When I flew out, I was really troubled. I knew the Army collectively was not prepared to deal with irregular warfare. I said to my guys [he was vice chief of staff at the time], we simply are not prepared to do this.[70]

Keane had been a platoon leader and company commander in the 101st Airborne in Vietnam. When he returned to the CONUS as a younger officer, he had studied the literature of counterinsurgency and concluded, "I and others [including a later protégé, Petraeus] came to the conclusion that we had been conducting a conventional war against an irregular enemy."[71] As he explained his learning process to Ricks, "'We'd studied the history, we'd learned the doctrine, and some of us had the experience. . . .' After the [Vietnam] war, the Army 'purged' that knowledge,' he said. But 'I kept the memory, especially the idea that you must protect the population.'"[72]

In September 2006, Keane had bluntly presented his case to Rumsfeld in his Pentagon office:

> "We are edging toward strategic failure. . . . Despite capturing Saddam Hussein, killing his two sons, holding three elections, writing a constitution, installing a permanent government, beginning to develop a capable ISF [Iraqi Security Force], killing Zarkawi[73]—the level of violence has increased every year in the contested areas. Security and stability is worse today than it has been since the insurgency started. It threatens the survival of the government and the success of our mission. . . . You have to come to grips with that." . . . Next, he said, start employing classic counterinsurgency practice: "The only way to do this is the way that it's been done in the past, using proven COIN practices—and that is by protecting the people and permanently isolating the insurgents from the population."[74]

Ricks indicated that General Peter Pace, the chairman of the JCS, invited Keane to his Pentagon office for a private meeting as a follow-up to the Rumsfeld meeting. During the meeting, Pace asked Keane, during the fall of 2006, what grade he could give him as CJCS. "F" was Keane's reply. Pace was taken aback and asked what Keane meant: "'Well, Pete, the number one national security priority we have is Iraq, and it's the number one priority in the Pentagon . . . [but] you're absorbed in so many other things. . . . You've got to get into this full time.'" Ricks explains Pace's hands-off approach to Iraq "on the grounds that his plate was full with the rest of the world and that two other four-star generals, Abizaid and Casey, were on the case." General John P. Abizaid was the eighth CINCENT, an Arabic speaker and knowledgeable officer, who had succeeded General Franks in July 2003 and was General Casey's boss as commander, MNF-I. Pace may have assumed that these two officers were closer to the situation in Iraq and therefore in a better position to make more informed decisions. Ricks's implicit point is that Pace was higher in the chain of command as CJCS and therefore was in a position at the top to demand accountability for a strategy that was increasingly perceived as a failed one.[75]

General Keane recommended that MNF-I needed to stop conducting vehicle-borne patrols out of the main operating bases and instead deploy coalition forces among the population, patrolling specific, contested areas on foot, setting up traffic-control points, issuing identity cards, conducting a census of the local population—all classical measures to channel and track movements of a population with violent insurgents in its midst. His most controversial recommendation was that Rumsfeld order everyone to stop talking about drawing down troop levels in Iraq and replace the existing military leadership (General Casey in particular) with new generals and hold them accountable. General Keane concluded: to live among the Iraqis and drain the sea in which the insurgents were swimming, the army would need more troops. And it would need to focus them initially on Baghdad.

Ricks's reconstruction of the politics and personalities involved in the Iraq strategy identifies multiple participants in various forums both inside and outside the government. Three groups worked concurrently: (1) the "Council of Colonels" tasked by CJCS chairman General Pace, including Colonels McMaster and Mansoor (both soon to serve with Petraeus in Iraq);[76] (2) an ad hoc group at the American Enterprise Institute (AEI) under the leadership of Dr. Frederick W. Kagan[77] that brought together academics, knowledgeable hawks who had served in previous administrations, and retired military officers including General Keane; and (3) General Petraeus and selected staff who began to visit Washington in October to lay the groundwork for rolling out his new COIN manual.

The AEI group during the first week in December 2006 engaged in a three-day exercise to devise an alternative military approach for Iraq. They had to determine how to redeploy American troops in Iraq so that they could protect the population. That had been a major theme in General Keane's critique of the Casey main-operating-base/transition-to-the-Iraqis approach. The alternative that this group developed evolved into the surge ordered the following month.

By design the group chose to follow a back-to-front military planning process: define a problem, develop a solution, identify a sequence of logical steps to reach the solution, and then calculate the logistical requirements specifying the troops and matériel needed. The solution was a seven-brigade surge in US forces in Iraq, five from the army and two from the marine corps. It was not enough simply to define military strength in terms of seven additional brigades. The AEI team also had to be realistic: Where were these additional troops to be found? Were they at the required combat readiness levels? Were they deployable according to a credible schedule? They examined the army's planned rotation schedule and figured out how many combat brigades the army could send to Iraq. They also "red teamed" the plan—that is, they reviewed the proposed operation from the enemy's point of view: How would al Qa'ida in Iraq react? What would the Shiite militias do? What would the Sunni insurgents do?

Within days, on December 11, 2006, the White House invited General Keane to a council-of-war meeting in the Oval Office along with Professor Eliot Cohen, Dr. Stephen Biddle, and retired army generals Barry McCaffrey and Wayne A. Downing.[78] As Ricks describes the meeting, Cohen spoke first and cut to the chase:

> "Mr. President, I'm going to be very blunt," he began. "I don't mean to cause offense, but this is wartime, and I feel I owe it to you." . . . Cohen hit the issue of generalship squarely. It was time to get a new team and a new strategy in Iraq, he advised. "It's not enough to say these are good guys—of course they are good guys [referring to Generals Casey and his number two, Lieutenant General Chiarelli[79]]. The question is, are they the *right* [italics in original] guys?" He said he didn't think so. He urged the president to hold them accountable.[80]

General Keane spoke second:

> "Mr. President, to my mind, this is a major crisis. . . . Time is running out." We need more troops, he said. . . . "For the first time, we will secure the population, which is the proven way to defeat an insurgency. . . . In time the troops will be more secure, but I can't hide from you that the casualties will initially go up. In any counteroffensive operation that we have ever done, from Normandy to the island-hopping campaign in the Pacific, Inchon in Korea, multiple ones in Vietnam, casualties always go up, because you are bringing more troops and more firepower to bear on the problem."[81]

Keane was addressing the essential disagreement between General Casey and his civilian superiors in Washington. Mansoor indicates that Casey firmly believed that progress in political reconciliation between Sunnis and Shia should be a prerequisite for any surge of forces into Iraq. Casey had only requested two army brigades and two marine battalions in his own early December 2006 request for more forces. The Bush White House meanwhile recognized that lowering the violence by protecting the Iraqi population was a prerequisite for reconciliation. "There was no way to square this circle without a change of commanders in Iraq."[82]

Everyone had a chance to speak. Generals McCaffrey and Downing disagreed with Keane's proposed surge of more troops, while the two academics, Cohen and Biddle, supported it. President Bush then asked the group what he should do with their advice. He particularly wanted to know what general he was supposed to pick to replace General Casey. Cohen answered, "Petraeus." Retrospectively, his reasoning was straightforward, quoting Michael Howard: "All armies get it wrong at the beginning—the question is who adapts fastest."[83] Cohen believed that Petraeus was the right general to appoint. Petraeus while serving in Iraq in earlier assignments had demonstrated the best ability to adapt. Bush decided on the surge and endorsed the recommendation of selecting Petraeus to command it.

The Oval Office meeting that started the process for changing the strategic architecture of War IV is extraordinary because of the meeting participants and what was on the agenda, the government's failed strategy in Iraq. All were outside the chain of command. The military officers present were all retired generals, Keane, Downing, and McCaffrey. The other three were civilians holding no position in the government, Cohen, Biddle, and Kagan. Ricks writes that "about a dozen high-level note takers—Karl Rove [a close presidential political advisor], National Security Advisor Stephen Hadley, and some of his staffers—sat in the outer circle."[84] No one from Defense, State, or the JSC was present, no one in the military chain of command.

Colonel Peter Mansoor picked up the story in his own account of the surge, written years later. He wrote, "General Keane's role in the meeting was pivotal." He then indicates that Keane gave a more thorough briefing along the same lines to Vice President Richard W. Cheney. Two days after the Oval Office meeting, on December 13, 2006, President Bush, Cheney, and Hadley all traveled to the Pentagon because "they had to get the Joint Chiefs on board or there would be public dissension."[85] Secretary Gates described his impression of this meeting. It was six days before he was sworn in as Rumsfeld's successor as secretary of defense.

Bush raised the ideas of more troops going to Iraq. All of the chiefs unloaded on him, not only questioning the value of the additional forces but expressing concern about the impact on the military if asked to send thousands of more troops. They worried about "breaking the force." . . . I was struck in the meeting by the service chiefs' seeming detachment from the wars we were in and their focus on future contingencies and stress on the force. Not one uttered a single sentence on the need for us to win in Iraq. It was my first glimpse of one of the biggest challenges I would face throughout my time as secretary—getting those whose offices were in the Pentagon to give priority to the overseas battlefields. Bush heard them out respectfully but at the end simply said, "The surest way to break the force is to lose in Iraq." I would have to deal with all the legitimate issues the chiefs raised that day, but I agreed totally with the president.[86]

Gates's description of this Pentagon meeting revealed the depth of division between the White House and the JCS on the misalignment between policy, strategy, and operations. The top leadership of the armed forces of the United States was not behind the surge that President Bush wanted to pursue. This is not how effective strategic architectures are supposed to work.

President Bush in December 2006 ended up overruling the advice of his commander in Iraq (General Casey), relieving him and appointing a new one (General Petraeus), and, in the process, overruling most on the JCS, many in the Pentagon generally, and some in the White House to impose an alignment of policy, strategy, and operations.

Over the next month, the surge strategy was approved, Gates was sworn in as the new secretary of defense, and a new commander of forces in Iraq (General Petraeus) had been appointed. The Bush administration recognized that it needed a realignment of its policy of regime change and a strategy for defeating the violence so that Prime Minister Maliki's leadership could establish itself on a solid foundation of effective civil governance. No longer were the administration and the Rumsfeld Pentagon directing drawdowns of deployed brigades. The White House and the Gates Pentagon were doing the reverse: committing surge forces to a COIN mission in which they wanted a dramatic reduction in the violence to enable a longer endgame in Iraq. After his Senate confirmation hearing, General Petraeus met with President Bush in the Oval Office. The president observed that he had doubled down on the US war effort in Iraq. "'This isn't double down, Mr. President,' Petraeus replied. 'It's all in.'"[87]

OPERATIONS

General Petraeus arrived in Baghdad two months later in February 2007 to take command of MNF-I. He met his number two there, Lieutenant General Raymond T. Odierno, commander of Multi-National Corps–Iraq (MNC-I), who had commanded day-to-day military operations and had succeeded General Chiarelli in December 2006. Two "anomalies" characterized the way Petraeus and Odierno assembled their command staffs. The first anomaly was that the Petraeus team was dominated by military officers who among their military credentials possessed not only combat experience in Iraq but in many cases doctorates from top-flight universities in fields directly germane to counterinsurgency. Thomas Ricks and Linda Robinson described it as a "brain trust."[88] The second anomaly was that it was an unorthodox military organization in the sense that it was populated by a group of combat veterans with proven command experience in Iraq, including many who were published authors on COIN operations. Most were skeptics and some were foreigners; others were civilians. Their names, positions, qualifications, and backgrounds are summarized in table 27.1. While this table is not a complete representation of all the essential functions on a theater command staff, it is intended to convey the extent to which Petraeus wanted to take advantage of COIN expertise, academic knowledge of Iraq, and combat experience inside his MNF-I command organization. He wanted a different organizational mind-set to plan and execute the surge.

General Petraeus selected Colonel Peter Mansoor as his executive officer to lead his transition team and help put together the staff. "Petraeus valued three attributes above all else: intelligence, prior experience in Iraq, and commitment. He did not want people serving on the MNF-I staff for three to six months and then leaving once their résumé cards were punched." Mansoor offers the most comprehensive published firsthand account of the MNF-I staff composition. Neither Mansoor's narrative nor table 27.1 identifies everyone whose contribution was critical, but the "specific expertise" of those identified is representative of the scope of talent sought.[89]

Ambassador Crocker arrived at his post in Baghdad in March 2007. He, too, staffed his embassy with an "A-team" of experienced professional Foreign Service officers, including three serving ambassadors and three deputy chiefs of mission with their expertise and experience matched to their assignments (table 27.1). He also sent the State Department a blunt request to staff his embassy with fully qualified personnel.[90]

The American civil-military relationship in Iraq improved dramatically when Petraeus and Crocker arrived in Baghdad. In a formal sense, Petraeus was responsible for military matters while Crocker had primary leadership responsibility over the political, economic, and diplomatic lines of operation. In that sense, nothing formally changed in the command-and-control structure under which previous leaders had operated under NSPD 36. However, Petraeus and Crocker formed a strong working partnership. When needed, together they created multiple interagency "fusion cells" to deal with "big issues" of governance and economics, such as oil exports and electrical power. As Mansoor observed, "Four years into the conflict, the U.S. Embassy and Multi-National Force–Iraq had finally integrated the non-kinetic [noncombat] lines of operation at the strategic level."[91]

Table 27.1. General Petraeus's Brain Trust

The Petraeus MNF-I staff was unique in its composition, combining combat command experience with COIN expertise and its close partnership with Ambassador Crocker's Embassy Baghdad staff.

Name, Rank, Position (in 2007)	Position, Qualifications, Combat Experience, Education, and Publications
General David H. Petraeus, US Army	Commander, Multi-National Force–Iraq; West Point; PhD, political science, Princeton Univ., Woodrow Wilson School, dissertation: "The American Military and the Lessons of Vietnam" (1987)
Colonel Peter R. Mansoor, US Army	Executive officer (XO), commander "Ready First Combat Team," 1st Brigade, 1st Armored Division (2003–2004); West Point; PhD, military history, Ohio State Univ.; *Surge: My Journey with General David Petraeus and the Remaking of the Iraq War* (2013), published six years after the surge as an insider's account; *Baghdad at Sunrise* (2008); and *The GI Offensive in Europe* (1999)
Colonel Derek J. Harvey, US Army (Ret.)	Chief, Commander's Assessments and Initiatives Group/senior intelligence analyst for MNF-Iraq, prior service in DIA, Arabist; PhD, Islamic political thought and jurisprudence
Colonel (later lieutenant general and later national security advisor under President Trump between February 2017 and March 2018) H. R. McMaster, US Army	Chief, Joint Strategic Assessment Team (JSAT), Silver Star, Gulf War I, commander 3rd Armored Cavalry Regiment, Battle of Tal Afar, COIN expert; PhD, history, Univ. N. Carolina (Chapel Hill); his dissertation became a book, *Dereliction of Duty: Lyndon Johnson, Robert McNamara, the Joint Chiefs of Staff, and the Lies That Led to Vietnam* (1997). The JSAT brought together twenty COIN experts, officers, Embassy Baghdad officials, and academics to meet daily in one of Saddam's former palaces to develop planning details for Petraeus's campaign plan.
Lieutenant Colonel David Kilcullen, Royal Australian Army (Ret.)	Sr. COIN advisor; lieutenant colonel, Australian Army (Ret.); State Dept. counterterrorism coordinator; PhD, political anthropology, Univ. S. Wales; *The Accidental Guerrilla: Fighting Small Wars in the Midst of a Big One* (2009); *Counterinsurgency* (2010); *Out of the Mountains: The Coming of Age of the Urban Guerrilla* (2013).
Lieutenant Colonel John A. Nagl, US Army	Advisor, platoon commander, 1st Cav Div, Gulf War I, and operations officer, Task Force 1-34 Armor in Khalidiyah, War III; PhD, Oxford Univ., dissertation became a book: *Learning to Eat Soup with a Knife: Counterinsurgency Lessons from Malaya and Vietnam* (2002), military aide to Dep. Defense Secretary Paul Wolfowitz
Lieutenant Colonel William E. Rapp, US Army	Director, Commander Initiatives Group, commanded an airborne engineer company in Operations *Desert Shield* and *Desert Storm* in War I and the 555th Combat Support Brigade, attached to the 101st Airborne Division in War IV; served previous tour in Iraq that ended in October 2006; PhD, Stanford Univ., dissertation addressed reliability of democracies in war-fighting alliances

Name, Rank, Position (in 2007)	Position, Qualifications, Combat Experience, Education, and Publications
Lieutenant Colonel Charles Miller, US Army	Deputy Director, Commander's Initiatives Group; served in 3rd Battalion of 187th Infantry Regiment where his commanding officer was Lieutenant Colonel Petraeus; in 2004, served as Petraeus's executive officer in Multi-National Security Transition Command, responsible for training Iraqi security forces; PhD, political science, Columbia Univ., dissertation about doctrinal changes in US Army
Colonel (later brigadier general) Mark S. Martins, US Army	MNF-I staff judge advocate; a lawyer and holdover from General Casey's staff, Petraeus asked him to stay on; Martins had earlier advised Petraeus on use of seized Iraqi funds to jump-start reconstruction, a CERP precursor, and wrote the legal appendix to the new COIN manual, FM 3-24, in 2006; had served in Petraeus's airborne battalion in 1990–1991 at the time of Petraeus's shooting accident in 1991
Colonel Michael J. Meese, US Army	Advisor, chairman, Social Science Dept. (West Point), combat service in the Balkans; served as Petraeus's chief of staff in Balkans peacekeeping mission; PhD, economics, Princeton Univ.
Lieutenant Colonel Douglas A. Ollivant, US Army	Chief of plans for Multi-National Division Baghdad during the surge; led the team that wrote the Baghdad Security Plan; operations officer, 1st Battalion of 5th Cavalry Regiment in Baghdad, Najaf, and Fallujah; later, chief of plans of Multi-National Division in Baghdad; PhD, political science, Indiana Univ.
Lieutenant Colonel (later colonel) Suzanne C. Nielson, US Army	Intelligence officer, served in Germany, Balkans, Korea, and Iraq; PhD, Harvard Univ., dissertation on military organizational change, won American Political Science Association's Lasswell Award for best public-policy dissertation in 2002–2003; *American National Security*, 6th ed., coauthor, and *American Civil-Military Relations: The Soldier and the State in a New Era*, coeditor (2009)
Lieutenant Colonel Conrad C. Crane, US Army	Advisor; director, US Army Military History Institute; West Point classmate of Petraeus; PhD, history, Stanford Univ.; principal author, FM 3-24, US Army/USMC Counterinsurgency Field Manual; *Bombs, Cities, and Civilians: American Airpower Strategy in World War II* (1993)
Captain (later major) Jeanne F. Godfroy (née Hull), US Army	Intelligence officer; military service in the Balkans; MA, PhD candidate, Princeton Univ., Woodrow Wilson School; now a serving major; dissertation title, "'Civil' Warriors: A Study on Military Intervention and Key Leader Engagement in Iraq"
Sadi Othman	Advisor and Petraeus's interpreter, Palestinian born in Brazil, raised in Jordan; a Sunni Muslim, Univ. of Amman; eventually became a US citizen after attending Hesston College, a Mennonite institution in Kansas; became Petraeus's translator and daily envoy to Maliki and other top Iraqi leaders, including emissaries from Moqtada al-Sadr, who after the 2005 elections had become politically powerful; Petraeus had met Othman while commanding the 101st Airborne in Mosul during his first tour

(continued)

Table 27.1. *Continued*

Name, Rank, Position (in 2007)	Position, Qualifications, Combat Experience, Education, and Publications
Emma Sky	Chief political advisor to Odierno; formerly a member of the British Council in Manchester as a governance advisor, managing projects globally on governments, justice, and access to security; specialist in Third World economics with experience in the West Bank and Israel; Arabic and Hebrew speaker; appointed under the CPA as governorate coordinator for Kirkuk, and then governance advisor to CPA North, 2003–2004; Odierno encountered her there while he commanded the 4th ID; a "fiercely antiwar expert on the Middle East," according to Ricks, she resisted his 2007 job offer initially but soon agreed; it would become a chemistry of opposites, and she would become one of Odierno's strongest defenders; *The Unraveling: High Hopes and Missed Opportunities in Iraq* (2015)
Ambassador Crocker's Embassy Staff	
Ambassador Ryan C. Crocker	Ambassador, Iraq; reassigned from post as ambassador to Pakistan; senior career Arabist in State Dept.; assignments to Lebanon, Kuwait, and Syria (as ambassador) from 1990 to 2001; Arabic and Farsi speaker; graduate studies at Princeton Univ.
Meghan L. O'Sullivan	Deputy national security advisor for Iraq and Afghanistan assigned by President Bush to return to Iraq in May 2007 to serve with Crocker; deputy director of the governance section of CPA, 2003–2004; involved in many key decisions relating to early transfer of sovereignty to the Iraqis and assisting the Iraqis in writing their interim constitution; also in 2006 a surge proponent; PhD, politics, Oxford Univ.; *Shrewd Sanctions: Statecraft and State Sponsors of Terrorism* (2003); edited volume (with Richard Haas), *Honey and Vinegar: Incentives, Sanctions, and Foreign Policy* (2000)
Patricia A. Butenis	Deputy chief of mission, a career Foreign Service officer reassigned from post as ambassador to Bangladesh and deputy chief of mission in Pakistan (under Crocker); MA, international relations, Columbia Univ.
Marcie B. Ries	Minister-counselor for political-military affairs overseeing liaison with coalition forces and security issues; multiple overseas postings; languages include Turkish, Spanish, and French; MA, international affairs, Johns Hopkins Univ.
Charles P. Ries	Coordinator for economic transition in Iraq at Embassy Baghdad; formerly ambassador to Greece; MA, international affairs, Johns Hopkins Univ.
Matthew H. Tueller	Political minister counselor; Arabist with previous assignments across the Middle East; MPP (MA, public policy), Harvard Univ., JFK School of Government
Philip T. Reeker	Counselor to the ambassador for public affairs; a career Foreign Service officer with multiple overseas postings; BA, Yale Univ., MBA, Thunderbird School of International Management
Phyllis M. Powers	Director of the Office of Provincial Affairs, oversight of all Provincial Reconstruction Teams; multiple postings across the Middle East

Many COIN experts believed that unity of command was vital to mission success. One model was the CORDS program in Vietnam, which combined military officers and civilians in the same chain of command. Although Petraeus decided against formal integration at the top, he initiated two important advances in unity of command at lower echelons. The military advisory teams assigned to each Iraqi battalion were placed under the operational control of the American brigade in charge of the area so that the two groups could be more tightly controlled and coordinated. The new Provincial Reconstruction Teams (PRTs) in Baghdad were also embedded at each brigade headquarters.[92]

Petraeus and Crocker became effective partners over 2007–2008, creating a close working relationship that was the converse of the dysfunctional relationship between General Sanchez and Ambassador Bremer after War III. They worked hard to achieve "unity of effort." As Ricks describes the chemistry, "Where Bremer had been a control freak, Crocker could be self-effacing. Where Sanchez dove into minutiae, Petraeus strove constantly to keep his head above water, to focus on the big picture."[93]

Petraeus's team began each day with the one-hour MNF-I Battlefield Update and Assessment (BUA) at 0730. The BUA was a large conference that included representatives from all the various staff sections and commands in Iraq, most of them participating via secure video teleconference. It would begin with staff updates of the preceding twenty-four hours on a broad range of subjects, including insurgent/terrorist attacks, media coverage of events, logistical statuses, progress (or lack thereof) on key pieces of Iraqi legislation, and the organization and training of Iraqi forces, as well as an exchange of information on dozens of other topics displayed on large video screens. Six days a week, Petraeus presided over the BUA in the al-Faw palace at Camp Victory (General Odierno's MNC-I HQ), the coalition military base near Baghdad International Airport. On Thursdays, Petraeus and his immediate staff would fly to the Green Zone to convene the BUA in the Republican Palace where a broader group from Embassy Baghdad could participate directly. Subjects would focus on nonsecurity issues such as oil production, electricity, agriculture, and other governmental functions in which the embassy had the lead. Whether the BUA was convened at Camp Victory or in the Green Zone, these two locations and many others were securely teleconferenced on large plasma screens, usually displaying briefing slides in PowerPoint. The BUA was one of the methods Petraeus used to oversee the complex political-military-economic battlefield of Iraq. "PowerPoint slides [now ubiquitous in both military and business environments] were tools to allow General Petraeus to drill down into issues, emphasize priorities, and impart guidance."[94]

Petraeus used the daily BUA as a much more proactive management tool than his predecessors had to elevate persistent problems. One example Robinson and Mansoor cite was the problem of restoring electrical power generation in Iraq at least to pre–Gulf War levels.[95] Power generation had fallen steadily in Iraq from 9,000 megawatts in 1991 at the end of War I to 4,400 at the start of War III. In the spring of 2007, Baghdad received power on average 8.4 hours per day and the rest of the country about 14.5 hours per day. Petraeus latched onto the case of Tower 57, a high-voltage power pylon in a rural area south of Baghdad that had been damaged in a recent attack and was a critical node in Baghdad's electrical grid. Fixing it required Iraqi workers to make repairs in a violent insurgent area without adequate security. It took months to repair Tower 57, finally requiring Petraeus to write a letter to Prime Minister Maliki suggesting that the electricity ministry was not doing its job. The pylon was finally repaired in September 2007. Petraeus knew the importance of making visible progress during the surge.

Another regular BUA agenda item was Colonel McMaster's Joint Strategic Assessment Team (JSAT). It was one of the first cooperative activities between Petraeus and Crocker to achieve a "unity of effort" as called for in the COIN FM 3-24 manual: to fuse the Embassy Baghdad and MNF-I staffs under the dual leadership of Petraeus and Crocker. The JSAT reviewed the strategic environment, assessed the evolving campaign plan on an ongoing basis, and recommended adjustments to it. Led by McMaster, it was staffed by two dozen senior officers and diplomats, including Colonel Harvey and David Kilcullen (table 27.1) and many other handpicked experts. The team focused on the key issues of War IV and challenged the assumptions on which the US and Iraqi governments were basing their strategy. They asked fundamental questions: What were the root causes of the insurgency and continuing violence? Was the Iraqi government essential to reducing the sectarian violence, or was it part of the problem? As Mansoor explained,

> one of the major outcomes of the JSAT was the lowering of the bar for what success in Iraq would look like. . . . Iraq had devolved into a low-grade civil war that would take a generation or more to resolve. Gone were visions of Jeffersonian democracy; they were replaced by the concept of "sustainable stability."[96]

The Petraeus-Crocker partnership established a routine of meeting jointly and regularly (at least once a week) with Prime Minister Maliki so they could broaden their partnership in unity of effort to include the Iraqi government from the top down.[97] Maliki was every inch a Shia politician who, left to his own devices, wanted to settle scores with Ba'athist Sunnis. In their meetings with Maliki, the general and ambassador would take turns sitting next to him. As Robinson describes their modus operandi,

> When Crocker finished presenting his agenda to the prime minister, he would switch places with Petraeus. They developed something of a "good-cop, bad-cop" routine. Crocker admitted that he played this card, telling Maliki or other Iraqi

leaders that "if you don't agree to this, you're going to have to deal with him," jerking his thumb in Petraeus' direction. Whereas Crocker was the model diplomat with a perpetually modulated voice, Petraeus had a sharper temperament that could turn fiery. Petraeus also confessed that he simulated anger on occasion, when he felt it would make his point more persuasively.[98]

Petraeus and Crocker doggedly pressed Maliki to make decisions that would benefit Sunnis in al Anbar Province where Colonel (now Lieutenant General) Sean B. MacFarland, the brigade commander in the capital city of Ramadi, had persuaded thirty-five Sunni tribes and subtribes to join the "Anbar Awakening." The formation of the Anbar Awakening, the grouping of Anbari tribes and former insurgents opposed to al Qa'ida's Taliban-like rule, traces back to 2006, when al Qa'ida in Iraq conducted its campaign of murder and intimidation throughout al Anbar Province. Sheikhs and their allies among the tribes and anti-AQI insurgent groups began forming alliances in the spring and summer of 2006. The tribal groups began working more closely with coalition forces and establishing ties with the Iraqi government.[99]

Petraeus recognized that steps had to be taken to institutionalize the progress in Anbar where attacks had averaged thirty to thirty-five per day in February 2007 and by summer averaged less than one per day. MacFarland had succeeded in getting eighteen thousand Anbaris to help US and Iraqi forces by getting them hired as police on CERP contracts. Anbar had undergone an extraordinary turnaround as a result of co-opting participation by local tribes, where al Qa'ida in Iraq violence against the local population had alienated virtually everyone. Three steps were necessary to integrate large numbers of Anbar's Sunni population into the security forces, many of whom had been former insurgents. First, Maliki had to agree to raise the official quota for Anbar's police force to twenty-one thousand. A second step was to give the Ramadi tribal sheikhs a role in the political process. A third was for the central government to open its financial coffers to the Anbar provincial government. Like most of the country's provinces, Anbar had received virtually none of its 2006 allocated funding because of the paralysis in forming Maliki's government; his ministries were barely functional. Petraeus worked to break this logjam, convincing Maliki that by agreeing to the three steps he could demonstrate a commitment by the central government to enfranchise Sunnis to select their own local leaders and give them resources to administer the province.

In Petraeus's mind, this approach was the only viable option to enable Maliki's government to broaden political reconciliation to the national level. He was piecing together the puzzle diagram, the "Anaconda" chart that he would display during a congressional hearing in the spring of 2008, reporting on the progress of the surge (figure 27.1). He envisioned that other pieces of the Iraqi governmental puzzle would join Anbar over the coming two years.

"You have some of the pieces in place in 2008, you get a few more in 2009. . . . They are not yet all united but at least you get [Iraqis who have] found ways to live with each other."[100] This was the way Iraqis could begin to resolve some of the bigger political issues about representation, sharing of oil revenues, and use of resources locally.

These steps were an adaptive departure from the COIN manual that had been published in December 2007, two months before Petraeus assumed command of MNF-I. Though a champion of the manual, Petraeus knew that its usefulness as a how-to playbook was more limited than was commonly thought. He personally believed that adaptive leadership was more important than adherence to specific doctrinal principles. The most difficult challenges lay not in identifying principles but in putting them into practice and making them successful. He observed, "The basic concepts and principles are not rocket science or brain surgery, but they can be very hard to apply."[101]

Generals Petraeus and Odierno launched the MNF-I Baghdad Security Plan (BSP) in February 2007. It emphasized the assignment of US troops to small American-Iraqi outposts, similar to those previously used in Tal Afar, Al Qaim, and Ramadi by Colonels McMaster and MacFarland. They dispersed the presurge soldiers away from the large, remote forward operating bases (FOBs) to joint security stations (JSSs) and combat outposts (COPs) located in Baghdad's neighborhoods. The contested, high-violence neighborhoods in the capital's northeastern and northwestern districts initially received the most attention during the first months.

In 2006, most American combat forces had been concentrated on the FOBs, from where they would "commute" to the contested zones and patrol violent areas. These operations were reactive rather than proactive, episodic rather than sustained and continuous. Rather than conducting COIN operations, they often relied on ineffective checkpoints. As a result, security for Iraqi residents in Baghdad increased or decreased throughout neighborhoods without ever lasting. The solution that Petraeus envisaged was embodied in the Baghdad Security Plan. Building on what General Casey had started during 2006, US forces had moved off their FOBs into Baghdad to construct smaller fortified positions in the neighborhoods. Petraeus expanded Casey's COIN concept by building and manning joint security stations and combat outposts throughout Baghdad's neighborhoods, along with Iraqi army and police personnel.[102]

Although the BSP's dispersion of large numbers of additional troops was consistent with two of the COIN FM 3-24 principles—that forces should be deployed across the population and that they should maintain a permanent presence—it ran contrary to a third: that the presence of foreign forces should be minimized (General Casey's concept of gradual disengagement) to promote host-nation self-reliance and forestall xenophobia.[103] By the beginning of 2007, many army and marine units were living among the people, patrolling on foot,

and engaging in numerous nonmilitary COIN activities, as they had been doing in some cases for several years. Petraeus changed the allocation of these
forces. He wanted American units involved more intensively in population
security because they outclassed most Iraqi units in initiative, resilience, and
respect for the population.

However, the commitment of forces locally was not the only aspect of the
surge. Petraeus wanted to control the military initiative and deny the insurgents and AQI sanctuary. Petraeus, Odierno, and their subordinate commanders assigned a substantial number of American troops, including many of the
arriving surge forces, to raids and sweeps against AQI hideouts and staging
areas. Some of these operations were large and "kinetic,"[104] involving multiple
battalions or brigades, in seeming contravention of COIN doctrine, which
viewed large military operations as inherently futile. FM 3-24 eschewed conventional military operations and firepower, yet Petraeus used both.

Colonel Gian P. Gentile, who commanded a combat battalion in Iraq in
2006 and later directed West Point's military history program, made the same
point in a trenchant critique of the COIN surge. He argued that there was
more operational continuity between General Casey's clear-and-hold strategy
and the Petraeus surge than is generally realized.

> The [COIN] triumph narrative pushes the notion that before the surge the
> American army had hunkered down on large bases, content to let the violence
> outside the wire soar. But then Petraeus arrives, and lectures his troops that we
> "can't commute to the fight." However, the narrative wrongly sensationalizes a
> purported change in operational method from being hunkered down on large
> bases to living among the population.[105]

The difference was not operational method. Kinetic and COIN clear-and-
hold operations had preceded Petraeus's arrival in Iraq. The difference was
in the changes the Bush administration made to the strategic architecture
in committing to the surge. The administration recognized that it needed a
realignment of its policy of regime change and a strategy for defeating the violence coupled with key staffing changes, including a new secretary of defense
(Gates) and a new commander of MNF-I (Petraeus).

By the spring and summer of 2007, MNF-I had launched multiple operations not only in and around Baghdad but also beyond the enemy-dominated
"Baghdad Belts" surrounding the city (map 27.1).[106] They began with shaping operations and an established presence in eastern Baqubah, thirty miles
northeast of Baghdad, in May. US forces began by taking control of terrain
from Baqubah to Balad in the Diyala River valley, from Tamiya north of
Baghdad on the Tigris to Fallujah west of Baghdad, and from the Euphrates
to the Tigris south of Baghdad.

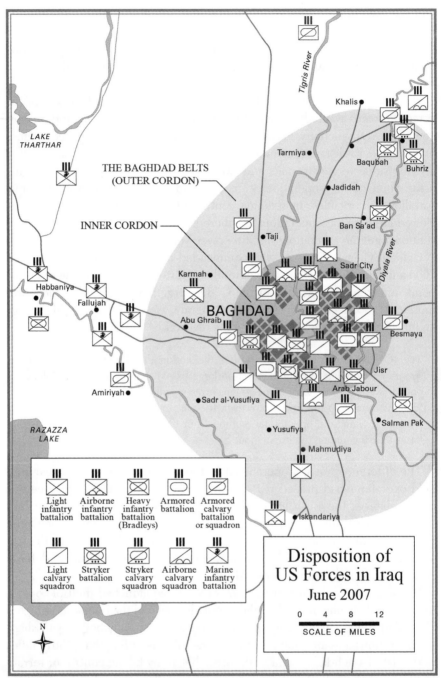

Map 27.1. MNF-I launched shaping operations around Baghdad against the enemy-dominated "Baghdad Belts" surrounding the city.

Source: Institute for the Study of War (ISW), http://www.understandingwar.org/iraq-project/maps.

This shaping of the large battle space around Baghdad then resulted in the launch of Operation *Phantom Thunder* in two phases, the first to clear Baqubah, Arab Jabour, Fallujah, and the Doura neighborhood of Baghdad between June 15 and July 15, 2007, followed by the second phase to take control of the Mahmudiya–Musayyib highway south of Baghdad with forces clearing Karma between Fallujah and Baghdad and maintaining security in Baqubah and its environs (map 27.1).[107]

At the conclusion of *Phantom Thunder*, Iraqi and coalition forces had conducted 142 battalion-level joint operations. They had detained 6,702 suspects, killed 1,196 insurgents, wounded 419 others, and killed or captured 382 high-value targets. Additionally, they found and neutralized more than two thousand IEDs and VBIEDs and discovered 1,113 weapons caches.[108]

Operation *Phantom Strike* followed *Phantom Thunder* on August 13, with offensives in the north to clear the Diyala River valley to Lake Hamrin and strike insurgents along the Tigris and between the Tigris and Zaab Rivers. In the south, MNF-I forces attacked insurgents from Salman Pak to Suwayrah and in Diwaniya and Karbala.[109] The synchronicity of these larger-scale military operations was designed to complement security operations within Baghdad itself where the real surge was about to get underway in June (map 27.2). During the first half of 2007, Petraeus and Odierno had been conducting the shaping operations around Baghdad because al Qa'ida in Iraq had attacked the capital repeatedly with IEDs and VBIEDs to undermine American and Iraqi forces and break the will of the Maliki government. As long as AQI could maintain its support in the Baghdad Belts, it could continue to conduct its lethal car-bombing campaign. AQI had conducted a spectacular attack in west Baghdad's Mansour district in February, killing sixteen and wounding forty. There was another particularly violent suicide bomb attack at the historic Mutanabi book *souq* (market) in central Baghdad's Karkh district in March near the Green Zone, killing forty and wounding more than one hundred.[110] There were more car bomb attacks in the turbulent neighborhoods of Doura in eastern Rashid. During February and March, as part of the initial execution of the Baghdad Security Plan, units had erected temporary concrete security barriers to control vehicle traffic, reduce the likelihood of car bombings, and revive neighborhood economies that had flourished in earlier periods during War IV before sectarian violence had overtaken them. The construction of a similar concrete barrier wall around the Adhamiyah neighborhood in northern Baghdad in April and May contributed to the security of east Baghdad. In March and April, AQI focused its VBIED attacks against the Shia population in Sadr City.

The initial goals of the Baghdad Security Plan were to fragment AQI operations simultaneously inside the Baghdad Belts and in the city itself. AQI's bombing campaign relied on an extensive support network outside the city to supply stolen and stripped vehicles and to operate VBIED bomb-making

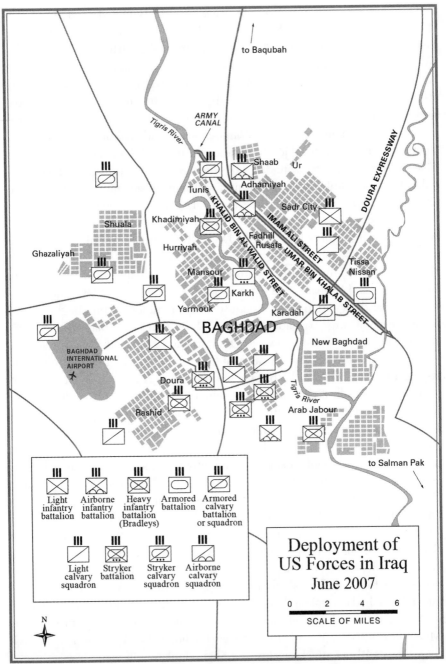

Map 27.2. The real surge began inside Baghdad during June 2007 where nearly seventy joint security stations and combat outposts were located and manned by MNF-I forces in Baghdad's neighborhoods.

Source: Institute for the Study of War (ISW), http://www.understandingwar.org/iraq-project/maps.

shops. Petraeus and Odierno, along with their deployed brigade and battalion commanders, were determined to disrupt the enemy's mobility in the network of roadways, rivers, and other LOCs in Baghdad's inner and outer belts out to a thirty-mile radius around the city.

In the southern arc of belts, al Qa'ida had been able to operate across an arc southeast along the Euphrates to the Tigris, often by boat, from Fallujah to Sadi al-Yusifiya to Mahmudiya. Coalition forces had cleared Mahmudiya during the winter months, but AQI and *Jaish al-Mahdi* (JAM), Shia cleric Moqtada al-Sadr's Iraqi paramilitary Mahdi Army, continued to combat one another for control of these areas of the city.[111] The southern arc through which AQI infiltrated used the canals in the farmlands stretching from Mahmudiya toward Salman Pak, fifteen miles south of Baghdad where no US forces had been stationed for three years before the surge brigades arrived. Salman Pak had become an AQI stronghold, so US surge forces targeted car bomb factories there during the first half of 2007. By reducing the number of factories, MNF-I could begin to disrupt the routes AQI used to channel bombs, terrorists, and weapons north from Salman Pak to Sadr City.

This encirclement of the city by MNF-I battalions was the most significant military development during the first six months of the surge. It enabled more discrete operations to secure individual neighborhoods, accompanied by the fanning out of troops into Baghdad. From February through June, five of the surge brigades deployed within Baghdad, concentrated on some of the most violent areas (avoiding Sadr City), hardened vehicle routes, and then built and inhabited nearly seventy joint security stations and combat outposts located in Baghdad's neighborhoods by the end of 2007. The combat outposts required foresight, planning, and combat engineering to make them viable and defensible. They included vehicle barriers and guard towers; as the surge progressed, more outposts were equipped with Rapid Aerostat Initial Deployment (RAID) towers and aerostats (helium-filled dirigibles tethered to the ground) in which were mounted daylight cameras and forward-looking infrared (FLIR) thermal-imaging devices to put more of the city's neighborhoods under continuous surveillance.[112]

Robinson describes the experience of a Stryker brigade that conducted clearing operations in Mansour and Amiriyah. The 3rd Stryker Brigade Combat Team, 2nd ID, was commanded by Colonel Stephen J. Townsend (later lieutenant general).[113] Half of the soldiers in this unit had gained experience during their first tour in Mosul in 2004–2005. Now, in their second tour, battalions in Townsend's brigade conducted clearing operations in Shaab and Ur, opening up JSSs and COPs. Once the local residents saw that the Americans were there to stay, to help and to control the Iraqi forces and police, often living with them side by side, Townsend's soldiers began to pick up useful intelligence tips about where insurgents could be found. It was a protracted, often building-by-building process, but it produced results. They destroyed abandoned houses where homemade explosives were being manufactured and raided another where thousands of electronic components were found that were assembled for making IEDs and VBIEDs.[114] It was a start.

Soldiers in Colonel Townsend's brigade used the automated FBCB2 (Force XXI Battle Command Brigade and Below), a networked, secure, wireless command-and-control system, accessible from computer laptops used for receipt and use of graphics, overlays, and threat data provided by unmanned aerial vehicles and other intelligence sources. They also carried HIDE (Handheld Interagency Identification Detection Equipment), which enabled soldiers to take photographs, fingerprints, and biometric (retinal) scans of young men, enabling the unit to create a registry of military-age males in insurgent areas. The FBCB2 and Biometric Automated Toolsets enabled intelligent use of state-of-the-art technologies to learn about the populations they were protecting and to reduce combat risk.

Another army battalion, with a long history of service dating back to the Indian Wars, World Wars I and II, Vietnam, and the Balkans, was one of the first to pull a fifteen-month extended tour. It was the 1st Battalion, 26th Infantry Regiment, the 1-26, known as the Blue Spaders, commanded by Lieutenant Colonel Eric O. Schacht (later colonel), a taciturn, unflappable, hands-on officer who knew every soldier in his battalion. The Blue Spaders found themselves entering an "inferno" when they were assigned to secure the Adhamiyah district in northern Baghdad. They had arrived in-country in August 2006, initially deploying daily from two FOBs on the southeast edge of the city (FOBs Rustamiyah and Loyalty) to Adhamiyah. In April 2006, Shia militias had attacked Sunnis in Adhamiyah, who found themselves under siege. "The once-proud neighborhood was a portrait of dilapidation and destruction. Gracious buildings were pockmarked with bullet holes, especially around the mosque where the fiercest fighting [had] occurred. . . . An average of ten dead bodies turned up on the streets each day."[115] One company of the 1-26 moved into Combat Outpost Apache, a small compound on the banks of the Tigris where an Army Special Forces team had been the lone US presence since 2003. The rest of the battalion suffered casualties on the dangerous daily commute from the FOBs; eleven soldiers were killed, mostly by EFPs (explosively formed penetrators, which the Iranians had been supplying to the Shia militias).

The 1-26 was confronting the violent militias that were consuming Adhamiyah. Midway into its tour, in early 2007, the 1-26 had become a combat-hardened battalion engaged in repeated firefights to protect contractors, repel attacks on JSSs and COPs, and engage in the painstaking, intelligence-driven hunt for AQI and rogue Shia militias. They faced the panoply of urban threats, including elements of Moqtada al-Sadr's *Jaish al-Mahdi* militia, because

Adhamiyah was contiguous with Sadr City. As 1-26 companies and platoons attacked the AQI network in Adhamiyah in March, the battalion was also overseeing and protecting the construction of a wall of twelve-foot concrete barriers around the entire neighborhood.

When it was completed, six kilometers (nearly four miles) of barriers ran along the eastern and southern borders of Adhamiyah to protect the population from Shia militia attacks. The wall was controversial, but it was an adaptive, desperate approach because it was the one tactic that had not yet been tried to stem the enemy's bombing campaign. It had an immediate and visible effect on reducing Iraqi deaths: the number of dead bodies declined to two a week from the daily average of ten. The Adhamiyah wall and the constant patrolling reduced the violence in the surrounding areas because the Sunnis who had left Adhamiyah to fight the encroaching JAM militias were now unable to move freely. Car bombings also abated dramatically.

In early May, one 1-26 platoon was on patrol in a small convoy of Humvees that drove into an ambush set up by the enemy with an IED explosion. This triggered a firefight requiring medevac helicopters to evacuate the wounded. A highly regarded NCO died of his wounds, others were grievously wounded and burned, and the entire platoon entered a mental health clinic to recover from the shock. 1-26 platoons started patrolling in Bradley infantry fighting vehicles, the army's tank-like, nearly twenty-eight-ton armored personnel carrier. On a patrol in June, the enemy detonated a deeply buried IED directly underneath a Bradley with such force that an entire street appeared to have been blown up, tossing the Bradley into the air and flipping it upside down where it caught fire. The effect stunned everyone. A combat-loaded Bradley weighs thirty-five tons with its stock of munitions and special reactive armor tiles. Again, medical rescue and reinforcement efforts produced more casualties; a Humvee was hit by an IED.[116]

Petraeus, who had been monitoring the 1-26's increasing casualties, knew that Lieutenant Colonel Schacht's battalion was in the inferno; he attended the memorial service for the dead. The carnage affected the entire battalion. Bradleys had been regarded as invincible, having performed effectively in previous operations in Sadr City, the Blackwater contractor recovery battle, and countless other missions. Now the 1-26 felt naked. Yet they continued to patrol. Eventually there was a turning point in the battle for Adhamiyah when two relatives of a prominent sheikh were killed. This sheikh had been an imam at the Abu Hanifa mosque, preaching resistance to Americans for years. He had been on the Americans' list of "bad guys" since Colonel Peter Mansoor's (in 2007–2008 Petraeus's executive officer on his second tour) brigade of the 1st ID had patrolled Adhamiyah in 2003–2004. When insurgents refused to allow the sheikh to bury his relatives at the Abu Hanifa cemetery, the outraged sheikh denounced the "terrorists" being harbored at the mosque. As a result, eighty members of the sheikh's clan forced their way into the grounds of the mosque. A melee broke out, and a responding Iraqi army unit discovered a massive cache of small arms, mortars, rockets, mines, IEDs, and explosives.

It surprised no one that the sheikh was the uncle of the Iraqi general who was directing the Baghdad Security Plan in the eastern half of the city. The sheikh's home was bombed a few days later and he was seriously wounded, and three more of his relatives were killed. The mosque's chief imam fled to Syria. A guest imam arrived and adopted a far less belligerent tone. By late August, there was a trickle of Sunni volunteers who came forward to work as security guards on CERP contracts. They had shunned Colonel Schacht's earlier attempts to recruit them into the Iraqi army, but the CERP effort at engagement meant recruits could remain in Adhamiyah. The first thirty were put through a training course at Combat Outpost Apache. The platoon that had taken the casualties in the Humvee convoy ambush in May was now patrolling the area around the mosque. Bomb factories, militia members, and insurgents continued to be found, but the population in the area started extending traditional Iraqi hospitality to the soldiers who came to ask questions and search their homes because the residents knew the violence was being reduced by their presence.

By the end of the 1-26 Blue Spaders' tour of fifteen months, they became the first active-duty unit to serve the full extended tour, necessitated by the surge. Nearly every day, there was a combat patrol. Of Schacht's eight-hundred-man battalion, 35 had been killed and 122 wounded, three times the casualty rate of the 1-26's previous deployment in 2004–2005. It was the highest casualty rate any battalion had suffered since the Vietnam War. Six soldiers had lost one or both legs, and many more would suffer lifelong injuries. This combat tour in Baghdad caused an exponential increase in stress and the potential for PTSD (posttraumatic stress disorder) upon return to the CONUS. The battalion worked hard to prepare the men for the return. Robinson's book offers two chapters of moving combat narratives of units like Schacht's. They are not breezy reading. Petraeus agreed with Robinson that

Adhamiyah was probably the toughest nut to crack in all of Baghdad. He shared the officers' [of the 1-26] skepticism about whether a local peace was possible there. "It seemed to have an extremist fervor to it that other areas didn't have," he said. "It was such a tough place to get established in. We had to fight to get the JSS in, and fight AQ [al Qa'ida] continually. They were very hard core, very resilient. It really appeared to be one of those areas, candidly, where you wonder if you can solve it with the resources you have."[117]

Petraeus's comment about Adhamiyah reflected seemingly contradictory aspects implicit in his COIN strategy: "You can't kill your way out of an insurgency," a phrase he would use repeatedly. The flip side to this assertion is that there are some combatants who are so extreme that there is no alternative but to kill them. Another recurring term was *kinetic*, the euphemistic adjective he used with some frequency in public and during congressional testimony in the fall of 2007 to explain the necessity of larger-scale combat operations—what Race a generation earlier identified as the "reinforcement" strategy in Vietnam.[118]

By the summer of 2007, both General Petraeus and Ambassador Crocker knew that they faced a political reckoning with Congress. In May, Congress had passed a war-funding bill that required the Bush administration to report by September 15, 2007, whether eighteen benchmarks were being met in Iraq.[119] This legislation set a clock ticking in Washington to produce tangible results or declare the surge a failure. There was another clock ticking in Baghdad where Petraeus and Crocker needed to buy time to create the necessary military and political conditions inside Iraq to show that the surge strategy was making headway on Iraqi governance, the economy, provincial reconstruction, and above all sectarian reconciliation.

The *Initial Benchmark Assessment Report* made public in July indicated that "unsatisfactory progress" had been made on ten of the eighteen benchmarks, including the most important items on the political-reconciliation agenda. The report bluntly stated that sectarian behavior was rife within the top levels of the Maliki government. It found

> sectarian bias in the appointment of senior military and police commanders, which in turn gives rise to suspicions that political considerations may be behind Iraqi commanders' decisions on which operations to undertake or support. Prime Minister Maliki is willing to take action when evidence of this is clear. Seven of nine National Police Brigade Commanders and sixteen battalion commanders have been relieved in the past seven months due to concerns over sectarian activities.[120]

Throughout the summer, political pressure was mounting in Washington for Petraeus to recommend an end to the surge in September.

Since June, Petraeus and Odierno had been analyzing what they described as the "battlefield geometry"[121] in weekly meetings, along with their chiefs of plans and operations, including Colonels Rapp and Meese. The statistics on sectarian violence had not changed appreciably during the first six months of the surge, and although they dropped off somewhat in July, they were still nearly double the average number of daily attacks during 2004–2005. The first significant change in the trend of a downward slope would appear only after the August data had been collected and analyzed. The August data were not available in time to be included in the initial government and congressional reports, but Petraeus testified to the positive reduction in the sectarian violence shown in the August data as we shall see.

There was a battle inside the government during August over the substance and recommendations that were to be presented in Petraeus and Crocker's report. General Pace and the Joint Staff wanted a quick drawdown and transition to noncombat missions. General Casey, by then elevated to the position of army chief of staff, had made his antisurge views known to Congress. The CENTCOM commander, Admiral William J. Fallon, also strongly advocated a substantial drawdown.

In late August, Petraeus gave his presentation to Secretary Gates, who

> was also personally in favor of a drawdown on a more modest path, but he was not inclined to overrule Petraeus. The views of Petraeus, as commander on the ground, should carry enormous weight, the secretary believed. But he also believed that CENTCOM and the Joint Staff should be heard directly by the president, so he constructed a process that allowed each to have his say.[122]

On August 31, Petraeus presented his case to President Bush. The previous night, in an unplanned session, Admiral Fallon had flown to Washington and presented his position to the president, arguing that the US Armed Forces should not take on more risk in Iraq. He believed Petraeus's approach was too cautious about the pace of withdrawal and that a mission change would force an accelerated withdrawal. Toward the end of the two-hour meeting the next day at the White House, with General Petraeus, the Joint Chiefs, Secretary Gates, Admiral Fallon, and other National Security Council principals present, the president asked Fallon during the last ten minutes of the meeting if he had anything else to add. Fallon "repeated his view about having a different risk calculus and said he was concerned about other [unspecified] contingencies."[123] The president listened but endorsed Petraeus's recommendations. President Bush and General Petraeus, even eight months into the surge, were still having to work to keep the military chain of command, including Petraeus's CENTCOM boss, Admiral Fallon, aligned with the administration's Iraq policy, the surge strategy, and MNF-I operations in Iraq.

The release of the Government Accountability Office (GAO) report about Iraq a week before Petraeus and Crocker were scheduled to testify before congressional committees did not report promising statistics on one of the key benchmark parameters, the reduction of sectarian violence: "The average number of daily attacks against civilians remained about the same over the last six months [February–July 2007]."[124] The GAO relied on the same data as MNF-I, but it included data only through July. A sharp decline in violence only occurred when the August data were included, but the GAO published its report without this information to meet a publication deadline.

Moreover, the GAO report assessed that only seven of the eighteen benchmarks had been met, whereas the administration's assessment reported that ten had been met.[125]

The congressional testimony by General Petraeus and Ambassador Crocker in September 2007 was unprecedented in the annals of World War II, Korea, Vietnam, or Iraqi Wars I–III. Generals Eisenhower, MacArthur, Ridgway, Westmoreland, Abrams, Schwarzkopf, and Franks had never been summoned to Washington as theater commanders in the middle of major combat operations and subjected to such intensive questioning by members of Congress.[126] The legislative atmosphere had not been promising for months. At a press conference on April 19, 2007, Senate Majority Leader Harry Reid declared, "I believe myself that the secretary of state, secretary of defense and—you have to make your own decisions as to what the president knows—[know] this war is lost and the surge is not accomplishing anything."[127] A week after Senator Reid's remarks, General Petraeus presented a preliminary report on the surge in classified testimony to the House and Senate. Colonel Mansoor accompanied Petraeus and observed the following:

> As usual, I sat directly behind him as he discussed the situation in Iraq with U.S. lawmakers. Although they were respectful to him in the closed sessions away from the glare of TV cameras and reporters, it was clear that many lawmakers, like Senator Reid, had already made up their minds concerning the fate of the U.S. war effort in Iraq. It was somewhat amusing to hear a few of the congressmen and senators give what amounted to stump speeches for and against the war, until reminded by their peers that there were no reporters present.[128]

This was the backdrop to the congressional demand for a public accounting of the surge in September. The legacies of Vietnam had taken the demands for military accountability within both the executive and legislative branches of government to a whole new level of scrutiny. Mansoor quoted journalist Mark Bowden: "It was an inquisition."[129]

The heated political debate over the surge peaked on the first day of Petraeus's testimony when MoveOn.org, the antiwar group, bought a full-page advertisement in the *New York Times* with the headline "General Petraeus or General Betray Us? Cooking the Books for the White House," citing the GAO report. While congressmen and senators repeatedly distanced themselves from any association with the MoveOn.org advertisement, Petraeus and Crocker still found themselves subjected to blunt questions and unpleasant remarks. New York senator Hillary R. Clinton declared, "Despite what I view as your rather extraordinary efforts in your testimony both yesterday and today, I think that the reports that you provide to us really require the willing suspension of disbelief. In any of the metrics that have been referenced in your many hours of testimony, any fair reading of the advantages and disadvantages accruing post-surge, in my view, end up on the downside."[130] Petraeus and Crocker accepted this mauling with equanimity. Both remained unfailingly phlegmatic and responded with data-driven answers. Crocker did not try to sugarcoat the reality that there had been no major breakthroughs in political reconciliation among Iraq's warring sectarian factions. But he did assert, "The cumulative trajectory is upwards but the curve is not steep. . . . I cannot guarantee success but I believe it is attainable."[131]

The hearings were televised gavel to gavel on the public broadcasting networks, and highlights were shown repeatedly on the major commercial news channels. People were impressed by their calm demeanor and deferential, professional bearing, if not, perhaps, convinced by the substance. Their performance was a triumph of sangfroid. They were educating the American public that the surge was moving in the right direction. In short, the public reacted favorably to the performance, accepting it for what it was: masterful. Petraeus and Crocker had bought themselves, and the Bush administration, some more time. They had rebalanced the Washington-Baghdad clocks, at least for another six months until their next scheduled testimony. Both gave numerous media interviews after the hearings concluded. Petraeus gave a press conference at the National Press Club followed by twenty-three more interviews before returning to his command.

As Petraeus and Crocker returned to Iraq, the momentum of the surge continued to shift favorably. Insurgent attacks entered into a steep decline, falling from 180 per day in June to 60 per day in November 2007, with Baghdad and al Anbar showing the largest drops in violence. One reason for this dramatic change was that the MNF-I troop surge, with the arrival of all combat brigades completed in June, enabled MNF-I to conduct more offensive operations and population security operations in the Baghdad area. Another reason was an increase in initiative and determination among Iraqi Security Force leaders, the result of command changes that the Americans had pushed the Maliki government to make. Under assault virtually everywhere, AQI contracted rapidly in the second half of the year, allowing MNF-I and the ISF to devote more resources to combating the Shiite militias. The arrest and killing of significant numbers of Mahdi Army or JAM militiamen led to Maliki's repudiation of the Mahdi Army. That threatened Moqtada al-Sadr's political position with respect to influencing the government, so Sadr ordered Mahdi Army units to stop fighting because he calculated that he could get more through political action than military confrontation. Not all units obeyed, but during the final months of 2007, the Shiite militias had to abandon control of much of Baghdad to MNF-I and ISF forces.

As General Keane had predicted in the Oval Office meeting in December 2006, the surge was purchased at a price: 901 members of the US military died in Iraq during 2007, the highest annual casualty count since the war began. Thousands of Iraqis had also died. The rate of Iraqi deaths peaked during the spring and early summer months and then started to decline steadily. By the end of the year, overall attacks were down by more than 60 percent over the preceding nine months, and civilian deaths were 72 percent lower over the preceding seven months. The total number of IED incidents followed a similar trajectory over the same time period.[132]

Security continued to improve in the first quarter of 2008. In March, the Maliki government faced a crucial test in the south. In the southern city of Basra, where armed criminals and militias were running out of control against local police through threats and repeated attacks, Maliki sent ISF units from other parts of the country to reestablish control, triggering intense fighting, especially in neighborhoods dominated by Sadr's Mahdi Army. Initially, some of the forces sent by Maliki fought poorly or refused to fight at all because their officers were weak or were sympathetic to the groups they had been ordered to suppress. Determined to prevail, Maliki traveled to Basra himself. He fired 1,300 soldiers and policemen, including thirty-seven senior officers, for their unwillingness to engage. The Americans helped identify those deserving of removal, drawing upon reports from US intelligence agencies and advisory teams including the PRTs. Maliki, with extensive American advice, intelligence, and logistical support, succeeded by installing more effective combat commanders and drawing upon the best-led Iraqi units from around the country. They pushed into the city and killed enough of the insurgents to convince the survivors to negotiate an end to the fighting.[133]

In their second round of congressional testimony on April 8–9, 2008, General Petraeus and Ambassador Crocker presented a case that significant progress had been made. Violence had declined at least 70 percent since the summer of 2007, but Petraeus acknowledged that this progress was still "fragile and reversible." This assertion was intended as a hedge against pressure to reduce troop levels. Petraeus wanted force levels to remain at fifteen combat brigades (about 140,000 troops) until mid-September 2008. Army chief of staff General Casey had become even more vocal about the need to decrease troop levels to reduce stress on the army. Admiral Fallon, the CENTCOM commander, continued to speak openly about the need for forces for other missions and contingencies in the Middle East. However, on March 11, 2008, Admiral Fallon abruptly resigned after an article appeared in *Esquire* that painted him as the main bulwark against administration hawks lobbying for a military strike on Iran to neutralize its nuclear weapons program. The Iran contretemps may have been the trigger, but the Petraeus-Fallon tensions had been building for over a year.[134]

During the hearings, most legislators did not dispute that progress had been made, although many believed that the gains were ephemeral. Then senator Barack H. Obama asked Petraeus and Crocker whether their definition of success was unrealistic. Petraeus replied that neither he nor Ambassador Crocker was holding out for "Jeffersonian democracy." Crocker added, "I think that when Iraq gets to the point that . . . they can drive it [governance] forward themselves without significant danger of having the whole thing slip away from them again, then, clearly, our profile, our presence diminishes markedly." Members of Congress were asking a question Petraeus himself had raised during his first tour in 2003: "Tell me how this ends." The war would end, in Petraeus's and Crocker's minds, "when the Iraqi competition over power and resources had been resolved."[135]

In 2007–2008, the conflict in Iraq had undergone a major shift as a result of the surge. The leadership of Petraeus and Crocker was a discriminator because of their knowledge, determination, and the way they deployed military and diplomatic personnel. Petraeus introduced strategic and tactical innovations to fighting War IV flowing from the broad principles in the COIN manual: the increase in manpower and the deployment of combat brigades and battalions into Baghdad's urban neighborhoods. These actions led to a chain of events that were positive: the painstaking development of better local intelligence, which in turn enabled direct outreach to the armed insurgents. The kinetic catalyst was often operations that the COIN conventional wisdom eschewed: the simultaneous conduct of large-scale combat operations in the Baghdad Belts and beyond into the Tigris, Euphrates, and Diyala River valleys. These operations had been designed to push Sunni insurgents, Shiite militiamen, and Sadrists in the Mahdi Army out of areas where they could intensify violence. Simultaneous with the military effort, Crocker's Embassy Baghdad staff worked hard to field effective PRTs.[136]

The insertion of thirty thousand combat troops in the surge brigades along with PRT enablers was the measurable input of the surge. So was the addition of one hundred thousand new Iraqi soldiers and policemen into the areas of conflict. However, the way in which this manpower was employed was much more important than the numbers. Each battalion and company made it a priority to develop relationships with local Iraqis and to reach out to "reconcilable antagonists." Petraeus spent considerable time with battalion and company commanders empowering them to make pragmatic deals with Iraqi insurgents when they could, to wade into the local politics of tribal and local council meetings, and to offer, often with CERP funds, to put many former insurgents on their security payrolls. As Robinson describes this approach, "The measure most directly responsible for reducing violence was the recruitment of 73,000 volunteers. It literally turned enemies into allies, increasing the number of those providing security and intelligence and decreasing the ranks of those fighting against the Americans and the Iraq government and supporting the insurgency overtly or tacitly."[137]

These kinds of measures were a significant departure from the CORDS and Phoenix playbook in Vietnam a generation earlier. Here, combat-hardened US soldiers were being directed and encouraged by Petraeus to meet with sheikhs, imams, and other local intermediaries where the objective was to recruit young, military-age males onto the government side in the conflict. In many cases, they were offering paid work but also protection and recognition. In effect, the Americans in many of the JSS and COP outposts were placing themselves between the warring parties and absorbing the brunt of the violence until the warring factions decided to take a risk and use their weapons in furtherance of effective local governance. Combat units focused their actions on working with people as they found them in Baghdad's neighborhoods, talking to them, and drawing them back into their communities. Instead of sweeps and searches that inevitably alienated local residents, they worked to build confidence among local Iraqis by living in their midst, sharing the same daily risks. This kind of presence started producing intelligence that units could use more directly. Most important, Petraeus tried to impress upon everyone in MNF-I that staying in local neighborhoods, often in isolated outposts where "life outside the wire" was totally and dangerously different than life on a forward operating base, ensured that insurgent groups and militias could not easily return and start intimidating those areas again. This approach, as it intensified in the summer and fall of 2007, created the window of opportunity that few presurge skeptics would have thought possible. Petraeus and Crocker worked in 2008 to exploit it.

Petraeus and Crocker had been working since January 2008 to convince Maliki to pass national reconciliation legislation. Their tenacity broke the stalemate between the American and Iraqi governments on this issue; they had mounted a full-court press. Petraeus had directed the MNF-I staff to track the process of this legislation through the Iraqi parliament. He enlisted Sadi Othman, his translator and advisor (table 27.1), in this effort, in effect to act as a vote counter and where needed to persuade legislators to support it.[138] Directing this kind of political and lobbying activity is very unusual for a general operating in the field, but Petraeus's experience from his two prior tours in Iraq where he intensively engaged with Iraqi officials and politicians in the field made it a natural task for him to perform. Other legislative accomplishments included the provincial-powers statute, an amnesty bill, and the 2008 budget, all monitored and bundled together into another milestone in February 2008.[139] Both Petraeus and Crocker were looking toward more favorable reporting on meeting more of the eighteen benchmarks.

They started discussions with the Maliki government on a status-of-forces agreement. They knew that Iraqis in the government were eager for the United States to provide a security blanket during and after the critical period of the surge. They also knew that the Iraqis wanted to maximize their control over the US forces that remained in Iraq. There remained the very sensitive issue of whether the United States would allow its military personnel to be subject to Iraqi jurisdiction rather than US federal law in cases of troop misconduct. This issue festered for several more years without satisfactory resolution.

Iraqi security forces were growing substantially during this period. Some eight hundred army officers were graduating every six months as part of an overall plan to increase Iraq's total armed forces to 580,000 by the end of 2008 and later to 640,000. Similarly, the national police organization was getting an overdue overhaul. Over the previous two-year period, all of the national police brigade commanders and seventeen of the twenty-seven battalion commanders had been replaced. There had been a purge of eighteen thousand lower-level police officials as well.

By June 2008, Iraq was a much calmer society than it had been since April 2004. War IV was not over, but it had reached a new stage. Petraeus, with Crocker's help, pulled Iraq back from the brink of a civil war and created an opportunity for the next administration "to bring the war to a soft landing."[140]

CONCLUSIONS

General Petraeus's COIN doctrine and its adaptation by his command of MNF-I supported by Ambassador Crocker's strengthened Embassy Baghdad staff were the leadership discriminators that produced the dramatic turnaround of the surge by 2008. Petraeus's planning and execution of the surge, the adaptability and pragmatism he encouraged among his brigade-and-below combat commanders, and the calculated and focused deployment of brigades and battalions in the belts around Baghdad and beyond enabled the military turnaround. Petraeus and Crocker undertook a full-scale, interagency mobilization of in-country resources by matching the requisite staffing expertise, knowledge, and technical and political skills of their subordinates to practical accomplishments that could directly enable sectarian reconciliation to begin.

As War IV grew in violence, President Bush was finally wise enough to absorb the realistic counsel he received from retired senior military officers like General Keane. What is most interesting about events as they unfolded in 2006 and 2007 is how a group of officers in the US Army and Marine Corps had educated themselves in a new generation of COIN principles to take responsibility for planning and executing the surge. They became known as "COINinistas," a term not intended to be complimentary. Fred Kaplan describes the proponents of COIN as engaged in a "battle of ideas" with army traditionalists.

The stakes were very high. It was no longer an esoteric quarrel over history and theory, but a struggle whose outcome meant life or death, victory or defeat. . . . It was a battle for how the Pentagon does business and how America goes to war.[141]

The doctrinal debate within the army is an ongoing and complex one. Colonel Gentile is one of the most informed and articulate among those who challenge COIN on its historical merits. Gentile, a Stanford PhD in history, published his own scholarly work in 2013 that argues that COIN and nation building in Iraq and Afghanistan constitute a "myth."

It is entirely possible . . . that if President Bush had never appointed General Petraeus as commander in Iraq but had kept General Casey in command, violence would have declined in the same way that it did in 2007. This conclusion is based on extending the trajectory of the conditions that were already developing—the Sunni Awakening and the climax of sectarian violence in 2006. Because Casey was not advocating a quick withdrawal from Iraq and because the operational framework for the military in Iraq before 2007 was and continued to be counterinsurgency, it is certainly possible that the level of violence would have fallen in the same way as it did after the actual Petraeus surge. Extending this hypothetical to Afghanistan, it is also entirely possible that without the surge triumph narrative constructed around Petraeus' surge and the mythical belief that COIN worked in Iraq, the discussions [about Afghanistan] . . . might have been tempered by focusing on other, more limited options. . . . American strategy has failed [writing twenty-two pages later about Afghanistan] because it has become trapped by the promise that counterinsurgency can work if only it is given enough time and tactical tweaking. But in war, time is a factor in the overall calculation of strategy, and lots and lots of time is needed for American counterinsurgency to succeed in Afghanistan.[142]

Colonel Gentile is certainly correct about the time factor in strategic architectures. General Petraeus and Ambassador Crocker could not bring the Iraqi War IV to a victorious conclusion on their watches alone. But they believed that they had created the conditions for a successful geopolitical endgame. Gentile indicated that Secretary Gates's successor, Charles T. "Chuck" Hagel, took "a cautionary view of the use of American power to transform foreign societies—a notable change from the dominant view of counterinsurgency."[143]

The Brookings Iraq Index pointed to positive security, economic, and quality-of-life indicators: that war-related violence "declined more than tenfold," electricity production increased to seven thousand megawatts from a prewar level of four thousand megawatts, and that GDP had increased nearly eightfold to $108 billion in 2011 from $14 billion in 2003.[144]

By 2011, the Obama administration's Iraq policy was the decision to withdraw all military combat forces from that country by the end of 2011. This decision represented Obama's fulfillment of a 2008 campaign promise to end the war in Iraq. It did not end the war. There remained serious political and military issues that needed to be resolved.

Prime Minister Maliki's coalition government in the wake of the postsurge parliamentary elections remained a weak one. Negotiating a status-of-forces agreement with the Americans apparently was beyond either Maliki's own policy preferences or was too difficult to get through a contentious legislative process. When it became clear that Iraqi politicians, with long memories mindful of the residual Iraqi anger over American abuses at Abu Ghraib prison and elsewhere, could not publicly approve of letting American soldiers have immunity from arrest, as any American administration negotiating status-of-forces agreements since the 1950s would insist, the talks broke down, and plans for a rapid and complete withdrawal began in earnest.

Like the ARVN in 1972–1975, the Iraqi army was not a fully integrated, combined-arms force that could defend Iraq's sovereignty without foreign help. Its officers were still not demonstrably skilled in multidivision, multiechelon operations, much less COIN principles. Its logistical capability was limited and dependent on American support. The same was true of its capability in the air. Its police units were still in need of major reform, training, and internal discipline and control.

The Economist pointed out after the Obama withdrawal decision was announced, "Those with most to lose from the withdrawal may be American diplomats, who are engaged in the biggest military-to-civilian switch since the time of the Marshall Plan in Europe after the second world war."[145] Embassy Baghdad in 2011 was the largest in the world, employing sixteen thousand people, including nearly five thousand private contractors to take the place of US Armed Forces in securing the embassy, training the Iraqi military, and providing secure convoys for diplomats and helping to supply PRT members who continued, at reduced numbers, to work in most of Iraq's eighteen provinces.[146] Another consequence was that the State Department took over, also in a much reduced capacity, the training of Iraqi police.

Reliance on contractors as a substitute for understaffed State and USAID billets is not a proven solution, not unless their preparation, training, cultural knowledge, and linguistic proficiencies are equivalent to or exceed those of government personnel. Contractor competence, with the possible exception of those tasked to highly specialized missions like security and body guarding, is rarely equivalent to what the military services can provide. Contractor outsourcing, particularly for COIN tasks and military or law enforcement training of host-nation armies and police forces, has been a growing business since the Vietnam War. Contractor personnel had been present in Iraq since War I commenced. In War III, they peaked at over 160,000 personnel in the first quarter of 2008 during the surge and had declined to 45,000 in the first two quarters in 2011.[147] Managing and evaluating the effectiveness of such large numbers of contractor personnel without DoD's procurement help and management oversight tends to be beyond State's "usual remit." Auditors raised fears that the diplomats were unprepared to handle the contractors and have no real plan for training the police. Without the US Armed Forces to fly helicopters and man convoys, their activities were severely reduced.

Lieutenant General H. R. McMaster, who served multiple tours of duty in Iraqi Wars I, III, and IV and in Afghanistan, years later broadly reflected on the consequences of architectures that do not align back-to-front with national policy, military strategy, and field operations:

> I think the study of military history has been the most important preparation for every position I've had in the last twelve years or so . . . we often start by determining the resources we want to commit or what is palatable from a political standpoint. We confuse activity with progress, and that's always dangerous, especially in war. In reality, we should first define the objective, compare it with the current state, and then work backward: what is the nature of this conflict? What are the obstacles to progress? . . . Our doctrine is still catching up. We have the counterinsurgency manual, the stability-operations manual, and the security-force-assistance manuals, but I don't think we have put the politics at the center of those manuals. So, for example, we assume in our doctrine that the challenges associated with developing indigenous security forces are mainly about building capacity, when, in fact, they're about trying to develop institutions that can survive and that will operate in a way that is at least congruent with our interests.[148]

General McMaster and Colonel Gentile both might agree that politics is at the center of the Iraqi Wars, as it was at the center of the Vietnam War. Gentile told the *New York Times* in 2012 that America's COIN wars in Iraq and Afghanistan were "certainly not worth the effort. In my view."[149] Like the Vietnam War, the same question remains over a generation later: can strategic architectures be designed for the long game that span across multiple administrations?

28

IRAQI WAR V, THE RISE OF ISIS

A New, More Violent Enemy

Three years after the withdrawal of US combat forces from Iraq, Iraqi War IV transformed into War V as ISIS emerged as a menacing threat. The Kagans viewed War IV as a defeat after the American withdrawal from Iraq at the end of 2011. Then they watched with alarm the growth of the ISIS threat during the spring and summer of 2014. Tim Arango three years later had written a front-page article in the *New York Times* explaining how Iran became the principal economic, cultural, military, and political beneficiary of the US withdrawal: "From Day 1, Iran saw . . . a chance to make a client state of Iraq. . . . In that contest, Iran won, and the United States lost."[1]

After 2011 the Maliki government's marginalization of Sunni leaders and growing domination of sectarian command of the Iraqi Security Forces spurred an antigovernment protest movement, primarily in the Sunni provinces of al Anbar and Saladin. Joel Rayburn summarized Maliki's rule after 2011 succinctly:

> Iraq's parliamentary democracy [had] evolved into an authoritarian regime, whose control over state institutions has grown as time passed. The Iraqi state that the United States and its allies worked hard to decentralize and democratize after 2003 has reverted under Nouri al-Maliki to its old form: An Arab oil power ruled by one sect, one party, one man.[2]

As a result, al Qa'ida in Iraq began a dramatic recovery. By 2013 a new more violent and militant enemy had emerged identifying itself as the Islamic State of Iraq and Syria (ISIS). By March 2015, ISIS controlled a wide swath of ter-

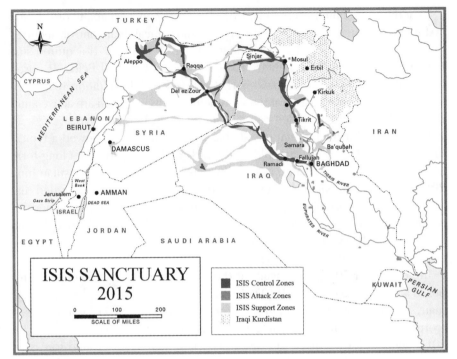

Map 28.1. ISIS by December 2015 had overrun a territory that currently stands at about one-third of both Iraq and Syria.

Source: Jessica Lewis McFate, ISIS Sanctuary Map (Washington, DC: ISW, May 2015), http://www.understandingwar .org/report/isis-defense-iraq-and-syria-countering-adaptive-enemy.

ritory in Mesopotamia running from Aleppo in Syria to Mosul in Iraq (map 28.1). With ease, it overran the cities of Fallujah, Ramadi, Tikrit, Mosul, and many others and virtually surrounded Baghdad.[3] Its leader and self-appointed caliph, Abu Bakr al-Baghdadi, declared that ISIS constituted a reclaimed caliphate and renamed ISIS the Islamic State.

It is significant that al-Baghdadi added Abu Bakr to his name. Abu Bakr was Muhammad's most trusted advisor and companion who became the Muslim world's first caliph after the Prophet's death in AD 632. One of the principal doctrinal treatises defining ISIS strategy, *The Management of Savagery*, places a narrow and deliberate focus on violence. The beheadings, mass executions, and slaughter of apostates are not whimsical, crazed acts of fanaticism but are designed to shock ISIS enemies; they are considered part of an integral strategy that advances in three stages, from "vexation operations," to the creation of a "fighting society," to the consolidation of the caliphate.[4] *The Management of Savagery* is part of the ISIS organizational curriculum and is widely read among provisional commanders and rank-and-file fighters to justify the Islamic basis of escalating violence in religious and sharia texts. "Savagery is part of ISIS's ideological DNA."[5]

In addition to military conquest, ISIS demonstrated a capability of "holistic system governance" that included religious and educational control, security, public administration, and a broad range of public services.[6] It acquired sustained financing from the military takeover of banks and oil fields. It raised $2–4 million per day from black-market sales of oil.[7] In addition to ISIS, a large number of other armed antigovernment groups were and are active amid the complicated and unsettled political landscape in Iraq and Syria.

Examination of operational digests has shown that ISIS followed a typical insurgency strategy of "clear, hold, and build" and demonstrated a long-term planning and military execution capability behind the capture of Mosul in June 2014, the capital of Nineveh Province in Iraq. Richard Barrett concluded that "this is not the work of neophyte enthusiasts inspired by their imagined rewards of martyrdom; it is clearly the result of detailed planning by people who know Iraq well, have prior experience and training, and are able to manage an organization with discipline and secrecy."[8]

In September 2014, the Kagans at the Institute for the Study of War proposed a strategy to defeat ISIS. Their strategy proposed the deployment of as many as twenty-five thousand ground forces in Iraq and Syria "in a dispersed footprint."[9] President Obama in his address to the nation on September 10, 2014, about the ISIS threat refused to consider significant ground forces on this scale: "We will not get dragged into another ground war in Iraq."[10]

At the end of 2011, the United States remained in Iraq with an embassy complement of sixteen thousand people but no US armed forces remained to bolster State's or USAID's operations or logistics. By early 2012, State's numbers began to diminish. The *New York Times* reported that State estimated 50 percent personnel and contractor reductions and that not many who remained in Baghdad were venturing outside the Green Zone.[11] The *Wall Street Journal* similarly reported that the CIA was reducing its in-country presence by 40 percent.[12]

The ambassador who succeeded Crocker was Christopher R. Hill, sent to Baghdad by the Obama White House in early 2009. Emma Sky described him as having not wanted the job and as uninterested in engaging with the Iraqis at a key transition point separating the Bush and Obama presidencies. "It was," Sky wrote, "frightening how a person could so poison a place. Hill brought with him a small cabal who were new to Iraq and marginalized all those with experience in the country."[13]

In 2010, the State Department had elevated its Office of Coordinator for Reconstruction and Stabilization to the Bureau of Conflict and Stabilization. State's first Quadrennial Diplomacy and Development Review asserted that it was time for change:

> It is time for a new approach. We start by embracing crisis and conflict prevention and resolution; the promotion of sustainable, responsible, and effective se-

curity and governance in fragile states; and fostering security and reconstruction in the aftermath of conflict as a central national security objective and as a core State mission that must be closely supported by USAID and many other U.S. government agencies.[14]

This conclusion came long after the unity of effort that the Petraeus-Crocker partnership implemented during the surge in Iraq. The boilerplate language and innumerable bullet points in State's quadrennial review declared intention but specified nothing about the need for increased budgets and staffing. The organizational upgrade of the department's reconstruction and stabilization mission from an office to a bureau[15] is not remotely on the scale of the resources required.[16] Kori N. Schake noted that the "current director of State's Office of the Coordinator for Reconstruction and Stabilization, a genuinely outstanding twenty-seven-year veteran of the Foreign Service and career ambassador, received no training at all other than language."[17]

An article in the *Washington Post* in 2011 described the kind of effective State performance by skilled people in the field necessary to achieve stabilization:

Carter Malkasian, who had been the State Department's representative in Garmser [a district in Afghanistan's Helmand Province] . . . is perhaps the only foreign official in the country to have been so widely embraced as a *sahib*, an Urdu salutation once used to address British colonial officials that Afghans now employ as a term of honor and respect. . . . Seeing his role more as a proconsul than adviser, he single-handedly cajoled influential tribal leaders and mullahs to return to the district, correctly betting that it would lead others to follow. He won the trust of skeptical residents through countless meetings and roadside conversations, persuading them to reject the insurgency and support their government. And he provided vital institutional memory in a mission that has generally forced Afghans to build fresh relationships with new waves of Americans each year. He also shaped the Marine campaign here in a way no civilian has in other parts of the country. He served as a counselor to each of the battalion commanders [five during his two consecutive tours], influencing decisions about when to use force, and helping them calibrate it with a political engagement strategy. He built such credibility with the Marines—the result of spending so much time in Garmser—that if he urged a different course of action, they almost always complied. "We need a Carter Malkasian in every district of Afghanistan," said Major General Larry Nicholson, a former top Marine commander in Afghanistan.[18]

Given that places like Afghanistan and Iraq comprise administrative divisions numbering thirty-four provinces and 361 districts in Afghanistan's case and eighteen provinces and 102 districts in Iraq's,[19] the creation of an organization capable of fielding five hundred Carter Malkasians should not be beyond the capability of the United States to recruit, train, and deploy.

Malkasian published his own account of the two years he spent in Garmser. He modeled his own book on Jeffrey Race's seminal Vietnam book, *War Comes to Long An*, about "one small place" as part of the larger conflict that has engulfed Afghanistan for more than thirty years. In his concluding chapter, he asserted that "U.S. and Allied strategy in regard to Garmser generally improved," but he acknowledged that,

> of greater importance, we shied away from large structural (and admittedly more intrusive) changes that might have reduced infighting within the government. The common refrain was to stay out of internal Afghan politics, for it was their business, not ours. Yet those politics were what really mattered. We should have established a hierarchical chain of command between governors, police chiefs, and other officials. . . . Appointments were not based on willingness to fight. They were based on political connections and bribes, which allowed weak leaders to hold important positions. Solving the problem required that the United States and Great Britain dig deeper into Afghan sovereignty, checking that strong leaders were going to the districts and preventing them from being removed. Too often we assisted whoever was sent down under the argument that we were building the government and had to respect its decisions. We should have linked our support and our projects to a leader's combat performance rather than unconditionally to his office.[20]

Race's and Malkasian's accounts stand as generational bookends in the COIN literature bracketing the Vietnam and Afghanistan conflicts.

The State Department, and its subsidiary, USAID, need to rethink their operational cultures if they are serious about supporting foreign interventions with the same kind of audacity and continuing education, training, and professionalism that the military services have routinely demonstrated for decades.[21] Schake contrasts the military and diplomatic cultures:

> Warfare is a team sport. An individual is not considered successful unless everyone around them is successful, which means that military leaders are fundamentally teachers. It's a culture built to make a lot out of very little: the military takes young people with generally only a high school education, gives them the self-discipline, self-respect and skills to make them contributors while in the service. . . . The institution invests in them, identifying practices to help them succeed at future needs and both educating and training them for the responsibilities to come. It studies intensively what has worked in the past [lessons learned] and how differences between the present and future might require different approaches. . . . It provides extensive education at many different points across a career. . . . The State Department makes no such investment in its talented people.[22]

Similarly, the Central Intelligence Agency needs to modify its operational culture so that it can recruit and train more foreign-born agents who are able to infiltrate enemies.[23] These agencies need to redesign their missions and organizations with respect to how their personnel are recruited and trained during their careers so that they are prepared and ready for future assignments.

The Obama administration's DoD policy in January 2012 declared diminished priority for military deployments:

> U.S. forces will nevertheless be ready to conduct limited counterinsurgency and other stability operations if required, operating alongside coalition forces wherever possible. Accordingly, U.S. forces will retain and continue to refine the lessons learned, expertise, and specialized capabilities that have been developed over the past ten years of counterinsurgency and stability operations in Iraq and Afghanistan. *However, U.S. forces will no longer be sized to conduct large-scale, prolonged stability operations* [italics in original].[24]

It is surprising that the Obama administration required the Department of Defense to express itself so nebulously about priorities.[25] The detailed parsing of the strategic architectures of the last seventy-five years clearly shows that present leaders and their counselors have not learned, have forgotten, or have willfully ignored the emergent lessons since 1945. They will have to be relearned again by a future administration.

In the late spring of 2014, two weeks after delivering the commencement address to graduating cadets at West Point on the limits of American power,[26] President Obama faced a collapsing situation in Iraq. By the fall of 2014, ISIS had conquered and was in control of large swaths of Iraq and Syria. The American strategic architecture in Iraq, which evolved in fits and starts over four presidencies, was headed for failure. That is what happens to presidents who fail to think through what a successful strategic architecture requires.

29

THE STRATEGIC ARCHITECTURES
OF THE IRAQI WARS

Like the Vietnam War, the Iraqi Wars encompassed new and old aspects of warfare. Wars I–III bore the familiar characteristics of combatant states and armies engaged in conventional battles. The transition from War III into War IV brought back memories of the frustrations the United States had experienced in Southeast Asia. War V shows that the defeat of ISIS is now a mission for the Trump administration or a future administration.

The first Bush administration's decision to liberate Kuwait in War I was a straightforward and initially high-risk response where there was a clear casus belli, Saddam's invasion of one major oil-producing state and his threat to another, Saudi Arabia. Twenty-five years ago, the team of President Bush, Secretary Baker, Secretary Cheney, and Generals Schwarzkopf and Powell produced a winning result, despite post–War I commentary about the lost opportunity for regime change. President Bush in 1990–1991 understood the importance of Arab, European, and international participation in War I to liberate Kuwait. He and Secretary Baker implemented a global full-court press to bring a total of thirty-five states to contribute forces and matériel to *Desert Storm*. President Bush understood the limits of what he could effectively accomplish, listened to his staff and generals, and accepted the outcome.

Neither Bush nor Schwarzkopf could predict that War I would turn into a cakewalk; sixteen thousand body bags had been warehoused in the theater in anticipation of high casualties. With those kinds of casualty projections, no one was thinking beyond the liberation of Kuwait, certainly not of regime change. To have proposed such a goal would have undermined the international coalition Bush and Baker had so carefully assembled. And their strategic architecture did not include the kind of postwar planning that would have been required had regime change been the goal. Historians may eventually realize the wisdom of Bush's restraint once Saddam was defeated. In fundamental geopolitical terms, President Bush protected much of the world's petroleum energy supplies from a brute-force takeover by a tyrant.

General Schwarzkopf's military triumph achieved its stated aim of the liberation of Kuwait in War I, but President Bush failed to provide Schwarzkopf and CENTCOM with specific policy guidance at the Safwan armistice. In a PBS *Frontline* broadcast transcript in February 1997, former prime minister Margaret Thatcher and Bush's national security advisor, General Scowcroft, retrospectively said the following years later:

> PBS NARRATOR. The Iraqi generals got exactly what Saddam wanted, to the astonishment of some of the civilian architects of the war.
>
> THATCHER. They should have surrendered their equipment, the lot. When you're dealing with a dictator, he has got not only to be defeated well and truly, but he's got to be seen to be defeated by his own people so that they identify the privations they've had to go through with his actions. And we didn't do that.
>
> SCOWCROFT. I think what we should have insisted upon is Saddam Hussein come to Safwan. That was our mistake because that allowed him to blame his generals for the defeat and not he himself.[1]

War II evolved out of the unresolved issues of War I's flawed termination at Safwan, which left Saddam as a surviving dictator of a major Middle East oil-producing state and a potential future hegemon who could covertly develop WMDs. The Clinton administration that succeeded Bush entered office with much more modest ambitions and assumptions about the application of military power.

War III was born out of the failure of international efforts to compel Saddam's satisfactory compliance with UN resolutions throughout the 1990s decade. When UN WMD inspection policy crumbled, President George W. Bush decided to invade Iraq because of the perceived menace of Saddam possessing WMDs after the events of 9/11 had elevated international awareness of terrorist threats. Yet invasion was not the worst decision; it was the insistence that it was not necessary to plan and prepare to occupy, secure, and rebuild Iraq. The administration's willful denial that such a massive undertaking might be necessary led to War IV.

The decision to invade Iraq a second time to overthrow Saddam and his Ba'athist government committed the error of relying on front-to-back military planning where the assumptions about the geopolitical outcome turned out to be wrong. President George W. Bush launched Operation *Iraqi Freedom* based on a military plan for regime change with optimistic postwar assumptions. Had the president insisted on a fully defined postwar end state before-hand, he could have ensured better and more immediately executable postwar planning after Saddam's defeat. It very well might have influenced the size and composition of the CENTCOM force that Secretary Rumsfeld and General Franks sent into Iraq in March 2003.

Secretary Rumsfeld by War III believed that the inclusion of allies did not weigh decisively in the military scales because the Americans and their prin-cipal ally, Britain, possessed ample conventional combat manpower, weapons platforms, and matériel. He was convinced that participation by European allies had become unnecessary to achieving military success because of the revolution in military affairs (RMA). Rumsfeld believed in the superiority of American advanced technology. Specifically, a faster, lighter, more agile force with a smaller footprint, deployed with network-centric and RMA technolo-gies, rendered a European military contribution irrelevant.[2] It took President George W. Bush nearly three years before he realized that his decision to in-vade Iraq required a major change of course. The Bush War III strategic archi-tecture failed to develop a realistic postwar plan with the necessary resources.

President Bush was honest and wise enough to eventually recognize that War IV required a new approach. It was fortuitous that there were enough senior officers in the US Army who had prepared themselves for the daunting mission they undertook in 2007. Petraeus and his colleagues recommended and then executed the surge. As Colonel Mansoor, Petraeus's executive officer, observed, "the most important surge was the surge of ideas, not the surge in forces. . . . The most important of the 'big ideas' was that the U.S. and Iraqi forces had to focus on securing the people."[3] It was also a surge in effective leaders.

General Petraeus and the men and women that he and Ambassador Crocker recruited were not conventional military or diplomatic careerists. They were students who had spent decades studying, writing, and learning from America's mistakes. Americans continued to believe that prevailing in Wars I through III required the application of their firepower, airpower, tech-nology, and mobility. As War IV developed, General Petraeus implemented a balanced combination of COIN doctrinal concepts and kinetic operations to break the violence of the insurgency. The application of force had to be traded between earning the confidence of the local populations in Baghdad's districts and in the belts around the city and the risks of collateral damage from exces-sive use of firepower and airpower.

On the military and diplomatic levels, the Petraeus-Crocker team demon-strated what a group of focused, determined, and informed soldiers and civil-ian experts could accomplish: reverse a very bad situation and create more time to enable Iraq's sectarian factions to reconcile themselves to a plausible future where Shias, Sunnis, and Kurds could govern themselves, resolve dis-putes without violence, and rebuild a shattered economy. That was the vision. They reversed what many had already written off as a hopeless expeditionary war. Their watch, however, did not end the violence of War IV. An effective endgame required a political, whole-of-government strategic architecture.

The Obama administration's decision to bring War IV to a "soft landing" by withdrawing all US military forces by the end of 2011 was not an effective end of the American military mission in Iraq. In the fall and winter of 2011–2012, the Kagans reinforced their view that the withdrawal decision was a "defeat."[4] In a series of articles starting in late 2011 to the present, they began by viewing the breakdown of the status-of-forces negotiations as a diplomatic failure of the Obama administration.[5]

The Obama administration had its own difficulties in constructing effective strategic architectures, the good war versus the bad war. At various times, between 2002 and 2009, Obama characterized Afghanistan as the "good war"[6] and the "war of necessity"[7] and Iraq as "the dumb war . . . the rash war."[8] Once in office, President Obama discovered that he too was unwilling to sustain a protracted war in Afghanistan with its long-haul implications for de facto nation building, even as the "war of necessity." He wanted to be done with both wars because he believed the American people remain unconvinced and sharply divided over the strategic merits for expeditionary war in Iraq or Afghanistan.

Polling data about how well the war was going in Iraq ranged from 90 percent agreeing with "very or fairly well" in March 2003 to only 30 percent by February 2007.[9] Polling data in late 2011 indicated that the American public was evenly divided between 50 percent believing that the United States had achieved its goals in Iraq and 47 percent saying the United States had not achieved its goals.[10] With the killing of Osama bin Laden on May 2, 2011, and pressures mounting on federal fiscal policy, the Obama administration was more interested in fulfilling its campaign promises of withdrawal from Iraq than maintaining a long-term, military commitment to help build a new Iraq in the heart of Mesopotamia.

The Bush administration, before it left office in early 2009, had already agreed to a timetable for the withdrawal of military forces from Iraq by 2011 because it could not conclude a status-of-forces agreement (SOFA) with adequate jurisdictional provisions regarding legal exposure of American personnel to Iraqi rather than US law. President Obama then readily implemented this timetable based on the failure of either Bush or his own administration to achieve a SOFA with Iraq so that US military forces could continue to provide security after 2011.[11]

Neither the Bush nor the Obama administration was prepared to plan and implement a long-haul, whole-of-government approach to defining a nation-building strategic architecture.[12] Had either administration been serious about a sustained whole-of-government intervention in Iraq, negotiating a workable SOFA or finessing its jurisdictional sticking points with a diplomatic instrument would have been an incidental detail to an overarching strategy with an extended, preferably indefinite, schedule for the presence of US combat forces.[13]

Whatever one's geopolitical judgment about whether Wars III–V should have been fought, or whether they were follies similar to what had happened in Vietnam, Iraq involved much higher stakes. Iraq contains the fifth-largest oil reserves in the world and ranks as the sixth-largest exporter of petroleum liquids, with daily production at 2.9 million bbl per day and potentially much higher volumes.[14]

On the tenth anniversary of Wars III and IV in 2013, the nation's two premier newspapers ran front-page stories and op-ed pieces about the continuing sectarian violence in Iraq (a barrage of car bombs killing dozens and wounding 177 people in Baghdad). The *New York Times* opined,

> The Iraq war was unnecessary, costly and damaging on every level. It was based on faulty intelligence manipulated for ideological reasons. The terrible human and economic costs over the past ten years show why that must never happen again.

The *Wall Street Journal* made this observation about the future:

> As long as the United States remains a great power, it will eventually have to fight such a war again. When that day comes, let's hope our political and military leaders will have learned the right lessons from this bitter but necessary war.[15]

Five years later, the fight against ISIS continues and the search for the "right lessons" persists.

Years earlier, Ambassador Crocker had offered this prescient criterion: "In the end, what we leave behind and how we leave will be more important than how we came."[16]

In January 2015, former secretary of state Henry Kissinger, in testimony before the US Senate Armed Services Committee, characterized the consequences of the US military withdrawal from Iraq. He defined the emerging threat of ISIS as a new competitor for power in the region. ISIS should be viewed as an organization "explicitly designed to undermine all of the existing weapons of legitimacy" on which the post-1945 international system depends. If ISIS were to succeed as a governing authority within the Middle East, it could directly challenge "the current international order—based on respect for sovereignty, rejection of territorial conquest, open trade, and encouragement of human rights—primarily a creation of the West," for a world order based on "universal theocracy."[17]

This view of ISIS as a threat changed over the next two years. ISIS may no longer be viewed as an expanding governing force. However, the price for this result is Iran's deep penetration into Mesopotamia, as Arango's *New York Times* reporting in the summer of 2017, cited in chapter 28, made all too clear to a world paying little attention to Iraq or Syria.

Iraqi Wars

(1) Retreating Iraqi soldiers left behind ruined vehicles like this T-55 main battle tank on the highway between Kuwait City and Basra (left). (2) Kuwaiti oil wells on fire, set by defeated Iraqis, causing massive environmental and economic damage (right). US Army photos

(3) Tapline Road convoy, prior to *Desert Storm* launch. US Army photo

(4) Abandoned Iraqi armored personnel carrier (left). (5) "Highway of Death," the six-lane highway between Kuwait and Iraq, officially known as Highway 80 running north from Kuwait City to the border towns of Abdali and Safwan and then east to Basra; photo taken on April 19, 1991 (right). US Army photos

Iraqi Wars

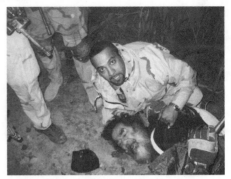

(1) General David Petraeus, commanding general of Multi-National Forces–Iraq during the surge, meets with a local sheikh to discuss security, the neighborhood guard, and revitalization of the surrounding community on June 4, 2008. (2) Iraqi-American soldier pinning deposed Saddam Hussein to the ground during his capture in Tikrit on December 13, 2003. US Army photos

(3) Lieutenant Raymond Odierno, commander of Multi-National Corps–Iraq (right), conferring with Iraqi brigadier general and Sadr City police chief at local Joint Security Station in March 2007 (left). US Army photo by Sgt. Curt Cashour, MNC-I Public Affairs (4) An Iraqi police vehicle damaged by shrapnel from a vehicle-borne improvised explosive device (VIBED), which blew up just inside the entrance to the police station in Bayji, Iraq, on January 17, 2005 (middle). US Army photo by Spc. Elizabeth Erste (5) Soldiers from Stryker Brigade Combat Team cordon and search houses in Buhriz, Iraq, in March 2007 (right). US Air Force photo by Staff Sgt. Stacy L. Pearsall

(6) General Petraeus and Ambassador Crocker during congressional testimony in April 2008. *New York Times* photo

PART VI

STRATEGIC ARCHITECTURES: THE ENDGAME

Strategic architectures are more likely to succeed when policy, strategy, and operations are in alignment. Alignment means that these three elements are arranged realistically so that operations achieve a successful geopolitical result. This is the thesis that this work set out to illuminate.

The World War II chapters in part II showed that Allied alignment was superior to Axis alignment. The Allies defined policies, designed strategies, and executed operations in each of the ten critical battles and campaigns that cumulatively led to the defeat of their Axis enemies. The Allies defined policies that focused on priorities (Europe First) and imposed a 70/30 allocation of resources between the European and Pacific theaters. Within weeks of Pearl Harbor, they started to create the necessary leadership institutions (Combined Chiefs of Staff and subordinate joint collegial structures) so they could fight together effectively. The Allies created a progression of winning strategic architectures that balanced what was achievable in various theaters with realistic military objectives. By the middle years of the war, they were able to design strategies and execute operations back-to-front that enabled them to win every major campaign after 1942. After the Axis surrenders, the Allies executed well-planned, well-led, and well-funded occupations of their Axis enemies that restored Germany and Japan to peaceful and prosperous participation in the international system. The occupations lasted longer than the war itself.

By contrast, by mid-1941, Axis misalignments between policy, strategy, and operations became a growing problem for Germany and by mid-1942 for Japan. Axis policy and strategy misalignments in theater after theater ultimately led to war-losing deficits everywhere. Enemy air forces could not project power, armies became outnumbered, and navies could not win decisive battles or produce enough submarines to sink Allied shipping.

The World War II alignment threads that ran through the ten critical battles and campaigns reveal a consistent series of increasingly effective architectures demonstrating how the Allies defined policy, developed strategy, and executed operations to win strategic victories in the European, Mediterranean, and Pacific theaters. This same consistency of alignment also created immense and unprecedented military power. It is this consistency of alignment that renders World War II as such an impressive historical benchmark.

The Korean War chapters in part III show that the US government's failure to provide clear policy guidance in the early months of the war resulted in the misalignment of policy goals, military strategy, and operational execution. When General MacArthur's Inchon counterstroke changed the military balance of forces three months after Kim Il Sung's invasion, the Truman administration over the summer of 1950 had not aligned policy, strategy, and operations for a limited war. It failed to take advantage of the council-of-war meeting at Wake Island to think through the risks and military requirements to reunify Korea as a democratic, noncommunist state versus restoration of the status quo for South Korea. President Truman accepted General MacArthur's confidence that the war had been won. It had not. It was only beginning once the Chinese entered the conflict six weeks later. By Christmas of 1950, MacArthur had to cable Washington that "we face an entirely new war." The United States and the UN Command then had to draw the boundaries of a limited war around the Korean conflict, driven by the potential dangers of Cold War nuclear escalation that were recognized by both sides. The realignment of policy, strategic, and operational choices imposed strict constraints on the scope of military operations by the winter of 1950–1951. Two and a half years later, the war ended in a stalemate where it began. For more than sixty years since the armistice in 1953, the continuous presence of combat-ready US forces in South Korea has guaranteed the peace between the North and the South.

The Vietnam War chapters in part IV show that a successful strategic architecture required US-GVN agreement on aligning four things: (1) a clearly stated policy that made a compelling case to the American and South Vietnamese people for why the GVN deserved such a massive American national commitment to nation building, which resulted in the sacrifice of nearly 60,000 American lives, 260,000 ARVN lives, and over 5 million Vietnamese casualties; (2) a political strategy that undermined the revolutionary movement's preemptive social and economic policies with GVN policies that were at least equally preemptive and compelling in the areas of land reform, taxes, military recruitment, and rural administration; (3) a military strategy that integrated MACV, CORDS, ARVN, and GVN ministries into joint organizations where they could plan and operate together; and (4) execution that balanced conventional and COIN operations because, as events showed, the ARVN had to be capable of both.

Alignment of policy, strategy, and operations would have required putting politics at the center of the enterprise. Sometime between 1963 and 1965, the US government could have proposed to the Diem government (or its soon-to-be successors after the November 1963 coup) that the United States was prepared to risk thousands of soldiers' lives and provide billions of dollars in aid if the GVN agreed to formalize the US–host government relationship in the form of a diplomatic instrument. The US government could have specified a major role in the formulation of a policy to defeat the revolutionary movement. The instrument could have addressed how the two governments would work together to achieve effective joint resolution of major policy issues, including provincial administration, military and intelligence operations, military recruitment and promotion, land distribution, taxation, and so on. American negotiators could have made explicit that Americans would work in a collocated environment with their Vietnamese counterparts to ensure that the distribution of economic and military support was corruption free and accountable to both governments with transparency.

There was the World War II precedent for preparing and executing plans jointly. The creation of the wartime Combined Chiefs of Staff and SHAEF included American, British, and many other Allied officers. This jointness made sense during World War II under the exigent necessity of winning battles and campaigns.

Vietnam was the last conflict where nation building was part of the accepted American policy vocabulary. After 1975, nation building was judged a failure. It would take more than a quarter century before Americans in the field realized that once again, in Iraq and Afghanistan, they were engaging in de facto nation building.

Ironically, North Vietnam succeeded in its own efforts at nation building. If ever there was a case of effective "armed nation building," it was the NLF/NVA operating in South Vietnam for over thirty years. Some Vietnam historians have argued that US-GVN nation-building dissimilarities did not render collaboration impossible, but for such collaboration to succeed they had to speak each other's languages to achieve a common understanding of why the communist revolutionary movement's preemptive policies were so effective and then respond with a strategic architecture that aligned in a common effort. This never happened.

The Iraqi Wars chapters in part V show that Wars I–V encompassed new and old aspects of warfare. The five consecutive wars that were fought did not follow a coherent, long-haul strategic architecture that ensured Iraq would become a peaceful polity within the international system. Wars I–III were conventional conflicts. The War I strategic architecture liberated Kuwait but did not attempt regime change for reasons that at the time were prudent. However, the armistice provisions General Schwarzkopf imposed at Safwan left enough loopholes for Saddam and his Ba'athist dictatorship to survive and continue for thirteen more years. War II's architecture was a series of ad hoc actions to enforce UN resolutions but to no satisfactory and lasting effect. The transition from War III into War IV brought back memories of the frustrations the United States had experienced in Vietnam in failing to design a winning strategic architecture.

Midway into Iraqi War IV, General Petraeus implemented a combination of COIN doctrinal concepts and military operations that he believed were required to break the violence of the Iraqi insurgency. The application of force had to be balanced between, on the one hand, earning the confidence of the local populations in Baghdad's districts and in the belts around the city and, on the other hand, the risks of collateral damage from excessive use of firepower and airpower. The Petraeus-led surge operated on the doctrinal premise embedded in the newly published COIN field manual: "An effective counterinsurgent force is a learning organization." But what did learning mean for an integrated US whole-of-government approach? That would have required a strategic architecture in which alignment of policy, strategy, and operations meant that Iraqi leaders would change their behaviors to create a government that could autonomously reconcile its warring sectarian factions, defend itself against either internal or external threats, and govern its provinces and districts with sufficiently diverse consent from a plurality of its people to establish legitimacy.

Nearly a century has elapsed since the Sykes-Picot agreement divided the Middle East into imperial spheres of influence. ISIS has filmed its jihadists bulldozing the border posts between Syria and Iraq. Abu Bakr al-Baghdadi's "caliphate" in 2014 was inhabited by an estimated six to eight million people in a territory larger than the United Kingdom, right in the heart of the Middle East. ISIS represented the final blow to the imperial ambitions of Britain and France a century ago. Al-Baghdadi declared that his caliphate was "a state where the Arab and non-Arab, the white man and black man, the easterner and westerner are all brothers. . . . Syria is not for the Syrians, and Iraq is not for the Iraqis. The Earth is Allah's."[1]

Nearly a quarter century has transpired as a succession of five American presidencies has tried to design and implement a series of flawed strategic architectures to address Iraq as a major American national security problem. Iraq, Syria, and the Middle East still remain a serious problem. The emergence of Iraqi War V shows that the complete defeat of ISIS may very well have to be a task for the Trump administration or its successors.

The richness of the historical record and the data and evidence from many of the participants themselves in these conflicts is so voluminous and persuasive that it merits high-level summarization. A distillation of the evidence in these pages reduces to a small set of guidelines for strategic thought.

Since World War II ended, four simple American imperatives emerge. Wise statesmen and generals, when contemplating military expeditionary missions in remote parts of the world, before everything else need to:

1. Define a successful geopolitical outcome, in keeping with American core interests. Then, plan backward. Frederick Kagan's recommendation of back-to-front thought processes is very sound.
2. Define a strategy as a sequence of political-military operations to achieve the end state. If statesmen and generals cannot do this, or if the range of acceptable alternatives cannot be defined or is unknowable, the enterprise is a hostage to fortune and likely doomed.
3. Define a set of executable plans for the sequence of operations and specify the resources necessary to produce the end state. If a government is unprepared to do this at the outset, it invites failure. When statesmen and generals think a conflict might be protracted, defining an exit strategy is an oxymoron. Exit is what happens after governments and armies prevail and win; then Americans come home. That is why World War II is such a compelling benchmark.
4. Execute plans where comprehensive, whole-of-government operations and resources are identified in detail with realistic schedules. Successful execution means a well-thought-out endgame.

These four imperatives make the case for strategic architectures that align an overseas mission goal with America's core interests, define back-to-front how to achieve the goal, and sequence operations that achieve that goal. If alignment fails, the mission risks failure beyond America's control.

The historical records of the four conflicts over the last seventy-five years form the evidentiary basis behind these imperatives that drive a successful strategic architecture. The postwar presidents did not define end states in Korea, Vietnam, or Iraq in terms of victory or perseverance to play a long endgame to achieve strategic geopolitical success. The strategic architectures of these conflicts failed in the realistic alignment of policy, strategy, and operations.

President Truman in Korea ignored the four imperatives. His police action in Korea failed to achieve an early winning result for restoring the status quo because he unwisely accepted General MacArthur's confident assurances and gambled on a bigger prize, a unified Korea. Instead, he got a long, bloody, unpopular war of attrition that ended in stalemate.

President Johnson neither followed the imperatives nor did he pay close attention to the mounting evidence of risk, out of fear that he might be voted out of office. In the event, he lost both power and Vietnam. President Johnson and President Nixon could not define an end state in Vietnam that led to plans that MACV, CORDS, State, USAID, and the CIA could execute effectively. Despite the massive expenditures of lives and material aid, the US government failed to change a host nation's behavior enough so that it could achieve victory against the revolutionary movement.

Presidents George H. W. Bush, William J. Clinton, George W. Bush, and Barack H. Obama were confronted with the challenge of defining a successful end state in Iraq but did not immerse themselves in the relevant intricacies of effective, long-haul execution. In Iraqi Wars I through V, Clausewitzian friction, the fog of war, was inevitable. No plan can be executed the way it is initially conceived. Armies need to be prepared for the unexpected, as General Garner and his successor, Ambassador Bremer, discovered when their assumptions about postwar reconstruction and governance in Iraqi War III turned out to be wrong. Years later General Petraeus and the MNF-I command staff were prepared for the unexpected in War IV because they knew they had to be flexible and ready to adapt. They knew that the FM 3-24 playbook was only a very rough COIN outline. They found themselves having to combine a mix of kinetic operations in the belts around Baghdad to keep AQI, the JAM militias, and the Sunni insurgents off balance before they could begin to effectively pacify Baghdad's tough urban districts. FM 3-24 eschewed conventional military operations and firepower, yet Petraeus used both. And once the MNF-I surge units had deployed into Baghdad's urban districts, they found, as Lieutenant Colonel Schacht's Blue Spaders did in Adhamiyah, that they had to engage in hard fighting at the same time they were trying to win the confidence of the local population.

All of the postwar presidents were heirs to the World War II policy of unconditional surrender that enabled Americans to use the power they gained after victory to remodel Germany and Japan as democracies. The Soviets of course had similar claims of their own with a very different ideological design.

James Q. Whitman recently asserted that "it is by no means clear that the practices of World War II are the practices we should still be following today." He goes on to argue that his analysis of victory "does not lie in vindicating high ideals like democracy. It lies in creating a framework for negotiation" where combatant "parties find a way to accommodate each other." Applying military power to a conflict can create conditions and opportunities "that the parties can then bargain over. That is how the classic *jus victoriae* worked: it accorded rights to victors in such a way that deals could be cut."[2] Cutting deals was very much a part of what General Petraeus and Ambassador Crocker did during Iraqi War IV. Similarly, President Johnson, MACCORDS ambassador Komer, and General Westmoreland might have used the leverage of deployed American military power in Vietnam to convince their GVN counterparts that effective collaboration required transparency and mutual trust at all operational levels.

A president cannot outsource the tasks of defining a successful end state: he sets the direction of policy. He participates in the key military and diplomatic staffing decisions—the only way to impose accountability. His job is to direct the mobilization of DoD, State, and the intelligence community for coordinated, effective execution of whole-of-government plans. His job is to define chains of accountability to whomever he places in charge.[3] He must communicate policy and strategy clearly to his key subordinates in the White House. Then he must explain all of this directly to the American people with honesty about the risks and costs. Proposing to commit the armed forces of the United States to expeditionary wars is a dreadful mistake if such a strategic architecture cannot be defined. Vietnam, Korea, and Iraqi Wars I through V all suffered from flawed strategic architectures. Even now in Iraq or Afghanistan, no one can answer General Petraeus's question, "Tell me how this ends."

When the surprise of 9/11 immersed the Pentagon in military operations in two states, Thomas P. M. Barnett proposed that the United States needed to start thinking and planning for two kinds of armies. He defined a "Leviathan Army," which emerged out of World War II, Korea, Vietnam, and Iraqi Wars I and IV, and a "System Administrator Army."[4] Both kinds of armies are needed in Afghanistan and Iraq. These states are where the presence of organizations like al Qa'ida, the Taliban, ISIS, and similar transnational jihadist groups can disrupt the international system. Barnett put his case for the two different armies this way:

> I propose that America truly needs two separate types of military force: one to serve as warfighting . . . Leviathan, and one to serve as peacekeeping System Administrator that organizes and facilitates . . . security. . . . In short, we need a force for *might* and a force for *right*. When our . . . allies see that America is serious about generating both types of military power, we will see the usual bandwagoning[5] effect—meaning, friendly nations will join coalitions they know are certain to succeed. *Build it and they will come*, as they say, but they will come only if we decide to build both forces [italics in original].[6]

Barnett has put the issue squarely: Should the United States seriously consider designing two different kinds of institutions for exercising power with different missions, what some have called "soft" and "hard" power?[7] And should both missions be vested with the armed forces of the United States? One point favoring the military services, as Barnett does, is that the army and marine corps have demonstrated that they can function as effective learning institutions and pass on operational learning from one generation of leaders to the next, who in turn study, learn, and adapt. The military services have also demonstrated that they, more than any other governmental institution, are skilled at developing realistic operational plans, either on their own initiative or in response to governmental direction.

Barnett's System Administrator proposal is really asking whether the United States since the Vietnam era is capable of creating a CORDS-like institution that could be deployed "off the shelf"—a "global CORDS."[8] If it were innovatively structured and staffed to enable Americans, sent to the field with the right training, language preparation, communications skills, infrastructure support, and risk-taking incentives, could it succeed in convincing foreigners to change rule sets in places like Afghanistan and Iraq?

Carnes Lord is the most recent political scientist to revisit the CORDS experience in Vietnam and addresses the problem of directing a multiagency government effort:

> The historical record shows that this has sometimes been finessed by the devel-opment of close working relationships between the senior military and civilian officials in a theater [like General Petraeus and Ambassador Crocker working closely together during Iraqi War IV]. . . . Is there a workable alternative? In the American historical experience, one stands out: CORDS. . . . [It] was a unique experiment in truly integrated interagency operations. It intermixed military officers and civilians from various agencies at every echelon and ensured real integration by giving civilians authority to write performance evaluations of their military subordinates and the other way around. It was headed by a civilian of ambassadorial rank but was embedded in a military structure [MACV] to ensure tight coordination between the pacification effort and regular military operations. There is no reason why this model could not be adapted for use today.[9]

Lord's praise of the CORDS model as an institutional recommendation ignores one basic fact. CORDS was never designed specifically to change Viet-namese governing behavior. It was designed to administer development inputs and then measure outputs using automated systems like HES. As Lord ex-plained, CORDS effectiveness during the Vietnamization years (1969–1972) depended on the commitment by the Abrams-Bunker-Colby triad to work closely together. Lord's proposing CORDS as an institutional model would require a much more fundamental change in American strategic thinking, be-ginning top down by specifying the contingent incentives such an interagency organization could deploy to change the behavior of Iraqi or Afghan military commanders or government officials. The Departments of Defense and State have only been paying lip service to sweeping institutional innovation.

When confronted with these kinds of conflicts, it is difficult if not impossi-ble for American leaders to discuss a successful strategic architecture without reference to nation building or postwar governance. Nadia Schadlow's most recent contribution to the tiny, modern literature on nation building opens by discussing "American denial syndrome" this way:

> The absence of a sustained discussion of governance operations in official and unofficial army histories reflected the prevailing view that such operations were separate and distinct from the prosecution of war as a whole. Many of the problems related to the reconstruction efforts in Operation Iraqi Freedom and

Operation Enduring Freedom in Afghanistan demonstrated the consequences of this denial of governance operations as integral to war.[10]

It is equally difficult to eliminate the institutional stovepiping among DoD, State, USAID, Homeland Security, and the CIA where both the executive and legislative branches regard nation building as a taboo subject, even where it might be undertaken with a smaller, different kind of military and civilian footprint.[11]

Nation building has been the "elephant in the room" since the end of the World War II occupations. No prominent American leader is willing to discuss it publicly except to deny its relevance as a basis for any ongoing or future strategic architecture. Yet General Petraeus and Ambassador Crocker both found themselves leading military, diplomatic, aid, and intelligence organizations directly engaged in nation building—twice in the last decade. Both deployed first to Iraq during the surge under President Bush and later to Afghanistan under President Obama.[12] Indeed, nation building is what the Vietnam and Iraqi Wars were about.

Failure of American strategic architectures can cost tens of thousands of lives. Successful strategic architectures demand that leaders define necessary geopolitical outcomes clearly, appoint winning military commanders, and formulate and execute feasible plans with a full spectrum of national resources and institutional coherence. Successful presidents need to hold all in key leadership positions accountable, shape and accommodate key domestic and international constituencies, and communicate with their countrymen convincingly and often. In other words, these tasks to build effective strategic architectures are very hard to perform successfully, as Hanson outlined in a 2017 Hoover monograph.*

Four years earlier, David Kilcullen, who served as a COIN advisor on Petraeus's surge command staff in Iraq, wrote an insufficiently noticed book that added specificity to the difficulty of designing effective strategic architectures of the future. He identified four "megatrends" of population

---

*Hanson formulated six caveats that apply to ambitious, interventionist, strategic architectures that become protracted: (1) Zealous hawks for intervention often become the greatest "I-told-you-so" critics of an unpopular war. (2) Ground forces deployed in such interventions are often left "to fend for themselves in dirty alleyways figuring out who wants to blow them up." (3) Such a protracted unpopular war will "certainly end up being a political football in the next election." (4) Congressional approval, authorizing UN resolutions, NATO participation, and EU support mean nothing compared to a quick American victory. (5) Americans have no great interest in foreign affairs, but voters "gravitate to perceived inexpensive victory and loathe, as they should, costly defeat." (6) The armed forces of the United States "can ultimately accomplish any mission [that] is asked. But increasingly if deployed on the ground in tribal fighting, with legalistic and politically correct rules of engagement, in haphazard fashion and for political abstractions . . . concerned more with global than U.S. interests . . . will pay a cost that is more than Americans are willing to pay . . . for a cause the public deems not worth the effort." Hanson, "The Tar Pits Abroad" (online monograph, Hoover Institution, April 21, 2017), http://www.hoover.org/research/tar-pits-abroad.

growth, urbanization, littoralization, and digital connectivity in the world's most densely populated coastal cities in the Mediterranean basin, Middle East, South Asia, Africa, Latin America, and even Europe and North America that are vulnerable to infiltration by nonstate terrorists and criminal syndicates and to the breakdown of state and local governance. Many of these "megacities," with populations ranging from one million to over twenty million, are rapidly deteriorating into "feral cities."

By 2050, 75 percent of the world's population will be concentrated in these types of conurbations. All are vulnerable to acts of terrorism; all are susceptible to the breakdown of governance and law and order because many of these megacities represent concentrations of "the world's poorest areas—a recipe for conflict, for crises in health, education, and governance, and for food, energy, and water scarcity."

Everyone with a handheld digital device has seen reports of the mayhem that can happen in cities like Mumbai, Mogadishu, Karachi, Calcutta, Delhi, Cairo, New York, London, Boston, Los Angeles, Lagos, Jakarta, Tokyo, Manila, and Bangkok. All have been targets of terrorist attacks. Kilcullen singles out Mogadishu, Karachi, and Mumbai as examples of feral environments where large urban tracts are dominated by competing militias, criminal syndicates, and/or terrorist groups.

He is not sanguine about how Western constitutional governments can respond effectively to these future threats where hit-and-run attacks, ambushes, and bombings have become regular occurrences.

> Governments that draw sharp distinctions between warfare and law enforcement and between domestic and overseas legal authorities will experience great difficulty, and may find it impossible to act with the same agility as irregular actors who can move across these artificial [boundaries] at will.[13]

Constitutional republics like the United States are slow to recognize and effectively respond to this kind of peril while simultaneously accelerating adherence to the strategic imperatives. That is why it is so important to keep studying the record of how and why the United States succeeded or failed in earlier conflicts.

Since 1940, more than thirty-two million American men and women have served in the armed forces of the United States. In the four conflicts, 507,184 of them sacrificed their lives and 975,156 sustained wounds, many of them grievous.[14] Their accomplishments have made the United States the preeminent power in the world. Their sacrifices, documented in the preceding chapters, demonstrate why the study of the four historical strategic architectures of World War II, Korea, Vietnam, and Iraq can inform and help prepare leaders in future American governments.

ACRONYMS AND SELECTED GLOSSARY

A-1E	A-1E Skyraider, propeller-powered, tactical attack aircraft, USN, USMC, and USAF
A-7E	A-7E Corsair II, carrier-based, subsonic, light attack aircraft, flown during *Desert Storm* and earlier in Vietnam, USN
A-10	A-10 Warthog, close air support fighter-bomber, USAF
AA	antiaircraft
Abwehr	German intelligence service
ACR	armored cavalry regiment
AEI	American Enterprise Institute
AFSA	Armed Forces Security Agency (later NSA)
AH-64	AH-64 Apache, attack helicopter
AirLand Battle	army doctrine of the AirLand Battle where four tenets drove planning and offensive action: initiative (change the terms of battle through aggressive action), depth (fight deep, close, and rear battles simultaneously), agility (think and act faster than the enemy), and synchronization (arrange battlefield activities in time, space, and purpose to concentrate the greatest possible combat power at the decisive point)
AK-47	Officially known as *Avtomat Kalashnikova*, the AK-47 is a selective-fire, gas-operated, 7.62 mm assault rifle, first developed in the USSR by Mikail Kalashnikov; easy to mass produce, it has been sold globally in quantities of tens of millions
ALCM	air-launched cruise missile
AO	area of operation or holding area
AP	armor-piercing

APC (M-113)	armored personnel carrier
AQI	al Qa'ida in Iraq (Iraqi Wars III and IV)
Arc Light	Code name given to the use of B-52 strategic bombers in Southeast Asia
ARDF	airborne radio direction finding (ARDF) aircraft
Armeegruppe	army group (German)
ARPA	Advanced Research Projects Agency (until 1972), DoD
ARVN	Army of Vietnam (South Vietnam)
ASW	antisubmarine warfare
ASWORG	Anti-Submarine Warfare Operations Research Group
ATO	air tasking order
Auftragstaktik	mission tactics, element of German military doctrine, a flexible command-and-control system that enabled subordinate commanders to assess a situation quickly and act equally on their own
AV-8B	AV-8B Harrier II, single-engine, VSTOL (vertical short takeoff and landing), tactical attack aircraft, USMC
AVRE	armored vehicle, Royal Engineers
AWACS	Airborne Warning and Control System, USAF
B-1	B-1 Lancer, four-engine, variable-sweep wing, strategic bomber, USAF
B-2	B-2 Spirit, subsonic, twin-engine, low-observable (stealth) strategic bomber designed to deliver nuclear and conventional weapons, USAF
B-17	B-17 Flying Fortress, long-range, four-engine, World War II bomber flown mostly in ETO, built by Boeing, USAAF
B-24	B-24 Liberator, heavy, four-engine World War II bomber, USAAF, USN
B-29	B-29 Superfortress, advanced-design, long-range, four-engine, World War II bomber used to bomb Japan, 1944–1945, and also flown during the Korean War; built by Boeing, USAAF and later USAF
B-52	B-52 Stratofortress, long-range, subsonic, high-altitude, jet-powered, nuclear-capable strategic bomber, configured and flown as B-52G in Vietnam and Iraq to drop conventional bombs
BBC	British Broadcasting Corporation
bbl	barrel
BCCF	Baghdad Central Confinement Facility (Abu Ghraib)
BDA	bomb damage assessment
B-dienst	*Beobachtungs und Entzifferungs Dienst*, observation and cryptanalytic service, the German navy's SIGINT service
Bewegungskrieg	war of movement (and maneuver)
Blitzkrieg	lightning war
Bocage	A mass of small, irregularly shaped farm fields in Normandy separated by hedgerows consisting of earthen banks, several feet high, topped with a mass of tangled vegetation; the *bocage* provides natural cover, concealment, and ready-made engagement areas—a patchwork quilt ideal for the defense.

BSP	Baghdad Security Plan (Iraqi War IV)
BUA	Battlefield Update and Assessment (Iraqi Wars III and IV)
C^3	command, control, and communications
C^3I	command, control, communications, and intelligence
C^4/ISR	command, control, communications, and computers/intelligence, surveillance, reconnaissance
CAP	combat air patrol (WWII) or Combined Action Platoon (Vietnam)
CBO	Congressional Budget Office
CCS	Combined Chiefs of Staff, Allied
CENTCOM	US Central Command
CEP	circular error probable
CERP	Commander's Emergency Response Program (Iraqi Wars III and IV)
Chicom	Chinese communist
CHOP	change of operational control
CIA	Central Intelligence Agency
CINC	commander in chief, pronounced "sink"
CINCCENT	commander in chief, Central Command
CINCFE	commander in chief, Far East
CINCPAC	commander in chief, Pacific Fleet
CINCUNC	commander in chief of the United Nations Command (Korea)
CJCS	chairman, Joint Chiefs of Staff
CJTF-7	Combined Joint Task Force–7 (Iraqi War IV)
CMH	Center of Military History, US Army
CNN	Cable News Network
CNO	chief of naval operations
COIN	Counterinsurgency
COM Z	Communications Zone, the forward logistical headquarters for US forces operating in Northwest Europe during World War II
COMSOPAC	commander, South Pacific
COMUSMACV	commander, US Military Assistance Command Vietnam
CONUS	Continental United States
COP	combat outpost (Iraqi War IV surge)
CORDS	Civil Operations and Revolutionary Development Support (Vietnam)
COSSAC	chief of staff to the supreme Allied commander
COSVN	Central Office for South Vietnam. This organization served as the headquarters of the Lao Dong Party in South Vietnam. It directed the military and political activities of the communist insurgency. Until 1967, it was located inside South Vietnam but was driven into eastern Cambodia and US military forces. (Finlayson, *Rice Paddy Recon*, glossary, 297)
CPA	Coalition Provisional Authority
CSO	Bureau of Conflict and Stabilization Operations (State Department)

CSR	Office of the Coordinator for Construction and Stabilization (State Department)
CTZ	Corps Tactical Zone (Vietnam)
DARPA	Defense Advanced Research Projects Agency (after 1972)
DCI	director of central intelligence
Deutsches Afrikakorps	German Africa Corps, deployed to North Africa in 1941 with General Rommel in command and became *Panzergruppe Afrika*, consisting of both German and Italian divisions, of which the DAK was a part; it then became *Panzerarmee Afrika* (January–October 1942), and then subsequently went through another evolution of more grandiose designations inversely proportional to their military success. At the time of the Alamein defeat, Axis forces became *Deutsche-Italienische Panzerarmee.*
DGSE	*Direction générale de la sécurité extérieure* (French intelligence service)
DIA	Defense Intelligence Agency
DMZ	demilitarized zone
DoD	Department of Defense, United States
DOS	Department of State
DPRK	Democratic People's Republic of Korea
EA-6B	EA-6B Prowler, electronic warfare aircraft, USN and USMC
E-8A	E-8A Joint STARS aircraft, USAF
EF-111A	EF-111A Raven, electronic warfare aircraft, USAF
ECB	engineer combat battalion
ECCM	electronic counter-countermeasure
ECM	electronic countermeasure
EFP	explosively formed penetrator, enhanced IED or VBIED causing more lethality and damage when detonated, supplied by Iranians to Iraqi insurgent groups; EFP roadside bombs looked like large coffee cans with a precisely milled copper disc at one end; when activated by a passive infrared sensor, explosives in the can detonated, propelling the disc forward and turning it into a mass of molten copper that could penetrate through heavy armor (Gordon and Trainor, *The Endgame*, 151)
Einsatzgruppen	German special-operations groups tasked to eliminate designated racial groups in *Mitteleuropa*, especially Jews
Elektroboot	advanced German submarine design
Enigma	Allied encryption equipment derived from Polish mathematicians breaking into German message traffic in the 1930s
EOGB	electro-optically guided bomb
ePRT	embedded PRT (Iraqi War IV)
ERP	European Recovery Program
Erprobungsgruppe	operational trials wing, special *Luftwaffe* unit
Erprobungskommandos	operational test commands
ESG	Executive Steering Group (George W. Bush era)
ETO	European theater of operations

EW	electronic warfare
F	Fahrenheit
F-4 or F-4 G	F-4 Phantom or F-4G Wild Weasel, flown in *Desert Storm* for enemy radar suppression mission
F-14	F-14 Tomcat, tactical attack aircraft, USN
F-15	F-15 Eagle, all-weather, tactical attack aircraft; F-15 C/D, improved model for tactical strike missions; F-15E Strike Eagle, an improved and enhanced version of earlier models, USAF
F-16	F-16 Fighting Falcon, tactical attack aircraft, USAF
F/A-18	F-18 Hornet, supersonic, twin-engine, all-weather, carrier-capable, tactical attack aircraft designed for interception and ground-attack missions, USN
F-86	US Sabre jet fighter flown in Korea, built by North American Aviation, USAF
F-111 E/F	F-111 E/F Aardvark, supersonic, medium-range interdictor and tactical attack aircraft, flown in Vietnam, with later E/F variants with more advanced engines and avionics, flown in *Desert Storm*
F-117A	F-117 Nighthawk advanced stealth fighter
flak	*Flugzeug Abwehr Kanonen*, antiaircraft artillery (German)
FLIR	forward-looking infrared
FM	field manual, US Army
FOB	forward operating base
Fortitude	Operation *Fortitude* was an Allied deception: the creation of the bogus First United States Army Group (FUSAG) under the command of a general known and respected by the German officers, Lieutenant General George S. Patton Jr.
FRUS	Foreign Relations of the United States, US official diplomatic documents
FSB	Federal Intelligence Service (Russian intelligence service)
FUSAG	First United States Army Group
G3	Alpha-numeric designator for staff responsible for military operations
GAO	US Government Accountability Office
Gauleiter	party leader of a regional branch of the NSDAP
GC&CS	Government Code and Cypher School, UK (Bletchley Park)
GCHQ	Government Communications Headquarters, UK
GDP	gross domestic product
Generalplan Ost	German plan for the Germanization of usable, arable lands in the east, the wholesale relocation and reallocation of national populations according to German criteria of population density, and the relocation and genocide of Jewish populations everywhere in Europe
Gestapo	*Geheimnestaatpolizei*, secret state police
GHQ	general headquarters
GIGO	garbage in/garbage out

Glückliche Zeit	happy time, German expression when U-boats were successful off the US eastern seaboard
Goldfasane	"Golden Pheasants," pejorative term referring to top National Socialist party members
GPO	US Government Printing Office
GPS	Global Positioning System
GRC	General Research Corporation
GRT	gross registered tonnage
GVN	Government of (South) Vietnam
GWAPS	*Gulf War Air Power Survey*
hamlet	The smallest administrative entity in South Vietnam, usually a small grouping of houses within the larger entity of a village. Hamlets varied in size from one hundred to one thousand people.
HE	high-explosive
Heeresgruppe	army group, German
HES	Hamlet Evaluation System
HF	high frequency
HF/DF	high-frequency direction-finding equipment, pronounced "huff-duff"
HIDE	Handheld Interagency Identification Detection Equipment
HMMWV	high-mobility multipurpose wheeled vehicle
HMS	His Majesty's Ship or Her Majesty's Ship, depending upon the British monarch's gender at the time of service
HUMINT	human intelligence
Hunger Plan	plan to implement German policy to uproot between thirty-one and forty-five million people from their homes in what became a murderously violent process of dispossession to enable Germanization of conquered territories
IAEA	International Atomic Energy Agency
ID	infantry division
IEA	International Energy Agency
IED	improvised explosive device (Iraqi Wars III and IV)
IGC	Interim Governing Council to submit a plan for drafting a constitution and electing a government established by the CPA during Iraqi War IV
Igloo White	code name for classified program for the aerial insertion of electronic sensors to detect and interdict vehicle and personnel traffic along the Ho Chi Minh Trail in Laos and Vietnam
IJA	Imperial Japanese Army
IJN	Imperial Japanese Navy
IMINT	imagery intelligence
ISAF	International Security Assistance Force (Afghanistan)
ISF	Iraqi Security Forces
ISI	Inter-Services Intelligence directorate (Pakistani intelligence service)

ISIL	Islamic State of Iraq and the Levant (used interchangeably with ISIS during the Obama administration to avoid explicit identification of Syria)
ISIS	Islamic State of Iraq and al-Sham (Syria)
JAM	*Jaish al-Mahdi*, also known as the Mahdi Army, an Iraqi paramilitary force, created by Iraqi Shia cleric Moqtada al-Sadr
JCS	Joint Chiefs of Staff
JFC-E	Joint Forces Command–East (Iraqi War I)
JFC-N	Joint Forces Command–North (Iraqi War I)
JN 25	Japanese Naval Code 25, cracked by American code breakers
JSAT	Joint Strategic Assessment Team (Iraqi War IV)
JSS	joint security stations (Iraqi War IV surge)
JSTARS or Joint STARS	Joint Surveillance and Target Attack Radar System (Iraqi Wars I–IV)
Ju-88	Junkers 88, German two-engine, medium bomber
kamikaze	Japanese word for "divine wind," referring to a systematic campaign to sink Allied ships by flying one-way combat sorties where pilots crashed conventional fighter, bomber, and torpedo planes into ships. Also refers to any Japanese piloting a boat or submarine on a suicide mission against a target.
KBR	Kellogg Brown & Root (Wars II and IV contractor consortium in Iraq)
Kesselschlacht	cauldron battle
KIA	killed in action
Kido Butai	Mobile Unit/Force, was IJN's Combined Fleet tactical designation for its carrier strike force
km	kilometer
KMAG	US Army Korean Military Advisory Group
KPA	Korean People's Army (North Korea)
Kriegsmarine	German navy
KTB	*Kriegstagebüch*, daily war diary
KTO	Kuwait theater of operations
lb.	pound
LC	landing craft
LCA	landing craft assault
LCI	landing craft infantry
LCM	landing craft mechanized
LCT	landing craft tank
Lend-Lease	US program to provide war matériel to Allies
LGB	laser-guided bomb
LIC	low-intensity conflict
LOC	line of communication
LORAN	long-range navigation
LST	landing ship tank
Luftflotte	air fleet, German
Luftwaffe	German air force

LZ	landing zone (helicopter)
M2/M3	Bradley fighting vehicle
M-16	officially known as rifle, caliber 5.56 mm, the M-16 is the US military designation for the AR-1 Armalite rifle adapted for semiautomatic, three-round burst, and full automatic fire, built by Colt Manufacturing Company
MAAF	Mediterranean Allied Air Force
MAAG-V	Military Assistance Advisory Group–Vietnam
MACCORDS	Military Assistance Command Vietnam, Civil Operations and Revolutionary Development Support
MACV	Military Assistance Command Vietnam
madrassa	Islamic boarding school in Pakistan that teaches mostly Islamic subjects but in many cases may serve as a indoctrination and training center for jihad
Magic	Allied cryptanalysis project during World War II, principally undertaken by US code-breaking units
MAP	Master Air Plan (Iraqi War I)
MARCENT	Marine Central Command (Iraqi War I)
Marine-Funkschlüssel-Maschine M	German radio naval decryption machine
Me-109	Messerschmitt 109, German fighter
Me-262	Messerschmitt 262, advanced German jet fighter design, flown in combat during last months of the war
MEF	Marine Expeditionary Force
Metox	French firm (also Grandin) that produced the electronic equipment that could receive signals over some radar frequency ranges; *Metox* receiver sets were called FuMB for *Funkmessbeobachtergerät*, radar observer device
MI6	British Secret Intelligence Service
MiG	Soviet military aircraft design bureau, Mikoyan-and-Gurevich Design Bureau; the *MiG* prefix was placed in front of numbered fighter models
MiG-15	Soviet jet fighter, circa Korean War
MiG-29	Soviet jet fighter, circa Iraqi Wars I–III
MILES	Multiple Integrated Laser Engagement System
Mitteleuropa	German term for central Europe
MLR	Main Line of Resistance
MLRS	M270 Multiple Launch Rocket System
mm	millimeter, generally referring to rifle, gun, or artillery calibers
MNC-I	Multi-National Corps–Iraq (Iraq War IV)
MNF-I	Multi-National Force–Iraq (Iraqi War IV)
MOBA	military operation in a built-up area
Montagnard	French term meaning "people from the mountain," referring to the indigenous, non–ethnic Vietnamese population inhabiting the Central Highlands of Vietnam; used routinely by Americans in Vietnam
MOUT	military operation in urban terrain

MP	military police
MR	Military Region (Vietnam)
MRAP	mine-resistant ambush-protected vehicle
MTO	Mediterranean theater of operations
Mulberry	code name for artificial floating harbor, several of which were deployed for the D-Day Normandy landings
NARA	National Archives and Records Administration
NATO	North Atlantic Treaty Organization
NAVSHIPS	Bureau of Ships, USN
NBC	nuclear, biological, chemical
NCO	noncommissioned officer
Nebelwerfer	"fog thrower," a German five-barreled multiple rocket launcher mounted on a towed carriage
NFZ	no-fly zone
NKIDP	North Korea International Documentation Project (Woodrow Wilson Center)
NKP	Nakhon Phanom (province in northeastern Thailand)
NKVD	Narodnyy Komissariat Vnutrennikh Del, People's Commissariat for Internal Affairs, Soviet secret police organization during the Stalinist era
NLF	National Liberation Front
NSA	National Security Agency
NSC	National Security Council
NSC-XX	National Security Council directives from Truman era, generally designated by NSC, followed by the number of the directive
NSDAP	National Socialist German Workers' Party, Nationalsozialistische Deutsche Arbeiterpartei
NSDD	National Security Decision Directive (Reagan era)
NSPD	National Security Presidential Directive (Bush era)
NSSM	National Security Study Memorandum (Nixon era)
NVA	North Vietnamese Army
OB	order of battle
OB West	Oberbefehlshaber West, commander in chief, West, German high command designation for Western Front
Oberbefehlshaber der Kriegsmarine	commander in chief of the German navy
OER	Officer Efficiency Report
OIC	Operational Intelligence Center
OKH	Oberkommando der Herres, high command of German army
OKW	Oberkommando der Wehrmacht, high command of German armed forces
OpFor	opposing force
OPSEC	operational security
ORC	Opinion Research Corporation
ORHA	Office of Reconstruction and Humanitarian Assistance (Iraqi War IV)
ORSA	operations research and systems analysis

OSD	Office of the Secretary of Defense
Ostheer	German army on Eastern Front
OV-10	OV-10 Bronco, twin-turboprop, light attack and observation aircraft, USAF, USMC, flown in *Desert Storm* and earlier in Vietnam
OW	*On War*
P-38	P-38 Lockheed Lightning, World War II twin-engine fighter interceptor, built by the Lockheed Corporation
P-47	P-47 Thunderbolt, World War II fighter, built by Republic Aviation
P-51	P-51 Mustang, World War II, long-range fighter built by North American Aviation, developed to escort bombers in ETO and provide close air ground support; operated globally and during Korean War
Panzer	German term for tank
Panzerarmee	German tank army
Panzerfaust	German antitank weapon
PAVN	People's Army of Vietnam (formal term for NVA)
PDD	Presidential Decision Directive (Clinton era)
PF	Popular Force (Vietnam)
Pfc	private first class
PGM	precision-guided munition
Phoenix	The American name for the South Vietnamese pacification program called *Phung Hoang*. The Phoenix program began in 1967 aimed at defeating the communist political infrastructure in the villages of South Vietnam by forcing all of the American and South Vietnamese organizations involved with defeating the VCI to cooperate and coordinate their efforts at every administrative level of the GVN.
Pillenwerfer	Submarine decoy, a bubble ejector, consisting of a perforated metal cylinder about the size of a standard container of tinned vegetables, released by a submerged U-boat through a special vent. It contained calcium hydride which, when mixed with seawater, produced a dense column of hydrogen bubbles.
PLA	People's Liberation Army (PRC)
PLO	Palestine Liberation Organization
PLUTO	pipeline under the ocean
POL	petroleum, oil, and lubricants
POW	prisoner of war
PPS	Policy Planning Staff (State Department)
PRC	People's Republic of China
PROVN	Program for the Pacification and Long-Term Development of South Vietnam, army staff study in 1966
PRT	Provincial Reconstruction Teams (Iraqi War IV) or Provincial Reconnaissance Team (Vietnam)
PTSD	posttraumatic stress disorder

puzzle diagram	PowerPoint chart, presented by General David H. Petraeus, attempting to display graphically the interrelationships among political, economic, military, and security measures (Iraqi War IV)
Pvt	private
R&D	research and development
RAF	Royal Air Force
RAID	Rapid Aerostat Initial Deployment
RDC	Revolutionary Development Cadre (Vietnam)
RDT&E	research, development, test, and evaluation
Reichskriegsministerium	Reich War Ministry
Reichsminister für Rüstung und Kriegsproduktion	Reich minister for armaments and war production
Reichsminister für Volksaufklärung und Propaganda	Reich minister for public enlightenment and propaganda
RF	radio frequency or Regional Force (Vietnam)
RF-4C	RF-4C Phantom II, tactical reconnaissance aircraft, flown during *Desert Storm*
RMA	revolution in military affairs
RMK-BRJ	Raymond International, Morrison-Knudsen International, Brown & Root, and J. A. Jones Construction Company, joint venture of contractors in Vietnam
RN	Royal Navy
ROAD	Reorganization Objective Army Division
ROK	Republic of Korea
ROKA	Republic of Korea Army (South Korea)
Route Package	Authorizations and designations of routes for ingress and egress for naval and air force bombing missions during Vietnam War
RPG	rocket-propelled grenade (Vietnam and Iraqi Wars)
S-3 (US Army staff position)	operations officer (battalion level)
S-3 (aircraft)	S-3 Viking, twin-engine, turbofan jet aircraft designed for ASW and USN surface warfare missions, USN, flown in *Desert Storm*
S-5	civil affairs officer (battalion level)
SAC	Strategic Air Command
SAM	surface-to-air missile
SBN	"Dauntless" dive-bomber, built by Douglas Aircraft Corporation
SCAP	supreme commander, Allied powers (in the Far East)
Schnorchel	snorkel, a tall tube rising from a submarine's conning tower to above the ocean surface so that a U-boat could take in fresh air while running submerged with its diesel engines
Schwerpunkt	heavy or main point of attack
SHAEF	Supreme Headquarters Allied Expeditionary Force
SHAPE	Supreme Headquarters Allied Powers Europe
SIGINT	signals intelligence

SIM	*Servicio Informazione Militare*, Italian military intelligence service
SINCGARS	Single Channel Ground and Airborne Radio System, US Army tactical radio
situational awareness	ability to identify, process, and comprehend critical elements of information about what is happening in a combat environment; more simply, it is knowing what is going on around you
SNAFU	"situation normal all fucked up," American World War II colloquial expression
SOFA	status-of-forces agreement
sonar	sound navigation and ranging, Allied submarine detection equipment
sortie	individual operational flight by a pilot
SS	*Schutzstaffel*, protection echelon (literally); SS initially served as Hitler's praetorian guard and later evolved into the *Waffen-SS*, an elite force that fielded by 1944 almost six hundred thousand men (thirty-eight divisions by 1945)
Stabschwarm	staff flight, German
Staffel	flight (*Luftwaffe*) or echelon (more general)
Stavka	Russian supreme military command (*Stavka Verkhovnogo Komandovaniya*)
Stellungskrieg	positional, defensive warfare
SVN	South Vietnam
T-34	Soviet medium battle tank, used during World War II and Korean War by communist forces
T-72	Soviet state-of-the-art main battle tank, circa 1990
T-82	Soviet state-of-the-art main battle tank, circa 1990
TAOR	tactical area of operational responsibility
TBD-1	American "Devastator" torpedo bombers, built by Douglas Aircraft Corporation
TERCOM	terrain contour matching guidance system
TF	task force
TLAM	Tomahawk land-attack cruise missile
TNT	trinitrotoluene was a common explosive material used in World War II and Korea, a chemical compound ($C_6H_2[NO_2]_3CH_3$)
TOE	table of organization and equipment
TOW	tube-launched, optically tracked, wire-guided missile
TRADOC	Training and Doctrine Command
UAV	unmanned aerial vehicle, aka "drone"
U-boat	*Unterseeboot*, German submarine
UH-60	US "Blackhawk" transport helicopter
UK	United Kingdom
Ultra	code name for British code-breaking intelligence products
UN	United Nations
UNDRO	United Nations Disaster Relief Organization (Iraqi War II)

UNMOVIC	United Nations Monitoring, Verification and Inspection Commission (Iraqi War II)
UNSCOM	United Nations Special Commission (Iraqi War II)
US	United States
USA	US Army
USAAF	US Army Air Force (until 1947)
USAF	US Air Force (after 1947)
USAFFE	US Army Forces, Far East
USAID	US Agency for International Development
USIA	US Information Agency
USMA	US Military Academy
USMC	US Marine Corps
USMM	US Merchant Marine
USN	US Navy
USSBS	US Strategic Bombing Survey (World War II)
USSR	Union of Soviet Socialist Republics
V-1	*Vergeltungswaffe-1*, German retaliation weapon, colloquially known in Britain as the "Buzz Bomb" or "Doodlebug." It was an early pulse-jet-powered unmanned aerial vehicle, built by Fieseler.
V-2	*Vergeltungswaffe-2*, German retaliation weapon, the first short-range ballistic missile used in armed conflict
VB	abbreviation for USN dive-bomber squadron
VBIED	vehicle-borne IED (Iraqi Wars III and IV)
VCI	Viet Cong Infrastructure
Vernichtungsschlacht	battle of annihilation
VF	abbreviated designation for a USN fighter squadron followed by the squadron number
VHF	very high frequency
village	A grouping of hamlets that constituted the basic rural administrative entity in South Vietnam. Villages ranged in size from one thousand to ten thousand people.
VLR	very long range
VS	abbreviation for USN scouting squadron
VT	abbreviation for a USN torpedo bombing squadron followed by the squadron number
WDF	Western Desert Force, British North African army designation, circa 1941
Wehrmacht	German armed forces
Westheer	German army on Western Front
WMD	weapon(s) of mass destruction
XO	executive officer

NOTES

PART I: STRATEGIC ARCHITECTURES

1. Lawrence Freedman, *Strategy: A History* (Oxford: Oxford University Press, 2013), xi–xii.

2. Freedman, *Strategy*, 611.

3. Eliot A. Cohen, *Supreme Command: Soldiers, Statesmen and Leadership in Wartime* (New York: Free Press, 2002), 1–2.

4. Two sets of cultural lenses are referenced in later chapters to help explain conflict outcomes. Adrian R. Lewis, *The American Culture of War: The History of U.S. Military Force from World War II to Operation Enduring Freedom* (New York: Routledge, 2012), 1–2, passim. Lewis traces evolving practice to five factors: the United States becoming a superpower in 1945, the advent of *"artificial limited war"* (italics in original), the technological revolution in warfare, expanded American expectations from life in peacetime, and "a new American militarism." Brian A. Linn, *The Echo of Battle: The Army's Way of War* (Cambridge, MA: Harvard University Press, 2007), 5, passim. Linn delineates three "martial philosophies" that have shaped American military thinking within the US Army: Guardians, Heroes, and Managers.

5. Cohen, *Supreme Command*, 109, 132.

6. Cohen, *Supreme Command*, 109–10.

7. Frederick W. Kagan, *Finding the Target: The Transformation of American Military Policy* (New York: Encounter Books, 2006), 371.

8. Eldad Eilam, *Reversing: Secrets of Reverse Engineering* (Indianapolis, IN: Wiley, 2005), 3–4.

9. Carl (Philipp Gottfried) von Clausewitz, *On War*, ed. and trans. Sir Michael Eliot Howard and Peter Paret (Princeton, NJ: Princeton University Press, 1984), 87, Book I, chap. 1, para. 24 (hereafter cited as *OW* by page, book, chapter, and para., e.g., *OW*, 87, I:1:24).

10. The text at *OW* 87, I:1:24, reads, "We see, therefore, that war is not merely an act of policy but a true political instrument, a continuation of political intercourse, carried on with other means. What remains peculiar to war is simply the peculiar nature of its means."

11. Sun Tzu, *The Art of War*, trans. Lionel Giles (Lexington, KY: BN Publishing, 2007), 7, chap. I, paras. 1 and 2 (hereafter cited as *Art of War* by page, chapter, and para., e.g., *Art of War*, 7, I:1, 2); and Sun-Tzu Ping-Fa, *The Essential Art of War*, trans. and commentaries by Ralph D. Sawyer (New York: Basic Books, 2005), 1.

12. Martin van Creveld, *The Art of War: War and Military Thought* (London: Cassell, 2000), 119.

13. Van Creveld, *The Art of War*, 119.

14. Clausewitz, *OW*, 579, VIII:2.

15. Clausewitz in his "sketches" for Book VIII ("War Plans") mentions the benefit of allies in his chapter 9 discussion of a conflict between Prussia and Austria fighting France (*OW*, 619, VIII:9). There are numerous references to allies in seven of the eight books of *On War* but no explicit systematic discussion of the benefits of securing allies. Sun Tzu mentions allies in his exposition of the "nine situations" (*Art of War*, 53, 54, XI:12).

16. Churchill read *The Prince* early in his education as a statesman. Roosevelt certainly was aware of Machiavelli from his Groton prep school education and his Uncle Theodore Roosevelt's mentoring. Niccolò Machiavelli, *The Prince*, trans. Hill Thompson (Norwalk, CT: Easton Press, 1980), 161–62, chap. 21, "How a Prince Should Bear Himself," first published in Italy in 1532; and James MacGregor Burns, *Roosevelt: The Lion and the Fox, 1882–1940* (1956; repr., New York: Harcourt, 1984), 15, 80, and 472.

17. Winston S. Churchill, *The Best of Winston Churchill's Speeches* (New York: Hyperion, 2003), 289–90.

18. Churchill, *The Best of Winston Churchill's Speeches*, 289.

19. Mark McNeilly, *Sun Tzu and the Art of Modern Warfare* (New York: Oxford University Press, 2001), 28, 191–96.

PART II: WORLD WAR II

1. Fest records Dr. Paul K. Schmidt's (German foreign minister von Ribbentrop's chief interpreter) description of his delivery of the British diplomatic note to the Reich Chancellery: "Hitler sat immobile, staring into space. . . . After an interval, which seemed an eternity to me, he turned to Ribbentrop who had remained standing frozen by the window. 'What now?' Hitler asked his Foreign Minister with a furious glare." Joachim C. Fest, *Hitler* (New York: Harcourt, 1974), 601.

2. Richard Overy, *Why the Allies Won* (London: Pimlico, 1995), 1–3.

3. Mark Harrison, "Counting Soviet Deaths in the Great Patriotic War: Comment," *Europe-Asia Studies* 55, no. 6 (2003): 939–44; for civilian deaths, see G. F. Krivosheev and M. F. Filimoshin, "Poteri vooruzhennykh sil SSSR v Velikoi Otechestvennoi voine" [Losses of Soviet armed forces in World War II], in *Naselenie v XX veke. Ostoricheskie orcheriki. Tom 2. 1940–1959*, ed. V. B. Zhiromskaia (Moscow: Rosspen, 2001), 30–31. Harrison asserts that "Krivosheev's data are the best we have" and adds that for the complete armed forces the total military personnel losses are 11.9 million. Harrison, "Counting Soviet Deaths," 939ff.

4. The US Army in the 1970s and 1980s studied the German army in World War II. In 1976, General William H. DuPuy, a combat-tested officer during World War II and commander of an infantry division in Vietnam, wrote much of the new Field Manual (FM) 100-5, *Operations*, the army's premier tactical doctrine manual of the time. FM 100-5

emphasized the speed with which decisive actions would transpire on modern battlefields and enhanced awareness of the increased lethality of modern weapons. This evolved into the AirLand Battle Doctrine of the 1980s. Richard W. Stewart, ed., *American Military History*, vol. 2, *The United States Army in a Global Era, 1917–2003*, CMH Pub. 30-22 (Washington, DC: US Army Center of Military History, 2005), 378 and chap. 12, "Rebuilding the Army, Vietnam to Desert Storm."

5. The ninety-division gamble was "a decision based more on the erroneous belief that American industry could not give up more manpower to the military without incurring shortfalls than on any rational calculation of American needs on the battlefield." Peter R. Mansoor, *The GI Offensive in Europe: The Triumph of American Infantry Divisions, 1941–1945* (Lawrence: University Press of Kansas, 1999), 10–11, 15.

6. Organizzazione per la Vigilanza e la Repressione dell'Antifascismo (OVRA), "Organization for Vigilance and Repression of Anti-Fascism."

7. Congressional Budget Office, *The Budget and Economic Outlook: Fiscal Years 2013 to 2023* (Washington, DC: Congress of the United States, February 2013), 2, fig. 1.

8. The reference librarian of the Humanities and Social Sciences Division, Library of Congress, estimates that the World War II collection includes two hundred thousand titles (email from Rodney P. Katz, August 12, 2009).

CHAPTER 1. BATTLE OF BRITAIN

1. First speech to the House of Commons, May 13, 1940, https://www.winstonchurchill.org/learn/speeches/speeches-of-winston-churchill/92-blood-toil-tears-and-sweat.

2. Second speech to the House, June 4, 1940, https://www.winstonchurchill.org/learn/speeches/speeches-of-winston-churchill/128-we-shall-fight-on-the-beaches.

3. Retired French general Maxime Weygand, a World War I veteran, had been called back into service to command the Allied armies in France.

4. Third speech to the House, June 18, 1940, http://www.winstonchurchill.org/resources/speeches/1940-the-finest-hour/their-finest-hour.

5. Denmark, Norway, Holland, Belgium, Luxembourg, and France.

6. John Lukacs, *Five Days in London, May 1940* (New Haven, CT: Yale University Press, 1999), 2, 194. Churchill acquired his set of talents during a lifetime of long, deep service in government. Three times during World War I, he served the Crown, as First Lord of the Admiralty already in office when the war started and, after the failure of the Dardanelles and Gallipoli campaigns of 1915, as an infantry officer on the Western Front in 1916, and then later in 1917 as minister of munitions. In that post, "Not allowed to make the plans. I was set to make the weapons." Churchill streamlined the fifty large departments operating under the ministry, grouped them into ten large enterprises under heads who became direct reports to him, and created a Munitions Council to coordinate everything collegially; the result was a huge increase in the mass-production capacity of Britain's war industries that delivered the "mountains" of munitions to the Western Front in time to stop Ludendorff's offensive the following year. It was experience like this that he brought to No. 10 Downing Street in May 1940 where he imposed his will on institutions large and small until World War II ended in victory. He wrote about what he did in illuminating detail. Winston S. Churchill, *The World Crisis, 1911–1918*, abridged and rev. ed. (New York: Free Press, 1931), 722ff, chap. 47.

7. Richard Overy, *The Battle of Britain: The Myth and the Reality* (New York: Norton, 2000), 58ff; and Andrew Roberts, *The Storm of War: A New History of the Second World War* (London: Allen Lane, 2009), 106.

8. James Holland, *The Battle of Britain: Five Months That Changed History, May–October 1940* (London: Bantam, 2010), 59.

9. High-frequency (HF) radios were prone to communication distortion and operated over shorter ranges; very-high-frequency (VHF) sets enabled better voice transmission and reception over longer ranges. Only Fighter Command late in the battle had VHF sets in its fighter cockpits.

10. Performance comparisons between the Spitfire and Me-109 are the subject of endless debate. See "Spitfire Mk. I versus Me-109 E: A Performance Comparison," http://www.spitfireperformance.com/spit1vrs109e.html. For production figures, also see Overy, *Battle of Britain*, 159, table 1; and Stephen Bungay, *The Most Dangerous Enemy* (London: Aurum, 2000), 372.

11. Holland, *Battle of Britain*, 106ff.

12. Roberts, *Storm of War*, 95.

13. The eight wing-mounted Browning .303 machine guns in Spitfires could fire for 14.7 seconds versus 55 seconds for Me-109s with four MG-17s; James Holland, *The Rise of Germany, 1939–1941: The War in the West* (New York: Atlantic Monthly Press, 2015), 303, 333; and Geoffrey Wellum, *First Light: The True Story of the Boy Who Became a Man in the War-Torn Skies above Britain* (Hoboken, NJ: Wiley, 2002) 165, 168, 195, 336.

14. Overy, *Battle of Britain*, 44–45.

15. Williamson Murray and Allan R. Millett, eds., *Military Innovation in the Interwar Period* (Cambridge: Cambridge University Press, 1996), 284; and David E. Fisher, *A Summer Bright and Terrible: Winston Churchill, Lord Dowding, Radar, and the Impossible Triumph of the Battle of Britain* (Washington, DC: Shoemaker and Hoard, 2005), 73–75.

16. Roberts, *Storm of War*, 96.

17. Fisher, *Summer Bright and Terrible*, 62.

18. Bungay, *Most Dangerous Enemy*, 380–81.

19. Roberts, *Storm of War*, 99.

20. Bungay, *Most Dangerous Enemy*, 64; and Peter Townsend, *Duel of Eagles*, paperback ed. (New York: Simon & Schuster, 1971), 176ff.

21. Bungay, *Most Dangerous Enemy*, 114–15; and Derek Robinson, *Invasion, 1940: The Truth about the Battle of Britain and What Stopped Hitler* (New York: Carol and Graf, 2005), 249.

22. Eighty percent of the German army's entire transport was horse drawn.

23. Robinson, *Invasion*, 205–6.

24. Bungay, *Most Dangerous Enemy*, 130.

25. By September, Park abandoned the "vic" formation, telling his pilots to fly in the looser, line-abreast formation of four. Holland, *Battle of Britain*, 545.

26. Bungay, *Most Dangerous Enemy*, 368; and Overy, *Battle of Britain*, 128.

27. Bungay, *Most Dangerous Enemy*, 379.

28. Williamson Murray, *Military Adaptation in War: With Fear of Change* (Cambridge: Cambridge University Press, 2011), 182–83; and Roberts, *Storm of War*, 100.

29. Peter Caddick-Adams, *Snow and Steel: The Battle of the Bulge, 1944–45* (Oxford: Oxford University Press, 2015), 62.

30. Richard Overy, *The Air War, 1939–1945* (Washington, DC: Potomac, 2005), 110.

31. Len Deighton, *Fighter: The True Story of the Battle of Britain* (1977; repr., New York: HarperCollins, 1994), 256–57.

32. Operation *Felix* never got beyond the staff study stage. Walther Hubatsch, *Hitlers Weisungen für die Kriegführung, Dokumente des Oberkommandos der Wehrmacht* (Frankfurt: Bernard and Graefe Verlag, 1962), 72–75, Weisungen Nos. 18a and 19.

33. Bungay, *Most Dangerous Enemy*, 386, citing Drew Middleton, *The Sky Suspended* (London: Secker and Warburg, 1960), 230.

34. B. H. Liddell Hart, *The German Generals Talk* (New York: Quill, 1979), 153.

CHAPTER 2. BATTLE OF THE ATLANTIC

1. Peter Padfield, *War beneath the Sea: Submarine Conflict during World War II* (New York: Wiley, 1995), 25.

2. John Keegan, *The Second World War* (New York: Penguin, 1990), 105.

3. Williamson Murray and Allen R. Millett, *A War to Be Won: Fighting the Second World War* (Cambridge, MA: Harvard University Press, 2000), 235.

4. Murray and Millett, *War to Be Won*, 235–36.

5. Adam Tooze, *The Wages of Destruction: The Making and Breaking of the Nazi Economy* (New York: Viking Penguin, 2006), 121–22, 338, 435–36, 613ff.

6. John Terraine, *Business in Great Waters: The U-boat Wars, 1916–1945* (London: Leo Cooper, 1989), 361–62, 409.

7. For the fall of 1942, Offley's U-boat numbers are much higher than Terraine's: 80–100 U-boats at sea in the North Atlantic for mass wolfpack attacks. Edward Offley, *Turning the Tide: How a Small Band of Allied Sailors Defeated the U-boats and Won the Battle of the Atlantic* (New York: Basic Books, 2011), x, xxvi. Westwood reports much larger numbers of U-boats by 1943: "368 boats in all, 193 operational and 175 in training and working-up." David Westwood, *The U-boat War: The German Submarine Service and the Battle of the Atlantic, 1935–1945* (Philadelphia, PA: Casemate, 2005), 73.

8. Murray and Millett, *War to Be Won*, 249.

9. Padfield's 1942 operational numbers are comparable: thirty U-boats at sea in the Atlantic at any one time. Padfield, *War beneath the Sea*, 149.

10. Murray and Millett, *War to Be Won*, 238; David K. Brown, *Atlantic Escorts, Ships, Weapons and Tactics in World War II* (Annapolis, MD: Naval Institute Press, 2008), 46–47, tables 2.2 and 2.3 for corvettes on order; and John Lambert and Les Brown, *Flower Class Corvettes* (Barnsley, UK: Seaforth, 2008), 7, 65–72; launch and completion numbers were extracted from the "Corvette Building List."

11. Michael L. Dockrill and Brian J. C. McKercher, *Diplomacy and World Power: Studies in British Foreign Policy, 1890–1950*, paperback ed. (Cambridge: Cambridge University Press, 2002), 205. Keegan defines minimal import tonnage at fifty-five million. Keegan, *Second World War*, 105.

12. Winston S. Churchill, *The Second World War*, vol. 2, *Their Finest Hour* (London: Cassell, 1949), 529.

13. Keegan limits the sea space to nine million square miles of "operational waters." John Keegan, *Intelligence in War: Knowledge of the Enemy from Napoleon to Al-Qaeda* (New York: Knopf, 2003), 237.

14. Westwood, *The U-boat War*, 267–76.

15. Clay Blair, *Hitler's U-boat War*, vol. 1, *The Hunters, 1939–45* (New York: Random House, 1986), 244–45; and Terraine, *Business in Great Waters*, 501–2.

16. Winston S. Churchill, *The Second World War*, vol. 5, *Closing the Ring* (London: Cassell, 1951), 6.

17. Padfield, *War beneath the Sea*, 117–18, 328.

18. Blair, *Hitler's U-boat War*, 1:247.

19. Stephen Budiansky, *Blackett's War: The Men Who Defeated the Nazi U-boats and Brought Science to the Art of Warfare* (New York: Knopf, 2013), 182–83.

20. Offley, *Turning the Tide*, 180, 445.

21. Keegan, *Intelligence in War*, 244.

22. Paul Kennedy, *Engineers of Victory: The Problem Solvers Who Turned the Tide in the Second World War* (New York: Random House, 2013), 55–57.

23. Metox and Grandin were French firms that produced radar countermeasure equipment. Padfield, *War beneath the Sea*, 366.

24. Keegan, *Intelligence in War*, 253–54.

25. Murray and Millett, *War to Be Won*, 259.

26. Murray and Millett, *War to Be Won*, 239–40; and Keegan, *Intelligence in War*, 244.

27. Keegan, *Intelligence in War*, 235; and Len Deighton, *Blood, Tears and Folly: An Objective Look at World War Two* (New York: HarperCollins, 1993), 56–57.

28. Murray, *Military Adaptation*, 192.

29. Budiansky, *Blackett's War*, 214 (force multiplier), 224–25 (convoy size: a sixty-ship convoy was better and safer than a forty-ship one), 246 (Bay of Biscay VLR surveillance).

30. Budiansky, *Blackett's War*, 221.

31. Winston S. Churchill, *The Second World War*, vol. 3, *The Grand Alliance* (Boston: Houghton Mifflin, 1950), 100–101.

32. Budiansky, *Blackett's War*, 242.

33. Bernard Ireland, *Battle of the Atlantic* (Annapolis, MD: Naval Institute Press, 2003), 111. Ireland defines the climax period as January–July 1943. Keegan puts the "critical point" in July 1942, *Intelligence in War*, 113. Murray and Millett have the tables turning "irrevocably" in April–May 1943, *War to Be Won*, 256. Dockrill and McKercher put victory in the summer of 1943, *Diplomacy and World Power*, 205.

34. Keegan, *Intelligence in War*, 149–50, 237–42; and Murray and Millett, *War to Be Won*, 244–45.

35. Between February and December 1942, Bletchley Park lost its way into Enigma altogether, with a calamitous effect on sinkings. It was compounded by the *B-dienst*'s breakthrough into British naval codes. Keegan, *Intelligence in War*, 123. Offley's chapter 5, "The Battle of the Codes," is the best and most recent account written about the Bletchley–*B-dienst* competition, with clear exposition of the competing technologies. Offley, *Turning the Tide*.

36. A new convoy code, Cipher No. 5, was ordered into service in June 1943 that remained unbroken for the rest of the war. Offley, *Turning the Tide*, 100; and Budiansky, *Blackett's War*, 243.

37. Padfield, *War beneath the Sea*, 149, 170–71, 306, 314.

38. Keegan, *Intelligence in War*, 242; Blair, *Hitler's U-boat War*, 1:424; and Blair, *Hitler's U-boat War*, vol. 2, *The Hunted, 1939–45* (New York: Random House, 1988), 712.

39. Keegan, *Intelligence in War*, 240.

40. Offley, *Turning the Tide*, 375.

41. Offley, *Turning the Tide*, 212–26, 374–75, and 418.

42. American Merchant Marine at War, website presenting statistics on Battle of the Atlantic losses from multiple sources, http://www.usmm.org/battleatlantic.html. As used in the text, Nathan Miller puts North Atlantic losses at 2,742 ships sunk, *War at Sea: A Naval History of World War II* (New York: Scribner, 1995), 534, appendix 2; authoritative estimates vary but are comparable: Terraine's number of sinkings is 2,265, *Business in Great Waters*, 559; Blair's is about 2,900, *Hitler's U-boat War*, 2:813, appendix 16; and Offley's is 2,653, *Turning the Tide*, xxiv, 382.

43. Karl Dönitz, *Memoirs: Ten Years and Twenty Days* (1958 in German; Annapolis, MD: De Capo, 1997), 341.

CHAPTER 3. INVASION OF RUSSIA

1. Roberts, *Storm of War*, 608.
2. Tooze, *Wages of Destruction*, 487.
3. Richard J. Evans, *The Third Reich at War* (New York: Penguin, 2008), 173.
4. Tooze, *Wages of Destruction*, 465–66.
5. Tooze, *Wages of Destruction*, 464–80.
6. Two works document Stalin's surprise in detail: David E. Murphy, *What Stalin Knew: The Enigma of Barbarossa* (New Haven, CT: Yale University Press, 2005); and Constantine Pleshakov, *Stalin's Folly: The Tragic First Ten Days of WWII on the Eastern Front* (Boston: Houghton Mifflin, 2005). The Red Army on the eve of war fielded three million Soviet soldiers, fourteen to fifteen thousand tanks, thirty-four thousand artillery tubes, and eight to nine thousand fighter aircraft. Andrew Nagorski, *The Greatest Battle: Stalin, Hitler, and the Desperate Struggle for Moscow That Changed the Course of World War II* (New York: Simon & Schuster, 2007), 47; and David M. Glantz, ed., *The Initial Period of War on the Eastern Front, 22 June–August 1941* (London: Routledge, 1993), 29–31.
7. Richard Overy, *Russia's War: Blood upon the Snow* (New York: Penguin Putnam, 1997), 255.
8. By the spring of 1942, Soviet industrial facilities relocated to the Urals and further east began producing massive quantities of military equipment. Evans, *Third Reich at War*, 403.
9. Nagorski, *The Greatest Battle*, 2; David M. Glantz, "The Soviet-German War 1941–1945: Myths and Realities; A Survey Essay" (paper presented at Clemson University, October 11, 2001), 104, http://sti.clemson.edu/publications-mainmenu-38/commentaries -mainmenu-211/cat_view/33-strom-thurmond-institute/153-sti-publications-by-subject -area/158-history; David M. Glantz and Jonathan M. House, *The Battle of Kursk* (Lawrence: University Press of Kansas, 1999), 337–38; and David M. Glantz, *Colossus Reborn: The Red Army at War, 1941–1943* (Lawrence: University Press of Kansas, 2005), 621.
10. Rodric Braithwaite, *Moscow 1941: A City and Its People at War* (New York: Random House, 2006), 9, 327–28, citing Grigoriy F. Krivosheev, ed., *Rossia I SSSR v Voinakh XX Veka: Statisticheskoe Issledovanie* [Russia and the Soviet Union in 20th-century war: Armed forces losses, statistical investigation] (Moscow: Olma Press, 2001), 273, 276, 277, the source for the figures for Russian losses between September 30, 1941, and April 20, 1942; Braithwaite puts British World War II losses at 264,443, total British dead, including civilians, at 357,116, citing W. Franklin Mellor, ed., *Casualties and Medical Statistics* (London: HMSO, 1972), 829–39. The Congressional Research Service (CRS) of the US Congress reports 291,557 US battle casualties and 113,842 "other deaths," Hannah Fischer et al., *American War and Military Operations Casualties: Lists and Statistics* (Washington, DC: CRS, May 2008), 3, table 1.
11. Lincoln's saturnine phrase mentioned in Victor Davis Hanson, *The Soul of Battle* (New York: Anchor, 1999), 127, 208.
12. Keith Cummins, *Cataclysm: The War on the Eastern Front, 1941–45* (Solihill, UK: Hellion, 2011), 296, passim, citing Rüdiger Overmans, *Deutsche militärische Verluste im Zweiten Weltkrieg* (München: Oldenbourg Verlag, 2000), 265, 272.

13. Axis casualty sources: Overmans, *Deutsche militärische Verluste im Zweiten Welt-krieg*; Italy: *Ufficio Storico dello Stato Maggiore dell'Esercito* (Commissariato generale C.G.V., Ministero della Difesa—Edizioni 1986); Romania: Krivosheev, *Rossiia i SSSR v voinakh XX veka*, tables 200–203; Hungary: Krivosheev, ibid., tables 200–203.

14. Krivosheev, *Rossia I SSSR v Voinakh XX Veka*, tables 115 (26.6 million total Russian military and civilian casualties) and 133 (11.3 million Red Army casualties). English translation, http://translate.google.com/translate?hl=en&sl=ru&tl=en&u=http%3A%2F%2Flib .ru%2FMEMUARY%2F1939-1945%2FKRIWOSHEEW%2Fpoteri.txt.

15. Glantz puts the number at 34,476,700 in his "Myths and Realities" paper, 9.

16. OKW was the high-command organization of the German armed forces. OKH was the high command of the army.

17. Robert M. Citino, *Death of the Wehrmacht: The German Campaigns of 1942* (Lawrence: University Press of Kansas, 2007), 18.

18. Clausewitz, *OW*, 179, III:1.

19. Citino, *Death of the Wehrmacht*, 6–7.

20. Timothy W. Ryback, *Hitler's Private Library: The Books That Shaped His Life* (2008; repr., New York: Vintage, 2010), 201; and Caddick-Adams, *Snow and Steel*, 49.

21. Directive No. 21, *Operation Barbarossa, Führer* Headquarters, December 18, 1940, OKW/WFSt./Abt.L(I) Nr.33 408/40 g.Kdos, http://www.rajajoki.com/directive21.htm.

22. Nagorski, *The Greatest Battle*, 23.

23. *Intelligence Bulletin*, "German Horse Cavalry and Transport" (Washington, DC: War Department, Military Intelligence Service, March 1946); and Overy, *Why the Allies Won*, 5, 210, 215–18, 227.

24. Deighton, *Blood, Tears and Folly*, 439.

25. Deighton, *Blood, Tears and Folly*, 445–46, citing Martin van Creveld, *Supplying War: Logistics from Wallenstein to Patton* (Cambridge: Cambridge University Press, 1977), 148–55.

26. Van Creveld, *Supplying War*, 150–51, citing Josef Windisch, *Die deutsche Nach-schubtruppe im Zweitem Weltkrieg* (München: Rosenheim, 1953), 38–39. Germany produced 279,487 trucks between the launch of *Barbarossa* and the Allied invasion of France and lost 39 percent of the fleet, equal to its entire production in 1943. James F. Dunnigan and Albert A. Nofi, *Dirty Little Secrets of World War II: Military Information No One Told You about the Greatest, Most Terrible War in History* (New York: Morrow, 1994), 175. Atkinson indicates that Germany produced seventy thousand trucks in the last eighteen months of the war versus Allied production of over one million. Rick Atkinson, *The Day of Battle: The War in Sicily and Italy, 1943–1944* (New York: Henry Holt, 2007), 451.

27. Deighton, *Blood, Tears and Folly*, 445. Van Creveld adds that German locomotives did not have their water pipes built inside the boilers so that 80 percent of them froze and burst when the early winter ensued. *Supplying War*, 153, 173.

28. Murray and Millett, *War to Be Won*, 119; and Van Creveld, *Supplying War*, 150.

29. Deighton, *Blood, Tears and Folly*, 445; and Van Creveld, *Supplying War*, 152.

30. Deighton, *Blood, Tears and Folly*, 437; Robert Kirchubel, *Operation Barbarossa 1941 (2): Army Group North* (Oxford: Osprey, 2005), 15.

31. Van Creveld, *Supplying War*, 159, 163, 166.

32. Deighton, *Blood, Tears and Folly*, 443.

33. Murray and Millett, *War to Be Won*, 37.

34. Citino, *Death of the Wehrmacht*, 35.

35. Citino, *Death of the Wehrmacht*, 39–40.

36. Franz Halder, Charles Burdick, and Hans-Adolf Jacobsen, eds., *The Halder War Diary, 1939–1942* (Novato, CA: Presidio, 1988), 446, 506.

37. Halder was not exaggerating the size of the Soviet order of battle. Sources include Citino, *Death of the Wehrmacht*, 40; Walter S. Dunn Jr., *Stalin's Keys to Victory: The Rebirth of the Red Army in World War II* (Westport, CT: Praeger Security International, 2006), 69, citing James M. Goff, "Evolving Soviet Force Structure, 1941–45," *Journal of Soviet Military Studies* (September 1991), who estimated that 229 rifle and motorized divisions were available on June 22, 1941, and 483 new divisions were formed during the war, for a total of 712.

38. Pleshakov, *Stalin's Folly*, 258–60; and Nagorski, *The Greatest Battle*, 219–21.

39. Ian Kershaw, *Fateful Choices: Ten Decisions That Changed the World, 1940–1941* (New York: Penguin, 2007), 247–48, citing Dmitri A. Volkogonov, *Stalin, Triumph and Tragedy* (New York: Grove, 1991), 369.

40. David Stahel, *Kiev 1941: Hitler's Battle for Supremacy in the East* (Cambridge: Cambridge University Press, 2012), 302.

41. Van Creveld, *Supplying War*, 177.

42. Kagan, *Finding the Target*, 316–17.

43. Allen F. Chew, "Fighting the Russians in Winter: Three Case Studies" (Leavenworth Papers No. 5, Combat Studies Institute, Fort Leavenworth, Kansas, December 1981), 31–42.

44. Dunn, *Stalin's Keys to Victory*, 63; and Murray and Millett, *War to Be Won*, 56, 133–34.

45. Nagorski, *The Greatest Battle*, 226.

46. Anthony Eden, *The Reckoning* (Boston: Houghton Mifflin, 1965), 336.

47. The Red Army created four major waves of new divisions. Dunn, *Stalin's Keys to Victory*, 63, passim.

48. Citino, *Death of the Wehrmacht*, 41; and Kennedy, *Engineers of Victory*, 188–90, 371.

49. Glantz, "Myths and Realities" paper, 65.

50. Joel Hayward, "Too Little, Too Late: An Analysis of Hitler's Failure in August 1942 to Damage Soviet Oil Production," *Journal of Military History*, 64, no. 3 (July 2000): 769–94, 793.

51. Dunn, *Stalin's Keys to Victory*, viii, 1, 93–96.

52. Evans, *Third Reich at War*, 196.

53. Overy, *Why the Allies Won*, 208ff.

54. Overy, *Russia's War*, 237; and Murray and Millett, *War to Be Won*, 388, for comparable Lend-Lease data.

55. Overy, *Russia's War*, 239.

56. Glantz, "Myths and Realities" paper, 106; and William Manchester and Paul Reid, *The Last Lion: Winston Spencer Churchill, Defender of the Realm, 1940–1965* (New York: Little, Brown, 2012), 673.

57. Overy, *Russia's War*, 289.

58. Steven Zaloga, *Bagration 1944: The Destruction of Army Group Centre* (London: Osprey, 1996), 7.

59. Overy, *Russia's War*, 289.

60. Lieven identified the tsarist roots of Russia's capacity to raise mass armies. Dominic Lieven, *Russia against Napoleon: The Battle for Europe, 1807–1814* (London: Allen Lane, 2009), 345, chap. 10, "Rebuilding the Army."

CHAPTER 4. BATTLE OF EL ALAMEIN AND OPERATION *TORCH*

1. The Battle of the Kerch Peninsula was launched in the eastern Crimea on May 8 and concluded on May 18, 1942, with the near complete destruction of the Soviet defending forces and 175,000 Soviets killed or taken prisoner. Murray and Millett, *A War to Be Won*, 276.

2. Murray and Millett, *A War to Be Won*, 277.

3. Jon Latimer, *Alamein* (Cambridge, MA: Harvard University Press, 2002), 52.

4. Rommel's command in North Africa was originally designated *Deutsches Afrikakorps* in February 1941. Later it acquired more grandiose designations inversely proportional to its military success: *Panzergruppe Afrika* (August 1941); then *Panzerarmee Afrika* (January 1942–October 1942); then, by Alamein, *Deutsche-Italienische Panzerarmee* (October 1942–February 1943); and finally, by the Tunisian surrender, *Heeresgruppe Afrika* (February 1943–May 1943). Latimer, *Alamein*, 27–28, 35, 39.

5. Martin J. Bradley, *The British Army 1939–45 (2): Middle East & Mediterranean* (Oxford: Osprey, 2002), 2–3.

6. B. H. Liddell Hart, ed., *The Rommel Papers* (Pennington, NJ: Collectors Reprints, The Great Commanders Series, originally published in 1953 by Harcourt, Brace and Co., 1995), xiii.

7. Rommel is referring to Sicily as an Axis-dominated chokepoint in the Mediterranean, which forced the Allies to take the much longer passage around the Cape of Good Hope of Africa until late 1942.

8. One US Army official history described the "Persian Corridor," which at its peak involved the deployment of thirty thousand US Army engineering and transportation personnel. The estimate of American deliveries to Russia was sufficient by US Army standards to maintain sixty Soviet divisions. T. H. Vail Motter, *United States Army in World War II: The Middle East Theater; The Persian Corridor and Aid to Russia*, CMH Pub. 8-1 (Washington, DC: Center of Military History, 1952), 6, 10, 346–447, http://www.history.army.mil/books /wwii/persian/index.htm#contents.

9. Liddell Hart, *Rommel Papers*, 511–12.

10. Liddell Hart, *Rommel Papers*, 514–15.

11. Latimer, *Alamein*, 23.

12. Latimer, *Alamein*, 194.

13. Latimer, *Alamein*, 7.

14. Van Creveld, *Supplying War*, 193. Cf., American maturation of automotive mass production by the mid-1920s and concurrent creation of innovative organizations to manage such production accelerated the conversion of the peacetime economy to full-scale wartime production; it took less than a year. In 1941, Detroit produced more than 3.5 million automobiles. After Pearl Harbor, automotive production quickly shifted to trucks, tanks, and armored vehicles. German truck production averaged sixty-two thousand trucks during each year of the war. Germany's highly skilled workforce with its high standards of craft production in incremental batches rather than assembly-line production was no match against the "Arsenal of Democracy." John Paxton, "Myth vs. Reality: The Question of Mass Production in World War II," *Economics & Business Journal: Inquiries & Perspectives* 1, no. 1 (October 2008): 92, 99, 101, 103; and for German truck production: *Waffenamt* production data, OKH, http://www.panzerworld.com/truck-production-numbers.

15. John Bierman and Colin Smith, *The Battle of Alamein: Turning Point in World War II* (New York: Viking, 2002), chap. 15, and 171.

16. Winston S. Churchill, *The Second World War*, vol. 4, *The Hinge of Fate* (New York: Houghton Mifflin, 1950), 359–60.

17. Latimer, *Alamein*, 63.

18. Latimer, *Alamein*, 98.

19. Latimer, *Alamein*, 98–99.

20. Latimer, *Alamein*, 1–2; and Murray and Millett, *War to Be Won*, 271, where they identify more favorable Allied/Axis force advantages: 230,000 British Commonwealth versus 80,000 German troop strength, 1,500 vs. 500 tanks, and 1,200 vs. 350 aircraft.

21. Citino, *Death of the Wehrmacht*, 273.

22. Liddell Hart, *Rommel Papers*, 297.

23. Citino, *Death of the Wehrmacht*, 280–82.

24. Citino, *Death of the Wehrmacht*, 285.

25. Liddell Hart, *Rommel Papers*, 320.

26. Liddell Hart, *Rommel Papers*, 321.

27. In a speech to the Lord Mayor's Luncheon, Mansion House, London, November 10, 1942.

28. The 70/30 allocation reflected army personnel more than matériel. Louis Morton, *The United States Army in World War II: The War in the Pacific; Strategy and Command; The First Two Years* (Washington, DC: Department of the Army, US Government Printing Office, 1962), 377, chap. 18, "The Pacific in Grand Strategy"; and Mark A. Stoler, *Allies and Adversaries: The Joint Chiefs of Staff, the Grand Alliance, and U.S. Strategy in World War II* (Chapel Hill: University of North Carolina Press, 2000), 99.

29. Mansoor, *GI Offensive*, 84–85.

30. Mark Perry, *Partners in Command: George Marshall and Dwight Eisenhower in War and Peace* (New York: Penguin, 2007), 77.

31. Ed Cray, *General of the Army: George C. Marshall, Soldier and Statesman* (New York: Norton, 1990), 175; Jack Uldrich, *Soldier, Statesman, Peacemaker: Leadership Lessons from George C. Marshall* (New York: AMACOM, 2005), 83, 164, 166–67; Christopher R. Gabel, *The U.S. Army GHQ Maneuvers of 1941* (Washington, DC: US Government Printing Office, 1991), 116–18, 187; and Eric Larrabee, *Commander in Chief: Franklin Delano Roosevelt, His Lieutenants, and Their War* (New York: Harper and Row, 1987), 101.

32. Linn, *Echo of Battle*, 5, passim.

33. Thomas E. Ricks, *The Generals: American Military Command from World War II to Today* (New York: Penguin, 2012), 7.

34. Rick Atkinson, *An Army at Dawn: The War in North Africa, 1942–1943* (New York: Henry Holt, 2002), 536.

35. Mansoor, *GI Offensive*, 85.

36. Atkinson, *Army at Dawn*, 4, passim.

37. Douglas A. Macgregor, *Breaking the Phalanx: A New Design for Landpower in the 21st Century* (Westport, CT: Praeger, 1997), 158–60.

38. Mansoor, *GI Offensive*, 96–99.

39. Liddell Hart, *Rommel Papers*, 523.

CHAPTER 5. BATTLES OF MIDWAY AND GUADALCANAL

1. Masatake Okumiya and Jiro Horikoshi, *Zero*, with Martin Caidin (New York: Dutton, 1956), 61; Peter G. Tsouras, ed., *Rising Sun Victorious: An Alternate History of the Pacific War; It Could Have Happened . . . and Nearly Did* (New York: Presidio, 2007), 38; and

Mark Harrison, ed., *The Economics of World War II: Six Great Powers in International Comparison* (Cambridge: Cambridge University Press, 1998), 11, 228. Harrison's time-series plots of real GDPs of the World War II combatants (1938–1945) showed that the US/Japan GDP ratio, in 1941 already 5.5:1 (in favor of the United States), escalated to 7:1 in 1943 and peaked at 7.5:1 in 1944.

2. Tomoyuki Ishizu and Raymond Callahan, "The Rising Sun Strikes," in *The Pacific War: From Pearl Harbor to Hiroshima*, ed. Daniel Marston (Oxford: Osprey, 2010), 53; and Jonathan Parshall and Anthony Tully, *Shattered Sword: The Untold Story of the Battle of Midway* (Washington, DC: Potomac, 2007), 411, citing David C. Evans and Mark R. Peattie, *Kaigun: Strategy, Tactics, and Technology in the Imperial Japanese Navy, 1887–1941* (Annapolis, MD: Naval Institute Press, 1997), 282–86.

3. The Imperial Japanese Navy began the war with nine aircraft carriers. The six carriers that attacked Pearl Harbor—*Akagi, Kaga, Sōryū, Hiryū, Shōkaku*, and *Zuikaku*—were the IJN's largest fleet carriers. The US Navy began the war with seven carriers, only three of which—*Enterprise, Hornet*, and *Yorktown*—fought at Midway. Parshall and Tully, *Shattered Sword*, 40–41, 63, 93, 418–21; and H. P. Willmott, *The Great Crusade: A New Complete History of the Second World War*, rev. ed. (Washington, DC: Potomac, 2008), 314. By war's end, the US Navy had added 110 aircraft carriers to the US fleet, including eighteen new Essex-class fleet carriers. Ernest J. King, *U.S. Navy at War, 1941–1945* (Washington, DC: US Navy Department, 1946), 253–57, http://www.ibiblio.org/hyperwar/USN/USNatWar/USN-King-B.html. After the IJN's Midway loss of four carriers, the IJN began a series of ambitious projects to build more fleet carriers, only three of which saw service, and all were sunk by 1944, including the 29,300-ton *Taihō* with an armored, heavy-steel deck. Ian W. Toll, *The Conquering Tide: War in the Pacific Islands, 1942–1944* (New York: Norton, 2015), 2:427.

4. Roger J. Spiller, *In the School of War* (Lincoln: University of Nebraska Press, 2010), 91–95, 102–5, 107, citing John W. Dower, *War without Mercy: Race and Power in the Pacific War* (New York: Random House, 1988), 204–5.

5. Dennis Showalter, "Storm over the Pacific," in Marston, *Pacific War*, 28.

6. Fireside chat of February 23, 1942; John T. Wooley et al., American Presidency Project, http://www.presidency.ucsb.edu/ws/index.php?pid=16224.

7. Hadley Cantril, *The Human Dimension: Experiences in Policy Research* (Piscataway, NJ: Rutgers University Press, 1967), 48, chart VI; and Peter Clarke, *Mr. Churchill's Profession: The Statesman as Author and the Book That Defined the "Special Relationship"* (New York: Bloomsbury, 2012), 250.

8. Overy, *Why the Allies Won*, 18.

9. Edwin T. Layton, Roger Pineau, and John Layton Costello, *"And I Was There": Pearl Harbor and Midway—Breaking the Secrets* (Old Saybrook, CT: Morrow, 1985), 337.

10. Murray and Millett, *War to Be Won*, 190.

11. Overy, *Why the Allies Won*, 43.

12. The 250 first-line Japanese pilots averaged seven hundred hours of flight time; American pilots averaged three hundred hours of flight time. Dallas W. Isom, *Midway Inquest: Why the Japanese Lost the Battle of Midway* (Bloomington: Indiana University Press, 2007), 52; and Alvin Kernan, *The Unknown Battle of Midway: The Destruction of the American Torpedo Squadrons* (New Haven, CT: Yale University Press, 2005), 58.

13. H. P. Willmott, *The Barrier and the Javelin: Japanese and Allied Pacific Strategies, February to June 1942* (Annapolis, MD: Naval Institute Press, 1983), 518.

14. Isom, *Midway Inquest*, 52.

15. Parshall and Tully, *Shattered Sword*, 420.

16. Parshall and Tully, *Shattered Sword*, 219. Nimitz already knew that he could have *Yorktown* back in three days because the repair superintendent and his team had been flown out to the carrier the day before its arrival at Pearl Harbor and had already made an assessment based on priorities for Midway. C.f., Ian W. Toll, *Pacific Crucible: War at Sea in the Pacific, 1941–1942* (New York: Norton, 2012), 396–97.

17. Parshall and Tully, *Shattered Sword*, 33–34.

18. Overy, *Why the Allies Won*, 37, citing Mitsuo Fuchida and Masatake Okumiya, *Midway: The Battle That Doomed Japan; The Japanese Navy's Story* (Annapolis, MD: Bluejacket Books, 2001), 92–100; and Ronald Lewin, *The American Magic: Codes, Ciphers and the Defeat of Japan* (New York: Farrar, Straus & Giroux, 1982), 109.

19. John A. Adams, *If Mahan Ran the Great Pacific War: An Analysis of World War II Naval Strategy* (Bloomington: Indiana University Press, 2008), 118.

20. Adams, *If Mahan Ran the Great Pacific War*, 9, 135; and Parshall and Tully, *Shattered Sword*, 159–60.

21. Overy, *Why the Allies Won*, 41.

22. Isom, *Midway Inquest*, 169–73.

23. Richard R. Frank, *Guadalcanal: The Definitive Account of the Landmark Battle* (New York: Penguin, 1990), 86.

24. VT is the abbreviated designator for a USN torpedo bombing squadron followed by the squadron number.

25. VF is the designator for a fighter squadron.

26. Isom, *Midway Inquest*, 193–96, 206–8.

27. The SBN "Dauntless" dive-bomber, designed and built by Douglas Aircraft Corporation, was the most capable aircraft aboard the American carriers at Midway. In Isom's judgment, "without the Dauntless, the American navy would have lost the Battle of Midway and been knocked out of the Pacific, at least for the first year of the war." Isom, *Midway Inquest*, 51.

28. VB is the designator for a dive-bomber squadron.

29. VS is the designator for a scouting squadron.

30. Walter J. Boyne, *Clash of Titans: World War II at Sea* (New York: Simon & Schuster, 1995), 190.

31. *Yorktown*'s quick repairs of battle damage were sufficient after the earlier Japanese strike because it continued air operations until two torpedoes struck it from an enemy submarine (*I-168*). It remained afloat but sank the following day.

32. Murray and Millett, *Military Innovation*, 225.

33. Toll, citing Kernan, notes that the early 1942 carrier raids on the Marshall Islands before Midway involving the carriers *Enterprise*, *Lexington*, and *Yorktown* taught their pilots "the skills they needed to win the Battle of Midway." Toll, *Pacific Crucible*, 229ff.

34. James D. Hornfischer, *Neptune's Inferno: The U.S. Navy at Guadalcanal* (New York: Bantam, 2011), 13.

35. Hornfischer, *Neptune's Inferno*, 20.

36. Hornfischer, *Neptune's Inferno*, 220.

37. Marston, *Pacific War*, 186–89.

38. Hornfischer, *Neptune's Inferno*, xxi.

39. Hornfischer, *Neptune's Inferno*, 89.

40. Trent Hone, "U.S. Navy Surface Battle Doctrine and Victory in the Pacific," *Naval War College Review* 62, no. 1 (Winter 2009): 67–105. In June 1943, Pacific Fleet published a manual of tactical principles as the basis for training light forces (including cruisers and destroyers): *Current Tactical Orders and Doctrine: U.S. Pacific Fleet*, known as PAC-10.

41. Hornfischer, *Neptune's Inferno*, 136.

42. Hornfischer, *Neptune's Inferno*, 22–25.

43. Hornfischer, *Neptune's Inferno*, 247.

44. Hornfischer, *Neptune's Inferno*, 198–99.

45. Hornfischer, *Neptune's Inferno*, 208–9.

46. Evan Thomas, *Sea of Thunder: Four Commanders and the Last Great Naval Campaign, 1941–1945* (New York: Simon & Schuster, 2006), 1–2.

47. Hornfischer, *Neptune's Inferno*, 221.

48. The carriers *Zuikaku* and *Junyō*, though not seriously damaged, were forced home to Japan for lack of pilots to fly their planes. Hornfischer, *Neptune's Inferno*, 235.

49. Hornfischer, *Neptune's Inferno*, 231.

50. Murray, *Military Adaptation*, 67; and Robert Coram, *Brute: The Life of Victor Krulak, U.S. Marine* (New York: Little, Brown, 2010), 61–62.

51. Hornfischer, *Neptune's Inferno*, xxi. He puts the major warship losses as even for both the Allied and Japanese navies: twenty-four each.

52. Hornfischer, *Neptune's Inferno*, xxi.

53. Hornfischer, *Neptune's Inferno*, xxi.

54. Hornfischer, *Neptune's Inferno*, xxi.

55. Warren M. Bodie, *The Lockheed P-38 Lightning: The Definitive Story of Lockheed's P-38 Fighter* (Hiawassee, GA: Widewing Publications, 1991), 113–14.

CHAPTER 6. STRATEGIC BOMBING OFFENSIVE

1. Albert Speer, *Spandau: The Secret Diaries* (New York: Macmillan, 1976), 339–40.

2. Evans, *Third Reich at War*, 461.

3. Overy, *Air War*, 75.

4. Richard Overy, *The Bombers and the Bombed: Allied Air over Europe, 1939–1945* (New York: Viking, 2014), xii.

5. Overy, *Why the Allies Won*, 131.

6. Randall Hansen, *Fire and Fury: The Allied Bombing of Germany, 1942–1945* (New York: New American Library, 2009), 287.

7. Overy, *Air War*, 120.

8. Overy, *Air War*, 120.

9. Overy, *Air War*, 179–80. Caddick-Adams observed that design and production inefficiencies were not limited to aircraft. "German designers tended to over-engineer. . . . For example, the sixty-ton Tiger tank took 300,000 man hours to manufacture compared to 55,000 for a Panther, 48,000 for a Sherman—and only 10,000 for a Russian T-34." *Snow and Steel*, 65, citing "these hotly debated figures" from recent online debates; see chap. 5 and note 11.

10. Overy, *Air War*, 120, citing Wesley F. Craven and James L. Cate, eds., *Army Air Forces in WW II* (Chicago: University of Chicago Press, 1948–1958), 6:152; and Central Statistical Office, *Statistical Digest of the War* (London: HMSO, 1951), 152.

11. Heinrich Hecht, *The World's First Turbojet Fighter—Messerschmitt Me 262* (Atglen, PA: Schiffer, 1990).

12. Albert Speer, *Inside the Third Reich: Memoirs* (New York: Macmillan, 1970), 364–65.

13. The V-1 was an early pulse-jet-powered, unmanned, aerial vehicle launched from "ski" launch sites along the French and Dutch coasts. More than 9,500 were launched against southeast England. The V-2 was the first short-range ballistic missile used in armed

conflict. Over 3,000 V-2s were launched against urban targets in Britain and on the Continent. Speer noted in his memoirs, "Hitler wanted 900 of these produced monthly. The whole notion was absurd." Speer, *Memoirs*, 364–65. The V-2 cost one-fourth of the Manhattan Project ($2 billion). Murray, *Military Adaptation*, 240, citing Michael J. Neufeld, *The Rocket and the Reich: Peenemünde and the Coming of the Ballistic Era* (Cambridge, MA: Harvard University Press, 1996), 273.

14. A. J. Baime, *The Arsenal of Democracy: FDR, Detroit, and an Epic Quest to Arm an America at War* (Boston: Houghton Mifflin Harcourt, 2014), 95–96, 99, 131–32, 134, passim, and chaps. 10 and 11; and Overy, *Why the Allies Won*, 196–97.

15. Richard M. Baughn, "The P-51: USAAF's WWII Stepchild" (unpublished, undated white paper), 3–4, http://www.au.af.mil/au/aunews/archive/2009/0422/Articles /BaughNo110422.htm, and monograph (no author cited) about P-51 total production and combat performance available online at The Aviation History Online Museum accessible at http://www.aviation-history.com/north-american/p51.html.

16. Ralph H. Nutter, *With the Possum and the Eagle: The Memoir of a Navigator's War over Germany and Japan* (Denton: University of North Texas Press, 2002), 11.

17. The full text of LeMay's memorandum is presented in Nutter, *With the Possum and the Eagle*, 292–300, appendix A.

18. Norman Longmate, *The Bombers: The RAF Offensive against Germany, 1939–1945* (London: Hutchinson, 1983), 131, citing Charles Webster and Noble Frankland, *The Strategic Air Offensive against Germany* (London: HMSO, 1961), 1:331. After the war operations, researchers discovered how exaggerated Lindemann's conclusions were. Budiansky, *Blackett's War*, 200–201.

19. Donald L. Miller, *Masters of the Air: America's Bomber Boys Who Fought the Air War against Nazi Germany* (New York: Simon & Schuster, 2006), 183; and Hansen, *Fire and Fury*, 48.

20. Overy, *Air War*, 122, 129; and Evans, *Third Reich at War*, 446.

21. Hansen, *Fire and Fury*, 280.

22. Goebbels is referring to Karl Kaufmann, the National Socialist regional leader in Hamburg. Evans, *Third Reich at War*, 248, 446.

23. Evans, *Third Reich at War*, 227. Stout points out that German flak guns shot down more heavy bombers (B-17s and B-24s) than fighters did: 3,752 bombers by flak and 3,299 bombers by fighters. Jay A. Stout, *The Men Who Killed the Luftwaffe: The U.S. Army Air Forces in World War II* (Mechanicsburg, PA: Stackpole, 2010), 201.

24. Overy, *Why the Allies Won*, 129.

25. Stout, *Men Who Killed the Luftwaffe*, 193.

26. Kennedy, *Engineers of Victory*, 130. German loss figures come from Anthony Furse, *Wilfred Freeman: The Genius behind Allied Survival and Air Supremacy, 1939–1945* (Staplehurst, UK: Spellmount, 1999).

27. *United States Strategic Bombing Survey* (USSBS), "Summary Report, European War" (September 30, 1945).

28. Overy, *Why the Allies Won*, 130.

29. Tooze, *Wages of Destruction*, 597–98, and 625.

30. Evans, *Third Reich at War*, 438–58.

31. Michael Burleigh, *The Third Reich: A New History* (New York: Hill and Wang, 2000), 745–47.

32. The Schweinfurt factories accounted for almost half of Germany's ball-bearing production (45 percent). Murray and Millett, *War to Be Won*, 413.

33. Speer, *Memoirs*, 284.

34. Hansen, *Fire and Fury*, 129.

35. Evans, *Third Reich at War*, 442.

36. Speer, *Memoirs*, 285.

37. Speer, *Memoirs*, 286.

38. Overy, *Why the Allies Won*, 121–22; and Wesley F. Craven and James L. Cate, eds., *The Army Air Forces in World War II: Services around the World* (Washington, DC: Office of Air Force History, January 2012), 7:312, http://www.ibiblio.org/hyperwar/AAF/VII /AAF-VII-11.html#fn312-2.

39. Miller, *Masters of the Air*, 201.

40. Stout explains that deep bombing penetrations of Germany stopped between mid-October and the end of December 1944, largely because of bad weather, not USAAF orders to refrain from deep attacks. Stout, *Men Who Killed the Luftwaffe*, 153–54.

41. Overy, *Air War*, 81.

42. Overy, *Air War*, 8.

43. *United States Strategic Bombing Survey. Statistical Appendix to Over-All Report, European War* (Washington, DC: US Government Printing Office, 1947), table 1.

44. Rob Morris, *Untold Valor: Forgotten Stories of American Bomber Crews over Europe in World War II* (Dulles, VA: Potomac, 2006), xi, citing Walter J. Boyne, *Clash of Wings* (New York: Simon & Schuster, 1995), 306.

45. Speer's entry in his diary on August 12, 1959, reads as follows: "As far as I can judge from the accounts I have read, no one has yet seen that this war was the greatest lost battle on the German side." Speer, *Spandau*, 285.

CHAPTER 7. INVASION OF ITALY

1. US Department of State, Foreign Relations of the United States (FRUS), *The Conferences at Washington, 1941–1942, and Casablanca, 1943* (Washington, DC: US Government Printing Office, 1941–1943), 581, http://digicoll.library.wisc.edu/cgi-bin/FRUS /FRUS-idx?id=FRUS.FRUS194143.

2. The Quebec Conference in August 1943 reinforced President Roosevelt's strong commitment to *Overlord* as the highest military priority. Perry, *Partners in Command*, 214ff.

3. Atkinson, *Day of Battle*, 20–21.

4. FRUS, 512.

5. Atkinson, *Day of Battle*, 21.

6. Willmott, *Great Crusade*, 338.

7. Willmott, *Great Crusade*, 340.

8. Andrew J. Birtle, *Sicily: The U.S. Army Campaigns of World War II*, brochure, CMH Pub. 72-16 (Washington, DC: US Army Center of Military History, 1993), 3, 8, 25–27.

9. Birtle, *Sicily*, 27.

10. Atkinson, *Day of Battle*, 129, 181.

11. Martin Blumenson, *U.S. Army in World War II: Mediterranean Theater of Operations, Salerno to Cassino* (Washington, DC: US Army Center of Military History, 1993), 118–32, http://www.ibiblio.org/hyperwar/USA/USA-MTO-Salerno/index.html.

12. Atkinson, *Day of Battle*, 233; and Willmott, *Great Crusade*, 343.

13. Atkinson, *Day of Battle*, 254–55.

14. Perry, *Partners in Command*, 231.

15. Atkinson, *Day of Battle*, 256.

16. Atkinson, *Day of Battle*, 255–56.

17. John Ellis, *Cassino, the Hollow Victory: The Battle for Rome, January–June 1944* (London: Aurum, 1984), 37.

18. Roberts, *Storm of War*, 386, 387, 390.

19. Atkinson, *Day of Battle*, 354–55.

20. Atkinson, *Day of Battle*, 354–55.

21. Winston S. Churchill, *The Second World War*, vol. 5, *Closing the Ring* (1951; repr., New York: Houghton Mifflin, 1985), 432.

22. John Keegan, "Anzio (1944)," in *The Mammoth Book of Battles: The Art and Science of Modern Warfare*, ed. Jon E. Lewis (New York: Carroll and Graf, 1999), 320.

23. Keegan points out that Cassino and Anzio were too far apart (seventy miles) for 6th Corps and 5th Army to mutually assist one another. Keegan, "Anzio (1944)," 329–30.

24. Kesselring after the Anzio landing called up his *Alarmeinheiten* (alarm units), paper units formed from clerks, drivers, and men returning from leave. Keegan, "Anzio (1944)," 324; and Peter Caddick-Adams, *Monte Cassino: Ten Armies in Hell* (Oxford: Oxford University Press, 2013), 53–54.

25. 6th Corps fired a total of 158,000 rounds during the German counterattack, a ten-to-one Allied firepower advantage over the Germans. Atkinson, *Day of Battle*, 424, 428, 431.

26. Atkinson, *Day of Battle*, 431.

27. Atkinson, *Day of Battle*, 431.

28. Martin Blumenson, *U.S. Army in World War II: Mediterranean Theater of Operations, Salerno to Cassino* (Washington, DC: US Army Center of Military History, 1993), 454, http://www.ibiblio.org/hyperwar/USA/USA-MTO-Salerno/index.html; and Atkinson, *Day of Battle*, 583.

29. Michael Howard, "A Bloody Place," *Times Literary Supplement*, June 12, 2008, 12, reviewing Atkinson's *Day of Battle*.

CHAPTER 8. D-DAY AND THE BATTLE FOR NORMANDY

1. Rick Atkinson, *The Guns at Last Light: The War in Western Europe, 1944–1945* (New York: Henry Holt, 2013), 18, 21–41.

2. Willmott, *Great Crusade*, 349.

3. Olivier Wieviorka, *Normandy: The Landings to the Liberation of Paris*, trans. M. B. DeBevoise (Cambridge, MA: Harvard University Press, 2008), 1.

4. Mansoor, *GI Offensive*, 170, 176.

5. Geoffrey Best, *Churchill: A Study in Greatness* (London: Hambledon and London, 2001), 201–3.

6. Nearly half of the British supply tonnage by August arrived through the restored Mulberry. Atkinson, *Guns at Last Light*, 116.

7. Atkinson, *Guns at Last Light*, 240–41.

8. Luc Braeuer, *The Atlantic Wall in France, 1940–1944* (Côte Sauvage: Editions Le Grand Blockhaus, 2010), 11–15, 46, 58.

9. Willmott, *Great Crusade*, 352; John C. Masterman, *The Double Cross System* (New Haven, CT: Yale University Press, 1972); Ben Macintyre, *Double Cross: The True Story of D-Day* (New York: Crown, 2012); and Stephan Talty, *Agent Garbo: The Brilliant, Eccentric Secret Agent Who Tricked Hitler and Saved D-Day* (New York: Houghton Mifflin Harcourt, 2012).

10. Allied invasion of southern France from Mediterranean landings, Operation *Anvil* (later designated *Dragoon*) in August 1944 by the US 7th and the French 1st Armies. John Keegan, *Six Armies in Normandy* (New York: Penguin, 1982), 57.

11. Adrian R. Lewis, *Omaha Beach: A Flawed Victory* (Chapel Hill: University of North Carolina Press, 2001), 5–7.

12. Conrad Black, *Franklin Delano Roosevelt: Champion of Freedom* (New York: PublicAffairs, 2003), 805–6; Alfred D. Chandler, ed., *The Papers of Dwight David Eisenhower: The War Years* (Baltimore, MD: Johns Hopkins University Press, 1971), 1:75; and Keegan, *Six Armies*, 36.

13. Carlo D'Este, *Decision in Normandy: The Real Story of Montgomery and the Allied Campaign*, 60th D-Day anniversary rev. ed. (1983; repr., London: Penguin, 2004), 32, 34–38.

14. The D-Day ship totals vary from historian to historian. Wieviorka's numbers, citing the official naval source, are in the text. Wieviorka, *Normandy*, 186, citing Admiral Ramsay, "Report by the Allied Commander in Chief, Expeditionary Force on Operation Neptune," October 16, 1944, NARA, RG 331, entry 279, box 4. Keegan's total is smaller: 5,000, *Six Armies*, 56–57. Willmott's total is 3,183, *Great Crusade*, 349. The official US Army source indicates more than five thousand ships and thirteen thousand aircraft, US Army official website, http://www.army.mil/d-day.

15. D'Este, *Decision in Normandy*, 105, 213.

16. Willmott, *Great Crusade*, 359 (encirclements, destruction of divisions, and *Bagration*), 365 (ten offensives identified).

17. Roberts, *Storm of War*, 425–26, citing David M. Glanz and Jonathan M. House, *The Battle of Kursk* (Lawrence: University Press of Kansas, 1999), 281.

18. Willmott, *Great Crusade*, 374.

19. Willmott, *Great Crusade*, 374.

20. Willmott, *Great Crusade*, 374.

21. Willmott, *Great Crusade*, 387.

22. Willmott, *Great Crusade*, 351.

23. Murray, *Military Adaptation*, 249, citing Air Historical Branch, "Air Attacks against German Rail Systems during 1944," *Luftwaffe* Operations Staff/Intelligence, No. 2512/44 (March 6, 1944).

24. Liddell Hart, *Rommel Papers*, 486; and Russell A. Hart, *Clash of Arms: How the Allies Won in Normandy* (London: Lynne Rienner, 2001), 385, table 10.2.

25. Willmott, *Great Crusade*, 351–52.

26. Robin Neillands, *The Battle for the Rhine* (Woodstock: Overlook Press, 2005), 56.

27. Willmott, *Great Crusade*, 352.

28. City Museum and Records Office, Museum Road Portsmouth PO1 2LJ, UK, http://www.ddaymuseum.co.uk/contact.htm.

29. Laurent Lefebvre, "D-Day Documents, 29th Infantry Division, 116th Regiment, 1st Battalion, Able Company, Group Critique Notes," http://www.americandday.org/Documents/29th_ID-116th_IR-1st_Bn-A_Company-Group_Critique_Notes.html. Also see Laurent Lefebvre, *They Were on Omaha Beach: 213 Eyewitnesses; D-Day Told by Veterans*, American D-Day 3rd ed. (France: Imprimerie Henry, France, 2007).

30. Lewis, *Omaha Beach*, 26–27.

31. Anthony Beevor, *D-Day: The Battle for Normandy* (New York: Viking, 2009), 100–101.

32. Beevor, *D-Day*, 101.

33. Major General Robert R. Ploger (US Army, Ret.) told the author in July 1999 that he was a lieutenant colonel on D-Day in command of the 121st Engineering Combat Battalion in the 29th Division on *Omaha* Beach in the first wave. Also see Barry W. Fowle, "The Normandy Landing," *Army History*, PB-20-94-3, no. 30 (Spring 1994): 443.

34. Wieviorka, *Normandy*, 212ff.

35. Beevor, *D-Day*, 266–73.

36. Wieviorka, *Normandy*, 229–34.

37. Neillands, *Battle for the Rhine*, 156.

38. D'Este, *Decision in Normandy*, 322.

39. D'Este, *Decision in Normandy*, 338, citing Martin Blumenson, "Some Reflections on the Immediate Post-Assault Strategy," in *D-Day: The Normandy Invasion in Retrospect*, Eisenhower Foundation (Lawrence: University Press of Kansas, 1971).

40. Keegan, *Six Armies*, 232.

41. John Prados, *Normandy Crucible: The Decisive Battle That Shaped World War II in Europe* (New York: Nal Caliber, 2011), appendix A, 271–80.

42. Willmott, *Great Crusade*, chapter 5, "Time, Space and Doctrine."

43. Mansoor, *GI Offensive*, 134.

44. Mansoor, *GI Offensive*, 180.

45. Hitler ordered the Ardennes offensive, desperately planned and executed four months later in December 1944. The *Wehrmacht* could still be locally powerful and lethal.

46. Linn, *Echo of Battle*, 5–7.

47. Michael D. Doubler, *Busting the Bocage: American Combined Arms Operations in France, 6 June–31 July 1944* (Fort Leavenworth, KS: US Army Command and General College, Combat Studies Institute, 1955), 37–38.

48. Linn, *Echo of Battle*, 6.

49. Liddell Hart, *Rommel Papers*, 522–23.

50. Mansoor, *GI Offensive*, 170; and Wieviorka, *Normandy*, 291.

51. "The *bocage* is a mass of small, irregularly shaped farm fields separated by hedgerows that have grown over the centuries into formidable barriers. The hedgerows consist of earthen banks, several feet high topped with a mass of tangled vegetation. Each hedgerow forms a natural breastwork and obstacle to movement. . . . The *bocage* provides natural cover, concealment, and ready-made engagement areas—a patchwork quilt ideal for the defense." Mansoor, *GI Offensive*, 142.

52. Mansoor, *GI Offensive*, 154.

53. Hart, *Clash of Arms*, 387, table 10.7.

54. Keegan, *Six Armies*, 316–17.

55. Prados, *Normandy Crucible*, 262.

56. Kershaw answers the question, why and how did the Reich and the *Wehrmacht* continue fighting even though everyone knew Hitler was driving Germany to destruction? The leadership of the "quadrumvirate" of Martin Bormann, Joseph Goebbels, Heinrich Himmler, and Albert Speer displayed remarkable powers of tenacity, organization, and desperate ingenuity. Ian Kershaw, *The End: The Defiance and Destruction of Hitler's Germany, 1944–1945* (New York: Penguin, 2011), xvii, 379.

CHAPTER 9. BATTLE FOR THE RHINE

1. Antwerp lay sixty-five miles inland from the sea, up the winding waterway and banks of the estuary at the western end of the Scheldt River basin. Much of the southern bank of the estuary was still occupied by the German 15th Army. Neillands, *Battle for the Rhine*, 53–54.

2. Van Creveld, *Supplying War*, 224.

3. Van Creveld's logistical arithmetic concluded that eighteen divisions were available for the Ruhr heavy punch. He judged that these divisions were a "small number, admittedly,

but one which would in all probability have sufficed to break through the weak German opposition in early September." Van Creveld, *Supplying War*, 227–28.

4. Van Creveld, *Supplying War*, 228.

5. Mansoor, *GI Offensive*, 181.

6. COM Z was the handiwork of General John C. H. "Court House" Lee, a controversial figure who ran a vast logistical bureaucracy; one in every four soldiers in the ETO was in the COM Z supply services. After the liberation of Paris, Lee requisitioned 315 hotels for himself and COM Z personnel. Atkinson, *Guns at Last Light*, 236–41.

7. Neillands, *Battle for the Rhine*, 156; *Dwight David Eisenhower: The Centennial*, booklet (Washington, DC: Center of Military History, 1990), 6, http://www.history.army .mil/brochures/ike/ike.htm; for an explanation of Eisenhower's philosophy underpinning how he performed his supreme command tasks, see Prados, *Normandy Crucible*, 50ff.

8. At fifty-four divisions ashore and with each requiring 700–750 tons of supplies per day, the logistical math of 40,500 tons per day underscored Antwerp's strategic importance. Neillands put Antwerp's port capacity at only forty thousand tons per day (*Battle for the Rhine*, 157) and Caddick-Adams at eighty to one hundred thousand tons per day (Caddick-Adams, *Snow and Steel*, 120); and Van Creveld, *Supplying War*, 205–12, 228.

9. In Mansoor's judgment, "without Antwerp in Allied hands, Operation *Market Garden* was doomed to failure." Mansoor, *GI Offensive*, 180.

10. Neillands, *Battle for the Rhine*, 155.

11. Neillands, *Battle for the Rhine*, 173.

12. Flyable days in the fall of 1944 ranged from 61 percent for heavy bombers attacking German industrial targets and occasionally targets in support of ground operations, to 51 percent for medium and light bombers flying tactical missions, to a best case of 79 percent for fighters flying tactical missions. Computed from daily entries about weather and air missions after extraction into a spreadsheet from Kit C. Carter and Robert Mueller, *The Army Air Forces in World War II: Combat Chronology, 1941–1945* (New York: Arno, 1980), 439ff.

13. Many German divisions, after heavy losses from the fighting on the Western Front in 1944, were broken up into *Kampfgruppen* trained for quick-reaction operations. Max Hastings, *Armageddon: The Battle for Germany, 1944–1945* (New York: Knopf, 2004), 16; and Chris Bishop, *SS: Hell on the Western Front* (St. Paul, MN: Amber, 2003), 146ff.

14. Mansoor, *GI Offensive*, 180.

15. Van Creveld, *Supplying War*, 222; and Caddick-Adams, *Snow and Steel*, 24.

16. Willmott, *Great Crusade*, 427.

17. Mansoor, *GI Offensive*, 180.

18. Mansoor, *GI Offensive*, 184–85.

19. Neil Short, *Germany's West Wall: The Siegfried Line* (Oxford: Osprey, 2004), 17.

20. Martin van Creveld, *Fighting Power: German and U.S. Army Performance, 1939–1945* (Westport, CT: Greenwood, 1982), 75.

21. Mansoor, *GI Offensive*, 251–52, table 11.1.

22. Mansoor, *GI Offensive*, 194; for a general exposition of combat trauma, see Ben Shephard, *A War of Nerves: Soldiers and Psychiatrists in the Twentieth Century* (Cambridge, MA: Harvard University Press, 2001), 330–38; and John E. Talbott, "Soldiers, Psychiatrists, and Combat Trauma," *Journal of Interdisciplinary History* 27, no. 3 (Winter 1997): 437–54.

23. Mansoor drew a sharper conclusion a decade later about combat experience in Iraq: "Entry-level training received by new soldiers must be lengthy, thorough, and rigorous enough to prepare them for combat upon integration into their [receiving] units. To do less is to consign some of those soldiers to unnecessary wounds or death in battle, whether

the battlefield be the Normandy beaches or the streets of Baghdad." Peter R. Mansoor, *Baghdad at Sunrise: A Brigade Commander's War in Iraq* (New Haven, CT: Yale University Press, 2008), 16.

24. Mansoor, *GI Offensive*, 11.

25. Mansoor, *GI Offensive*, 15, 31.

26. Van Creveld, *Supplying War*, 229.

27. The German order of battle was between five and eight *Panzer* divisions. *Ardennes-Alsace: The U.S. Army Campaigns of World War II*, brochure, CMH Pub. 72-26 (Washington, DC: US Army Center of Military History, 2003), 10–27, http://www.history.army.mil/brochures/ardennes/aral.htm; and Hugh M. Cole, *United States Army in World War II: European Theater of Operations; The Ardennes: The Battle of the Bulge*, 50th anniversary paperback ed. (1965; repr., Washington, DC: US Army Center of Military History, 2009), 650, http://www.history.army.mil/books/wwii/7-8/7-8_7.htm; and Neillands, *Battle for the Rhine*, 273. Caddick-Adams's most recent Bulge history indicates that a total of forty-three "fresh" divisions (mostly *Volksgrenadier*) were raised by November 1944. Caddick-Adams, *Snow and Steel*, 193ff.

28. Roger Cirillo, *Ardennes-Alsace: The US Army Campaigns of World War II*, CMH Pub 72-26 (Washington, DC: US Army Center of Military History, 1995), 4–9, https://archive.org/stream/Ardennes-Alsace/Ardennes-Alsace_djvu.txt.

29. Liddell Hart, *German Generals Talk*, 77.

30. Within the Ardennes forest there is a plateau from which protrudes three distinct ridges or ranges, the central one being called the Schnee Eifel (Snow Mountain). Cole, *Ardennes*, 137.

31. Neillands, *Battle for the Rhine*, 219, 276; Caddick-Adams, *Snow and Steel*, 169.

32. Neillands, *Battle for the Rhine*, 275–76; and Carlo D'Este, *Eisenhower: A Soldier's Life* (New York: Henry Holt, 2002), 637; D'Este points out that Allied intelligence staffs had been getting indications since October that the Germans had assembled 6th *Panzerarmee* in the area east of Aachen. Colonel Oscar W. Koch (later brigadier general), Patton's astute 3rd Army G-2 intelligence chief, was alert to the threat. On 9 December, Koch briefed Patton. Patton told his staff that he wanted to be in a position to meet whatever happens. Koch's intelligence assessment helped Patton to be well prepared at the Allied meeting at Verdun ten days later on December 19. For a comprehensive account of "who knew what," see Caddick-Adams, *Snow and Steel*, chap. 9.

33. Between December 16 and 24, 1944, when the German offensive was at full strength, the US 9th Air Force was hampered by severe winter weather. Carter and Mueller, *Combat Chronology*, 439ff.

34. Stanley Weintraub, *15 Stars: Eisenhower, MacArthur, Marshall; Three Generals Who Saved the American Century* (New York: NAL Caliber, 2008), 280–81.

35. Cole, *Ardennes*, 649.

36. D'Este, *Eisenhower*, 645ff.

37. D'Este, *Eisenhower*, 646.

38. Mansoor, *GI Offensive*, 229.

39. Willmott, *Great Crusade*, 430.

40. Cole, *Ardennes*, 670.

41. Willmott's estimate is one hundred thousand (*Great Crusade*, 431); Caddick-Adams's more recent estimate is eighty-five thousand (*Snow and Steel*, 635).

42. Caddick-Adams, *Snow and Steel*, 635.

43. David Reynolds, *Summits: Six Meetings That Shaped the Twentieth Century* (New York: Basic Books, 2007); Serhii M. Plokhy, *Yalta: The Price of Peace* (New York: Viking,

2010); and Fraser J. Harbutt, *Yalta 1945: Europe and America at the Crossroads* (Cambridge: Cambridge University Press, 2010).

44. Plokhy, *Yalta*, 81–82.

45. Churchill in May 1945 ordered contingency plans to be drawn up for a possible war against the USSR where the objective was British-American hegemony in Eastern Europe to get a better political deal for Poland. The chief of the Imperial General Staff, General Brooke, and his planning team concluded that any quick success would be the result of surprise alone and that such a war would likely be total and protracted, with force ratios favoring the Soviets of four to one in manpower and two to one in tanks, similar to Germany's strategic situation at the beginning of Operation *Barbarossa*. "Operation *Unthinkable*" was quietly shelved. Caddick-Adams, *Snow and Steel*, 687.

46. Caddick-Adams, *Snow and Steel*, 106–7, citing Jonathan R. Adelman, *Prelude to the Cold War: The Tsarist, Soviet, and U.S. Armies in the Two World Wars* (Boulder, CO: Lynne Rienner, 1988), 128. A total Allied casualty breakdown can be summarized as follows: A total of nearly twenty-seven million Soviet citizens were casualties in World War II, 11.3 million killed or missing and 15.3 million civilian deaths (chap. 3, note 14, supra). The total number of US battle casualties was 291,557 and 113,842 "other deaths." The total number of British dead, including civilians, was 357,116 (chap. 3, note 10, supra).

47. The Kennan "long telegram" became the basis of Kennan's famous "X" article in a 1947 issue of *Foreign Affairs*, titled "The Sources of Soviet Conduct," *Foreign Affairs* 25, no. 4 (1947): 566–82.

48. The Truman Doctrine stated that the United States would support Greece and Turkey with economic and military aid to prevent their falling into the Soviet sphere. Both countries eventually became part of the North Atlantic Treaty Organization (NATO). "Special Message to the Congress on Greece and Turkey: The Truman Doctrine" (Truman Library Public Papers, March 12, 1947), https://trumanlibrary.org/publicpapers/index.php?pid=2189&st=&st1.

CHAPTER 10. BATTLE OF OKINAWA AND THE BOMBING OF JAPAN

1. Richard B. Frank, *Downfall: The End of the Imperial Japanese Empire* (New York: Penguin, 1999), 30 (see footnote on "Saipan ratio"), 342. Casualty estimates were "best guesses," with ranges from five hundred thousand to one million depending on which casualty models were used. D. M. Giangreco, "A Score of Bloody Okinawas and Iwo Jimas," in *Hiroshima in History: The Myths of Revisionism*, ed. Robert J. Maddox, 76–115 (Columbia: University of Missouri Press, 2007).

2. Stalin knew about the atomic bomb project as early as 1941, but he did not appreciate the military significance of the atomic bomb until it was dropped on Hiroshima years later. David Holloway, *Stalin and the Bomb: The Soviet Union and Atomic Energy, 1939–1956* (New Haven, CT: Yale University Press, 1994), 82–84, 122.

3. Victor Davis Hanson, *Ripples of Battle: How Wars of the Past Still Determine How We Fight, How We Live, and How We Think* (New York: Doubleday, 2003), 56.

4. In October 1944, Japanese airmen defending the Philippines discovered that Zeros, fitted with five-hundred-pound bombs and crashed headlong into targets, especially ships, wreaked massive damage. Thus the kamikaze was born, the Japanese word for "divine wind," which quickly entered the vernacular of World War II.

5. Hanson, *Ripples*, 22.

6. Bruce I. Gudmundsson, "Okinawa," in *No End Save Victory*, ed. Robert Cowley (New York: Putnam, 2001), 631; and Max Hastings, *Retribution: The Battle for Japan, 1944–45* (New York: Knopf, 2008), 377.

7. Gudmundsson, "Okinawa," 632.

8. Hanson, *Ripples*, 20; Hastings, *Retribution*, 371; Charles S. Nichols Jr. (Major, USMC) and Henry I. Shaw, *Okinawa: Victory in the Pacific* (Washington, DC: Historical Branch, G-3 Division, Headquarters, US Marine Corps, 1955), 64; and Roy E. Appleman et al., *United States Army in World War II: The War in the Pacific; Okinawa: The Last Battle* (Washington, DC: US Army Center of Military History, 1948), 44, 49, http://www.history.army.mil/books/wwii/okinawa/chapter2.htm#b3 (posted December 10, 2001).

9. Hanson, *Ripples*, 20.

10. Cowley, *No End Save Victory*, 628–29.

11. Hanson, *Ripples*, 27.

12. Hastings, *Retribution*, 377.

13. Cowley, *No End Save Victory*, 626. American artillery expenditures were enormous: over one million 105 mm howitzer shells and another six hundred thousand rounds of various calibers from 75 to 115 mm. Hanson, *Ripples*, 22.

14. For combat veteran tone and realism, see William Manchester, *Goodbye Darkness: A Memoir of the Pacific War* (Boston: Little, Brown, 1979), 367–68; and Eugene B. Sledge, *With the Old Breed: At Peleliu and Okinawa* (New York: Oxford University Press, 1990), 298.

15. Cowley, *No End Save Victory*, 635.

16. Hanson, *Ripples*, 29.

17. *Ripples*, 29, 41–43.

18. Willmott, *Great Crusade*, 408. USN official statistics corroborate Willmott's numbers. Navy Department, Bureau of Ships, NAVSHIPS A-3 (420), *Summary of War Damage to U.S. Battleships, Carriers, Cruisers, Destroyers, Destroyer Escorts, 8 December 1943 to 7 December 1944* (Washington, DC: US Hydrographic Office, June 1, 1945), 3, table II.

19. Naval Historical Center, "Casualties: U.S. Navy and Coast Guard Vessels, Sunk or Damaged beyond Repair during World War II, 7 December 1941–1 October 1945," June 1, 2004, https://www.history.navy.mil/research/histories/ship-histories/casualties-navy-and-coast-guard-ships.html.

20. Mitscher had to move his flag to the carrier *Enterprise*, which was hit three days later by a wave of twenty-six kamikazes inflicting such heavy damage that it had to be withdrawn from operations. This was the last fast carrier loss of the war. Hastings, *Retribution*, 400.

21. Hanson, *Ripples*, 42–43.

22. Hanson, *Ripples*, 19, 56; and Cowley, *No End Save Victory*, 638.

23. US Navy losses were 4,907, the army 4,675, and the marines 2,928, a total of 12,510 US combat deaths. There were 44,613 combat casualties and 36,000 nonbattle casualties, many of them combat-fatigue cases. Hastings, *Retribution*, 402. A Japanese shell killed Buckner on June 18, 1945. Generals Ushijima and Cho committed suicide a week later. Hanson, *Ripples*, 28.

24. Hanson, *Ripples*, 29–30; Cowley, *No End Save Victory*, 638; and Hastings, *Retribution*, 402.

25. Carter and Mueller, *Combat Chronology*, 594.

26. Wesley F. Craven and James L. Cate, *The Army Air Forces in World War II: The Pacific Matterhorn to Nagasaki, June 1944 to August 1945* (Chicago: University of Chicago Press, 1953), 5:xx, http://www.ibiblio.org/hyperwar/AAF/V/index.html.

27. Editorial Staff, *Air Victory over Japan*, paperback reprint of the final issue of impact of strategic bombing of Japan produced by the Office of the Assistant Chief of Air Staff, September–October, 1945 (Whitefish, MT: Kessinger, 2006), 90.

28. John T. Correll, "Daylight Precision Bombing," *Air Force Magazine*, October 2008, 64.

29. St. Clair McKelway, "A Reporter with the B-29s," *New Yorker*, June 23, 1945, 26–39.

30. McKelway, "A Reporter with the B-29s," 37.

31. Editorial Staff, *Air Victory*, 90.

32. Editorial Staff, *Air Victory*, 90.

33. Michael S. Sherry, *The Rise of American Air Power: The Creation of Armageddon* (New Haven, CT: Yale University Press, 1987), 209.

34. David A. Anderson, *B-29 Superfortress at War* (New York: Scribner, 1978), 153.

35. Craven and Cate, *Army Air Forces in World War II*, 5:xx–xxi.

36. Conrad C. Crane, *Bombs, Cities, and Civilians: American Airpower Strategy in World War II* (Lawrence: University Press of Kansas, 1993), 162.

37. The name painted on the fuselage of the B-29 that bombed Hiroshima was the Christian name of the mother of Colonel Paul W. Tibbets who flew the mission.

38. Edward T. Linenthal, "Anatomy of a Controversy," and Michael S. Sherry, "Patriotic Orthodoxy and American Decline," in *History Wars: The Enola Gay and Other Battles for the American Past*, ed. Edward T. Linenthal and Tom Engelhardt (New York: Holt, 1996), 1–8, 97ff; Barton J. Bernstein, "The Struggle over History: Defining the Hiroshima Narrative," in *Judgment at the Smithsonian*, ed. Barton J. Bernstein (New York: Marlowe, 1995), 127ff; and Wilson D. Miscamble, *The Most Controversial Decision: Truman, the Atomic Bombs, and the Defeat of Japan* (Cambridge: Cambridge University Press, 2011), 1–2.

39. Japanese policy making centered on the Supreme Council for the Direction of the War created in 1944. Known as the "Big Six," the membership consisted of five generals or admirals and one civilian diplomat and operated under a decision rule of unanimity.

40. The Potsdam Declaration on July 26, 1945, demanded Japan's unconditional surrender and specified further terms of military occupation, limitation of sovereignty, prosecution of war criminals, and guarantees for "fundamental human rights." The declaration was silent about Hirohito's personal future.

41. Tsuyoshi Hasegawa, *Racing the Enemy: Stalin, Truman, and the Surrender of Japan* (Cambridge, MA: Harvard University Press, 2005), 4, 291, 297ff, passim.

42. Hasegawa, *Racing the Enemy*, 290–98. Hasegawa analyzed eight counterfactuals to reach this conclusion that Soviet entry was decisive in forcing the surrender.

43. Frank, *Downfall*, 345.

44. Hasegawa, *Racing the Enemy*, 297.

45. Frank, *Downfall*, 349.

46. Frank, *Downfall*, 332–34, 355–56; also see online monographs, "American Military Leaders Urge President Truman Not to Drop the Atomic Bomb," https://www.colorado.edu/AmStudies/lewis/2010/atomicdec.htm, citing "The Decision to Use the Atomic Bomb," Gar Alperovitz and the H-Net Debate, at Doug Long website, "The Decision the Atomic Bomb," http://www.doug-long.com/debate.htm.

47. Frank, *Downfall*, 303–4ff.

48. In 1941, the average citizen consumed about 2,000 calories daily, just 6.3 percent above subsistence levels. Americans in 1941 consumed a diet of 3,400 calories per day. By 1944 the Japanese caloric average had fallen to 1,900, and by 1945 it had dropped to 1,680. Frank, *Downfall*, 350–55.

49. Walter R. Borneman, *The Admirals: Nimitz, Halsey, Leahy, King—The Five-Star Admirals Who Won the War at Sea* (New York: Little Brown, 2012), 372.

50. Major General Leslie R. Groves Jr. (later lieutenant general) is the most well known of the World War II generation of Guardians. A colonel in 1940, Groves was an engineering officer whose reputation as a "doer, a driver, and a stickler for duty" oversaw the rapid design and construction of the Pentagon, completed in May 1942. Groves then directed the Manhattan Project. Lenore Fine and Jesse A. Remington, *The Corps of Engineers: Construction of the United States* (Washington, DC: US Army Center of Military History, 1972), 157–59.

51. Harrison, *Economics of World War II*, 10, table 1.3.

52. Paul Fussell, *Thank God for the Atom Bomb and Other Essays* (New York: Summit Books, 1988), 28.

53. William B. Hussey, *Uncommon Good Fortune: A Memoir*, privately published book (Santa Barbara, CA: Alternative Digital Printing, 2012), 155.

CHAPTER 11. THE STRATEGIC ARCHITECTURES OF WORLD WAR II

1. "It must never be forgotten that the present rulers of Russia are blood-stained criminals and here we have the dregs of humanity. . . . In Russian Bolshevism we ought to recognize the kind of attempt which is being made by the Jew in the 20th century to secure domination of the world." Note: These types of rants by Hitler pervade the text of chap. 14 of *Mein Kampf*, "Germany's Policy in East Europe." Adolf Hitler, *Mein Kampf*, trans. James Murphy, unexpurgated ed. (1939; repr., London: Hurst and Blackett, 1942), 364–65.

2. Gordon Fraser, *The Quantum Exodus: Jewish Fugitives, the Atomic Bomb and the Holocaust* (New York: Oxford University Press, 2012), 241–49.

3. The Zossen-Wunsdorf complex consisted of three huge underground bombproof bunker systems, named Maybach I and II and Zeppelin; buildings were disguised aboveground to look like farm buildings. Hitler never used it. Hans-Albert Hoffmann, *Die Deutsche Herresführung im II.Weltkrieg* (Berlin: self-published by Holga Wende, 2006); Hans George Kampe, *The Underground Military Command Bunkers of Zossen, Germany: Construction History and Use by the Wehrmacht and Soviet Army, 1937–1994* (Atglen, PA: Schiffer, 1996); and Neil Short, *The Führer's Headquarters: Hitler's Command Bunkers, 1939–45* (Oxford: Osprey, 2010).

4. Ian Kershaw, *Hitler, 1936–1945 Nemesis* (New York: Norton, 2000), 311, 573.

5. Caddick-Adams, *Snow and Steel*, 41–42.

6. Eri Hotta, *Japan 1941: Countdown to Infamy*, e-book ed. (New York: Knopf, 2013), quoted from "Prologue: What a Difference a Day Makes." Hotta illuminates the strategic predicament facing the Japanese government in 1941. She indicates that even Tojo was "ambivalent" about starting the war.

7. James M. McPherson, *The War That Forged a Nation: Why the Civil War Still Matters* (Oxford: Oxford University Press, 2015), 2, 54, chap. 4.

8. Caddick-Adams, *Snow and Steel*, 645.

9. Lincoln relieved Generals Irvin McDowell, George B. McClellan, John Pope, McClellan again, Ambrose E. Burnside, Joseph Hooker, and George G. Meade. Ricks, *Generals*, 22.

10. John L. Gaddis, "He Made It Look Easy," *New York Times Book Review*, April 22, 2012, 14, reviewing Jean Edward Smith, *Eisenhower in War and Peace* (New York: Random House, 2012).

11. Max Hastings, *The Secret War: Spies, Ciphers, and Guerrillas, 1939–1945* (New York: Harper, 2016).

12. Lewis makes this very useful distinction between defeat and surrender. John D. Lewis, *Nothing Less Than Victory: Decisive Wars and the Lessons of History* (Princeton, NJ: Princeton University Press, 2010), 272–73.

13. Earl F. Ziemke, *The U.S. Army in the Occupation of Germany, 1944–1946* (Washington, DC: US Army Center of Military History, US Government Printing Office, 1990), 5–6, http://www.globalsecurity.org/military/library/report/other/us-army_germany_1944-46_index.htm#contents.

14. Tony Judt, *Postwar: A History of Europe since 1945* (New York: Penguin, 2005), 5; and Timothy Snyder, *Bloodlands: Europe between Hitler and Stalin* (New York: Basic Books, 2010). Snyder shifts the geographical focus away from the combatant countries to *Mitteleuropa*, the "bloodlands" where they first colluded and then collided.

15. Alan Bullock, *Ernest Bevin: Foreign Secretary* (London: Heinemann, 1983; repr., Oxford: Oxford University Press, 1985); Richard Bessell, *Germany 1945: From War to Peace* (London: Simon & Schuster, 2009); Nicholas Pronay and Keith Wilson, eds., *The Political Re-education of Germany and Her Allies after World War II* (London: Croom Helm, 1985); and John Ramsden, *Don't Mention the War: The British and the Germans since 1890* (London: Little, Brown, 2006).

16. The US Army was the executive agency for military government until 1949. In March 1946 the Office of Military Government in Berlin was headed by General Lucius D. Clay. Ziemke, *Occupation of Germany*; and Carnes Lord, *Proconsuls, Delegated Political-Military Leadership from Rome to America Today* (Cambridge: Cambridge University Press, 2012), 232. Lord assessed Clay's performance: "In the case of military occupations following the defeat of an enemy by military means, the American experience . . . [is] best exemplified by Lucius Clay in postwar Germany."

17. Seventeen European states benefited from the Marshall Plan: Austria, Belgium, Denmark, France, Germany, Greece, Iceland, Ireland, Italy and Trieste, Luxembourg, the Netherlands, Norway, Portugal, Sweden, Switzerland, Turkey, and the United Kingdom.

18. Tony Judt writing in Martin A. Schain, ed., *The Marshall Plan: Fifty Years After* (New York: Palgrave, 2001), 2.

19. US Department of Commerce, Bureau of Economic Analysis, http://www.data360.org/dsg.aspx?Data_Set_Group_Id=230.

20. Use of an inflation calculator indicates that $25 billion in 1945 had the same buying power as $332 billion in 2016. Present values computed at http://www.dollartimes.com/calculators/inflation.htm.

21. Benn Steil, *The Marshall Plan: Dawn of the Cold War* (New York: Simon & Schuster, 2017), 342. Steil estimates total Marshall Plan aid at $800 billion and Mutual Security Agency assistance at $46 billion over the four-year period (1948–1952); see note 13.

22. Frederick Taylor, *Exorcising Hitler: The Occupation and Denazification of Germany* (New York: Bloomsbury, 2011), xviii.

23. US Army official histories, http://www.globalsecurity.org/military/agency/army/8army-history.htm.

24. Ruth Benedict, *The Chrysanthemum and the Sword: Patterns of Japanese Culture* (1946; repr., Boston: Houghton Mifflin, 1974), 298–99.

PART III: THE KOREAN WAR

1. Robert Leckie, *Conflict: The History of the Korean War, 1950–1953* (New York: Avon, 1962), 50–51; and Warren Kozak, *LeMay: The Life and Wars of General Curtis LeMay*,

paperback ed. (Washington, DC: Regnery, 2011), 272. The US Air Force had 218 combat-ready groups in 1945; it was down to 52 groups by 1950.

2. Max Hastings, *The Korean War* (New York: Simon & Schuster, 1987), 50.

3. Carter Malkasian, *The Korean War, 1950–1953* (Oxford: Osprey, 2001), 7–8.

4. Bruce Cumings, *The Korean War: A History* (New York: Random House, 2010), xv–xvii; and Hastings, *The Korean War*, 25.

5. Don Oberdorfer, *The Two Koreas*, rev. ed. (New York: Basic Books, 2001), 6; Leckie, *Conflict*, 26; Roy E. Appleman, *South to the Naktong, North to the Yalu, June–November 1950* (1961; repr., Washington, DC: US Army Center of Military History, US Government Printing Office, 1992), 3; and James F. Schnabel, *United States Army in the Korean War: Policy and Direction; The First Year*, CMH Pub. 20-1-1 (1972; repr., Washington, DC: US Army Center of Military History, US Government Printing Office, 1992), 9, http://www.history.army.mil/books/p&d.htm.

6. The reference librarian of the Humanities and Social Science Division, Library of Congress, estimates that the Korean War collection includes twenty thousand titles about this "unknown" war (email from Rodney P. Katz, June 1, 2011).

7. Stephen Turnbull, *Samurai Invasion: Japan's Korean War, 1592–98* (London: Cassell, 2002), 52ff, 75ff; Turnbull, *The Samurai Invasion of Korea, 1592–98* (Oxford: Osprey, 2008), 80–81, 91; Mary E. Berry, *Hideyoshi*, Harvard East Asian Monographs, paperback ed. (1982; repr., Cambridge, MA: Council on East Asian Studies, Harvard University, 1989); and Kitami Masao, *The Swordless Samurai: Leadership Wisdom of Japan's 16th Century Legend—Toyotomi Hideyoshi* (New York: St. Martin's, 2005). Note: A shogun ("commander of a force") was one of the military dictators of Japan from 1192 to 1867.

8. Hodge had served on Okinawa, was promoted to lieutenant general in August 1945, and became the commander of the 24th Corps of the US 10th Army. The units he brought to Korea were combat outfits. Hastings, *The Korean War*, 29–30.

9. Hastings, *The Korean War*, 33.

10. Leckie, *Conflict*, 30–31.

11. Hastings, *The Korean War*, 57.

12. David Halberstam, *The Coldest Winter: America and the Korean War* (New York: Hyperion, 2007), 1.

13. Cumings, *The Korean War*, 72, citing Bradley K. Martin, *Under the Loving Care of the Fatherly Leader: North Korea and the Kim Dynasty* (New York: Thomas Dunne, 2004), 63.

14. In 1963, Harold Adrian Russell "Kim" Philby was revealed as a member of the spy ring now known as the Cambridge Five, along with Donald Maclean, Guy Burgess, Anthony Blunt, and John Cairncross. Philby, a high-ranking intelligence officer in the British Secret Intelligence Service (MI6), served in the British embassy in Washington as the British liaison officer to the CIA. His espionage is considered to have been very successful in providing secret information to the Soviet Union during 1950–1951.

15. Cumings, *The Korean War*, 72–73.

16. John Lewis Gaddis, *The Cold War: A New History* (New York: Penguin, 2005), 42.

17. Cumings, *The Korean War*, 51–65.

18. Burritt Sabin, "They Came, They Saw, They Democratized," *Japan Times*, April 28, 2002. For an assessment of MacArthur's proconsular accomplishments in Japan, see Lord, *Proconsuls*, chap. 5.

19. Appleman, *South to the Naktong*, 9.

20. William J. Webb, *The Korean War: The Outbreak*, CMH Pub. 19-6 (Washington, DC: US Army Center of Military History, 2006), 7, http://www.history.army.mil/brochures/KW-Outbreak/outbreak.htm. As the Korean War began, North Korea had about 180 Soviet aircraft.

21. Hastings, *The Korean War*, 68.

22. Stanley Weintraub, who served as a US Army lieutenant during the Korean War, told an interviewer upon publication of his book, *MacArthur's War: Korea and the Making of an American Hero* (New York: Free Press, 2008), that MacArthur "didn't stay overnight one night in Korea. He ran the war from the American embassy in Tokyo where he lived and from the Dai Ichi [building] across from the Emperor's Palace in Tokyo." Online site of journalist Geoff Metcalf, http://www.geoffmetcalf.com/qa/19638.html.

23. Schnabel, *U.S. Army in the Korean War*, 77–78, citing archived radio message Rad, C 56942, CINCFE to JCS, June 30, 1950.

24. UN Security Council Resolution 83, https://documents-dds-ny.un.org/doc/RESO LUTION/GEN/NR0/064/96/IMG/NR006496.pdf?OpenElement.

25. Hastings, *The Korean War*, 238–39, 365–68, with the appendix listing military forces and resources provided by UN members.

26. Hastings, *The Korean War*, 9.

27. Appleman, *South to the Naktong*, 9, 17–18.

28. Cumings, *The Korean War*, 11; and Leckie, *Conflict*, 43.

29. Leckie, *Conflict*, 43, 51; Appleman, *South to the Naktong*, 32; and Robert K. Sawyer, *Military Advisers in Korea: KMAG in Peace and War*, CMH Pub. 30-3 (1962; repr., Washington, DC: US Army Center of Military History, US Government Printing Office, 1988), 126, note 32; and General Park Chung-hee's newspaper account of the "Hangang Bridge Massacre," excerpted from *Chosun Ilbo* ("Spit on My Grave"), is "the Korean version" of what happened; http://english.chosun.com/site/data/html_dir/1999/05/14/1999051461374.html.

30. Leckie, *Conflict*, 44; and Webb, *The Korean War*, 7.

31. Principal among these diplomats was the Indian ambassador to Peking, Dr. Kavalam M. Panikkar, who warned Western capitals that the PRC would intervene in force should the UN move north. Acheson was unimpressed: "Such warnings were the 'mere vaporings of a panicky Panikkar.'" Halberstam, *The Coldest Winter*, 334–37; and Hastings, *The Korean War*, 134–35, 367.

32. Matthew Ridgway, *The Korean War* (Garden City, NY: Doubleday, 1967), 151.

33. Appleman, *South to the Naktong*, 7; and Richard W. Stewart, ed., *American Military History: The United States Army in a Global Era, 1917–2003*, CMH Pub. 30-22 (Washington, DC: US Army Center of Military History, 2005), 2:232, http://www.history.army.mil /books/AMH-V2/AMH-V2-PDF.htm. Soviet pilots flew MiG-15 interceptors from bases in Manchuria protected by Soviet antiaircraft units.

34. Cumings, *The Korean War*, xvii–xviii.

CHAPTER 12. BATTLE OF THE PUSAN PERIMETER

1. MacArthur remarked to roving ambassador John Foster Dulles during a visit to Korea a week before the invasion "that if he could put the 1st Cavalry Division into Korea, 'why, heavens, you'd see these fellows scuttle up to the Manchurian border so quick, you would see no more of them.'" Cumings, *The Korean War*, 14.

2. Hastings, *The Korean War*, 69–70, cited in note 16 as Hastings interview with Colonel Jonathan F. Ladd, October 1985.

3. Bevin Alexander, *Korea: The First War We Lost* (New York: Hippocrene, 2003), 55–56.

4. Alexander, *Korea*, 55.

5. Appleman, *South to the Naktong*, 59–81; Halberstam, *The Coldest Winter*, 144–48; Hastings, *The Korean War*, 9–22; Leckie, *Conflict*, 52–60; and John Garrett, *Task Force Smith: The Lesson Never Learned*, paperback (BiblioScholar Publishing, 2012). A search of

the US Army War College's website reveals two critiques, William J. Davies, "Task Force Smith—A Leadership Failure?" (Military Studies Program Paper, US Army War College, Carlisle Barracks, PA, 1992); and a tank availability critique, Arthur W. Connor Jr., "The Armor Debacle in Korea, 1950: Implications for Today," *Parameters* 67–76 (Summer 1992).

6. Webb, *The Korean War*, 19.

7. Halberstam, *The Coldest Winter*, 158.

8. Hastings, *The Korean War*, 84. Walker's fight-or-die order echoed another 8th Army commander eight years earlier: General Montgomery telling his staff before El Alamein, "We will stand and fight here. If we can't stay here, then let us stay here dead." Latimer, *Alamein*, 98–99.

9. Stewart, *American Military History*, 2:230.

10. Malkasian, *The Korean War*, 24.

11. Within the first four months after Japan's surrender in 1945, the army and navy COMINT organizations lost 80 percent of their personnel. AFSA, created in 1947, the predecessor organization to the later creation of the National Security Agency (NSA) in 1952, quickly recovered from the June 1950 North Korean surprise. Matthew M. Aid, *The Secret Sentry: The Untold Story of the National Security Agency* (New York: Bloomsbury, 2009), 8–9.

12. Aid, *The Secret Sentry*, 27.

13. Halberstam, *The Coldest Winter*, 255.

14. Appleman, *South to the Naktong*, 425ff.

CHAPTER 13. INCHON—OPERATION *CHROMITE*

1. Throughout the weeks of the summer of 1950, MacArthur's staff had been diverting too many of the best field officers and units to the Inchon buildup rather than to Walker's 8th Army around the Pusan Perimeter. Halberstam, *The Coldest Winter*, 156 and 270; and John C. Chapin, *Fire Brigade: U.S. Marines in the Pusan Perimeter* (Washington, DC: Marine Corps Historical Center, Korean War Commemorative Series, 2000), 64.

2. Schnabel, *U.S. Army in the Korean War*, 142, citing Rad, C 58473, CINCFE to DA (for JCS), July 23, 1950.

3. Hastings, *The Korean War*, 101–2; and Halberstam, *The Coldest Winter*, 300. Appleman's CMH account is less colorful but describes subsequent message traffic between MacArthur and Washington; Appleman, *South to the Naktong*, 494–95.

4. Hastings characterized this fleet that sailed from Yokohama on September 5 as a "makeshift transport fleet"; Hastings, *The Korean War*, 105.

5. Halberstam, *The Coldest Winter*, 304–5; and Chen Jian, *China's Road to the Korean War: The Making of the Sino-American Confrontation* (New York: Columbia University Press, 1994), 269n42.

6. Halberstam, *The Coldest Winter*, 129; and Hastings, *The Korean War*, 104.

7. D'Este, *Eisenhower*, chaps. 18–21.

8. Halberstam, *The Coldest Winter*, 128.

9. Aid, *Secret Sentry*, 28–29.

10. Alexander points out that KPA logistics depended heavily on the only single double-tracked railroad line in Korea, which ran through Seoul; Alexander, *Korea*, 249–50.

11. Almond's World War II record in the ETO was blemished. Atkinson, *Day of Battle*, 383; T. R. Fehrenbach, *This Kind of War: The Classic Korean War History*, 50th anniversary ed. (Washington, DC: Potomac, 2001), 163; and Appleman, *South to the Naktong*, 490.

12. *Military operation in a built-up area* (MOBA) was the term used by the US military to describe urban warfare until approximately 1980. Lilita I. Dzirkals, Konrad Kellen, and Horst Mendershausen, *Military Operations in Built-Up Areas: Essays on Some Past, Present, and Future Aspects*, R-1871-ARPA (Santa Monica, CA: Rand, 1976). Then *MOBA* was superseded by *military operation in urban terrain* (MOUT) in 1998. Marine Corps Warfighting Publication 3-53.3, *Military Operations on Urbanized Terrain* (Washington, DC: Headquarters, US Marine Corps, 1998).

13. Fehrenbach, *This Kind of War*, 166–67; and Hastings, *The Korean War*, 112.

14. David Rees, *Korea: The Limited War* (London: Macmillan, 1964), 90.

15. Richard W. Stewart, *Staff Operations: The X Corps in Korea, December 1950* (Fort Leavenworth, KS: US Army Command and General Staff College, Combat Studies Institute, 1991), 1–2.

16. Hastings, *The Korean War*, 309.

17. Stewart, *Staff Operations*, 1–2.

18. Hastings, *The Korean War*, 114.

19. Eliot A. Cohen and John Gooch, *Military Misfortunes: The Anatomy of Failure in War* (New York: Free Press, 1990), 166, citing JCS 92985, dated September 29, 1950, Secretary of Defense to CINCFE, in *Foreign Relations of the United States 1950*, vol. 7, *Korea* (Washington, DC: US Government Printing Office, 1976), 826; and Appleman, *South to the Naktong*, 608, also citing JCS 92985.

CHAPTER 14. CROSSING THE 38TH PARALLEL AND DRIVING NORTH TO THE YALU

1. General Almond at the time of his appointment to command 10th Corps became "double hatted" because he still continued serving as MacArthur's chief of staff.

2. Halberstam, *The Coldest Winter*, 312.

3. Halberstam, *The Coldest Winter*, 313.

4. Goulden points out that terrain was a factor in the CINCFE split-command decision. The Taeboek mountain range above the Seoul–Wonsan corridor forms "an almost trackless mountainous waste in the direction of the Manchurian frontier." MacArthur thought that Wonsan would make a more efficient supply base than Pusan because the US Air Force had bombed every railroad and highway bridge north of the perimeter. Joseph C. Goulden, *Korea: The Untold Story of the War* (New York: McGraw-Hill, 1982), 240.

5. Halberstam, *The Coldest Winter*, 11; and Hastings, *The Korean War*, 154.

6. Cohen and Gooch, *Military Misfortunes*, 177.

7. Mao Tse Tung, *The Art of War*, ed. James H. Ford, trans. Foreign Language Press, Peking, special ed. (El Paso: El Paso Norte Press, 2005), 19, 58, 240–42, 283.

8. Mao Tse Tung, *Quotations from Mao Tse Tung* (Peking: Peking Foreign Languages Press, 1966; Mao Tse Tung Internet Archive [marxists.org], 2000), chap. 5, "War and Peace," citing "On Protracted War," *Selected Works*, 2:152–53.

9. Halberstam, *The Coldest Winter*, 364–65.

10. Truman first used the term on June 27, 1950, two days after the North Korean attack, in response to a reporter's question. Hastings, *The Korean War*, 60; Halberstam, *The Coldest Winter*, 2; Leckie, *Conflict*, 77; and Cumings, *The Korean War*, 228.

11. The date of the Wake Island meeting fell two weeks before the 1950 midterm congressional elections. Hastings, *The Korean War*, 122.

12. David McCullough, *Truman* (New York: Simon & Schuster, 1990), 801; Halberstam, *The Coldest Winter*, 365–66; Hastings, *The Korean War*, 122; and Merle Miller, *Plain Speaking: An Oral Biography of Harry S. Truman* (New York: Putnam, 1974).

13. Alexander, *Korea*, 247–48.

14. Omar N. Bradley, General of the Army, Chairman of the JCS, *Substance of Statements Made at Wake Island Conference on October 15, 1950*, prepared for the use of the Committee on Armed Services and the Committee on Foreign Relations, US Senate (Washington, DC: Government Printing Office, 1951).

15. Bradley, *Substance of Statements Made at Wake Island*, 1.

16. UN aircraft flew over one million aerial sorties during the Korean War, most in close air ground support or fighter cover missions. The bombing campaign focused on cutting the enemy's supply lines. "Notwithstanding the all-out efforts of the air force in Korea, there was never a day when the trains did not run and the trucks did not roll behind the enemy lines in North Korea." Hastings, *The Korean War*, 256, 268, and 286–87, citing for the airpower assessment Melvin B. Vorhees, *Korean Tales* (London: Secker and Warburg, 1953), 170; Cumings, *The Korean War*, 158–60; and Crane, *Bombs, Cities, and Civilians*, 147–50.

17. The Russians were capable of delivering technological shocks on American forces. The appearance of MiG-15 jet fighters over Korea in November 1950 sent shockwaves through the US Air Force. Some fifty MiGs, flown by Chinese and Soviet pilots, were initially deployed. Within six months, there were 445 MiGs. By 1953 there were 830, mostly flown by Chinese pilots operating from the political sanctuary of air bases north of the Yalu. Hastings, *The Korean War*, 258.

18. Bradley, *Substance of Statements Made at Wake Island*, 5; Appleman, *South to the Naktong*, 760.

19. Appleman, *South to the Naktong*, 767, citing multiple Far East Command (FEC) intelligence digests.

20. Text of National Security Council Report, "United States Courses of Action with Respect to Korea," NSC 81/1, September 9, 1950, para. 15, 4, http://digitalarchive.wilson center.org/document/116194.

21. National Security Council Report, "United States Courses of Action with Respect to Korea," para. 7, 4.

22. Ridgway, *The Korean War*, 151.

23. Aid, *Secret Sentry*, 29–32, citing Ridgway interview, Office of the Secretary of Defense Historical Office, oral history, "Interview with General M. B. Ridgway," DoD FOIA (Freedom of Information Act) Reading Room, Pentagon, Washington, DC (April 18, 1984), 20–21; and Cohen and Gooch, *Military Misfortunes*, 169.

24. Halberstam, *The Coldest Winter*, 25–27, 41.

25. Hastings, *The Korean War*, 139–40.

26. Cohen and Gooch, *Military Misfortunes*, 168, citing CINCFE to JCS C69953, November 28, 1950, FRUS, 1950, 7 and 1237.

27. Cohen and Gooch, *Military Misfortunes*, 168.

28. Yu Bin, "What China Learned from Its 'Forgotten' War," in *Chinese Warfighting: The PLA Experience since 1949*, ed. Mark A. Ryan, David M. Finkelstein, and Michael A. McDevitt (Armonk, NY: M. E. Sharpe, 2003), 127.

29. Cohen and Gooch, *Military Misfortunes*, 173–74.

30. Steven W. Nerheim (Captain, USN), *NSC 81/1 and the Evolution of U.S. War Aims in Korea, June–October 1950* (Carlisle Barracks, PA: US Army War College, 2000), 15, 10–24.

31. For an excellent narrative of 1st Marine Division and 10th Corps withdrawal from Chosin, see Martin Russ, *Breakout: The Chosin Reservoir Campaign, Korea, 1950* (New York: Fromm International, 1999).

32. Cohen and Gooch, *Military Misfortunes*, 172.

33. Cohen and Gooch, *Military Misfortunes*, 175–86.

34. Cohen and Gooch, *Military Misfortunes*, 191, fig. 7.1.

35. *OW*, 88–89, I:1.

36. Cohen and Gooch, *Military Misfortunes*, 192–93, citing Robert F. Futtrell, *The United States Air Force in Korea, 1950–1953* (Washington, DC: Office of Air Force History, 1983), 71, 91, 186.

37. Cohen and Gooch, *Military Misfortunes*, 192–93.

38. Cohen and Gooch, *Military Misfortunes*, 192–93, citing Samuel B. Griffith, *The Chinese People's Liberation Army* (New York: McGraw-Hill, 1967), 73.

39. Cohen and Gooch, *Military Misfortunes*, 188, citing Lynn Montross and Nicholas A. Canzona, *U.S. Marine Operations in Korea, 1950–1953: The Chosin Reservoir Campaign* (Washington, DC: US Government Printing Office, 1957), 3:351–54.

40. By this time, the 10th Corps staff had become much more proficient, having recovered from its earlier weak pre-Inchon planning performance.

41. Stewart, *Staff Operations*, 7–8.

42. Cohen and Gooch, *Military Misfortunes*, 189, citing Ridgway, *The Korean War*, 88.

43. Ricks, *Generals*, 185.

CHAPTER 15. OPERATIONS *RIPPER* AND *KILLER*

1. Ricks, *Generals*, 189.

2. Hastings, *The Korean War*, 190.

3. James D. Clayton, *The Years of MacArthur*, vol. 3, *Triumph and Disaster, 1945–1964* (Boston: Houghton Mifflin, 1985), 590; and Michael D. Pearlman, *Korean War Anthology: Truman and MacArthur; The Winding Road to Dismissal* (Fort Leavenworth, KS: US Army Command and General Staff College, Combat Studies Institute, CSI Press, 2003), 12.

4. Halberstam, *The Coldest Winter*, 616.

5. Aid, *Secret Sentry*, 36–37.

6. Aid, *Secret Sentry*, 36–37.

7. Malkasian, *The Korean War*, 40–41.

8. Alexander, *Korea*, ix, xi.

CHAPTER 16. THE STRATEGIC ARCHITECTURES OF THE KOREAN WAR

1. Stephen Crabtree, "The Gallup Brain: Americans and the Korean War" (online monograph, February 4, 2003), 3, figure titled "Views on the Korean War: July 1950–September 1951," http://www.gallup.com/poll/7741/gallup-brain-americans-korean-war.aspx.

2. Cumings, *The Korean War*, 19–21.

3. For a vivid account, see Andrew Salmon, *To the Last Round: The Epic British Stand on the Imjin River, Korea 1951* (London: Aurum, 2009).

4. Malkasian, *The Korean War*, 46, passim.

5. Malkasian, *The Korean War*, 231–32.

6. Stewart, *American Military History*, 2:240.

7. Hastings, *The Korean War*, 333.

8. Halberstam, *The Coldest Winter*, 499.

9. Goulden, *Korea*, 233–34, citing as sources in notes 3 and 4: Draft memorandum, "U.S. Courses of Action in Korea," Joint Strategic Planning Committee, JCS (July 31, 1950), and Draft memorandum, untitled, Policy Planning Committee, Department of State (July 25, 1950).

10. Crabtree, "The Gallup Brain," 2, figure titled "February 1951–January 1953."

11. Malkasian, *The Korean War*, 88; and website, "The Korean War," http://www.cotf .edu/ete/modules/korea/kwar.html.

12. *The World Factbook 2016* (Washington, DC: Central Intelligence Agency, 2016), https://www.cia.gov/library/publications/the-world-factbook/geos/ks.html.

PART IV: THE VIETNAM WAR

1. The reference librarian of the Humanities and Social Science Division, Library of Congress, estimates that the Vietnam War collection includes twenty-five thousand titles (email from Rodney P. Katz, February 8, 2011).

2. Sophie Quinn-Judge, *Ho Chi Minh: The Missing Years, 1919–1941* (Berkeley: University of California Press, 2003), 11; and Fredrik Logevall, *Embers of War: Fall of an Empire and the Making of America's Vietnam* (New York: Random House, 2012), 4, 11, 85.

3. Talbott opens his history of the French colonial war in Algeria with a brief recitation of the French defeat in Indochina resulting in heavy French casualties: 92,000 killed, 114,000 wounded, and 30,000 POWs, higher than US casualties in Vietnam. John E. Talbott, *The War without a Name: France in Algeria, 1954–1962* (New York: Knopf, 1980), 6.

4. Bernard B. Fall, *Hell in a Very Small Place: The Siege of Dien Bien Phu*, paperback ed. (New York: Vintage, 1968), vii, 379; and Talbott, *War without a Name*, 403–25, 445–53, 510–46.

5. Douglas Porch, *Counterinsurgency: Exposing the Myths of the New Way of War* (Cambridge: Cambridge University Press, 2013), 205.

6. President Eisenhower's News Conference, April 7, 1954, *Public Papers of the Presidents*, 382, https://www.mtholyoke.edu/acad/intrel/pentagon/ps11.htm.

7. John F. Kennedy Presidential Library and Museum, https://www.jfklibrary.org/Re search/Research-Aids/Ready-Reference/JFK-Quotations/Inaugural-Address.aspx.

8. Porch described the etymology of *counterinsurgency*. "While it still retained colonial small wars roots, by 1962, 'counterrevolutionary warfare' had been modernized, refined, and rebranded as 'counterinsurgency,' in part to eliminate the heroic 'revolutionary' subtext. COIN was defined as a war waged 'amongst the people' by governments against non-state 'national liberation movements.'" Porch, *Counterinsurgency*, 208.

9. Porch, *Counterinsurgency*, 208.

10. Transcript of President Kennedy's CBS television interview on Vietnam, September 2, 1963, http://www.mtholyoke.edu/acad/intrel/kentv.htm.

11. Edward Miller, *Misalliance: Ngo Dinh Diem, the United States, and the Fate of South Vietnam* (Cambridge, MA: Harvard University Press, 2013), 119–23.

12. Jeffrey Race, forty years after he published *War Comes to Long An*, reflected retrospectively on the limitations of the Diem regime and by implication those that followed after his execution in 1963. Michael J. Montesano, "*War Comes to Long An*, Its Origins and Legacies: An Interview with Jeffrey Race," *Journal of Vietnamese Studies* 6, no. 1 (2011): 164.

13. Shelby L. Stanton, *Order of Battle: A Complete Illustrated Reference to U.S. Army Combat and Support Forces in Vietnam, 1961–1973* (Mechanicsburg, PA: Stackpole, orig. 1981, 2003), 7 (table I-5) and 333 (appendix A).

14. Richard A. Rinnaldi, *U.S. Naval Forces in Vietnam* (unpublished monograph, 2008), 1–6.

15. John T. Cornell, *The Air Force in the Vietnam War* (Arlington, VA: Aerospace Education Foundation, 2004), 4–9, http://higherlogicdownload.s3.amazonaws.com/AFA/6379b747 -7730-4f82-9b45-a1c80d6c8fdb/UploadedImages/Mitchell%20Publications/The%20Air%20 Force%20and%20the%20Vietnam%20War.pdf.

16. The RMK-BRJ joint venture consisted of Raymond International, Morrison-Knudsen International, Brown and Root, and the J. A. Jones Construction Company.

17. Morrison-Knudsen company history, http://www.fundinguniverse.com/company -histories/Morrison-Knudsen-Corporation-Company-History.html.

18. Based on online inflation calculator, calculating value of $1.9 billion in 1966 to equivalent in 2016 of $14 billion, http://www.dollartimes.com/calculators/inflation.htm.

19. Andrew F. Krepinevich Jr., *The Army and Vietnam* (Baltimore, MD: Johns Hopkins University Press, 1986), 73–99. Krepinevich was a major in the US Army at the time he wrote *The Army and Vietnam*.

20. John A. Nagl, *Learning to Eat Soup with a Knife: Counterinsurgency Lessons from Malaya and Vietnam* (Chicago: University of Chicago Press, 2002), 137.

21. Nagl, *Learning to Eat Soup with a Knife*, 136, fig. 6.1.

22. Harold P. Ford, *CIA and the Vietnam Policymakers: Three Episodes, 1962–1968*, historical document (Washington, DC: CIA, Center of Intelligence, posted March 19, 2007); see Annex, "III, The Domino Thesis," citing Pentagon Papers (*New York Times* edition), 253–54; https://www.cia.gov/library/center-for-the-study-of-intelligence/csi-publications/books-and -monographs/cia-and-the-vietnam-policymakers-three-episodes-1962-1968/anex1.html.

23. *Viet Minh* is a Vietnamese abbreviation for "League for the Revolution and Independence of Viet-Nam." The movement was abolished in 1951, but the name stuck to the communist North Vietnamese regime during the 1950s. Viet Minh operatives later became Viet Cong cadres. Bernard B. Fall, *Street without Joy: From the Indochina War to the War in Vietnam*, 4th ed. (Harrisburg, PA: Stackpole, 1967), 25 (see endnote).

24. The formal term for the North Vietnamese Army is People's Army of Vietnam (PAVN), but the use of NVA is so widespread in the literature that it is used throughout the text.

25. Lien-Hang T. Nguyen, *Hanoi's War: An International History of War for Peace in Vietnam* (Chapel Hill: University of North Carolina Press, 2012), 2, 5.

26. Le Duan, *The Vietnamese Revolution: Fundamental Problems, Essential Tasks* (1970; repr., Honolulu: University Press of the Pacific, 2005), 64, passim, "The Revolution in South Viet Nam and the People's War against U.S. Aggression for National Salvation."

27. For an excellent exposition of Le Duan's "strategic empathy," see Zachary Shore, *A Sense of the Enemy: The High-Stakes History of Reading Your Rival's Mind* (Oxford: Oxford University Press, 2014), chap. 6, "Hanoi's New Foe: Le Duan Prepares for America," and chap. 7, "Counting Bodies: The Benefits of Escalation."

28. Mao Tse Tung, *Selected Military Writings* (Peking: Foreign Languages Press, 1968), 210–11; Vo Nguyen Giap, *People's War, People's Army* (New York: Praeger, 1962); Chinh Truong, *Primer for Revolt: The Communist Takeover in Viet-Nam* (New York, Praeger, 1963); and as discussed in Fall, *Street without Joy*, 401, 403.

29. Jeffrey Race, *War Comes to Long An: Revolutionary Conflict in a Vietnamese Province* (Berkeley: University of California Press, 1972), x, later republished in a 2nd edition, *War Comes to Long An: Revolutionary Conflict in a Vietnamese Province*, updated and expanded ed. (Berkeley: University of California Press, 2010). Race ironically observed that

Vietnam is the most "researched" war in our history, but with the American government as the sole sponsor and consumer of the research. This effort has been handicapped in two important ways. First, the shortage of researchers qualified in both the Vietnamese language and in the understanding of revolutionary social movements has severely limited the reliability of the research effort. Second, and equally significant, is the fact that government research has been concentrated on trivial areas of study only marginally relevant to the basic issues of the conflict. Those engaged in the research have felt it either inappropriate or inexpedient to object to this preoccupation with triviality.

Scholarship two generations later would confirm Race's assertion that government-sponsored social science research was only "marginally relevant."

30. *Corps* was an abbreviated form of designation for each of four Corps Tactical Zones (CTZs). Each was Roman numbered: I Corps, in the north abutting the 17th parallel where the marines fought in the northern tier of provinces; II Corps for the Central Highlands; III Corps for the war zones around the capital, Saigon; and IV Corps for the Mekong River delta. Before 1954, Vietnam was divided into four Military Regions (MRs) numbered I–IV. In 1961, *Corps* or *CTZ* became synonymous with *MR*. CTZs later became MRs again during the Vietnamization phase of the war. Spencer C. Tucker, ed., *Encyclopedia of the Vietnam War: A Political, Social, and Military History* (Santa Barbara: ABC-CLIO, 1998), 1:339–440.

31. Race, *War Comes to Long An*, ix, 2.

32. Race described a 1971 invitation from Dr. Chester L. Cooper, director of the Institute for Defense Analyses (IDA), in Washington to join a seminar on "lessons learned in pacification." Race argued that if the lessons were broadened beyond pacification to include consideration of new variables such as the distribution of political power in Vietnam, or the distributive issues he had laid out in *War Comes to Long An* (land reform, tax policies, and the like), then something useful could be learned. Cooper heatedly responded that "IDA's charter did not permit consideration of [such] lessons." Cooper et al. later published a three-volume IDA report in 1972, identifying Race as a participant in the "Long An Province seminar." Chester L. Cooper et al., *The American Experience with Pacification in Vietnam: An Overview of Pacification* (Arlington, VA: Institute for Defense Analyses, 1972). Race, "War Comes to Long An: Back Story to the Writing of a Military Classic," *Small Wars Journal*, January 2010, 6–7, http://smallwarsjournal.com/jrnl/art/war-comes-to-long-an-back-story-to-the-writing-of-a-military-classic.

33. Krepinevich, *Army and Vietnam*, 271–75.

34. Robert H. Berlin, *Historical Bibliography No. 8*, "Military Classics" (Fort Leavenworth, KS: US Army, Command and General Staff College, January 1998).

35. *U.S. Army Marine Corps Counterinsurgency Field Manual*, US Army Field Manual No. 3-24, Marine Corps Warfighting Publication No. 3-33.5, foreword by General David H. Petraeus and Lieutenant General James F. Amos (Chicago: University of Chicago Press, 2007). In 2005, an annotated Naval War College reading list had this entry about *War Comes to Long An*: "If one wishes to understand the Vietnam conflict and why the United States lost, start here." Jeffrey Race, "What the Vietnam War and the Buddha Can Teach about Researching, Teaching, and Writing on Controversial Subjects," *World History Connected* 10, no. 1 (February 2013): online text citing note 11, http://worldhistoryconnected.press.illinois.edu/10.1/race.html.

36. Race, *War Comes to Long An*, ix.

37. Race, *War Comes to Long An*, 141.

38. For an exposition of these concepts, see Race, *War Comes to Long An*, chaps. 3 and 4.

39. Race, *War Comes to Long An*, 146–47, 277ff.

40. Race, *War Comes to Long An*, 174.

41. Race's analysis of land-use records in Long An in 1968 revealed that 79 percent of the farm families in Long An had no land of their own, and an additional 11 percent rented some land; only 10 percent farmed their own land exclusively. As Race drolly commented, "Thus, it is hard to see how the government's land reform could have fulfilled its announced purpose of turning a dissatisfied peasantry into a satisfied one, even if it had been implemented to the fullest." Race, *War Comes to Long An*, 58–60; and Logevall, *Embers of War*, 683. A half century later, *The Economist*'s "Banyan" columnist pointed to "a voluminous literature" where land reform enabled "sustained bounding growth for decades" of Asian economies that successfully implemented land reform, including Japan, Hong Kong, Singapore, Taiwan, and the PRC (after 1978). Banyan concluded, "When weighted against the costs, land reform, done well, starts to look cheap." *The Economist*, October 14, 2017, 36.

42. Race, *War Comes to Long An*, 167–68.

43. Andrew R. Finlayson, *Rice Paddy Recon: A Marine Officer's Second Tour in Vietnam, 1968–1970* (Jefferson, NC: McFarland, 2014), 166, chap. 10, "Qua's Story: The Life of a Viet Cong Guerrilla."

44. Race, *War Comes to Long An*, 136, table 2, and 155–56.

45. Logevall, *Embers of War*, 685, citing Fall's unpublished paper "The Anatomy of Insurgency in Indochina, 1946–64" (delivered March 20, 1964, at the Industrial College of the Armed Forces in Washington, DC). Source: Box P-1, Series 1.5, "Papers and Reports by Dr. Fall," Bernard Fall Collection, John F. Kennedy Library.

46. Race, *War Comes to Long An*, 157.

47. Krepinevich, *Army and Vietnam*, 57, quoting Lieutenant General Lionel C. McGarr, commander of the Military Assistance Advisory Group–Vietnam (MAAG-V), 1960–1962, and citing Commander, MAAG-V, *Tactics and Techniques for Counterinsurgent Operations*, I:3 (February 10, 1952).

48. Race, *War Comes to Long An*, 193–209.

49. Jon Tetsuro Sumida, *Decoding Clausewitz: A New Approach to "On War"* (Lawrence: University Press of Kansas, 2008), 187–88.

50. Harry G. Summers, Jr., Colonel, US Army (Ret.), *On Strategy: A Critical Analysis of the Vietnam War* (Novato, CA: Presidio, 1982), 88–89, 102, 124.

51. Finlayson, *Rice Paddy Recon*, 290–93.

52. Alexander, *How Wars Are Won*, 33.

53. Nagl, *Learning to Eat Soup*, 174.

54. The Advanced Research Projects Agency (ARPA), part of the Office of the Secretary of Defense (OSD), Department of Defense, was established in 1958 and known as ARPA; in 1972, ARPA became DARPA, Defense Advanced Research Projects Agency.

55. Nagl, *Learning to Eat Soup*, 175, citing ARPA Order 1108-68, "Village Defense Study—Vietnam, Vol. I" (Santa Barbara, CA: General Research Corporation, November 1968). Note: Originally classified Secret, this study has now been downgraded to "For Official Use Only" (FOUO) but remains accessible only to Department of Defense employees and military contractors. The author was a member of the research team in Vietnam in 1968 and wrote sections of it. A copy is archived at the US Army Military History Institute, US Army War College, Carlisle Barracks, PA.

56. Ricks, *Generals*, 53, 77.

57. "Nation: Patton's Peer," *Time*, April 14, 1967, http://www.time.com/time/magazine/article/0,9171,836935,00.html.

58. Andrew J. Birtle, *U.S. Army Counterinsurgency and Contingency Operations Doctrine, 1942–1976*, CMH Pub. 70-98 (Washington, DC: US Army Center of Military History, 2006), 368.

59. Birtle, *U.S. Army Counterinsurgency*, 371.

60. Birtle, *U.S. Army Counterinsurgency*, 371.

61. Gian Gentile, *Wrong Turn: America's Deadly Embrace of Counterinsurgency* (New York: New Press, 2013), 71.

62. Porch, *Counterinsurgency*, 220–21.

63. Birtle, *U.S. Army Counterinsurgency*, 372, 374; Gentile, *Wrong Turn*, 74; and Porch, *Counterinsurgency*, 220–21.

64. Porch, *Counterinsurgency*, 219–21.

65. Porch, *Counterinsurgency*, 219–21, citing James H. Lebovic, *The Limits of U.S. Military Capability: Lessons from Vietnam and Iraq* (Baltimore, MD: Johns Hopkins University Press, 2010), 38–39, 207; and Eric M. Bergerud, *The Dynamics of Defeat: The Vietnam War in Hau Nghia Province* (Boulder, CO: Westview, 1993), 327–28.

CHAPTER 17. BATTLE OF THE IA DRANG VALLEY

1. William Gardner Bell et al., *American Military History*, rev. ed. (Washington, DC: US Army Center of Military History, 1989), 658.

2. Martin van Creveld, *The Age of Airpower* (New York: PublicAffairs, 2011), 385–86.

3. Bell, *American Military History*, 658.

4. Van Creveld, *Airpower*, 385–86.

5. Operation *Arc Light* was the code name given to the use of B-52 strategic bombers in Southeast Asia; http://www.cc.gatech.edu/~tpilsch/AirOps/arclight.html.

6. Bell, *American Military History*, 659; John A. Cash et al., "Fight at Ia Drang: Seven Firefights in Vietnam" (Washington, DC: Office of the Chief of Military History, US Government Printing Office, first published 1970, 1985), 40, http://www.history.army.mil/books/Vietnam/7-ff/Ch1.htm; and Harold G. Moore, *We Were Soldiers Once . . . and Young: Ia Drang—the Battle That Changed the War in Vietnam* (New York: Random House, 1992), 346.

7. Stewart, *American Military History*, 2:310.

8. Stewart, *American Military History*, 2:309.

9. Merle L. Pribbenow, trans., *Victory in Vietnam: The Official History of the People's Army of Vietnam, 1954–1975*, foreword by William J. Duiker (Lawrence: University Press of Kansas, 2002), xiii, 158–60.

10. The Center for the Study of the Vietnam Conflict and Vietnam Archive at Texas Tech University, Lubbock, has created an online Military Operations Database that includes over 1,300 operations. The time frame covers 1965 through 1973. The database is accessible at http://www.vietnam.ttu.edu/QuickSearch.php?srch=operations%20database.

11. Porch, *Counterinsurgency*, 325.

CHAPTER 18. BOMBING CAMPAIGN AND HIGH-TECH INITIATIVES

1. Van Creveld's data (3.4 million sorties and 8 million bomb tons) are used in the text because he cites more recent and comprehensive work; Van Creveld, *Airpower*, 384, 397. Van Creveld cites as his source Mark Clodfelter, *The Limits of Airpower: The American Bombing of North Vietnam* (New York: Free Press, 1989), 129.

2. Crane indicates that "target lists grew to 240 and then 427 fixed objectives, and priorities ranking interdiction, oil, industry, and electrical power fluctuated"; Crane, *Bombs, Cities, and Civilians*, 151.

3. Earl H. Tilford Jr., "Rolling Thunder," in *Encyclopedia of the Vietnam War: A Political, Social, and Military History*, ed. Spencer C. Tucker (Santa Barbara, CA: ABC-CLIO, 1998), 2:619.

4. Tilford, *Vietnam Encyclopedia*, 2:619. The "panhandle" refers to where North and South Vietnam narrow into a panhandle on either side of the 17th parallel.

5. Crane, *Bombs, Cities, and Civilians*, 151.

6. "Clearance procedures [for the targeting process] that extended from MACV in Saigon through CINCPAC in Honolulu to the Pentagon, State Department, and White House were not unusual," Tilford, *Vietnam Encyclopedia*, 2:619. James C. Thompson's analysis of the civilian and military organizations charged with managing *Rolling Thunder* is more extensive; Thompson, *Rolling Thunder: Understanding Policy and Program Failure* (Chapel Hill: University of North Carolina Press, 1980), 74.

7. Thompson, *Rolling Thunder*, 76–77; and Van Creveld, *Airpower*, 388–90.

8. Thompson, *Rolling Thunder*, 72.

9. Tilford, *Vietnam Encyclopedia*, 2:619–20.

10. Tilford, *Vietnam Encyclopedia*, 2:666; and Van Creveld, *Airpower*, 391–92.

11. Bernard C. Nalty, *The War against Trucks: Aerial Interdiction in Southern Laos, 1968–1972* (Washington, DC: US Air Force History and Museums Program, 2005), 8–16, 185.

12. Nalty, *The War against Trucks*, 300.

13. Nalty, *The War against Trucks*, 5–6.

14. Jacob Van Staaveren, *Interdiction in Southern Laos, 1961–1968* (Washington, DC: Center of Air Force History, 1993), 255; and Nalty, *War against Trucks*, 19–20. Also see http://wn.com/Operation_Igloo_White, an online link to a video about *Igloo White* operations.

15. Nalty, *War against Trucks*, 340.

16. Peter W. Brush, "Igloo White," in *Vietnam Encyclopedia*, 1:417.

17. Nalty, *War against Trucks*, 297. One former air force intelligence officer wrote to the author about the effectiveness of bombing North Vietnamese trucks. He reports that finding enemy trucks on the Ho Chi Minh Trail was never the problem. During the day, they could be seen from the air. Hitting them was the problem, particularly if jet fighter bombers were used instead of World War II–vintage, propeller-driven Douglas A-1 Skyraiders. He doubted that the *Igloo White* sensors helped with electronic geolocation and radar bombing of targets because other aircraft dropped flares at night to illuminate attacking them. Peter Haslund, former captain assigned to the 56th Air Commando Wing, email to the author, April 9. 2014.

18. Van Creveld, *Airpower*, 393–94.

CHAPTER 19. THE PACIFICATION PROGRAM (1967–1968)

1. Nagl, *Learning to Eat Soup*, xvi.

2. Thompson and others published books about the British counterinsurgency effort in Malaya: Robert G. K. Thompson, *Defeating Communist Insurgency: Experiences from Malaya and Vietnam* (New York: Praeger, 1966), *No Exit from Vietnam* (London: Chatto and Windus, 1969), and *Peace Is Not at Hand* (London: Chatto and Windus, 1974); Richard L. Clutterbuck, *The Long, Long War: The Emergency in Malaya, 1948–1960* (London: Cassell, 1966), and *Riot and Revolution in Malaya and Singapore* (London: Faber and Faber, 1973); and John Cloake, *Templer, Tiger of Malaya: The Life of Field Marshal Sir Gerald Templer* (London: Herrap, 1985).

3. Nagl, *Learning to Eat Soup*, 75.

4. Porch, *Counterinsurgency*, 255.

5. Porch, *Counterinsurgency*, 254.

6. Birtle, *Counterinsurgency*, 229–30.

7. David French, *The British Way in Counter-Insurgency, 1945–1967* (Oxford: Oxford University Press, 2011), 7–8, 254.

8. Miller, *Misalliance*, 248–49.

9. Pribbenow, *Victory in Vietnam*, 109–10, 115.

10. Ngo Dinh Nhu was Ngo Dinh Diem's younger brother who remained in Indochina during Diem's lengthy exile. He labored tirelessly to promote his brother's political fortunes among anticommunist Vietnamese. After Diem became president, Nhu wielded immense political power, commanding private armies and secret police, even though he held no formal executive position in the GVN. The Ngo brothers were Catholic, a faith that appealed to their American patrons. Ngo in 1943 married Tran Le Xuan from a wealthy aristocratic family in Hanoi in French Indochina. She later became known to the world as "Madame Nhu," the de facto First Lady of South Vietnam; her presidential brother-in-law was a bachelor. All of the Ngos lived in the Gia Long Presidential Palace. It was the Buddhist crisis in 1963 that precipitated the Ngos' fall from power.

11. Miller, *Misalliance*, 248–49.

12. Race, *War Comes to Long An*, 192–93.

13. Rufus Phillips, *Why Vietnam Matters: An Eyewitness Account of Lessons Not Learned* (Annapolis, MD: Naval Institute Press, 2008), 307.

14. Krepinevich, *Army and Vietnam*, 217; and Nagl, *Learning to Eat Soup*, 165–66.

15. Frank L. Jones, *Blowtorch: Robert Komer, Vietnam, and American Cold War Strategy* (Annapolis, MD: Naval Institute Press, 2013), 3; and Phillips, *Why Vietnam Matters*, 283.

16. Phoenix was responsible for "capturing, killing, or persuading to defect . . . more than 80,000 cadres during 1968–72." William Rosenau and Austin Long, *The Phoenix Program and Contemporary Counterinsurgency* (Santa Monica, CA: Rand, 2009), 13; and Dale Andradé, *Ashes to Ashes: The Phoenix Program and the Vietnam War* (Lexington, MA: Lexington Books, 1990), vii, 282, 287, table A-1.

17. Robin D. Meyer, "Provincial Reconstruction Teams Aren't for Everyone" (paper submitted to the Department of Joint Military Operations, Newport, Rhode Island, Naval War College, October 31, 2008), 7; and Krepinevich, *Army and Vietnam*, 222.

18. A short list of scholars who have examined CORDS includes Bergerud, *Dynamics of Defeat*; David W. P. Elliott, *The Vietnamese War: Revolution and Social Change in the Mekong Delta, 1930–1975*, 2 vols. (London: M. E. Sharpe, 2003); Gentile, *Wrong Turn*; David Kilcullen, *Counterinsurgency*, paperback ed. (Oxford: Oxford University Press, 2010); Krepinevich, *The Army and Vietnam*; Nagl, *Learning to Eat Soup*; Phillips, *Why Vietnam Matters*; Race, *War Comes to Long An*; Lewis Sorley, *A Better War: The Unexamined Victories and Final Tragedy of America's Last Years in Vietnam* (New York: Harcourt, 1999); and Richard A. Hunt, *Pacification: The American Struggle for Vietnam's Hearts and Minds* (Boulder, CO: Westview, 1995); Hunt wrote the "Pacification" entry in Tucker's *Vietnam Encyclopedia*, 1:545–49.

19. Robert W. Komer, *Bureaucracy Does Its Thing: U.S.-GVN Performance in Vietnam*, R-967-ARPA (Santa Monica, CA: Rand, August 1972).

20. Komer, *Bureaucracy Does Its Thing*, chap. 4, "Institutional Constraints on U.S. Performance"; chap. 5, "Institutional Obstacles to the Learning Process"; chap. 6, "Lack of Unified Management"; and chap. 9, "What Institutional Lessons Can Be Learned."

21. Race in 1976 explained how unreceptive senior officials like Komer were to analyses that departed from the MACV and MACCORDS official views. He describes Brigadier

General Herbert's encounter with Komer in 1971 in the Pentagon corridor. Komer told Herbert he had just read Race's 1970 *Asian Survey* article titled "How They Won," which had preceded publication of *War Comes to Long An* by two years; Race, "How They Won," *Asian Survey* 10, no. 8 (August 1970): 628–50. He asked Herbert, "Had Herbert ever heard of Jeff Race, and had Race ever visited Long An?" Race would comment, "Jim Herbert and I had a good laugh about this, but the serious point is that Komer, 'with the personal rank of ambassador,' as he was always described, and reading all the secret intelligence reports from the field, could not imagine how anyone who had ever visited Long An province could write the analysis that I wrote—so different was his map of reality and the issues he considered important. . . . With his cognitive map, Vietnam was a technical problem, not a human one, and technological means were the way to solve it." Jeffrey Race, "The Unlearned Lessons of Vietnam," *Yale Review* 66, no. 2 (December 1976): 173.

22. William R. Corson, *The Betrayal* (New York: Norton, 1968), 232–33; John D. Root's entry about HES in Tucker's *Vietnam Encyclopedia*, 1:263–64; and Sorley's description of HES, *A Better War*, 70–71. The General Research Corporation Village Defense Study team in Vietnam in March 1968 discovered that one troubling aspect was the HES instrument itself. A high development score could offset a low security score.

23. Colby acknowledged, "Many of [the district advisors] don't speak Vietnamese very well, many of them haven't been there very long, so it's an imperfect system. But it's just an awful lot better than anything we used to use." Sorley, *A Better War*, 70–71.

24. Krepinevich points out that one analysis, performed by DoD's Office of Systems Analysis based on HES data, showed that "big-unit sweeps [by US Army or ARVN units] did not promote pacification—you had to stay in an area; otherwise the VC would come in right behind you and undo any pacification gains you had made." Krepinevich, *Army and Vietnam*, 222.

25. Larry Berman, *Lyndon Johnson's War: The Road to Stalemate in Vietnam* (New York: Norton, 1989), 120.

26. Sorley, *A Better War*, 72.

27. Phillips, *Why Vietnam Matters*, 280–90; Lord, *Proconsuls*, 163; and Sorley, *A Better War*, chaps. 21–23.

28. Root, *Vietnam Encyclopedia*, 1:264.

29. David W. P. Elliott, *The Vietnamese War: Revolution and Social Change in the Mekong Delta, 1930–1975* (London: M. E. Sharpe, 2003), 2:857–58.

30. Corson, *The Betrayal*, 233–34.

31. Corson, *The Betrayal*, 235–36.

32. Harry R. Yager, *Strategy and the National Security Professional: Strategic Thinking and Strategy Formulation in the 21st Century* (Westport, CT: Greenwood, 2008), 109.

CHAPTER 20. THE TET OFFENSIVE (1968)

1. Lien-Hang T. Nguyen, *Hanoi's War*, 87–101, which indicates that Hanoi's strategic deliberations concerning the Tet Offensive are "still shrouded in mystery." She notes that Vietnam expert Merle Pribbenow portrays the genesis of the Tet Offensive as a "Faustian bargain" between Le Duan and General Dung (100), citing Merle L. Pribbenow, "General Vo Nguyen Giap and the Mysterious Evolution of the Plan for the 2968 Tet Offensive," *Journal of Vietnamese Studies* 3, no. 2 (Summer 2008): 1–33; also see Pribbenow, *Victory in Vietnam*, chap. 9.

2. James H. Willbanks, *The Tet Offensive: A Concise History*, paperback ed. (New York: Columbia University Press, 2007), 83. Bui Tin, a former colonel who served on the general staff of the NVA, concurs with General Tran Do's Tet assessment; Bui Tin, *Following Ho Chi Minh: The Memoirs of a North Vietnamese Colonel* (Honolulu: University of Hawaii Press, 1995), 62. Lien-Hang Nguyen cautions that Bui Tin, who defected to France in the 1990s, wrote a "memoir [that] must be read more as gossip, with perhaps a nugget of truth buried deep in its pages." Bui Tin's Tet view may be such a nugget. Lien-Hang, *Hanoi's War*, 319n41. Despite her caveat about reliability, Lien-Hang cites Bin Tui as a source (fifteen times) in *Hanoi's War*.

3. Douglas Pike, *PAVN: People's Army of Vietnam* (Novato, CA: Presidio, 1986), 332.

4. President Johnson's poll numbers dropped from 48 percent to 36 percent; James L. Ray, *American Foreign Policy and Political Ambition*, e-book (Washington, DC: CQ Press, 2008), fig. 8.1 (interpolated from a plot of "Public Support for Lyndon Johnson and the Toll of Vietnam, 1965–1968"); and William C. Gibbons, *The U.S. Government and the Vietnam War: Executive and Legislative Roles and Relationships*, vol. 4, *July 1965–January 1968* (Princeton, NJ: Princeton University Press, 1995), 337, histogram ("Public Approval of the Johnson Administration's Handling of the Vietnam War, 1965–1968"), 334–43.

5. Tucker, *Vietnam Encyclopedia*, 2:679.

6. In his *Rice Paddy Recon* book, Finlayson described the Tay Ninh source whose knowledge of COSVN's plans was extensive and highly accurate. He warned the United States about the Tet Offensive, but "CIA analysts had doubts about the [Tay Ninh] source's reasons for the communist Tet Offensive." According to the Tay Ninh source, one of the NVA reasons for attacking Khe Sanh and launching the Tet Offensive was fear that Khe Sanh would become "the main logistical base for [what the enemy believed to be] the planned invasion of Laos and that is why [the NVA] attempted to overrun it prior to the Tet Offensive and devoted so much combat power to that effort." Finlayson concluded, "Hanoi's leaders knew the bulk of the manpower and almost all of the weapons and ammunition needed by the communist forces in South Vietnam came through the panhandle of southern Laos. Any American barrier anchored on the Mekong River in Laos would effectively isolate their forces south of the DMZ . . . [and] cutting the Ho Chi Minh Trail was an existential threat to the communist plans to unite North and South Vietnam." Finlayson, *Rice Paddy War*, 234–36.

7. Aid credits a "tiny" USMC detachment belonging to the 1st Radio Battalion and an attached ARVN SIGINT outfit, which had been operating a radio intercept site inside Khe Sanh since 1967, as one reason the marines fought so effectively. Aid, *Secret Sentry*, 122–23.

8. As the war developed between 1965 and 1967, the communists established a pattern of cease-fire activity that was repeated during the truces declared in 1967 for Buddha's birthday, Christmas, and New Year's. James J. Wirtz, *The Tet Offensive: Intelligence Failure in War* (Ithaca, NY: Cornell University Press, 1991), 109.

9. Aid records that, between 1961 and 1969, the NSA had enhanced the nation's robust recovery of its SIGINT establishment from 59,000 military and civilian personnel, with a budget of $654 million, to 93,067. In 1969, the NSA's budget was $1 billion. Aid, *Secret Sentry*, 128.

10. Aid, *Secret Sentry*, 118.

11. Aid, *Secret Sentry*, 119.

12. Tucker, *Vietnam Encyclopedia*, 2:679.

13. Provided to the author and Village Defense Study colleagues by a US Army intelligence officer briefer at the Combined Intelligence Center Vietnam (CICV) adjacent to MACV headquarters in March 1968.

14. David T. Zabecki, "Tet Offensive: Overall Strategy" and "The Saigon Circle," in Tucker, *Vietnam Encyclopedia*, 2:680, where he amplifies, "After Tet 1968 the war was run entirely by the North. The VC were never again a significant force on the battlefield. When Saigon fell in 1975, it was to four PAVN [People's Army of Vietnam] corps."

15. On January 21, 1969, Henry Kissinger, President Nixon's national security advisor, sent out National Security Study Memorandum (NSSM) 1 to the secretaries of state and defense and the director of central intelligence (DCI) asking for responses to twenty-five questions about the situation in Vietnam. Question number 8 asked, "What controversies persist on the estimate of VC Order of Battle?" Henry A. Kissinger, "Situation of Vietnam," NSSM 1 (Washington, DC: White House, declassified from Secret, January 21, 1969), 3.

16. Sorley, *A Better War*, 144.

17. In fairness, Eddie Adams, the AP photographer, would deliver a eulogy about General Loan reported in *Time* on July 27, 1998: "The general killed the Viet Cong; I killed the general with my camera. Still photographs are the most powerful weapon in the world. . . . They are only half-truths." Retrieved online at http://www.time.com/time/magazine /article/0,9171,988783,00.html.

18. Computed from data available compiled by Theodore J. Hull, "Statistical Information about Casualties of the Vietnam War" (College Park, MD: US National Archives at College Park, Electronic and Special Media Records Services Division, December 2002), http://www.archives.gov/research/military/vietnam-war/casualty-statistics.html#year; Nagl's January rates for 1968 are comparable, *Learning to Eat Soup*, 173.

19. On February 28, 1968, General Earle Wheeler, chairman of the JCS, returning to Washington from Saigon after conferring with General Westmoreland, requested in writing authorization from the Johnson administration for two hundred thousand more soldiers in Vietnam. The story went public in the *New York Times* on March 10, 1968. To provide that many troops to MACV would have required activating 280,000 reservists; it was a fork in the road.

CHAPTER 21. VIETNAMIZATION

1. Henry A. Kissinger, "The Vietnam Negotiations," *Foreign Affairs* 47, no. 2 (January 1969): 214.

2. Kissinger, "The Vietnam Negotiations," 233.

3. Gideon Rose, *How Wars End: Why We Always Fight the Last Battle* (New York: Simon & Schuster, 2010), 193; based on the secret Nixon White House taping system in the Oval Office. The president's daily diary for August 3, 1972, logs a twenty-nine-minute meeting between Nixon and Kissinger, http://nixontapes.org/chron4.html.

4. Jeffrey Kimball, *Nixon's Vietnam War* (Lawrence: University of Kansas Press, 1998), xii–xiii, chaps. 8–13.

5. Online timeline, University of California, Berkeley, Social Activism and Sound Recording Project, partnership between the UC Berkeley Library and the Pacifica Foundation, http://www.lib.berkeley.edu/MRC/pacificaviet.html#copyright; David L. Anderson and John Ernst, eds., *The War That Never Ends: New Perspectives on the Vietnam War* (Lexington: University Press of Kentucky, 2007), 235, 259, 301.

6. Melvin Small, *The Presidency of Richard Nixon* (Lawrence: University Press of Kansas, 1999), 73–75.

7. Penny Lewis, *Hardhats, Hippies, and Hawks: The Vietnam Antiwar Movement as Myth and Memory* (Ithaca, NY: ILR Press, imprint of Cornell University Press, 2013), 15–17.

8. Lewis, *Hardhats, Hippies, and Hawks*, 50 (poll numbers), 53 (protester composition and public-opinion segments).

9. Henry A. Kissinger, "Memorandum for the President, Top Secret/Sensitive, Exclusively Eyes Only, Subject: Contact with the Chinese" (Washington, DC: White House, declassified by authority EO 12958 by WDP, NARA dated January 4, 2002 [September 12, 1970]), http://china.usc.edu/ShowArticle.aspx?articleID=2483&AspxAutoDetectCookieSupport=1.

10. Nagl, *Learning to Eat Soup*, 171.

11. Transcript of President Kennedy's CBS television interview with Walter Cronkite on Vietnam, September 2, 1963.

12. J. Lawton Collins Jr., Brigadier General, *Vietnam Studies: The Development and Training of the South Vietnamese Army, 1950–1972*, CMH Pub. 90-10 (1975; repr., Washington, DC: US Army Center of Military History, US Government Printing Office, 1991), 128–29.

13. Nagl, *Learning to Eat Soup*, 173, fig. 7.2.

14. Tucker, *Vietnam Encyclopedia*, 2:799.

15. Douglas S. Blaufarb, *The Counterinsurgency Era: U.S. Doctrine and Performance, 1950 to the Present* (New York: Free Press, 1977), 253.

16. Nagl, *Learning to Eat Soup*, 172; and Krepinevich, *Army and Vietnam*, 254–55.

17. Krepinevich, *Army and Vietnam*, 257.

18. Tucker, *Vietnam Encyclopedia*, 1:97.

CHAPTER 22. THE FINAL YEARS (1969–1975)

1. Norman B. Hannah, *The Key to Failure: Laos and the Vietnam War* (New York: Madison, 1987), 299, citing Stanley Karnow, *Vietnam: A History* (New York: Viking, 1983), 663; and Van Creveld, *Airpower*, 394.

2. Van Creveld, *Airpower*, 394.

3. Tucker, *Vietnam Encyclopedia*, 1:185–86.

4. Van Creveld, *Airpower*, 394.

5. Dale Andradé, *America's Last Vietnam Battle: Halting Hanoi's 1972 Easter Offensive* (1995; repr., Lawrence: University Press of Kansas, 2001), 151–64.

6. G. H. Turley, Colonel, USMCR (Ret.), *The Easter Offensive: Vietnam, 1972* (Annapolis, MD: Naval Institute Press, 1985), chaps. 8–17. Turley acted as chief advisor to the 3rd ARVN Division.

7. Andradé, *Last Vietnam Battle*, 488–89; and Turley, *Easter Offensive*, 2, 22ff.

8. By March 1972, almost all American infantry, armor, and artillery units had left South Vietnam. Frederick F. Lash Jr., "Tet with Tanks—The NVA Easter Offensive, 1972," *Armchair General* (2007), http://www.armchairgeneral.com/tet-with-tanks-the-nva-easter-offensive-1972.htm.

9. Brigadier General Alexander M. Haig Jr., a decorated Korean War and Vietnam War veteran who had commanded a battalion in the 1st ID between 1966 and 1967, was serving in the Nixon White House as deputy assistant to the president for national security affairs.

10. Van Creveld, *Airpower*, 394–95.

11. Tilford, *Vietnam Encyclopedia*, 1:379.

12. Tilford, *Vietnam Encyclopedia*, 1:379.

13. As Van Creveld qualified, "whether such an operation would have led to the desired results (as the wrecking of some dams in Korea had not) remains uncertain." Van Creveld, *Airpower*, 397.

14. Van Creveld concluded, "Airpower . . . was able to prevent the guerrillas from switching from Mao's second stage to the third." Van Creveld, *Airpower*, 399.

15. The War Powers Resolution of 1973, Public Law 93-148, 93rd Congress, H.J. Resolution S42, was codified as 50 USC 1541–1548 and was simply known as the War Powers Act. Online at http://www.fordlibrarymuseum.gov/museum/exhibits/watergate_files /content.php?section=2&page=a and http://www.archives.gov/research/guide-fed-records /groups/460.html#460.3.

16. Harry G. Summers Jr., "America's Bitter End in Vietnam," originally published in the April 1975 issue of *Vietnam* magazine, http://www.vnafmamn.com/bitter_end.html.

17. Tucker, *Vietnam Encyclopedia*, 1:553.

18. Pike, *PAVN*, 225.

19. Sorley, *A Better War*, 380–81, citing Ngo Quang Trong, Lieutenant General, *RVNAF and U.S. Operational Cooperation and Coordination* (Washington, DC: US Army Center of Military History, 1980), 183.

20. Tucker, *Vietnam Encyclopedia*, 1:58.

21. Sorley, *A Better War*, 288–89. Veith authoritatively amplifies on Sorley's narrative. George J. Veith, *Black April: The Fall of South Vietnam, 1973–75* (New York: Encounter Books, 2012), 2, 6, 172ff, 181, 498.

22. Sorley recounts that President Thieu years earlier had admitted to Ambassador Bunker "that he had little experience in command above division level," which helps explain the military decisions he imposed on General Truong that led to the collapse of the GVN in the spring of 1975. Sorley, *A Better War*, 381.

23. Nguyen Cao Ky, *Buddha's Child: My Fight to Save South Vietnam*, with Marvin J. Wolf (New York: St. Martin's, 2002), 334–37. A few years before Ky published his memoir, Duong Van Mai Elliott recounted her own experience of the Vietnam War within the broader context of the generational history of her own family. The last six chapters of her book document her own observations of the social disintegration of South Vietnamese society as the war continued year after year, based in part on describing her job in Saigon interviewing Viet Cong defectors and prisoners as part of the Rand Corporation's Morale and Motivation research program. She explains how the American military deployment to Vietnam economically skewed traditional values and turned the social order upside down: "In the old days, the social order was expressed in the saying 'scholars first, peasants second, artisans third, and merchants fourth.' But now . . . this saying . . . changed to 'prostitutes first, *cyclo* drivers second, taxi drivers third, and maids fourth.' Money, not intellectual achievements or social usefulness, had become the yardstick of success." Her contribution to the literature about the revolutionary conflict is compelling reading. Duong Van Mai Elliott, *The Sacred Willow: Four Generations in the Life of a Vietnamese Family* (New York: Oxford University Press, 1999), 314, chaps. 12–17.

24. Wolf, who assisted Ky in writing his memoirs, observed in a corroborating email sent to Race and forwarded by Race to the author (October 1, 2011), "Ky had a healthy ego, but he knew very well who he was and didn't pretend otherwise. . . . In general, and in every particular that I can recall, Ky recalled his thoughts and described his goals and his actions without false modesty. I believe that it was important for him to be known to posterity as his own man, as nobody's puppet, but I also believe that this was exactly how he felt and acted at the time."

25. Section 30 of the Foreign Assistance Act of 1973 specified that "No funds authorized or appropriated under this or any other law may be expended to finance military or paramilitary operations by the United States in or over Vietnam, Laos or Cambodia" (P.L. 93-189; 87 Stat. 714).

26. Sorley, *A Better War*, 380.

27. Bui Tin, *From Enemy to Friend: A North Vietnamese Perspective on the War*, trans. Nguyen Ngoc Bich (Annapolis, MD: Naval Institute Press, 2002), 95.

28. Sorley, *A Better War*, 381; Bui Tin, *From Enemy to Friend*, 95; and Finlayson, *Rice Paddy War*, 290–93.

29. Congress had halved President Gerald R. Ford's request for military aid to South Vietnam in 1975. By contrast, the Soviet Union and the PRC together had provided over $1 billion of aid to North Vietnam's military in 1974 and 1975.

30. In fact, US Army advisory strength to the ARVN reached a peak of 9,430 in 1968. By 1972, this strength, even under Vietnamization, had decreased to 1,000. Andradé, *Last Vietnam Battle*, 484.

31. Sorley certainly has the professional qualifications to make such a statement. He is a third-generation graduate of the US Military Academy with a Johns Hopkins PhD in history who served in the US Army and later as a senior official in the Central Intelligence Agency.

32. Sorley, *A Better War*, 384–85.

33. Sorley, *A Better War*, 384–85.

34. Sorley, *A Better War*, 386. General Westmoreland himself had drawn similar conclusions about inadequacy a decade earlier. In mid-1965, as President Johnson was debating whether to commit more US combat forces to Vietnam, Secretary McNamara asked Westmoreland for his suggestions on winning the war. Moyar amplifies,

> "Short of decision to introduce nuclear weapons against sources and channels of enemy power, I see no likelihood of achieving a quick, favorable end to the war," the general informed the secretary of defense. "The fabric of GVN civil functions and services has been rendered so ineffective and listless by successive coups and changes, and the military arm is in such need of revitalization, that we can come to no other conclusion." Final victory was not dependent on American exertions, Westmoreland contended, but on the development of a strong South Vietnamese government. In the interim, nevertheless, U.S. troops would need to move out of their own enclaves to engage the big Viet Cong and North Vietnamese Army units. (Mark Moyar, *Triumph Forsaken: The Vietnam War, 1954–1965* [New York: Cambridge University Press, 2006], 407)

35. Douglas Pike, *Viet Cong: The Organization and Technique of the National Liberation Front of South Vietnam* (Cambridge, MA: MIT Press, 1966).

36. Pike, *Viet Cong*, 1.

37. Pike explains the term *cadre* this way: "There is no equivalent to the cadre in non-Marxist societies, either within the government bureaucracy (with its three forms of service—military, foreign, civil), or outside government among activist-volunteer organizations. The closest counterpart, perhaps, is the old-time U.S. trade union organizer." Pike, *Viet Cong*, 180.

38. Pike, *Viet Cong*, 189.

39. Race, *War Comes to Long An*, 172, 189–92, 208, and 229; and Montesano, "*War Comes to Long An*, Its Origins and Legacies," 174–75.

CHAPTER 23. THE STRATEGIC ARCHITECTURES OF THE VIETNAM WAR

1. Nagl, *Learning to Eat Soup*, 60.

2. Le Duan, *The Vietnamese Revolution*, 64, passim. For COSVN details, see Lien-Hang T. Nguyen, *Hanoi's War*, 26, 37, 49–50.

3. President Johnson in a televised address at Johns Hopkins University on April 7, 1965, referred to the international system almost as an afterthought. "We are there [in Vietnam] because we have a promise to keep. Since 1954 every American president has offered support to the people of South Vietnam." Gregory A. Olson, ed., *Landmark Speeches on the Vietnam War* (College Station: Texas A&M University Press, 2010), 46.

4. The author vividly recalls an official visit to the Political Section, Office of the Counselor for Political Affairs, US Embassy, Saigon, in early May 1968, as a member of the ARPA-sponsored Village Defense Study team. He showed a senior embassy staff member a copy of his DD Form 173 "theater orders," addressed to COMUSMACV and referencing the requisite CINCPAC authorization for "the theater request and [security] clearances for entrance to Vietnam" (Sec Def Msg 0330304 dtd 020346Z Feb 68 and CINCPAC Msg 0330304 dtd 020346Z Feb 68). He requested any written, succinct documentation stating what the US national security interest was in Vietnam. Despite polite embarrassment and befuddlement in response to fulfilling this request, the embassy staff neither understood what he was talking about nor how to produce any documented response.

5. The late Richard C. Holbrooke entered the US Foreign Service in 1962 out of college and spent six years in Vietnam, first in the Mekong delta as a civilian representative for the Agency for International Development. He then moved to Embassy Saigon where he became a staff assistant to Ambassadors Maxwell E. Taylor and Henry Cabot Lodge Jr.

6. Excerpt from Kissinger's address to the conference, "The American Experience in Southeast Asia, 1946–1975," conducted at the Department of State, Washington, DC, September 29, 2010, http://history.state.gov/conferences/2010-southeast-asia/ambassador -holbrooke.

7. Excerpt from keynote address by Holbrooke, ibid.

8. Excerpt from Secretary Clinton's opening address, ibid.

9. "Statistical Information about Casualties of the Vietnam War, Electronic and Special Media Records Division Reference Report" (College Park, MD: National Archives), http:// www.archives.gov/research/military/vietnam-war/casualty-statistics.html#branch.

10. US Military Operations, Casualty Breakdown, http://www.globalsecurity.org/mili tary/ops/casualties.htm.

11. US Military Operations, Casualty Breakdown.

12. The South Vietnamese number in the text is the average of Rummel's low and high values. Rudolph J. Rummel, *Freedom, Democracy, Peace; Power, Democide, and War* (Honolulu: University of Hawaii System, 1997), table 6.1A, "Vietnam Democide: Estimates, Sources, and Calculations," (GIF). PBS's Vietnam website estimates military and civilian casualties as follows: "In 15 years, nearly a million NVA and Viet Cong troops and a quarter of a million South Vietnamese soldiers have died. Hundreds of thousands of civilians had been killed," http://www.pbs.org/battlefieldvietnam/timeline/index4.html.

13. Translation of text of Agence France-Presse news release of April 4, 1995, about the North Vietnamese government's release of official figures of dead and wounded during the Vietnam War. Text reads, "The Hanoi government revealed on April 4 that the true civilian casualties of the Vietnam War were 2,000,000 in the north, and 2,000,000 in the south. Military casualties were 1.1 million killed and 600,000 wounded in twenty-one years of war. These figures were deliberately falsified during the war by the North Vietnamese Communists to avoid demoralizing the population." Retrieved online at http://www.rjsmith .com/kia_tbl.html#press.

14. Nagl, *Learning to Eat Soup*, 177–81.

15. Fredrik Logevall, *Choosing War: The Lost Chance of Peace and the Escalation of War in Vietnam* (Berkeley: University of California Press, 1999), xix–xx, xxii.

16. Michael Beschloss, *Newsweek*, November 12, 2001, reporting on the thousands of audiotapes President Johnson recorded on his covert White House taping system between 1964 and 1965.

17. Doris Kearns Goodwin, *Lyndon Johnson and the American Dream* (1976; repr., New York: St. Martin's, 1991), 234.

18. H. R. McMaster, *Dereliction of Duty: Lyndon Johnson, Robert McNamara, the Joint Chiefs of Staff, and the Lies That Led to Vietnam* (New York: HarperCollins, 1997), 297; originally written as a doctoral dissertation at the University of North Carolina while a serving lieutenant colonel and later published as a book. A respected combat veteran, beginning with his performance as a decorated captain at the Battle of 73 Easting during the Persian Gulf War in 1991 (for which he was awarded the Silver Star), he was not selected for promotion twice before being promoted to brigadier general. Now a lieutenant general, he demonstrates that outspoken departure from established orthodoxy may be career delaying but not career ending.

19. David Halberstam, *The Best and the Brightest* (1969; repr., New York: Ballantine, 1992), 512.

20. Gordon M. Goldstein, *Lessons in Disaster: McGeorge Bundy and the Path to War in Vietnam* (New York: Henry Holt, 2008), 29.

21. Halberstam, *The Best and the Brightest*, x–xi, xix, 59, chap. 4 (38–63), 224, passim. Halberstam, prior to writing *The Best and the Brightest*, had written a long magazine piece about Bundy in *Harper's* titled "The Very Expensive Education of McGeorge Bundy," in which he had used and liked the phrase "best and brightest."

22. Bob Woodward and Gordon M. Goldstein, "The Anguish of Decision," *Washington Post*, October 18, 2009.

23. James C. Thompson Jr., "How Could Vietnam Happen?—An Autopsy," *The Atlantic*, April 1968, http://www.theatlantic.com/past/issues/68apr/vietnam.htm. Thompson was an East Asia specialist and an assistant professor of history at Harvard at the time he wrote the article.

24. Logevall, *Choosing War*, xix–xx, xxii.

25. Moyar, *Triumph Forsaken*, xxiii.

26. Race proposed a similar retrospective counterfactual in *War Comes to Long An* by suggesting that there was a chance in 1945 for a very different outcome in the South had a government implemented land reform under Law 003/70. However, he points out one sentence later that by 1970 the same land reform was perceived as neither revolutionary nor preemptive because the movement a quarter century before had already carried it out de facto. Race, *War Comes to Long An*, 273. In the interview in 2011 after the second edition of *War Comes to Long An* was published, he expressed discomfort about counterfactuals because they create false historical contexts and are by their very nature improvable. Montesano, "*War Comes to Long An*, Its Origins and Legacies," 171.

27. Miller, *Misalliance*, 324.

28. Fifty years ago, nation building was an accepted and respected part of political science in the subfields of international politics or comparative politics. Students at top universities studying political science were routinely assigned to read selections from this literature, whether it was labeled nation building or modernization. A dominant theme in this literature was that for nation building to be successful, it had to address "people problems." It had to relate to what social scientists were observing in developing states: the challenge of changing cultural, civic, political, administrative, and military behaviors. A small sample of some of the seminal works included in a course syllabus would have included the following: Daniel Lerner, *The Passing of Traditional Society: Modernizing the Middle East* (New York: Free Press, 1958); W. W. Rostow, *The Stages of Economic Growth:*

A Non-Communist Manifesto (Cambridge: Cambridge University Press, 1960); Lucian W. Pye, *Politics, Personality, and Nation Building* (New Haven, CT: Yale University Press, 1966); Gabriel A. Almond and Sidney Verba, *The Civic Culture: Political Attitudes and Democracy in Five Nations* (Princeton, NJ: Princeton University Press, 1963). One review of the more recent and limited nation-building literature identifies a Rand publication by Ambassador James F. Dobbins as one that offers a specific definition of *nation building*: "the use of armed force as part of a broader effort to promote political and economic reforms with the objective of transforming a society emerging from conflict into one at peace with itself and its neighbors." Zoe Scott, *Literature Review on State Building* (Birmingham, UK: Governance and Social Development Resource Center, University of Birmingham, May 2007), 20, citing J. Dobbins, S. Jones, K. Crane, and B. C. DeGrasse, *The Beginner's Guide to Nation-Building*, MG557 (Santa Monica, CA: Rand, National Security Research Division, May 2007), xvii.

29. Miller, *Misalliance*, 324.

30. Miller, *Misalliance*, 94.

31. For example, in 1973, the United States sent $2.3 billion in aid to South Vietnam. The ARVN required an annual operating budget of $3 billion. Andrew Wiest, *The Vietnam War, 1956–1975* (Oxford: Osprey, 2002), 80.

32. K. W. Taylor, *A History of the Vietnamese* (Cambridge: Cambridge University Press, 2013), 589–90, 602.

PART V: THE IRAQI WARS

1. Albert Hourani, Philip Khoury, and Philip Wilson, eds., *The Modern Middle East*, 2nd ed. (London: I. B. Tauris, 2005), 513.

2. Victor Davis Hanson, "The Iraqi Wars: Our 15-Year Conflict with Iraq," *National Review*, July 11, 2005.

3. Steven Metz, *Iraq and the Evolution of American Strategy* (Washington, DC: Potomac, 2008), xxii.

4. Metz, *Iraq and the Evolution*, chap. 4, "Transformation and Containment."

5. David Fromkin, *A Peace to End All Peace* (New York: Avon, 1989), 25.

6. Phebe Marr, *The Modern History of Iraq* (Boulder, CO: Westview, 2012), 3–6.

7. Marr, *Modern History of Iraq*, 5.

8. "'Narratives' here mean the accounts people give of themselves and others in relation to the state." Charles Tripp, *A History of Iraq*, 3rd ed. (Cambridge: Cambridge University Press, 2007), 1.

9. Tripp, *A History of Iraq*, 1.

10. Sean McMeekin, *The Origins of the First World War* (Cambridge, MA: Harvard University Press, Belknap, 2011), 233, passim.

11. Karl E. Meyer and Shareen Blair Brysac, *Kingmakers: The Invention of the Modern Middle East* (New York: Norton, 2008), 106–7; for more detail on the terms of Sykes-Picot, see Fromkin, *A Peace to End All Peace*, 188–203.

12. Fromkin, *A Peace to End All Peace*, 25. Former secretary of defense Robert M. Gates underscored Fromkin's point about frontier lines in a Charlie Rose PBS interview on May 16, 2012: "Any time you see a straight-line boundary in the Middle East, Churchill probably drew it in 1920." Retrieved online at https://charlierose.com/videos/18540.

13. Meyer and Brysac, *Kingmakers*, 202.

14. It was ibn Saud who skillfully maneuvered the British into subsidizing his conquest of what became Saudi Arabia, ruled by the House of Saud to the present day. As a result

of the British deal with Saud, Whitehall had to find some other suitable throne for Faisal, starting with Syria and eventually settling upon Iraq.

15. Kedourie includes a three-page appendix that reads like today's newspapers, the "Proclamation by the Executive Committee of the Shiahs in Iraq," dated February 11, 1932. Elie Kedourie, *The Chatham House Version and Other Middle Eastern Studies* (1970; repr., Chicago: Ivan R. Dee, 2004), 236–85.

16. Originally the Emirate of Transjordan, subsequently the Hashemite Kingdom of Jordan. The British, ever practical, established Jordan to placate another of Sherif Hussein's sons, his second son, Abdullah, because his younger brother, Faisal, had been placed on the throne of Iraq following his expulsion from Syria by the French.

17. The Balfour Declaration, written by British foreign secretary Arthur J. Balfour in November 1917, favored the establishment in Palestine of a national home for the Jewish people. The letter was incorporated into the Palestine Mandate of 1922.

18. General Sir Edmund Henry Hynman Allenby (later field marshal) had been sent to Egypt in 1917 as CINC of the Egyptian Expeditionary Force during World War I. The Arab revolt, which Lawrence aided and abetted with British arms and sterling, swept from Aqaba to Jerusalem, to Damascus, and later to Baghdad with Allenby's Middle East armies. Allenby became high commissioner for Egypt and the Sudan after the war until 1926. Meyer and Brysac, *Kingmakers*, chap. 7, 228–29.

19. Fromkin, *A Peace to End All Peace*, 18.

20. The received historical view of Faisal's reign is that it was a failure because the British-backed monarchy was swept away in 1958 by a military coup. Ali A. Allawi, making use of Arabic as well as British sources, portrayed Faisal as a more complex figure who had a humane vision for a modern and tolerant Iraq. He judged him as more of a statesman and nation builder. Allawi contended that Faisal toward to end of his life saw himself as a liberator devoted to the "cause of Arab renascence" with the goal of Iraq as an independent state free of British imperial influence. Ali A. Allawi, *Faisal I of Iraq* (New Haven, CT: Yale University Press, 2014), 561.

21. The Arab socialist Ba'ath Party mixes Arab nationalist and socialist ideas, opposes Western imperialism, and calls for the renaissance or resurrection of the Arab world. Two Syrian intellectuals founded the party in Damascus in 1946. Ba'athists hold power in Syria to the present day and dominated Iraq until 2003. Created as a cell-based organization, with hierarchical lines of compartmentalized control, this feature ensured that the Ba'ath Party in Iraq was difficult to infiltrate. As the United States and its allies were to discover in 2003, the cell structure made the party highly resilient as an armed resistance organization.

22. In July 1979, just five days into his tenure as Iraq's new president, Saddam called a meeting of over three hundred Ba'ath Party senior leaders to read out a list of plotters allegedly trying to overthrow him and his new regime. There were sixty-one names identified among those assembled; they were led away into custody to face firing squads. Saddam demanded that the surviving delegates volunteer to serve on the firing squads. Williamson Murray and Robert H. Scales Jr., *The Iraq War: A Military History* (Cambridge, MA: Harvard University Press, 2003), 16–17.

CHAPTER 24. IRAQI WAR I, PERSIAN GULF WAR

1. CIA, Iraq Economic Data (1989–2003), Annex D, Foreign Debt, fig. 11 (April 23, 2007), https://www.cia.gov/library/reports/general-reports-1/iraq_wmd_2004/chap2_annx D.html.

2. Based on 1989 data from the US Energy Information Administration: 2.9 million bbls/day for Iraq and 1.9 million bbls/day for Kuwait. Retrieved online at http://www.eia .gov/cfapps/ipdbproject/iedindex3.cfm?tid=5&pid=57&aid=6&cid=SA,&syid=1990&eyid =1991&unit=BB.

3. Ibid., based on 2010 proven Iraqi oil reserves, 113 billion bbls, 2010 proven Kuwaiti oil reserves, 104 billion bbls, and world total proven reserves of 1.33 trillion bbls.

4. Bob Woodward, *The Commanders* (1991; repr., New York: Touchstone, 2002), 11.

5. Dan Goodgame, "In the Gulf: Bold Vision—What If We Do Nothing," *Time*, January 7, 1991. Goodgame provides context:

> The prevailing attitude among the group, recalled one White House official, was "Hey, too bad about Kuwait, but it's just a gas station, and who cares whether the sign says Sinclair or Exxon? Anyway, what can we do? Doesn't Iraq have the Middle East's largest army, and aren't we a long way from the scene?" There was little sense that big U.S. interests were at stake—until the President spoke. He asked a simple question that decisively shifted the debate: "What happens if we do nothing?"

6. Woodward, *The Commanders*, 226. Had Saddam invaded Saudi Arabia, he would have controlled 41 percent of the world's oil supply.

7. Unlike the situation in Korea forty years before when the Soviet Union had boycotted the Security Council, the USSR as a permanent member of the Security Council in 1990 voted for the resolution imposing sanctions and later the coalition's armed response against Iraq.

8. Atkinson recounts that President Bush and Secretary of State James A. Baker initiated a "166-day blitzkrieg of 'coercive diplomacy.'" This "diplomatic juggernaut" secured military contributions from thirty-eight nations. Rick Atkinson, *Crusade: The Untold Story of the Persian Gulf War* (Boston: Houghton Mifflin, 1993), 53–54. The coalition of Persian Gulf War countries, listed alphabetically showing those with significant contributions of military personnel, included thirty-five nations: Afghanistan, Argentina, Australia, Bahrain, Bangladesh, Belgium, Canada, Czechoslovakia, Denmark, Egypt (30,200), France (16,000), Germany, Greece, Honduras, Hungary, Italy, Kuwait (11,000), Morocco, the Netherlands, New Zealand, Niger, Norway, Oman (25,000), Pakistan, Poland, Qatar, Romania, Saudi Arabia (50,000), South Korea, Spain, Syria (14,000), Sweden, the United Arab Emirates (40,000), the United Kingdom (53,000), and the United States (527,000).

9. Cohen, *Supreme Command*, 185.

10. Powell served two tours in Vietnam, first as a captain, and was awarded the Purple Heart and Bronze Star; Schwarzkopf also served two tours in Vietnam, first as a major, and was awarded the Purple Heart, the Silver Star three times, and the Bronze Star with Combat V (for valor) three times.

11. Max Boot, *War Made New: Technology, Warfare, and the Course of History, 1500 to Today* (New York: Gotham, 2006), 334.

12. "At one press conference, he mordantly announced, 'Now you're going to see the luckiest man alive,' just before playing a video clip of an Iraqi vehicle that had barely cleared a bridge before the bridge was struck by a laser-guided bomb." Boot, *War Made New*, 334–35.

13. Powell would appear in a Pentagon press briefing room six days after the air campaign had begun and said this: "We're in no hurry. . . . We are not looking to have large numbers of casualties," operationally articulating one of his cardinal principles, about casualties, from his doctrine. Pointing to a map of Kuwait and Iraq on an easel, he then said, "Our strategy in going after this army is very, very simple: first, we're going to cut it off,

and then we're going to kill it," adding another of his doctrinal principles, the application of overwhelming force. Atkinson, *Crusade*, 162.

14. Boot, *War Made New*, 330.

15. Based on data from the US Energy Information Administration, Saudi Arabia oil reserves: 258 bbls; world reserves: 1,002 bbls. Retrieved online at http://www.eia.gov /cfapps/ipdbproject/iedindex3.cfm?tid=5&pid=57&aid=6&cid=SA,&syid=1990&eyid=199 1&unit=BB.

16. Atkinson, *Crusade*, 55.

17. Boot, *War Made New*, 337.

18. Atkinson, *Crusade*, 53–54.

19. Boot, *War Made New*, 337.

20. Diane T. Putney, *Airpower Advantage: Planning the Gulf War Air Campaign, 1989–1991* (Washington, DC: Air Force History and Museums Program, US Air Force, 2004), 183–84, 212–17.

21. Considered wildly controversial when it was first drafted and discussed in the mid-1970s, the 1982 edition of the army's *Operations Field Manual*, FM 100-5, identified combat success in terms of speed and violence, leveraging technology and firepower to specific missions, rapid decision making, flexibility and reliance on the initiative of junior leaders, indirect approaches and deception, clearly defined objectives and operational concepts, a clearly designated main effort, and deep attack.

22. Atkinson, *Crusade*, 60–61; and Putney, *Airpower Advantage*, 131.

23. Atkinson, *Crusade*, 111.

24. Both Atkinson, *Crusade*, 111, and Boot, *War Made New*, 337, mention this phrase. Everyone in the US Armed Services recognizes its pejorative, suicidal connotation.

25. Putney, *Airpower Advantage*, 219 (Schwarzkopf's admonition), 220 (chart text), citing H. Norman Schwarzkopf, *It Doesn't Take a Hero* (New York: Bantam, 1992), 359; and Briefing, CENTCOM Offensive Campaign, October 11, 1990, in CENTCOM J-5 After Action Report and Supporting Documents, NA 259, GWAPS (*Gulf War Air Power Survey*), AFHRA.

26. Atkinson, *Crusade*, 111.

27. Atkinson, *Crusade*, 109.

28. This approval was kept secret until November 8, 1990, after the congressional midterm elections.

29. Atkinson, *Crusade*, 113.

30. Lieutenant General William "Gus" Pagonis, Schwarzkopf's logistics chief, and his staff would use a combination of computers, cellular telephones, and 3×5 in. index cards to coordinate a vast infrastructural network involving the movement from multiple CONUS and European bases of more than 12,000 tracked vehicles, 117,000 wheeled vehicles, 122 million meals, and 1.3 billion gallons of fuel to the KTO. Boot, *War Made New*, 338.

31. CENTCOM Military News Briefing, February 27, 1991, https://www.c-span.org /video/?16795-1/us-centcom-military-news-briefing.

32. Boot, *War Made New*, 338; and Richard Stewart, *War in the Persian Gulf: Operations Desert Shield and Desert Storm, August 1990–March 1991*, CMH Pub. 70-117-1 (Washington, DC: US Army Center of Military History, 2010), 41.

33. For example, huge truck convoys ferried personnel, equipment, and armor hundreds of miles west on the two-lane, asphalt Trans-Arabian Pipeline highway called the Tapline Road running parallel to the Kuwaiti-Saudi-Iraqi border "straight as a gunshot toward Jordan." This deployment did not commence until the coalition had achieved air supremacy. Then General Schwarzkopf directed 18th Airborne and 7th Corps to move 250 and 150

miles, respectively, west into the desert along Tapline. A total of two hundred thousand troops and sixty-five thousand vehicles moved west. This force deployed at night under radio silence after the initial phase of the air campaign had neutralized Iraqi air reconnaissance. CENTCOM logistical organizations built multiple supply bases and depots in the Saudi western desert at the same time to support the 18th Airborne and 7th Corps Left Hook offensive. Atkinson, *Crusade*, 257, 323; and Richard P. Hallion, *Storm over Iraq: Air Power and the Gulf War* (Washington, DC: Smithsonian Institution Press, 1992), 227.

34. James Fallows, *National Defense* (New York: Random House, 1981), 172.

35. Enhanced MILES combat training kits continue to be used by the army's training establishment. Lockheed Martin, "Live Training Capabilities," marketing pamphlet.

36. The B-2 stealth bomber had been developed and flown by 1989, but it was not used in War I.

37. AWACS data retrieved online at http://www.af.mil/AboutUs/FactSheets/Display /tabid/224/Article/104504/e-3-sentry-awacs.aspx.

38. The first two developmental JSTARS aircraft (on a modified Boeing 707-300 airframe) were deployed in 1991 to support *Desert Storm*. Retrieved online at http://www .af.mil/AboutUs/FactSheets/Display/tabid/224/Article/104507/e-8c-joint-stars.aspx. In 1991, JSTARS was the most advanced airborne C⁴/ISR targeting and battlement platform in the world. From a standoff position, it could detect, locate, classify, track, and target hostile maneuvering ground forces communicating real-time information through secure data links with US Air Force and Army command posts.

39. The Global Positioning System is a space-based global navigation satellite constellation that provides precise location and time information in all weather, anywhere on or near the earth, where there is an unobstructed line of sight to four or more GPS satellites. The first experimental Block I GPS satellite was launched in 1978; by 1985, ten Block I satellites had been launched in orbit. Retrieved online at http://www.af.mil/AboutUs/FactSheets /Display/tabid/224/Article/104610/global-positioning-system.aspx. By 1994, a full constellation consisted of twenty-four satellites.

40. Atkinson, *Crusade*, 21.

41. Putney, *Airpower Advantage*, 362.

42. CENTCOM air sorties totaled 109,876 over the forty-three-day air campaign. Of those, more than twenty-seven thousand sorties were tasked to strike enemy Scuds, airfields, air defenses, electrical power, biological and chemical weapons caches, headquarters, intelligence assets, communications, the Iraqi army, and oil refineries. Retrieved online at http://www.u-s-history.com/pages/h2020.html.

43. Edwin E. Moïse, "Limited War, the Stereotypes" (online monograph, revised, November 22, 1998), http://www.clemson.edu/caah/history/FacultyPages/EdMoise/limit1 .html. The War I bomb tonnages were dwarfed by the air ordnance dropped by the millions of tons in World War II, Korea, and Vietnam.

44. While the B-52Gs delivered much more tonnage, accuracy from high altitude was low. Jon Lake, *B-52 Stratofortress Units in Operation Desert Storm* (Oxford: Osprey, 2004), 6–7, 75.

45. BDA was a source of controversy soon after the initial combat air sorties were flown because the methods and assets used by intelligence agencies in Washington versus those in the theater were different. Putney concludes that CENTCOM reported that the destruction percentages were "fairly accurate." Eliot A. Cohen, *Gulf War Air Power Survey (GWAPS)*, vol. 2, part 2, "Operations and Effects and Effectiveness" (Washington, DC: Department of the Air Force, December 16, 1993), 207–26, 259–64, 459, citing GWAPS figures in note 81.

46. Originally designed as a Cold War antiaircraft defense system in 1969, the Patriot during *Desert Storm* was assigned to intercept and shoot down Iraqi Scuds even though the design at the time had not been optimized for a missile defense mission. "The Patriot radars detected eighty-eight Scuds but only fifty-three entered areas defended by Patriot launchers. Of these, fifty-one were engaged, and the army assessed that twenty-seven had been successfully engaged." Steven J. Zaloga, *Scud Ballistic Missile Launch Systems, 1955–2005* (New York: Osprey, 2006), 37. Campbell adds,

> When videotape was examined after the war, it was concluded that no evidence existed that the Patriot missile intercepted any [Scud] warheads. Most of what was hit by the Patriot was the Scud missile bodies that reentered along with the warhead. The missile bodies broke up as they reentered and created a larger target for the Patriot's radar. The smaller warhead among all the debris was hardly, if ever, hit by the Patriot missile. The Patriots were designed to explode close to a target and use shrapnel to destroy it. (John T. Campbell, *Desert War: The New Conflict between the U.S. and Iraq* [New York: New American Library, 2003], 45)

47. Atkinson, *Crusade*, 2.

48. Boot, *War Made New*, 343.

49. Stewart, *War in the Persian Gulf*, 42.

50. General Schwarzkopf was impatient with the speed at which 7th Corps advanced, even though he had moved up their attack schedule by nearly a full day, telling the mild-mannered General Franks, with phraseology that might have been straight out of Patton's playbook, that he did not "want a slow, ponderous pachyderm mentality . . . I want 7th Corps to slam into the Republican Guard. The enemy is not worth shit. Go after them with audacity, shock action, and surprise." Atkinson, *Crusade*, 344. Schwarzkopf's impatience became a moot point when the war ended less than two days later.

51. An "easting" is a north–south grid line on a military map. H. R. McMaster, "Battle of 73 Easting, monograph by Captain H. R. McMaster, Eagle Troop, 2nd Squadron, 2nd Armored Cavalry Regiment (during the war with Iraq on 26 February 1991)," 34, identified for the author by Lieutenant General H. R. McMaster for online retrieval from the Donovan Research Library, Fort Benning, Georgia. McMaster wrote this account shortly after the battle to prepare future soldiers for what "a pitched armored battle at the small unit level" is like.

52. McMaster's account reports what his Eagle Troop accomplished: "Our Bradleys and tanks destroyed over thirty enemy tanks, approximately twenty personnel carriers and other armored vehicles, and about thirty trucks. The artillery strike had destroyed another thirty enemy trucks, large stocks of fuel, ammunition, and other supplies and several armored vehicles." McMaster, "Battle of 73 Easting," 29. He was awarded a Silver Star for his aggressive combat leadership.

53. Atkinson reports that after the war, approximately 1,500 destroyed vehicles were counted on the highway and another 400 on the secondary parallel coastal road and in the adjacent desert. Only 2 percent were tanks or APCs. The remainder was civilian cars, trucks, and buses commandeered by the Iraqis. Atkinson, *Crusade*, 451.

54. Michael T. Kelly, "Highway to Hell," *New Republic*, April 1, 1991, 11–14.

55. Atkinson notes that after Schwarzkopf agreed to allow military helicopter overflights, General Sultan Hashim Ahmad al-Tai was quick to seek clarification: "So you mean even armed helicopters can fly in Iraqi skies?" Schwarzkopf's reply was this: "I will instruct our Air Force not to shoot at any helicopters that are flying over the territory of Iraq." Atkinson, *Crusade*, 9.

56. Atkinson, *Crusade*, 476.

57. Atkinson, *Crusade*, 453 (twenty divisions), 476–77 (equipment).

58. Daniel J. Castellano, "Down the Memory Hole: Shifting Narratives of U.S. Policy in Iraq" (online monograph, 2007–2009), http://www.arcaneknowledge.org/histpoli/iraq.htm.

59. Boot, *War Made New*, 349. The exception was the Soviet-built T-72 designed in 1967 and put into service in 1973.

60. Atkinson, *Crusade*, 109, 183; and Boot, *War Made New*, 341, 347.

61. Boot, *War Made New*, 349.

62. Historical plot of Gallup confidence trends, http://www.gallup.com/poll/148163 /americans-confident-military-least-congress.aspx.

63. Atkinson, *Crusade*, 493.

CHAPTER 25. IRAQI WAR II, THIRTEEN-YEAR AIR CONFLICT

1. Retrieved online at http://www.un.org/Depts/unscom/Chronology/chronologyframe .htm.

2. Gordon W. Rudd, *Humanitarian Intervention: Assisting the Iraqi Kurds in Operation Provide Comfort, 1991*, CMH Pub. 70-78-1 (Washington, DC: US Army Center of Military History, 2004), 34, 243.

3. The first NFZ in the north was established shortly after War I ended from the 36th parallel northward. In August 1992, the NFZ in the south was added to extend south from the 32nd parallel, later expanded in 1996 to the 33rd parallel.

4. Ricks indicates that a total of 408,000 sorties were flown in the southern and northern no-fly zones. Thomas E. Ricks, *Fiasco: The American Military Adventure in Iraq* (New York: Penguin, 2006), 43.

5. Daniel L. Byman and Matthew C. Waxman, *Confronting Iraq: U.S. Policy and the Use of Force since the Gulf War* (Santa Monica, CA: Rand, 2000), 68.

6. Jay E. Hines, command historian, *History of the Persian Gulf War, and Subsequent Actions of the U.S. Central Command* (online monograph), http://www.daveross.com/cent com.html.

7. Jeffrey A. Meyer and Mark G. Califano, *Good Intentions Corrupted: The Oil for Food Scandal and the Threat to the U.N.*, intro. by Paul A. Volker (New York: PublicAffairs, 2006), xxxvi.

8. Stephen Black, "Verification under Duress: The Case of UNSCOM," in *Verification Yearbook*, ed. Trevor Findlay (London: VERTIC, 2000), 126.

CHAPTER 26. IRAQI WAR III, INVASION OF IRAQ

1. T. V. Paul, *Asymmetric Conflicts: War Initiation by Weaker Powers* (Cambridge: Cambridge University Press, 1994), 20. Paul defines asymmetric conflict as "a conflict involving two states with unequal overall military and economic power resources."

2. Boot, *War Made New*, 391.

3. Madrassas are Islamic boarding schools in Pakistan, Afghanistan, and Iran that teach mostly Islamic subjects but in many cases serve as indoctrination and training centers for jihad. The number of madrassas exploded in Pakistan during President Mohammad Zia-ul-Haq's rule (1978–1988). From two hundred in 1947, the madrassas grew to an estimated forty thousand by 2008, supported by private funding from radical sheikhs in Saudi Arabia.

Kamila Hyat, "No Room for Doubt and Division," *News International*, September 25, 2009, the largest English-language, tabloid-size newspaper in Pakistan; cf., Christopher Candland, "Pakistan's Recent Performance in Reforming Islamic Education," in *Education Reform in Pakistan: Building for the Future*, ed. Robert M. Hathaway (Washington, DC: Woodrow Wilson Center for Scholars, 2005), 151, passim. The *New York Times* reported that similar private funding by radical Saudi and other Persian Gulf sheikhs quadrupled the number of Taliban madrassas in Afghanistan from one thousand in 2001 to more than four thousand today. Carlotta Gall, "Saudis Fund Taliban and Back Government, Too," *New York Times*, December 7, 2016, A13.

4. Kagan, *Finding the Target*, 290.

5. Within a year, the term *CINC* disappeared as a military designation. On October 24, 2002, Secretary of Defense Donald H. Rumsfeld announced that in accordance with Title 10 of the US Code, the title of commander in chief would thereafter be reserved for the president, consistent with the terms of Article II of the Constitution. Thereafter, the military CINCs would be known as "combatant commanders," as heads of the Unified Combatant Commands.

6. Gary Berntsen, *Jawbreaker: The Attack on Bin Laden and Al-Qaeda; A Personal Account by the CIA's Key Field Commander* (New York: Crown, 2005), 307–8. Berntsen was the veteran CIA intelligence officer who led the teams. He asserts that "a number of al-Qa'ida detainees later confirmed that bin Laden escaped with another group of 200 Saudis and Yemenis by a . . . route over difficult snow-covered passes into the Pashtun tribal area of Parachinar, Pakistan."

7. Kagan, *Finding the Target*, 296.

8. Kagan, *Finding the Target*, 296.

9. Ethnic groups include the Pashtun, Tajik, Dari, Hazara, Uzbeki, Turkmani, Baluchi, Pashai, Pamiri, and Nuristani tribes.

10. Judith Miller, a former *New York Times* reporter who was embedded with one of the WMD search teams in 2003, reported years later that "more than 6,000 chemical weapons or remnants of them—some containing mustard gas and sarin made before the 1991 war—were found and . . . sickened some American soldiers and Iraqis. While . . . these were not the weapons for which America had invaded, Saddam's failure to acknowledge or account for them violated his pledges to the United Nations and was part of the [Bush] administration's justification for war." Judith Miller, *The Story: A Reporter's Journey* (New York: Simon & Schuster, 2015), xii.

11. Joint Resolution to Authorize the Use of United States Armed Forces against Iraq, Public Law 107–243, H. J. Res. 114. For text, see press release, White House, Office of the Press Secretary (October 2, 2002), http://georgewbush-whitehouse.archives.gov/news/releases/2002/10/print/20021002-2.html.

12. Among them, Fouad Ajami, "Iraq and the Arabs' Future," *Foreign Affairs* 82, no. 1 (January/February 2003): 12; Ajami put the case for War III this way: "For *pax americana*, Iraq may be worth the effort and the risks"; and John Lewis Gaddis, *Surprise, Security, and the American Experience* (Cambridge, MA: Harvard University Press, 2004), 14–22. Gaddis pointed out that preemption had deep historical roots linked to American security and continental expansion.

13. Kagan, *Finding the Target*, 300.

14. Kagan, *Finding the Target*, 324–25.

15. Bob Woodward, *Plan of Attack: The Definitive Account of the Decision to Invade Iraq* (New York: Simon & Schuster, 2004), 40, passim.

16. Boot, *War Made New*, 7–16.

17. Shinseki retired on June 11, 2003, after the expiration of his four-year JCS term ended thirty-eight years of military service.

18. Boot, *War Made New*, 390.

19. State's Future of Iraq Project produced thirteen volumes that ran to 2,500 pages. One expert who read it concluded, "It was unimplementable. It was a series of essays to describe what the future could be" (Dr. David A. Kay, an Iraq Survey Group weapons inspector). James Dobbins, Michele A. Poole, Austin Long, and Benjamin Runkle, *After the War: Nation-Building from FDR to George W. Bush* (Santa Monica, CA: Rand, MG716, 2008), 109.

20. Kagan, *Finding the Target*, 324–25.

21. Kagan, *Finding the Target*, 326.

22. Kagan, *Finding the Target*, citing Woodward, *Plan of Attack*, 63, 101, 184, 260, passim.

23. Kagan, *Finding the Target*, 330–31.

24. Van Creveld, *Airpower*, 333.

25. Eric Peltz, John M. Halliday, Marc L. Robbins, and Kenneth J. Girardini, *Sustainment of Army Forces in Operation Iraqi Freedom: Battlefield Logistics and Effects on Operations* (Santa Monica, CA: Rand, MG344, 2005), xxiii, http://www.rand.org/content/dam/rand/pubs/monographs/2006/RAND_MG344.pdf.

26. Boot, *War Made New*, 402.

CHAPTER 27. IRAQI WAR IV, THE INSURGENCY AND THE SURGE (2007–2008)

1. Dobbins et al., *After the War*, 117–18.

2. Dobbins defines *nation building* "as the use of armed forces in the aftermath of a conflict to promote an enduring peace and a transition to democracy." Dobbins et al., *After the War*, 2.

3. Dobbins et al., *After the War*, xiii. Dobbins might have added that in the case of Iraq in 2003 the Bush administration chose the wrong paradigm with Germany as the "gold standard." Mansoor points out that the occupations of Italy in 1943 and Korea in 1945 were better guides to the liberation of Iraq. Peter R. Mansoor, *Surge: My Journey with General David Petraeus and the Remaking of the Iraq War* (New Haven, CT: Yale University Press, 2013), 7.

4. Most CPA personnel were initially headquartered in one of Saddam's former palaces, nestled along the Euphrates River inside the International Zone, more popularly known as the "Green Zone," a secure area encompassing over a square mile. CPA staff traveled to ministries and other destinations with security guards or in military convoys. As violence increased in mid-2003 and 2004, providing security for CPA personnel traveling to and from downtown Baghdad and to points outside the city became a major task for CJTF-7, the military command that assumed postwar military responsibility in Iraq. James Dobbins, Seth G. Jones, Benjamin Runkle, and Siddharth Mohandas, *Occupying Iraq: A History of the Coalition Provisional Authority*, MG847 (Santa Monica, CA: Rand, 2009), 23–27.

5. Dobbins et al., *After the War*, xx–xxi.

6. *Frontline* interview, PBS, "Nation-Building 101: An Interview with James Dobbins," about his 2003 study, Dobbins et al., *America's Role in Nation-Building: From Germany to Iraq*, MR1753 (Santa Monica, CA: Rand, 2003), http://www.pbs.org/wgbh/pages/frontline/shows/truth/stake/dobbins.html.

7. Dobbins et al., *After the War*, xxiv–xxv, 137.

8. Dobbins et al., *After the War*, 111. Moyar is blunter, quoting one of Feith's associates: "Feith can't manage anything, and he doesn't trust anyone else's judgment." Mark A. Moyar, *A Question of Command: Counterinsurgency from the Civil War to Iraq* (New Haven, CT: Yale University Press, 2009), 214. Chandrasekaran corroborates Moyar's assessment. Rajiv Chandrasekaran, *Imperial Life in the Emerald City: Inside Iraq's Green Zone* (New York: Knopf, 2006), 29, 35.

9. Rumsfeld, for example, specifically refused to assign the organizer of State's Future of Iraq Project to the ORHA staff. When Garner pushed back, Rumsfeld told him he was acting under instructions from "higher authority." Moyar, *Question of Command*, 214.

10. Chandrasekaran, *Imperial Life*, 33.

11. Moyar, *Question of Command*, 33, 94–97.

12. Dobbins et al., *After the War*, 115.

13. Bob Woodward, *State of Denial: Bush at War, Part III* (New York: Simon & Schuster, 2006), 166. Garner himself acknowledges that DoD had been upfront with him at the start of his assignment about early replacement; PBS *Frontline* interview, October 17, 2006, http://www.pbs.org/wgbh/pages/frontline/yeariniraq/interviews/garner.html.

14. Moyar, quoting Diamond, *Question of Command*, 216.

15. Larry Diamond, *Squandered Victory: The American Occupation and the Bungled Effort to Bring Democracy to Iraq* (New York: Henry Holt, 2005), 303–5.

16. Diamond, *Squandered Victory*, 303–5.

17. The US Army in 2005 had seven civil affairs brigades, mostly in reserve units, consisting of approximately thirteen thousand personnel. Retrieved online at http://www.usar.army.mil/Commands/Functional/USACAPOC/USACAPOC-Units. An army civil affairs officer wrote in 2005, "Despite assertions by past and current White House residents that the United States is not in the business of nation-building, the Army's experience in Afghanistan and Iraq convinces us otherwise. . . . Despite the force's successes, there is a strong perception that the Army does not have enough CA [civil affairs] operators." Mark L. Kimmey, Lieutenant Colonel, US Army Reserve (Ret.), "Transforming Civil Affairs," *Army Magazine*, March 2005, http://www.socnet.com/showthread.php?t=47686.

18. Lord and Mansoor elaborated on Bremer's errors. Lord, *Proconsuls*, 203–4; and Mansoor, *Surge*, 7, 266.

19. The other three Ds were demilitarization, decartelization, and democratization.

20. Whether Bremer was the creator of CPA-1 and CPA-2 or merely the mouthpiece is a moot point. His name is associated with their execution even though he had been presented with their substance in Washington as a fait accompli before his departure to Iraq.

21. Only seven thousand Iraqi soldiers became POWs during Operation *Iraqi Freedom*. The Iraqi generals who surrendered had no troops remaining on duty. Dobbins et al., *After the War*, 120.

22. Moyar, *Question of Command*, 217. To General Garner's credit, there were serious demilitarization, demobilization, and reintegration (DDR) proposals developed by ORHA, fulfilling the intent of Diamond's counterfactual action 5. Office of Reconstruction and Humanitarian Assistance, "Rehabilitation and Development Center Brief (*Markaz Al-Ta'heel wa Al-atweer*)" (PowerPoint briefing developed by an ORHA contractor, RONCO Consulting Corporation, May 11, 2003).

23. "Sanchez alienated Bremer, other senior U.S. officials, his subordinates, the press, and numerous Iraqis . . . micromanaged one small issue at a time, leaving most other matters to subordinate commanders. He allowed his division commanders to select counterinsurgency approaches in their areas, a sensible policy. . . . But Sanchez neglected a

critical element of decentralized command—oversight. . . . Seldom checking on divisions commanders, not to mention brigade or battalion commanders, Sanchez was unable to determine how well they were leading." Moyar, *Question of Command*, 219.

24. Dobbins et al., *After the War*, 122; and Ricks, *Fiasco*, 174.

25. Ricks, *Fiasco*, 187.

26. Michael R. Gordon and Bernard E. Trainor, *The Endgame: The Inside Story of the Struggle for Iraq, from George W. Bush to Barack Obama* (New York: Pantheon, 2012).

27. AQI was initially established as *Jama'at al-Tawhid wa-al Jihad* (Unity and Jihad Group) in the early 2000s by longtime Jordanian jihadist Abu Musab al-Zarqawi. In October 2004, Zarqawi came to an agreement with Osama bin Laden and formally joined al Qa'ida, renaming his organization Tanzim Qaidat al-Jihad fi Bilad al-Rafidayn Zarqawi, known as al Qaeda in Iraq (AQI) in English. AQI by 2013 evolved into the Islamic State of Iraq. Retrieved online at http://web.stanford.edu/group/mappingmilitants/cgi-bin/groups/view/1.

28. Gordon and Trainor, *Endgame*, 21, identifying the title of Colonel Harvey's assessment as "Sunni Arab Resistance: Politics of the Gun."

29. Gordon and Trainor, *Endgame*, 132–33.

30. Gordon and Trainor, *Endgame*, 13. Bremer "pored over Dobbins' Rand study of classic nation-building efforts in Germany and Japan."

31. According to Fred Kaplan, in 2006, of the one thousand US officials in Embassy Baghdad, "just 33 spoke Arabic, only six of them fluently." Fred Kaplan, *The Insurgents: David Petraeus and the Plot to Change the American Way of War* (New York: Simon & Schuster, 2013), 206.

32. Robinson describes Petraeus's chart. The puzzle diagram was a PowerPoint chart attempting to display graphically the interrelationships among political, economic, military, and security measures, showing a series of concentric rings and circles arranged in a Venn-diagram configuration, surrounded by clouds labeled to identify interagency, nonkinetic, detainee, intelligence, political, and kinetic operations. Robinson mentions it in multiple contexts. The chart was named "Anaconda" after the snake that squeezes its prey to death. Linda Robinson, *Tell Me How This Ends: General David Petraeus and the Search for a Way Out of Iraq* (New York: PublicAffairs, 2008), 275, passim. Mansoor adds that Petraeus selected Anaconda after the Civil War plan to blockade the Atlantic and Gulf Coasts, cut the Confederacy in two along the Mississippi River, and squeeze the South through simultaneous offensives at multiple points along its borders. Mansoor, *Surge*, 172.

33. Dobbins et al., *After the War*, 124.

34. Dobbins et al., *After the War*, 126.

35. General Casey's command, MNF-I, succeeded General Sanchez's command, CJTF-7, in May 2004.

36. Anthony H. Cordesman, "The Iraqi Insurgency and the Risk of Civil War: Who Are the Players" (working draft, revised, Center for Strategic and International Studies, Washington, DC, March 1, 2006), 2–4; and Bruce R. Pirnie and Edward O'Connell, *Counterinsurgency in Iraq (2003–2006), Rand Counterinsurgency Study, Vol. 2*, MG595.3 (Santa Monica, CA: Rand, National Defense Research Institute, 2008), 2, 9–10, http://www.rand.org/pubs/monographs/2008/RAND_MG595.3.pdf.

37. Officially the High Mobility Multipurpose Wheeled Vehicle (HMMWV).

38. Mansoor, *Surge*, 210.

39. Boot, *War Made New*, 416.

40. The sites were companycommand.com and platoonleader.org that the army by 2004 had started underwriting and supporting, rendering them more secure (these sites are no

longer available online without access through military networks: http://cc.army.mil/index
.htm and http://platoonleader.army.mil).

41. Moyar, *Question of Command*, 221.

42. Petraeus was later promoted twice, to lieutenant general and then general, receiving
his fourth star. As general, he was appointed commander, MNF-I; then CINCENT; then
commander, International Security Assistance Force (ISAF), Afghanistan; and, as a retired
officer in 2011, director of central intelligence.

43. Roger J. Spiller taught classes to professional officers, mostly majors, for twenty-five
years. He wrote, "For years after the war in Vietnam the college offered no courses on it,
as if the school's managers would do anything to avoid referring to the war. It might as well
have been fought on Mars." *School of War*, 5.

44. David H. Petraeus, "The American Military and the Lessons of Vietnam: A Study of
Military Influence and the Use of Force in the Post-Vietnam Era" (Princeton University,
1987), 132, 312, 315, 316.

45. CERP was funded to give military commanders money that could be disbursed
quickly on small-scale economic and infrastructure projects that would immediately help
a local Iraqi community. "The program was designed to avoid the volumes of bureaucratic
red tape most large-scale U.S. civilian and military aid projects required. . . . CERP projects
were judged by the U.S. special inspector general for Iraq to be the most effective aid the
U.S. provided in the postwar period." Robinson, *Tell Me How This Ends*, 69.

46. Robinson, *Tell Me How This Ends*, 69.

47. Moyar, *Question of Command*, 223–24.

48. Quoted by Moyar, *Question of Command*, 223–24, citing Eliot A. Cohen, "Conclusion," in *War in Iraq: Planning and Execution*, ed. Thomas G. Mahnken and Thomas A.
Keaney (New York: Routledge, 2007), 252.

49. George Packer, "The Lesson of Tal Afar," Letter from Iraq, *New Yorker*, April 10, 2008.

50. Michael Yon was a forty-one-year-old former Green Beret who wrote a series of
highly regarded blogs (web logs), available at www.michaelyon-online.com. He published
four books, the most recent of which is *Moment of Truth in Iraq* (Minneapolis, MN: Richard Vigilante Books, 2008), 36–45, in which he describes Colonel Kurilla's exceptional
leadership. Kurilla's 1st Battalion, 24th Infantry Regiment, 1st Stryker Brigade, 25th ID,
sustained heavy casualties, 25 percent killed or wounded, including Kurilla himself, who
was seriously wounded in close combat.

51. Moyar, *Question of Command*, 235.

52. Moyar, *Question of Command*, 236.

53. The MNF-I database, compiled from military reporting, included all attacks such
as small-arms fire, antiaircraft fire, indirect fire, and IED and later VBIED attacks against
coalition forces, as well as against civilian "neutrals" and Iraqi security forces. The data ag-
gregated on annual centers June 2003 to June 2004 showed the quadrupling.

54. Dobbins et al., *Occupying Iraq*, 93–94.

55. These events happened on General Sanchez's watch while in command of CJTF-7.
Sanchez had already ordered a US Army Criminal Investigation Command investigation
led by Major General Antonio M. Taguba. The investigation, made public in May 2004,
found that "between October and December 2003, at the Abu Ghraib Baghdad Central
Confinement Facility (BCCF), numerous incidents of sadistic, blatant, and wanton criminal
abuses were inflicted on several detainees." This systemic and illegal abuse of detainees
was intentionally perpetrated by several members of the military police guard force (372nd
Military Police Company, 320th MP Battalion, 800th MP Brigade) at the BCCF. The wide-

spread media coverage did much to destroy public confidence worldwide in the American-led occupation and policies.

56. Petraeus completed his assignment as the first commander of the Multi-National Security Transition Command Iraq responsible for training, equipping, and mentoring Iraq's growing army, police, and other security forces as well as developing the associated infrastructure.

57. US Army and Marine Corps, *The U.S. Army Marine Corps Counterinsurgency Field Manual*, U.S. Army Field Manual No. 3-24, Marine Corps Warfighting Publication No. 3-33.5, foreword by General David H. Petraeus and Lieutenant General James F. Amos (Chicago: University of Chicago Press, 2007), http://www.fas.org/irp/doddir/army/fm3-24.pdf.

58. John Nagl wrote in the foreword to the Chicago edition of FM 3-24, "Petraeus [turned] to his West Point classmate Lieutenant Colonel Conrad C. Crane (Ret). Crane, with a doctorate in history from Stanford University, called on the expertise of both academics and army and marine corps veterans of the conflicts in Afghanistan and Iraq." The core writing team was assembled at Fort Leavenworth in December 2005, and FM 3-24 was first issued a year later on December 15, 2006. US Army and Marine Corps, *The U.S. Army Marine Corps Counterinsurgency Field Manual*, xvi, University of Chicago 2006 edition of FM 3-24. Mansoor reports that "Petraeus read every word of the manual and personally edited and reedited key sections of it—30 drafts of the first two chapters alone." Mansoor, *Surge*, 38.

59. FM 3-24, xlvii.

60. For the US Army, FM 90-8, *Counterinsurgency Operations* (August 29, 1986), cited in FM 3-24, 399; and for the marine corps cited as a "classic," the *Small Wars Manual*, with the annotation, "originally published in 1940; covers lessons learned from the Corps' experience in the interwar years," republished by the USMC (Washington, DC: US Government Printing Office, 1987).

61. A line General Petraeus would use frequently in public after publication of FM 3-24: "You can't kill your way out of an insurgency."

62. FM 3-24, 41 (I-128 and I-126), 45 (I-141), and 47 (I-147).

63. Thomas E. Ricks, *The Gamble: General David Petraeus and the American Military Adventure in Iraq, 2006–2008* (New York: Penguin, 2009), 36. Ricks presents a detailed reconstruction of the strategic debate that ensued in the summer and fall of 2006, a dissection of the political and military issues, and the many public and private personalities involved, both inside and outside the Bush administration. It is a follow-on to *Fiasco: The American Military Adventure in Iraq*, published three years earlier.

64. Kimberly Kagan, *The Surge: A Military History* (New York: Encounter Books, 2009), 8–9, citing press briefing by Major General (later lieutenant general) William B. Caldwell IV, spokesman for Multi-National Force–Iraq, topic: Security Operations in Iraq, location: Combined Press Information Center, Baghdad, September 6, 2006.

65. Observed by Colonel Mansoor, who would soon become General Petraeus's executive officer after the latter assumed command of MNF-I in early 2007. Ricks, *The Gamble*, 37.

66. For example, retired Major General John R. S. Batiste had declined a promotion to lieutenant general to return to Iraq because he no longer wished to serve under Secretary Rumsfeld. Major General Charles H. Swannack Jr., who had commanded the 82nd Airborne Division in Iraq between 2002 and 2004, laid responsibility for the Abu Ghraib scandal at Rumsfeld's feet, claiming it was the result of top-level pressure to step up interrogations. Retired General Anthony Zinni, the fifth CINCCENT, and Major General John

M. Riggs were questioning the handling of the war. A retired army vice chief of staff, General John "Jack" Keane, was becoming increasingly concerned. Retired air force general Charles F. Wald, a Vietnam veteran, would say that the Iraq war "makes Vietnam look like a cakewalk," adding that "worst-case scenarios are the most likely thing to happen." Ricks, *The Gamble*, 39–40, 57–58, 76.

67. Ricks, *The Gamble*, 76.

68. The Iraq Study Group was a ten-person, bipartisan panel appointed in March 2006 by Congress, charged with evaluating US policy and strategy in Iraq and making policy recommendations.

69. Ricks, *The Gamble*, 79–80.

70. Ricks, *The Gamble*, 80.

71. Ricks, *The Gamble*, 81.

72. Ricks, *The Gamble*, 81.

73. Abu Musab al-Zarqawi was the AQI leader in Iraq and led it until his death by US forces in June 2006.

74. Ricks, *The Gamble*, 88–89.

75. Ricks, *The Gamble*, 89–90; and for more historical detail on Keane's growing role, see Kaplan, *Insurgents*, 224ff, passim.

76. Mansoor, himself a member of the Council of Colonels, indicates that it was the brainchild of General Pace, who had been prodded by retired General Keane. Mansoor, *Surge*, 41.

77. AEI is a public-policy think tank based in Washington. Kagan was a resident fellow at AEI, the author of multiple books about strategy and the revolution in military affairs, and had written extensively about Iraq policy. His front-to-back versus back-to-front distinction about strategic planning, explained in *Finding the Target*, is particularly trenchant. Mansoor indicates that the AEI report gained traction because of the influence of General Keane. Mansoor, *Surge*, 52.

78. Cohen is professor of strategic studies at Johns Hopkins University. Biddle's academic background included stints at the US Army War College, University of North Carolina, and the Institute for Defense Analyses (IDA). McCaffrey had commanded the 24th Mechanized ID in the 18th Airborne Corps in War I as major general. Downing, an officer with extensive airborne and special operations command experience, came out of retirement between 2001 and 2003 to serve as a counterterrorism advisor to the national security advisor and the director of homeland security.

79. In fairness, Ricks discusses Chiarelli's role in Iraq, Casey's commander of day-to-day operations, as occupying an "ambiguous position in this tale." He had done a creditable job as a division commander and understood COIN principles better than most of his peers, but he was publicly supportive of Casey despite rumors of disagreement. Ricks, *The Gamble*, 52; and Kaplan, *Insurgents*, 185.

80. Ricks, *The Gamble*, 98–99.

81. Ricks, *The Gamble*, 100.

82. Mansoor, *Surge*, 54.

83. Ricks, *The Gamble*, 100. Cohen was referring to Sir Michael E. Howard, British military historian, decorated World War II veteran (Italy), and author of more than twenty books.

84. Ricks, *The Gamble*, 98.

85. Mansoor, *Surge*, 52.

86. Robert M. Gates, *Duty: Memoirs of a Secretary at War* (New York: Knopf, 2014), 39–40.

87. Mansoor, *Surge*, 62.

88. Ricks, *The Gamble*, 133, passim; and Robinson, *Tell Me How This Ends*, 98–99.
89. For Mansoor's account of how the staff was formed, see *Surge*, 57–61.
90. Robinson, *Tell Me How This Ends*, 170.
91. Mansoor, *Surge*, 92, 102–3.

The relationship between General Petraeus and Ambassador was critical to the successful outcome of the surge. Although unity of command is the ideal for military and civilian agencies participating in a COIN operation, political considerations usually dictate division of the necessary authorities among a variety of actors. Division of civil and military power places a premium on the creation of a clear, common understanding of the political and security goals and how the counterinsurgent forces and agencies intend to achieve them. Only then does unity of effort become a viable substitute for unity of command.

Mansoor asserts that it was the personal relationship these two men developed that achieved unity of effort.

92. Robinson, *Tell Me How This Ends*, 116. By March 2008, there were thirty-one PRTs in Iraq with about eight hundred total staff. Catherine Dale, *Operation Iraqi Freedom: Strategies, Approaches, Results, and Issues for Congress*, CRS Report for Congress, updated, RF34376 (Washington, DC: Congressional Research Service, March 28, 2008), 97.
93. Ricks, *The Gamble*, 139.
94. The BUA was broadcast every day in real time over secure communications links accessible by anyone with a SIPRNet (Secret Internet Protocol Router Network) terminal. SIPRNet is DoD's system of classified, interconnected computer networks. Subordinate commands in Iraq could link into the BUA via the SIPRNet. "The Iraq War being the hottest topic in U.S. foreign policy in 2007, thousands of people scattered across the globe from Iraq to Europe to Tampa [CENTCOM HQ] to Washington, DC, viewed the BUA each day." Mansoor, *Surge*, 92–93; and Robinson, *Tell Me How This Ends*, 90–91, passim; 149; and 173.
95. Robinson, *Tell Me How This Ends*, 92–93. Mansoor's surge account corroborates the importance of repairing Tower 57. "During the eight-month saga of its repair, Tower 57 became a metaphor for the progress of the surge." Mansoor, *Surge*, 91–92, 119.
96. Kaplan, *Insurgents*, 260ff; and Mansoor, *Surge*, 104.
97. Lord assesses the Petraeus-Crocker partnership as follows: "The military leadership of General David Petraeus and, perhaps as important, Petraeus' fruitful collaboration with Ryan Crocker, the very able U.S. ambassador to Baghdad, has demonstrated that effective proconsular leadership is possible in a very unpromising setting." Lord, *Proconsuls*, 21. For Mansoor's description of how these meetings evolved and improved, see *Surge*, 77–79, 99, 217.
98. Robinson, *Tell Me How This Ends*, 150.
99. Bill Roggio, "Drawing the Battlelines in Anbar," *Long War Journal*, September 2006, http://www.longwarjournal.org/archives/2006/09/drawing_the_battleli.php; and Mansoor, *Surge*, chap. 5, "The Awakening."
100. Robinson, *Tell Me How This Ends*, 275.
101. Moyar, *Question of Command*, 247.
102. Kagan, *Surge*, 32, passim; and Moyar, *Question of Command*, 246, passim.
103. Moyar, *Question of Command*, 247.
104. *Kinetic* in military jargon describes violent combat operations, often large-scale, requiring considerable application of combined-arms firepower.
105. Gentile, *Wrong Turn*, 97.
106. Three army majors on General Odierno's intelligence staff, Nichoel Brooks, Ketti Davison, and Monica Miller, analyzed data from more than three hundred intelligence

officers, fifty of them embedded with combat brigades. Their work added credibility to reports of insurgent activities in the cities and villages encircling Baghdad, the Baghdad Belts. Kaplan, *Insurgents*, 257.

107. Operation *Arrowhead Ripper* was part of *Phantom Thunder*, launched on June 19, 2007, consisting of simultaneous supporting operations in the Khalis Corridor against AQI, clearing of western Baqubah, and supporting operations in Khan Bani Sa'ad to dislodge enemy insurgents, followed by a second phase of *Arrowhead Ripper* on July 17 with a Khalis tribal reconciliation meeting, more clearing of Baqubah, and Operations *Ithaca* and *Olympus* to drive AQI from Haimer, Abu Nasim, Jamil, and Anbakia in the Diyala River valley northeast of Baghdad, capped by a reconciliation agreement by eighteen important sheikhs on August 12, 2007. Kagan, *Surge*, extracted from color-coded maps and tables presented in front matter.

108. Online monograph posting, Institute for the Study of War (December 6, 2007), http://www.understandingwar.org/operation/operation-phantom-thunder.

109. Online monograph posting, ISW.

110. Mansoor, *Surge*, 87.

111. The *Jaish al-Mahdi* (JAM), as MNF-I intelligence discovered, was a mosaic of various military Shia groups operating under Moqtada al-Sadr. The most dangerous of the militias were "Special Groups" of JAM, armed, trained, equipped, and funded, and in some cases directed by, the Quds force, a special branch of the Iranian Revolutionary Guards Corps. Quds is the Arabic name for Jerusalem. "Iran's goals was nothing less than to create a client proxy force out of portions of the JAM, much as it had formed Hezbollah in Lebanon to do Iranian bidding in that state. . . . By late 2006 Quds force personnel were plying their trade inside Iraq itself, a fact that would soon become apparent." The Iranians through the Quds force were supplying explosively formed penetrators used in IEDs and VBIEDs, the most lethal munitions in Iraq that were responsible for hundreds of American deaths. Mansoor, *Surge*, 82–83, 167.

112. Kagan, *Surge*, 76, 97, passim; Robinson, *Tell Me How This Ends*, 234; and Mansoor, *Surge*, 71.

113. The Stryker is a twenty-one-ton, eight-wheeled armored fighting vehicle with a top speed of sixty miles per hour, carrying high-tech information systems that provide situational awareness, and with an ungainly appearance. It was the vehicle of choice during the surge because it had better armor than the thin-skinned Humvee. Robinson, *Tell Me How This Ends*, 127–34; and Mansoor, *Surge*, 76, passim. Mansoor cautioned in his *Surge* narrative that "despite the manifest success of the program, biometric identity devices were at best a partial technological solution to lifting the veil of insurgent anonymity as [insurgents] attempted to blend in with the local population."

114. Robinson, *Tell Me How This Ends*, 134–35.

115. Robinson, *Tell Me How This Ends*, 183.

116. Robinson, *Tell Me How This Ends*, 199. Mansoor indicates that some Iranian-supplied explosively formed penetrators (EFPs), when detonated, projected a semimolten slug of copper that could slice through even the thickest armor of the M1/A1 Abrams tank. "Some of these devices, buried in the ground, were deadly enough to flip 68-ton tanks upside down." Mansoor, *Surge*, 150.

117. Robinson, *Tell Me How This Ends*, 210–16. For moving military narratives of what surge operations were like for American combat soldiers in some of Baghdad's worst neighborhoods, see Robinson's chaps. 8, "The Blue Spaders in the Inferno," and 9, "The Knights of Amiriyah."

118. Kagan, *Surge*, 200.

119. George W. Bush, *Initial Benchmark Assessment Report* (Washington, DC: White House, July 12, 2007), http://georgewbush-whitehouse.archives.gov/news/re leases/2007/07/20070712.html.

120. Bush, *Initial Benchmark Assessment Report*.

121. Mansoor indicates that battlefield geometry refers to the changing of unit boundaries within areas of operation and the stability of local relationships that would be affected by shifts in forces. Iraqis were much more forthcoming with cooperation and intelligence when they believed that US forces were committed to areas where they lived and worked. "Iraq was a geographic and cultural kaleidoscope, which made [military] planning incredibly complex." Mansoor, *Surge*, 181.

122. Robinson, *Tell Me How This Ends*, 294.

123. Robinson, *Tell Me How This Ends*, 296.

124. David M. Walker, *Securing, Stabilizing, and Rebuilding Iraq: Iraqi Government Has Not Met Most Legislative, Security, and Economic Benchmarks*, GAO-07-1195 (Washington, DC: Government Accountability Office, September 2007), 51, 52, fig. 5.

125. Robinson attributes the differences to "the GAO applying a more rigorous standard of what constituted 'satisfactory progress.'" Robinson, *Tell Me How This Ends*, 297.

126. General Westmoreland addressed a joint session of Congress in April 1967. His thirty-minute speech was interrupted nineteen times by applause, but congressional and popular support for the Vietnam War thereafter continued to decline.

127. Mansoor, *Surge*, 89, citing "Senator Reid on Iraq: This War Is Lost," *CBS News*, April 20, 2007, http://www.cbsnews.com/stories/2007/04/20/politics/main2709229.shtml.

128. Mansoor, *Surge*, 89–90.

129. Mansoor, *Surge*, 207, citing Mark Bowden, "The Professor of War," *Vanity Fair*, May 2010, http://www.vanityfair.com/politics/features/2010/05/petraeus-201005.

130. Seven years later, Secretary Gates recorded in his memoirs that Senator Clinton admitted in a White House conversation with President Obama that her opposition to the surge was "political." She asserted, "The Iraq surge worked." Gates, *Memoirs*, 376.

131. Robinson, *Tell Me How This Ends*, 300.

132. Dale, *Operation Iraqi Freedom*, 103–5; and Robinson, *Tell Me How This Ends*, 322–23. Dale's CRS report defined "overall attacks" as a specified metric that included attacks against Iraqi infrastructure and facilities; bombs found and exploded; small-arms attacks including snipers, ambushes, and grenades; and mortar, rocket, and surface-to-air attacks.

133. Moyar, *Question of Command*, 252–54; and Robinson, *Tell Me How This Ends*, 341–42.

134. Thomas P. M. Barnett, "The Man between War and Peace," *Esquire*, April 2008; and Thom Shanker and David Stoudt, "Top U.S. Commander in Mideast to Retire Early," *New York Times*, March 11, 2008.

135. Robinson, *Tell Me How This Ends*, 343–44, 345ff.

136. As Crocker would tell an interviewer on January 10, 2008, "That [referring to the deployment of Provincial Reconstruction Teams] has been a tremendous success in the course of 2007." Retrieved online at http://iraq.usembassy.gov/pr_01102008b.html.

137. Robinson, *Tell Me How This Ends*, 324–25. For Mansoor's more complete account, see *Surge*, chap. 8, "Power Politics."

138. Mansoor describes Sadi Othman's role in multiple contexts. He summarizes, "Sadi was a key adviser throughout General Petraeus' time in Iraq. . . . As General Petraeus' alter ego, he was constantly on the phones with Iraqi interlocutors at all hours of the day and night. He would convey messages from General Petraeus and relay messages to him in return. The Iraqis trusted Sadi, trust that went a long way in enhancing General Petraeus' relations with his Iraqi counterparts." Mansoor, *Surge*, 229.

139. Robinson, *Tell Me How This Ends*, 331–35.

140. Robinson, *Tell Me How This Ends*, 345ff.

141. Kaplan, *Insurgents*, 4, passim.

142. Gentile, *Wrong Turn*, 110, 132.

143. Gentile, *Wrong Turn*, 140.

144. Michael E. O'Hanlon and Ian Livingston, *Iraq Index: Tracking Variables of Reconstruction & Security in Post-Saddam Iraq* (Washington, DC: Brookings Institution, November 30, 2011), 3, 23, 24. The *New York Times* in mid-2012 reported a 20 percent jump in Iraqi oil production with exports of nearly 2.5 million bbls per day. Tim Arango and Clifford Krauss, "Oil Output Soars as Iraq Retools," *New York Times*, June 3, 2012, 1.

145. "Now Please Go," *The Economist*, October 29, 2011, 59–61.

146. *New York Times*, January 15, 2012, 1, http://www.nytimes.com/2012/01/16/world/middleeast/asserting-its-sovereignty-iraq-detains-american-contractors.html?ref=todays paper&pagewanted=print. Additional reporting a month later would indicate that the military vs. contractor numbers were also changing in Afghanistan. By January 2012, there were 113,491 employees of defense contractors in Afghanistan, compared with about 90,000 American soldiers, according to Defense and Labor Department statistics; http://www.acq .osd.mil/log/PS/CENTCOM_reports.html. Between 2001 and 2017, 6,750 American troops were killed in Iraq (4,400) and Afghanistan (2,350); at least 3,200 contractors died over the same period in Iraq and Afghanistan. Defense Base Act Summary by Nation, Office of Workers' Compensation Programs, Department of Labor (Washington, DC, March 31, 2017), https://www.dol.gov/owcp/dlhwc/dbaallnation.htm#content.

147. Commission on Wartime Contracting in Iraq and Afghanistan, *Transforming Wartime Contracting: Controlling Costs, Reducing Risks* (Arlington, VA: Commission on Wartime Contracting, August 2011), 200, fig. E-1; 202; and 205, figs. E-3 and E-5. A very small number of contractors (1 percent) were engaged in training, and another 16 percent were engaged in security tasks by mid-2011; the remaining 83 percent were engaged in communication support, transportation, translation, construction, and base support. There were nearly one hundred thousand contractors in Afghanistan by mid-2011.

148. Andrew Erdman, "How Militaries Learn and Adapt: An Interview with Major General H. R. McMaster," *McKinsey on Defense*, no. 8 (McKinsey & Company, April 2013), http://www.mckinsey.com/insights/public_sector/how_militaries_learn_and_adapt.

149. Elisabeth Bumiller, "West Point Is Divided on a War Doctrine's Fate," *New York Times*, May 27, 2012, 1.

CHAPTER 28. IRAQI WAR V, THE RISE OF ISIS

1. Frederick W. Kagan, Kimberly Kagan, and Marisa C. Sullivan, "Defeat in Iraq: President Obama's Decision to Withdraw U.S. Troops Is the Mother of All Disasters," *Weekly Standard* 17, no. 8 (November 7, 2011); Tim Arango, "Iran Dominates in Iraq after U.S. Opened Door, Projecting Economic and Military Influence in One-Time American Foothold," *New York Times*, July 16, 2017, 1.

2. Joel Rayburn, *Iraq after America: Strongmen, Sectarians, Resistance* (Stanford, CA: Hoover Institution Press, 2014), 243.

3. Iraqi government forces recaptured Tikrit on April 17, 2015; Ramadi on February 9, 2016; Fallujah on June 28, 2016; and Mosul on July 9, 2017. However, all these cities sustained extensive damage, many residents fled during the fighting, and cleanup and bomb and IED defusing operations continue to the present day.

4. Written around 2004, *The Management of Savagery* evolved out of the al Qa'ida in Iraq (AQI) strategy developed by Abu Musab al-Zarqawi, the AQI leader anointed by Osama bin Laden in 2003 who was killed by CENTCOM forces in Iraq in 2006. Its author, an anonymous jihadi ideologue, also added Abu Bakr to his name, Abu Bakr Naji. Alastair Crooke, a British diplomat and former MI6 intelligence officer, explained that, like the communist people's war tracts in Southeast Asia, the document defines three stages: (1) conduct "vexation operations" in Syria and the northern Euphrates valley, (2) create a "fighting society," and (3) consolidate people and territory into a caliphate. Alastair Crooke, "The ISIS' 'Management of Savagery' in Iraq," *Huffington Post*, June 30, 2014, updated August 30, 2014, http://www.huffingtonpost.com/alastair-crooke/iraq-isis-alqaeda_b_5542575.html. Also see Abu Bakr Naji, *The Management of Savagery: The Most Critical Stage through Which the Ummah Will Pass* [Idārat at-Tawahhush: Akhtar marhalah satamourrou bihalummah] (Cambridge, MA: Institute for Strategic Studies, Harvard University, May 2006), https://azelin.files.wordpress.com/2010/08/abu-bakr-naji-the-management-of-savagery-the-most-critical-stage-through-which-the-umma-will-pass.pdf.

5. Michael Weiss and Hassan Hassan, *ISIS: Inside the Army of Terror* (New York: Regan Arts, 2015), chap. 4. "Ideological DNA" quote, widely repeated on blogs, originated with Hassan.

6. Charles C. Caris and Samuel Reynolds, "ISIS Governance in Syria" (online monograph, Middle East Security Report 22, Institute for the Study of War, Washington, DC, September 2014), 4, http://www.understandingwar.org/sites/default/files/ISIS_Governance.pdf.

7. Karen Leigh (Syria Deeply), "ISIS Makes Up to $3 Million a Day Selling Oil, Say Analysts," ABC News, http://abcnews.go.com/International/isis-makes-million-day-selling-oil-analysts/story?id=24814359; and Richard Barrett, "The Islamic State" (monograph, Soufan Group, New York, NY, November 2014), 47–48, http://soufangroup.com/wp-content/uploads/2014/10/TSG-The-Islamic-State-Nov14.pdf.

8. Barrett, "The Islamic State," 37–38.

9. Kimberly Kagan, Frederick W. Kagan, and Jessica D. Lewis, "A Strategy to Defeat the Islamic State" (monograph, Middle East Security Report 23, Institute for the Study of War, Washington, DC, September 2014), 5, http://www.understandingwar.org/report/strategy-defeat-islamic-state.

10. "Statement by the President on ISIL [Islamic State of Iraq and the Levant]," http://www.whitehouse.gov/the-press-office/2014/09/10/remarks-president-barack-obama-address-nation.

11. Tim Arango, "U.S. Planning to Slash Iraq Embassy Staff by as Much as Half," *New York Times*, February 8, 2012, 1; and Arango, "U.S. May Scrap Costly Efforts to Train Iraqi Police," *New York Times*, May 13, 2012, 1.

12. Siobhan Gorman and Adam Entous, "CIA Prepares Iraq Pullback: U.S. Presence Has Grown Contentious; Backers Favor Focus on Terror Hot Spots," *Wall Street Journal*, June 5, 2012, 1.

13. Emma Sky, *The Unraveling: High Hopes and Missed Opportunities in Iraq* (New York: PublicAffairs, 2015), 312.

14. *Leading through Civilian Power: The First Quadrennial Diplomacy and Development Review* (Washington, DC: US Department of State and US Agency for International Development, 2010), 123–24, http://www.state.gov/documents/organization/153142.pdf.

15. The website of the Bureau of Conflict and Stabilization Operations (CSO) does not indicate the size of its budget, the number of its personnel, or offer much specificity about its assigned mission. Its first sentence reads, "The [CSO] is a vital part of the ambitious U.S. effort to be more effective in helping prevent conflict and supporting post-conflict nations recover." In 2012, it reported that it focused 80 percent of its effort on Burma, Honduras,

Kenya, and Syria. No mention was made of Iraq or Afghanistan. The current website is less informative: http://www.state.gov/j/cso/index.htm. The State Department's FY 2011 Agency Financial Report made no mention of the CSO bureau. Department of State, *Leadership in a Time of Change* (Washington, DC: US Department of State Publication, November 2011); it is no longer available online.

16. Department of State, *Congressional Budget Justification*, vol. 1, *Department of State Operations, Fiscal Year 2012* (Washington, DC: Department of State, February 2011), 22, 115, 355, 450.

17. Kori N. Schake, *State of Disrepair: Fixing the Culture and Practices of the State Department* (Stanford, CA: Hoover Institution Press, 2012), 38, passim.

18. Rajiv Chandrasekaran, "In Afghanistan's Garmser District, Praise for a U.S. Official's Tireless Work," *Washington Post*, August 13, 2011. The article described Malkasian's background and preparation for his assignment to Garmser. He had earned a doctorate in the history of war at Oxford. His dissertation focused on the Korean and Vietnam conflicts and why, as Malkasian put it to the *Washington Post*, "people fight long, grueling wars." Most important, he had learned to speak Pashto, the language of southern Afghanistan. Malkasian conversed fluently, engaging in rapid-fire exchanges with tribal elders. Also see Chandrasekaran, *Little America: The War within the War for Afghanistan* (New York: Knopf, 2012), 184, passim.

19. "Afghanistan," in *The World Factbook* (Washington, DC: CIA, November 21, 2016), https://www.cia.gov/library/publications/the-world-factbook/geos/af.html; and "Iraq," in *The World Factbook* (Washington, DC: CIA, November 21, 2016), https://www.cia.gov/library/publications/the-world-factbook/geos/iz.html.

20. Carter Malkasian, *War Comes to Garmser: Thirty Years of Conflict on the Afghan Frontier* (Oxford: Oxford University Press, 2013), 268–69.

21. For an incisive analysis of State's operational model, the inadequacy of the QDRR, and how to rebuild USAID, see Schake, *State of Disrepair*, 43–60, 72–77, chap. 4.

22. Schake, *State of Disrepair*, 47–48.

23. Reuel Marc Gerecht, a former Farsi-speaking intelligence officer, published a trenchant op-ed in 2006 in the *Wall Street Journal*:

> The CIA has stubbornly refused to move away from stations and bases within official facilities overseas, where most American operatives pose as fake diplomats. . . . This official-cover deployment, combined with a promotion system premised overwhelmingly on a "head-count" of "recruited" agents, had atrociously poor results during the Cold War, producing hundreds of assets on the books with no real intelligence value, except as means for case-officer advancement and cash performance awards. Foreign intelligence services, if minimally competent, can identify and track these officers when they choose to focus their surveillance resources, which has happened much more frequently since the end of the Cold War. It is simply absurd to believe that these officially covered operatives, who still represent a preponderant majority of case officers stationed overseas, have much value against an Islamic terrorist target or any hard target protected by a competent counterespionage service. (Reuel Marc Gerecht, "Intelligence Deficit Disorder," *Wall Street Journal*, May 9, 2006)

Peritz and Rosenbach observed that in 1995 the FBI had more special agents in New York City than the CIA had case officers worldwide. Aki Peritz and Eric Rosenbach, *Find, Fix, and Finish: Inside the Counterterrorism Campaigns That Killed bin Laden and Devastated al Qa'ida* (New York: PublicAffairs, 2012), 23–24.

24. Department of Defense, *Sustaining U.S. Global Leadership: Priorities for 21st Century Defense* (Washington, DC: Department of Defense, January 2012), 6, http://www.defense.gov/news/Defense_Strategic_Guidance.pdf.

25. Charles Hill, a retired career Foreign Service officer, observed six months later in a *Wall Street Journal* interview,

What amazes Mr. Hill is how much of a break the Obama foreign policy represents compared with the bipartisan consensus stretching back to Truman. That culminated in President George W. Bush's second inaugural address, which he likens to an "emancipation proclamation for the world." But, he says, "The democracy wave that began twenty years ago [at the end of the Cold War] is now turning backward." Why? "The conduct of the Obama administration." . . . The message remains dead serious. The "battle" for liberal democracy and some semblance of international order "has been being won because the U.S. has been putting out the effort for it," he says. "And now we're not." (Robert L. Pollock, "The Empire Strikes Back," *Wall Street Journal*, July 28–29, 2012, A15)

26. Relevant Obama excerpts included the following:

Here's my bottom line: America must always lead on the world stage. If we don't, no one else will. The military that you have joined is, and always will be, the backbone of that leadership. But U.S. military action cannot be the only, or even primary, component of our leadership in every instance. Just because we have the best hammer does not mean that every problem is a nail. . . . First, let me repeat a principle I put forward at the outset of my presidency: The United States will use military force, unilaterally if necessary, when our core interests demand it: when our people are threatened; when our livelihoods are at stake; when the security of our allies is in danger. . . . In these circumstances, we still need to ask tough questions about whether our actions are proportional and effective and just. International opinion matters, but America should never ask permission to protect our people, our homeland or our way of life. (*New York Times*, "Transcript of President Obama's Commencement Address at West Point," May 28, 2014, http://www.nytimes.com/2014/05/29/us/politics/transcript-of-president-obamas-commencement-address-at-west-point.html)

CHAPTER 29. THE STRATEGIC ARCHITECTURES OF THE IRAQI WARS

1. *Frontline*, show 1408T, aired February 4, 1997, http://www.pbs.org/wgbh/pages/front line/gulf/script_b.html. Two years later, President Bush and General Scowcroft wrote that they had considered forcing Saddam personally to accept the terms of the Iraqi defeat at Safwan. They concluded that the risk of Saddam refusing was too great because if he refused, they were faced with two unpalatable options: "continue the conflict until he backed down or retreat from our demands." George H. W. Bush and Brent Scowcroft, *A World Transformed* (New York: Vintage, 1999), 489–90.

2. Mansoor years later made this observation about Rumsfeld's emphasis on small military footprints, RMA, net-centric warfare, and technology: "Defense Secretary Rumsfeld viewed Afghanistan and Iraq as laboratories in which to validate [these concepts]. But advanced sensors and precision-guided munitions are tactical and operational capabilities—they are not a strategy." Mansoor, *Surge*, 274.

3. Mansoor, *Surge*, 69.

4. Kagan et al., "Defeat in Iraq"; Kagan et al., "Is Iraq Lost?," *Weekly Standard* 17, no. 16 (January 9, 2012); Kagan et al., "Losing Iraq: We Face a Strategic Debacle," *National Review* 64, no. 19 (October 15, 2012); and Kagan, "Iraq War Is Not Over," *Weekly Standard* 18, no. 40 (July 1, 2013).

5. The Kagans argued that requiring Iraqi parliamentary approval was an unnecessary formality because the United States has negotiated status-of-forces agreements with other countries without parliamentary approval. For a review of the SOFA issue, see R. Chuck Mason, *U.S.-Iraq Withdrawal/Status of Forces Agreement: Issues for Congressional Oversight*, R40011 (Washington, DC: Congressional Research Service, July 13, 2009), 4–5, 10, http://www.fas.org/sgp/crs/natsec/R40011.pdf.

6. During the 2008 campaign, then presidential candidate Obama "campaigned on the basis of Afghanistan being the 'good war' and needing reinforcements." Council on Foreign Relations (CFR) interview of Stephen Biddle, CFR senior fellow, by Roger Hertog, senior fellow for defense policy, http://www.cfr.org/afghanistan/ending-afghan-war/p27668.

7. In a speech to the Veterans of Foreign Wars on August 18, 2009, in Phoenix, President Obama said about Afghanistan, "This is not a war of choice. This is a war of necessity." Reported in the *Los Angeles Times*, http://articles.latimes.com/2009/aug/18/nation/na-obama-vfw18.

8. National Public Radio transcript of the remarks by then state senator Obama delivered on October 2, 2002, at Federal Plaza in Chicago, http://www.npr.org/templates/story/story.php?storyId=99591469.

9. Scott Keeler, "Trends in Public Opinion about the War in Iraq, 2003–2007" (online monograph, Pew Research Center, Washington, DC, March 15, 2007), http://pewresearch.org/pubs/431/trends-in-public-opinion-about-the-war-in-iraq-2003-2007.

10. Cable News Network (CNN)/Opinion Research Corporation (ORC) Poll, November 18–20, 2011, 9, http://i2.cdn.turner.com/cnn/2011/images/11/22/rel19c.pdf; polling results based on a sample taken on November 18–20, 2011, N = 1,019 adults nationwide, with margin of error of ± 3 percent.

11. Michael R. Gordon, "Failed Efforts and Challenges of America's Last Months in Iraq," *New York Times*, September 23, 2012, 1.

12. Retrospectively, Mansoor evaluated the surge and describes its aftermath this way:

> Because the surge succeeded, the competition for power and resources in Iraq moved into the political realm, underpinned by the new distribution of power in Baghdad. Consolidation of the gains made during the surge, however, required a long-term commitment by the United States to stability in Iraq and a deft handling of the diplomacy and politics required to moderate the sectarian instincts of many in the Iraqi government. This commitment regrettably has not been forthcoming. . . . The new [Obama] administration in Washington saw the withdrawal of U.S. forces from Iraq as the fulfillment of a campaign promise to its domestic base, so it acquiesced in the withdrawal of U.S. forces from Iraq at the end of 2011 without protest. When the last U.S. troops departed at the end of 2011, the United States lost much of its leverage with the Iraqi government, and Iraq lost the one force in the country that for nine years had tried to keep a lid on sectarian bloodletting. (Mansoor, *Surge*, 271–72)

On the definition, purpose, and scope of "whole-of-government" operations, see Schake, *State of Disrepair*, 5–6, passim.

13. In June 2014, the Obama administration accepted an immunity agreement in the form of a "diplomatic note" from the Iraqi government of Nouri al-Maliki so that three hundred special operations troops could be sent to Iraq to help combat the growing Islamic State of Iraq and Syria (ISIS) insurgency. It did so without the formality of a SOFA. Peter Baker, "Diplomatic Note Promises Immunity from Iraqi Law for U.S. Advisory Troops," *New York Times*, June 24, 2014. Schake's explanation of the Obama administration's SOFA failure is more direct: "The Obama administration refused the Maliki government assurances [of immunity from Iraqi law for US troops], insisting instead on approval from the

Iraqi parliament. In doing so, it succeeded in raising the bar high enough that there would be no renegotiation of the agreement to allow U.S. military forces to remain in Iraq past 2011." Schake, *State of Disrepair*, 54.

14. In 2012, Iraq's crude oil production averaged 2.98 million barrels per day (bbl/d), almost 25 percent above 2008 levels, and above its prewar production capacity level of 2.8 million bbl/d in 2003. US Energy Information Administration, Independent Statistics and Analysis, http://www.eia.gov/countries/country-data.cfm?fips=iz. The International Energy Agency (IEA) projected in its "Central Scenario" in 2012 that Iraq's oil production would more than double to six million bbl/d by 2020 and reach 8.3 million bbl/d by 2035. "Iraq Energy Outlook, Executive Summary," Paris, International Energy Agency (November 12, 2013), http://www.iea.org/publications/freepublications/publication/weoiraqexcerptsum maryWEB-1.pdf. A June 2014 IEA update revised upward the 2035 projection to nine million bbl/d, noting that "in the long term Iraq is set to become one of the main pillars of global oil export and will become the largest contributor to global oil export growth . . . surpassing Saudi Arabia as the region's largest exporter." IEA, "World Energy Investment Outlook, Special Report" (Paris: IEA, June 3, 2014), 68, http://www.iea.org/publications/freepublications/publication/WEIO2014.pdf.

15. *New York Times* and *Wall Street Journal*, March 20, 2013.

16. Excerpt from Ambassador Crocker's April 2008 congressional testimony. Two years later, Crocker explained why the United States needs to remain engaged with Iraq if it wants to leave behind an inclusive, effective representative government: "The Shia are afraid of the past—that a Sunni dictatorship will reassert itself. The Sunnis are afraid of the future—an Iraq in which they are no longer ascendant. And the Kurds, with their history of suffering, are afraid of both the past and the future." Ryan Crocker, "Dreams of Babylon," *National Interest*, July–August 2010, http://nationalinterest.org/print/article/dreams-of-babylon-3541.

17. Henry A. Kissinger, testimony before the US Senate Armed Services Committee, "Global Challenges and the U.S. National Security Strategy," January 29, 2015, http://www.c-span.org/video/?323996-1/hearing-national-security-strategy.

PART VI: STRATEGIC ARCHITECTURES

1. Patrick Cockburn, *The Rise of Islamic State: ISIS and the New Sunni Revolution* (London: Verso, 2015), preface in Kindle edition.

2. James Q. Whitman, *The Verdict of Battle: The Law of Victory and the Making of Modern War* (Cambridge, MA: Harvard University Press, 2012), 260.

3. Lord's seminal study of American intervention reveals a deep history of presidential appointments of "proconsuls" during and after conflicts. He characterizes proconsular rule as the "delegated political military leadership that rises in the best case to statesmanship." Presidents over the last century have appointed "proconsuls" to achieve "unity of command in the field." Their record of achievement is mixed, but Lord judges the balance sheet to be "respectable." Lord opens *Proconsuls* with the vocabulary of empire. While denying that the United States is operating an empire, he uses the term *proconsular leadership* to describe and assess American "imperial governance," defined in its broadest and most positive sense as "the best way to deal with international troublemakers and failed states." The last sentence of *Proconsuls* is telling: "Suffice it to say that proconsular leadership, which so plainly offers dangers as well as opportunity, is an instrument in need of adult supervision at the imperial center." Lord, *Proconsuls*, 3–5, 9, 230–31, 239.

4. Barnett defines the System Administrator Army as "the 'second half' blended force that wages peace after the Leviathan force has successfully waged war." Operationally, the SysAdmin force would be staffed with civil security and law enforcement personnel, as well as civilian personnel with expertise in rebuilding networks, infrastructure, and social and political institutions. "While the core security and logistical capabilities are derived from uniformed military components, the SysAdmin force is fundamentally envisioned as a standing capacity for interagency . . . and international collaboration in nation-building." Thomas P. M. Barnett, *Blueprint for Action: A Future Worth Creating* (New York: Putnam, 2005), xix.

5. *Bandwagoning* refers to weaker states joining a stronger power or coalition within a balance-of-power or collective-security arrangement in international politics. The term was coined by Philip Quincy Wright in *A Study of War* (Chicago: University of Chicago Press, 1942) and popularized by Kenneth N. Waltz, *Theory of International Politics* (New York: McGraw-Hill, 1979).

6. Thomas P. M. Barnett, *The Pentagon's New Map: War and Peace in the Twenty-First Century* (New York: Putnam, 2004), 315.

7. Nye coined the phrase *soft power* in 1990. Joseph S. Nye Jr., *Bound to Lead: The Changing Nature of American Power* (New York: Basic Books, 1990). He developed the concept in *Soft Power: The Means to Success in World Politics* (New York: PublicAffairs, 2004). Kagan explained the shift in European interest from hard to soft power in Robert Kagan, *Of Paradise and Power: America and Europe in the New World Order* (New York: Knopf, 2003), 33, 37, 65. One US air force colonel, a decorated (Bronze Star) Vietnam veteran, after he read this part of the text wrote to the author, "There is no such thing as soft power; there is just strength or weakness." Robert V. Schwartz, Colonel, USAF (Ret.), in email to the author on July 26, 2012.

8. Kilcullen uses the phrase "global CORDS" in *Counterinsurgency*, 217; also see Gentile, *Wrong Turn*, 115, passim.

9. Lord, *Proconsuls*, 234ff, 236.

10. Nadia Schadlow, *War and the Art of Governance: Consolidating Combat Success into Political Victory* (Washington, DC: Georgetown University Press, 2017), 15.

11. Gates's memoirs recounted President Obama's "AfPak" strategy speech on April 27, 2009, calling for a "dramatic increase in the U.S. civilian effort—agricultural specialists, educators, engineers, and lawyers—to advance security, opportunity, and justice" in Afghanistan. In early May, neither State nor other federal agencies could provide the hundreds of civilian experts needed at the provincial and district levels in Afghanistan. Gates told State and the NSS (National Security Staff) that he was "prepared to provide several hundred civilian experts from Defense and from the military reserve to fill vacancies. State did not respond to the offer. Gates urged Ambassador Holbrooke and USAID officials to reach out to universities and offer to help. "There wasn't any interest at State or AID." Gates, *Memoirs*, 343, 347–48. For a discussion of security with a "lighter footprint," see Rufus Phillips, "Fostering Positive Political Change: The Key to Stabilizing Vulnerable States" (working paper, National Strategy Information Center, Washington, DC, 2013).

12. President Obama asked General Petraeus to serve as commander, International Security Assistance Force (ISAF), Afghanistan, and commander, US Forces Afghanistan (USFOR-A), between July 4, 2010, and July 18, 2011. General Stanley A. McChrystal, who had been commander ISAF, was removed by President Obama over controversial remarks to a journalist reported in *Rolling Stone*. General Petraeus at the time was his boss commanding CENTCOM. Petraeus agreed to a step down from CENTCOM to ISAF, at Obama's behest, to succeed McChrystal. Obama asked Ambassador Crocker to return to

the diplomatic service from private life to serve as the US ambassador to Afghanistan for two years from July 2011 to July 2013. His nomination in April 2011 and Senate confirmation in June 2011 allowed some collaboration with Petraeus, but this brief overlap did not afford the same intensity as their partnership in Iraq during the surge.

13. David Kilcullen, *Out of the Mountains: The Coming Age of the Urban Guerrilla* (New York: Oxford University Press, 2013), 28; 30n28; 52, passim; 112.

14. Casualty data (killed in action and other nonhostile deaths) computed from official and secondary sources for World War II, Korea, Vietnam, and Iraq. For a single-point source for casualties during World War II (405,399), Korea (36,574), Vietnam (58,220), and Iraqi War I (383), see Nese F. DeBruyne and Anne Leland, *American War and Military Operations Casualties: Lists and Statistics*, CRS 7-5700 (Washington, DC: Congressional Research Service, January 2015), http://www.fas.org/sgp/crs/natsec/RL32492.pdf.

For Iraqi War III and War IV casualties and Afghanistan, see Michael O'Hanlon and Ian S. Livingston, "Brookings Index, Tracking Variables of Reconstruction and Security," https://www.brookings.edu/wp-content/uploads/2016/07/index20130726.pdf for Iraq (January 31, 2012): 4,487 US military deaths; and Ian S. Livingston and Michael O'Hanlon, "Afghanistan Index," https://www.brookings.edu/wp-content/uploads/2016/07/21csi_20161031_afghanistan_index.pdf for Afghanistan (October 31, 2016): 2,383 US military deaths.

SELECTED BIBLIOGRAPHY

STRATEGIC ARCHITECTURES: INTRODUCTION AND WORLD WAR II

Alexander, Bevin. *How Hitler Could Have Won World War II: The Fatal Errors That Led to Nazi Defeat*. New York: Crown, 2000.

———. *How Wars Are Won: The 13 Rules of War—from Ancient Greece to the War on Terror*. New York: Crown, 2002.

Atkinson, Rick. *An Army at Dawn: The War in North Africa, 1942–1943*. New York: Henry Holt, 2002.

———. *The Day of Battle: The War in Sicily and Italy, 1943–1944*. New York: Henry Holt, 2007.

———. *The Guns at Last Light: The War in Western Europe, 1944–1945*. New York: Henry Holt, 2013.

Beevor, Anthony. *D-Day: The Battle for Normandy*. New York: Viking, 2009.

Bungay, Stephen. *The Most Dangerous Enemy*. London: Aurum, 2000.

Burleigh, Michael. *The Third Reich: A New History*. New York: Hill and Wang, 2000.

Caddick-Adams, Peter. *Monte Cassino: Ten Armies in Hell*. Oxford: Oxford University Press, 2013.

———. *Snow and Steel: The Battle of the Bulge, 1944–45*. Oxford: Oxford University Press, 2015.

Carter, Kit C., and Robert Mueller. *The Army Air Forces in World War II: Combat Chronology, 1941–1945*. New York: Arno, 1980.

Citino, Robert M. *Death of the Wehrmacht: The German Campaigns of 1942*. Lawrence: University Press of Kansas, 2007.

Cohen, Eliot A. *Supreme Command: Soldiers, Statesmen and Leadership in Wartime*. New York: Free Press, 2002.

Cole, Hugh M. *United States Army in World War II: European Theater of Operations; The Ardennes: The Battle of the Bulge*. 1965. 50th anniversary paperback ed. Washington, DC: US Army Center of Military History, 2009. http://www.history.army.mil/books/wwii/7-8/7-8_7.htm.

Cowley, Robert, ed. *No End Save Victory*. New York: Putnam, 2001.

Crane, Conrad C. *Bombs, Cities, and Civilians: American Airpower Strategy in World War II*. Lawrence: University Press of Kansas, 1993.

Deighton, Len. *Blood, Tears and Folly: An Objective Look at World War Two*. New York: HarperCollins, 1993.

Dunn, Walter S., Jr. *Stalin's Keys to Victory: The Rebirth of the Red Army in World War II*. Westport, CT: Praeger Security International, 2006.

Eilam, Eldad. *Reversing: Secrets of Reverse Engineering*. Indianapolis, IN: Wiley, 2005.

Evans, Richard J. *The Third Reich at War*. New York: Penguin, 2008.

Frank, Richard B. *Downfall: The End of the Imperial Japanese Empire*. New York: Penguin, 1999.

Fussell, Paul. *Thank God for the Atom Bomb and Other Essays*. New York: Summit Books, 1988.

Glantz, David M. *Colossus Reborn: The Red Army at War, 1941–1943*. Lawrence: University Press of Kansas, 2005.

Hansen, Randall. *Fire and Fury: The Allied Bombing of Germany, 1942–1945*. New York: New American Library, 2009.

Hanson, Victor Davis. *Ripples of Battle: How Wars of the Past Still Determine How We Fight, How We Live, and How We Think*. New York: Doubleday, 2003.

———. *The Savior Generals: How Five Great Commanders Saved Wars That Were Lost—from Ancient Greece to Iraq*. New York: Bloomsbury, 2013.

———. *The Second World Wars*. New York: Basic Books, 2017.

Hastings, Max. *Armageddon: The Battle for Germany, 1944–1945*. New York: Knopf, 2004.

———. *Retribution: The Battle for Japan, 1944–45*. New York: Knopf, 2008.

———. *The Secret War: Spies, Ciphers, and Guerrillas, 1939–1945*. New York: Harper, 2016.

———. *Winston's War: Churchill, 1940–1945*. New York: Knopf, 2010.

Holland, James. *The Battle of Britain: Five Months That Changed History, May–October 1940*. London: Bantam, 2010.

Hornfischer, James D. *Neptune's Inferno: The U.S. Navy at Guadalcanal*. New York: Bantam, 2011.

Hotta, Eri. *Japan 1941: Countdown to Infamy*. New York: Knopf, 2013.

Howard, Michael. *War in European History*. 1976. Updated ed. Oxford: Oxford University Press, 2009.

Ireland, Bernard. *Battle of the Atlantic*. Annapolis, MD: Naval Institute Press, 2003.

Isom, Dallas W. *Midway Inquest: Why the Japanese Lost the Battle of Midway*. Bloomington: Indiana University Press, 2007.

Judt, Tony. *Postwar: A History of Europe since 1945*. New York: Penguin, 2005.

Kagan, Frederick W. *Finding the Target: The Transformation of American Military Policy*. New York: Encounter Books, 2006.

Kahn, David. *The Code Breakers: The Comprehensive History of Secret Communications from Ancient Times to the Internet*. Rev. and updated ed. New York: Scribner, 1996.

Keegan, John. *Intelligence in War*. New York: Knopf, 2003.

———. *The Second World War*. New York: Penguin, 1990.

Kennedy, Paul. *Engineers of Victory: The Problem Solvers Who Turned the Tide in the Second World War*. New York: Random House, 2013.

Kershaw, Ian. *The End: The Defiance and Destruction of Hitler's Germany, 1944–1945.* New York: Penguin, 2011.

———. *Fateful Choices: Ten Decisions That Changed the World, 1940–1941.* New York: Penguin, 2007.

Latimer, Jon. *Alamein.* Cambridge, MA: Harvard University Press, 2002.

Lewis, Adrian R. *The American Culture of War: The History of U.S. Military Force from World War II to Operation Enduring Freedom.* New York: Routledge, 2012.

Lewis, John D. *Nothing Less than Victory: Decisive Wars and the Lessons of History.* Princeton, NJ: Princeton University Press, 2010.

Linn, Brian A. *The Echo of Battle: The Army's Way of War.* Cambridge, MA: Harvard University Press, 2007.

Macgregor, Douglas A. *Breaking the Phalanx: A New Design for Landpower in the 21st Century.* Westport, CT: Praeger, 1997.

Manchester, William. *Goodbye Darkness: A Memoir of the Pacific War.* Boston: Little, Brown, 1979.

Mansoor, Peter R. *The GI Offensive in Europe: The Triumph of American Infantry Divisions, 1941–1945.* Lawrence: University Press of Kansas, 1999.

Marston, Daniel, ed. *The Pacific War: From Pearl Harbor to Hiroshima.* Paperback ed. Oxford: Osprey, 2010.

McNeilly, Mark. *Sun Tzu and the Art of Modern Warfare.* New York: Oxford University Press, 2001.

Murray, Williamson, and Allen R. Millett. *A War to Be Won: Fighting the Second World War.* Cambridge, MA: Harvard University Press, 2000.

Neillands, Robin. *The Battle for the Rhine.* Woodstock: Overlook Press, 2005.

Offley, Edward. *Turning the Tide: How a Small Band of Allied Sailors Defeated the U-boats and Won the Battle of the Atlantic.* New York: Basic Books, 2011.

Overy, Richard. *Why the Allies Won.* London: Pimlico, 1995.

Parshall, Jonathan, and Anthony Tully. *Shattered Sword: The Untold Story of the Battle of Midway.* Washington, DC: Potomac, 2007.

Perry, Mark. *Partners in Command: George Marshall and Dwight Eisenhower in War and Peace.* New York: Penguin, 2007.

Plokhy, Serhii M. *Yalta: The Price of Peace.* New York: Viking, 2010.

Prados, John. *Normandy Crucible: The Decisive Battle That Shaped World War II in Europe.* New York: Nal Caliber, 2011.

Reynolds, David. *Summits: Six Meetings That Shaped the Twentieth Century.* New York: Basic Books, 2007.

Ricks, Thomas E. *The Generals: American Military Command from World War II to Today.* New York: Penguin, 2012.

Roberts, Andrew. *The Storm of War: A New History of the Second World War.* London: Allen Lane, 2009.

Rose, Gideon. *How Wars End: Why We Always Fight the Last Battle.* New York: Simon & Schuster, 2010.

Sledge, Eugene B. *With the Old Breed: At Peleliu and Okinawa.* New York: Oxford University Press, 1990. First published by Presidio (New York), 1981.

Snyder, Timothy. *Bloodlands: Europe between Hitler and Stalin.* New York: Basic Books, 2010.

Speer, Albert. *Inside the Third Reich: Memoirs.* New York: Macmillan, 1970.

Steil, Benn. *The Marshall Plan: Dawn of the Cold War.* New York: Simon & Schuster, 2017.

Sumida, Jon Tetsuro. *Decoding Clausewitz: A New Approach to "On War."* Lawrence: University Press of Kansas, 2008.

Sun Tzu. *The Art of War.* Translated by Lionel Giles. Lexington, KY: BN Publishing, 2007.

Taafe, Stephen B. *Marshall and His Generals: U.S. Army Commanders in World War II.* Lawrence: University Press of Kansas, 2011.

Tooze, Adam. *The Wages of Destruction: The Making and Breaking of the Nazi Economy.* New York: Viking, 2006.

Van Creveld, Martin. *The Age of Airpower.* New York: PublicAffairs, 2011.

———. *Supplying War: Logistics from Wallenstein to Patton.* Cambridge: Cambridge University Press, 1977.

Wieviorka, Olivier. *Normandy: The Landings to the Liberation of Paris.* Translated by M. B. DeBevoise. Cambridge, MA: Harvard University Press, 2008.

Willmott, H. P. *The Great Crusade: A New Complete History of the Second World War.* Rev. ed. Washington, DC: Potomac, 2008.

THE KOREAN WAR

Aid, Matthew M. *The Secret Sentry: The Untold Story of the National Security Agency.* New York: Bloomsbury, 2009.

Alexander, Bevin. *Korea: The First War We Lost.* New York: Hippocrene, 2003.

Appleman, Roy E. *South to the Naktong, North to the Yalu, June–November 1950.* Washington, DC: US Army Center of Military History, US Government Printing Office, 1992. http://www.history.army.mil/books/korea/20-2-1/toc.htm.

Chen Jian. *China's Road to the Korean War: The Making of the Sino-American Confrontation.* New York: Columbia University Press, 1994.

Cohen, Eliot A., and John Gooch. *Military Misfortunes: The Anatomy of Failure in War.* New York: Free Press, 1990.

Cumings, Bruce. *The Korean War: A History.* New York: Random House, 2010.

Eberstadt, Nicholas. *The North Korean Economy: Between Crisis and Catastrophe.* New Brunswick, NJ: Transaction Publishers, 2007.

Fehrenbach, T. R. *This Kind of War: The Classic Korean War History.* 50th anniversary ed. Washington, DC: Potomac, 2001.

Gaddis, John Lewis. *The Cold War: A New History.* New York: Penguin, 2005.

Griffith, Samuel B. *The Chinese People's Liberation Army.* New York: McGraw-Hill, 1967.

Halberstam, David. *The Coldest Winter: America and the Korean War.* New York: Hyperion, 2007.

Hastings, Max. *The Korean War.* New York: Simon & Schuster, 1987.

Leckie, Robert. *Conflict: The History of the Korean War, 1950–1953.* New York: Avon, 1962.

Malkasian, Carter. *The Korean War, 1950–1953.* Essential Histories Series. 2001. Oxford: Osprey, 2010.

Oberdorfer, Don. *The Two Koreas.* Rev. ed. New York: Basic Books, 2001.

Pearlman, Michael D. *Korean War Anthology, Truman and MacArthur: The Winding Road to Dismissal.* Fort Leavenworth, KA: US Army Command and General Staff College, Combat Studies Institute Press, 2003.

Ridgway, Matthew B. *The Korean War.* Garden City, NY: Doubleday, 1967.

Russ, Martin. *Breakout: The Chosin Reservoir Campaign, Korea, 1950.* New York: Fromm International, 1999.

Stueck, William W. *Rethinking the Korean War: A New Diplomatic and Strategic History*. Princeton, NJ: Princeton University Press, 2004.

Webb, William J. *The Korean War: The Outbreak*. CMH Pub. 19-6. Washington, DC: US Army Center of Military History, 2006.

THE VIETNAM WAR

"The American Experience in Southeast Asia, 1946–1975." Conference conducted at the Department of State, Washington, DC, September 29, 2010. http://history.state.gov/conferences/2010-southeast-asia/ambassador-holbrooke.

Andradé, Dale. *America's Last Vietnam Battle: Halting Hanoi's 1972 Easter Offensive*. 1995. Lawrence: University Press of Kansas, 2001.

Bergurud, Eric M. *The Dynamics of Defeat: The Vietnam War in Hau Nghia Province*. Boulder, CO: Westview, 1993.

Berman, Larry. *Lyndon Johnson's War: The Road to Stalemate in Vietnam*. New York: Norton, 1989.

Birtle, Andrew J. "PROVN, Westmoreland, and the Historians: A Reappraisal." *Journal of Military History* 72 (October 2008): 1213–47. http://viet-studies.info/kinhte/PROVN_Westmoreland.pdf.

———. *U.S. Army Counterinsurgency and Contingency Operations Doctrine, 1942–1976*. CMH Pub. 70-98. Washington, DC: Center of Military History, 2006.

Cash, John A., et al. "Fight at Ia Drang." In *Seven Firefights in Vietnam*. 1970. Washington, DC: Office of the Chief of Military History, US Government Printing Office, 1985. http://www.history.army.mil/books/Vietnam/7-ff/Ch1.htm.

Clutterbuck, Richard L. *Riot and Revolution in Malaya and Singapore*. London, Faber and Faber, 1973.

Corson, William R. *The Betrayal*. New York: Norton, 1968.

Daddis, Gregory A. *No Sure Victory: Measuring U.S. Army Effectiveness and Progress in the Vietnam War*. New York: Oxford University Press, 2011.

Elliott, David W. P. *The Vietnamese War: Revolution and Social Change in the Mekong Delta, 1930–1975*. Vols. 1 and 2. London: M. E. Sharpe, 2003.

Fall, Bernard B. *Hell in a Very Small Place: The Siege of Dien Bien Phu*. Paperback ed. New York: Vintage, 1968.

———. *Street without Joy: From the Indochina War to the War in Vietnam*. 4th ed. Harrisburg, PA: Stackpole, 1967.

Finlayson, Andrew R. *Rice Paddy Recon: A Marine Officer's Second Tour in Vietnam, 1968–1970*. Jefferson, NC: McFarland, 2014.

French, David. *The British Way in Counter-Insurgency, 1945–1967*. Oxford: Oxford University Press, 2011.

Gentile, Gian. *Wrong Turn: America's Deadly Embrace of Counterinsurgency*. New York: New Press, 2013.

Giap, Vo Nguyen. *People's War, People's Army*. New York: Praeger, 1962.

Goldstein, Gordon M. *Lessons in Disaster: McGeorge Bundy and the Path to War in Vietnam*. New York: Henry Holt, 2008.

Goodwin, Doris Kearns. *Lyndon Johnson and the American Dream*. 1976. New York: St. Martin's, 1991.

Halberstam, David. *The Best and the Brightest*. 1969. New York: Ballantine, 1992.

Hannah, Norman B. *The Key to Failure: Laos and the Vietnam War*. New York: Madison, 1987.

Hunt, Richard A. *Pacification: The American Struggle for Vietnam's Hearts and Minds*. Boulder, CO: Westview, 1995.

Jones, Frank L. *Blowtorch: Robert Komer, Vietnam, and American Cold War Strategy*. Annapolis, MD: Naval Institute Press, 2013.

Kimball, Jeffrey. *Nixon's Vietnam War*. Lawrence: University of Kansas Press, 1998.

Kissinger, Henry A. "The Vietnam Negotiations." *Foreign Affairs* 47, no. 2 (January 1969).

Krepinevich, Andrew F., Jr. *The Army and Vietnam*. Baltimore, MD: Johns Hopkins University Press, 1986.

Ky, Nguyen Cao. *Buddha's Child: My Fight to Save South Vietnam*. With Marvin J. Wolf. New York: St. Martin's, 2002.

Logevall, Fredrik. *Embers of War: Fall of an Empire and the Making of America's Vietnam*. New York: Random House, 2012.

McMaster, H. R. *Dereliction of Duty: Lyndon Johnson, Robert McNamara, the Joint Chiefs of Staff, and the Lies That Led to Vietnam*. New York: HarperCollins, 1997.

Miller, Edward. *Misalliance, Ngo Dinh Diem, the United States, and the Fate of South Vietnam*. Cambridge, MA: Harvard University Press, 2013.

Moyar, Mark. *Triumph Forsaken: The Vietnam War, 1954–1965*. New York: Cambridge University Press, 2006.

Nagl, John A. *Learning to Eat Soup with a Knife: Counterinsurgency Lessons from Malaya and Vietnam*. Chicago: University of Chicago Press, 2002.

Nalty, Bernard C. *The War against Trucks: Aerial Interdiction in Southern Laos, 1968–1972*. Washington, DC: US Air Force History and Museums Program, 2005. http://www.scribd.com/doc/1451015/US-Air-Force-WarAgainstTrucks.

Nguyen, Lien-Hang T. *Hanoi's War: An International History of War for Peace in Vietnam*. Chapel Hill: University of North Carolina Press, 2012.

The Pentagon Papers: The Defense Department History of United States Decision-Making on Vietnam. Senator Gravel Edition. Boston: Beacon Press, 1971.

Phillips, Rufus. *Why Vietnam Matters: An Eyewitness Account of Lessons Not Learned*. Annapolis, MD: Naval Institute Press, 2008.

Pike, Douglas. *PAVN: People's Army of Vietnam*. Novato, CA: Presidio, 1986.

Porch, Douglas. *Counterinsurgency: Exposing the Myths of the New Way of War*. Cambridge: Cambridge University Press, 2013.

Pribbenow, Merle L., trans. *Victory in Vietnam: The Official History of the People's Army of Vietnam, 1954–1975*. Foreword by William J. Duiker. Lawrence: University Press of Kansas, 2002.

Race, Jeffrey. *War Comes to Long An: Revolutionary Conflict in a Vietnamese Province*. Berkeley: University of California Press, 1972. Later republished in a 2nd edition. *War Comes to Long An: Revolutionary Conflict in a Vietnamese Province, Updated and Expanded*. Berkeley: University of California Press, 2010.

Sorley, Lewis. *A Better War: The Unexamined Victories and Final Tragedy of America's Last Years in Vietnam*. New York: Harcourt, 1999.

Summers, Harry G., Jr. *On Strategy: A Critical Analysis of the Vietnam War*. Novato, CA: Presidio, 1982.

Taylor, K. W. *A History of the Vietnamese*. Cambridge: Cambridge University Press, 2013.

Thompson, James C. *Rolling Thunder: Understanding Policy and Program Failure*. Chapel Hill: University of North Carolina Press, 1980.

Thompson, Sir Robert G. K. *Defeating Communist Insurgency: Experiences from Malaya and Vietnam*. New York: Praeger, 1966.

Tucker, Spencer C., ed. *Encyclopedia of the Vietnam War: A Political, Social, and Military History*. Santa Barbara, CA: ABC-CLIO, 1998.

THE IRAQI WARS AND STRATEGIC ARCHITECTURES: CONCLUSIONS

Ajami, Fouad. "Iraq and the Arabs' Future." *Foreign Affairs* 82, no. 1 (January/February 2003).

Allawi, Ali A. *Faisal I of Iraq*. New Haven, CT: Yale University Press, 2014.

Atkinson, Rick. *Crusade: The Untold Story of the Persian Gulf War*. Boston: Houghton Mifflin, 1993.

Barnett, Thomas P. M. *The Pentagon's New Map: War and Peace in the Twenty-First Century*. New York: Putnam, 2004.

Berntsen, Gary. *Jawbreaker: The Attack on Bin Laden and Al-Qaeda; A Personal Account by the CIA's Key Field Commander*. New York: Crown, 2005.

Boot, Max. *War Made New: Technology, Warfare, and the Course of History, 1500 to Today*. New York: Gotham, 2006.

Chandrasekaran, Rajiv. *Imperial Life in the Emerald City: Inside Iraq's Green Zone*. New York, Knopf, 2006.

———. *Little America: The War within the War for Afghanistan*. New York: Knopf, 2012.

Cordesman, Anthony H. "The Iraqi Insurgency and the Risk of Civil War: Who Are the Players." Working draft, revised. Washington, DC, Center for Strategic and International Studies, March 1, 2006.

Diamond, Larry. *Squandered Victory: The American Occupation and the Bungled Effort to Bring Democracy to Iraq*. New York: Henry Holt, 2005.

Dobbins, J., S. Jones, K. Crane, and B. C. DeGrasse. *The Beginner's Guide to Nation-Building*. Santa Monica, CA: Rand, National Security Research Division, MG557, May 2007.

Dobbins, James, Seth G. Jones, Benjamin Runkle, and Siddharth Mohandas. *Occupying Iraq: A History of the Coalition Provisional Authority*. Santa Monica, CA: Rand, MG847, 2009.

Fromkin, David. *A Peace to End All Peace*. New York: Avon, 1989.

Gaddis, John Lewis. *Surprise, Security, and the American Experience*. Cambridge, MA: Harvard University Press, 2004.

Gates, Robert M. *Duty: Memoirs of a Secretary at War*. New York: Knopf, 2014.

Gerecht, Reuel Marc. "Intelligence Deficit Disorder." *Wall Street Journal*, May 9, 2006.

Gordon, Michael R., and Bernard E. Trainor. *The Endgame: The Inside Story of the Struggle for Iraq, from George W. Bush to Barack Obama*. New York: Pantheon, 2012.

Kagan, Kimberly. *The Surge: A Military History*. New York: Encounter Books, 2009.

Kagan, Robert. *Of Paradise and Power: America and Europe in the New World Order*. New York: Knopf, 2003.

Kaplan, Fred. *The Insurgents: David Petraeus and the Plot to Change the American Way of War*. New York: Simon & Schuster, 2013.

Katz, Mark N. *Leaving without Losing: The War on Terror after Iraq and Afghanistan*. Baltimore, MD: Johns Hopkins University Press, 2012.

Kedourie, Elie. *The Chatham House Version and Other Middle Eastern Studies*. 1970. Chicago: Ivan R. Dee, 2004.

Keegan, John. *The Iraq War*. New York: Knopf, 2004.

Kilcullen, David. *Counterinsurgency*. Paperback ed. Oxford: Oxford University Press, 2010.

Lewis, Bernard. *What Went Wrong? The Clash between Islam and Modernity in the Middle East*. Oxford: Oxford University Press, 2002.

Lord, Carnes. *Proconsuls: Delegated Political-Military Leadership from Rome to America Today*. Cambridge: Cambridge University Press, 2012.

Malkasian, Carter. *War Comes to Garmser: Thirty Years of Conflict on the Afghan Frontier*. Oxford: Oxford University Press, 2013.

Mansoor, Peter R. *Baghdad at Sunrise: A Brigade Commander's War in Iraq*. New Haven, CT: Yale University Press, 2008.

———. *Surge: My Journey with General David Petraeus and the Remaking of the Iraq War*. New Haven, CT: Yale University Press, 2013.

Marr, Phebe. *The Modern History of Iraq*. Boulder, CO: Westview, 2012.

Metz, Steven. *Iraq and the Evolution of American Strategy*. Washington, DC: Potomac, 2008.

Meyer, Karl E., and Shareen Blair Brysac. *Kingmakers: The Invention of the Modern Middle East*. New York: Norton, 2008.

Moten, Matthew, ed. *Between War and Peace: How America Ends Its Wars*. New York: Free Press, 2011.

Moyar, Mark. *A Question of Command: Counterinsurgency from the Civil War to Iraq*. New Haven, CT: Yale University Press, 2009.

Murray, Williamson, and Robert H. Scales Jr., Major General. *The Iraq War: A Military History*. Cambridge, MA: Harvard University Press, 2003.

Rayburn, Joel. *Iraq after America: Strongmen, Sectarians, Resistance*. Stanford, CA: Hoover Institution Press, 2014.

Ricks, Thomas E. *Fiasco: The American Military Adventure in Iraq*. New York: Penguin, 2006.

———. *The Gamble: General David Petraeus and the American Military Adventure in Iraq, 2006–2008*. New York: Penguin, 2009.

Robinson, Linda. *Tell Me How This Ends: General David Petraeus and the Search for a Way Out of Iraq*. New York: PublicAffairs, 2008.

Sanger, David E. *Confront and Conceal: Obama's Secret War and Surprising Use of American Power*. New York: Random House, 2012.

Schadlow, Nadia. *War and the Art of Governance: Consolidating Combat Success into Political Victory*. Washington, DC: Georgetown University Press, 2017.

Schake, Kori N. *State of Disrepair: Fixing the Culture and Practices of the State Department*. Stanford, CA: Hoover Institution Press, 2012.

Schwarzkopf, H. Norman. *It Doesn't Take a Hero*. New York: Bantam, 1992.

Suri, Jeremi. *Liberty's Surest Guardian: American Nation-Building from the Founders to Obama*. New York: Free Press, 2011.

West, Owen. *The Snake Eaters: An Unlikely Band of Brothers and the Battle for the Soul of Iran*. New York: Free Press, 2012.

Whitman, James Q. *The Verdict of Battle: The Law of Victory and the Making of Modern War*. Cambridge, MA: Harvard University Press, 2012.

Woodward, Bob. *Obama's Wars*. New York: Simon & Schuster, 2010.

———. *State of Denial: Bush at War*. New York: Simon & Schuster, 2006.

Yon, Michael. *Moment of Truth in Iraq*. Minneapolis, MN: Richard Vigilante Books, 2008.

INDEX